Reconceptualizing Language Norms in Multilingual Contexts

Sarah Jones
University of Toronto, Canada

Rebecca Schmor
University of Toronto, Canada

Julie Kerekes
University of Toronto, Canada

A volume in the Advances in Educational Technologies and Instructional Design (AETID) Book Series

Published in the United States of America by
    IGI Global
    Information Science Reference (an imprint of IGI Global)
    701 E. Chocolate Avenue
    Hershey PA, USA 17033
    Tel: 717-533-8845
    Fax: 717-533-8661
    E-mail: cust@igi-global.com
    Web site: http://www.igi-global.com

Copyright © 2024 by IGI Global. All rights reserved. No part of this publication may be reproduced, stored or distributed in any form or by any means, electronic or mechanical, including photocopying, without written permission from the publisher.
Product or company names used in this set are for identification purposes only. Inclusion of the names of the products or companies does not indicate a claim of ownership by IGI Global of the trademark or registered trademark.
    Library of Congress Cataloging-in-Publication Data

Names: Jones, Sarah, 1983 September 18- editor. | Schmor, Rebecca, 1996- editor. | Kerekes, Julie, 1965- editor.
Title: Reconceptualizing language norms in multilingual contexts / edited by, Sarah Jones, Rebecca Schmor, and Julie Kerekes.
Description: Hershey PA : Information Science Reference, 2024. | Includes bibliographical references and index. | Summary: "This book critically expands on existing scholarly literature in intercultural communication, interlanguage pragmatics, second language pragmatics, sociolinguistics, and applied linguistics. It challenges the traditional assumptions about mono-cultures and mono-languages, creating space for a diversity of perspectives and arguments. Furthermore, it explores the implications of its findings for language education and language policy, paving the way for a more inclusive and nuanced approach to language in multilingual societies"-- Provided by publisher.
Identifiers: LCCN 2023026441 (print) | LCCN 2023026442 (ebook) | ISBN 9781668487617 (hardcover) | ISBN 9781668487655 (paperback) | ISBN 9781668487624 (ebook)
Subjects: LCSH: Multilingualism--Social aspects. | Intercultural communication. | LCGFT: Essays.
Classification: LCC P115.45 .R43 2023 (print) | LCC P115.45 (ebook) | DDC 306.44/6--dc23/eng/20230621
LC record available at https://lccn.loc.gov/2023026441
LC ebook record available at https://lccn.loc.gov/2023026442

This book is published in the IGI Global book series Advances in Educational Technologies and Instructional Design (AETID) (ISSN: 2326-8905; eISSN: 2326-8913)

British Cataloguing in Publication Data
A Cataloguing in Publication record for this book is available from the British Library.

All work contributed to this book is new, previously-unpublished material. The views expressed in this book are those of the authors, but not necessarily of the publisher.
For electronic access to this publication, please contact: eresources@igi-global.com.

Advances in Educational Technologies and Instructional Design (AETID) Book Series

Lawrence A. Tomei
Robert Morris University, USA

ISSN:2326-8905
EISSN:2326-8913

Mission

Education has undergone, and continues to undergo, immense changes in the way it is enacted and distributed to both child and adult learners. In modern education, the traditional classroom learning experience has evolved to include technological resources and to provide online classroom opportunities to students of all ages regardless of their geographical locations. From distance education, Massive-Open-Online-Courses (MOOCs), and electronic tablets in the classroom, technology is now an integral part of learning and is also affecting the way educators communicate information to students.

The **Advances in Educational Technologies & Instructional Design (AETID) Book Series** explores new research and theories for facilitating learning and improving educational performance utilizing technological processes and resources. The series examines technologies that can be integrated into K-12 classrooms to improve skills and learning abilities in all subjects including STEM education and language learning. Additionally, it studies the emergence of fully online classrooms for young and adult learners alike, and the communication and accountability challenges that can arise. Trending topics that are covered include adaptive learning, game-based learning, virtual school environments, and social media effects. School administrators, educators, academicians, researchers, and students will find this series to be an excellent resource for the effective design and implementation of learning technologies in their classes.

Coverage

- Digital Divide in Education
- Curriculum Development
- Bring-Your-Own-Device
- E-Learning
- Classroom Response Systems
- Hybrid Learning
- Instructional Design Models
- Game-Based Learning
- Online Media in Classrooms
- Virtual School Environments

> IGI Global is currently accepting manuscripts for publication within this series. To submit a proposal for a volume in this series, please contact our Acquisition Editors at Acquisitions@igi-global.com or visit: http://www.igi-global.com/publish/.

The Advances in Educational Technologies and Instructional Design (AETID) Book Series (ISSN 2326-8905) is published by IGI Global, 701 E. Chocolate Avenue, Hershey, PA 17033-1240, USA, www.igi-global.com. This series is composed of titles available for purchase individually; each title is edited to be contextually exclusive from any other title within the series. For pricing and ordering information please visit http://www.igi-global.com/book-series/advances-educational-technologies-instructional-design/73678. Postmaster: Send all address changes to above address. Copyright © 2023 IGI Global. All rights, including translation in other languages reserved by the publisher. No part of this series may be reproduced or used in any form or by any means – graphics, electronic, or mechanical, including photocopying, recording, taping, or information and retrieval systems – without written permission from the publisher, except for non commercial, educational use, including classroom teaching purposes. The views expressed in this series are those of the authors, but not necessarily of IGI Global.

Titles in this Series

For a list of additional titles in this series, please visit: http://www.igi-global.com/book-series/advances-educational-technologies-instructional-design/73678

Architecture and Technological Advancements of Education 4.0
Rajiv Pandey (Amity University, Uttar Pradesh, India) Nidhi Srivastava (Amity University, Uttar Pradesh, India) and Parag Chatterjee (National Technological University Buenos Aires, Argentina)
Information Science Reference • © 2024 • 320pp • H/C (ISBN: 9781668492857) • US $225.00

Handbook of Research on Shifting Paradigms of Disabilities in the Schooling System
Hlabathi Rebecca Maapola-Thobejane (University of South Africa, South Africa) and Mbulaheni Obert Maguvhe (University of South Africa, South Africa)
Information Science Reference • © 2023 • 535pp • H/C (ISBN: 9781668458006) • US $270.00

Perspectives on Digital Burnout in Second Language Acquisition
Ali Kurt (Istanbul Esenyurt University, Turkey)
Information Science Reference • © 2023 • 293pp • H/C (ISBN: 9781668492468) • US $215.00

Instructional Leadership Efforts and Evidence-Based Practices to Improve Writing Instruction
Jennifer VanSlander (Columbus State University, USA)
Information Science Reference • © 2023 • 346pp • H/C (ISBN: 9781668486610) • US $215.00

Converting Ideas to Innovation With Lean Canvas for Invention
Arabella Bhutto (Mehran University of Engineering and Technology, Pakistan)
Information Science Reference • © 2023 • 156pp • H/C (ISBN: 9781668483411) • US $215.00

AI-Assisted Special Education for Students With Exceptional Needs
Ashish Kumar (Bennett University, India) Anand Nayyar (Duy Tan University, Vietnam) Rohit Kumar Sachan (Bennett University, India) and Rachna Jain (Bhagwan Parshuram Institute of Technology, India)
Information Science Reference • © 2023 • 335pp • H/C (ISBN: 9798369303788) • US $215.00

Teaching Methodologies in Pacific School Systems
Victor Mafone Alasa (Fiji National University, Fiji) Unaisi Nabobo-Baba (Fiji National University, Fiji) Taraivini Raiula (Fiji National University, Fiji) Cresantia Frances Koya-Vaka'uta (SPC and The University of the South Pacific, Fiji) and Ratish Chand (Fiji National University, Fiji)
Information Science Reference • © 2024 • 330pp • H/C (ISBN: 9781668467770) • US $215.00

701 East Chocolate Avenue, Hershey, PA 17033, USA
Tel: 717-533-8845 x100 • Fax: 717-533-8661
E-Mail: cust@igi-global.com • www.igi-global.com

Editorial Advisory Board

Yaseen Ali, *OISE, University of Toronto, Canada*
Pablo Robles-García, *University of Toronto Mississauga, Canada*
Nicola Townend, *University of Toronto Schools, Canada*
Shawna-Kaye Tucker, *OISE, University of Toronto, Canada*
Mélissa Villella, *Université du Québec en Abitibi-Témiscamingue, Canada & University of Ottawa, Canada*

List of Reviewers

Reshara Alviarez, *OISE, University of Toronto, Canada*
Gulnigar Baham, *OISE, University of Toronto, Canada*
Stephen Bahry, *OISE, University of Toronto, Canada*
Rosalia Cha, *OISE, University of Toronto, Canada*
David Cooper, *OISE, University of Toronto, Canada*
Karla Culligan, *University of New Brunswick, Canada*
Leonard Danglli, *Yorkville University, Canada*
Celine de Almeida, *George Brown College, Canada*
Selcuk Emre Ergut, *OISE, University of Toronto, Canada*
Dilruba Jahan, *OISE, University of Toronto, Canada*
Claudio Jaramillo Yanquepe, *OISE, University of Toronto, Canada*
Ye Jia, *OISE, University of Toronto, Canada*
Hannah Keim, *McGill University, Canada*
Ivan Lasan, *OISE, University of Toronto, Canada*
Li Peng, *McGill University, Canada*
Ma Guadalupe Sanchez Sandoval, *OISE, University of Toronto, Canada*
Andre Scholze, *OISE, University of Toronto, Canada*
Lorenzo Sclocco, *University of Toronto, Canada*
Kanza Tariq, *OISE, University of Toronto, Canada*
Serikbolsyn Tastanbek, *University of British Columbia, Canada*
Jennifer Walsh Marr, *University of British Columbia, Canada*
Linda Ward, *OISE, University of Toronto, Canada*

Table of Contents

Preface xvi

Section 1
Identity

Chapter 1
"Queer English" and "Heteronormative German": Negotiating Linguistic Repertoires and Identity in a Queer Activist Context in Berlin 1
Vroni Zieglmeier, Freie Universität Berlin, Germany

Chapter 2
Negotiating Language and Cultural Identity in Multicultural Contexts in Canada 23
Ariel Quinio, University of Toronto, Canada

Section 2
Translanguaging

Chapter 3
Translanguaging in the Multilingual Language Classroom 54
Laura E. Mendoza, University of Texas at El Paso, USA

Chapter 4
Translingual and Transcultural Engagement: Imagining, Maintaining, and Celebrating Collaboration, Agency, and Autonomy in a US University 68
Sibylle Gruber, Northern Arizona University, USA
Nancy G. Barrón, Northern Arizona University, USA

Section 3
Technology and Language Learning

Chapter 5
Embracing Advances in AI-Based Language Tools in EAP Programs: Towards a Plurilingual Shift . 88
Elena Danilina, University of Toronto, Canada
Emmanuelle Le Pichon, University of Toronto, Canada

Chapter 6
Digital Technology and Language Learning: How Does Digital Technology Change Our Perspectives on Language Learning?.. 108
Yasuyo Tomita, University of Toronto, Canada

Section 4
Teacher Practices

Chapter 7
Reconceptualizing Language Education With Mediation: Perspectives From Israel........................ 131
Leor Cohen, The Open University, Israel
Ingrid Barth, The Open University, Israel

Chapter 8
Bilingualism in Cuba: Social and Economic Impact of English Among Teachers 149
Ali Borjian, San Francisco State University, USA

Section 5
International Migration

Chapter 9
Teachers' Mindsets About Their Role in Shaping the Norms of Students' L1 Use in Greek Classrooms.. 165
Eftychia Damaskou, University of Thessaly, Greece

Chapter 10
Challenging the Monoglossic Ideology in English-Medium Higher Education in Türkiye 186
Talip Gülle, Bartın University, Turkey
Yavuz Kurt, Marmara University, Turkey

Section 6
Intranational Migration

Chapter 11
Migration and Language Dynamics: Reflections From the University of Education Community, Ghana 211
Esther Yeboah Danso-Wiredu, University of Education, Winneba, Ghana
Emma Sarah Eshun, University of Education, Winneba, Ghana

Chapter 12
Leaving Out No One: Multilingualism and Inclusiveness in Public Health Awareness Campaign Messages in Nigeria.. 225
Saheed Omotayo Okesola, University of Freiburg, Germany

Section 7
Dialectical Language Use

Chapter 13
Promoting US-Based Pre-Service ESOL Teachers' Understanding of Language Variation in Multidialectical Settings 247
Brian Hibbs, Dalton State College, USA

Chapter 14
Construction of Dialogue: The Language of an American Black Man Working in Higher Education 269
Lavon Davis, University of Maryland, Baltimore County, USA

Section 8
Speaker Agency

Chapter 15
Turkish Heritage Speakers' Reasons for Code-Switching in the United States 284
Didem Koban Koç, İzmir Democracy University, Turkey

Chapter 16
Interrogating "Filter Bubbles" Within Content Areas and Language Choices for Multilingual Learners in US Classrooms... 301
Karen L. Terrell, Loyola University Maryland, USA
Luciana C. de Oliveira, Virginia Commonwealth University, USA
Allessandra Elisabeth dos Santos, Sergipe Federal University, Brazil
Joy Beatty, Virginia Commonwealth University, USA
Tara Willging, Virginia Commonwealth University, USA
Silvia Hoyle, Virginia Commonwealth University, USA
Jia Gui, Clarkson University, USA

Conclusion 313

Afterword 317

Compilation of References 321

About the Contributors 372

Index 377

Detailed Table of Contents

Preface xvi

Section 1
Identity

Chapter 1
"Queer English" and "Heteronormative German": Negotiating Linguistic Repertoires and Identity
in a Queer Activist Context in Berlin 1
    Vroni Zieglmeier, Freie Universität Berlin, Germany

This chapter explores linguistic identity construction by L2 speakers in a multilingual context. It is based on an ethnographic field study about the indexical use of English in a queer community of practice (CofP), a queer activist group in Berlin. The chapter analyzes ethnographic interview data with members of the group, focusing on metapragmatic and metadiscursive statements. The main result is that in the group context, English and German are juxtaposed alongside a "queer" versus "heteronormative" dichotomy, leading to the use of English as constitutive of the members' and the group's cosmopolitan queer identity. More generally, the chapter combines 3rd wave variationist perspectives on linguistic indexicality with a contemporary approach to multilingualism and language contact and emphasizes the importance of including L2 speakers to the study of multilingualism and linguistic identity production in order to fully account for the plurality of multilingual experiences.

Chapter 2
Negotiating Language and Cultural Identity in Multicultural Contexts in Canada 23
    Ariel Quinio, University of Toronto, Canada

This chapter aims to explore and examine the role of language in the integration to the community of practice (CoP) of a culturally diverse group of participants, the Internationally Educated Professionals (IEPs) in Canada. Based on interpretive qualitative research and Bourdieu's theory as a lens, an in-depth interview, survey questionnaire and policy document data were analyzed using critical discourse analysis and the grounded theory. A selection of 30 IEP participants were divided into three categories according to their year of arrival. Findings reveal four different classes of IEPs and explain how they negotiate their language and cultural identity to integrate in their CoP post-migration. Results offer implications for reconceptualizing language norms, policies and practices in multicultural contexts.

Section 2
Translanguaging

Chapter 3
Translanguaging in the Multilingual Language Classroom 54
Laura E. Mendoza, University of Texas at El Paso, USA

Given today's culturally diverse classrooms, incorporating new perspectives and pedagogies must be considered of value. This should be primarily considered in the language classroom. Considering multilingualism as a rule, but simultaneously also considering how marginalized many individuals have been, especially in the language classroom; the inclusion of newer pedagogies which resist, and conjointly empower, emergent bilinguals, should be considered. The current chapter aims to highlight relevant literature which may enlighten the use of translanguaging practices in the language classroom.

Chapter 4
Translingual and Transcultural Engagement: Imagining, Maintaining, and Celebrating
Collaboration, Agency, and Autonomy in a US University 68
Sibylle Gruber, Northern Arizona University, USA
Nancy G. Barrón, Northern Arizona University, USA

This chapter uses an epistemological framework rooted in feminism, post-colonialism, and deconstruction to situate discussions of how knowledge is created, and how collaborative knowledge creation extends our understanding of the shifting and inter-connected cultural, social, and language realities that we experience in our lives. The authors show that these collaborative efforts construct meaning, expand meaning, and change previously accepted meaning. They show how they interrogate the normalization of this discipline, how they address the need for continuously re-examining and re-thinking approaches to translingual and transcultural collaboration as a way to construct new meaning, and how collaborative work continues to address and redefine the norms and realities of the dominant academic culture so that our contributions can lead to much-needed change in how we understand our roles as participants and stakeholders in translingual and transcultural collaborations.

Section 3
Technology and Language Learning

Chapter 5
Embracing Advances in AI-Based Language Tools in EAP Programs: Towards a Plurilingual Shift. 88
Elena Danilina, University of Toronto, Canada
Emmanuelle Le Pichon, University of Toronto, Canada

The chapter calls for a change in language teaching and learning methodologies to keep pace with recent technological advances. It acknowledges the prevalence of conversational artificial intelligence tools like Chatbots, including ChatGPT and Bing. Many students and teachers are already using these tools, albeit discreetly. Instead of ignoring or dismissing, the authors argue for their integration into teaching practices. They discuss both opportunities and challenges associated with the implementation of AI tools, considering the current debate surrounding their controversial use and the dominance of a monolingual orientation in English for Academic Purposes courses. By proposing a shift in current practices, the authors advocate for an asset-based, language-friendly, and technology-enriched pedagogy. This new pedagogical approach aims to promote learner autonomy, linguistic and cultural inclusion, and more individualized instruction. By implementing such a pedagogy, teachers can better meet the individual needs of their students leveraging the benefits of these technologies to enhance learning.

Chapter 6
Digital Technology and Language Learning: How Does Digital Technology Change Our Perspectives on Language Learning?... 108
    Yasuyo Tomita, University of Toronto, Canada

The advancement of digital technologies allows us to communicate in plurilingual contexts without learning additional languages. This makes the author wonder what learning languages means in today's technologically advanced environment. Therefore, this chapter explores the meaning of learning languages and taking language courses from multiple theoretical perspectives, including ecology, digital nature, agency and emotions in the action-oriented approach, and instructed second language acquisition. Using the concept of digital nature, the chapter argues that technology has provided us with freedom from the pressure to memorize and process a great deal of information owing to "our" externally existing knowledge (i.e., the internet) and magical tools such as real-time translation apps. The chapter discusses how this freedom allows us to exert our agencies, utilize noise for creativity and innovation, and take risks to learn languages through the fine-tuned delicate art of work, or teaching, valued in digital nature.

Section 4
Teacher Practices

Chapter 7
Reconceptualizing Language Education With Mediation: Perspectives From Israel 131
    Leor Cohen, The Open University, Israel
    Ingrid Barth, The Open University, Israel

The central argument in this chapter is that mediation is not simply a fourth mode of communication sitting alongside the other three modes of communication in the CEFR-CV, but should continue to evolve to become a core principle of the framework and a powerful engine for reconceptualizing language education. The central goal of this chapter is to support wide-scale implementation of mediation by putting forward possible paths for helping practitioners overcome some prevalent misunderstandings regarding mediation. To provide language educators with a deeper understanding of the entangled relationship between language and context, the authors borrow the concept of context from linguistic anthropology, as well as concepts such as positioning, roles and relationships. The overlapping, yet widely differing mediation activities described in the CEFR-CV are distilled down to just two groups - single context and double context - each with its own set of student-centered competences. Practitioner-friendly recommendations are provided for classroom use.

Chapter 8
Bilingualism in Cuba: Social and Economic Impact of English Among Teachers 149
   Ali Borjian, San Francisco State University, USA

This chapter considers the impact of English in a context where it is not a predominant language. For decades, the post-revolutionary Cuban government has recognized the importance of English in the economic advancement of the country. Although other world languages, especially Russian, have been promoted in Cuba, English has remained the most popular second language for the Cuban population. How Cuban teachers of English became interested in learning English and factors that contributed to their high level of proficiency in English is examined, and the social and economic impact of this language in their lives is investigated. Obstacles teachers face and their recommendations for ways to enhance English language development in Cuba are presented. Factors that keep them in the teaching profession or could force them to leave are also revealed.

Section 5
International Migration

Chapter 9
Teachers' Mindsets About Their Role in Shaping the Norms of Students' L1 Use in Greek
Classrooms 165
   Eftychia Damaskou, University of Thessaly, Greece

In Greece, mainstream classes consist of linguistic and cultural mosaics, where pupils face problems related to the absence of their L1. Teachers play a significant part in this, as when L1 is welcome, the sense of belonging increases, being highly influenced by their mindsets, in terms of values, teaching attitudes and methods. The chapter explores teachers' mindsets about their role in handling the presence and set the norms of different L1 use in class, presenting the findings of a qualitative research conducted as part of a doctoral thesis on the production of multilingual teaching material for the awakening of first-schoolers to linguistic diversity. The data was collected through semi-structured interviews, exploring 60 teachers' mindsets about their role in promoting the use of L1 in class. All interviews were recorded, transcribed, and processed through thematic analysis. Encouraging the L1 use, adopting integrative routines, creating conditions of cooperation, and cultivating values among pupils are the main axes that set the norms of students' L1 use in class.

Chapter 10
Challenging the Monoglossic Ideology in English-Medium Higher Education in Türkiye 186
   Talip Gülle, Bartın University, Turkey
   Yavuz Kurt, Marmara University, Turkey

Türkiye has witnessed exponential growth in the number of English-medium instruction (EMI) programs and an influx of international students — changes that are accompanied by challenges and opportunities. This chapter examines the discrepancy between the prevailing English-only policy and the increasing linguistic and cultural diversity in EMI higher education institutions in Türkiye. While the chapter focuses more on EMI programs, similar challenges in Turkish-medium (TMI) programs are also examined. The chapter argues for a shift in perspective that recognizes and embraces language diversity, and proposes the development of inclusive language policies to facilitate student interaction and involvement. It also calls for further research on multilingualism in EMI and TMI programs to inform policymaking, curriculum development, and teacher training. Overall, it argues for a comprehensive understanding of actual language needs and practices in linguistically diverse classrooms to develop policies that better serve the increasingly multilingual student body in Türkiye's universities.

Section 6
Intranational Migration

Chapter 11
Migration and Language Dynamics: Reflections From the University of Education Community, Ghana 211
Esther Yeboah Danso-Wiredu, University of Education, Winneba, Ghana
Emma Sarah Eshun, University of Education, Winneba, Ghana

Many different cultural traits are assimilated through migration; one such trait is language. In the processes of migration, many languages are moved from their ecological domain to new ecologies. About 60 known languages are spoken in the country of Ghana, and language experts argue that at the initial stages of migration, migrants might keep their indigenous languages. However, with time, the intents of maintaining the original language become wobbly. This study examines language dynamics in migration at University of Education, a multilinguistic community with diverse migrants. This case study uses a mixed methods approach. Findings indicate evidence of code-switching, code-mixing, dilution of original language, language shift, and total loss of original language and development of a new language. Negotiation of language use among migrants is paramount in or during migration so that existing indigenous languages will be saved from extinction as well as to maintain their vitality and the identity of the people who owns it.

Chapter 12
Leaving Out No One: Multilingualism and Inclusiveness in Public Health Awareness Campaign Messages in Nigeria 225
Saheed Omotayo Okesola, University of Freiburg, Germany

The COVID-19 pandemic altered human activities in several ways. It affected how people communicate and use language. Nigeria, with over 500 languages and just one official language, exploited multilingual resources to fight the COVID-19 pandemic. This chapter examines multilingualism and linguistic diversity in the discourse of COVID-19 public health awareness campaign messages in Nigeria. Thirty COVID-19 campaign messages in form of posters, audio jingles, videos, brochures, and sociolinguistic field interviews (30 unstructured one-on-one interviews) with some selected members of rural communities were analyzed. The study found that indigenous languages, multimodality, and translations were utilized as mass mobilization tools to promote inclusion. The study concludes that multilingualism and multimodality deliver COVID-19 sensitization messages effectively, increase access, and promote inclusiveness. It further suggests the localization of public health crisis in line with the sociolinguistic dynamics in multilingual settings.

Section 7
Dialectical Language Use

Chapter 13
Promoting US-Based Pre-Service ESOL Teachers' Understanding of Language Variation in
Multidialectical Settings 247
Brian Hibbs, Dalton State College, USA

This chapter outlines the elements of a course unit on language variation within a culture and education ESOL course intended to support the development of pre-service elementary education teacher candidates' awareness of language variation writ large and, more specifically, their knowledge concerning the nature of American English dialects, along with their understanding and appreciation of their future students' home dialects/languages. The chapter begins with a discussion of various theories that frame the course unit (challenging language norms, heteroglossia, critical applied linguistics, language-as-problem/right/resource, and language variation) and provides an overview of several prevailing attitudes concerning dialectical variation and how the course unit works to counter these narratives. The chapter then highlights the resources, activities, and assignments that constitute the course unit along with an examination of how and why they are included and utilized in the unit.

Chapter 14
Construction of Dialogue: The Language of an American Black Man Working in Higher
Education 269
Lavon Davis, University of Maryland, Baltimore County, USA

The ways dialogue is constructed is influenced by a myriad of factors—institution, context, the multiple identities people hold. Based on these factors, people bring with them varied experiences that inform the way they communicate with one another, both consciously and subconsciously. This chapter takes an in-depth look at how dialogue is constructed in the higher education setting. Utilizing a discourse analysis lens, the author conducted a 45-minute-long interview to obtain information about the experience of one Black male professional in higher education. During this interview, the author sought to investigate his usage of multiple varieties of English that showcased how a professional in higher education employed racial linguistic practices as a bridge between faculty/staff norms and student dynamics and interactions. Through this process, the author takes a look at how language shifts and switches play a role to develop the legitimacy, connection, and sharing that takes place in a higher education environment for students and staff.

Section 8
Speaker Agency

Chapter 15
Turkish Heritage Speakers' Reasons for Code-Switching in the United States 284
Didem Koban Koç, İzmir Democracy University, Turkey

The present study explores first- and second-generation Turkish speakers' reasons for code-switching in the United States (U.S.) as well as the effects of social variables (age of arrival and length of residence in the U.S.) on the speakers' reasons for code-switching. The speeches of Turkish speakers were analyzed via interviews, focusing on their reasons for code-switching. A total of 20 Turkish speakers participated in the study. The study adopted a qualitative research approach to determine the reasons for code-switching. The data were based on spontaneous corpus data consisting of 10 hours of interviews with the Turkish speakers. According to the results, the participants used code-switching for the following reasons: lexical need, emphasizing and clarifying a particular point, and filling a gap in speech. Significant effects of length of residence on the use of code-switching were also observed suggesting that the longer the speakers lived in the U.S., the less items they recalled in Turkish.

Chapter 16
Interrogating "Filter Bubbles" Within Content Areas and Language Choices for Multilingual Learners in US Classrooms 301
    Karen L. Terrell, Loyola University Maryland, USA
    Luciana C. de Oliveira, Virginia Commonwealth University, USA
    Allessandra Elisabeth dos Santos, Sergipe Federal University, Brazil
    Joy Beatty, Virginia Commonwealth University, USA
    Tara Willging, Virginia Commonwealth University, USA
    Silvia Hoyle, Virginia Commonwealth University, USA
    Jia Gui, Clarkson University, USA

Filter Bubbles refer to a state of intellectual isolation that can result from people becoming encapsulated in streams of data. When considering factors that contribute to the language choices of multilingual learners (MLs), specifically in the primary content areas of schooling, the Filter Bubble concept easily transposes into the field of education. According to Quintos, "multicultural educators focus on an education for a more democratic and socially just society" (p. 238). However, standards of learning chosen by states and their school districts represent the values of those who sit in positions of power and govern the concepts to which students are exposed. This chapter endeavors to respond to these questions within the intersections of societal constructs and the schooling contexts of English language arts, science, social studies, and mathematics, and to determine possibilities in which MLs can be provided optimal language choices and afforded the spaces to exercise these choices.

Conclusion 313

Afterword 317

Compilation of References 321

About the Contributors 372

Index 377

Preface

Most of what we do in communication involves language strategies: decisions we make about how to say what we mean and get what we want; how to interpret and how to negotiate. Most of these choices involve some kind of orientation to language norms. Language norms provide interpersonal frames of reference, establishing a space of shared understanding. At the same time, resisting or manipulating norms is a way to assert agency, spur creativity, and spark diversity. Traditional studies on language norms have focused on single, isolated languages and communities, and yet the reality is that single languages and communities do not exist in isolation. Indeed, the defining characteristics of contemporary societies are cultural and linguistic diversity, migration, and dynamism. What remains to be done is to document and engage with how language reflects and is reflected by that plurality. The purpose of this book is to take a step in this direction and begin to re-examine and reconceptualize normative language practices in multilingual and multicultural contexts.

The Canadian city of Toronto, where we three editors currently live and work, is a unique example of a contemporary metropolitan center. While Canada has long been a top educational destination for language students seeking immersive programs in English or French, it is also host to one of the world's most multicultural and multilingual social landscapes. According to the Statistics Canada 2021 Census Profile (Statistics Canada, 2023), 47% of Toronto's population was born outside of Canada. Nearly half, or 42%, of Toronto residents were raised speaking a language that is neither French nor English, and over half, or 56%, reported knowledge of a language other than English or French. In a city thousands visit every year for English language education, only 53% reported using English regularly at home.

While demographic statistics such as these are, by their very nature, reductive and overly simplistic, the numbers also hint at the reality of Toronto's linguistic and cultural repertoire, one characterized by fluidity, migration, and a multiplicity of shifting language practices. The three of us are no different: While our linguistic and cultural histories are distinct, none of us was born in this city; our personal and professional lives have been shaped by migration of varying degrees, and by our ongoing individual relationships to our own language repertoires. The reality of living in a city like Toronto is one of constant exposure to linguistic diversity, a diversity that undoubtedly has an impact on languages and language users. It is that very relationship - the reciprocal impact that language practices and language users have on each other - that sparked the idea for this edited volume.

Taking both multilingualism and multiculturalism as the rule, rather than the exception, this book challenges the assumption that languages, cultures, and norms are stable or stationary. Instead, we position them as ever-changing and dependent on the people who use them. This idea is not new: In an article on World Englishes, Braj Kachru (2017) makes the important point that "users of [a language] do not use the language to make meanings in identical ways" (p. 276). In sociolinguistics, Deborah Cameron has

Preface

long been calling for a reevaluation, or what she refers to as "demythologizing," of her field, specifically targeting what she views as problematic approaches to norms:

Sociolinguists make casual but significant use of notions like 'norm' and 'social identity' in order to explain the variation and attitudes they observe. And I have argued that one of the problems with this is that we are left with no account of where the norms 'come from' and how they 'get into' individual speakers - it is not good enough simply to situate them in some vague and ill-defined 'society', as though society were homogenous, monolithic and transparent in its workings, and as if individual language users were pre-programmed automata. (2014, pp. 91-92)

While much has been published on language norms and multilingualism as separate areas, this book looks at where they intersect. If we can agree with Kachru (and we do) that speakers manipulate and navigate language in different ways, and we recognize, as Cameron does, that norms emerge and develop from speakers in real-life language practices worthy of empirical examination, what do these actual language practices look like? The voices in this book open a door to the multiplicity of language practices that can begin to address this question.

In working towards *Reconceptualizing Language Norms in Multilingual Contexts*, this book brings together the work of 27 authors spanning diverse international and professional contexts and affiliations. The 16 chapters in this book explore the various ways language norms emerge, change, and shape communication in contemporary global - and local - societies, marked by linguistic and cultural diversity. Conveyed across its pages are research and reflections on language education, higher education, and teacher education; on communities, workplaces, and nations, represented - at risk of simplification - by the geographical descriptors American, Austrian, Canadian, Cuban, German, Ghanaian, Greek, Israeli, Japanese, Nigerian, and Turkish. Some of these chapters are position papers, while others are critical reflections or explorations. Others are empirical studies representing a wide range of methodological approaches. Together, they showcase voices from unique contexts around the globe.

The book is divided into 8 overlapping subthemes, each containing a pair of chapters. While many of the themes are consistent across multiple chapters, each section focuses on a particular aspect of language use. The first two chapters by Zieglmeier and Quinio deal with how language practices reflect and are reflected by identity, the former in a queer community in Berlin and the latter a typology of voices from newcomer professionals in Canada. The second theme, translanguaging, is discussed both in the educational classroom by Mendoza and within a translingual framework where two educators, Gruber and Barrón, share personal stories of growth. Next, the role of technology in language learning is explored, through a discussion of including AI tools in the classroom (Danilina and Le Pichon) as well as an exploration of the tensions between digital technologies and traditional language learning (Tomita). Two perspectives on the practices of teachers come from Borjian's discussion of teachers in Cuba, and the role of mediation in teacher practices from Israel by Cohen and Barth. The broad theme of migration is included in two sections: as migration across national borders, in the chapters from Damaskou and from Gülle and Kurt, and migration within national borders, as reflected in Ghana by Danso-Wiredu and Eshun and in Nigeria by Okesola. Next, two chapters discussing dialectical variation come from Hibbs' chapter on pre-service teacher training, and a discussion from Davis on dialectical language choice and racial identity. The final section, dealing with speaker agency, brings the concept of "filter bubbles" (Terrell et al.) into conversation with code-switching choices made by Turkish speakers living in the US (Koban Koç). In arranging the chapters as themed pairs, our hope is to highlight the multiplicity of

xvii

perspectives demonstrated across and within various aspects of language use in multilingual contexts. What follows is a brief description of each chapter, in the order that they appear in this volume.

In the chapter "'Queer English' and 'Heteronormative German': Negotiating Linguistic Repertoires and Identity in a Queer Activist Context in Berlin," Vroni Zieglmeier explores the language choices of members of a queer community who share German as a first language but choose to communicate in English, demonstrating how English represents an unmarked norm in this community and connotes values of diversity, modernity, and accessibility in affective processes of group identity construction, despite its members' critiquing the hegemony of the English language. Reflective of the complexity of multilingual language norms, Zieglmeier finds that English indexes positive qualities within the group, and negative ones outside of the group.

An exploration of the complexity of linguistic identity construction continues in Ariel Quinio's chapter, entitled "Negotiating Language and Cultural Identity in Multicultural Contexts in Canada." Focusing on the experiences of internationally educated professionals in Canada, Quinio theorizes a typology of professional experiences, ranging from high achieving and collaborating to low achieving and avoiding. In doing so, he stresses the role of linguistic identity and other sociolinguistic factors in contributing to the integration and satisfaction of internationally educated professionals.

Sociolinguistic perspectives also inform Laura Mendoza's chapter, "Translanguaging in the Multilingual Language Classroom." Mendoza guides readers through the historical and pedagogical tenets of translanguaging approaches, outlining opportunities for multilingual scaffolding, identifying cognates, using translations, paraphrasing, collaborating, writing autoethnographies, and conducting community member interviews.

More models for transforming pedagogical practices through pluralistic perspectives are found in Sibylle Gruber and Nancy G. Barrón's chapter, "Translingual and Transcultural Engagement: Imagining, Maintaining, and Celebrating Collaboration, Agency, and Autonomy in a US University." Through an autoethnographic exploration of the authors' personal and professional experiences, the chapter juxtaposes shared shifts from internalized linguistic stigmatization to the creation of critical translingual curricula.

Plurilingual shifts in education are also explored in Elena Danilina and Emmanuelle Le Pichon's chapter, "Embracing Advances in AI-Based Language Tools in EAP Programs: Towards a Plurilingual Shift." Drawing on the context of English for Academic Purposes, Danilina and Le Pichon exemplify how educators can incorporate artificial intelligence tools to help expand learners' plurilingual repertoires, increase metacognitive awareness, and afford multimodality.

Yasuyo Tomita continues the exploration of the intersection of plurilingualism and technology in the chapter, "Digital Technology and Language Learning: How Does Digital Technology Change Our Perspectives on Language Learning?" Conceptualizing technology as an extension of self and environment, Tomita theorizes reasons for learning the Japanese language despite the availability of digital translation tools that make language learning seemingly unnecessary. In doing so, she identifies how language learning affords experiences that technology itself does not embody, including emotion, creativity, risk-taking, and agency.

Insights into agency and language learning are further mediated in Leor Cohen and Ingrid Barth's chapter, "Reconceptualizing Language Education with Mediation: Perspectives from Israel," which positions the concept of mediation as the foundation of all modes of communication. Incorporating reflections from facilitating teacher education workshops in Israel, the authors propose a series of approaches to make the notion of mediation more accessible for practitioners. These include, among others, a move

Preface

from the notion of acquisition to socialization through an understanding of context, and a consideration of a spectrum of in/appropriate and in/effective language choices.

Ali Borjian explores teacher development in another part of the world, in "Bilingualism in Cuba: Social and Economic Impact of English Among Teachers." First contextualizing motivations to learn English within the socioeconomic history of Cuba, Borjian reveals how Cuban teachers of English have both instrumental and integrative language learning motives. With this, he details how these teachers value the role of positive attitudes toward the English language in motivating learners, while also recommending the use of Spanish to scaffold English language instruction.

Teachers' attitudes and learners' languages remain central themes in Eftychia Damaskou's chapter, "Teachers' Mindsets about their Role in Shaping the Norms of Students' L1 Use in Greek Classrooms." In this chapter, Damaskou analyzes opportunities for including languages other than Greek in primary school classrooms in Greece, emphasizing the integral role of teachers in fostering linguistic diversity, cultivating attitudes and values such as empathy and inclusion, and overcoming the discrepancy between emerging plurilingual policies and enduring monolingual practices.

Talip Gülle and Yavuz Kurt advance a critical analysis of the discrepancy between multilingual realities and monolingual policies in their chapter, "Challenging the Monoglossic Ideology in English-Medium Higher Education in Türkiye." Complexifying the envisioned monolingual space of English-medium instruction, the authors reveal how higher education institutions in Türkiye are in fact characterized by linguistic diversity and educational translanguaging. With this, they advocate for a shift - both in policy and practice - from English-medium instruction to translanguaging as a medium of education, for the benefit of all students; in particular, those who arrived as refugees from Syria.

Moving from contexts of international to *intra*national migration, Esther Danso-Wiredu and Emma Sarah Eshun explore the influence of migration on language loss and change in their chapter, "Migration and Language Dynamics: Reflections from University of Education Community, Ghana." Through this study, the authors exemplify how the adoption of new regional languages - often at the expense of other languages - mainly stems from marriage and migration, arguing that intentional maintenance of family languages is required at school and at home.

The maintenance of national linguistic diversity is further advocated for in Saheed Okesola's chapter, "Leaving Out No One: Multilingualism and Inclusiveness in Public Health Awareness Campaign Messages in Nigeria." Critically analyzing language-based access to public health information during the COVID-19 pandemic in Nigeria, Okesola positions multilingualism and multimodality as features of (indigenous) language rights, demonstrating how most people prefer to access public health information in their own native language, and how multimodality offers increased accessibility in contexts of low literacy.

Brian Hibbs also takes up themes of language variation and language rights in the chapter, "Promoting US-Based Pre-Service ESOL Teachers' Understanding of Language Variation in Multidialectical Settings." Critiquing the monolingual bias in educational contexts in the United States, Hibbs presents a teacher course unit on dialectal variation as a way to position multilingualism as the norm, even within a named language. Promoting a positive, additive view towards dialects, he argues, can help to reduce the societal eradication of dialectal languages and associated identities, commonly rooted in racialized communities.

The intersection of language and race is, once again, present in Lavon Davis' chapter, "Construction of Dialogue: The Language of a Black Man Working in Higher Education." In this chapter, Davis investigates the relationship between race, gender, language, and privilege in the professional and linguistic choices of a Black man who speaks (White) mainstream English and African American English, showing how this individual draws on the African American variety along with Black cultural references to support Black students in the United States.

The intersecting themes of the previous chapters come together in the chapter "Turkish Heritage Speakers' Reasons For Codeswitching In The United States," written by Didem Koban Koç. In this study, the author draws on a sociolinguistic framework to identify how code-switching from Turkish to English serves four main functions, including lexical need, clarification of a point, emphasizing a point, and filling a gap. This study, in turn, fills a gap in research on Turkish code-switching in the context of the United States.

Finally, agency in language choices remains a central theme in "Interrogating 'Filter Bubbles' within Content Areas and Language Choices for Multilingual Learners in US Classrooms," written by Karen Terrell, Luciana C de Oliveira, Allessandra Elisabeth dos Santos, Joy Beatty, Tara Willging, Silvia Hoyle, and Jia Gui. With a critical lens on educational and societal discourses, the authors draw on the concept of filter bubbles - a state of intellectual isolation which reinforces discriminatory biases - to exemplify the relationship between language and power in education. The authors share how, in the role of gatekeepers, teachers can provide access to linguistic codes of power and, for instance, help students add the code of academic English to their repertoire while recognizing the value of their existing linguistic knowledge.

In engaging with the discussions of norms present across these chapters, we also had to consider the norms of the editorial process of publishing a volume in (academic) English. We set out to curate a scholarly book about how language practices in multilingual spaces have fluid norms; at the same time, we chose to lean into the tensions around the multiple norms represented by the authors in this book in light of the prescriptive nature of the book's academic discourse genre. In this process, we were reminded that, while norms do indeed exist, language users ultimately decide what we do with them. To quote Gleick (1987), "The act of playing the game has a way of changing the rules" (p. 24). This book, too, plays the academic discourse game, but, in its discussion of normative practices and diversity of authorial voices, also works to resist, subvert, challenge, and otherwise reconceptualize those very norms.

With its diversity of perspectives and arguments, the book takes an important step toward gathering and disseminating research that reflects the realities of language use and language users in diverse linguistic and cultural contexts. On, within, and beyond its pages, implications can be found for educators, researchers, policy makers, and students engaged in the very broad fields of multilingualism and applied linguistics.

As editors, our hope is that this book sheds light on real language practices in multilingual and multicultural spaces, reflecting how language practices are enacted, resisted, and reimagined by the rich, diverse, multi-voiced people who embody them.

Sarah Jones
University of Toronto, Canada

Rebecca Schmor
University of Toronto, Canada

Julie Kerekes
University of Toronto, Canada

REFERENCES

Cameron, D. (2014). Demythologizing sociolinguistics: why language does not reflect society. In J. E. Joseph & T. J. Taylor (Eds.), *Ideologies of language* (Vol. 4, pp. 79–94). Routledge., doi:10.4324/9781315880341_6

Gleick, J. (1987). *Chaos: Making a New Science.* Viking Press.

Kachru, Y. (2017). World Englishes, pragmatics, and discourse. In M. Filppula, J. Klemola, & D. Sharma (Eds.), *The Oxford handbook of World Englishes* (pp. 272–290). Oxford University Press.

Statistics Canada. (2023, February 1). *2021 Census Profile - Toronto [Census metropolitan area], Ontario.* Statistics Canada. https://www12.statcan.gc.ca/census-recensement/2021/dp-pd/prof/details/page.cfm?Lang=E&SearchText=Toronto&GENDERlist=1%2C2%2C3&STATISTIClist=1%2C4&DGUIDlist=2021S0503535&HEADERlist=0

Section 1
Identity

Chapter 1
"Queer English" and "Heteronormative German":
Negotiating Linguistic Repertoires and Identity in a Queer Activist Context in Berlin

Vroni Zieglmeier
Freie Universität Berlin, Germany

ABSTRACT

This chapter explores linguistic identity construction by L2 speakers in a multilingual context. It is based on an ethnographic field study about the indexical use of English in a queer community of practice (CofP), a queer activist group in Berlin. The chapter analyzes ethnographic interview data with members of the group, focusing on metapragmatic and metadiscursive statements. The main result is that in the group context, English and German are juxtaposed alongside a "queer" versus "heteronormative" dichotomy, leading to the use of English as constitutive of the members' and the group's cosmopolitan queer identity. More generally, the chapter combines 3rd wave variationist perspectives on linguistic indexicality with a contemporary approach to multilingualism and language contact and emphasizes the importance of including L2 speakers to the study of multilingualism and linguistic identity production in order to fully account for the plurality of multilingual experiences.

INTRODUCTION

Shortly before our interview, Chris had attended a queer-feminist demonstration in Berlin. It was March 8th, International Women's Day. As a queer activist, participating in queer and feminist protests is part of Chris's daily life. This time, however, something was off. During the speeches, they realized that the only German speech in a series of otherwise English-language contributions was translated into English. The other contributions, on the other hand, were not translated into German. While Chris's first language is German, understanding, speaking, and chanting English is not an issue: They study English

DOI: 10.4018/978-1-6684-8761-7.ch001

at university, lived in England for a few months during high school, and have plans to work and study abroad in New Zealand and Canada over the next couple of years. The fact that the organizers of the demonstration seemed to assume that all participants understand English, but not German, would probably not even have occurred to Chris if they hadn't happened to be at the demo with two friends who are not part of their political collective, and who feel significantly less comfortable speaking English than their first language German. In Chris's friend group, these two friends are somewhat exceptional. English, a language which Chris and most people they know had first learned in high school, is a central repertoire for their everyday social and political life.

English competence is a highly valued resource in Berlin. The growing presence of the language is a consequence of a series of national policies in the Federal Republic of Germany after WW2 and urban policies in the reunited Berlin after 1989. As Heyd and Schneider suggest, four groups contribute to the visibility of English in the German capital: educated upwardly mobile native German speakers, tourists and the tourist-based industry, hypermobile wealthy, mostly white expats and refugees and more precarious migrants (Heyd & Schneider, 2019, 149–150). The wealthy expats in particular have received much public and media attention in the last decades. Through the marketing of Berlin as a hip and artsy "place to be" in the post-reunification era (Farrell, 2019) and, more recently, as a start-up location and destination for so-called digital nomads, the presence of English has been synonymous with the gentrification of the city and the displacement of underprivileged communities and communities of color (Baines, 2015; Malmgren, 2011; Mendoza, 2011). As such, English in Berlin has been met with skepticism from both conservative (Spahn, 2017) and leftist voices (Hilal & Varatharajah, 2022). In the meantime, the diverse linguistic practices of the first group of English speakers identified by Heyd and Schneider—and the group that best describes Chris and their friends: upwardly mobile L1 German speakers—have received little media and scholarly attention until now.

This chapter is concerned with the role of English in the identity construction of queer L1 German and L2 English speakers[1] in Berlin. It is based on an ethnographic field study conducted in 2021–2022 with members of a community of practice (CofP) (Eckert & McConnell-Ginet, 1992), a queer political collective which operates in English. Drawing on qualitative interviews with members of the CofP, it explores identity-based motivations for repertoire management and the semiotic processes of language ideology that underlie these motivations. In order to determine the semiotic aspects of English use in the participants' identity construction, the study is primarily concerned with their metapragmatic reflections on the use of English and German. The discussion focuses on the opposing indexical meanings of English usage in and outside of the group and on the affective dimension of L2 usage in identity construction.

LITERATURE REVIEW

Repertoire, Code-Switching, and Repertoire Management

Associated with early ethnographic research in sociolinguistics, the term *repertoire* denotes "the totality of linguistic resources [...] available to members of particular communities" (Gumperz, 1972, 20–21). Thus, the notion refers to an individual's linguistic experience and expertise constituted by linguistic features and resources from a broad range of varieties, languages, and linguistic practices. Alternating between subsystems of the linguistic repertoire (sociolects, dialects, or languages) is commonly referred to as 'code-switching'. The mechanisms of code-switching, in turn, are determined by the context of the utterance and the social role of the interlocutors. Fishman (1965, 1967) argues that speakers compartmentalize their repertoires by domain, while Blom and Gumperz (1972) distinguish between situational switching, whereby the code switch includes a change in topic or interlocutors, and metaphorical switching, whereby it impacts the social role relations of the interlocutors. Building on this, the markedness model of code-switching, introduced by Myers-Scotton (1995, 1998), systematizes socio-indexical motivations for code-switching by establishing that there is an "unmarked choice" in every linguistic interaction. The 'unmarked choice' is the linguistic form that does not change or threaten the social roles of the speakers involved and could thus either be to codeswitch or not to codeswitch, according to the situation. The establishment of an 'unmarked choice' does not mean that speakers always and necessarily decide to use it, but rather that the decision whether to meet or violate these normative linguistic expectations involves social trade-offs. Finally, in order to conceptually frame regularly occurring code-switching acts, Matras uses the term *repertoire management*, referring to an individual speaker's ability to map parts of their repertoire onto addressee constellations and activity domains (Matras, 2009).

Linguistic Identity Construction and Language Ideologies

It is well-established in contemporary sociolinguistics that identity emerges through language (among other semiotic practices). In other words, language serves to *construct* identity instead of merely *reflecting* it (Barrett, 2002, 28). As Bucholtz and Hall (2005) argue, the mechanism central to linguistic identity production is indexicality. Broadly speaking, indexicality refers to the semiotic relationship between language and social meaning. Speakers use a particular linguistic form that indexes (points to) a social group or persona in order to position themselves as a particular kind of person. These indexical uses of language can be straightforward, i.e., in a statement such as "I am gay", which explicitly names an identity label, or indirect, through the use of linguistic features that are associated with specific personas or groups (Bucholtz & Hall, 2005, 594). The indexical sign relationship between linguistic feature and social meaning is not immediate, but indirect. As Ochs (1992) determines, linguistic signs do not index social persons or groups, but rather stances, acts, and activities, which in turn are associated with the person or group. As a means of illustration, a speaker who uses a lot of tag questions might seem insecure, shy, and unassertive, qualities which, in turn, are associated with femininity (Lakoff, 1973; Ochs, 1992, 340; but cf. also Dubois & Crouch, 1975). Adding to this, Eckert (2008) emphasizes that the indexical meanings of a variable constitute an indexical field, a constellation of potential, ideologically related social meanings, "any one of which can be activated in the situated use of the variable" (Eckert, 2008, 454; cf. also Silverstein, 2003).

In language contact settings particularly, the use of one language instead of another is a common vector for socio-indexical meaning. For instance, Besnier (2004) reports that interlocutors at a market in Tonga use English instead of Tongan in order to appear modern and cosmopolitan (as cited in Bucholtz & Hall, 2005, 598). However, the fact that English is linked to modernity and cosmopolitan (and Tongan is not) is not a given: These associations are the result of what is widely referred to as language ideologies. Language ideologies, in broad terms, are underlying ideas about the characteristics of individual languages and their speakers (Irvine & Gal, 2000). Like other ideologies, language ideologies are shaped by political culture and reflect the systems of power of the societies in which they come into being. Following Irvine and Gal, language ideologies emerge from linguistic difference, that is, from speakers and groups speaking differently in different contexts. For instance, a speaker might explain their use of a Standard German at work as opposed to Bavarian at home by saying that the former is simply better suited for professional communication, backing up this statement with assumptions and ideas about the typical speakers and the linguistic properties of the varieties. As a consequence, linguistic features are understood to express and reflect characteristics associated with individuals, social groups, and activities (Irvine & Gal, 2000). In Eckert's words, "linguistic variation constitutes an indexical system that embeds ideology in language and that is in turn part and parcel of the construction of ideology" (Eckert, 2008, 454).

Language ideologies are negotiated and reflected in metapragmatic discourse. These reflections occur, for example, when a speaker anecdotally reports on linguistic difference or evaluates the linguistic behavior of others. In her considerations on Pittsburghese, Johnstone (2006) emphasizes the analytical productivity of the personal narrative for the study of linguistic ideologies. As "one of the discursive practices through which certain speech features that can be heard locally are typified as signals of localness, and normative instructions about how to hear and use this (imagined) vernacular variety are disseminated" (Johnstone, 2006, 48), she argues that personal narrative is a central vehicle for language-ideological differentiation.

Queer English

Through terms such as *pride*, *coming out* or *queer*, English as the language of the Anglo-American LGBT movement is echoed in queer languages and communities worldwide. On the lexical level alone, one can infer the enormous influence of the commodified and globalized urban American queer history on communities worldwide. But this commodification and globalization process is far from limited to lexical aspects. Leap (2010) uses the term "gay English" to refer to these globalized linguistic, but also other semiotic and discursive practices—including symbols like the rainbow flag, the imperative of coming out, and a collective memory of the milestones of the American LGBT movement, especially of the Stonewall Riots.

The use of English and English-based linguistic practices in queer communities of practice around the world has been subject to a considerable amount of study. In Tonga, for instance, Besnier (2002) observes that English is the default language at a beauty pageant with transfeminine performers. Because English and Tongan are dichotomized as modern versus traditional, the author argues, the use of English helps the participants to perform an eloquent, modern, cosmopolitan femininity. Still, the performers reject Western ideas about gay and lesbian identities "and are highly selective in their adoption of symbols and indexes of a globalizing modernity as constitutive of their transgendered [sic] [...] selves" (Besnier, 2002, 559). Leap (2005) states that in the townships of Cape Town in the 1990s, English identity labels like *gay* and *lesbian* were associated with a metropolitan and cosmopolitan understanding of gender-sexuality.[2] Their use connected the speakers to the subculture in the city center rather than to local township discourse. Whether a speaker used or rejected the terms, then, also indicated their positioning in the cultural understanding of the "center" versus the "township" in Cape Town. The use of identity labels is also relevant to Hall's (2009) exploration of English and Hindi in a sexual health center in New Delhi. Hall studied two groups that frequent the center: the female-identified *lesbians* and the transmasculine *boys*. Similar to what Besnier (2002, 2004) has attested for Tonga, Hall finds that English and Hindi are mapped onto *progressive* and *traditional* domains of talk. Both groups see the traditional Hindi as more masculine than the progressive English. The lesbians, Hall observes, find English to be the most appropriate language for gender-sexuality related discussions, while the boys prefer Hindi. Whether speakers in the center use English or Hindi, the author notes, reveals a range of other ideological polarizations, including "upper class vs. lower class, femininity vs. masculinity, and lesbian vs. boy" (Hall, 2009, 142).

The negotiation of English versus non-English in globalized queer communities seems to necessarily involve questions of belonging in local discourse and of the relationship to the Western, especially Anglo-American world (Hall, 2009, 143; Leap, 2010, 571; Massad, 2002). In the postcolonial contexts of Tonga, Cape Town, and New Delhi, the status of English as the colonizer language is ideologically tied to an understanding of race, ethnicity, and culture (whiteness and Western-ness) that is not necessarily reflected in European contexts, where English meets other languages tied to colonizing and imperialist nations.

In Berlin, English remains without an official status, but rather serves as a transnational resource (Heyd & Schneider, 2019; Schneider, 2012). As such, it inhabits the in-between of the local and the non-local and thus, as the following analysis will show, it can index both "us" and "them". A study by Minning (2004), which explores the idea of a "Lavender German" (a queer variety of the German language), points to an undeniable presence of English-based language practices in queer communities in Berlin around the turn of the millennium. She reports that in German-speaking conversational contexts, English terms such as *pride*, *pink*, or *community* can index specifically queer meaning while their German counterparts (*Stolz*, *rosa*, *Gemeinschaft*) do not (Minning, 2004, 59–60). Despite this rather intriguing finding, the author's focus on English-based words as part of a queer German lexicon leads to some still unanswered questions, in particular about the potential influence of the linguistic ecology in Berlin at the time of the data collection and of social and biographical factors on the speakers' use of English-based language.

Methodology and Ethnographic Insight

My ethnographic field study is based on queer and feminist insights into linguistic and anthropological fieldwork (Besnier & Philips, 2012; Rooke, 2010; Sauntson, 2022) and draws on semi-structured ethnographic interviews conducted in 2021 with five members of a queer CofP in Berlin.

The CofP (henceforth: the group) is a queer collective which varies in group size, but at the time of the interviews, around 20 people attended the weekly plenaries. The group organizes non-violent direct action in Berlin and online, such as marches, vigils, raffles, and kiss-ins. The first chapter of the group was founded in New York in 2018; chapters in London and Berlin followed in 2019. The political work of the Berlin chapter focuses on topics specific to the German context such as the *Selbstbestimmungsgesetz* ('self-determination act') as well as inter- and transnational causes. The use of English is the unmarked norm in the group: As the participants report, weekly plenary meetings and subgroup meetings are held in English, internal communication in chat groups is in English, and the group's postings on social media are either in English or in English and German. Further, the group members state that on the rare occasions that subgroups do switch to German, everyone present has to affirm that they feel comfortable with it. The plenary is never held in German. In addition, all participants report that they had never thought about why the group is operating in English and not German before our conversation.

All five participants were university students at the time of the interview, the youngest in their second semester and the oldest in the course of finishing their master's thesis. All are white L1 German speakers who learned English in their teens and state to be fluent in both languages at the moment of the data collection. Fundamentally, the participants all have a strong connection to the English language. They report using English frequently in their day-to-day life. Some have lived in anglophone countries or plan on doing so, others study or work in English, all consume media in English and have friends and partners they speak English with. Next to German, they say that English is the language that they speak most, most readily, and most confidently. Because this study's main concern is with the category *queer* as a self-designation and group identity and the ways in which this is reflected in linguistic practice, the participants' specific gender and sexual identity are not relevant to the analysis and thus omitted. To further ensure their anonymity, the participants' names are replaced with gender-neutral pseudonyms: Charlie, Chris, Kim, Luka, and Robin. The term *queer* has been adopted from the self-designation of the group and its members and is to be understood as synonymous with the abbreviation *LGBTQIA+* (lesbian, gay, bisexual, transgender, queer, intersex, asexual, and more), referring to various types of non-normative gender-sexuality.

My initial contact with the group and written correspondence with the participants was in English. After asking the participants in the beginning which language they would be most comfortable with, the interviews were conducted in German on the videocall platform *Webex*, recorded, transcribed in *f4transkript* (Pehl & Dresing, 2015a), and coded using *f4analyse* (Pehl & Dresing, 2015b). The transcriptions loosely follow the standards established by Selting et al. (2011), avoiding orthographic capitalization and using (-) and (---) for short and long pauses, respectively. Non-lexical linguistic material, such as laughter, is marked with two parentheses: ((laugh)). The translations of the interview excerpts discussed in this chapter were done by me.

The starting point of the interviews were biographical questions about the participants' origin, their coming of age and coming out, and moving to and living in Berlin. We further discussed their motivations for joining the group (in particular with reference to the pandemic, the interviews were done while Germany was in the second Covid-19 lockdown). Other data collection strategies included me mentioning specific activities and social media postings of the group and asking the participants for their group internal insight about the activities and inquiring about their use of language at home, with family, at work, university, and in the group. I was aiming to first understand which language they associate with which domain and, in a next step, if applicable, to elicit their judgments of "appropriate" and "inappropriate" uses of one language instead of the other.

The qualitative analysis was inspired by Braun and Clarke's thematic analysis (2006, 2019, cf. also Guest et al., 2016) which involves several close readings of the data, the identification of patterns, a thematic coding system and the distillation of underlying themes and arguments. The analysis centers around indexical use of language (Bucholtz & Hall, 2005) and aims at understanding the linguistic ideologies (Irvine & Gal, 2000) emerging from the participants' multilingual experience as queer activists in Berlin. In the participants' metapragmatic statements, four major underlying themes were identified: cosmopolitanism and diversity, modernity and media, openness and accessibility, and youth and progressiveness. These themes form the basis of the following analysis of the indexical use of English in the group.

Findings

The participants' general affinity for English is in line with the tendency of young, educated, upwardly mobile individuals and communities in Berlin to use English rather than German in order to index openness, cosmopolitanism, and progressiveness (Farrell 2019, Heyd & Schneider 2019, Schneider 2020). However, they explicitly link their personal use of English and the dominance of English in the group to their queer identity. Through the four major themes identified in the interviews, the next sections will explore this connection between English and queerness against the backdrop of theories of language ideology and linguistic indexicality.

Cosmopolitanism and Diversity

After the participants had established that English was the dominant language in the group, I asked them what the reason for this might be. In response to this, several of my interlocutors pointed to the group's origins in New York City. Kim, for example, explains it as follows:

Excerpt One

V: und ähm, wie kommt es, dass [die gruppe] auf englisch stattfindet?

Kim: *also (---) generell ist [group] 'ne internationale (---) gruppe so, gegründet auch von 'nem (---) new yorker (-) und ich glaub das gibt's noch in london und in new york (-) und (-) dadurch dass das ein arm davon ist glaub ich erst mal deswegen andererseits aber auch weil's einfach international ist, also weil da auch wirklich (-) ja leute von ganz verschiedenen (-) hintergründen mit drin sind und (-) bei den meisten ist halt wirklich englisch nochmal glaub ich einfach viel einfacher als deutsch (-) ich bin mir gar nicht sicher ob da wirklich (-) auch mitglieder mit dabei sind die gar kein deutsch sprechen oder verstehen, ich glaube das tun schon alle zu 'nem gewissen grad (-) aber, ja, die hauptsprache ist dadurch englisch, dass es glaub ich einfach zugänglicher sein soll*

V: and um, how come that [the group] takes place in english?

Kim: *so, in general [group] is an international group, founded by a new yorker and i think it also exists in london and in new york and because it is a chapter of that so i think first of all because of that but also because it is just international, like because there really are people from very different backgrounds in it and for most of them english is just much easier than german. i'm not sure if there are actually members who don't speak or understand german at all, i think they all do to a certain degree but, yes, the main language is english, so that it becomes more accessible i think.*

Kim connects the use of English in the group to a sense of cosmopolitanism, both in the group's history and in its composition. This understanding touches upon the status of English as the language of Anglo-America as well as an international lingua franca, available to large parts of the world. The use of English establishes a connection to the group's origins in New York City, thus confirming its substantive ties to the place widely mystified as the birthplace of the modern LGBT movement. In addition, English is seen as inclusive of a wide range of people with different (that is, non-German) backgrounds, which comes back to its status as a dominant language of the global circulation of cultural and economic capital and, presumably, also due to its status as a "foreign language" in Berlin. By speaking English in Berlin (and not the local majority language, German), the group members become cosmopolitan agents. English becomes synonymous with diversity, cosmopolitanism, and accessibility, and German, by implication, with uniformity, provincialism, and inaccessibility.

The assumption implicit in Kim's account—that queer people are more likely to speak English than others—is made more explicit by Chris:

Excerpt Two

V: du meintest aber vorhin dass du auch in deinem freundeskreis relativ viel englisch sprichst

Chris: *<<affirm.>hm> also eher so (-) mit den [group]-leuten oder mit so ja anderen queeren, also, wenn man sich irgendwie doch mal trifft mit queeren leuten dann wird meistens englisch gesprochen weil einfach (-) ich glaub die wahrscheinlichkeit höher ist dass da auch (-) leute da sind die nur englisch sprechen können und nicht auch deutsch*

V: but earlier you said that also speak a lot of english with your friends

Chris: *<<affirm.>hm> like mostly like with the [group]-people or with like yeah other queer, like, when you do hang out with queer people somehow then it's mostly english-speaking because i guess it's just more likely that there are also people there who only speak english and not also german*

Chris reports that they speak English more often in queer than in non-queer groups, because at least in their social environment, queer people are more likely not to speak German than non-queer people. Through this statement, Chris seems to directly connect English to queerness. However, at closer inspection, Chris first and foremost states that queer people are more likely to be non-German, thus connecting queerness to diversity and cosmopolitanism, which is similar to what Kim said in Excerpt 1.

Robin, while critically reflecting on the tendency to use English on dating apps in Berlin, also states that something about the queer community is more international:

Excerpt Three

Robin: *auf ner app wie grindr wird man tatsächlich nur auf englisch angeschrieben [...] und das find ich schon auch tatsächlich 'n bisschen irritierend. weil das eine ist natürlich 'ne englische infrastruktur zu haben aber das andere irgendwie standardmäßig davon auszugehen dass alle menschen anglophon sind hier ist halt auch wild. also weißt du? wo ich mir so denke naja also ist schon auch bisschen gewagt jetzt zu denken alle menschen würden halt nur englisch sprechen (-) und das ist glaub ich aber so in der queeren community schon auch nochmal (---) weiß nicht vielleicht irgendwie präsenter weil halt sehr viele (-) queere personen auch irgendwie aus'm ausland nach berlin ziehen*

Robin: *on an app like grindr[3] you will only get contacted in english [...] and that's actually a bit irritating for me. because one thing is to have an english infrastructure of course but another thing is to assume by default that everyone here is anglophone that's also just wild. like you know? where i think to myself like it is also a bit daring now to think all people would speak english. but that's i think in the queer community yet again i don't know maybe kind of more present because just a lot of queer people move to berlin from abroad*

Starting off by criticizing the tendency to use English on dating apps, Robin proceeds to explain the presence of English as an unmarked norm by suggesting that the queer community is more diverse than other parts of Berlin. While this is not far-fetched—considering that sexual orientation and gender identity are still reasons for displacement and persecution in many countries and that Berlin is mystified as an *El Dorado* for queer communities—, Robin's back and forth between criticizing and rationalizing the use of English also shows that the social acceptability of English is highly contested in Berlin. Two contradictory ideological roles that English inhabits in the lives and perceptions of the participants collide: the role of the progressive, diverse and international language of queer liberation on the one hand and that of the languages of gentrification and uprooting in Berlin on the other. As cosmopolitan queers and members of an English-speaking political group, English is central to the participants' sense of belonging in a queer community and in queer activism. In this context, to speak English is to form a bridge to urban America, connecting the speakers to the imagined transnational queer community (Anderson, 2006). Moreover, the persistent association of English with non-locality and 'foreignness' in the Berlin context and, by implication, of German with locality and sameness leads to the use of English to index greater diversity than German. Presumably, this is enhanced by the global spread of American-inspired movements of racial justice such as Black Lives Matter and Critical Race Theory. In Berlin, this globalized discourse of diversity, however, competes with a local counter-discourse, which has become ever more audible in recent years. Critics argue that racial inequality has a different history in Germany and the fight for equity and equality has to be informed by the specifics of local cultural and racial hegemonies (see e.g., Perinelli 2019). Further, activists and scholars like Hilal and Varatharajah point out that the dominance of English in discussions about racial justice and diversity in Berlin runs the risk of obscuring the histories and realities of non-English speaking people of color, especially non-white Germans (Hilal & Varatharajah, 2022). Not surprisingly, concerns about English and racial inequality were also raised in the interviews. Luka, for example, points out the ideological hypocrisy that comes with the use of English in Berlin:

Excerpt Four

Luka: also ich kenn auch tatsächlich leute die hier her gezogen sind und (-) immer noch kein deutsch sprechen und schon 'n paar jahre hier wohnen also ich glaub in berlin, kommt auch nochmal an was für 'n job man machen will irgendwie manche davon sind dann halt auch einfach baristas irgendwo in (-) mitte oder kreuzberg wo eh alle englisch sprechen auch irgendwie ((laugh)) um ihren hafer latte zu bestellen aber ja also ich glaub je nachdem was für 'n job man haben will kommt man schon über die runden aber (-) es ist natürlich auch privilegiert also das sind dann auch noch oft weiße leute

[…] und wobei bei der sache mit den jobs muss man auch sagen […] dass es dann voll okay ist wenn leute englisch sprechen aber sobald du dann türk-, also nicht du aber, jemand dann türkisch spricht oder so ist es dann so ah warum sprichst du nicht deutsch oder so

Luka: *so i actually know people who moved here and still don't speak german and have been living here for a few years so i think in berlin it also depends on what kind of job you want to do somehow some of them are just baristas somewhere in mitte or kreuzberg where everyone speaks english anyway also somehow ((laugh)) to order their oat latte but yes so i think depending on what kind of job you want you can get by but of course it's also privileged so these are then often white people as well*

[…] and although with the job thing you also have to say […] that it's completely okay if people speak english but as soon as you speak turk-, like not you, but somebody speaks turkish then it's gonna be like ah why don't you speak german or something like that

Luka points out two discursive tendencies in which it becomes visible that English has a privileged status as a foreign language in Berlin: On the one hand, Luka argues, English is more readily accepted when it is used white immigrants than when it is used by non-white immigrants, and on the other hand, the use of English (and not German) is more widely tolerated than the use of other, especially non-white immigrant languages such as Turkish. In this context, speaking English in Berlin is a privilege reserved for white immigrants, whereas nonwhite immigrants face stronger pressure to learn and speak German. Fundamentally, English use in Berlin outside of the group is discussed and criticized as a separate issue and is met with significantly more skepticism than English use in the group. The openness and diversity that English undoubtedly indexes in the group is a highly context-specific indexical meaning. A central part of the participants' repertoire management skills is the awareness of the different social meanings that different languages have according to context. In their metapragmatic reflections, the participants signal that they understand the linguistic norms and expectations in and outside of the group and know how to navigate and make use of the rivaling indexical meanings that English has in these contexts. As such, the apparent contradiction—English is open and inclusive, but also discriminatory and excluding—is compensated by the compartmentalization of language use.

Progressiveness and Modernity

The interviews also touched upon the participants' experience as English language learners. Although they had encountered English as a school subject, the participants report that they acquired most of their language skills through their interest for English language media in their teenage years, like movies, books, and TV shows. Even at the time of the interview, they counted media-related activities among their central hobbies: one participant runs a queer book blog on a social media platform, another is interested in zine culture, and another engages with art films in their cinema studies degree and beyond. Crucially, in conversations about these activities and the way the participants link them to their English skills, the Anglophone sphere is mystified as the production site of large parts of globally circulating mass media, especially media that represents and speaks to the experiences of queer youth worldwide. For instance, Chris explained their and their friends' English skills through the absence of German-language queer media:

Excerpt Five

V: und was glaubst du, wieso können so viele leute in deinem umfeld so gut englisch?

Chris: *hm (---) ich (-) also ich glaube das liegt tatsächlich so 'n bisschen da dran dass einfach (-) ich weiß nicht <<laughing>queere menschen> sich mehr mit so englischen medien befassen mehr (-) einfach weil's vielleicht auch nicht so (-) im deutschen raum so viele (-) sachen gibt die man da (-) ja, die man (---) gucken kann, lesen kann, keine ahnung.*

V: and why do you think so many people in your environment speak english that well?

Chris: *hm i, well i think that's actually a bit because i don't know queer people spend more time with english media simply because there's not so many things in german you can watch or read, i don't know.*

Interestingly, the participants make a point to consume these media in the original language (English) rather than in the German translation. In fact, they report feeling uncomfortable and awkward when watching the German dubbed versions of movies or TV shows. In this context, the association of English with globalized mass media and progressive discourse around gender-sexuality intersects with a cosmopolitan understanding of 'authentic' media consumption. Further, the dominance of anglophone queer media is framed as a sign for the apparent suitability of English for the expression and representation of queer identities and discourse.

Openness and Accessibility

The aforementioned association of English with media consumption and subsequently also with queerness also is touched upon in Kim's account of the "special relationship" that queer communities have with the language:

Excerpt Six

Kim: [...] aber ich hab schon auch das gefühl dass queere communities (-) mehr 'nen bezug zum englischen haben (-) dadurch dass sie auch (---) glaub ich dieses bewusstsein und diese community durch das internet irgendwie gelernt (-) haben oder dadurch dass das da entstanden ist, so wie ja auch viele begriffe die es im deutschen erst mal nicht gibt einfach übernommen werden aus'm englischen genau so wie pronomen selbst also (-) das kommt jetzt glaub ich kommen jetzt 'n paar bücher raus wo tatsächlich auch dieses they als genderneutrale pronomen einfach so übernommen wird aus dem englischen

Kim: [...] but i do have the feeling that queer communities have more of a connection to english because they also i guess they have learned this awareness and this community through the internet somehow or because it emerged there, just like many terms that don't exist in german at first are simply taken over from english even pronouns. like i think there are going to be a couple of books who are released now where the "they" as a gender-neutral pronoun is actually adopted from english

The connection that Kim establishes between queerness and the internet is exceptionally fundamental, as they argue that speakers encounter queer discourse on the internet in the first place. Psychological and social science research has established that online spaces are of particular importance to queer youth (Byron et al., 2019; Cserni & Talmud, 2015; Hillier & Harrison, 2007). In the participants' narratives, however, their experiences as queer youth on the internet is directly linked to their English skills and the use of English in the group. The connection of queerness with the internet adds to the indexical linking of English with modernity and media addressed in the previous section.

Zooming in on the excerpt from Kim's interview, the underlined phrase, "because it emerged there", is particularly interesting. The speaker illustrates this statement with the adoption of the gender-neutral pronoun *they* into German. However, in re-reading the interview, I noticed that the referents of *es* ('it') and *da* ('there') are somewhat ambiguous. While *es* could refer to "this awareness and this community," *da* could refer both to the aforementioned Internet or, more abstractly, to the anglophone world. Either way, according to Kim, queer discourse and sense of community does not emerge locally. Based on linguistic variation in their everyday lives, where queer spaces versus non-queer spaces coincide with foreign language versus domestic language, the participants categorize queerness as "not from here."

German becomes synonymous with the familiar, established, heteronormative mainstream and English with the foreign, innovative, queer subculture. In Kim's statement about the adoption of the gender-neutral pronoun *they* into German, iconization, a semiotic process of language ideology defined by Irvine and Gal (2000), comes into play. Iconization refers to a change in the sign relationship from index (indicative) to icon (representative), which "entails the attribution of cause and immediate necessity to a connection (between linguistic features and social groups) that may only be historical, contingent, or conventional" (Irvine & Gal, 2000, 37). In the present example, the existence of singular *they* is seen as an iconic representation of queerness, which is thus understood as inherent to the English language and English-speaking spheres and absent from German and German-speaking spaces. As a consequence, it ideologically becomes necessary to 'import' linguistic features from the queer (-friendly) English into the heteronormative German.

Charlie also cited singular *they* as an example for the openness of English towards queerness:

Excerpt Seven

V: *[...] und wie ist das für dich, so auf 'ner anderen sprache als auf deutsch aktivistisch tätig zu sein?*

Charlie: *hm, ich find's auf englisch fast (-) einfacher würde ich sagen (-) grade was queere themen angeht weil es einfach sprachlich sehr viel einfacher glaub ich ist menschen anzusprechen. also zum beispiel they (-) gibt's im deutschen einfach nicht so, dass man das nutzen kann und auch wenn ich halt mit freunden oder über freunde sprech die they im englischen benutzen dann (-) dödelt man sich da immer so rum benutzt tausendmal den namen versucht irgendwie (-) die person zu sagen oder so. und im englischen ist es halt einfacher weil man einfach they benutzt und dann hat sich das so*

V: *ja*

Charlie: *deswegen glaube ich grade was queere themen angeht ist englisch (-) einfacher so*

V: *[...] and how is it for you to do activist work in another language than german?*

Charlie: *hm, i would even say it's easier in english i would say especially concerning queer issues because it's just linguistically much easier i think to address people. like for example they doesn't exist in german in a way where you can use it and also when i talk to friends or about friends who use they in english then you always muddle around using the name a thousand times trying to say die person or something.[4] and in english it's just easier because you just use they and then that's it like*

V: *yeah*

Charlie: *that's why i think especially when it comes to queer issues english is easier like*

What resonates in Charlie's assertion—that English is easy and flexible, and German is awkward and bulky—is the idea that English is open to queer discursive needs and German is not. More explicitly than in the previous excerpts, English and German are set against each other, which is common for linguistic identity production. In Eckert's words: "Local identity claims are about what it means to be from 'here' as opposed to some identified 'there.'" (2008, 462). In the case of the group, the ideological "here" claims transnationality and otherness and contrasts with the "there" of the heteronormative German mainstream. What is ultimately a linguistic phenomenon—singular *they*—is located as "part of, and evidence for" (Irvine & Gal, 2000, 37) the difference between open, inclusive queer communities and inaccessible, cis-heteronormative communities.

Part of this ideological conception of English as 'queer' and German as 'not queer' is that contradicting linguistic and extralinguistic phenomena are ignored ("erased") (Irvine & Gal, 2000, 38). For instance, singular *they* without an antecedent is a relatively recent phenomenon in English and remains controversial in some spaces, and the German-speaking trans movement has been and is giving impulse to de-gender the German language (Baumgartinger, 2007; s_he, 2010).

Youth and Subversiveness

It becomes evident that the participants strongly link the English part of their repertoire to their queer identity and queer activism. When German queer vocabulary was mentioned in the interviews, the participants distanced themselves from the terms: Luka laughed at *kesser Vater* (a German word for masculine lesbians), and Chris reported that saying the word *lesbisch* felt significantly more awkward to them than using the English equivalent *lesbian*. When talking about their study abroad experience in Paris, Robin brought up the term *schwul* (gay):

Excerpt Eight

Robin: *[...] und ich finde (-) es hat mich auch fasziniert wie selbstbewusst auch viele leute so mit französisch als ihrer sprache umgehen und auch so wie krass kreativ und (-) wie sehr damit irgendwie gespielt wird. weil dagegen ist deutsch halt schon echt (---) sperrig und irgendwie angestaubt und man weiß nie ((laugh)) also man hängt immer wieder so konstruktionen dran. ja und so ist es halt mit queeren begriffen irgendwie auch. also davon abgesehen dass queer schon mal 'n englischer begriff ist (---) aber auch so wenn ich jetzt sage okay man ist schwul zum beispiel also das ist auch so ich würde mal sagen die konnotation ist halt (-) ist halt auch so 'n bisschen angestaubt. also ich finde so schwulsein ist in deutschland schon auch so 'n bisschen konnotiert mit (-) keine ahnung so 'n bisschen die ära halt so achtziger neunziger so klaus wowereit so ((laugh))*

V: *((laugh)) hape kerkeling*

Robin: *ja genau so hape kerkeling. und das ist ist (---) das trifft's halt nicht mehr so genau für jüngere personen*

Robin: *[...] it also fascinated me how confidently many people deal with french as their language and also how blatantly creative and how much they play with it somehow. because in comparison german is just really bulky and kind of dusty and you never know ((laugh)) like you always append like constructions to it. yeah and it's the same with queer terms somehow. like apart from the fact that queer is an english term but also like when i say okay someone is schwul ['gay'] for example like that's also so i would say the connotation is just, is just also a bit dusty. like i think that being schwul in germany is also a bit connotated with i don't know like the eighties nineties era like klaus wowereit ((laugh))*

V: *((laugh)) hape kerkeling*

Robin: *yes exactly like hape kerkeling. and that is that's just not that accurate for younger people anymore*

In comparing French and German, Robin shares a common perception of the German language—that it is bulky and full of long and complicated words. Adding to this, Robin calls German "dusty", implying that the language is less modern than French. When talking about queer terms after this, however, Robin goes back to opposing German to English (instead of French), still asserting that German is "dusty". A word like *schwul*, they argue, is associated with outdated German gay discourse, which they underline by mentioning Berlin's former mayor Klaus Wowereit, who was among the first openly gay German politicians after his coming out in 2001. When I signaled my understanding by bringing up the comedian Hape Kerkeling, who was publicly outed in the 1990s, Robin agreed and stated that being *schwul* like Wowereit and Kerkeling (as opposed to *queer* like Robin) is antiquated. After this exchange, Robin expanded on what they associated with being *schwul*, which in particular is a gay political discourse that strives for recognition by the heteronormative mainstream through gay marriage and legal equality of gay parents. Robin, on the contrary, wants to subvert and contradict mainstream conceptions of gender-sexuality, love, and family. They attach this political claim to the use of the English word *queer* as opposed to the German *schwul*. In this way, the opposition salient on the intergroup level—between the English-speaking queer community and the German-speaking heteronormative mainstream—is projected onto the intracommunity level, a process which Irvine and Gal name fractal recursivity (2000, 38). German queer discourse is less open, less subversive, less modern, in short: less queer than its English equivalent.

Discussion

Indexical Meanings of English in the Group

As indicated by the data, English has context-specific indexical meanings in the group, some of which overlap with, and some of which differ from those of English in other communities in Berlin and in other cosmopolitan queer communities elsewhere. The participants' assessments of the appropriateness of code-switching within and outside of the communities reveal the strong metapragmatic awareness inherent in their repertoire management skills. In addition, their considerations of why English is so central to the group and to their personal lives reflect the semiotic processes (iconization, erasure, fractal recursivity) (Irvine & Gal, 2000) by which linguistic variation is 'charged' with social meaning.

Ultimately, the act of speaking English (and not German) is a manifestation of various related but distinct ideological oppositions. While they might seem contradictory at first, the positive connotation of English as the language of an open-minded, liberal cosmopolitanism and the negative association of English with an elitist, privileged imperialism, are ideologically related and their understanding depends on the situated use of the repertoire. As Eckert argues, which indexical meaning of a linguistic variable the hearers will understand in a specific context "will depend on both the perspective of the hearer and the style in which it is embedded – which includes not only the rest of the linguistic form of the utterance but the content of the utterance as well" (Eckert, 2008, 466).

While the participants directly link their relationship to English and the use of the language in the group to queerness, I would argue that the queer indexical meaning is actually constituted indirectly, through stances and qualities associated with contemporary transnational queer movements and individuals. In Ochs' words, the use of English "index[es] social meanings […], which in turn helps to constitute [gender-sexuality] meanings" (Ochs, 1992, 341). Speaking English in the group, then, does not index queerness per se, but activates the part of the indexical field of English that comprises the positive stances and qualities that the participants associate with queerness. When English is used outside of the group, that is, in non-queer contexts or by out-group speakers, the indexicality of English changes for the participants. Figure 1 is an illustration of the stances and qualities associated with English (in small caps) and German in and outside of the group encountered in the participants' evaluations of language use.

Figure 1. Indexical field of English and German in and outside of the group

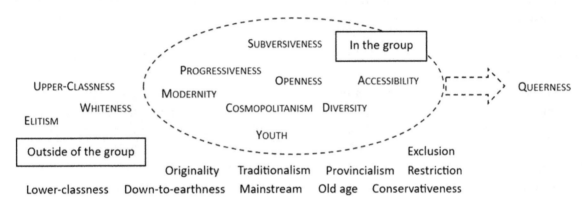

A key difference between the positive and negative connotation with English use seems to be whether the speakers see themselves as part of the group that speaks English or not. In the context of the group, English is a central language of belonging, a social cement that binds the group together in an us versus them mentality. Outside of discussions of queerness, English is understood as the language of the others, and the participants may be more likely to identify with the local majority language and their L1, German.

L2 Identity Construction

Certainly, the status of English as an L2 for the participants and as a "foreign language" in the Berlin context is of central importance for the indexical use of the language. As indicated above, the status of English as a "foreign language" also affects its indexical use in the group, precisely because it is not-German and, as such, not-familiar and not-same. At the same time, it is not as directly linked to an ethnically or culturally distinct group in Berlin, but rather to a network of detached groups and discourses. The use of English as a language of an abstract Otherness in a majority German-speaking context, then, likely contributes to its socio-indexical meaning of "different" and "not mainstream" and provides a surface onto which the speakers can project their concept of queer identity.

Second language acquisition researchers have established that identity construction and membership in imagined communities is a central motivation for language learners, especially in the context of schools and immigration processes (Block, 2007; Kanno & Norton, 2003; Norton, 2000; Norton, 2006; Pavlenko & Norton, 2007; Peirce Norton, 1995; Tsung, 2015). As Peters maintains, "[t]he L2 speaker's investments in language learning or use are dependent upon the identities available to them in the L2, where they may find unusual outlets of self-representation, adopting stances to assimilate to the community or be active in multiple or mixed communities, creating mixed sociolinguistic identities, or reject them altogether, finding them incompatible" (Peters, 2016, 182–183). This is supported by my findings, where the participants report to have found large parts of their intrinsic motivation to acquire English through their queer identity and directly or indirectly related engagements with media and online communities. Coming of age and coming out are often seen as processes of departure and detachment from family and context of origin. As a consequence, the participants' recollection of learning English as part of their search for belonging during and after these formative years might play a role in the ideological linking of English with queerness and German with heteronormativity.

Further, as Minning (2004) points out, the use of English terms in taboo subject areas such as gender-sexuality allows German speakers to be less direct and, thus, less provocative. Research on affective dimensions of L2 usage suggests that the L1 is more strongly associated with direct emotional involvement of the speaker, while languages acquired in the teenage years allow speakers to keep a cooler head (Dewaele & Pavlenko, 2002). In the context of non-normative sexual identities, indirectness is known as an important face-saving strategy. For instance, Provencher reports that the queer imam and theorist Ludovic-Mohamed Zahed adopts face-saving strategies when talking about his gender-sexuality by saying that he is "going out with guys" or "with men" and not using more direct statements such as "I am a homosexual", "I am gay" or "I sleep with men" (Provencher, 2017, 115). In Berlin, English terms for gender-sexuality do not have the same discursive history as in English-speaking contexts. A word like *queer*, for instance, has a history of linguistic reclamation in English and remains subject to controversy and discussion today (Butler, 2011; Stollznow, 2020). In German, however, *queer* simply means "not heterosexual" (Duden, n.d.). The indexical meaning and affective dimension of language use is influenced by this discursive history, as language historically associated with particular groups, registers, and opinions may elicit stronger reactions than a borrowing, code-switch, or change of repertoire. Thus, through the use of English and English-based terms, discourses and terms that might threaten the heteronormative order can stay under the radar and provocation is avoided.

CONCLUSION

In this chapter, I have analyzed the use of English as constitutive of the queer identity of members of a queer community of practice in Berlin, Germany. Through the semiotic charging of English with social meanings associated with transnationalism, mobility, and openness, English and German are juxtaposed alongside a variety of ideological dichotomies, the sum of which result in the dichotomy queer vs. heteronormative in the context of the group. The multilingual context of early 2020s Berlin—where English, while omnipresent in some areas, is still considered a "foreign language"—and the fact that English is an L2 for the participants allows the use of English to be a way for them to distance themselves linguistically from the majority language, German, and ideologically from the heteronormative mainstream society. Further, the participants report feeling less emotionally comfortable with German queer vocabulary than with English terms, suggesting that the affective dimension of the L2 impacts the participants' language use and, as a result, their language ideology.

Focusing on queer identity-based motivations for repertoire management in a community of practice where the unmarked standard is an L2 for the members raises some interesting conceptual questions. While sociolinguistic, especially variationist research often relies on locally situated concepts of identity and community, the participants of this study have a concept of identity and community that significantly feeds on the global and the transnational. They construct their local authenticity as cosmopolitan queers precisely by being non-authentic and non-local. What's more, the line between "native language" and "foreign language", considered outdated by many in the discipline (Birkeland et al., 2023) is blurred in a particular way. All participants are L1 German speakers and live in a seemingly predominantly German-speaking context. Yet, studying their use of German would not have surfaced the questions of English versus German which seem to make up large parts of their day-to-day negotiations of language use.

Rapid globalization and the propagation of digital capitalism serve as a catalyst for the emergence of more and more dynamic phenomena of language contact—of which the use of English by a group of queer L2 speakers in Berlin is only a tiny sliver. In light of this, researchers and language workers alike are required to rethink their theoretical frameworks and analytical concepts. One thing is certain: In order to fully account for the plurality of multilingual experiences, it is essential to include language learners and L2 speakers.

ACKNOWLEDGMENT

Thanks to my consultants whose insights allowed me to explore a unique facet of L2 use in Berlin and share it with a wider audience. I am deeply grateful for their openness and vulnerability in this process, and hope that I have done justice to their accounts. Thanks to Helen Sauntson, Ferdinand von Mengden, and Laura S. Griffin for their valuable feedback on this project. Thanks to the audience at Lavender Languages & Linguistics 28 in Catania, where I presented an earlier version of this research. Lastly, thanks to the editors of this volume and to the anonymous reviewers whose comments were a tremendous help in finishing this chapter.

REFERENCES

Amin, K. (2022). We are all nonbinary: A brief history of accidents. *Representations (Berkeley, Calif.)*, *158*(1), 106–119. doi:10.1525/rep.2022.158.11.106

Anderson, B. (2006). *Imagined communities. Reflections on the origin and spread of nationalism* (Revised Edition). Verso.

Baines, C. (2015). Seven rules for not being 'one of those' expats in Berlin. *Xtra**. https://xtramagazine.com/travel/seven-rules-for-not-being-one-of-those-expats-in-berlin-68725

Baumgartinger, P. P. (2007). Geschlechtergerechte Sprache? Über queere widerständige Strategien gegen diskriminierenden Sprachalltag. *Stimme von und für Minderheiten*, *62*, 16–17.

Besnier, N. (2002). Transgenderism, locality and the Miss Galaxy beauty pageant in Tonga. *American Ethnologist*, *29*(3), 534–566. doi:10.1525/ae.2002.29.3.534

Besnier, N. (2004). Consumption and cosmopolitanism: Practicing modernity at the secondhand marketplace in Nuku'alofa, Tonga. *Anthropological Quarterly*, *77*(1), 7–45. doi:10.1353/anq.2004.0002

Besnier, N., & Philips, S. U. (2014). Ethnographic methods for language and gender research. In S. Ehrlich, M. Meyerhoff, & J. Holmes (Eds.), *The Handbook of Language, Gender, and Sexuality* (2nd ed., pp. 123–140). Wiley-Blackwell. doi:10.1002/9781118584248.ch6

BirkelandA.BlockA.CraftJ. T.SedarousY.WuA.NamboordiripadS. (2022). Towards a linguistics free of "native speakerhood". Psyarxiv. https://psyarxiv.com/ektmf/ doi:10.31234/osf.io/ektmf

Block, D. (2007). Second Language Identities. *Continuum*.

Blom, J., & Gumperz, J. J. (1972). Social meaning in linguistic structure: Code-switching in Norway. In J. J. Gumperz & D. Hymes (Eds.), *Directions in Sociolinguistics. The Ethnography of Communication* (pp. 407–434). Holt, Rinehart and Winston.

Blommaert, J. (2012). Supervernaculars and their dialects. *Dutch Journal of Applied Linguistics*, *1*(1), 1–14. doi:10.1075/dujal.1.1.03blo

Braun, V., & Clarke, V. (2006). Using thematic analysis in psychology. *Qualitative Research in Psychology*, *3*(2), 77–101. doi:10.1191/1478088706qp063oa

Braun, V., & Clarke, V. (2019). Reflecting on reflexive thematic analysis. *Qualitative Research in Sport, Exercise and Health*, *11*(4), 589–597. doi:10.1080/2159676X.2019.1628806

Bucholtz, M., & Hall, K. (2005). Identity and interaction: A sociocultural linguistic approach. *Discourse Studies*, *7*(4/5), 585–614. doi:10.1177/1461445605054407

Butler, J. (2011). Critically queer. In *Bodies that matter: On the discursive limits of sex* (pp. 169–185). Routledge. doi:10.4324/9780203828274-15

Byron, P., Robards, B., Hanckel, B., Vivienne, S., & Churchill, B. (2019). "Hey, I'm having these experiences": Tumblr use and young people's queer (dis)connections. *International Journal of Communication*, *13*, 2239–2259.

Cserni, R. T., & Talmud, I. (2015). To know that you are not alone: The effect of internet usage on LGBT youth's social capital. In L. Robinson, S. R. Cotton, & J. Schulz (Eds.), *Communication and information technologies annual: Politics, participation, and production* (pp. 161–182). Emerald. doi:10.1108/S2050-206020150000009007

Dewaele, J.-M., & Pavlenko, A. (2002). Emotion vocabulary in interlanguage. *Language Learning*, *52*(2), 263–322. doi:10.1111/0023-8333.00185

Dubois, B. L., & Crouch, I. (1975). The question of tag questions in women's speech: They don't really use more of them, do they? *Language in Society*, *4*(3), 289–294. https://www.jstor.org/stable/4166832. doi:10.1017/S0047404500006680

Duden. (n.d.). Queer. *Duden online*. https://www.duden.de/rechtschreibung/queer

Eckert, P. (2008). Variation and the indexical field. *Journal of Sociolinguistics*, *12*(4), 453–476. doi:10.1111/j.1467-9841.2008.00374.x

Eckert, P., & McConnell-Ginet, S. (1992). Think practically and look locally: Language and gender as community-based practice. *Annual Review of Anthropology*, *21*(1), 461–490. doi:10.1146/annurev.an.21.100192.002333

Farrell, E. (2019). Language, economy, and the international artist community in Berlin. In T. Heyd, B. Schneider, & F. v. Mengden (Eds.), *The Sociolinguistic Economy of Berlin. Cosmopolitan Perspectives on Language, Diversity and Social Space* (pp. 145–166). De Gruyter. doi:10.1515/9781501508103-007

Fishman, J. A. (1965). Who speaks what language to whom and when? *La Linguistique* 1(2), 67–88. https://www.jstor.org/stable/30248773

Fishman, J. A. (1967). Bilingualism with and without diglossia; diglossia with and without bilingualism. *The Journal of Social Issues*, *23*(2), 29–38. doi:10.1111/j.1540-4560.1967.tb00573.x

Guest, G., MacQueen, K. M., & Namey, E. E. (2012). *Applied thematic analysis*. Sage. doi:10.4135/9781483384436

Gumperz, J. J. (1972). Introduction. In J. J. Gumperz & D. Hymes (Eds.), *Directions in Sociolinguistics. The Ethnography of Communication* (pp. 1–26). Holt, Rinehart and Winston.

Hall, K. (2009). Boys' talk: Hindi, moustaches and masculinity in New Delhi. In P. Pichler & E. Eppler (Eds.), *Gender and Spoken Language in Interaction* (pp. 139–162). Palgrave MacMillan. doi:10.1057/9780230280748_7

Heyd, T., & Schneider, B. (2019). Anglophone practices in Berlin: From historical evidence to transnational communities. In R. Hickey (Ed.), *English in the German-Speaking World* (pp. 143–164). Cambridge University Press. doi:10.1017/9781108768924.008

Hilal, M., & Varatharajah, S. (2022). *Englisch in Berlin. Ausgrenzungen in einer kosmopolitischen Gesellschaft/English in Berlin. Exclusions in a Cosmopolitan Society*. Wirklichkeit Books.

Hillier, L., & Harrison, L. (2007). Building realities less limited than their own: Young people practicing same-sex attraction on the Internet. *Sexualities*, *10*(1), 82–100. doi:10.1177/1363460707072956

Irvine, J. T., & Gal, S. (2000). Language ideology and linguistic differentiation. In P. V. Kroskrity (Ed.), *Regimes of Language: Ideologies, Polities, and Identities* (pp. 35–84). School of American Research Press.

Johnstone, B. (2006). A new role for narrative in variationist sociolinguistics. *Narrative Inquiry*, *16*(1), 46–55. doi:10.1075/ni.16.1.08joh

Johnstone, B., Andrews, J., & Danielson, A. E. (2006). Mobility, indexicality, and the enregisterment of "Pittsburghese". *Journal of English Linguistics*, *34*(2), 77–104. doi:10.1177/0075424206290692

Kanno, Y., & Norton, B. (2003). Imagined communities and educational possibilities: Introduction. *Journal of Language, Identity, and Education*, *2*(4), 241–249. doi:10.1207/S15327701JLIE0204_1

Lakoff, R. (1973). Language and woman's place. *Language in Society*, *2*(1), 45–80. https://www.jstor.org/stable/4166707. doi:10.1017/S0047404500000051

Leap, W. L. (2005). Finding the centre: claiming gay space in Cape Town, South Africa. In M. van Zyl & M. Steyn (Eds.), *Performing Queer: Shaping Sexualities 1992-2004* (pp. 235–266). Kwela Press.

Leap, W. L. (2010). Globalization and gay language. In N. Coupland (Ed.), *The Handbook of Language and Globalization* (pp. 555–574). Wiley-Blackwell. doi:10.1002/9781444324068.ch25

Leap, W. L. (2015). Queer linguistics as Critical Discourse Analysis. In D. Tannen, H. E. Hamilton, & H. Schiffrin (Eds.), *The Handbook of Discourse Analysis*. Wiley-Blackwell. doi:10.1002/9781118584194.ch31

Malmgren, S. (2011). Gentrification: Stop blaming foreigners! *Exberliner*. Retrieved on August 4, 2023 from https://www.exberliner.com/berlin/gentrification/

Massad, J. (2002). Re-Orienting desire: The gay international and the Arab world. *Public Culture*, *14*(2), 361–385. doi:10.1215/08992363-14-2-361

Matras, Y. (2009). *Language contact*. Cambridge University Press. doi:10.1017/CBO9780511809873

Mendoza, M. (2011). Neukölln Nasties. Foreigners Feel Accused in Berlin Gentrification Row. *Spiegel International*. https://www.spiegel.de/international/germany/neukoelln-nasties-foreigners-feel-accused-in-berlin-gentrification-row-a-750297.html

Minning, H. (2004). Qwir-English code-mixing in Germany: constructing a rainbow of identities. In T. Boellstorff & W. Leap (Eds.), *Speaking in Queer Tongues. Globalization and Gay Language* (pp. 46–71). University of Illinois Press.

Myers-Scotton, C. (1995). *Social motivations for code-switching: Evidence from Africa*. Oxford University Press.

Myers-Scotton, C. (Ed.). (1998). *Codes and consequences: Choosing linguistic varieties*. Oxford University Press.

Norton, B. (2000). *Identity and language learning: Gender, ethnicity, and educational change*. Longman.

Norton, B. (2006). Identity: Second language. Encyclopedia of Language & Linguistics, 5, 502–508.

Ochs, E. (1992). Indexing gender. In A. Duranti & C. Goodwin (Eds.), *Rethinking Context: Language as an Interactive Phenomenon* (pp. 335–358). Cambridge University Press.

Pavlenko, A., & Norton, B. (2007). Imagined communities, identity, and English language learning. In J. Cummins & C. Davison (Eds.), *International Handbook of English Language Teaching* (pp. 669–680). Springer. doi:10.1007/978-0-387-46301-8_43

PehlT.DresingT. (2015a). *f4transkript*. Audio Transkription. https://www.audiotranskription.de

Pehl, T. & Dresing, T. (2015b). *f4analyse*. Audio Transkripition. https://www.audiotranskription.de

Norton Peirce, B. (1995). Social identity, investment, and language learning. *TESOL Quarterly*, *29*(1), 9–31. doi:10.2307/3587803

Perinelli, M. (2019). Triggerwarnung! Critical Whiteness und das Ende antirassistischer Bewegung. In E. Berendsen, S.-N. Cheema, & M. Mendel (Eds.), *Trigger Warnung. Identitätspolitik zwischen Abwehr, Abschottung und Allianzen* (pp. 77–90). Verbrecherverlag.

Peters, M. A. (2016). Language attitudes and identity construction. A case study among two L2 attritors. In M. Fernández-Villanueva & K. Jungbluth (Eds.), *Beyond Language Boundaries. Multimodal Use in Multilingual Contexts* (pp. 179–199). De Gruyter. doi:10.1515/9783110458817-011

Provencher, D. (2017). *Queer Maghrebi French*. Liverpool University Press.

Rooke, A. (2010). Queer in the field: On emotions, temporality, and performativity in ethnography. In K. Browne & C. J. Nash (Eds.), *Queer Methods and Methodologies. Intersecting Queer Theories and Social Science Research* (pp. 25–41). Ashgate. doi:10.1080/10894160802695338

Sauntson, H. (2022). Reflexivity and the production of shared meanings in language and sexuality research. In S. Consoli & S. Ganassin (Eds.), *Reflexivity in Applied Linguistics Research: Opportunities, Challenges and Suggestions*. Routledge. doi:10.4324/9781003149408-10

Schneider, B. (2012). Is English a local language in Berlin? In *Language on the Move*. https://www.languageonthemove.com/is-english-a-local-language-in-berlin/

Schneider, B. (2020). Language in transnational communities of consumption. Indexical functions of English in third-wave coffee culture. In S. Rüdiger & S. Mühleisen (Eds.), *Talking about Food. The Social and the Global in Eating Communities* (pp. 79–96). Benjamins. doi:10.1075/impact.47.05sch

Selting, M., Auer, P., Barth-Weingarten, D., Bergmann, J.R., Bergmann, P., Birkner, K., Couper-Kuhlen, E., Deppermann, A., Gilles, P., Günthner, S., Hartung, M., Kern, F., Mertzlufft, C., Meyer, C., Morek, M., Oberzaucher, F., Peters, J., Quasthoff, U., Schütte, W., Stukenbrock, A. & Uhmann, S. (2011). A system for transcribing talk-in-interaction: GAT 2 (E. Couper-Kuhlen & D. Weingarten, Trans.). *Gesprächsforschung. Online-Zeitschrift zur verbalen Interaktion* 12, 1–51. (2009)

s_he (2010). Performing the Gap. Queere Gestalten und geschlechtliche Aneignung. *arranca!* 28(7).

Silverstein, M. (2003). Indexical order and the dialectics of sociolinguistic life. *Language & Communication*, 23(3-4), 193–229. doi:10.1016/S0271-5309(03)00013-2

Spahn, J. (2017). Berliner Cafés: Sprechen Sie doch deutsch! In *ZEIT online*. Retrieved on March 13, 2023, from https://www.zeit.de/2017/35/berlin-cafes-hipster-englisch-sprache-jens-spahn

Stollznow, K. (2020). Not that there's anything wrong with that. In On the Offensive: Prejudice in Language Past and Present (pp. 96–123). Cambridge University Press. doi:10.1017/9781108866637.004

Tsung, L. (2015). Multiple identities and second language learning in Hong Kong. In D. N. Djenar, A. Mahboob, & K. Cruickshank (Eds.), *Language and Identity Across Modes of Communication* (pp. 107–124). De Gruyter Mouton. doi:10.1515/9781614513599.107

ENDNOTES

[1] In the context of this chapter, I use "L2" to refer to a language acquired outside of the home and in adolescence or later.
[2] A term proposed by Amin, who argues that "the two are, in reality, indissociable" (2022, 107).

3   *Grindr* is a popular, mostly gay male mobile dating app.
4   To avoid gendered nouns or pronouns, some German speakers repeat the name of the referent or use *die Person* 'the person', as in: *Ich habe gestern Kim besucht. Kims Wohnung war sehr schön. Die Person interessiert sich sehr für Inneneinrichtung* ('I visited Kim yesterday. Kim's apartment was very nice. The person is very interested in interior design').

Chapter 2
Negotiating Language and Cultural Identity in Multicultural Contexts in Canada

Ariel Quinio
University of Toronto, Canada

ABSTRACT

This chapter aims to explore and examine the role of language in the integration to the community of practice (CoP) of a culturally diverse group of participants, the Internationally Educated Professionals (IEPs) in Canada. Based on interpretive qualitative research and Bourdieu's theory as a lens, an in-depth interview, survey questionnaire and policy document data were analyzed using critical discourse analysis and the grounded theory. A selection of 30 IEP participants were divided into three categories according to their year of arrival. Findings reveal four different classes of IEPs and explain how they negotiate their language and cultural identity to integrate in their CoP post-migration. Results offer implications for reconceptualizing language norms, policies and practices in multicultural contexts.

INTRODUCTION

This chapter aims to provide a deeper understanding of the role of language in negotiating the cultural identity of Internationally Educated Professionals (IEPs) in Canada, commonly known as "foreign-trained immigrants," identify the emerging themes that explain their employment successes or failures, and describe how their professional status has changed post-migration. Considering the new immigration plan to meet the current labour market shortages (IRCC, 2022), there continues a need for research studies to inform policy-makers on how immigrants over the past decades negotiate to integrate in the Canadian society and the economy. Based on a research study (Quinio, 2015), the role of the researcher as an IEP was to systematically explore and examine the hidden relationships between employment practices and the wider social structures as determined by policies on language use and ability (CIC, 2012). This study sought to investigate how such practices, events or texts were developed and ideologically shaped by social relations of power. Within this analytical framework (Guba & Lincoln, 1994; Fairclough, 1989, 1992),

DOI: 10.4018/978-1-6684-8761-7.ch002

the objective was to relate and corroborate the researcher's experiences with each study participant in comparable groups with whom they shared similar worldviews within the periphery of qualitative inquiry.

The study is situated in the context of a changing policy landscape, fluctuating economic conditions, and the increasing trends of globalization and migration. As a result of deteriorating conditions in periphery countries and a perceived advantage of living in more wealthy developed nations (Laquian & Laquian, 2008; McKay, 2002; Rodriquez, 2010), there has been an increasing trend in the migration of foreign-trained immigrants from the periphery nations to dominant countries with more developed economies (Apple, 2005). The influx of immigrants to the Global North with different knowledge and ways of seeing the world often results in contradictions within the dominant society (Gutmann, 2004), and can generate many forms of bias that serve as barriers for IEPs' socioeconomic integration and employment success. For the purpose of this book, this chapter is limited to answering two major research questions based on the study results: (1) How do different groups of IEPs negotiate their language backgrounds and cultural identities to integrate in their community of practice (CoP)? (2) What are the roles of language and the emerging themes that describe the integration experiences of IEPs, and explain the need to reconceptualize the existing language norms?

REVIEW OF LITERATURE AND THEORETICAL FRAMEWORK

Drawing from findings that the changing policies and macroeconomic conditions can impact the successful integration of immigrants in the socioeconomic arena of the host society (Alboim & MacIsaac, 2007; Boyd & Cao, 2009; Chiswick, Cohen, & Zach, 1997; Pendakur & Pendakur, 2012), this study seeks to explain the negotiation experiences of IEPs in employment as determined by many factors particularly their language and cultural identities at the time of their arrival over the two-decade period from 1988 to 2008. Although a consistent pattern emerged in the literature that language proficiency (Aydemir & Skuterud, 2004; Derwing & Waugh, 2012; Esser, 2006; Green & Worswick, 2004; Statistics Canada, 2005) and the contextual factors of employment (Block & Galabuzi, 2011; Picot & Hou, 2012; Reitz, 2001, 2007a, 2007b,) are among the dominant factors influencing the social and economic integration of immigrants in Canada, many of these related studies are purely quantitative and often positivistic in orientation. This study was designed to provide a rich narrative account of the IEPs' diverse cultural identities, language negotiation and integration experiences that seemed to be lacking in this area of interest.

The analytical approach used in this present study can be distinguished from the existing literature (Aydemir, 2003; McDonald & Worswick, 1997; Statistics Canada, 2005) in terms of the epistemological stance employed in previous studies with their positivist orientation such that the impact of macroeconomic conditions were controlled with the differences in the class composition of immigrant cohorts and their year of arrival. Although it is nearly impossible to determine the cohort effects of immigrants on their employment outcomes with the limited number of cases in this qualitative study, except with their level of income as an indicator of favourable or unfavourable economic conditions during their year of arrival, the rich narrative account of each individual participant according to their year of arrival can provide a meaningful basis for identifying the different employment barriers that different groups of immigrants may be confronting as they negotiate their different language backgrounds and cultural identities. Furthermore, the rich narrative account of each individual participant may not be captured adequately in the positivist approach, but such detail was made possible in this present study. These details may be useful in determining what particular policy will work for a particular group of immigrants.

Identity Negotiation and Cultural Frames

Previous studies show that language and accents of Native English Speakers (NES) are consistently and positively associated with higher income (Aydemir & Skuterud, 2004). Sources of work-related discrimination or unfair treatment (Kelly et al., 2009) provide a sound basis for conducting a study in this area. The knowledge of official languages was found to be significantly and positively associated with the probability of finding an appropriate job by new Canadian immigrants as revealed in the Statistics Canada (2005) study on Longitudinal Survey of Immigrants to Canada (LSIC). This result is important in the present study providing a solid theoretical framework which observed cohorts of immigrants over the span of four years after their arrival in Canada.

In this chapter, *negotiation* has been operationally defined as an assertion of an IEP in relation to individual factors including but not limited to language backgrounds and cultural identities for the purpose of finding employment in his/her intended profession. Thus, it could mean any attempt made by an IEP to integrate in his or her intended profession or community of practice or CoP (Wenger, 1998). The negotiation of language and cultural identity among the IEPs is akin to their specific traits or characteristics as presented in the emerging results of the present study. Kelly et al.'s (2009) findings on the work culture and racialization among Filipino IEPs informed this present research on how the employment experiences of this particular group of immigrants were positioned in their new working environment. This emerging theme in the literature is consistent with Jenkins' (2000) findings, which found differences in cultural frames of reference between work superiors and their subordinates. Cultural frames can be understood within the dynamics of interactional linguistics (Gumperz, 1992; Kerekes, 2005) involving employment practices of Canadian employers that could be an important factor influencing how the IEPs negotiate their language and cultural identities.

Language Norms and Employment Practices

Although human capital theory (Bowles & Gintis, 1975) is a widely accepted framework that puts great emphasis on the education and training of individual workers as a form of investment with the expectation of future economic success and better lives in the general population, Reitz (2005) adopted a more pragmatic view of this concept. Reitz implicates the actions of employers and the institutional process in the employment of immigrants. "When employers respond to information about the job-relevant skills presented by [job applicants], they are actually relying on a fairly elaborate set of institutional supports, which may not work as effectively when the applicants are skilled immigrants" (p. 5). Clearly, there is evidence suggesting that the underutilization of immigrants' skills can be traced from employers' biases, short-sightedness and failure to assess the productive value of foreign-trained immigrants for the perpetuation of the existing norms of Canadian employment that are based on postcolonial white supremacy and native English speakers' ideology. This argument - proposed in this chapter - is well supported in the literature (Gibb, 2008; Peters, 2011; Reis, 2011; Steinert, 2006).

Bourdieu's Theory

Given the context of the study, Bourdieu's (1977; 1984; 1986) theory of social and cultural reproduction was used to shape the nature of this inquiry. Bourdieu's theory explains that the individual's economic, cultural and social goods (*capital*) that he owns including his dispositions or ways of thinking resulting from his economic and cultural backgrounds (*habitus*) and the social context such as educational institution, a government body or workplace setting (*field*) with its own set of practices, values, rules or policies are capable of producing and reproducing similar practices and adopting similar stances resulting in class inequality (Harker et al., 1990).

As a theoretical lens, Bourdieu's theory informs this study and provides directions and insights into how to explore, examine and explain language negotiation and cultural identity among IEPs. The concept of social closure and exclusivity as status hierarchies, competition for honour, and standards of professional practice is explored in Bourdieu's (1977; 1984; 1986) theory of social and cultural reproduction using the concepts of class inequality, habitus, cultural capital, and field. Bourdieu's theory provides a useful framework for the analysis of the interviews and narratives of the IEP participants in this study.

Critical Discourse Analysis as Theory and Methodology

On the critical perspective, the epistemological stance of this inquiry was approached according to the tenets of Critical Discourse Analysis (CDA) as a theory and methodology (Fairclough, 1989; 1992; Fairclough & Wodak, 1997; Van Dijk, 1997; 1998). As a theory, CDA is "fundamentally interested in analyzing opaque as well as transparent structural relationships of dominance, discrimination, power and control as manifested to language" (Wodak & Meyer, 2009, p. 10). From this perspective, the goal of CDA is to critically investigate social inequality as it is expressed, constituted and legitimized by language use or discourse.

As a theoretical lens, CDA was used to critique and challenge existing language norms and policies as part of the immigration and employment of IEPs in Canada (federal government) and Ontario (provincial government) with the goal of achieving greater socioeconomic equity and promoting a more equitable social integration of visible ethnic minorities. This study inquired into the nature of power relations using narratives from in-depth interviews and survey data in the Canadian workplace. It examined how the existing language norms in multicultural contexts advance the increasing inequities in employment opportunities between IEPs and non-IEPs.

METHODS

To address the research questions set forth in this study, a variant of interpretive qualitative study design called the *multiple embedded case study* with essential components of *grounded theory* and *critical research* were used (Creswell, 1994). The *multiple embedded case study* (Yin, 2003), sometimes referred to simply as *multiple case studies,* also known as *comparative case study* (Merriam, 2009) or *collective case study* (Stake, 1995) is an in-depth and detailed description and analysis of categorically bounded systems (cases) through the collection of multiple sources of information. In this study, the multiple cases were primarily composed of IEPs who were bounded by the well-defined selection criteria and embedded into various categories and sub-categories as units of analysis for the purpose of comparison and contrast. In this design, the IEPs were divided into different categories according to their ethnicity (Filipino IEPs and IEPs from Other Cultures), integration into their community of practice (IEPs CoP and IEPs Non-CoP), year of arrival in Canada, and professional backgrounds (see Figure 1). *IEPs CoP* refers to participants who were members of their community of practice or those who have been integrated into their profession or found employment in their intended occupation in Canada. On the other hand,

IEPs Non-CoP are those participants who were not members of their community of practice or have not found employment in their intended profession even long after they arrived in Canada. According to specific selection criteria, a total of 30 IEP participants were selected within the Greater Toronto Area during the 8-month data collection period (August 2013 to March 2014) using the snowball sampling technique. An institutional research ethics board of the university approved the ethics review protocol for this study based on guidelines for collection of data involving human subjects.

Data Collection

There were two types of data collection instruments used, including the survey questionnaire called, *Employment Experiences Questionnaire (EEQ)* and a separate semi-structured *Interview Schedule*. The Employment Experiences Questionnaire is a 50-item rating scale designed to collect basic information on the socio-demographic background of the IEPs. The questionnaire was used to assess and evaluate their perceived levels of English language proficiency based on their level of confidence in spoken English and determine their level of job satisfaction, employment experiences, and how specific social, linguistic, cultural and contextual factors influenced their employment successes or failures since the time of their immigration to Canada. The individual responses of the IEP participants were used as a supplementary data collection tool that guided the researcher to further explore the employment negotiation and integration experiences of IEPs during in-depth interviews, in addition to the semi-structured interview schedule. The semi-structured interview schedule was the primary data collection tool and consisted of mainly open-ended questions intended to explore the negotiation and integration experiences of the IEPs. This was triangulated with the IEPs' responses from the EEQ to further substantiate and verify the information that they provided. To protect the privacy of the personal information of participants, a pseudonym was used for each respondent throughout the study according to the ethical standards of this research.

Figure 1. The interpretive qualitative multiple embedded case study showing the units of analysis

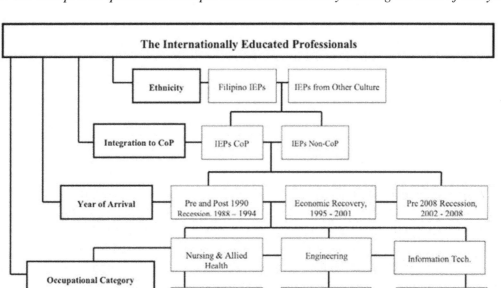

Analytic Procedures

A purely descriptive methodology using the interpretive qualitative analytic approach was employed in data analysis. The two basic qualitative analytic approaches used in this study were *critical discourse analysis* and *the constant comparative method* of grounded theory (Strauss & Glaser, 1967). Theoretical sampling and the constant comparative method were applied when analyzing other data sources including questionnaire and policy documents (see Appendix C) using *within-case* and *cross-case analysis*. In each approach, the data collected from survey questionnaires, in-depth interviews, field notes, and policy documents were pre-coded and presented in matrices and tabular formats. This facilitated the comparisons and contrasting of textual evidence according to patterns and common themes that emerged in participants' responses. Interviews were audio recorded and carefully transcribed in detail. A system of coding categories using the QSR NVivo 10 software was used to explore, examine and summarize the participants' responses based on the transcriptions of the in-depth interview for data reduction purposes.

FINDINGS

Participants were categorized according to group categories: CoP, employment trajectories, and the *study context*, which refers to the time or year of their arrival in Canada. A summary of the socio-demographic profile of the 30 IEP participants was presented in Appendix B including other characteristics such as gender, age group, ethnicity, educational attainment, and professional backgrounds. Moreover, participants were divided into three group categories according to the study context or year of their arrival in Canada where they were distributed in each of the seven-year periods: 1988–1994 (Pre and Post 1990 Recession), 1995–2001 (Economic Recovery), and 2002–2008 (Pre 2008 Recession).

Integration and Satisfaction: Negotiating Language and Cultural Identity According to Four Classes of IEPs

Results of the present study show that negotiating language and cultural identity that results in the employment success or failure among the IEPs can be determined not only by their employment trajectory and their resulting shifts in professional status, but also by their integration or lack of integration into their intended profession in conjunction with level of job satisfaction. In this study, the IEPs' employment trajectory can be described as either curvature or straight. The main difference between curvature and straight path employment trajectories depends on the direction of the employment experiences among the IEPs where *curvature path* refers to frequency of their job changes or movements, and a *straight path* is characterized by less and/or no movement in various occupational categories since their arrival in Canada from their first job to their present job. A notable finding revealed that not all of the IEPs who were integrated had a straight path employment trajectory; rather, many of them passed through a curvature path leading to their success. Therefore, it only makes sense that the criteria for success in negotiating language and cultural identities among the IEPs cannot be based solely on their employment trajectory and shift in professional status but most importantly on their integration or lack of integration into their profession. However, as this present study's results reveal, some IEPs who were not integrated or employed in unrelated occupations (UO) such as general labourers or warehouse workers had also reported a considerable level of satisfaction in their employment, meaning it is important to define success not only in terms of integration into the intended profession but also according to the individual's level of job satisfaction. Thus, negotiating language and cultural identities resulting in the employment success or failure among the IEPs cannot be explained solely in terms of their employment trajectories and shifts in professional status but results could rather be analyzed and interpreted according to their integration or lack of integration into their intended profession or CoP in relation to their level of job satisfaction or dissatisfaction. This basic analytical frame resulted in the categorization of IEPs according to their characteristics as determined by the four principles of integration-satisfaction: *integrated and satisfied, not integrated but satisfied, integrated but not satisfied,* and *not integrated and not satisfied.*

Figure 2 illustrates the four principles describing the fundamental relationships between integration into the intended profession and job satisfaction among IEPs that explained their language negotiation and cultural identities based on the study results. The principles suggest two important dimensions of integration among the IEPs: First, the "movements or directions of integration" as to either *moving to* (upward) or *moving away* (downward) from the intended profession; and second, the "levels or nature of job satisfaction" as to either *satisfied* (positive) or *not satisfied* (negative).

Figure 2. Negotiating language and cultural identity according to four classes of IEPs (Adapted from Quinio, 2015, p. 212)

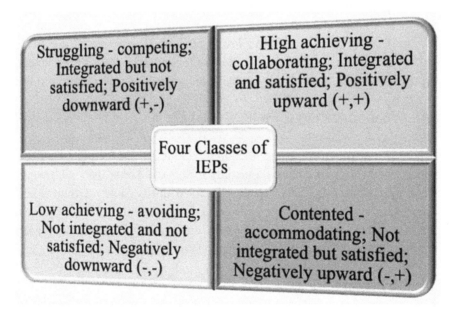

In this manner, the four principles of integration and satisfaction in employment among the IEPs can be drawn in a matrix describing the dimensions of the relationship; that is, the "directions" (movements) and "nature" (levels) of integration and satisfaction into four basic types: *positively upward* (integrated and satisfied), *positively downward* (integrated but not satisfied), *negatively upward* (not integrated but satisfied), and *negatively downward* (not integrated and not satisfied). The four principles describing the integration-satisfaction relationship resulted in four classes of IEPs, describing and explaining their negotiation strategies and distinguishing characteristics: First, the "high achieving - collaborating IEPs" include those who were integrated in their intended profession or CoP and at the same time satisfied with their job *(integrated and satisfied)*. The nature of their employment experiences can be described as positive and moving in an upward direction *(positively upward)*. Second, the "contented - accommodating IEPs" include those who are *not integrated but satisfied*. The nature and direction of their employment experiences tend to be *negatively upward*. Third, the "struggling - competing IEPs" refer to those who are *integrated but not satisfied*. The nature and direction of their employment experiences was *positively downward*. The fourth class of IEPs are "low achieving - avoiding" which include those who are *not integrated and not satisfied*.

They have negative employment experiences that are moving in a downward direction (negatively downward). The negotiation of language backgrounds and cultural identities according to these four classes of IEPs and their distinguishing characteristics are discussed with more details in the following discussions.

The High Achieving: Collaborating IEPs

Describing the information presented in Figure 2, the first category of IEPs is identified as high achieving - collaborating IEPs (Quadrant 1) who were *integrated and satisfied*. This is based on the study results showing that a number of IEPs who were integrated were also satisfied with their jobs. This can be explained with their most distinguishing characteristics that set them apart from other groups as evident in their strong ability to collaborate with others in a multicultural work environment resulting in their highly successful employment status, acceptable level of language proficiency or confidence in spoken English, having their first job related to their intended profession, receiving a high level of income, and possessing unique personal qualities such as perseverance, patience, and dedication to lifelong learning.

The Contented: Accommodating IEPs

The second group is categorized as contented - accommodating IEPs (Quadrant 4). These IEPs are categorized as *not integrated but satisfied* based on study results that some IEPs who were not integrated had also expressed job satisfaction. This can be explained not because of their socio-demographic characteristics (age, ethnicity, education), but because of their acceptable level of income, work culture, and contextual factors such as an accommodating work environment characterized by inclusiveness in the face of diversity, voice or freedom of expression, and equity as attributed to company unionization.

The Struggling: Competing IEPs

The third group of IEPs is described as struggling - competing IEPs (Quadrant 2) such as those who were *integrated but not satisfied*. Based on the present study results, although some IEPs had already been integrated in their CoP, they were not satisfied in their employment as they often faced competition with the dominant group to be recognized, and confronted issues of indifference, lack of belongingness or acceptance in the workplace. This had resulted in their feeling of inferiority or low self-esteem. The source of dissatisfaction among this group can be traced from the fact that their distinctive language and cultural identities were challenged by the dominant group. Results suggest that the challenges they had been facing in their employment can be attributed to their sociodemographic characteristics (ethnicity, education and professional status), individual factors (low level of income), and sociolinguistic factors (language ability and use, and linguistic and cultural differences). Moreover, contextual factors of the workplace such as exclusion among members within the CoP, and highly structured power relations established and sustained domination, subordination, and marginalization.

The Low Achieving: Avoiding IEPs

The fourth group of IEPs is identified as low achieving - avoiding IEPs (Quadrant 3); this group included those who were *not integrated and not satisfied*. Findings revealed that this group's feelings of avoidance and withdrawal resulted from their attempts to be integrated in their CoP and experiences of unfavourable employment situations. This group often lacks the means or economic resources to meet the requirements of the re-credentialing processes that they had failed in their attempts to be integrated. The source of their job dissatisfaction can be explained by their socio-demographic characteristics (age, ethnicity, education), individual factors such as low level of income, finding themselves in a precarious employment situation in their first job or staying in an unrelated occupation (UO) over an extended period of time. The combination of these factors often coalesced with this group finding themselves stuck in dead end jobs.

The Four Classes of IEPs: Employment Trajectory, Year of Arrival, Integration and Satisfaction

Table 1 is a direct translation of the integration-satisfaction matrix showing the four classes of IEPs and how each individual respondent is categorized according to their integration and satisfaction, year of arrival and employment trajectories. Additionally, Table 2 illustrates the frequency distribution of the four groups of IEPs according to their year of arrival and employment trajectories. This illustration serves as a useful guide in conducting a more detailed analysis of how the four groups of IEPs were impacted by the economic conditions during the time of their arrival based on their responses to survey questionnaires and in-depth interviews. A closer look at Table 1 and 2 indicate that a greater number of High Achieving IEPs (8) are recent arrivals during the years 2002-2008 and that many of them (10) had navigated a curvature employment trajectory. Although results seem to suggest that previous immigration policies (Immigration Act 1976, Multiculturalism Act 1988, and Immigration and Refugee Protection Act 2002, 2008) and the macroeconomic conditions during the pre-2008 recession had positively impacted on the integration of IEPs, the majority of respondents (60%) reported they had spent at least two years searching for jobs in their intended profession, 27% had spent up to 10 years looking for work opportunities in their related profession as mostly experienced among the Struggling IEPs, and 13% had already given up to be integrated in their CoP as in the case of the Low Achieving IEPs. During the process of integration, the IEPs reported that they had engaged in many forms of precarious employment despite the existence of the Fair Access to Regulated Profession Act 2006. Findings suggest that even if they were already integrated in their CoP, they continued to negotiate their cultural identities that is critical in meeting the daily challenges of their workplace as revealed in the succeeding discussions from the narratives and interview extracts of selected IEPs.

Table 1. Four classes of IEPs by employment trajectory, year of arrival, integration and satisfaction

	1988 – 1994 (n = 10)	1995 – 2001 (n = 7)	2002 – 2008 (n = 13)
High Achieving IEPs: Integrated and satisfied	Dr. Vera – curvature Helen – curvature Mary – straight Cathy – straight Ron – curvature Li – curvature	Pedro – straight Joe – curvature Pam – straight Tina – curvature	Allam – curvature Nena – straight Rose – straight Sarah – curvature Carlo – straight Alec – curvature Celia – straight Grace – curvature
Contented IEPs: Not integrated but satisfied	Maria – curvature	Ben – straight Rene – curvature Emma – curvature	
Struggling IEPs: Integrated but not satisfied	Vlad – curvature Anita – curvature		Martin – curvature Ann – curvature
Low Achieving IEPs: Not Integrated and Not Satisfied	Sindhu – straight		Mario – straight Mia – straight Singh – straight

Table 2. Distribution of the four classes of IEPs by year of arrival and employment trajectory

Four classes	Year of arrival			Employment trajectory	
	1988-1994	1995-2001	2002-2008	Curvature	Straight
High achieving (n = 18)	6	4	8	10	8
Contented (n = 4)	1	3		3	1
Struggling (n = 4)	2		2	4	
Low achieving (n = 4)	1		3		4
Total (N =30)	10	7	13	17	13

Sociolinguistics in Negotiating Language and Cultural Identity

To explore and examine how IEPs negotiate their language backgrounds and cultural identities, the interview data was analyzed using CDA and the constant comparative method. The methodological approach encompassing these two analytical tools has paved the way to answer the second question posed in this study, that is, to identify the roles of language and the emerging themes that explain the experiences of IEPs. Results suggest the importance of *sociolinguistic factors* in negotiating language and cultural identity among the participants. *Sociolinguistics* can be broadly defined as a descriptive study of the effect of any and all aspects of society, including cultural norms, expectations, and context in the way that language is used and the effects of language use on society. In this study, the term refers to the interplay of language use and ability (linguistic diversity, accentedness, pragmatic communicative competence, and knowledge of the official languages) and contextual factors (cross-cultural interactions, social support network, Canadian experience, work culture, practices of Canadian employers, role of Canadian Government and Ontario policies on employment, language education, and re-certification programs).

Role of Language

The literature review that laid the groundwork for this study posited the importance of second language proficiency in labour market access and social integration of the IEPs. Within the analytical framework of CDA and the constant comparative method, the next sections present the description (text analysis), interpretation (processing analysis), and explanation (social analysis) of the data collected in the form of narratives and interview extracts of selected participants to explore and examine how language negotiation and cultural identity played an important role in various emerging themes focusing on immigration, education, employment and integration experiences of the IEPs in multicultural contexts.

Language and Immigration

With the recent immigration policies (IRPA, 1976, 2002 and 2008; CIC, 2012), language has continuously become an important factor, not only in the process of immigration, but most importantly in the integration of IEPs in the society upon their arrival in Canada. This has been observed among the IEPs as narrated below in the case of Li, an IEP from the Other Cultures CoP who initially could not find employment in her field as a former bank financial analyst because of her distinctive Chinese accent:

In Canada, you don't start right away in a higher position. . . . I first worked as a waitress in a fast-food restaurant and as a part-time cashier in a grocery store. I didn't like my first job here, so I went back to Hong Kong. After a year, I returned to Canada but didn't work again as a waitress or cashier but got hired as a bank teller with the help of some friends.

According to Li, she was oftentimes discouraged from applying to jobs in her field because of her different language background. Due to this, she ended up working in precarious jobs upon her arrival in Canada in 1991. She went back to Hong Kong disappointed but returned back to Canada after one year. During this time, she used her network of friends to help her find employment in her related profession and fortunately landed in a bank teller position that required someone who was fluent in Mandarin to serve the bank's growing Chinese customers. In the case of Li, the diversity of Canada's labour market and the practices among firms and businesses to recognize multiculturalism in employment had turned into Li's favour to help her to find a suitable job.

Diversity and Multiculturalism

The practice of multiculturalism has been observed in some Canadian companies as in Rose's workplace where communication exchange among individuals is taking place without challenging their identities despite language differences and ethnicities. Rose commented on how cultural diversity is recognized in their workplace stating that:

Language plays a very important role. In my workplace, it does not matter whether you have an accent but the most important thing is you can express your message very clearly and you know how to organize your thoughts. There's a lot of Chinese and Indians in my office, they speak various types of accents but they are there. If you're fluent, yes, it helps a lot. But I observed that it does not matter if you have an accent. What is important is they understand what you're saying.

The observations that Rose recounted from her workplace can be compared with Allan's experiences with his present employment as a municipal engineer. Allan emphasized greater importance of the workplace-specific communication that requires ability to express oneself in a common language that is specific to their nature and type of work. Considering the technical nature of his job as an engineer, what is most important is one's knowledge of the professional language regardless of one's accent, cultural or ethnic background. Allan expresses his views on the role of language in his current job as follows:

The power to speak is the power to communicate. I work in a very professional environment. Unlike if you work in a restaurant with a Filipino employer as a cook, you need to communicate in a language that your employer can understand. In our case, fluency in English counts a lot. But it's more on how you express yourself regardless of your language background or accent.

The Language Negotiation and Integration of Immigrants

A similar success story depicting how language plays an important role in the integration of immigrants was observed in the case of Nena, a Filipino transmigrant nurse from Singapore and the UK before immigrating to Canada. For Nena, language symbolizes culture that one should embrace or adapt if they want to integrate and succeed in their areas of work. The following is an interview extract from Nena:

Extract One (Nena)
1 **Nena:** In my case, I don't see my language or accent as a problem//
2 I worked in Singapore and the UK
3 but I tried to EMBRACE their cultures –
4 **The Researcher**: What do you mean by that?
5 **Nena:** Let us say, you two are different,
6 and . . you don't have just to say . . . THAT'S ME!
7 That's difficult.
8 You really have to embrace their culture.
9 **The Researcher:** That's right, you embrace other people's culture.
10 **Nena:** Yeah, for example, when I was in Singapore,
11 they have different accent
12 because they are Chinese.
13 Then, when I was in U.K.,
14 I find it hard to understand BRITISH ACCENT//
15 **The Researcher:** Uh hmm
16 **Nena**: But I studied it myself because I need to adapt.
17 **The Researcher**: I see. In nursing certification,
18 do they require language proficiency tests?
19 **Nena**: They do//But in my case,
20 they didn't because I came from an English-speaking country.
21 **The Researcher**: I understand.
22 **Nena:** When I worked in [Hospital X], people are so MULTICULTURAL/
23 and I tried to mingle by studying their accents.
24 Every morning, when I arrived,
25 I listen to the news, and then I studied their HUMOR//
26 **The Researcher:** Oh, yeah?
27 **Nena:** Yeah, because I NEED to//
28 The problem is/ some people are stuck up
29 and they don't want to learn.
30 That's why it's hard for them/
31 to overcome their language barrier.
32 **The Researcher:** That's right!
33 **Nena:** I really studied different people's way

34 of communicating because I NEED to.

In this extract, the role of language in the negotiation and integration of IEPs has been articulated based on the experiences of Nena while working as a nurse in several employment contexts. What she narrated was more of a prescription of how to communicate with people in a workplace with diverse cultural and linguistic backgrounds. She pointed out the importance of collaborating and embracing the norms of the host society as a means of social inclusion in the context of her working environment (Line 3). She further elaborated as to what collaborating or embracing one's culture means, which according to her, is not just a matter of saying 'that's me'. Otherwise, it would be very difficult to get along well with others considering the differences among individuals (Lines 6–7). According to Nena, language barriers can be overcome by collaborating with others and learning other people's way of communication.

Language and Education

Whereas Nena shared her perspective on the role of language in the integration and employment of IEPs, Dr. Vera, a dentist by profession, had considered language as a means of differentiation, competition and selection among individuals.

Extract Two (Dr. Vera)
1 **Dr. Vera**: ". . . language is a barrier//
2 sometimes it's also the level of education.
3 When you come here to Canada
4 and you attended a university here,
5 I don't think there is not much a problem //
6 . . . However, when you come here
7 to Canada without higher education/
8 and worked here as an ordinary worker,
9 then, they really have problems on language//
10 **The Researcher:** Uh hmm . . .
11 **Dr. Vera:** I noticed that among Filipinos
12 who came to Canada through sponsorship//
13 They really have problems with communication.
14 But Filipino professionals can understand/
15 and speak English well.
16 **The Researcher:** But still, they cannot find jobs!
17 **Dr. Vera**: We'll . . hmm, because . . maybe our English
18 sounds differently from others . . .

For Dr. Vera, language is a barrier in the case of immigrants who cannot express themselves in English. The ability to speak in English is normally tied to one's level of educational attainment. Hence, language is not much of a problem among the Filipino IEPs. However, what is problematic are the cases of Filipino IEPs who despite their ability to speak in English cannot find employment in their professions.

Negotiating Language and Cultural Identity in Employment-Seeking

The hiring and selection of prospective employees for a vacant position normally takes place during a job interview. It is within job interviews where the identities of IEPs are most often challenged because of many factors including their ethnic backgrounds and being a Non-native English Speaker (NNES). Grace, a Filipino CoP, who is now a certified teacher and a permanent teacher shares the following employment-seeking experience in one of the job interviews she attended:

I attended a lot of interviews. In most of them, I failed . . . [in one of these interviews] there was a long line up of applicants waiting outside. I was not yet finished answering some of the questions. But . . . I felt like the principal [the interviewer] was already pushing me out of the door in favour of other job candidates. . . I felt like I came from a different planet.

Although there is no clarity in Grace's statement as to why the interviewer did not give her a chance to finish what she was saying, the interviewer should have treated her properly, by at the very least giving her an opportunity to complete her answers to the interview questions. The job interview could have been conducted more positively had the interviewer encouraged Grace to ask questions or seek any points of clarifications before the end of the job interview. The information that Grace provided in her narratives reveals her feelings of being treated unfairly because of her identity as an IEP with a different language background and ethnicity.

The discursive construction of the reality where the identities of individuals with different cultural backgrounds are challenged has been observed within the CoP among the teaching professionals. The role of language in shaping the identity of the IEPs is evident in the case of Ann, a certified occasional teacher, who shares the following narrative:

In the staff room, I heard two regular teachers talking to each other. One of the teachers was questioning why the board is letting occasional teachers who have strong accent to substitute for ESL classes. I was offended to hear that conversation because I have qualifications to teach ESL although I'm not a NES. "Is there anything wrong about that? . . . How come the teacher's college gave us certifications on specific subject areas but schools don't want to give us a job to teach the subject?" Our students are mostly immigrants too, and they can relate very well with us. In one of the schools I worked in, the children were mostly Asian immigrants and one of the students said: "We love to see you teachers in this school. Why don't we see many of you coming here?"

The compartmentalization among teachers who are qualified to teach specialized subject areas such as ESL has been brought forward in the narratives of Ann as an occasional teacher. The conversation of two teachers questioning the authority of NNES teachers to teach this specialized subject is a complex issue that challenges the cultural identity of teachers like Ann, who is a NNES. Although Ann is already qualified to teach ESL based on her teacher certification, some members of the teaching staff are apparently not in favour of allowing NNES teachers to teach ESL because of their different English accents. The dichotomization among teachers and their intolerance for difference based on language, to some extent, appears to be problematic. In the case of Ann, her legitimacy to teach ESL can be judged not only by her certifications but on the basis of the changing demographic composition of students who, like Ann, have different linguistic backgrounds and do thrive and survive in a multicultural environment.

Negotiating Language and Cultural Identity in Employment

Parallel with the cases of Dr. Vera, Grace and Ann, the role of language as a barrier in the negotiation and integration of IEPs and the visible and audible ethnic minorities has been revealed in the narratives of Ron, a former accountant from the Philippines who is now a Revenue Officer in one of Canada's largest public corporations. Ron said:

Sometimes we're not able to relate to and say what we want because English is not our first language. This is one of our barriers being a visible minority, we're too humble. However, we can get the attention of others by the quality of our work. Our hiring manager looks behind the colour of our skin. Instead, he looks at our potentials and our ability to lead the company. The problem at work is that many of them are native speakers and they can easily sell themselves, which often results in bragging. That makes it easier for them to go to the top.

For Ron, being a NNES is sometimes a barrier particularly when he is not able to relate to or say what he wants. He believes Filipinos are too humble and often they let other people step on them without saying a word. Despite this, Ron is well liked by his superior from whom he can always get attention for a job well done. Although he is fortunate to work in a company that does not discriminate against employees, Ron's work environment is dominated by NES, which he finds very challenging when they can easily get out of their way and make it to the top by selling or bragging about themselves.

The role of language as a barrier in the integration and employment of IEPs as NNES is more evident in the cases of Martin, a Filipino, and Vlad, an Eastern European, both occasional teachers. Based on the employment experiences of occasional teachers, the role of language was crystal-clear in their struggles to be integrated in the mainstream teaching profession. In the case of Martin, he mentioned how his students had once ridiculed him regardless of his best efforts on the job as he recalled:

I managed not to comeback in one of the schools I was assigned to teach when a Grade 9 boy in my class used to mimic my strong English accent [somewhat staccato sound] every time he spoke to me. I felt annoyed with that!... One time, I was writing on the board. I heard a group of students laughing at my back and then, suddenly one of them threw an apple on my desk to get my attention.

Whereas Martin recounts his integration experiences related to the performance of his work that sounds similar to Ron, Vlad shares his struggles in finding a permanent teaching job for more than 10 years. Vlad's experiences resonate more with employment-seeking experiences as presented earlier in the cases of Grace and Ann who are in the same field of teaching.

Vlad is an IEP from another culture CoP. He is in his late 50s, of European descent and works as an occasional teacher. The following interview extracts reveal how he negotiates his language and cultural identity in his employment and employment-seeking experiences:

Extract Three (Vlad)
1 **Vlad**: Language is a BIG issue....
2 based on my experience/ with the other
3 school board where I stayed for four years
4 as a supply teacher// I moved

5 to another board because
6 I also can't get a permanent job.
7 **The Researcher**: You can't get a permanent job?
8 **Vlad**: Yeah . . even here I can't get permanent . . .
9 **The Researcher**: Uh hmm . .
10 **Vlad**: They said my English is NOT very good . . .
11 But how about my MATH?
12 I'm a Math teacher, and for us/
13 the language issue should be taken separately.
14 I was not there to speak about Shakespeare//
15 . . . [but] Math is a universal language.

According to Vlad, his problem was he could not get a permanent teaching position, neither from his previous nor his present employer, as he continues to struggle with English. In Vlad's case, his employer seems not to favour his unique variety of speaking in English. As a middle-aged NNES with a bachelor's and a master's degree in engineering from his native country of Romania, Vlad has an accent that immediately places him as eastern European.

The main argument presented in Vlad's case was that he cannot get a permanent teaching position because of his not very good English (Line 10) and he was critical of the ambiguity and biases that he experienced in the hiring of NNES teachers. The ambiguity that existed in the hiring of NNES such as Vlad lies in the failure of the school system to delineate the teacher's content knowledge and expertise of the subject matter that they are supposed to teach. Instead, too much of the focus appears to be on other factors, such as the unique variety of English that Vlad brings to the classroom. In Lines 13–15, Vlad questions the biases of the school system in recognizing his expertise to teach the subject and he feels that his NNES status influences the recruitment and hiring process for occasional teachers to get permanent employment. Vlad made this explicit with his remark that he was trained to teach math - which is a universal language - and not to speak about the language of Shakespeare.

Language Ability and Use

In this study, *language ability* refers to the language proficiency among the IEPs as determined by their level of confidence in speaking English as a Second Language (ESL). Language ability or proficiency can also be determined using external criteria such as the government-mandated Canadian Language Benchmarks (CLB) and other recognized standardized methods of language assessments. Whereas language ability in the second language involves linguistic competence that includes mastery of vocabulary, grammar and pronunciation, *language use* is broader in scope, which refers to the individual's knowledge of a particular sociocultural context and their ability to use or speak the language in a given context or situation. Language use can be sometimes referred to as pragmatic communicative competence or sociolinguistic competence (Derwing & Waugh, 2012).

Sociolinguistic factors which are a broad set of factors encompassing both language ability and use (linguistic competence and pragmatic communicative competence) were examined among IEPs to further explore how they negotiate their language backgrounds and cultural identities. The analysis results as revealed in the succeeding discussions supported findings from the literature suggesting that linguistic competence is not all that matters. Sociolinguistic factors that include the immigrant's knowledge of the given context contributed more significantly to their social inclusion and integration into their CoP (Derwing & Waugh, 2012; Statistics Canada, 2005).

Education and Employment

In this section, the power of language to differentiate the IEPs according to their *language ability and use* was examined as observed in the areas of education and employment within Bourdieu's theoretical perspective. In this analytical component, the case of Tina illuminates how language ability and use become a powerful tool for negotiating cultural identity.

Schools as Complicit in Class Inequality

The narrative account of Tina was part of her experiences with the language education and re-credentialing program required to practice her teaching profession in Canada. Tina recalled:

I already passed all the oral and written language tests. When I went to the course orientation, there was an Indian lady who was assisting the orientation session. She approached me and asked where I came from. When I replied that I came from the Philippines, she said: . . . your language there is not English so you are not allowed to register for a course!

During the interview, Tina reflected on how the language education program and related policies became agents of social divide in the re-certification program for IEPs. She observed the marked discrepancy among the Canadian universities in the manner through which they accept or refuse applicants who are immigrants from diverse cultural and ethnic backgrounds. Whereas Tina was refused registration in a course by one Canadian university because of her language credentials from the Philippines, she was accepted by another university in the same field of study as part of her re-credentialing process. Tina's case contributed to the bodies of evidence in Bowles and Gintis' (1975) Marxian critique of the problem of human capital theory and Bourdieu's (1977; 1984; 1986) cultural capital suggesting the power of an educational institution to sort and divide students according to their different cultural and linguistic backgrounds. Schools who are agents of social justice are the same institutions that exercise class inequality and its perpetuation.

Bourdieu's Theory in Multicultural Contexts

The negotiation and integration experiences of IEPs in multicultural contexts is further examined with the application of Bourdieu's (1977; 1984; 1986) concept of habitus and institutional cultural capital to explain how the IEPs negotiate their language and cultural identity to earn membership in their CoP. Using the analytical component of the constant comparative method, specifically the *within-case analysis* of the narratives of IEPs who were members of CoP (Tina, Ann, Grace and Vlad) as presented in previous discussions can be explained within Bourdieu's concept of habitus and the institutional cultural capital theory. Looking into the case of Tina who was denied entry to a program of study leading to her teacher certification revealed the working of habitus that resides among educational institutions who reward students on the basis of their cultural capital and marginalizes others who do not possess it.

Although Tina had educational credentials, the Canadian university where she intended to study did not recognize it because of her status as an IEP. This perpetrated class inequality as a student like Tina who did not possess the required cultural capital such as language proficiency was denied access to a program of study because of the habitus of the Canadian educational institution that does not valorize the IEPs' language background and cultural identity.

The integration experience of Tina resonates with the case of Grace, a certified teacher who is now a teacher on a permanent status. In a similar account, Grace encountered the same scenario as part of her employment-seeking experiences when she was being interviewed for a teaching position. From Grace's previous narrative account, the principal who was interviewing her suddenly interrupted their conversion by abruptly ending her job interview in favour of other job candidates who were lined up outside.

The cases of Vlad and Ann revealed different scenarios for IEPs who have already been certified by a professional regulatory body but are continuously experiencing competition, marginalization, unfair treatment or being treated as different members of the teaching profession. The discourse of being treated as a different member of the profession on the basis of language or accent has been observed in the case of Vlad who failed in several job interviews because of his not being good in English (see Extract 3, Line 10).

Using *within-case analysis* for IEPs who were both members of CoP, the experiences of Vlad can be validated in the context of Ann's negotiation experiences as an occasional teacher. In a similar situation, Ann revealed how the members of the regular teaching staff in her workplace showed their negative perception towards ESL occasional teachers who have NNES background. The conversation between two regular teachers that Ann had encountered in the staff room was an explicit account of how the hegemonic work culture exercised exclusionary practices in schools and the manner how colleagues in the same profession interacted with the Internationally Educated Teachers (IETs) who were NNES and members of visible ethnic minorities. In Ann's narrative, the two teachers who were apparently NES were questioning the legitimacy of the NNES teachers to do substitute teaching for ESL classes. Results revealed that the contextual factors of employment such as the culture of the workplace characterized by an imbalance of power, the indifference of colleagues and employers as well as feeling of marginalization experienced by IEPs, replicated some findings on the negotiation and integration of foreign-trained immigrants in Canada (Kelly, 2006; Pollock, 2010; Reitz, 2001, 2007a, 2007b; Türegün, 2008). Türegün (2008) explained that this problem might be attributed to the labour market preferences that affect the integration of the IEPs because of their language barriers, accents, and the problem of person-organization fit. Furthermore, Reitz (2001) pointed out that this problem existed because of the power relations in the labour market where employers' decision was most likely influenced by the social, cultural, and political factors of the given work contexts which dictated the norms of employment and served as the basis for employers to decide who among job candidates would be selected.

Habitus of the Workplace

Bourdieu's theory of habitus, which refers to the disposition, system of internal structures, and scheme of perception and conception, was applied in the specific context of Ann's workplace. The concept of habitus appears to be influencing the embodied cultural capital (language, accent, ethnicity and race) among members of the teaching staff in this work scenario. The disposition commonly held by the majority in Ann's workplace recognized only the embodied cultural capital of the dominant group who were NES. On the other hand, members who did not possess this capital were considered as deficient and, therefore, subject to exclusion or marginalization.

In this context, the habitus which was in place among members of the teaching staff had important implications in the selection and hiring of ESL teachers by excluding the NNES to maintain the culture of the dominant group and, thus, to reproduce the cycle of class inequality. This only suggested that the internal structure of the work environment in Ann's case was not adapting to the changing multicultural student population of the school where children represented the majority of the immigrant population. The lack of representation if not exclusion of teachers with NNES background and visible ethnic minorities with physical resemblance of the majority of the student population was observed in the context of Ann's multicultural workplace based on the student's remarks as previously presented. The critical issue of class inequality was evident in the context of Ann's workplace where the composition of teaching staff may be dichotomized between NES who were predominantly permanent teachers, and NNES who were mostly IEPs and members of visible and audible ethnic minorities (Asians, Africans, Latin Americans) serving as a vast army of occasional teachers and surviving through precarious supply teaching jobs.

Multiculturalism and Habitus of the IEPs

Using *cross-case analysis,* results revealed that Bourdieu's theory of habitus with IEPs CoP (Grace, Martin, Vlad, Ann, Tina) can be replicated with multiple cases of IEPs who were Non-CoP (Mario, Maria, Ben, Emma). Regardless of membership to CoP, the analogy of the negotiation and integration experiences between IEPs CoP and Non-CoP can be interpreted in Bourdieu's theory as a form of symbolic violence that resulted from the imposition of different perception, treatment, systems of symbolism, culture and meaning upon certain groups or classes as a way of legitimizing class inequality and reproduction. The multilayer dimensions of the IEPs' narratives can be well understood within Bourdieu's concept of habitus depending on their characteristics including language background and cultural identity that influenced in one way or another their negotiation experiences to integrate in their CoP. Based on *within-case* (IEPs CoP) and *cross-case* (IEPs Non-CoP) analysis of the multiple cases presented, the habitus has been observed to mediate how the IEPs negotiate their language and identity as cultural capital, either institutional (educational credentials) or embodied (language, accent, or style), and thus, determined their employment success or failure in multicultural contexts.

SUMMARY OF FINDINGS

In consonance with the first research question posed in this study, the language negotiation and cultural identity in multicultural context can be summarized according to four classes of IEPs with their distinguishing characteristics that described and explained the movements of integration and levels of job satisfaction in their community of practice: high *achieving - collaborating IEPs* (integrated and satisfied), *contented - accommodating IEPs* (not integrated but satisfied), *struggling - competing IEPs* (integrated but not satisfied), and l*ow achieving - avoiding IEP*s (not integrated and not satisfied).

To explore and examine how IEPs negotiate their language backgrounds and cultural identities, the interview data was analyzed using CDA and the constant comparative method. The methodological approach encompassing these two analytical tools has paved the way to answer the second question posed in this study, that is, to identify the roles of language and the emerging themes that explain the negotiation and integration experiences of IEPs. The discussions of results were divided into two major sections. The *first section* identified the emerging themes focusing on the important role that language plays in the integration of IEPs, language in education, employment-seeking, and employment. The *second section* focused on language ability and use as observed in the areas of education and employment and interpreted from Bourdieu's theoretical perspective in the context of multiculturalism. Results suggest the importance of sociolinguistic factors in negotiating language and cultural identity among the IEPs.

Implication of Findings

Whereas the Ontario government recognizes the need for a new direction in immigration strategy through legislation of the Ontario Immigration Act 2014 (Government of Ontario, 2014), the employment- seeking experiences of the IEPs in this study and the actions of their prospective employers run contrary to the Canadian government policies of supporting newcomers to succeed and contribute to the economy and communities more favourably. The Government of Ontario (2014) once stated with their immigration strategy: *"We [also] need to help immigrants who are already here . . . we must do more to help them succeed by removing barriers to meaningful employment"* (p. 4). However, no matter what the immigration policy says to help immigrants to integrate in the Canadian economy, the IEPs will never succeed should there be no cooperation on the part of Canadian businesses and employers who are directly involved in the selection, hiring, selection, and employment of foreign-trained immigrants.

Notwithstanding the government programs and initiatives to educate the immigrants and provide them with the right information on how to access their professions in Canada, it shows that the government functions only in this limited capacity. The perfectly competitive labour market conditions suggest that the IEPs tend to be in the disadvantage position as the employer decides to hire job seekers as dictated by their own institutional demands. This means that the government has very little control of the labour market and that neither the government policies nor the human capital theory can explain why despite the IEPs educational credential, there is an existing gap in their employment. Results of this present study have relevant implications in resolving the gap in employment between the IEPs and the Canadian-born. However, this appears to be a challenge among Canadian employers because of the *habitus* – the unwritten rules of employment policies that create the double standard assessment of the IEPs' credentials. The unwritten rules generate the nature of realities prevailing and dictating the labour market, namely, the Canadian experience, soft skills requirements, and language proficiency in either one of Canada's two official languages (English and French) that emerged to be the most important rules of the game. This would explain why the playing fields in employment cannot be leveled off in Canada because the immigrants based on the results of this study were perceived to be lacking these requirements - wanting more Canadian work experience and being deficient in linguistic and cultural repertoire as non-native entities.

From the critical perspective, results of the study may serve as an eye-opener among policy-makers who failed to visualize the contradictions between the immigration policies notably, the Canadian Experience Class (CEC) category, a federally-sponsored program and the Ontario Human Rights Commission's (2013) policy on removing the Canadian experience barrier in the employment of IEPs for human rights considerations. Results of the present study had posed two critical questions, which may have been overlooked among government policy-makers that may have caused the problems and issues facing the IEPs and thus, shaping the contours of their employment trajectories: First, how can the employment gap between the Canadian-born and foreign-trained immigrant be reduced when the Canadian employers and professional regulatory bodies favoured specific group or class of job applicants with Canadian experience over the other? Second, how can the OHRC remove the Canadian experience barrier "when the Canadian government is institutionalizing this as a criterion in the immigration selection process, awarding credit to potential immigrants who already have work experience in this country - an opportunity not available to all[?]" (Sakamoto, 2013, para. 8)

Looking back to consider the economic conditions and the immigration policy ensembles from 2002 to 2015 with the legislation of Immigration and Refugee Protection Act (IRPA) 2002 and 2008 including the recent CEC category, the OHRC's (2013) policy, language policy (CIC, 2012), and the 2014 draft Ontario Immigration Act among others, the participants in this study, most particularly the Contented, Struggling and Low Achieving IEPs may have experienced more challenges in finding employment in their related professions had they arrived during this time period. This can be explained with the existing contradictions among different layers of government policy formulation and implementation including the federal and provincial governments.

Reconceptualizing Language Norms: Future Research Directions

Moving forward with the new immigration plan to meet the current labour market shortages (Immigration, Refugees and Citizenship Canada, 2022) spurred with Canada's population growth that reaches nearly 40 million mark during the first quarter of 2023 largely accounted to global migration in this post-pandemic period Statistics Canada (2023), it is imperative to collect new data since this study was conducted to re-evaluate how recently arriving immigrants over the past decade negotiate to integrate in the Canadian social and economic arena. Thus far, no related research has been conducted to advance the scholarship in this area and to substantiate results of this present study.

Whereas the most recently arrived IEPs may be more oriented to the changing labour market trends in Canada as a result of new government immigration policies, programs and initiatives that make them much easier to integrate in their professions, the government may be confronted with difficult challenges of how to deal with IEPs who have been in Canada for several years and are still struggling to negotiate and find employment that matches their education and training. Findings may offer suggestions for researchers and immigration policy makers for future directions among IEPs who are experiencing similar situations as revealed in this present study through the understanding of various factors that will assist the integration of different ethnic minorities into the Canadian labour market. These may include some preventative policy measures and remedies in the area of adult learning and continuing adult education and development, and changing the cultural practices in schools and the workplace through various training programs focusing on intercultural sensitivity.

The reconceptualization of language norms and promoting intercultural sensitivity in the light of present study results suggest shifting away from monolingual to translingual practices (Canagarajah, 2013) including translanguaging pedagogy (García, 2012) in language education programs where multilingualism and differences rather than sameness among individual learners should be normalized. The constant migration of people with different cultural backgrounds in multicultural contexts also suggest the importance of land-based pedagogy in curriculum design where "understandings of language are intertwined with indigenous concepts of land, identity, and thought, and as such, cannot be successfully compartmentalized and transmitted" (Hene-Ochoa et al., 2020, p. 482 cited in Canagarajah, 2021).

The government should strengthen their various initiatives and programs that are aligned with their existing policies in collaboration with employers, the business sectors, educational institutions, and various immigrant-serving organizations. A mechanism for monitoring policy implementation and program evaluation could be established including a system of incentives provided to various agencies and organizations to ensure best practices that promote inclusion in multicultural contexts.

CONCLUSION

The author's perspective based on the study results suggests the important role of language in negotiating the IEPs' cultural identities as determined by immigration policies in multicultural contexts. Language was a key to negotiation and integration. The different ways of speaking English among individuals of various ethnicities had also revealed the power of language to become a barrier to employment and a means for differentiation among the people of color. The language barriers facing IEPs can be overcome with the positive attitudes and some of the enduring qualities and traits among different ethnic groups as observed in negotiating their language and cultural identities.

The author's proposition that explains the need for the reconceptualization of language norms is anchored on present findings that although the present educational system in Canada is based on multicultural policy, the realities of the negotiation and integration of IEPs suggest that the system has not fully realized the ideals of a multicultural society. From the author's perspective, schools are responding to the ever changing economic, social and political environment within the constraints of habitus that prevails in various work organizations and educational institutions with hierarchical structure of power and internalized systems of discrimination and differentiation among different ethnic minorities through the neoliberal agenda of global competitiveness and the perpetuation of the dominant culture.

Many educational institutions nowadays are continuously offering courses to meet the demands of the global labour market and the increasingly competitive nature of employment. Consequently, schools teach students how to apply for jobs or respond successfully to job interview questions through a high level of language proficiency in the host dominant society. As part of neoliberal agenda, the employment-seeking strategies aim to translate the style, language, accent and other indigenous characteristics of the IEPs into the culture of the western colonialist's subjugation and domination. The manifestations of habitus as a cultural practice in schools have resulted in their own failure of maintaining balance of power among various members of society (Harker, 1984). The cultural practice in which the education system responds to the labour market demands entails the continued dominance of the group - capitalists, employers or owners of the factors of production, "whose habitus is embodied in schools" (p. 122). The continuous dominance of certain groups over non-dominant groups such as immigrant workers or IEPs is a "symbolic violence" (p. 122) that explains the legitimization of social inequality in Canadian multicultural society.

Results of the present study contributed to this existing knowledge in relation to the ways in which the education system sustains the reproduction of social inequality through cultural practices that do not consider the importance of human agency and the subjectivities of the minoritized group. The inequalities experienced among the IEPs necessitate changing the hegemonic cultural practices in schools and the ways that schools operate in relation to students and the community it serves. There is an urgent need to reconceptualize the language norms and change the conversation from the neoliberal rhetoric of domination and competition to the recognition of difference and diversity that the IEPs can contribute to a multicultural society. The education system can mediate the cycle of reproducing social inequalities by moving away from cultural practices that marginalize the knowledge and skills of foreign-trained immigrants. Schools are responsible for designing and developing curriculum and instructions to teach employers and future employers about the values of equity and inclusivity in increasingly diverse Canadian society.

REFERENCES

Alboim, N. & MacIsaac, E. (2007). Making the connections: Ottawa's role in immigrant employment. *IRPP Choices, 13*(3).

Apple, M. (2005). Are new markets in education democratic? In M. Apple, J. Kenway, & M. Singh (Eds.), *Globalizing education: Policies, pedagogies, & politics* (pp. 209–230). Peter Lang.

Aydemir, A., & Skuterud, M. (2004). Explaining the deteriorating entry earning of Canada's immigrant cohorts: 1966 – 2000. *Analytical Studies Branch Research Paper Series*. Statistics Canada.

Block, S., & Galabuzi, G. E. (2011). *Canada's colour coded labour market: The gap for racialized workers*. Policy Alternatives. http://www.policyalternatives.ca/

Bourdieu, P. (1977). *Outline of a theory of practice*. Harvard University Press. doi:10.1017/CBO9780511812507

Bourdieu, P. (1984). *Distinction: A social critique of the judgment of taste*. Harvard University Press.

Bourdieu, P. (1986). The forms of capital. In J. Richardson (Ed.), Handbook of theory and research in the sociology of education (pp. 241-258). Greenwood Press.

Bowles, S., & Gintis, H. (1975). The problem with human capital theory – A Marxian critique. *The American Economic Review, 65*(2), 74–82.

Boyd, M., & Cao, X. (2009). Immigrant language proficiency, earnings, and language policies. *Canadian Studies in Population, 36*(1–2), 63–86. doi:10.25336/P6NP62

Canagarajah, S. (2013). *Translingual practice: Global englishes and cosmopolitan relations*. Routledge. doi:10.4324/9780203120293

Chiswick, B. R., Cohen, Y., & Zach, T. (1997). The labour market status of immigrants: Effects of the unemployment rate at arrival and duration of residence. *Industrial & Labor Relations Review, 50*(2), 289–303. doi:10.1177/001979399705000206

Citizenship and Immigration Canada. (2012). *Canadian language benchmark: English as a second language for adults*. CIC. https://www.cic.gc.ca/english/pdf/pub/language-benchmarks.pdf

Creswell, J. W. (1994). Research design: Qualitative & quantitative approaches. *Sage (Atlanta, Ga.)*.

Derwing, T.M., & Waugh, E. (2012). Language skills and the social integration of Canada's adult immigrants. *IRPP Study, 31*.

Esser, H. (2006). Migration, language and integration. *Research Review 4*. Programme on Intercultural Conflicts and Societal Integration (AKI), Social Science Research Center Berlin. http://193.174.6.11/alt/aki/files/aki_research_review_4.pdf

Fair Access to Regulated Professions and Compulsory Trades Act. (2006). Service Ontario. e-Laws. http://www.e-laws.gov.on.ca/html/statutes/english/elaws _statutes_06f31_e.htm

Fairclough, N. (1989). *Language and power*. Longman.

Fairclough, N. (1992). *Discourse and social change*. Polity Press.

Fairclough, N., & Wodak, R. (1997). Critical discourse analysis. In T. Van Dijk (Ed.), *Discourse in social interaction* (pp. 258–284). Sage.

García, O. (2012). Theorizing translanguaging for educators. In C. Celic & K. Seltzer (Eds.), *Translanguaging: A CUNY- NYSIEB guide for educators* (pp. 1–6). City University of New York.

Gee, J. P. (2000). Identity as an analytic lens for research in education. In W. Secada (Ed.), *Review of Research in Education* (Vol. 25, pp. 99–126). American Educational Research Association. doi:10.2307/1167322

Gibb, T. L. (2008). Bridging Canadian adult second language education and essential skills policies, approach with caution. *Adult Education Quarterly*, 58(4), 318–334. doi:10.1177/0741713608318893

Government of Ontario (2014). *Strengthening immigration in Ontario: New legislation to help attract more skilled immigrants, boost economic growth*. http://news.ontario.ca/mci/en/2014/02/strengthening-immigration-in-ontario.html

Green, D., & Worswick, C. (2004). *Earnings of immigrant men in Canada: The roles of labour market entry effects and returns to foreign experience*. University of British Columbia Press.

Guba, E. G., & Lincoln, Y. S. (1994). Competing paradigms in qualitative research. In N. Denzin & Y. Lincoln (Eds.), Handbook of qualitative research (pp. 105-117). Sage Publications.

Gumperz, J. J. (1992). *Language and social identity*. Cambridge University Press.

Gutmann, A. (2004). Unity and diversity in democratic multicultural education: Creative and destructive tensions. In J. A. Banks (Ed.), *Diversity and citizenship education: Global perspectives* (pp. 71–96). Jossey-Bass.

Harker, R. K. (1984). On Reproduction, habitus and education. British Journal of Sociology of Education, 5(2), 117-127.

Henne–Ochoa, R., Elliott–Groves, E., Meek, B. A., & Rogoff, B. (2020). Pathways forward for Indigenous language reclamation: Engaging indigenous epistemology and learning by observing and pitching in to family and community endeavors. In S. Canagarajah (Ed), Rethinking mobility and language: From the global south (p. 580). Springer.

Immigration, Refugees and Citizenship Canada. (2022). *An immigration plan to grow the economy*. Immigration, Refugees and Citizenship Canada. https://www.canada.ca/en/immigration-refugees-citizenship/news /2022/11/an-immigration-plan-to-grow-the-economy.html

Jenkins, S. (2000). Cultural and linguistic miscues: A case study of international teaching assistant and academic faculty miscommunication. *International Journal of Intercultural Relations, 24*(4), 477–501. doi:10.1016/S0147-1767(00)00011-0

Kelly, P. F. (2006). Filipinos in Canada: Economic dimensions of immigration and Settlement. *CERIS Working Paper No. 48.* http://www.ceris.metropolis.net/wp-content/ uploads/pdf/research_publication/working_papers/wp48.pdf

Kelly, P. F., Astorga-Garcia, M., & Esguerra, E. F. (2009). Explaining the deprofessionalized Filipino: Why Filipino immigrants get low-paying jobs in Toronto. (CERIS Working Paper No. 75). CERIS. http://ceris.metropolis.net

Kerekes, J. A. (2005). Before, during, and after the event: Getting the job (or not) in an employment interview. In K. Bardovi-Harlig and B. Hartford (Eds.), Interlanguage pragmatics: Exploring institutional talk (pp. 99-131). Lawrence Erlbaum.

Laquian, E., & Laquian, A. (2008). *Seeking a better life abroad: A study of Filipinos in Canada 1957–2007.* Anvil Press.

McDonald, T., & Worswick, C. (1997). Unemployment incidence of immigrant men in Canada. *Canadian Public Policy, 23*(4), 353. doi:10.2307/3552069

Mckay, D. (2002). *Filipina identities: Geographies of social integration/exclusion in the Canadian Metropolis* (Working Paper Series, No. 02-18). Vancouver: Center of Excellence, Research on Immigration in the Metropolis.

Merriam, S. B. (2009). *Qualitative research: A guide to design and implementation.* Jossey-Bass.

Ontario Human Rights Commission. (2013). *Policy on removing the Canadian experience barrier.* OHRC. http://www.ohrc.on.ca

Pendakur, K., & Pendakur, R. (2012). Colour by numbers: Minority earnings in Canada 1996 –2006. *Journal of International Migration and Integration, 12*(3), 305–329.

Peters, C. (2011). *The bridging education and licensure of international medical doctors in Ontario: A call for commitment, consistency, and transparency.* [Dissertation, Ontario Institute for Studies in Education of the University of Toronto, Canada].

Picot, G., & Hou, F. (2012). How successful are second-generation visible minority groups in the Canadian labour market? *Canadian Diversity, 9*(1), 17–21.

Pollock, K. (2010). Marginalization and the occasional teacher workforce in Ontario: The case of Internationally Educated Teachers (IETs). *Canadian Journal of Educational Administration and Policy, 100.* http://www.umanitoba.ca/publications/cjeap/ pdf_files/pollock-iet.pdf

Quinio, A. (2015). *From Policy to Reality: A Study of Factors Influencing the Employment Trajectories of Internationally Educated Professionals* [Doctoral dissertation, University of Toronto]. TSpace Repository Database. https://hdl.handle.net/1807/71591

Reis, D. S. (2011). Non-native English-speaking teachers (NNESTs) and professional legitimacy: A sociocultural theoretical perspective on identity transformation. *International Journal of the Sociology of Language, 208*(208), 139–160. doi:10.1515/ijsl.2011.016

Reitz, J. G. (2001). Immigrant success in the knowledge economy: Institutional change and the immigrant experience in Canada, 1970-1995. *The Journal of Social Issues, 57*(3), 579–613. doi:10.1111/0022-4537.00230

Reitz, J. G. (2007a). Immigrant employment success in Canada, Part I: Individual and contextual causes. *The International Migration Review, 8*(1), 37–62. doi:10.100712134-007-0002-3

Reitz, J. G. (2007b). Immigrant employment success in Canada, Part II: Understanding the decline. *Journal of International Migration and Integration, 8*(1), 37–62. doi:10.100712134-007-0002-3

Rodriguez, R. M. (2010). *Migrants for export: How the Philippine state broker labor to the world*. University of Minnesota. doi:10.5749/minnesota/9780816665273.001.0001

Sakamoto, I. (2013). Tearing down the 'Canadian experience' roadblock. *The Star.* http://www.thestar.com/opinion/commentary/2013/07/16/tearing_down_the_canadian_experience_roadblock.html

Stake, R. E. (1995). The art of case study research. *Sage (Atlanta, Ga.).*

Statistics Canada. (2005). Knowledge of official languages among new immigrants: How important is it in the labour market? *Catalogue No. 89-624-XIE.* http://www.statcan.gc.ca /pub/89-624-x/89-624-x2007000-eng.pdf

Statistics Canada (2023). *Canada's population estimates, first quarter of 2023*. https://www150.statcan.gc.ca/n1/dailyquotidien/230628/dq230628c-eng.htm

Steinert, Y. (2006). *Building on diversity: A faculty development program for teachers of international medical graduates*. The Association of Faculties of Medicine of Canada.

Strauss, A., & Glaser, B. G. (1967). *The discovery of grounded theory: Strategies for grounded theory research*. Aldine Publishing.

Türegün, A. (2008). The politics of access to professions: Making Ontario's Fair Access to Regulated Professions Act, 2006. [CERIS Working Paper No. 70]. CERIS. http://www.ceris.metropolis.net/

Van Dijk, T. A. (Ed.). (1997). *Discourse as social interaction*. Sage.

Van Dijk, T. A. (1998). *Critical discourse analysis*. HUM. https://www.hum.uva.nl/teun/cda.htm

Wenger, E. (1998). *Communities of practice: Learning, meaning, and identity*. Cambridge University Press. doi:10.1017/CBO9780511803932

Wodak, R., & Meyer, M. (Eds.). (2009). *Methods of critical discourse analysis*. John Benjamin.

Yin, R. (2003). *Case study research: Design and methods* (3rd ed.). Sage.

KEY TERMS DEFINITIONS

Community of Practice: A system of relationships between people, activities, and the world which embodied certain beliefs and behaviours to be acquired; also known as "integration into one's profession".

Cultural Identity: Refers to anything that can be ascribed or assigned to a person including ethnic origin or skin colour, gender, language use, accentedness, education, employment or certain characteristics or connections based on what the person does and identifies with; sometimes used interchangeably in the context of the present study as "professional status."

Integration: refers to the IEPs' membership in his or her intended profession or community of practice.

Levels of Job Satisfaction: Refers to the "nature" or characteristics of integration as to either *satisfied* (positive) or *not satisfied* (negative) as depicted in the four quadrants of integration-satisfaction matrix.

Movements of Integration: Refers to the "direction" of one's intended profession described as either *moving to* (upward) or *moving away* (downward) from the intended profession or CoP.

Negatively Downward: Refers to movement of integration as depicted in the third quadrant of the integration-satisfaction matrix including the *Low Achieving IEPs* who are "not integrated and not satisfied;" they usually negotiate their language and cultural identity by avoiding attempts to be integrated due to lack of economic means.

Negatively Upward: Refers to movement of integration as depicted in the fourth quadrant of the integration-satisfaction matrix including the *Contented IEPs* who are "not integrated in their CoP but satisfied;" they usually negotiate their language and cultural identity by accommodating others in their work environment.

Periphery Country: Refers to a country characterized by a least developed or still in the process of developing the economy. They produce labor-intensive and low-skill products that are typically exploited as a source of cheap labor, raw materials, or agricultural production for those countries in the core or semi-periphery of the global trade.

Positively Downward: Refers to movement of integration as depicted in the second quadrant of the integration-satisfaction matrix including the *Struggling IEPs* who are "integrated in their CoP but not satisfied;" they usually negotiate their language and cultural identity by struggling to compete with other members of their CoP.

Positively Upward: Refers to movement of integration as depicted in the first quadrant of the integration-satisfaction matrix including the *Highly Achieving IEPs* who are "integrated and satisfied as members of CoP;" they negotiate their language and cultural identity through collaboration with other members of their work environment.

Positivist Approach: A term used to describe a scientific approach that relies on the collection of quantitative and statistical data using brief, clear, and objective discussions and interpretation of results, in contrast to using qualitative data, that uses descriptive narratives based on human feelings or subjective interpretation of facts, events or situations.

APPENDIX A

Interview Extracts Transcription Symbols

/ Non-final intonation contour, more words are coming
// Final intonation contour, closed off
? Final rising intonation
. Final falling intonation
! Lively tone to convey strong feelings
... Separate information as if heard from a different topic sentence
--- Separate information used to elaborate what was said earlier
CAPITALS Emphatic stress, extra loudness or pitch change
Italics Softer voice
    ◦ Talks interrupted, cut-off
(???) Blurred speech
    Audible breathing sounds
, Brief pause
.. Long pause
[ ] English translation of a foreign language,
transcriptor's substitution or interpretation of what was said.
() Connotation or description of what was said

APPENDIX B

Figure 3. Summary of the Socio-Demographic Profile of the Internationally Educated Professionals (N = 30)

Socio-demographic factors	General profile
Gender	13 male, 17 female
Age group	36 – 45 (n = 7), 45 – 55 (n = 18), 56 – 65 (n = 5)
Education	15 Bachelors, 13 Master's, 1 MD, 1 DDM
Professions in home country	7 teaching, 7 accounting/banking, 6 engineering, 5 nursing/allied health, 3 HR/admin, 2 IT,
Ethnicity	24 Filipinos, 3 Europeans, 1 Chinese, 1 Indian, 1 African
Integration to CoP	22 CoP, 8 Non-CoP
Group category/Ethnicity by CoP	18 Filipino CoP, 6 Filipino Non-CoP, 4 Other Culture CoP, 2 Other Culture Non-CoP
Group category/Year of arrival	1988 – 1994 (n = 10), 1995 – 2001 (n = 7), 2002 – 2008 (n = 13)

APPENDIX C

Language and Immigration Policy Documents

Bill 161 Ontario Immigration Act 2014
Canadian Experience Class (CEC)
Canadian Multiculturalism Policy 1971
Immigration Act 1976
Multiculturalism Act 1988
Immigration and Refugee Protection Act (IRPA) 2002
Fair Access to Regulated Professions Act (FARPA) 2006
Immigration and Refugee Protection Act (IRPA) 2008
Language Policy (CIC, 2012)
Ontario Human Rights Commission (OHRC)

Section 2
Translanguaging

Chapter 3
Translanguaging in the Multilingual Language Classroom

Laura E. Mendoza
https://orcid.org/0000-0001-8649-8775
University of Texas at El Paso, USA

ABSTRACT

Given today's culturally diverse classrooms, incorporating new perspectives and pedagogies must be considered of value. This should be primarily considered in the language classroom. Considering multilingualism as a rule, but simultaneously also considering how marginalized many individuals have been, especially in the language classroom; the inclusion of newer pedagogies which resist, and conjointly empower, emergent bilinguals, should be considered. The current chapter aims to highlight relevant literature which may enlighten the use of translanguaging practices in the language classroom.

INTRODUCTION

Given today's culturally diverse classrooms, incorporating new perspectives and pedagogies must be considered of value. This should be primarily considered in the language classroom. Considering multilingualism as a rule, but simultaneously also considering how marginalized many individuals have been (Palmer et al., 2014), especially in the language classroom, the inclusion of newer pedagogies that resist and conjointly empower emergent bilinguals should be considered. Therefore, the current chapter aims to highlight relevant literature which may enlighten the use of translanguaging practices in the language classroom.

For the purposes of the current chapter, translanguaging is to be understood as presented by García and Wei (2014). The authors state:

Translanguaging is the process of making meaning, shaping experiences, and gaining understanding and knowledge through the use of two languages. Translanguaging, for us, goes beyond the concept

DOI: 10.4018/978-1-6684-8761-7.ch003

of the two languages of additive bilingualism or interdependence. Translanguaging is the enaction of language practices that use different histories but are now experienced against each other in speakers' interactions as one new whole. (p. 20)

Building from this, García and Kleyn (2016) continued the conversation by explaining, "Translanguaging asserts that bilingual speakers draw from one integrated linguistic repertoire to make meaning with their environment. In contrast to code-switching, which assumes separate linguistic systems corresponding to each language" (García & Kleyn, 2016, p. 64). Consequently, for the current chapter, translanguaging will entail not only those practices (linguistic, social, and cultural) that emergent bilinguals and multilingual speakers engage in but also the contributions that such dynamic practices represent in the (language) classroom. In this sense, this chapter aims to reconceptualize emergent bilinguals' needs to present them as an asset rather than a deficiency.

BACKGROUND: A BRIEF HISTORICAL BACKGROUND OF TRANSLANGUAGING

Opposite to today's views of translanguaging, historically, the first conceptions of bilingualism were governed by the belief that languages were not meant to interact or be interrelated. Originally, "bilingualism was said to be additive, as if one autonomous language entity with explicit boundaries could be added to another. The two languages, corresponding to nation-states' sociopolitical construction, never met or interacted in the language of bilinguals" (García & Kleifgen, 2020, p. 3). This section of the chapter will illustrate how the perspectives about translanguaging have been evolving and the origins of such views.

The first instances where languages started to merge within minoritized societies were found amongst the Welsh, who proclaimed that their language was in decline for an extended period of time. Although bilingualism during the 20th century was evidently and strictly separative, some schools attributed their success to the inclusion of newer pedagogical approaches. Following these changes, in 1994, a Welsh educator named Cen Williams decided to start merging languages in a different way, where Welsh and English would interact during the same lesson, giving room for the creation of the term *trawsieithu* (García & Kleifgen, 2020; Goodman & Tastanbek, 2021). Like Williams, it was evident that academics and educators started questioning language separation in the classrooms at some point, leading researchers and practitioners to start working toward newer strategies and perspectives (Creese & Blackledge, 2010). In other words, the one-language-at-a-time perspective started to seem irrelevant (García & Kleifgen, 2020) and, more importantly, insufficient while caring for today's emergent bilinguals. During the early 2000s, authors (Lin & Martin, 2005; 2006) had already started showing the world some of the positive pedagogical implications of what, during those days, was known as code-switching. Soon after, Ofelia García started approaching the importance of multilingualism and pluriliteracies (García et al., 2007; García, 2008) to start theorizing about translanguaging (García & Kleifgen, 2020; García & Leiva, 2014; Kleyn & García, 2019; Vogel & García, 2017) in the ways which are presented in this chapter.

As addressed earlier, language teaching was historically based on monolingual approaches. Scholars (Kleyn & García, 2019; Lin, 2013) have noted how particularly the field of ESL (English as a Second Language) was initially inclined to focus on the mastery of native-like pronunciation and, perhaps, understanding too; the imitation and memorization (Raimes, 1983) of basic well-structured sentences represented the norm for years for many of these classrooms. Nevertheless, unfortunately, these teaching methods for language classrooms did not consider the fluidity emergent bilinguals were bringing with them. Similarly, these teaching methods did not have enough room for considering and integrating students' backgrounds and previous knowledge. The following paragraphs, then, will bring this historical path to our current days as they will present some of the most salient differences and similarities between code-switching and translanguaging, as research presented in the current chapter includes both terminologies at a given time.

Code-Switching and Translanguaging: Differences and Similarities

To fully acknowledge the relevance of adopting translanguaging pedagogies in the language classroom, the reader must be acquainted with the differences and similarities that different phenomena possess, as is in the case of *code-switching* and *translanguaging*. Even though both constructs are part of the current chapter, it is worth exemplifying how these terms have evolved over the last few years. Generally speaking, both constructs might be differentiated in terms of four main aspects: (1) their goals, (2) their focus on language boundaries, (3) their theoretical frameworks, and (4) their educational impetuses.

The first distinction between code-switching and translanguaging relates to their goals. Following García's (2009) views, Park (2013) establishes how translanguaging proposes the full utilization of languages, as flexible as these can be, in an effort to benefit students' experiences as they are becoming emergent bilinguals. This said, the practices mentioned above will allow minoritized students to freely socially navigate their linguistic resources while conjointly shaping their identities (Mendoza-Fierro, 2020). Translanguaging suggests a holistic perspective where individuals will be constantly using all their resources at hand in their meaning-making processes. On the other hand, code-switching remains purposeful; here, bilinguals with shared languages purposefully decide when to switch between these shared languages (Sahan & Rose, 2021).

Another significant variation between the constructs relies on their focus on language boundaries. For this reason, it is then relevant to follow Goodman and Tastanbek's (2021) words in order to gain a better understanding of the differences and overlapping of code-switching and translanguaging:

Through a translanguaging lens, what has previously been called alternation, mixing, hybridity, and fusion of codes is better understood as languaging practices that transcend named language boundaries. Translanguaging as a theory and pedagogical approach also adds greater emphasis on the use of language in classrooms for meaning making and identity formation. (p. 11)

In this sense, whereas code-switching emphasizes the existence of varied linguistic boundaries, translanguaging resists such notions. Similarly, while code-switching implies that individuals possess separate linguistic systems reigning with specific structures, translanguaging continues emphasizing the fluidity and hybridity of languages. Equally important, translanguaging emerged looking to diminish monolingual ideologies in reference to understanding bilingualism as additive, following the perspective that individuals must have an L1, probably their dominant language, and a separate L2 which represents another additional system; nevertheless, translanguaging suggests the use of language in a more accessible way in which individuals do not necessarily follow specific language rules, or more importantly, those mandated by several institutions (García & Kleifgen, 2020).

Another notable difference between code-switching and translanguaging relies on their theoretical framework. "Translanguaging markedly contrasts mainstream grammatical models of code-switching, which have historically focused on describing, examining, and predicting the grammatical structure of bi/multilingual speech" (Balam, 2021, p. 87). Creese and Blackledge (2015), following García and Wei's (2014) perspectives, remind us that translanguaging provides an ampler understanding of the linguistic repertoires people may have, as it understands people's practices as dynamic rather than static, which therefore can be adapted to varied contexts. Following Cook (2001), Park (2013) defines code-switching as "a bilingual-mode activity in which more than one language, typically speakers' native language and second language (L2), are used intrasententially or intersententially" (p. 50). In this sense, syntactic structures for monolinguals and bilinguals are highly relevant; therefore, from sociolinguistic and psycholinguistic perspectives, code-switching understands the use of language differently (Balam, 2021).

Furthermore, whereas translanguaging presupposes a more open view of the integration and co-construction of languaging, code-switching, as presented earlier, occurs intersententially or intrasententially (Balam, 2021; Cook, 2001; Park, 2013). Equally important to these distinctions is that code-switching follows monoglossic ideologies, and conversely, translanguaging follows heteroglossic ideologies. Not less importantly, code-switching constantly emphasizes the separation of languages, whereas translanguaging resonates with meaning-making and identity formation (Goodman & Tastanbek, 2021). Furthermore, Canagarajah (2011) explains how, for translanguaging, "Competence doesn't consist of separate competencies for each language, but a multicompetence that functions symbiotically for the different languages in one's repertoire" (p.1); in other words, translanguaging perceives all knowledge, and thus competencies, as relevant, allowing a more fluid and non-restrictive use of language.

Perhaps the most notable distinction between the two terms is their educational impetuses. As Lewis, Jones, and Baker (2012) reflected, code-switching was focused initially on the social practices of (bilingual) individuals, and then it moved to the description and analysis of educational settings. Opposingly, translanguaging started by focusing on educational settings, and then it started providing a lengthier understanding of diversified social practices. The historical turning point of the inclusion of code-switching views in terms of formal schooling was provided by McCarty in the early 1980s, who observed Native Americans and their linguistic practices; they were enrolled in a predominantly White school in Arizona, and McCarty noticed how Native Americans would use their languages as social identity (Goodman & Tastanbek, 2021; McCarty; 1980). The rest of the chapter will strategically present information regarding the inclusion of translanguaging in the language classroom as it may evoke various benefits for emergent bilinguals.

Translanguaging in Our Classrooms

The current chapter presents information regarding some of the studies mentioned above, paying particular attention to those where authors have highlighted a variety of pedagogical practices that positively impact the lives of emergent bilinguals (e.g., the inclusion of translanguaging in ESL classrooms). In the language classroom, using pedagogies like the inclusion of translanguaging can contribute to adding to the students' dynamic linguistic, social, and cultural practices instead of hindering them. It is then relevant for educators, policymakers, and administrators, in general, to continue considering the varied practices to be found as part of our current language classrooms.

Coming from Bakhtinian theories of heteroglossia (Bakhtin, 1981), translanguaging promotes the inclusion of (literacy) practices which provide better opportunities for minoritized students in our own classrooms; it draws attention to the conceptualization of multilingualism instead of bilingualism, and additionally, it promotes a positive perspective in regards to multilingualism (García & Kleifgen, 2020).

By sharing these perspectives, the present chapter aims to contribute to the literature that focuses on emergent bilinguals' meaning-making processes and identity-formation practices by including translanguaging pedagogies in our language classrooms.

It has been noted that, lamentably, many educators in the U.S. perceive their education to be fully in English, and perhaps and depending on the type of program they are involved in, sometimes happening in Spanish or another language entirely; in this way, educators continue perpetuating their monolingual perspectives generation after generation within their classrooms (García, 2020), leaving no room for emergent bilinguals to experience something better suited to their shared knowledge and practices outside of the classroom. Unfortunately, these preconceptions tend to hinder students' multilingualism and multiliteracies. Furthermore, because educators continue imposing these sociocultural perspectives primarily highlighted by certain institutions of power, emergent bilinguals avoid exploring all their linguistic, social, and cultural resources to represent what their own educators, who perhaps do not possess a broad cultural awareness of their students, expect from them. For these reasons, Goodman and Tastanbek (2021) make us reflect upon the importance for educators and researchers, especially those researchers who are focused on ESL education, to refrain from continuing to reproduce monoglossic views of language and start proposing more inclusive heteroglossic linguistic perspectives.

Conteh (2018), for example, reminds us of how important it is for policymakers and educators to understand that students' linguistic practices are not meant to be separated, but on the contrary, these are supposed to be integrated; when a separation occurs, students' home language practices are ignored, instead of empowered. By providing language learners with newer strategies and pedagogies, including the use of translanguaging practices, we can contribute to the maintenance of students' voices (Palmer et al., 2014); conjointly, we will be providing empowering spaces where students can feel safe and valued despite the messages that they might encounter outside the language classroom.

Similarly, García & Kleifgen (2020), based on Hornberger and Skilton-Sylvester (2000), remind us: "Biliteracy is better obtained when learners can draw on all points along the continua; for example, students would be best served by using their vernacular contextualized language at one end to support the attainment of literate decontextualized language at the other end" (p. 3). In this sense, if we provide emergent bilinguals with enough opportunities to embrace all their linguistic repertoires at hand, we can positively respond to their varied social, cultural, and political contexts in a way in which they can feel respected and valued. Additionally, appreciating their diversified practices, particularly their linguistic practices, may leverage their sense of belonging to their new communities (Mendoza-Fierro, 2020; Moran, 2019).

Therefore, the inclusion of translanguaging practices in a language classroom, like the ones summarized right after, presupposes various benefits as it continuously provides opportunities to explore diversity in emergent bilinguals' linguistic repertoires and should not be inhibited.

Possible Instructional Approaches

Although some educators remain enthusiastic about the inclusion of translanguaging pedagogies in their classrooms, many theoretical and practical concerns are still arising and unsolved (Canagarajah, 2011). In this section, different instructional approaches directly related to the use of translanguaging in the classroom and the proliferation of culturally responsive pedagogies are listed.

In the last decades, researchers (Cazden et al., 1996; García et al., 2007; García & Kleifgen, 2020; Kalantzis et al., 2003) have been proposing newer constructs (e.g., the terms multiliteracies and plurilitera-

Translanguaging in the Multilingual Language Classroom

cies) to gain a deeper understanding of the continua of bilingualism, and thus the continua of biliteracy, which is currently embedded in the fluid manners of emergent bilinguals; authors highlight that given the proliferation of innovative technologies, the sociocultural contexts surrounding us, and their practices, these are to be constantly merged linguistically in various ways. García & Kleifgen (2020) stated:

In 2007, García, Bartlett, and Kleifgen proposed the concept of pluriliteracies, an approach to literacy that privileges the acts of multilinguals, and attempted to capture not only the literacy continua with different interrelated axes but also an emphasis on literacy practices in sociocultural contexts, the fluidity of literacy practices especially afforded by new technologies, and the interrelation of languages and other semiotic resources (p. 3).

Newer constructs like those mentioned above provide educators with opportunities to welcome linguistic and literacy perspectives that would have been impossible in earlier days. Such perspectives allow us as language educators to engage ourselves in social, cultural, and linguistic practices that no longer hinder emergent bilinguals' roots but, opposingly, invite us to collectively co-construct meanings with our students. As a result, our role as educators and curriculum creators should be to embrace such newer perspectives and constructs to promote their inclusion and proper usage in the classrooms in order to provide spaces that better simulate outside-of-the-classroom global changes, which are positively impacting the emergent bilinguals in our classrooms.

In an effort to gain a broader and deeper understanding of the different ways in which translanguaging can be included in a language classroom, this section presents a variety of instances where educators and researchers have contributed to the inclusion of such practices and pedagogies. For instance, García, Lin, and May (2017) explain how educators may expect increasing proficiency in different languages when students do their readings from a textbook, the internet, or any particular worksheet in one language. However, the output of the lesson is in a language different than the first one, in this exact scenario, different from English. The authors explain: "This will produce a deeper and fuller understanding of the subject matter, develop oracy and literacy in both languages and better integrate language learning with content learning, as well as integrate children with different home languages in classroom activity" (p. 76). The authors highlight that although translanguaging may require some competency in both languages, scaffolding translanguaging remains beneficial.

Moreover, Carroll and Sambolín Morales (2016), for example, presented information regarding the use of translanguaging and its connection to literature circles. The authors stated that such a strategy helped promote collaborative learning while merging all students' linguistic repertoires. Others (Carroll & Sambolín Morales, 2016; Mazak & Herbas-Donoso, 2014) have provided their students, at the level of higher education, with lectures and exams using a mixture of both English and Spanish; this happened purposefully in a college classroom in Puerto Rico where emergent bilinguals are commonly found at all levels of education. The authors noted how these pedagogical practices are not commonly followed by other educators throughout the island. Carroll and Sambolín Morales (2016, p. 248), highlight: "Despite the fact that Spanish is overwhelmingly the first language of most islanders, English plays an influential role in students' experiences at tertiary institutions on the island." Similarly, transnational students who are currently living on the border, primarily the U.S.-Mexico border, are experiencing similar circumstances where although students are surrounded by Spanish, institutions still privilege the use of English if enrolled in an institution in the U.S.

Based on Ruiz's (1984) proposal of orientations toward language, Burton and Rajendram (2019) propose using translanguaging as a resource. The authors state that a way to validate students' diversified linguistic practices is to challenge monolingual perspectives; one way in which Burton and Rajendram (2019) suggest for this to happen is by creating pre-established groups in our classrooms that represent students' diverse linguistic practices. Following Flores and García (2013), the authors suggest building on project-based learning to open opportunities for emergent bilinguals to collaborate and, thus, raise awareness of peers' cultural and linguistic preferences. In the same manner, Cole (2019) suggests the implementation of collaborative translations in our classrooms.

Other strategies that have been used by educators who are following translanguaging pedagogies are the inclusion of home language cues, songs, or greetings, instead of just perpetuating English-only/one-language-only perspectives (Celic & Seltzer, 2011). To illustrate, given today's proliferation of reggaeton and trap, along with many other newer music genres, the inclusion of songs that freely and commonly participate in translanguaging practices in an authentic way could be more relevant. Many emergent bilinguals in today's society are acquainted with these fluid linguistic practices, given the current pop culture surrounding us. To illustrate, the students in a language classroom can collectively create a playlist that includes songs where singers/bands engage in translanguaging practices, and, as a follow-up, the emergent bilinguals in that classroom can corroborate the different meanings.

Moreover, authors like Esquinca, Araujo, and De la Piedra (2014) remind us of how important it is for us as language educators to help our emergent bilinguals to gain easier access to the understanding of specific topics while conjointly navigating their meaning-making processes. The authors note how, for example, the constant use of cognates, translations, and paraphrasing can help emergent bilinguals break down ideas or procedures to understand them easily. They also highlighted the importance of scaffolded translanguaging. Similarly, Berthele (2011) explored how students can expand their linguistic repertoires by guessing the meaning of unfamiliar cognates; the author states that by providing students with opportunities to listen to and engage in practices in all their languages, they can potentially become fluent soon in both languages which could help them interact with others in a more accessible manner.

Like the previous authors, Cole (2019) echoes the importance of including the use of cognates, especially in classrooms that are institutionally designated to teach and use academic English. Along the same lines, students in the language classroom can solve crossword puzzles where, for instance, the question from the crossword puzzle is a cognate in one language, and the answer is a cognate in another language. Educators must be cautious when using this approach, as they first must prescreen the linguistic diversity in their classroom. A piece of advice could be to assign students to specific teams in advance where they can build on one another's knowledge.

To continue the conversation and also support the use of cognates for emergent bilinguals, Cole (2019) says:

Many districts across the country provide vocabulary lists that students need to know, and a large proportion of the key vocabulary is based on Latinate cognates. Not only can teachers provide the district-mandated vocabulary list in multiple languages to facilitate student comprehension and parental engagement, but teachers can also actively help students draw connections across languages in ways that will support long-term vocabulary learning, as well as the kinds of meta-linguistic knowledge that is often valued on assessments that hold high stakes for students, such as the SAT (p. 246).

By providing lists in multiple languages, educators will be serving a variety of goals, as Cole (2019) states. On the one hand, educators will be providing equitable tools (e.g., multilingual vocabulary lists) that may provide different means for comprehension and clarification for emergent students in a classroom; on the other hand, educators will be opening spaces where students and their parents can participate in the learning process.

Providing opportunities for parents and caregivers to present clear connections to their children could alleviate the (school-home) disconnection many institutions still have when sharing knowledge. García, Lin, and May (2017) remind us about the previously mentioned importance of effectively including families and students' communities in their learning processes. The authors note: "[It] is not simply a matter of benefit to the children because of increased home participation; it benefits the production of knowledge because the lenses to understand the world are expanded by incorporating different perspectives and epistemologies embedded in the linguistic and cultural practices of local communities" (p. 11). For this reason, considering home participation in the language classroom can simultaneously provide safe spaces for the co-production of knowledge, and adhering to the current chapter's purpose, also provide safe spaces where emergent bilinguals and their families can use all their linguistic resources at hand to gain a deeper understanding of their experiences.

Alvarez (2014), guided by García's (2012) views, proposes the inclusion of the following assignments that clearly reflect the use of translanguaging. The author suggests including assignments like ethnographies or autobiographies where students can talk with and about their own communities; Alvarez notes that these activities allow students to pay attention to different accents, use different linguistic varieties, and, equally important, learn more about their backgrounds and communities. Furthermore, we should consider that by listening to our students' stories in their own words, we can foster a culture of respect and value in our language classrooms where all students feel equally appreciated. When conducting these projects, students can learn to listen to others' stories and start connecting with them in a more profound way based on their similar experiences. Opportunities to engage in culturally relevant pedagogies like the ones just presented can help us leverage our students' sense of community and belonging.

In a similar fashion, Alvarez (2014) highlights how important it is considering having assignments with detailed instructions, which can help minoritized students' parents to understand better what the assignment requires; in this sense, students will be provided with lengthier and better expectations, but conjointly, parents could be more aware of their children's needs. Alvarez (2014) notes: "Language minority parents are co-teachers of their children" (p. 329). The author continues, "Encouraging language brokering inside classrooms is the first step in recognizing it as a translanguaging tool." This said, a way for us as language educators to contribute to the inclusion of translanguaging pedagogies in the classroom can be as easy as starting to scaffold their linguistic practices. These translanguaging practices help them to negotiate their meanings constantly and, as a consequence, help them to highly value community-based functions (Alvarez, 2014; García, 2011). For emergent bilinguals, part of their roles in their communities is to constantly help as liaisons (e.g., as translators) for their family or other community members; this is what Orellana (2009) recognizes as language brokers and, simultaneously, it is also where connections to their real communities emerge. For this reason, by attending to these linguistic and cultural practices in our classroom, we are better bridging emergent bilinguals' homes with their academic endeavors.

Furthermore, when we draw from emergent bilinguals' previous knowledge and multicultural perspectives, we can help empower them by demonstrating that they have substantial knowledge to share with the rest of the class instead of viewing them as those with limited English proficiency (Celic & Seltzer,

2011). Ultimately, these practices can increase our cultural awareness to be more culturally responsible in our language classrooms. To illustrate, we can also encourage our students in the language classroom to create multiple connections, likely home connections, when reading a text and discussing it (Carroll & Sambolín Morales, 2016); therefore, if they make use of all their linguistic repertoire while participating in these discussions as mentioned earlier, we can potentially ensure success for them inside and outside the language classroom. By implementing culturally relevant pedagogies and materials in our language classrooms, we can help our emergent bilinguals to find safe spaces to share their experiences in a variety of ways (e.g., linguistically and rhetorically).

Additionally, other strategies that have been noted are those that can be mediated through the use of technology. For instance, a common way in which emergent bilinguals can make use of translanguaging in an academic setting is by using Google Translate (Celic & Seltzer, 2011; Mendoza-Fierro, 2020). These opportunities should be created in an effort to create multilingual environments that are more welcoming for emergent bilinguals. Another way to incorporate translanguaging in our language classroom is to assign tasks where the students can interview members of their family, who probably speak a different language, and report back to the class (Alvarez, 2014). The author also suggests that students can interview their own peers in their classroom to become more aware of their literacies and languaging practices; more importantly, Alvarez (2014) finishes by adding how important it is to provide opportunities to discuss translanguaging as a topic by having a variety of workshops.

For these reasons, the present chapter proposes the inclusion of translanguaging practices in the language classroom as a means of resisting the continuous integration of curricula, which, on the one hand, are not culturally responsive and, on the other hand, are not promoting social justice. Literature based on a culturally responsive pedagogy highlights how, although valuing students' funds of knowledge as well as their cultural competencies is relevant, these types of pedagogies are less helpful if the curriculum remains the same (Buck, 2016; Sleeter, 2011). Svensson (2021), for example, highlights how critical it is for educators and administrators to count on a curriculum that includes social justice; in this particular context of a language classroom, this social justice can be represented by implementing translanguaging and re-evaluating the respect provided to students' cultures and knowledge.

FUTURE RESEARCH DIRECTIONS

It is worth mentioning that although research regarding translanguaging and its pedagogical approaches is taking a more enlightening perspective recently, limitations in terms of such research are evident. For example, research is mainly dedicated to exploring the experiences of young students and not adults (Esquinca et al., 2014); specifics in relation to the use of translanguaging practices in ESL are still very limited (Mendoza-Fierro, 2020); and, equally important, much of the research relates face-to-face experiences but very limited research is available concerning other multimodal genres such as social media (Canagarajah, 2011). Other potential research opportunities include the comparison of varied contexts where translanguaging is used although not promoted versus others where translanguaging is highly encouraged; equally relevant would be to compare and contrast the use of translanguaging across generations.

CONCLUSION

Feasibly, the ongoing resistance of many (language) educators and curriculum creators to more freely integrate translanguaging as a pedagogy lies in how challenging this could be. Nevertheless, although adopting these more culturally relevant pedagogies (e.g., a translanguaging pedagogy) could be more demanding, its inclusion can be beneficial even when educators need to learn better all their students' linguistic resources (Cole, 2019). As a consequence, the present chapter aims to continue contributing to the literature, which is entirely devoted to promoting the inclusion of newer pedagogies, like translanguaging, to simultaneously invite educators, curriculum creators, and researchers to adopt such views. However, more importantly, the chapter aims to invite colleagues to adopt such pedagogies to help emergent bilinguals better navigate their meaning-making processes.

Based on Hornberger and Link (2012), Creese and Blackledge (2015) highlight how educators may build from students' mobile communicative repertoires to build a translanguaging culture. The authors state: "Educators recognize, value, and build on the multiple, mobile communicative repertoires of students and their families" (p. 26). By welcoming these linguistic practices in the language classroom, the students can not only use their linguistic repertoires at hand, but simultaneously, they can also be comfortable sharing their previous experiences and knowledge as they can feel valued and respected. As a closing remark, this chapter wants to emphasize how translanguaging allows emergent bilinguals to bridge their knowledge and language practices at home and school (Celic & Seltzer, 2011), favoring the creation of safer spaces for them where they can learn to better navigate all their social, cultural, and linguistic resources in varied contexts.

Sayer (2013) notes, "The emphasis on maintaining linguistic boundaries in the classroom has led educators to overlook the potential pedagogical benefits of language mixing" (p. 68). As presented earlier, many (language) classrooms were built on such an approach where purism in language darkened any sort of diversity. However, today's culturally diverse classrooms require a more diversified perspective where students can fully utilize their entire repertoires. Therefore, the chapter's purpose was to present evidence that resonates with the inclusion of more welcoming methods, particularly translanguaging, to diminish the hostile social and educational environments that emergent bilinguals may have to navigate constantly.

In a similar fashion, it has been noted how, as a means of building community, (language) educators can go further than only accepting and tolerating students' languages and social practices, but more importantly, they can provide a safe space to integrate them (Creese & Blackledge, 2010; Kleyn & García, 2019). Pitkänen-Huhta (2021) encourages us as educators not only to continue this relevant conversation of bringing translanguaging practices to the classroom but, more importantly, the author proposes a *translanguaging mindset* which should provide a smoother transition at the time of caring for all students equally. García and Kleifgen (2020) remind us: "Translanguaging transforms our understandings of language, bi/multilingualism, and pedagogical approaches to support multilingual learners' use and further expansion of their unique meaning-making repertoire" (p. 2). That being the case, by opposing the inclusion of such dynamic linguistic practices in our own classroom, we are perpetuating the unequal treatment of language and literacy and, consequently, perpetuating having students who feel powerless and devalued. As illustrated here, the current chapter intentionally presents arguments that should positively contribute to having a deeper understanding of the benefits that translanguaging can add to a language classroom.

REFERENCES

Alvarez, S. (2014). Translanguaging tareas: Emergent bilingual youth as language brokers for homework in immigrant families. *Language Arts*, *91*(5), 326–339.

Bakhtin, M. M. (1981). *The dialogic imagination: Four essays* (C. Emerson & M. Holquist, Eds. & Trans.). University of Texas Press.

Balam, O. (2021). Beyond differences and similarities in codeswitching and translanguaging research. *Belgian Journal of Linguistics*, *35*(1), 76–103. doi:10.1075/bjl.00065.bal

Berthele, R. (2011). On abduction in receptive multilingualism: Evidence from cognate guessing tasks. *Applied Linguistic Review*, *2*, 191–220. doi:10.1515/9783110239331.191

Buck, B. (2016). Culturally responsive peace education: A case study at one urban Latino K-8 Catholic school. *Journal of Catholic Education*, *20*(1), 32–55. doi:10.15365/joce.2001022016

Burton, J., & Rajendram, S. (2019). Translanguaging-as-resource: University ESL instructors' language orientations and attitudes toward translanguaging. *TESL Canada Journal*, *36*(1), 21–47. doi:10.18806/tesl.v36i1.1301

Canagarajah, S. (2011). Translanguaging in the classroom: Emerging issues for research and pedagogy. *Applied linguistics review*, *2*(1), 1-28.

Carroll, K. S., & Sambolín Morales, A. N. (2016). Using university students' L1 as a resource: Translanguaging in a Puerto Rican ESL classroom. *Bilingual Research Journal*, *39*(3-4), 248–262. doi:10.1080/15235882.2016.1240114

Cazden, C., Cope, B., Fairclough, N., Gee, J., Kalantzis, M., Kress, G., & Nakata, M.The New London Group. (1996). A pedagogy of multiliteracies: Designing social futures. *Harvard Educational Review*, *66*(1), 60–92. doi:10.17763/haer.66.1.17370n67v22j160u

Celic, C., & Seltzer, K. (2011). *Translanguaging: A CUNY-NYSIEB Guide for Educators.* CUNY-NYSIEB.

Cole, M. W. (2019). Translanguaging in every classroom. *Language Arts*, *96*(4), 244–249. doi:10.58680/la201930003

Creese, A., & Blackledge, A. (2010). Translanguaging in the bilingual classroom: A pedagogy for learning and teaching? *Modern Language Journal*, *94*(1), 103–115. doi:10.1111/j.1540-4781.2009.00986.x

Creese, A., & Blackledge, A. (2015). Translanguaging and identity in educational settings. *Annual Review of Applied Linguistics*, *35*, 20–35. doi:10.1017/S0267190514000233

Flores, N., & García, O. (2013). Linguistic Third Spaces in education: Teachers' translanguaging across the bilingual continuum. In D. Lile, C. Leung, & P. Van Avermaet (Eds.), Managing diversity in education: Key issues and some responses (pp. 243–256). Clevedon, U.K.: Multilingual Matters.

García, O. (2008). Multilingual language awareness and teacher education. Encyclopedia of language and education, 6, 385-400.

García, O. (2009). *Bilingual education in the 21st Century: A Global Perspective*. Wiley-Blackwell.

García, O. (2011). *Bilingual education in the 21st century: A global perspective.* Wiley and Blackwell.

García, O. (2012). Theorizing translanguaging for educators. In C. Celic & K. Seltzer (Eds.), *Translanguaging: A CUNY- NYSIEB guide for educators* (pp. 1–6). City. University of New York.

García, O. (2020). Translanguaging and Latinx bilingual readers. *The Reading Teacher, 73*(5), 557–562. doi:10.1002/trtr.1883

García, O., Bartlett, L., & Kleifgen, J. (2007). From biliteracy to pluriliteracies. Handbook of multilingualism and multilingual communication, 5, 207-228.

García, O., & Kleifgen, J. A. (2020). Translanguaging and literacies. *Reading Research Quarterly, 55*(4), 553–571. doi:10.1002/rrq.286

García, O., & Kleyn, T. (2016). *Translanguaging with multilingual students. Learning from classroom moments.* Routledge. doi:10.4324/9781315695242

García, O., & Leiva, C. (2014). Theorizing and enacting translanguaging for social justice. *Heteroglossia as practice and pedagogy*, 199-216.

García, O., Lin, M. Y., & May, S. (2017). Bilingual and multilingual. *Springer International Publishing, 10*, 978–3.

García, O., & Wei, L. (2014). *Language, bilingualism and education.* doi:10.1057/9781137385765_4

Hornberger, N. H., & Link, H. (2012). Translanguaging and transnational literacies in multilingual classrooms: A biliteracy lens. *International Journal of Bilingual Education and Bilingualism, 15*(3), 261–278. doi:10.1080/13670050.2012.658016

Hornberger, N. H., & Skilton-Sylvester, E. (2000). Revisiting the continua of biliteracy: International and critical perspectives. *Language and Education, 14*(2), 96–122. doi:10.1080/09500780008666781

Kalantzis, M., Cope, B., & Harvey, A. (2003). Assessing multiliteracies and the new basics. *Assessment in Education: Principles, Policy & Practice, 10*(1), 15–26. doi:10.1080/09695940301692

Kleyn, T., & García, O. (2019). Translanguaging as an act of transformation: Restructuring teaching and learning for emergent bilingual students. The Handbook of TESOL in K-12, 69-82.

Lewis, G., Jones, B., & Baker, C. (2012). Translanguaging: Origins and development from school to street and beyond. *Educational Research and Evaluation, 18*(7), 641–654. doi:10.1080/13803611.2012.718488

Lin, A. (2013). Toward paradigmatic change in TESOL methodologies: Building plurilingual pedagogies from the ground up. *TESOL Quarterly, 47*(3), 521–545. doi:10.1002/tesq.113

Lin, A. M. Y., & Martin, P. (2005). (Eds.). Decolonisation, globalisation: Language-in-education policy and practice. Clevedon, U.K.: Multilingual Matters.

Mazak, C. M., & Herbas-Donoso, C. (2014). Translanguaging practices at a bilingual university: A case study of a science classroom. *International Journal of Bilingual Education and Bilingualism, 18*(6), 1–17.

McCarty, T. L. (1980). Language use by Yavapai-Apache students with recommendations for curriculum design. *Journal of American Indian Education, 20*(1), 1–9.

Mendoza-Fierro, L. E. (2020). *The Digital Literacy Practices of Transfronterizx ESOL College Students: Los De ESOL* [Doctoral dissertation, The University of Texas at El Paso].

Moran, L. (2019). *Belonging and becoming in a multicultural world: Refugee youth and the pursuit of identity*. Rutgers University Press.

Orellana, M. F. (2009). *Translating childhoods: Immigrant youth, language, and culture*. Rutgers University Press.

Palmer, D. K., Martínez, R. A., Mateus, S. G., & Henderson, K. (2014). Reframing the debate on language separation: Toward a vision for translanguaging pedagogies in the dual language classroom. *Modern Language Journal, 98*(3), 757–772. doi:10.1111/j.1540-4781.2014.12121.x

Park, M. S. (2013). Code-switching and translanguaging: Potential functions in multilingual classrooms. Working Papers in *TESOL & Applied Linguistics, 13*(2), 50–52.

Pitkänen-Huhta, A. (2021). Multilingualism in Language Education: Examining the Outcomes in the Context of Finland. In P. Juvonen & M. Källkvist (Eds.) Pedagogical Translanguaging: heoretical, Methodological and Empirical Perspectives (pp. 226-245). Multilingual Matters. https://doi.org/10.21832/9781788927383-014

Raimes, A. (1983). Tradition and revolution in ESL teaching. *TESOL Quarterly, 17*(4), 535–552. doi:10.2307/3586612

Ruíz, R. (1984). Orientations in language planning. NABE. *The Journal for the National Association for Bilingual Education, 8*(2), 15–34. doi:10.1080/08855072.1984.10668464

Sahan, K., & Rose, H. (2021). Translanguaging or code-switching? Re-examining the functions of language in EMI classrooms. *Multilingual perspectives from Europe and beyond on language policy and practice*, 45-62.

Sayer, P. (2013). Translanguaging, TexMex, and bilingual pedagogy: Emergent bilinguals learning through the vernacular. *TESOL Quarterly, 47*(1), 63–88. doi:10.1002/tesq.53

Sleeter, C. E. (2011). An agenda to strengthen culturally responsive pedagogy. *English Teaching, 10*(2), 7–23.

Svensson, G. (2021). 5. Developing Pedagogical Translanguaging in a Primary and Middle School. In P. Juvonen & M. Källkvist (Eds.) Pedagogical Translanguaging: Theoretical, Methodological and Empirical Perspectives (pp. 76-94). Multilingual Matters. https://doi.org/10.21832/9781788927383-007

KEY TERMS AND DEFINITIONS

Culturally Relevant Pedagogy: A pedagogy with a focus on empowerment; a culturally relevant pedagogy constantly looks for student success without diminishing the importance of maintaining and appreciating their own cultures and heritages. This type of pedagogy contributes to the acknowledgment of home communities as well as their knowledge and practices.

Emergent Bilingual: The current chapter prefers the term emergent bilinguals over other standardized terminologies such as Language Learner in an effort to decrement the instances where individuals are perceived, and/or treated, based on their linguistic abilities.

Heteroglossic Ideology: An ideology which perceives languaging practices as diversified and multiple; it recognizes the constant validation, creation, and re-creation of identities since linguistic practices from this view are mobile and non-traditional.

Linguistic Repertoire: The linguistic repertoire an individual possesses refers to all the linguistic resources such an individual has accumulated during life, and which he/she is able to utilize, mobilize, and re-construct as needed.

Monoglossic Ideology: An ideology which presupposes that proper linguistic practices are exclusively legitimized by monolinguals as they are able to perform in a way which is broadly socially and culturally accepted.

Pluriliteracies: The ability to comprehend and/or produce diverse messages using linguistic and non-linguistic codes, but most importantly, incorporating a variety of modalities.

Translanguaging: For the purposes of the current chapter, translanguaging should be understood by the reader as the act of resisting monoglossic monolingual ideologies which devalued the linguistic practices of emergent bilinguals. Translanguaging reflects upon the use of language in a fluid and hybrid manner which constantly allows social, cultural, and linguistic flexibility.

Chapter 4
Translingual and Transcultural Engagement:
Imagining, Maintaining, and Celebrating Collaboration, Agency, and Autonomy in a US University

Sibylle Gruber
Northern Arizona University, USA

Nancy G. Barrón
Northern Arizona University, USA

ABSTRACT

This chapter uses an epistemological framework rooted in feminism, post-colonialism, and deconstruction to situate discussions of how knowledge is created, and how collaborative knowledge creation extends our understanding of the shifting and inter-connected cultural, social, and language realities that we experience in our lives. The authors show that these collaborative efforts construct meaning, expand meaning, and change previously accepted meaning. They show how they interrogate the normalization of this discipline, how they address the need for continuously re-examining and re-thinking approaches to translingual and transcultural collaboration as a way to construct new meaning, and how collaborative work continues to address and redefine the norms and realities of the dominant academic culture so that our contributions can lead to much-needed change in how we understand our roles as participants and stakeholders in translingual and transcultural collaborations.

INTRODUCTION

In an article on "Cultivating a Rhetorical Sensibility in the Translingual Classroom," Juan C. Guerra (2016) asks whether we should have explicit conversations about translingualism in our classrooms. He answers the question by arguing that we need to "engage in the process of explicitly demystifying

DOI: 10.4018/978-1-6684-8761-7.ch004

the various approaches to language difference – including the translingual – by inviting our students to consider how each of them influences the choices they make in the writing classroom" (p. 232). Guerra's (2016) comment reminded us of the many discussions we have had about the need for incorporating translingualism and transculturalism into the curriculum. It also reminded us of our own experiences as translingual and transcultural students and faculty, and the urgent need to expand current research and include attention to our own lived experiences in largely monolingual and monocultural academic environments where critical language awareness (Shapiro, 2022) was not part of any discussions on appropriate academic language use.

In this chapter, we focus on contextualizing our own experiences as translingual and transcultural individuals who have learned, through collaboration on curriculum development and research publications, that diverse cultural and language perspectives and practices can become a means to change current knowledge and create new and expanded knowledge. We use our experiences as an international faculty and a Latina faculty to address the benefits of transcultural and translingual collaboration. We use an epistemological framework rooted in feminism, post-colonialism, and deconstruction to situate our discussions of how knowledge is created, and how collaborative knowledge creation extends our understanding of the shifting and inter-connected cultural, social, and language realities that we experience in our lives. We show that our collaborative efforts as teachers and researchers – who grew up in different countries and whose backgrounds and experiences do not conform to dominant standards – construct meaning, expand meaning, and change previously accepted meaning. Such an understanding of collaboration in a dominant discourse system, we point out, has allowed us to work in an institutional setting that largely encourages heteronormative and hegemonic language and cultural discourses, and to redefine, realign, and reframe our roles as translingual and transcultural faculty who cannot and who do not want to claim participation in mainstream academic social realities devoid of our own realities. We address, overall, how we interrogate the normalization of our discipline, how we address the need for continuously re-examining and re-thinking our own approaches to translingual and transcultural collaboration as a way to construct new meaning and develop new agency, and how our collaborative work continues to address and redefine the norms and realities of the dominant academic culture so that our contributions can lead to much-needed change in how we understand our roles as participants and stakeholders in translingual and transcultural collaborations.

When we discussed the complex choices we would make when writing this article, we explored whether we would incorporate Spanish, Austrian German, Spanglish, or any of the dialects and vernaculars that we speak. We acknowledge the difficulty of our decision to focus on academic English. As translingual and transcultural professionals, we always make decisions based on purpose and intended audience. This affords us agency to determine which of our multiple and sometimes contradictory identities our audience can access. For this article, our intended audience is mostly English-speaking. We do not expect Spanish and Austrian German knowledge, nor do we expect in our audience a combination of the various dialects and vernaculars we speak. We are trained and find value in academic English when the communicative situation requires it. We also take seriously the need for critical reflections and continuous discussions of localized experiences. Our autoethnographic moments explore how we have continuously changed, adjusted, and reflected on our translingual and transcultural journeys, and how we have accepted that we need to take seriously our agency as individuals whose experiences are often outside or at the periphery of dominant educational, cultural, societal, and political systems.

Literature Review: Framing and Reframing Translingual and Transcultural Research

Beyond Speaking and Writing: Identity and Culture in Language Learning

In a recent publication on grounded literacies in a transnational setting, Jay Jordan (2022) argues that "language learning is rarely if ever linear, that transfer is complex and even idiosyncratic, that histories and trajectories are always relevant even if they are not immediately available for reflection" (p. 105). Jordan's (2022) argument reflects a growing concern with an institutionalized majority literacy that rejects "deviations" from a standardized language norm used and taught in educational settings. Learning a foreign language, in this monolingual understanding of language acquisition, is a stand-alone linguistic skill, devoid of any connections to students' past experiences, their fluency in other languages, or their positionalities within or outside a relatively homogeneous majority culture. In other words, linguistic competence, which includes knowledge of linguistic patterns and grammatical structures, is seen as the ultimate goal of language acquisition. Such a focus on decontextualized linguistic structures, as Amaral and Meurers (2008) explain, "has hindered the development of learner models that take into consideration the ability of students to perform language tasks; the strategies they must master to successfully use language in context; and their linguistic abilities relative to the linguistic context and the task" (p. 323).

The need for understanding language learning and language use within the context of discursive practices where speaking or writing is impacted by specific rhetorical situations has been explored as part of research on L1 speakers as well as L2 speakers. With it, we have learned much about the importance of paying attention to discourse communities in which language is used to communicate (Gee, 1987, 1999). According to Gee's (1987) early research, a discourse community is "a socially accepted association among ways of using language, of thinking, and of acting that can be used to identify oneself as a member of a socially meaningful group or 'social network'" (p. 3). As such, discourse is an "identity kit" that "comes complete with the appropriate costume and instructions on how to act and talk so as to take on a particular role that others will recognize" (p.3). This approach to communicating successfully in specific situations emphasizes that discourses are ideological and that they are "intimately related to the distribution of social power and hierarchical structure in society" (p. 5). Those in power positions are able to control what is accepted within different discourse communities and are, in effect, the keepers of "dominant discourses" (p. 5), discourses that are evident in workplace communications as well as in interactions in educational settings.

Dominant discourses, then, are discourses that have taken on the status of "standard," "normal," "legitimate," and "official." However, as Gee (1999) reminds us, our use of language is not stagnant and is "used in tandem with actions, interactions, non-linguistic symbol systems, objects, tools, technologies, and distinctive ways of thinking, valuing, feeling, and believing" (p. 11). In other words, our "social languages" allow us "to enact and recognize different identities in different settings" (p. 12). They are closely connected to "situated identities," defined by Gee (1999) as "different identities or social positions we enact and recognize in different settings" (p. 12). And although linguistic features of "standard English" – as diverse as standard English is in different parts of the world – are highlighted and expected in publications, formal schooling, many workplaces, and in language assessment practices, these standards are only abstracted from the dominant discursive practices used by those with political, economic, educational, and cultural capital.

Gee's (1999) discussion of social languages and situated identities is especially important to keep in mind when discussing discrimination based on communicative practices. As Rosina Lippi-Green (2012) points out, language "is the most salient way we have of establishing and advertising our social identities" (p. 3). In her research on the relationship between language and identity, Lippi-Green (2012) explores the "tyranny of the majority" (p. 3), a majority that is able to control language standards and our participation with the standards. She reminds us that language standardization promoted by prescriptivists neglects to address the continuous changes over time that languages go through. Standardization, then, is "an attempt to stop language change, or at least, to fossilize language by means of controlling variation" (p. 8). Such control is possible because we believe in the "myth of standard language," a myth that "is carefully tended and propagated, with huge, almost universal success" and which has led to an "ideology of standardization which empowers certain individuals and institutions to make these decisions and impose them on others" (p. 61).

When addressing the language subordination process, Lippi-Green (2012) highlights our complicity in the process. As she argues, "when speakers of devalued or stigmatized varieties of English consent to the standard language ideology, they become complicit in its propagation against themselves, their own interests and identities" (p. 69). Such complicity, she points out, is "surprising, even deeply disturbing" (p. 73) because "many individuals who consider themselves democratic, even-handed, rational, and free of prejudice, hold on tenaciously to a standard ideology which attempts to justify rejection of the other because of race, ethnicity, or other facet of identity that would otherwise be called racism" (pp. 73-74). Thus, although language variation is an intrinsic "feature of language" (p. 21) and often arises "from language as a creative vehicle of free expression" (p. 21), many adhere to and support a standard created to exclude and reject the many language variations used by discourse communities across the country and across the globe.

To show the irrationality and inequity of language subordination, Lippi-Green reminds us that "if as a nation we are agreed that it is not acceptable or good to discriminate on the grounds of skin color or ethnicity, gender or age," it is similarly intolerable "to discriminate against language traits which are intimately linked to an individual's sense and expression of self" (p. 332). Our socially situated identities, and with it our discursive practices (Gee, 1999), require us to look closely at the underlying reasons for dominant language ideologies, our complicity with the dominant system, our exclusion from it, and our willingness or unwillingness to take agency and expose and address the discriminatory and unjust sentiments of dominant language standards.

Communication Norms and Ideological Frameworks

Language variations in the U.S. include different Englishes based on dialects, accents, and languages spoken in the home, in schools, in the communities, and in the workplace. Subordinating languages to the language of a heteronormative majority, according to Lippi-Green (2012), "is about taking away a basic human right: to speak freely in the mother tongue without intimidation, without standing in the shadow of other languages and peoples" (p. 335). The many intersecting positionalities that are implicit in language discrimination create an intricate pattern of exclusion that goes beyond language use. Instead, language use is only one of many factors that create our situated identities within an established system and that determine our participation in majority or marginalized discursive communities. To counter intimidation and marginalization means to question and change the underlying epistemological framework that allows for and supports language discrimination and the many discriminatory behaviors against race, ethnicity, gender, LGBTQ+ individuals, internationals, cultural background, and economic and social status.

Changing an existing epistemological framework that is supported by those in positions of power is not an easy task because, as Louis Althusser (1968) points out in his work on ideology and our positions within an ideological framework, members of a community are "hailed" – what he calls interpellated – by the ideologies of those in power to perform according to established norms, rules and principles. Resistance to the accepted narrative of the community, he argues, can lead to exclusion and discrimination, which promotes continued support of established norms. In other words, it is easier to be hailed and interpellated – to be defined by others and to fit ourselves into a specific discursive community – than it is to resist hegemonic forces.

Established dominant ideologies, then, have the potential to define us and influence how we interpret reality and our position within an ideological reality. To escape interpellation by dominant ideologies, marginalized individuals and groups including women, BIPOC, LGBTQ+, and individuals with marginalized language modalities are asked to move beyond what is known and expected. Gloria Anzaldúa (1987), for example, suggests as one possibility to "disengage from the dominant culture, write it off altogether as a lost cause, and cross the border into a wholly new and separate territory" (p. 101). Such counteridentification, however, is only one part of addressing inequities because it continues a dualistic thinking pattern that, according to Anzaldúa (1987), "locks one into a duel of oppressor and oppressed" (p. 100). Instead, because of the many situated identities, we are part of many different communities, and we already understand that each individual "constantly has to shift out of habitual formations; from convergent thinking, analytical reasoning that tends to use rationality to move toward a single goal (a Western mode), to divergent thinking, characterized by movement away from set patterns and goals and toward a more whole perspective, one that includes rather than excludes" (p. 101). Anzaldúa's (1987) discussion of divergent thinking, and of holistic approaches to communicative practices, encourages us to look at frameworks which go beyond dualistic notions of assimilation or opposition, and which provide spaces that address dominant power structures from multiple and intersecting directions.

Anzaldúa's (1987) epistemological framework suggests that changing an unjust system is not the sole responsibility of those marginalized by the dominant language, social, or cultural system. Instead, those in positions of power and those marginalized need to develop "a tolerance for contradictions, a tolerance for ambiguity" (p. 101). This is especially important if we take into consideration that social identities and our ideologies develop, shift, and expand based on our experiences and our interactions with individuals and groups we encounter and interact with. An understanding that our identities and our ideological frameworks constantly shift is especially important to remember in our call for changing dominant language systems that seem static, but that also change based on the changes in political, social, cultural, and global power structures. In other words, we need to emphasize that change is not only necessary but inevitable, and that, as Stuart Hall (1997) explains, we make "meaning by forging links between three different orders of things: what we might broadly call the world of things, people, events and experiences; the conceptual world - the mental concepts we carry around in our heads; and the signs, arranged into languages, which 'stand for' or communicate these concepts." (p. 61). The production of meaning, then, exists within social, political, and cultural contexts and, among others, constructs language identities, national identities, gender identities, and ethnic and racial identities.

Individuals, according to Hall (1997), use language to communicate meaning. At the same time, users of language – as authors and audience – also reconstruct meaning and use specific lenses to interpret and define discursive actions. This means that our intersecting identities, transcultural interactions, and translingual practices influence and arbitrate our understanding and interpretation of communicative interactions. In addition, our understanding is also influenced by how well we can connect with individuals or with members of specific discourse communities. As Kenneth Burke (1969) argues, "you persuade a man [sic] only insofar as you can talk his language by speech, gesture, tonality, order, image, attitude, idea, *identifying* your ways with his" (p. 55, emphasis in original). Identification, the sharing of motives and common goals, in connection with communicative purpose, in other words, is necessary for successful communication.

In addition, to identify with or against something or somebody, as Burke (1965, 1966) reminds us in his discussion of what he calls "terministic screens," we use filters that impact our understanding of reality. Because of our filters and because of the frames we use, we reflect, select, and deflect reality (1966, p. 45). Translingual practices, seen in terms of Burke's (1965, 1966) terministic screens, can be considered through lenses that exclude the unexpected and that deflect realities that are different from what is known. The frames we use to see reality, Burke (1954, 1969) points out, promote the use of language to express positive and negative emotions – we eulogize or we dyslogize what we see, hear or read. For example, the language, dialect, or accent of a region or country we admire is eulogized and seen as superior – such as French and British accents – by many mainstream Americans. On the other hand, Spanish-speaking immigrants in the U.S. are often dyslogized – talked about in negative terms that express deficiency. From this epistemological framework, we reflect a reality that we believe exists. We also select specific parts of the reality that suit our own ideologies, and we deflect other parts of reality that we want to marginalize and exclude.

Theorizing the Issue: Paradigms of Imagining, Encouraging, and Celebrating Translingual and Transcultural Identities

Our role in discursive interactions is not simply the role of speaker and listener; instead, we participate in acts of communication that are impacted by our ideologies, cultural backgrounds, ethnicity, race, gender, sexuality, and language backgrounds. Kenneth Burke's (1965, 1966, 1969) discussion of how we identify with and identify against individuals and groups when we engage in communicative acts, and how we use terministic screens to eulogize or dyslogize, highlights the complexity of discussions on language and discursive practices. It also highlights how difficult it is to put into practice in our classrooms, our professional lives, and our personal interactions, what it is exactly that we are trying to implement in our lives and in our teaching practices. How do we, for example, bring together the interconnections of translingual practices and transculturalism? What do we tell students when they turn to us for support in expressing their concerns about addressing their sexuality with their immigrant parents and grandparents whose different opinions are based on differences in religious understandings, cultural upbringing, and dyslogized language used to describe LGBTQ+ individuals and groups? Questions on moving from theoretical attempts at understanding the complexity of translingual and transcultural identities to application and social justice action have begun to be addressed by teachers and researchers, and are an excellent starting point for in-depth explorations of how we can build on what we have learned over the last few years. This can help us move to a thorough investigation of explicit practices that shed light on how we can examine language diversity and difference from a non-deficit and eulogistic perspective.

The multidirectional and heterogeneous nature of language and culture, and the promises of what such an approach to language and culture can lead to, have been pointed out by researchers focusing on translingualism, on the impact of translingualism on language teaching, and on the connections between translingualism and identity development (Canagarajah, 2013; Cushman, 2016; De Costa, Singh, Milu, Wang, Fraiberg, & Canagarajah, 2017; Lee & Canagarajah, 2019a, 2019b; Lu & Horner, 2016). Lu and Horner (2016) highlight that a translingual approach is opposite "to what monolingualist ideology would have us understand normal language use, users, and relations to be" (p. 212). It is a counter to "using recognizable differences in language as justification for prejudicial treatment" (p. 213) of individuals and groups, and it transforms current monolingual and exclusionary language practices that consider language difference as a deficit and as outside the norm (see Lu & Horner, 2013).

As Keith Gilyard (2016) argues, the discussion of translingualism "galvanizes the multidimensional repudiation of monolingual curriculums and yields praxis informed by an understanding that language and language standards are situational, political, arbitrary, and palimpsestic" (p. 284). Similarly, Juan C. Guerra (2016) explains the promises of translingualism as "a concept that reflects the belief that every student needs to develop a critical awareness about what language does, rather than what it is, in the context of very specific circumstances informed … by a critical awareness of the choices made in the context of the various competing ideological approaches to language difference currently available to us" (p. 228).

Guerra (2016) sees translingualism and transculturalism at one end of a continuum, with multilingualism and multiculturalism in the middle, and monolingualism and monoculturalism at the other end (p. 228). Each approach is based on an ideological framework that, as Burke (1965, 1966) would argue, is influenced and limited by the terministic screens that we bring to the conversation. Guerra's (2016) suggestion is to alert students in our classes to the many competing ideologies at work in current writing and teaching approaches so that they understand the complexity of participating successfully in discursive practices (p. 232). And as Ellen Cushman (2016) argues, translingual practices can "help the process of decolonizing thought and everyday languaging practices" (p. 240) when "scholars, teachers, and students … begin working together to dwell in the borders created by the imperial difference" (p. 240).

Similar to Guerra's (2016) call for introducing students to the intricate processes of communication endeavors, and Cushman's (2016) call for decolonizing language, Canagarajah's (2013) teacher research addresses the promises of translingualism. Because a "translingual orientation moves literacy beyond products to the processes and practices of cross-language relations" (p. 40), it is necessary, according to Canagarajah (2013), that we see translingual literacy as "an understanding of the production, circulation, and reception of texts that are always mobile" (p. 41). He concludes that we need to teach students that literacy is negotiated on a "micro-social" level (p. 61), and that teaching and assessment needs to be based on "learning to find the right balance between authorial intentions and community expectations, writer's voice and readers' uptake, writerly designs and audience collaboration" (p. 64).

Lee and Canagarajah (2019a) also point out that translingual practices in connection with an increased understanding of transculturalism can encourage spaces where language diversity can be appreciated and where we can engage with "pluri-dialogic imaginations, globo-ethical positions and epistemological ecologies" (p. 14). Lee and Canagarajah (2019b) encourage us to look at "translingual dispositions" which they define as "an orientation towards language diversity and difference from a non-deficit perspective" (p. 352).

As can be seen from the research on identity and culture in language learning, and on communication norms and ideological frameworks that support standard language proponents, the need for encouraging, supporting, and carrying out practices that transform our understanding of standard and subordinate language ideologies is becoming ever more urgent if we want to resist and counter language discrimination and prejudice in schools, at work, and in community environments. New theories on translingualism and transculturalism are the beginning of shifting a standard language paradigm to one that embraces agency, difference, equity, and intersectionality. However, as Canagarajah (2013) argues, "theorization of translingual literacy has far outpaced pedagogical practices" (p. 41). In other words, now that we have arrived at the theoretical foundations of a new framework, it is important to continuously address the next steps in the process that leads us from theoretical frameworks to practical and localized applications. Transferring theoretical knowledge to workable actions is never an easy undertaking and is always fraught with complexities that cannot be predicted (see Canagarajah, 2013; Guerra, 2016; Hall & Horner, 2023; McDonald & DeGenero, 2017). To avoid the disconnect between theory and practice then, and to desist what Charles Bazerman (2023) calls the "slipperiness" of theoretical framing (p. 191), the next section explores our own localized translingual and transcultural practices and moves from the slipperiness of theory to positive and productive "coordinated action in the world" (p. 192).

From Theories to Opportunities of Application: Reframing Spaces for Translingual and Transcultural Interactions

In this autoethnographic portion of the chapter, we reflect on how our experiences as members of different discourse communities shape our understanding of how cultural constructs are created by us and also create us (see Canagarajah, 2012; Ellis & Bochner, 2000). This emphasis on socially situated practices allows for localized perspectives and experiences, and applies theory not as a top-down construct but as a result of lived, on-the-ground experiences. It affirms that we construct knowledge within an educational, cultural, social, and economic system that shapes how we see and interpret reality. Through autoethnography, we can take agency and relate our experiences as outside members of an insider environment from the perspective of the marginalized and dismissed without relying on the voices and descriptions of those in positions of power. As Mary Louise Pratt (1991) puts it, autoethnography provides opportunities for individuals to "describe themselves in ways that engage with representations others have made of them" (p. 35).

Our childhood encounters with language variations and cultural differences introduced us to an easy system of "us versus them." It meant that "we" were different and "they" were the norm that needed to be emulated. For Nancy, Spanish, spoken in the home and with other community members, was not accepted as an appropriate mode of communication by most teachers. Additionally, during Nancy's childhood and young adulthood, Mexican Spanish was not accepted in educational settings where Castellano was taught and where Castellano was the only accepted and appropriate Spanish for spoken and written communication. For Sibylle, Austrian dialect, used exclusively before the advent of elementary school, was replaced by a version of Austrian German that nobody in the community spoke outside the classroom walls. When English came into her life, the only acceptable English was standard British English until she studied in the U.S. where American academic English replaced British English, and where an accent modification program erased the Austrian German accent well known by many viewers of films featuring Arnold Schwarzenegger. Both of us were taught that there was a wrong and a right way to speak, and the wrong way was our family's way, and the right way was the school's way.

However, what is considered "standard" language, as Milroy and Milroy (1985) point out, is not a specific lived language. Instead, a standard language is "an idea in the mind rather than a reality – a set of abstract norms to which actual usage may conform to a greater or lesser extent" (pp. 22-23). In other words, instead of a wrong and a right way of communicating, communication happens in context and changes depending on the discourse communities that we belong to. Our families and community members understood this implicitly. They knew that literacy events, as Shirley Brice Heath mentions, "vary from situation to situation" and require "particular interpretive competencies on the part of the participants" (p. 350). At the same time, our families were also convinced that the normative language and pronunciation used and required by our teachers was the one to emulate to get a good job.

In our elementary school careers, we had no name for the normative practices of our teachers and of the school systems. We understood that their language use, and with it our cultural practices, did not conform to the normative requirements of the dominant culture. However, we saw the language of school not as better and only as different. Nancy, for example, knew that her interactions and her use of language needed to adjust to the rituals of Catholic mass. She knew that the store owner in Southern California was not a Spanish speaker and that the kids needed to translate for their Spanish-speaking parents. What neither of us knew at that time was that we were translanguaging, moving in and out of languages, vernaculars, and dialects and participating in diverse discourse communities that required us to shift, adjust, and rethink how we communicate with each other. We were, in other words, largely innocent to the machinations of a dominant social, political, and cultural system that devalued and marginalized the languages, customs, and knowledges of those who were excluded from the system.

Similar to Lippi-Green's (2012) argument that "children are systematically exposed to a standard language ideology by means of linguistic stereotypes in film or television entertainment (p. 101), we too were part of systemic language indoctrination through the entertainment industry. Even though such language indoctrination might be considered benevolent and without much impact, benevolent discrimination, as Romani, Holck, and Risberg (2019) point out, leads to "a subtle and structural form of discrimination that is difficult to see for those performing it, because it frames their action as positive, in solidarity with the (inferior) other who is helped, and within a hierarchical order that is taken for granted" (p. 371). Lippi-Green (2012) confirms this assertion by pointing out that the portrayal of normative languages as positive, and non-normative languages as problematic and negative, "is processed and added to the store of data on how things – and people – are categorized" (p. 104). Certainly, without consciously knowing that we were influenced by how film and media portray characters who speak standardized and non-standardized languages, we inadvertently were, as Althusser (1968) argues, hailed and "interpellated" by the messages sent through film and media. These messages or ideologies, according to Althusser (1968), are always connected to a larger and often normative narrative that, because repeated many times and presented as innocent and benevolent, can be hard to escape.

Normative English and normative Austrian German became the privileged languages of our early U.S. and Austrian college careers and became more and more dominant in our lives. By that time, we had been taught that we were part of communities who used marginalized languages and dialects, and that we needed to adopt standardized norms instead of marginalized languages if we wanted to succeed in academia. Teachers who were proponents of the normative ideological framework reinforced the belief that monolingualism strengthened a nation, and that any deviation needed to be pointed out and ridiculed in order to continue the belief in a uniform language system and a homogeneous society. The resulting stigmatization of other languages and vernacular language varieties had an impact far beyond language use in specific discursive contexts. No longer did we believe that the language of school was just another form of expressing ourselves. Instead, because it was billed as the superior form of communication that any educated person would want to emulate, we were trained to believe in a mythical and exclusive normative language that was supposed to become our own dominant language.

Much of our language learning through our undergraduate years was devoid of ideological context and did not consider the social, cultural, and political repercussions of language discrimination. Nor did it take into account the rhetorical situations complicated by social identity – gender, sexuality, race, ethnicity, nationality, region, socio-economic status, or religion. Certainly, what was valued, what was acceptable, and what was marginalized depended on an ideology of monolingualism and monoculturalism. We came to believe that those at the periphery could only join the ruling majority by consenting to the accepted norms and agreeing to the established social order. It was a time when we applied the rules of the majority to our own language use and quickly became prey to internalized language discrimination and subordination addressed by Lippi-Green (2012). We wanted to become part of the elusive academic community which seemed to own knowledge, culture, and language.

Because of the many times that our experiences as translingual, transcultural, and intersectional members in our educational communities were marginalized, criticized, and dismissed, we often focused on figuring out how to make it through the system. Our challenge as individuals within a monolingual and monocultural academic paradigm was not to enact the promises of translingual participation in learning environments; it was to survive an environment that did not see value in perspectives considered to be outside the acceptable academic norm, whether this involved teaching practices, research agendas, or local, national, and international participation in our fields of study. Even though both of us grew up in a translingual and transcultural world, where we switched in and out of languages, dialects, and vernaculars, and where we learned to rethink, revise, adjust, and redefine who we are, who we were, and who we wanted to be based on family values, community values, and school values, our backgrounds and experiences were discounted in the classroom, and were mocked in the hallways.

The constant reminders that we were not "normal" but "deviant" language practitioners influenced how we identified within and outside academia. For some years, we were convinced that our success as teachers and researchers was only possible if we immersed ourselves within an exclusive educational environment that had made it clear during our undergraduate careers that we needed to leave behind our home languages, our way to express ourselves, and any social and cultural affiliations that could get in the way of academic success. In other words, because of the consistent rejection of our home and community languages and cultural values, we were ready to at least partially re-identify with the language of the majority system. With our willingness to participate in the system, we assumed that our apartness and division from the dominant system would be mitigated by our ability to speak the language of the system.

However, joining a majority system is not a straightforward proposition. It involves a complex web of shifting perspectives that go beyond language use and include a deliberate effort to identify not only with a new community but to also identify against individuals, groups, and communities. As Burke (1969) reminds us, "identification is affirmed with earnestness precisely because there is division" (p. 22). Thus, embracing and identifying with, for example, an exclusionary academic community that expects specific language and social behaviors also means to adjust and change our ideological framework, our social and cultural identities, and our attitudes to others who are part of the system and who exist outside the system. It can create an environment of internalized linguistic discrimination in addition to internalized racism, sexism, homophobia, and genderism. Donna Bivens (2005) articulates the pervasive strain that accompanies the internalization of discrimination, when she points out that "we develop ideas, beliefs, actions and behaviors that support or collude" with ideological frameworks that support racism, homophobia, and language discrimination. Individuals outside the dominant culture, she continues, "are often unconsciously and habitually rewarded for supporting white privilege and power and punished and excluded when we do not. This system of oppression often coerces us to let go of or compromise our own better judgment, thus diminishing everyone as the diversity of human experience and wisdom is excluded" (p. 44). Biven's (2005) specific focus on internalized racism can be expanded to our own internalized language discrimination and our efforts to conform to an abstract standardized language system where we ignored and diminished our own language experiences and the language experiences of our families and communities.

Our understanding of what it meant to be part of an academic community took a little turn during our graduate studies where both of us were introduced to the work of Gloria Anzaldúa (1987), Judith Butler (1990), James Paul Gee (1987), Mary Louise Pratt (1991), Paulo Freire (2007), Shirley Brice Heath (1983, 1988), and Susan Dicker (2003), scholars who address the importance of paying attention to how linguistic, cultural, social, and political ideologies influence our positionalities in different discourse communities. They confirmed what we had learned during our early childhood: it was not a matter of fitting into a system that did not want us but a matter of understanding that we too had valuable contributions to make that would inevitably change not only us but that would require the establishment to change as well. We were no longer confined to remaining at the periphery of academia; instead, we could actively participate in creating new opportunities for all members of the educational environments in which we were working. We could acknowledge and be proud of our participation as translingual and transcultural members in many communities, taking ownership of the languages, dialects, and vernaculars we speak, and showing that our linguistic performance was always and will always be transformed by new experiences and interactions. In other words, we learned by slow process and over many years that academic English could become part of our translingual lives without erasing and negating the many other linguistic, cultural and social identities that defined us.

Our participation expanded beyond individual efforts to change academic teaching and research practices to collaborative translingual and transcultural endeavors where we could highlight our rhetorical and linguistic agency as well as our agency in resisting dominant language standards and address the importance of diverse approaches to student and faculty interactions and learning (Barrón & Gruber, 2007; Barrón, Gruber, & Grimm, 2006; Gruber & Barrón, 2020). From our own interactions, we learned the importance of contextualizing our knowledge and our experiences, and considering the local needs of students, faculty, and the community. In other words, we learned to expand and add to our terministic screens by shifting our focus to move beyond what is expected by an exclusionary framework that only focuses on one narrow and limiting screen. Instead, we learned to listen to individuals and groups at the periphery of educational institutions, and we learned to rethink our own practices as educators. We started to emphasize what can be modified and transformed, and we adjusted our teaching and research practices to address situational and localized processes of linguistic discrimination and exclusion. We applied Kenneth Burke's (1965) concept of terministic screens to move beyond what we considered the realities of academia. We reminded ourselves that terministic screens reflected, selected, and deflected reality based on filters influenced by language use, gender, sexuality, culture, politics, and nationality. This meant that we needed to evaluate how our screens filtered reality, and how we could participate in expanding narrow definitions of successful linguistic frameworks and acceptable social and cultural behaviors in educational environments.

When we started to revisit, revise, and transform our teaching practices and our integration of translingualism in our courses, we emphasized the importance of taking into consideration the educational, cultural, and social backgrounds of students. We also wanted to explore in-depth how we, as teachers and researchers, can provide an educational experience that takes into account the diverse needs, interests, and perspectives of our student populations while introducing and exposing them to a wide range of academic communication practices (Barrón, 2003; Gruber, 2007; Gruber, 2021; Gruber & Barrón, 2023). We emphasized in our work that "the same institution or field may well be interpreted, experienced, and embodied differently by diverse individuals, and these experiences might be in conflict within a single community or social group" (Navarro, 2023, p. 264). We wanted to reiterate the need to move from acculturation into a system that would encourage students to show their translingual and transcultural competencies, or what Navarro (2023) calls "critical and heteroglossic approaches" (p. 267) to communication practices.

This ongoing and constantly shifting process of creating sustainable and heteroglossic learning spaces for students resulted in a curriculum that embeds translingual practices within a wider network of addressing linguistic, cultural, political, and social justice. Much like Jamila Lyiscott (2014) in her TED talk on "3 Ways to Speak English," we emphasize that "the English language is a multifaceted oration subject to indefinite transformation" (1:11). We use it differently in our home, school, and community environments, and we know when to use which language, when to code-switch, and when to integrate different languages and dialects. We participate in what Lyiscott calls "linguistic celebration" (3:44) by consciously highlighting language diversity instead of language subordination.

Our autoethnographic reflections on our experiences emphasize an epistemological framework that expands what it means to create opportunities and participate successfully in language and knowledge communities. In our case, collaborative knowledge creation enlarged our understanding of the shifting and inter-connected cultural, social, political and language realities that we experience in our lives. We learned to appreciate the opportunities for co-constructing meaning, expanding meaning, and changing previously accepted meaning. Collaboration has allowed us to work in an institutional setting that encourages heteronormative and hegemonic language and cultural discourses, and to redefine, realign, and reframe our roles as translingual and transcultural faculty who cannot and who do not want to claim participation in mainstream academic social realities that marginalize the linguistic knowledge and resources of students whose language differences are considered a hindrance instead of a benefit in the academic classroom.

Recommendations and Research Directions: Taking on New Challenges

When we first started teaching and started to conduct research, we attempted to follow an academic paradigm whose epistemological foundation had remained separate from the ever-changing and ever-evolving student and faculty population. The exclusionary and often discriminatory academic agendas were – and still are – determined by the dominant culture and marginalized the perspectives of women, LGBTQ+ individuals and groups, BIPOC, and internationals. This system functioned because the members within the system participated in privileging a normative language, and it is through language, as Shapiro (2022) points out, that "we define our relationships, our communities, and our very identities" (p. 16). Now that we have collaborated and published on creating inclusive learning and teaching environments (Barrón, 2003; Gruber, 2007; Gruber, 2021; Gruber & Barrón, 2023), we recommend that teachers and researchers emphasize the importance of looking carefully at the interconnections of theoretical frameworks and specific localized situations. Instead of using theoretical concepts without attention to specific situations, we encourage individuals and groups to evaluate each situation carefully and to adapt and re-adapt theoretical frameworks to localized contexts.

We approach discussions of collaboration with other faculty and with students, and its impact on our explorations of dominant discourse, through the lens of participatory modeling used very successfully to bring together multiple stakeholders (Henly-Shepard, Gray, & Cox, 2015; Olivar-Tost, Valencia-Calvo, & Castrillón-Gómez, 2020). Participatory modeling directly involves stakeholders from academic communities including scientists and non-scientists, as well as local community members and decision makers, in discussions originally only addressed by a small number of outside experts. Local knowledge is integrated with expert knowledge, and co-learning and a shared understanding of the larger goals while remembering the local context become integral to the process. As rhetoricians, we can apply a similar process by involving faculty, students, and community stakeholders to make space for diverse knowledge experiences and knowledge creation. This encourages us to create a shared understanding of how explicit and implicit dominant discourses shape our interactions with systemic discriminatory ideologies. Our goal is to provide students, faculty, and community members to find confidence in their multiple and sometimes contradictory roles as students, friends, colleagues, and community members and to use their languages, dialects, and vernaculars to be successful individuals and members of their communities. Thus, instead of encouraging a universal definition of a standard language, it is important to show that such an approach allows for inequity and dismissal of experiences and of stakeholders' realities. Higher education works without much change if we avoid, deny, and refuse our stakeholders' realities and knowledges. Instead of creating student dependence on academic language limitations, we encourage teachers to create spaces that lead to critical thinking and to multidirectional sharing of knowledge while purposefully using linguistic skills most appropriate for specific rhetorical situations.

We also encourage teachers to take a close look at the interdependent concepts of language, social and cultural identity, and ideology. Translingualism does not exist outside of students' and teachers' lived experiences, and is connected to culture, gender, sexuality, socio-economic background, politics, religion, and nationality. This means that we need to learn about individual students or a group of students in order to understand how their languages, dialects, and vernaculars connect to their social and cultural identities, and how they influence their ideologies. It also means that we need to be explicit about the purpose of specific writing tasks, and the situational rhetoric in which writing takes place. When we understand students as stakeholders in defining writing for specific situations, then we can create a shared understanding of different kinds of purposes for written and oral communication, allowing for diverse languages, dialects, and vernaculars to show student autonomy in foregrounding and emphasizing the lived realities they want to share.

And although it is not easy to reframe current mainstream narratives, we find it essential to add to, adjust, and transform the limiting frames through which we see academic success. Instead, we need to constantly add to what is familiar to us, and we need to allow for the unfamiliar to teach us about new ways of thinking and understanding so that we can welcome who and what we might have considered outside the academic norm. Similar to Jamila Lyiscott (2014), we recommend that instead of marginalizing and diminishing students' multiple languages and dialects, we acknowledge them as equals and accept that language is "subject to indefinite transformation" (1:14). Thus, instead of diminishing one language and highlighting another, we can show that different rhetorical situations require us to use our translingual knowledge and foreground one of our many languages, dialects, and vernaculars to successfully communicate with our audience. As Lyiscott (2014) puts it, she knows when to use and foreground her many language skills because when the language she chooses does not fit the situation, she points out that "I feel crazy like … I'm cooking in the bathroom" (2:33). As long-term professors, we choose when to step away from traditional academic discourse and include the many other discourses we have incorporated into our lives. As professionals, we allow ourselves to use our languages, dialects, and vernaculars that might surprise students but that opens the door to discuss hegemonic expectations imposed on students and on faculty.

Much of our teaching and research takes into account our students' and our own linguistic diversity. We are aware of language subordination and have started to incorporate linguistic celebration into our teaching practices. *Wir sprechen Deutsch wenn ein Student oder Kollege uns auf Deutsch begrüßt und fragt, ob der Sound of Music genauso populär ist wie in Amerika. Respondemos en Español a los estudiantes que viven en la frontera y que están muy orgullosos de sus habilidades para aprender español e ingles perfectamente.* Future research projects can explore the successful incorporation of different languages, dialects, and vernaculars into a teaching or research environment. When, for example, is it important and necessary to include a teacher's translingual behaviors in the classroom, and when is a more complex approach to translingualism required – such as discussing and showing how languages are always connected in multiple ways to an individual's culture, gender, sexuality, social status, nationality, age, and religion? Studies that incorporate localized contexts will lend depth to current discussions of translingualism and transculturalism, and will shed light on how we, as teachers and researchers, can move forward and create environments where our theories of translingualism and transculturalism are revised, readjusted, and adapted for the purposes, audiences, and needs of specific communities.

We also continue to explore the dynamic complications that accompany individual understandings of hegemony, heteronormativity, and systemic exclusion and discrimination. We know that dominant ideological systems benefit a dominant group. We also know that interpellated hegemonic forces (Althusser, 1968) sustain the status quo. This means that when we make an effort to critically reflect on the problematic limitations imposed by dominant systems, we too are limited by the terministic screens that we have developed throughout our personal, professional, and educational careers. Our aim is to investigate how collaborative endeavors based on a classical and Hegelian dialectic can help us participate in changing current perspectives on translingual and transcultural discourse behaviors and can encourage translingual agency and autonomy. As members of a participatory community, we want to explore how participatory experts can engage in multiple and overlapping discourse communities to establish a shared understanding of our complex roles as teachers, researchers and practitioners.

CONCLUSION

When we started to interrogate the normalization of our discipline and the language acceptable to teach and research in our discipline, we learned that we needed to continuously re-examine and re-think our own approaches to translingual and transcultural collaboration as a way to construct and co-construct new meaning. We examined pragmatic questions on current student needs in order to succeed in academic and workplace situations, and we also paid attention to how we could incorporate a progressive approach that included students' linguistic diversity and opportunities for changing language discrimination and subordination in educational, cultural, political, and social situations. That is, we were especially interested in exploring how we could be pragmatic about current educational requirements while also exposing the injustices of those requirements and highlighting potential opportunities for addressing those injustices. Many teachers and researchers have addressed similar dichotomies in their teaching and scholarly work (Inoue, 2019; Lippi-Green, 2012; Shapiro, 2022). For example, Shapiro (2022), in her work on creating critical language awareness in the writing classroom, explores how we can "prepare student writers for today and also promote a more just world for tomorrow" (p. 7). In our research and teaching, we continue to move beyond to push against dichotomies and implement an approach that encourages and focuses, similar to Shapiro's (2022) discussion of critical language awareness, on "the intersections of language, identity, power, and privilege, with the goal of promoting self-reflection, social justice, and rhetorical agency among student writers" (p. 4).

Our collaborative work, whether as teachers or researchers, continues to address and question the norms and realities of dominant academic culture so that our contributions can lead to much-needed change in how we understand our roles as participants and stakeholders in translingual and transcultural collaborations. Instead of endorsing monolingual ideologies, we focus on creating what Shapiro (2022) calls critical language awareness, and with it linguistic and social justice. To participate in positive action, we continue to transform current practices and to support a pluralistic perspective on language practices and on concurrent knowledge practices influenced by our languages, race, ethnicity, culture, gender, sexuality, and nationality. Similar to Shapiro (2022), we believe that "when we foreground issues of language, identity, privilege, and power in both the content and the delivery of our curriculum, we begin to see and do our work differently" (p. 16). We do not see conclusions as a final moment; instead, we continue to experiment with and explore autoethnographic moments as part of our attempt to include diverse voices into the discussions on the complexities of translingual and transcultural endeavors.

REFERENCES

Ahluwalia, J. (2020). Both not half: How language shapes identity. *TED talk: Ideas worth spreading.* [Youtube]. https://www.youtube.com/watch?v=SP0bAQ8J6C0

Althusser, L. (1968). *Ideology and ideological state apparatuses in Lenin and philosophy and other essays*. New Left Books.

Amaral, L., & Meurers, D. (2008). From recording linguistic competence to supporting inferences about language acquisition in context. *Computer Assisted Language Learning*, *21*(4), 323–338. doi:10.1080/09588220802343454

Anzaldúa, G. (1987). *Borderlands/La frontera: The new mestiza*. Aunt Lute.

Barrón, N. G. (2003). Dear saints, dear stella: Letters examining the messy lines of expectations, stereotypes, and identity in higher education. *College Composition and Communication*, *55*(1), 11–37. doi:10.2307/3594198

Barrón, N. G., & Gruber, S. (2007). Diversity reconsidered: Teaching U.S. heterogeneity in a border state. *The International Journal of Diversity in Organisations, Communities and Nations*, *7*(4), 195–208. doi:10.18848/1447-9532/CGP/v07i04/58023

Barrón, N. G., Gruber, S., & Grimm, N. (Eds.). (2006). *Social change in diverse teaching contexts: Touchy subjects and routine practices*. Peter Lang.

Baxter Magolda, M. B. (2004). Evolution of a constructivist conceptualization of epistemological reflection. *Educational Psychologist*, *39*(1), 31–42. doi:10.120715326985ep3901_4

Bidens, D. (2005). What is internalized racism. In M. Potapchuk, S. Leiderman, D. Bivens, & B. Major, (Eds.), Flipping the script: White privilege and community building, pp. 43-52. Silver Spring, MD, and Conshohocken, PA: MP Associates and CAPD.

Burke, K. (1954). *Permanence and change: An anatomy of purpose*. University of California Press.

Burke, K. (1965). Terministic screens. *Philosophy and the Arts*, *39*, 87–102.

Burke, K. (1966). *Language as symbolic action: Essays on life, literature and method*. University of California Press. doi:10.1525/9780520340664

Burke, K. (1969). *A rhetoric of motives*. University of California Press.

Canagarajah, A. S. (2013). Negotiating translingual literacy: An enactment. *Research in the Teaching of English*, 40–67.

Cushman, E. (2016). Translingual and decolonial approaches to meaning making. *College English*, *78*(3), 234–242.

De Costa, P. I., Singh, J. G., Milu, E., Wang, X., Fraiberg, S., & Canagarajah, S. (2017). Pedagogizing translingual practice: Prospects and possibilities. *Research in the Teaching of English*, 464–472.

Dicker, S. J. (2003). *Languages in America: A pluralist view* (2nd ed.). Multilingual Matters. doi:10.21832/9781853596537

Ellis, C. S., & Bochner, A. P. (2000). Autoethnography, personal narrative, reflexivity: Researcher as subject. In N. K. Denzin & Y. S. Lincoln (Eds.), *Handbook of Qualitative Research* (pp. 733–768). Sage.

Freire, P. (2007). Pedagogy of the oppressed, translated by Myra Bergman Ramos. New York: Continuum.

Gee, J. P. (1987). What is Literacy? *Journal of Teaching and Learning*, *2*(1), 3–11.

Gee, J. P. (1999). *Introduction to discourse analysis: Theory and method*. Routledge.

Gilyard, K. (2016). The rhetoric of translingualism. *College English*, *78*(3), 284–289.

Gruber, S. (2007). *Literacies, experiences, and technologies: Reflective practices of an alien researcher*. Hampton Press.

Gruber, S. (2021). I am an immigrant: Cultural multiplicities in U.S. educational systems. In H. Ostman, H. Tinberg, & D. Martínez (Eds.), *Teaching writing through the immigrant story* (pp. 13–35). Utah State University Press. doi:10.7330/9781646421664.c001

Gruber, S., & Barrón, N. G. (2020). Redirecting failure: Controlling a sense of self. In A. D. Carr & L. R. Micciche. Failure Pedagogies: Learning and unlearning what it means to fail (pp. 83–95). Peter Lang.

Gruber, S., & Barrón, N. G. (forthcoming). Transcultural endeavors: Boundary crossers and writing transfer. In L. Tremain & L. Miller (Eds.), *Radical frameworks for writing transfer: Epistemological justice in the writing classroom*. Peter Lang.

Guerra, J. C. (2016). Cultivating a rhetorical sensibility in the translingual writing classroom. *College English*, *78*(3), 228–233.

Hall, J., & Horner, B. (2023) (Eds.), Toward a transnational university: WAC/WID across Borders of language, nation, and discipline. The WAC Clearinghouse; University Press of Colorado.

Hall, S. (Ed.). (1997). *Representation: Cultural representations and signifying practices*. Sage Publications.

Heath, S. B. (1983). *Ways with words: Language, life and work in communities and classrooms*. Cambridge University Press. doi:10.1017/CBO9780511841057

Heath, S. B. (1988). Protean shapes in literacy events: Ever-shifting oral and literate traditions. In E.R. Kintgen, B. M. Kroll, & M. Rose. (Eds.), Perspectives on literacy, 348-70. Carbondale and Edwardsville: Southern Illinois University Press.

Henly-Shepard, S., Gray, S. A., & Cox, L. J. (2015). The use of participatory modeling to promote social learning and facilitate community disaster planning. *Environmental Science & Policy, 45*, 109–122. doi:10.1016/j.envsci.2014.10.004

Inoue, A. B. (2019). How do we language so people stop killing each other, or what do we do about white language supremacy. *College Composition and Communication, 71*(2), 352–369. doi:10.58680/ccc201930427

Jordan, J. (2022). *Grounded literacies in a transnational WAC/WID ecology: A Korean-U.S. study*. WAC Clearinghouse & University Press of Colorado. doi:10.37514/INT-B.2022.1503

Lee, E., & Canagarajah, A. S. (2019a). The connection between transcultural dispositions and translingual practices in academic writing. *Journal of Multicultural Discourses, 14*(1), 14–28. doi:10.1080/17447143.2018.1501375

Lee, E., & Canagarajah, A. S. (2019b). Beyond native and nonnative: Translingual dispositions for more inclusive teacher identity in language and literacy education. *Journal of Language, Identity, and Education, 18*(6), 352–363. doi:10.1080/15348458.2019.1674148

Lu, M. Z., & Horner, B. (2013). Translingual literacy, language difference, and matters of agency. *College English, 75*(6), 582–607.

Lu, M. Z., & Horner, B. (2016). Introduction: Translingual Work. *College English, 78*(3), 207–218.

Lyiscott, J. (2014). 3 ways to speak English. *TED talk: Ideas worth spreading.* Retrieved from https://www.ted.com/talks/jamila_lyiscott_3_ways_to_speak_english

Milroy, J., & Milroy, L. (2012). *Authority in language: Investigating standard English*. Routledge. doi:10.4324/9780203124666

Navarro, F. (2023). Afterword. Translingual lives and writing pedagogy: Acculturation, enculturation, and emancipation. In J. Hall, & B. Horner, (Eds.), Toward a transnational university: WAC/WID across Borders of language, nation, and discipline, 261-278. The WAC Clearinghouse; University Press of Colorado.

Olivar-Tost, G., Valencia-Calvo, J., & Castrillón-Gómez, J. A. (2020). Towards decision-making for the assessment and prioritization of green projects: An integration between system dynamics and participatory modeling. *Sustainability (Basel), 12*(24), 10689. doi:10.3390u122410689

Pratt, M. L. (1991). Arts of the contact zone. *Profession, 91*, 33–40.

Romani, L., Holck, L., & Risberg, A. (2019). Benevolent discrimination: Explaining how human resources professionals can be blind to the harm of diversity initiatives. *Organization, 26*(3), 371–390. doi:10.1177/1350508418812585

Shapiro, S. (2022). *Cultivating critical language awareness in the writing classroom*. Routledge.

ADDITIONAL READING

Canagarajah, A. S. (2011). Codemeshing in academic writing: Identifying teachable strategies of translanguaging. *Modern Language Journal, 95*(3), 401–417. doi:10.1111/j.1540-4781.2011.01207.x

Canagarajah, A. S. (2012). *Translingual practice: Global Englishes and cosmopolitan relations*. Routledge. doi:10.4324/9780203073889

Canagarajah, A. S. (Ed.). (2013). *Literacy as translingual practice: Between communities and classrooms*. Routledge. doi:10.4324/9780203120293

Casanave, C. P. (2002). *Writing games: Multicultural case studies of academic literacy practices in higher education*. Routledge.

Dryer, D. B. (2016). Appraising translingualism. *College English, 78*(3), 274–283.

Faist, T., Fauser, M., & Reisenauer, E. (2013). *Transnational migration*. John Wiley & Sons.

Frost, A., Kiernan, J., & Malley, S. B. (2020). *Translingual dispositions: Globalized approaches to the teaching of writing*. WAC Clearinghouse & University Press of Colorado. doi:10.37514/INT-B.2020.0438

Hesford, W. S., & Schell, E. E. (2008). Introduction: Configurations of transnationality: Locating feminist rhetorics. *College English, 70*(5), 461–470.

Horner, B. (2023). Introduction. The transnational translingual university: Teaching academic writing across borders and between languages. In J. Hall & B. Horner (Eds.), *Toward a transnational university: WAC/WID across borders of language, nation, and discipline*. WAC Clearinghouse & University Press of Colorado. doi:10.37514/ATD-B.2023.1527.1.3

Horner, B., & Lu, M. Z. (2013). Translingual Literacy and Matters of Agency. In A. S. Canagarajah (Ed.), *Literacy as Translingual Practice: Between Communities and Classrooms* (pp. 26–38). Routledge.

Kiernan, J., Frost, A., & Malley, S. B. (Eds.). (2021). *Translingual pedagogical perspectives: Engaging domestic and international students in the composition classroom*. University Press of Colorado. doi:10.7330/9781646421121

Levitt, P., & Schiller, N. G. (2004). Conceptualizing simultaneity: A transnational social field perspective on society. *The International Migration Review, 38*(3), 1002–1039. doi:10.1111/j.1747-7379.2004.tb00227.x

Martins, D. S. (Ed.). (2015). *Transnational writing program administration*. Utah State University Press. doi:10.7330/9780874219623

Matsuda, P. K. (2013). It's the wild West out there: A new linguistic frontier in US college composition. In A. S. Canagarajah (Ed.), *Literacy as Translingual Practice: Between Communities and Classrooms* (pp. 128–138). Routledge.

Michael-Luna, S., & Canagarajah, A. S. (2007). Multilingual academic literacies: Pedagogical foundations for code meshing in primary and higher education. *Journal of Applied Linguistics, 4*(1), 55–77.

KEY TERMS AND DEFINITIONS

Collaboration: To work with others to achieve a common goal.

Discursive Practices: Recurring interactions that have social and cultural meaning in a communication exchange.

Language Autonomy: The ability of speakers to make language choices without coercion.

Language Ideology: A way to characterize beliefs and feelings about languages, speakers, and discursive practices in cultural, social, and political worlds.

Language Subordination: The process of discriminating against a language and/or accent in order to uphold a mythical language standard.

Translingual Agency: The ability of speakers to apply diverse languages, dialects, and vernaculars in specific discursive situations.

Transculturalism: Emphasizes the shaping of cultural experiences in an environment where individuals and groups continuously interact with each other and participate in cultural exchange of values, ideas, stories, and experiences.

Section 3
Technology and Language Learning

Chapter 5
Embracing Advances in AI-Based Language Tools in EAP Programs:
Towards a Plurilingual Shift

Elena Danilina
https://orcid.org/0009-0003-6666-8871
University of Toronto, Canada

Emmanuelle Le Pichon
University of Toronto, Canada

ABSTRACT

The chapter calls for a change in language teaching and learning methodologies to keep pace with recent technological advances. It acknowledges the prevalence of conversational artificial intelligence tools like Chatbots, including ChatGPT and Bing. Many students and teachers are already using these tools, albeit discreetly. Instead of ignoring or dismissing, the authors argue for their integration into teaching practices. They discuss both opportunities and challenges associated with the implementation of AI tools, considering the current debate surrounding their controversial use and the dominance of a monolingual orientation in English for Academic Purposes courses. By proposing a shift in current practices, the authors advocate for an asset-based, language-friendly, and technology-enriched pedagogy. This new pedagogical approach aims to promote learner autonomy, linguistic and cultural inclusion, and more individualized instruction. By implementing such a pedagogy, teachers can better meet the individual needs of their students leveraging the benefits of these technologies to enhance learning.

DOI: 10.4018/978-1-6684-8761-7.ch005

INTRODUCTION

Current globalization and migration trends have contributed to a growth of international student admissions in post-secondary education in Canada. According to the Canadian Bureau of International Education (2023), there was a 43 percent increase in international student enrollment between 2017 and 2022. Moreover, over the last decade, there was a nearly 170 percent increase in international student arrivals, representing the largest growth in Canadian higher education to date. To ensure that international students are well-prepared to embark on their studies in English, many Canadian colleges and universities offer English for Academic Purposes (from now on EAP) bridging programs. These programs typically range from two to twelve months in duration and aim to equip students with the necessary language and literacy skills to succeed in their academic trajectory. The successful completion of EAP courses can serve as proof of required language proficiency for university admissions, after which students are eligible to take university credit courses in the service of their degree. Despite COVID-19 related interruptions in international travel and shifts to online modes of instruction in higher education between 2020 and 2022, EAP bridging programs have remained instrumental for offering English language support to international students to adapt to the academic requirements of their chosen Canadian university.

Most English for Academic Purposes bridging programs are conducted prior to a student's eligibility to enroll in credit courses. In the event of failure, the student is typically required to retake the EAP course or to achieve a minimum accepted IELTS exam score; in some cases, this may result in a term of waiting before starting the next academic year. Due to these implications, these courses are considered high stakes.

Recent research conducted in Canada (see, for instance, Chen, 2019; Galante, 2018; Marshall & Moore, 2013, 2018) and worldwide (e.g., Canagarajah, 2011; Cenoz & Gorter, 2011; Garcia & Sylvan, 2011; Khote, 2018; Piccardo, 2018) suggests that *language friendly instruction* offers several advantages for the development of academic language skills. Language friendly pedagogy has been defined as the mobilization of learners' linguistic talents and achievements in the development of the target language skills (Le Pichon & Kambel, 2022). Language friendly instruction, also called *plurilingual instruction* (Piccardo, 2018), consists of leveraging students' overall linguistic abilities for the development of academic language skills (Le Pichon & Kambel, 2022; Piccardo, 2018). Additionally, incorporating students' home languages not only hold the potential to enhance their academic proficiency but also empowers them to express their agency and strengthen their sense of identity (Cummins & Early, 2015; Extra & Yagmur, 2012; Le Pichon & Kambel, 2022; Sierens & Van Avermaet, 2014). Despite these advantages, teachers of bridging EAP classes often neglect the inclusion of students' linguistic and/or cultural knowledge. Moreover, teaching exclusively in the target language, as advocated by Krashen's *comprehensible input hypothesis* (Krashen, 1985), can overwhelm learners cognitively and hinder their progress. To address this, teachers can alleviate cognitive overload by tapping into students' linguistic repertoires.

Instruction in EAP courses relies primarily on what Gogolin called *monolingual habitus* (Gogolin, 1997), which is a set of assumptions rooted in the belief that language learning should occur in the majority language. The notion of a monolingual habitus, traditionally reflected in monoglossic norms of most education systems in North America, fails to address the academic and social needs of the culturally and linguistically diverse language learner (Gogolin, 2006). The term *monoglossic* was introduced by Blommaert (2010) to characterize a system that can be either monolingual, bilingual or multilingual, but that upholds an educational framework where languages are kept separate from each other. In a monoglossic system, languages are treated as distinct entities with little interaction between them within the educational context (Benson & Elorza, 2015). Consequently, language instruction occurs in isolation: Each language is taught independently without cross-linguistic connections. This type of instruction reflects a belief of strict separation of languages, potentially overlooking the benefits of leveraging the linguistic resources that students bring to the class (see also Herzog-Punzenberger et al., 2017; Little & Kirwan, 2019; Little, 2020; 2022).

In post-secondary education, the literature on language learning emphasizes the importance of learners' linguistic repertoires and cultural knowledge within academic contexts (Canagarajah, 2018; Galante, 2018; Le Pichon & Ammouche-Kremers, 2022). It also highlights the need for reforms in institutional language policies to better serve the growing number of international students (Herzog-Punzenberger et al. 2017; Jenkins, 2013; Murray, 2016). However, despite this call for action, consistent implementation of plurilingual practices is lacking. English-only language classroom policies are still prevalent in academic English courses. This indicates a disconnect between theory and practical applications of plurilingualism (Ellis, 2017; Jenkins, 2013; Pauwels, 2014).

Consequently, in this chapter and building upon the work of Herzog-Punzenberger and colleagues (2017), we propose a shift towards linguistically and culturally inclusive approaches by integrating artificial intelligence (AI) tools into these pivotal courses. Our examination encompasses the current literature on the use or rejection of AI-driven tools within EAP bridging courses, analyzed through the lenses of plurilingualism, language-friendly pedagogies, multimodalities, and multiliteracies. Furthermore, we delve into the prospective implications of adopting AI-based tools, with the aim of offering all students from diverse linguistic and cultural backgrounds equitable learning opportunities within an inclusive educational framework.

Theoretical and Conceptual Frameworks: Language Friendly Pedagogies, Plurilingualism, Multimodalities, and Multiliteracies

Language Friendly Pedagogies and Plurilingualism

To address the challenge of offering culturally and linguistically diverse students equitable and inclusive learning opportunities, translingual frameworks have emerged in the last two decades. As proposed by the Council of Europe (Council of Europe, 2001; 2018), plurilingualism has been developed as a theoretical framework for language learning and teaching. Plurilingualism is referred as "the interrelation and interconnection of languages … in relation to the dynamic nature of language acquisition" (Council of Europe, 2001, p. 4). Plurilingualism is characterized by a desirable imbalance of linguistic resources and dynamic and creative construction of partial linguistic competences (Piccardo, 2018). Emphasizing the flexible use of the learners' linguistic resources, researchers in second language acquisition have developed several pedagogical approaches that prioritize linguistic diversity by making use of the various language skills and abilities that students possess in their repertoire (Le Pichon et al., 2021). The concept of an individual's linguistic repertoire, which holds a central position in the literature on language friendly and plurilingual language teaching, includes not only linguistic dimensions but also emotional aspects of language (see for instance, Blommaert & Backus, 2013; Busch, 2015; Creese & Blackledge, 2010). Within this school of thought, educators encourage their students to draw on their individual repertoires, which include the knowledge of languages, dialects, and registers (Council of Europe, 2018). This concept forms the foundation of those teaching approaches that embrace a positive perspective on plurilingualism. Learners are acknowledged as proficient speakers of their home language(s) in addition to being learners

Embracing Advances in AI-Based Language Tools in EAP Programs

of a target language. According to the Council of Europe (2018), plurilingual competence involves the flexible use of a diverse repertoire of languages or dialects highlighting the learner's role as a "social agent" (p. 26), emphasizing their independence and responsibility as active citizens in society. This shift towards learner autonomy has led to the promotion of autonomous language learning (Council of Europe, 2018) where learners "plan, implement, monitor and evaluate their own learning" (p. 64). By exercising their individual and collaborative agency (Little, 2020; 2022), they develop proficiency in the target language, which becomes a critical component of their plurilingual repertoire. Given the importance of learner autonomy in the development of plurilingual competence, autonomous learning should be an integral part of EAP classes to better prepare students for pursuing their studies in higher education.

Learner autonomy involves students engaging in autonomous learning through self-directed activities beyond the classroom. Initially, the concept was associated with self-access language learning settings (see, for instance, Morrison, 2008; Murray, 2018; Thornton, 2016). In these settings, learners employed computer language programs, reference resources, and readers' books in the target language(s). Research on autonomous language learning also emphasized the teacher's role as a facilitator in the learning process (Dam, 1995; Little et al., 2017; Little, 1991). With the integration of educational technologies, learner autonomy can now be exercised in a variety of settings, including formal classroom, blended, or online settings, adding complexity to its implementation in the language classroom (Chateau & Tassinari, 2021).

Complementary Principle of Plurilingual Competence

The *complementary principle*, first introduced and developed by Grosjean (1985), is particularly relevant to studying the question of language teaching taking into account the learners' whole linguistic repertoire. The complementary principle (CP) describes the ability to use languages for communication and individual needs. It emphasizes the imbalance and flexibility of plurilingual language learners. Plurilingual competence, in addition, requires the ability to interrelate "language", characterized by balance, and "languaging", often referred to as "a phase of chaos in acquiring a new language" (Piccardo, 2018, p.8). Through the lens of the complementary principle (Grosjean, 2015), plurilingual competence allows plurilingual speakers to explore their hybrid, constantly changing, and constructively unbalanced linguistic repertoires.

Multiliteracies

The concept of *multiliteracies pedagogy*, described in the work of the New London Group (1996) and Cummins (2009), is central for a theoretical framework of plurilingualism. The concept of multiliteracies was introduced to address the change in the learning and teaching needs and respond to increasing global diversity. To achieve these goals, the educators recognized the need to introduce a wider range of literacies to students. They proposed two ways to enhance the learning experience by developing critical thinking necessary for learners to create a more inclusive society and more fulfilling employment opportunities and promoting access to "the evolving language of work, power, and community" (New London Group, 1996, p. 60). These strategies of enhancing learning opportunities are equally relevant in today's culturally and linguistically diverse classrooms, and particularly in the post-pandemic world, in which social inequalities can be more apparent. These social inequalities have stemmed from a widening schooling opportunity gap given the rapidly increased technological demands of online education that was swiftly introduced in most countries as an effective measure to prevent the spread of COVID-19 (Ferreira, 2021).

The second important aspect of the pedagogy, proposed by the New London Group, was the inclusion of other approaches to learning beyond traditional teaching practices that relied mainly on reading and writing (New London Group, 1996). In a language classroom, a multiliteracies approach can involve multiple modes to engage learners in the acquisition of language skills by integrating multimedia resources. Given the affordability and the widespread use of online tools in students' and teachers' everyday lives, the integration of the multiliteracies approach in language learning is particularly relevant in today's language learning settings.

Expanding on the multiliteracies approach to pedagogy in the Canadian educational context, Cummins (2009) highlighted the relevance of this multi-layered approach to literacies in addressing the academic achievement gap of the low-income and culturally diverse student population. In his work, Cummins (2009) focused on the children's and youth's literacy skills as an indicator of academic achievement. The importance of Cummins's (2009) work was in offering practical teaching practices to educators that can be integrated in the classroom to address the needs of all students in the classroom. While this research focused mainly on learning in secondary education, educators at post-secondary institutions recognized this approach as appropriate and relevant for the multiliteracies approach for their language classrooms.

Although the application of the multiliteracies approach was first proposed for developing literacy in the first language, the integration of the multiliteracies approach to additional language learning has received a growing research interest in recent years (Stille & Cummins, 2013; Tan, 2008; Warner & Dupuy, 2018). These researchers also recognized that focusing on the use of multimodalities in language learning is a crucial part of developing multiliteracies.

Multimodalities

Multimodality is defined as the use of semiotic modes and their combination for co-constructing meaning (Kress & van Leeuwen, 2001). The researchers in technology-mediated second language acquisition also argue that the concept of multimodal learning is crucial for developing language skills (Hampel & Hauck, 2006). Given the increased globalization, language learners are expected to learn in multimodal environments not only in academic settings, but also within social settings outside of the classroom, and presently, even more so in online environments. The integration of diverse multimodalities to additional language learning offers affordances to learners as they can construct meaning through the enhanced exposure of input in the target language (Chapelle, 2003; Le Pichon et al., 2021).

Mobile-assisted learning is defined as multimodal since it relies on the use of multiple modalities, including the use of videos, visuals, audio recordings, and interactive content on the Internet. With the widespread use of mobile technologies, it is unsurprising that these tools have become increasingly integrated in language learning, and particularly to academic language learning (see, for instance, Marcel, 2020). However, little research exists on the use of AI-based tools in the English for Academic Purposes (EAP) context (Marcel, 2020). Thus, it is imperative to address this research gap by investigating the use of AI-based tools in EAP and the development of learner autonomy of culturally and diverse students for successful integration of culturally and linguistically inclusive practices in Canadian universities.

Artificial Intelligence in EAP Programs

The emergence of technology-mediated learning has provided learning opportunities for both language teachers and learners. Since the 1970s, the development of *computer-assisted language learning (CALL)* has enhanced the learning process by incorporating educational technologies (Bax, 2003; Warschauer, 2000). In the context of EAP courses, research in CALL has emphasized the integration of educational technologies into learning activities to leverage self-paced and personalized learning and to foster learner autonomy (Arno, 2012; Jarvis, 2009; Lawrence et al., 2020; Plastina, 2003). However, little research focuses on the application of these tools in EAP courses (Dashtestani & Krajka, 2020), and few systematic reviews have been conducted on the effective implementation of technology in these programs (Lawrence et al., 2020).

The shift from computers to mobile-assisted online platforms has led to the adoption of *mobile-assisted language learning (MALL)* platforms (Crompton, 2013). MALL involves the use of applications on devices - such as iPads, mobile phones, tablets, and laptops - for language learning anytime and anywhere (Duman et al., 2015; Reinders & Pegrum, 2015). As a result, learners are increasingly using mobile applications in the language classroom, creating a flexible learning environment and blurring the boundaries between in and out-of-class settings. Additionally, since the 1990s, the Internet has transitioned from a static to dynamic mode, offering users increased interaction and choice in web content. Technology-mediated learning has facilitated opportunities for students to collaborate with others in wikis or blogs, enabling them to actively participate in knowledge-making activities. In the 2000s, mobile devices improved in quality and affordability, resulting in the rise of language learning apps (Crompton, 2013).

The prevalence of artificial intelligence (AI) further boosted mobile language learning tools especially during the COVID-19 online education shift (Altavilla, 2020; Moorhouse & Wong, 2021). In this chapter, we adopt a definition of AI as systems capable to perform highly cognitive functions, such as generating or translating text, or providing human-like responses (Collins et al., 2021). These systems use large sets of training data to recognize and use language patterns, build algorithms, and produce outputs. The training datasets are important, as the systems will adopt and replicate any bias from these sets (Khockly, 2023). As AI is starting to be used in most educational technologies, we consider all the terms discussed in the chapter, such as *mobile-assisted learning*, *mobile applications*, and *language learning app*, to be AI-based. We use AI tools and AI-based tools interchangeably in the chapter, as AI has swiftly started to be infused in several language tools (e.g., GrammarlyGO). These tools have been reshaping current educational practices, prompting a reevaluation of current teaching and assessment practices. This re-evaluation emphasizes the need to rethink the resources language learners might use to develop their language skills and exercise their learner autonomy. AI has demonstrated the ability to perform teachers' and students' routine tasks, such as grading students' work, for example, using the major learning management systems, such as Moodle, searching research articles in databases like Zotero, or offering feedback on students' grammatical choices in writing through software like Grammarly. However, more recently developed AI tools such as ChatGPT (released in November 2022 by OpenAI) have the potential to substitute or partially replace more challenging tasks that traditionally required human-generated academic training, including generating academic texts. Human-like conversational chatbots, such as ChatGPT or Bing, can answer test questions or generate academic papers, offering language learners multiple opportunities to use these tools for leveraging their linguistic repertoires.

Current Debate on Artificial Intelligence in EAP Courses

While students may attempt to explore the affordance of AI-based tools, educators are concerned about incorporating AI-based learning tools into the learning and testing process (Cope & Kalantzis, 2023). These concerns encompass ethical and pedagogical considerations as they contemplate the potential impact on current educational practices, including language learning and testing, considering students' ubiquitous use of AI-based tools. On the one hand, researchers and teachers alike argue that these tools present risks to academic integrity if used inappropriately (Rogerson, 2020); on the other hand, they are widely used by language learners and scholars. Despite limited knowledge on the motivation behind using these tools, some studies have also suggested that language learners might use these tools as self-service in an attempt to avoid self-plagiarism (Loadsman & McCulloch, 2017; Rogerson, 2020). To ensure academic integrity, some educators resort to the rapidly emerging AI-detection writing tools. However, these educators have raised questions about the reliability of these tools, adding to more complexity in detecting AI-generated content in students' writing (D'Agostino, 2023). Moreover, some universities have recently proposed the inclusion of AI into class activities to better prepare students for a rapidly changing digital learning environment. For example, the University of Toronto released guidelines on the use of AI in the classroom. The guidelines suggest that the use of AI-detection tools should be discouraged in the classroom, as AI affordances for teaching and learning students are crucial for allowing students to experience "transformative learning" (University of Toronto, 2023). This transformation in learning allows learners to use their autonomy to leverage the use of AI-based tools to better manage their learning. While plurilingual students' use of AI tools such as ChatGPT may be considered an attempt to offer equal opportunities for language support, these tools offer corrective feedback that may be too general or inaccurate (Kasneci et al., 2023; Kohnke et al., 2023).

The incorporation of a linguistic correction function into online language tools, such as Grammarly, offers a significant benefit by addressing the issue of linguistic dominance, particularly concerning the English language. Nevertheless, when the learner's aim is to achieve proficiency in the target language, the provision of AI-generated feedback hampers the development of a comprehensive understanding of errors. Consequently, the learner merely reproduces corrected text without engaging in critical reflection, thus restricting opportunities for learning and growth. But will these drawbacks of using AI-generated feedback in language learning hold for long? Recent advances in AI have made it easier for automated systems to generate linguistic feedback. For example, Grammarly and, more recently, AI-based GrammarlyGO both offer corrections in grammar, vocabulary, mechanics, and language style supporting students in their writing and editing tasks. While only a few studies suggest that learners develop metacognitive skills through noticing (see, for instance, Koltovskaia, 2020), students have shown to be more satisfied with discussing their Grammarly-generated corrections with an academic learning advisor (O'Neill & Russell, 2019). Moreover, students at a lower level of language proficiency have shown overreliance on Grammarly-generated corrections (Koltovskaia, 2020; Zheng &Yu, 2018), which can be mitigated by implementing this tool in classes, helping learners develop effective editing strategies.

Potential Dangers of AI Tools

Students also need to be aware of the potential dangers of using these large language models, since these models, trained predominantly on English materials, may generate texts that reflect hegemonic worldviews, producing bias (Bender et al., 2021; Kohnke et al., 2023; Rettberg, 2022). For example, the authors of

Embracing Advances in AI-Based Language Tools in EAP Programs

OpenAI caution their users that ChatGPT may provide biased answers (OpenAI, 2022). Moreover, the training data in AI has been based mostly on written texts, often producing verbose language or overused phrases (OpenAI, 2022). It is crucial for students to understand both the affordances and the limitations of these tools. Implementing these tools in classes may offer more meaningful learning opportunities, allowing students to use the tools responsibly while developing a clear understanding of their benefits and constraints. In addition, the implementation of these tools in EAP courses may enable learners to critically reflect on AI-generated content and better prepare students to learn with AI.

Examples of AI-Based Tools

Table 1 offers a summary of some AI-based tools for academic language learning. We have chosen these tools as examples of AI-based tools that can offer learning opportunities to students in EAP courses. As shown in the table, these tools range from offering translation to providing paraphrases, summaries, and generating titles. While this table represents only a fraction of the AI-based tools, it shows how these tools provide students with assistance in understanding and using academic text. The functions and features of these tools, as stated on the tools' websites, may help teachers identify suitable tools that address their students' learning needs in their EAP courses.

Table 1. AI-based tools for academic language learning

Tool	Focus	Notable Features
DeepL	Translation	Offers nuanced translations Generates editing and paraphrasing suggestions Translates industry-specific jargon across languages
Ref-n-Write	Academic writing	Includes option for drag-and-drop documents Includes search option for subject-specific vocabulary Provides writing prompts for sections of the paper
Rewordify	Vocabulary building	Simplifies difficult English phrases Provides individualized multimodal vocabulary lessons Tracks and reports reading time, progress, and errors
Writefull	Academic writing	Generates titles and heading suggestions Provides examples of various academic papers Provides examples of language from published articles
Wordtune	General writing	Checks sentence length and complexity Generates paraphrasing suggestions Offers suggestions for tone, word choice, and flow

Current Practices in EAP Courses

As stated earlier, EAP bridging programs aim to provide students preparatory training in the application of academic conventions commonly used in Canadian universities, covering areas such as academic writing, communication, and research skills. For example, at an upper-beginner level, the EAP bridging course at a Toronto-based university focuses on key outcomes such as critical reading, paragraph writing, and the interpretation of tables, diagrams, and graphs (George Brown College, 2022). Alongside achieving these objectives, students enrolled in EAP bridging classes also familiarize themselves with conventions in academic communication and plagiarism policies specific to Canadian universities. Since these academic conventions may greatly differ from those of the academic contexts in which students received their previous training, learning about these conventions and academic topics is crucial for students' academic success in their undergraduate programs in Canada.

Recent research indicates that EAP instructors generally recognize the importance of including students' previous knowledge of academic conventions in their first language(s) or language(s) of study (see for instance, Canagarajah, 2011; Marshall et al., 2019). However, this integration is often carried out informally and not fully integrated in the EAP curriculum (Galante, 2018). The reasons for excluding students' whole linguistic repertoires in classroom activities may be attributed to the high-stakes nature of the courses and teachers' lack of understanding regarding how to implement plurilingual instruction in the classroom.

Teachers tend to introduce online language tools limited to vocabulary acquisition (e.g., Quizlet), citation engines such as Zotero, or tools under the accessibility umbrella, such as Reading Aloud and Immersive Reader. These accessibility tools are designed to eliminate barriers in learning and offer differentiated learning opportunities to all students. Teachers also incorporate online tools (for example, Mentimeter, Google Docs, or Google Slides) to foster a collaborative learning environment. However, the use of AI-based tools offering automated feedback, such as Grammarly, or those providing paraphrasing or text generating (for example, Rewordify) tend to be used mostly by students outside of class. The cautious approach of teachers towards integrating other artificial intelligence tools may stem from time constraints, lack of guidance or training, and challenges of identifying benefits of unfamiliar tools, especially the latest AI-based tools (Lawrence et al., 2020). Nevertheless, these tools are widely accessible on the Internet, and students may use them independently without specific instruction from their teachers.

Given the prevalence of AI language tools, teachers cannot ignore the likelihood that students are already using them. However, without proper support and training, students may rely too heavily on these tools or use them inappropriately, such as copying AI-generated content to their writing without critically reviewing it. The integration of AI tools in the classroom will help address these issues. It may also help circumvent illicit use of these tools (Le Pichon & Ammouche-Kremers, 2022). Le Pichon and Ammouche-Kremers observed in their study that teachers, despite their initial apprehensions, found reassurance in witnessing the positive impact of incorporating external tools (such as feedback from proficient language speakers) on learners. This integration led to significant improvements in target language texts, enhanced learner autonomy, and increased exposure time to the target language.

The integration of the AI-based tools into EAP courses is crucial, as most students use them extensively outside of classes, and instructors are unaware of whether students are developing effective learning strategies. By implementing these tools into EAP courses, students and teachers work collaboratively towards common learning goals leading to a transparent learning process.

Opportunities and Challenges

This section discusses the opportunities and challenges associated with the implementation of AI-based tools in EAP bridging programs. With a comprehensive understanding of the functionality and implementation of these tools, language researchers and practitioners may gain valuable insights into their design potential for the EAP courses.

Opportunities for Implementation of AI-Based Tools

Developing Learners' Metacognitive Awareness

Tools such as Grammarly, DeepL, Google Lens, Immersive Reader, Read Aloud, and, recently, ChatGPT, assist students with paraphrasing, translating, and simplifying academic language. They are meant to offer learners the opportunity to improve their text. By proposing different wording, they, in fact, encourage learners to make choices among formulations with a variety of grammatical, semantic, or pragmatic connotations; however, the learner is not necessarily able to measure to detect the significance of these nuanced differences. Understanding the rationale behind suggested changes is crucial for learners to enhance their text and competence in writing (Simonsen, 2021).

To fully leverage the potential of these tools, learners must go beyond accepting suggestions without reflection. In Simonsen's study (2021) in a Danish university, students found AI writers beneficial for pre-, mid-, and post- writing stages in an L2. The study concluded that students engage in highly cognitive and metacognitive processes when using AI writers for pre-, mid- and post-editing written texts. Moreover, the study offers three levels of implementing AI writers in developing writing skills in language learning: (1) working independently with an AI writer; (2) working with a peer tutor to edit AI-suggested text; and, finally, (3) addressing final revisions of the text with a teacher. Using this approach, students need to develop an understanding of the pragmatic, stylistic (including grammar or syntactic choices), or semantic implications of each of these choices, considerably enriching their learning. In sum, to use the full potential of the tools, learners need to address each of the following questions: Which tools are most relevant for enhancing my language skills? How can I set my own language learning goals using these tools? Which skills am I trying to improve? And how can I use them to make the most of my progress? Finally, how do I critically evaluate the appropriateness of the suggestions offered by the tools? Helping students elucidate each of the aforementioned questions should be the objective of each educator in EAP classes. All these questions will help generate a higher level of metacognitive awareness.

Metacognitive awareness was first introduced and defined by Flavell (1976) as an "individual's knowledge about his/her own cognitive process and employing this knowledge to inspect cognitive processes" (p. 232), later expanding to draw on cognitive processes (van Kleeck & Schuele, 1987). Since this shift includes drawing attention to the enhancement of the cognitive processes, metacognitive awareness has become one of the most important factors required to succeed in language learning (Kemp, 2007; Le Pichon-Vorstman et al., 2009; Oxford, 1990; Rubin, 1975; Stern,1975).

Research in AI tools, albeit scarce, suggests that the use of language applications may vary among learners (Kohnke et al., 2023; Simonsen, 2021). Those learners less inclined toward academia may choose the application randomly and tend to accept and implement the proposed solutions without further research, while an industrious learner may exhibit skepticism by seeking additional information. By consciously making decisions regarding their language learning process, learners exercise their autonomy. However, research shows that instructors often assume that students misuse these tools, particularly when used for paraphrasing purposes (Rogerson, 2020). The assumptions are linked to broader concerns about students' academic integrity in general; for example, plagiarism (Prentice & Kinden, 2018; Rogerson, 2020), and the reuse of previous assignments (Rogerson, 2020). We argue, however, that these tools are instead opportunities for learners to question the suggested outputs, test them on the Internet, or ask for advice (e.g., in an online forum). To be able to use the applications appropriately versus misusing them, learners need a certain amount of autonomy over their learning. However, one can only recognize the intrinsic value of language tools by integrating these tools in the classroom and investigating how learners use the tools to improve their language skills.

Co-Constructing Meaning With the Knowledgeable Other

Among the most prevalent theories in technology-mediated research are constructivism and sociocultural theory (Vygotsky, 1978). According to Vygotsky (1978), learning occurs through the development of learners' internal self-regulation by mediating with the more knowledgeable other. This process of self-regulation can be achieved through three stages: social speech, or interaction with the more knowledgeable other who models the input; egocentric speech, which is self-talk offering oneself instructions on applying this knowledge; and inner speech, which is self-talk guiding oneself and showing that the learner understands the input correctly and internalizes it (Hurd & Lewis, 2008). These stages can also be applied to language learning, in which educational technology serves as a more knowledgeable other. With the emergence of AI-based tools, learners can now co-construct knowledge by interacting with the content of these tools in the classroom setting.

Currently, AI-based tools for language learning offer a variety of interactive formats, including forums, chats, dictionaries, and links connecting to other resources that explain the learning content. These tools provide opportunities for learners to engage with the content or suggestions offered by the language tools, engagement which is further enriched through mediation with the teacher and other students. An extensive body of research identifies independent language learning, in which the more knowledgeable other is remote from the classroom, as particularly difficult for language learners (see, for instance, Bown, 2008; Jones, 1994; White, 1995). Since mobile-assisted learning enables learners to use the tools both in and out of classroom settings, the social interactions with the teacher or more competent peers in technology-mediated language learning can lower students' anxiety and help learners self-regulate potential negative emotions, including feelings of isolation (Bown, 2008). In technology-mediated language learning, social interactions with teachers and peers play a crucial role in helping learners address these feelings. The development of strategies that target the affective aspects of language learning is particularly relevant in current post-COVID-19 learning settings, where hybrid modes of the course delivery, offering both online and face-to-face interactions, have become common in universities across Canada.

Multimodal Affordances to Language Learning

Additionally, language learners are increasingly expected to engage and make meaning from multimodal environments not only in academic settings, but also in social settings, and even more so in online environments. The integration of various multimodalities into language learning provides learners with opportunities to construct meaning through increased exposure to target language input (Chapelle, 2003; Le Pichon et al., 2021). While the use of AI-based tools in EAP courses is still in its infancy (Marcel, 2020), by integrating these tools, educators may also enhance learners' multimodal competences and empower plurilingual students to leverage multimodal resources in language learning.

Challenges of Implementing AI-Based Tools

Teachers' and Students' Attitudes Towards Implementing AI-Based Tools

A significant area of concern in the systematic implementation of tools that allow for language-friendly practices is the negative or ambivalent perceptions held by language learners and educators regarding the efficacy of these practices. Code-switching or transitioning between languages is often regarded by language instructors as a practice that lacks effort or diligence. Due to the lack of appropriate teacher training and of support from leadership, many educators express concerns that students may rely on direct translation from their home languages, which can lead to reduced exposure and cognitive effort in performing in the target language (Galante, 2020; Wilson & González Davies, 2017). Teachers' resistance to using AI-based tools in classes may result in students hiding their use of these tools in the classroom for fear of not complying with teachers' instructions or permissions. These issues of teachers' resistance in integrating these language tools in these high-stakes EAP bridging courses need to be addressed urgently, as the learners' academic success in pursuing their university degrees depends on achieving the required proficiency in English.

Similarly, students often perceive their use of their home language(s) in academic language courses through a deficit-based lens during the learning process (Marshall et al., 2019; Chen, 2019). As research suggests, deeply rooted in behaviorism, monoglossic teaching practices remain prevalent in academic courses and changing these practices may be even more challenging if instructors encounter resistance from learners. Teachers and students alike need a deeper understanding of the efficacy of these tools on the students' language learning and on the appropriate pedagogical approach to integrate these language tools.

Power Dynamics and Equitable Learning Opportunities

The integration of AI-based tools in language teaching and learning raises important questions that may not have been fully explored yet. One such question is whether AI poses a threat to instructors in EAP courses. AI does introduce an equitable learning opportunities by challenging the hegemony of the English language. It provides access to developing high-level English language skills for everyone. This equitable distribution of language proficiency may disrupt the coercive power dynamics often present at the university level between fluent English speakers and English learners. The potential resistance from instructors could stem from these shifts in power dynamics. To gain a deeper understanding of the situation, it is necessary to explore the practices of the students and the ideologies of the teachers. By examining the actual practices of students in utilizing AI tools and understanding the underlying beliefs and perspectives of teachers, we can shed light on the factors contributing to potential resistance or acceptance of AI in language education.

CONCLUSION AND FUTURE DIRECTIONS

The emergence of rapidly evolving AI-based language tools has opened possibilities for autonomous language learning, particularly within plurilingual teaching and learning practices that are stimulated by the use of these tools. Despite the growing research interest in language learner autonomy, the integration of AI-based language tools in EAP bridging courses has encountered resistance. In Canada, EAP bridging courses rely predominantly on English-only classroom practices, extremely limiting the use of any form of AI. This chapter examined the reasons for this resistance, including concerns about academic integrity and reliability of the AI-generated content. While research highlights the benefits of language-friendly practices in technology-enhanced academic English classes, language educators, school stakeholders, and students require a deeper understanding of plurilingual teaching practices and expertise in working with AI-based tools to effectively utilize them in these critical high-stakes academic English courses.

Future Directions

To accomplish this goal of educational equity, it is imperative for researchers, teachers, policymakers, and students to collaborate and collectively explore the optimal utilization of these tools. By embracing language-facilitated teaching and learning practices and integrating AI-based technology in EAP, the potential for fostering genuine and meaningful dialogues between language teachers and students is heightened. Researchers can offer teachers and students a comprehensive framework that supports their endeavors in utilizing these tools effectively. Working together as a cohesive unit, these stakeholders can contribute to the advancement of educational equity in language education.

It is crucial for language teaching and learning research to prioritize further studies, including document analyses and case studies, on the implementation of culturally and linguistically inclusive pedagogies utilizing AI-based tools to fully capitalize on the potential of AI in language teaching. Effective plurilingual practices have the potential to enhance learning outcomes, address the disparities caused by language hegemony (such as English dominance) and the power dynamics between the languages, and foster innovative modes of communication and learning. However, as discussed in this chapter, it is essential for teachers to embrace these tools in their classrooms to tap into learners' practices fully. Under such conditions, teachers can guide students effectively towards the development of heightened metacognitive skills.

REFERENCES

Altavilla, J. (2020). How technology affects instruction for English learners. *Phi Delta Kappan*, *102*(1), 18–23. doi:10.1177/0031721720956841

Arno, E. (2012). The role of technology in teaching languages for specific purposes courses. *Modern Language Journal*, *95*(s1), 88–103. doi:10.1111/j.1540-4781.2012.01299.x

Bax, S. (2003). CALL—Past, present and future. *System*, *31*(1), 13–28. doi:10.1016/S0346-251X(02)00071-4

Bender, E. M., Gebru, T., McMillan-Major, A., & Shmitchell, S. (2021). On the dangers of stochastic parrots: Can language models be too big? *FAccT 2021 - Proceedings of the 2021 ACM Conference on Fairness, Accountability, and Transparency*, (pp. 610–623). ACM. 10.1145/3442188.3445922

Benson, C., & Elorza, I. (2015). Multilingual education for all (MEFA): Empowering non-dominant languages and cultures through multilingual curriculum development. In D. Wyse, L. Hayward & J. Zacher Pandya (Eds.), The SAGE Handbook of Curriculum, Pedagogy and Assessment (pp. 557-574). Sage. doi:10.4135/9781473921405.n35

Blommaert, J. (2010). *The sociolinguistics of globalization*. Cambridge University Press., doi:10.1017/CBO9780511845307

Blommaert, J., & Backus, A. (2013). Superdiverse repertoires and the individual. In I. Saint-Georges & J. J. Weber (Eds.), *Multilingualism and multimodality: Current challenges for educational studies* (pp. 11–32). Sense Publishers., doi:10.1007/978-94-6209-266-2_2

Bown, J. (2008). Locus of learning and affective strategy use: Two factors affecting success in self-instructed language learning. *Foreign Language Annals*, *39*(4), 640–659. doi:10.1111/j.1944-9720.2006.tb02281.x

Busch, B. (2015). Expanding the notion of the linguistic repertoire: On the concept of Spracherleben—the lived experience. *Applied Linguistics*, *36*(4), 1–20. doi:10.1093/applin/amv030

Canadian Bureau of International Education. (2023). *International Students in Canada*. CBIE. https://cbie.ca/infographic/

Canagarajah, S. (2011). Codemeshing in academic writing: Identifying teachable strategies of translanguaging. *Modern Language Journal*, *95*(3), 401–417. doi:10.1111/j.1540-4781.2011.01207.x

Canagarajah, S. (2018). Translingual practice as spatial repertoires: Expanding the paradigm beyond structuralist orientations. *Applied Linguistics*, *39*(1), 31–54. doi:10.1093/applin/amx041

Cenoz, J., & Gorter, D. (2013). Towards a plurilingual approach in English language teaching: Softening the boundaries between languages. *TESOL Quarterly*, *47*(3), 591–599. doi:10.1002/tesq.121

Chapelle, C. A. (2003). *English language learning and technology*. John Benjamins Publishing., doi:10.1075/lllt.7

Chateau, A., & Tassinari, M. G. (2021). Autonomy in language centres: Myth or reality? *Language Learning in Higher Education*, *11*(1), 51–66. doi:10.1515/cercles-2021-2002

Chen, L. (2019). Problematising the English-only policy in English for Academic Purposes: A mixed-methods investigation of Chinese international students' perspectives of academic language policy. *Journal of Multilingual and Multicultural Development*, *41*(8), 718–735. doi:10.1080/01434632.2019.1643355

Collins, C., Dennehy, D., Conboy, K., & Mikalef, P. (2021). Artificial intelligence in information systems research: A systematic literature review and research agenda. *International Journal of Information Management*, *60*, 102383. doi:10.1016/j.ijinfomgt.2021.102383

Cope, B., & Kalantzis, M. (2023). Education 2.0. In Z. Xudong & M. Peters (Eds.), *The future of teaching* (pp. 276–291). Brill., doi:10.1163/9789004538351_015

Council of Europe. (2001). *Common European Framework of Reference for Languages*. Council of Europe Publishing. https://rm.coe.int/1680459f97

Council of Europe. (2018). *Common European Framework of Reference for Languages: Learning, teaching, assessment-companion volume with new descriptors*. Council of Europe Publishing. https://rm.coe.int/cefr-companionvolume-with-new-descriptors-2018/1680787989

Creese, A., & Blackledge, A. (2010). Translanguaging in the bilingual classroom: A pedagogy for learning and teaching? *Modern Language Journal, 94*(1), 103–115. doi:10.1111/j.1540-4781.2009.00986.x

Crompton, H. (2013). A historical overview of mobile learning: Toward learner-centered education. In Z. Berge & L. Muilengurg (Eds.), *Handbook of mobile learning* (pp. 3–14). Routledge., doi:10.4324/9780203118764.ch1

Cummins, J. (2009). Multilingualism in the English-language classroom: Pedagogical considerations. *TESOL Quarterly, 43*(2), 317–321. doi:10.1002/j.1545-7249.2009.tb00171.x

Cummins, J., & Early, M. (2015). *Big ideas for expanding minds: Teaching English language learners across the curriculum*. Rubicon Publishing.

D'Agostino, S. (2023, January 19). AI writing detection: A losing battle worth fighting. *Inside Higher Education*. https://www.insidehighered.com/news/2023/01/20/academics-work-detect-chatgpt-and-other-ai-writing

Dam, L. (1995). *Learner autonomy 3: From theory to classroom practice*. Authentik.

Dashtestani, R., & Krajka, J. (2020). A call for reconciling EAP and CALL. *Teaching English with Technology, 20*(5), 1–5.

Duman, G., Orhon, G., & Gedik, N. (2015). Research trends in mobile assisted language learning from 2000 to 2012. *ReCALL, 27*(2), 197–216. doi:10.1017/S0958344014000287

Ellis, E. (2013). The ESL teacher as plurilingual: An Australian perspective. *TESOL Quarterly, 47*(3), 446–471. doi:10.1002/tesq.120

Extra, G., & Yagmur, K. (Eds.). (2012). Language rich Europe: Trends in policies and practices for multilingualism in Europe. British Council/Cambridge University Press.

Ferreira, F. (2021). Inequality and COVID-19. *International Monetary Fund. Finance & Development*, 20–23. https://www.imf.org/external/pubs/ft/fandd/2021/06/pdf/inequality-and-covid-19-ferreira.pdf

Flavell, J. (1976). Metacognitive aspects of problem-solving. In L. Resnick (Ed.), *The Nature of Intelligence* (pp. 231–235). Lawrence Erlbaum Associates.

Galante, A. (2018). *Plurilingual or Monolingual? A mixed methods study investigating plurilingual instruction in an English for Academic Purposes program at a Canadian university*. [Unpublished doctoral dissertation, University of Toronto]. https://hdl.handle.net/1807/91806

Galante, A. (2019). "The moment I realized I am plurilingual": Plurilingual tasks for creative representations in English for Academic Purposes at a Canadian university. *Applied Linguistics Review., 11*(4), 551–580. doi:10.1515/applirev-2018-0116

Galante, A. (2020). Pedagogical translanguaging in a multilingual English program in Canada: Student and teacher perspectives of challenges. *System, 90*, 1–10. doi:10.1016/j.system.2020.102274

García, O., & Sylvan, C. E. (2011). Pedagogies and practices in multilingual classrooms: Singularities in pluralities. *Modern Language Journal*, *95*(3), 385–400. doi:10.1111/j.1540-4781.2011.01208.x

George Brown College. (2023, August 30). *English for Academic Purposes Program Overview*. George Brown College. https://www.georgebrown.ca/preparatory-liberal-studies/english-as-a-second-language-esl/english-for-academic-purposes-eap-program-overview

Gogolin, I. (1997). The "monolingual habitus" as the common feature in teaching in the language of the majority in different countries. *Per Linguam*, *13*(2), 38–49. doi:10.5785/13-2-187

Gogolin, I. (2006). Linguistic habitus. In K. Brown (Ed.), *Encyclopedia of language & linguistics* (2nd ed., pp. 194–196). Elsevier. doi:10.1016/B0-08-044854-2/05270-6

Hampel, R., & Hauck, M. (2006). Computer-mediated language learning: Making meaning in multimodal virtual learning spaces. *The JALT CALL Journal*, *2*(2), 3–18. doi:10.29140/jaltcall.v2n2.23

Herzog-Punzenberger, B., Le Pichon-Vorstman, E., & Siarova, H. (2017). *Multilingual education in the light of diversity: Lessons learned*. NESET II Report, Luxembourg: Publications Office of the European Union. https://data.europa.eu/doi/10.2766/71255

Hockly, N. (2023). Artificial intelligence in English language teaching: The good, the bad and the ugly. *RELC Journal*, *54*(2), 445–451. doi:10.1177/00336882231168504

Hurd, S. & Lewis, T. (Eds.). (2008). Language Learning Strategies in Independent Settings. Multilingual Matters. doi:10.21832/9781847690999

Jarvis, H. (2009). Computers in EAP: Change, issues and challenges. *Modern English Teacher*, *18*(2), 51–54.

Jenkins, J. (2013). *English as a Lingua Franca in the international university: The politics of academic English language policy* (1st ed.). Routledge., doi:10.4324/9780203798157

Jones, F. R. (1994). The lone language learner: A diary study. *System*, *22*(4), 441–454. doi:10.1016/0346-251X(94)90001-9

Kasneci, E., Seßler, K., Küchemann, S., Bannert, M., Dementieva, D., Fischer, F., Gasser, U., Groh, G. L., Günnemann, S., Hüllermeier, E., Krusche, S., Kutyniok, G., Michaeli, T., Nerdel, C., Pfeffer, J., Poquet, O., Sailer, M., Schmidt, A., Seidel, T, & Kasneci, G. (2023). ChatGPT for good? On opportunities and challenges of large language models for education. *Learning and Individual Differences*, *103*, 2–9. doi:10.1016/j.lindif.2023.102274

Kemp, C. (2007). Strategic processing in grammar learning: Do multilinguals use more strategies? *International Journal of Multilingualism*, *4*(4), 241–261. doi:10.2167/ijm099.0

Khote, N. (2018). Translanguaging in systemic functional linguistics: A culturally sustaining pedagogy for writing in secondary schools. In R. Harman (Ed.), *Bilingual Learners and Social Equity* (pp. 153–178). Springer. doi:10.1007/978-3-319-60953-9_8

Kohnke, L, Moorhouse, B. L, & Zou, D. (2023). ChatGPT for Language Teaching and Learning. RELC Journal, 54(2), 537-550. doi:10.1177/00336882231162868

Koltovskaia, S. (2020). Student engagement with automated written corrective feedback (AWCF) provided by Grammarly: A multiple case study. *Assessing Writing*, *44*, 1–12. doi:10.1016/j.asw.2020.100450

Krashen, S. D. (1985). *The input hypothesis: Issues and implications*. Addison-Wesley Longman Limited.

Kress, G., & van Leeuwen, T. (2001). *Multimodal discourse: The modes and media of contemporary communication*. Edward Arnold.

Lawrence, G., Ahmed, F., Cole, C., & Johnston, K. P. (2020). Not more technology but more effective technology: Examining the state of technology integration in EAP Programmes. *RELC Journal*, *51*(1), 101–116. doi:10.1177/0033688220907199

Le Pichon, E., Cummins, J., & Vorstman, J. (2021). Using a web-based multilingual platform to support elementary refugee students in mathematics. *Journal of Multilingual and Multicultural Development*, 1–17. doi:10.1080/01434632.2021.1916022

Le Pichon, E., & Kambel, E. R. (2022). The Language friendly school: An inclusive and equitable pedagogy. *Childhood Education*, *98*(1), 42–49. doi:10.1080/00094056.2022.2020538

Le Pichon-Vorstman, E., & Ammouche-Kremers, M. (2022). Education, mobility and higher education: Fostering mutual knowledge through peer feedback. In R., Supheert, G., Cascio & J. D. ten Thije (Eds.) The Riches of Intercultural Communication (pp. 93-110). Brill. doi:10.1163/9789004522855_007

Le Pichon-Vorstman, E., De Swart, H., Ceginskas, V., & Van Den Bergh, H. (2009). Language learning experience in school context and metacognitive awareness of multilingual children. *International Journal of Multilingualism*, *6*(3), 258–280. doi:10.1080/14790710902878692

Little, D. (2007). Language learner autonomy: Some fundamental considerations revisited. *Innovation in Language Learning and Teaching*, *1*(1), 14–29. doi:10.2167/illt040.0

Little, D. (2020). Plurilingualism, learner autonomy and constructive alignment: A vision for university language centres in the 21st century. *Language Learning in Higher Education*, *10*(2), 271–286. doi:10.1515/cercles-2020-2019

Little, D. (2022). Language learner autonomy: Rethinking language teaching. *Language Teaching*, *55*(1), 64–73. doi:10.1017/S0261444820000488

Little, D., Dam, L., & Legenhausen, L. (2017). *The Linguistic, social and educational inclusion of immigrants: A new challenge for language learner autonomy*. Multilingual Matters., doi:10.21832/LITTLE8590

Little, D. G. (1991). *Learner autonomy: Definitions, issues and problems*. Authentik.

Loadsman, J. A., & McCulloch, T. J. (2017). Widening the search for suspect data – is the flood of retractions about to become a tsunami? *Anaesthesia*, *72*(8), 931–935. doi:10.1111/anae.13962 PMID:28580657

Marcel, F. (2020). *Mobile mixed reality technologies for language teaching and learning*. [Unpublished doctoral dissertation, University of Toronto]. http://hdl.handle.net/1807/103360

Marshall, S., & Moore, D. (2013). 2B or not 2B plurilingual: Navigating languages literacies, and plurilingual competence in postsecondary education in Canada. *TESOL Quarterly*, *47*(3), 472–499. doi:10.1002/tesq.111

Marshall, S., & Moore, D. (2018). Plurilingualism amid the panoply of lingualisms: Addressing critiques and misconceptions in education. *International Journal of Multilingualism*, *15*(1), 19–34. doi:10.1080/14790718.2016.1253699

Marshall, S., Moore, D., James, C. L., Ning, X., & Dos Santos, P. (2019). Plurilingual students' practices in a Canadian university: Chinese language, academic English, and discursive ambivalence. *TESL Canada Journal*, *36*(1), 1–20. doi:10.18806/tesl.v36i1.1300

Moorhouse, B. L., & Wong, K. M. (2021). Blending asynchronous and synchronous digital technologies and instructional approaches to facilitate remote learning. *Journal of Computers in Education*, *9*(1), 51–70. doi:10.100740692-021-00195-8

Morrison, B. (2008). The role of the self-access centre in the tertiary language learning process. *System*, *36*(2), 123–140. doi:10.1016/j.system.2007.10.004

Murray, G. (2018). Self-access environments as self-enriching complex dynamic ecosocial systems. *Studies in Self-Access Learning Journal*, *9*(2), 102–115. doi:10.37237/090204

New London Group. (1996). A pedagogy of multiliteracies: Designing social futures. *Harvard Educational Review*, *66*(1), 60–93. doi:10.17763/haer.66.1.17370n67v22j160u

ONeill, R, & Russell, A. (2019). Stop! Grammar time: University students' perceptions of the automated feedback program Grammarly. Australasian Journal of Educational Technology, 35(1). doi:10.14742/ajet.3795

Open A.I. (2022). Introducing ChatGPT. *OpenAI.* https://openai.com/blog/chatgpt

Oxford, R. (1990). *Language learning strategies: What every teacher should know*. Newbury House.

Pauwels, A. (2014). The teaching of languages at university in the context of super-diversity. *International Journal of Multilingualism*, *11*(3), 307–319. doi:10.1080/14790718.2014.921177

Piccardo, E. (2018). Plurilingualism: Vision, conceptualization, and practices. In P. Trifonas, & T., Aravossitas, (Eds.) Springer International Handbooks of Education. Handbook of Research and Practice in Heritage Language Education (pp. 207-226). Springer International Publishing. doi:10.1007/978-3-319-44694-3_47

Plastina, A. F. (2003). CALL-ing EAP Skills. *Teaching English with Technology*, *3*(3), 16–30.

Prentice, F. M., & Kinden, C. E. (2018). Paraphrasing tools, language translation tools and plagiarism: An exploratory study. *International Journal for Educational Integrity*, *14*(1), 1–16. doi:10.100740979-018-0036-7

Reinders, H., & Pegrum, M. (2015). Supporting language learning on the move: An evaluative framework for mobile language learning resources. In B. Tomlinson (Ed.), *SLA research and materials development for language learning* (pp. 116–141). Taylor & Francis. https://hdl.handle.net/10652/2991

Rettberg, J. W. (2022, December 6). ChatGPT is multilingual but monocultural, and it's learning your values. *jill/txt.* https://jilltxt.net/right-now-chatgpt-is-multilingual-but-monocultural-but-its-learning-your-values/

Rogerson, A. M. (2020). The use and misuse of online paraphrasing, editing and translation software. In T. Bretag (Ed.), *A Research Agenda for Academic Integrity* (pp. 163–174). Edward Elgar Publishing. doi:10.4337/9781789903775.00019

Rogerson, A. M., & McCarthy, G. (2017). Using Internet based paraphrasing tools: Original work, patchwriting or facilitated plagiarism? *International Journal for Educational Integrity*, *13*(2), 2. doi:10.100740979-016-0013-y

Rubin, J. (1975). What the good language learner can teach us. *TESOL Quarterly*, *9*(1), 41–51. doi:10.2307/3586011

Sierens, S., & Van Avermaet, P. (2014). Language diversity in education: Evolving from multilingual education to functional multilingual learning. In D. Little, C. Leung, & P. Van Avermaet (Eds.), *Managing diversity in education: Languages, policies, pedagogies* (pp. 204–222). Multilingual Matters., doi:10.21832/9781783090815-014

Simonsen, H. K. (2021). AI writers in language learning. *2021 International Conference on Advanced Learning Technologies (ICALT)*, (pp. 238–240). IEEE. 10.1109/ICALT52272.2021.00078

Stern, H. H. (1975). What can we learn from the good language learner? *Canadian Modern Language Review*, *31*(4), 304–318. doi:10.3138/cmlr.31.4.304

Stille, S., & Cummins, J. (2013). Foundation for learning: Engaging plurilingual students' linguistic repertoires in the elementary classroom. *TESOL Quarterly*, *47*(3), 630–638. doi:10.1002/tesq.116

Tan, J. P. L. (2008). Closing the gap: A multiliteracies approach to English language teaching for 'at-risk' students in Singapore. In A. Healy (Ed.), *Multiliteracies and diversity in education: New pedagogies for expanding landscapes* (pp. 144–167). Oxford University Press.

Tassinari, M. G. (2017). A self-access centre for learners and teachers: Promoting autonomy in higher education. In M. Jiménez, J. J. Martos, & M. G. Tassinari (Eds.), *Learner and teacher autonomy in higher education: Perspectives from modern language teaching* (pp. 183–208). Peter Lang.

Thornton, K. (2016). Evaluating language learning spaces: Developing formative evaluation procedures to enable growth and innovation. *Studies in Self-Access Learning Journal*, *7*(4), 394–397. doi:10.37237/070407

University of Toronto. (2023, September 10). *Generative Artificial Intelligence in the classroom*. University of Toronto. https://teaching.utoronto.ca/resources/generative-artificial-intelligence-in-the-classroom/

van Kleeck, A., & Schuele, C. M. (1987). Precursors to literacy: Normal development. *Topics in Language Disorders*, *7*(2), 13–31. doi:10.1097/00011363-198703000-00004

Vygotsky, L. (1978). *Mind in society: The development of higher psychological processes*. Harvard University Press.

Warner, C., & Dupuy, B. (2018). Moving toward multiliteracies in foreign language teaching: Past and present perspectives…and beyond. *Foreign Language Annals*, *51*(1), 116–128. doi:10.1111/flan.12316

Warschauer, M. (2000). The death of cyberspace and the rebirth of CALL. *English Teachers'. Journal, 53*(1), 61–67.

White, C. (1995). Autonomy and strategy use in distance foreign language learning: Research findings. *System, 23*(2), 207–221. doi:10.1016/0346-251X(95)00009-9

Wilson, J., & González, M. G. (2017). Tackling the plurilingual student/monolingual classroom phenomenon. *TESOL Quarterly, 51*(1), 207–219. doi:10.1002/tesq.336

Zheng, Y., & Yu, S. (2018). Student engagement with teacher written corrective feedback in EFL writing: A case study of Chinese lower-proficiency students. *Assessing Writing, 37*, 13–24. doi:10.1016/j.asw.2018.03.001

Chapter 6
Digital Technology and Language Learning:
How Does Digital Technology Change Our Perspectives on Language Learning?

Yasuyo Tomita
University of Toronto, Canada

ABSTRACT

The advancement of digital technologies allows us to communicate in plurilingual contexts without learning additional languages. This makes the author wonder what learning languages means in today's technologically advanced environment. Therefore, this chapter explores the meaning of learning languages and taking language courses from multiple theoretical perspectives, including ecology, digital nature, agency and emotions in the action-oriented approach, and instructed second language acquisition. Using the concept of digital nature, the chapter argues that technology has provided us with freedom from the pressure to memorize and process a great deal of information owing to "our" externally existing knowledge (i.e., the internet) and magical tools such as real-time translation apps. The chapter discusses how this freedom allows us to exert our agencies, utilize noise for creativity and innovation, and take risks to learn languages through the fine-tuned delicate art of work, or teaching, valued in digital nature.

INTRODUCTION

Tourist: "I want to go to Fukuoka Airport."
Station Staff: 「地下鉄とバスがございます。」 *("There is a subway and a bus.")*
(https://youtu.be/8Jjlv8VRBLk)

This dialogue is between a tourist and a station staff at a train ticket booth in Japan. In this dialogue, the tourist's utterances in English are automatically translated into Japanese and presented on a monitor screen between the tourist and the station staff. Similarly, the station staff's responses in Japanese are

DOI: 10.4018/978-1-6684-8761-7.ch006

automatically translated into English and presented on the monitor screen. As the dialogue shows, people can communicate using different languages in real time through digital technology, such as a monitor displaying automatically translated sentences, as in this dialogue, and smartphones. Such plurilingual or multilingual interactions have become part of everyday communication. Moreover, some may even use Google Maps in the above situation instead of communicating with others.

Similar phenomena have been observed in foreign or second language (L2) classrooms with rapid advancement in technology. Technology has been used in language education (Chapelle, 2003) and extensively researched in the fields such as computer-assisted language learning (CALL) (Grgurovic et al., 2013; Plonsky & Ziegler, 2016), online language learning (Rienties et al., 2018; Ushida, 2005), and mobile-assisted language learning (MALL) (Hsu, 2013; Karakaya & Bozkurt, 2022; Loewen et al., 2019). Recently, AI-based language learning has been discussed (Hockly, 2023; Jeon, 2022; Kohnke, Moorhouse, & Zou, 2023). Although I was aware of technological advancement in language education, I was completely amazed by the drastic change in students' use of technology in classrooms when I went back to teaching in-person after the COVID-19 pandemic. It was a first-year introductory Japanese course at a university in Canada. Reading materials in L2 Japanese were captured and instantly translated into their mother tongues (L1) on their smartphones; L2 listening activities turned into L1 reading activities using translated sentences on their phones; writing activities were completed with automatically suggested phrases on their tablets; hand-written sentences could also be shared instantly through tablets; and speaking performance, be it video-recorded monologues, dialogues, or group skits, could be edited for linguistic errors and adjusted for an appropriate speed. The current AI technology can create speech "as if you were a native speaker" (Reager, 2022, par. 7) with our own voice through voice cloning (Eleven Labs, 2023; OpenAI, 2023; Speechify, 2023).

By witnessing such useful digital tools for plurilingual and multilingual language use, I could not help wondering about the meaning of taking language courses. Why is it necessary to learn another language when there are various useful tools, including smartphones, that translate everything for us? Even for conversations, as presented above, digital technology makes it possible to have conversations in different languages. Contrary to my concerns, however, the number of language learners has been growing globally (LingoMelo, 2023). Let us take the number of Japanese language learners as an example. According to the surveys conducted every three years by the Japan Foundation (2022), the number of language learners – or, more specifically, Japanese language learners– has been increasing over the years. Although there was a slight drop in fiscal 2021 (3,794,714) from 2018 (3,851,774) by 1.5% (Japan Foundation, December 28, 2022), probably due to the COVID-19 pandemic, the number of learners of the Japanese language has increased by approximately thirty times since the first survey conducted in 1979 (Japan Foundation, December 15, 2022). The most recent survey also showed a change in language learners' motivation; the majority of the learners in the 1980s were studying Japanese for business, but the learners in recent years are more likely to become interested in the Japanese language due to the pop culture, such as anime and manga (Japan Foundation, December 15, 2022).

Speaking of motivation, I was recently surprised to see the results of the questionnaire I gave my students at the beginning of the course. I am currently teaching Japanese at a Canadian university and regularly give a questionnaire at the beginning of the term as part of a needs analysis to learn about students' purposes and goals for taking the Japanese course. Although this is a casual questionnaire, becoming able to communicate in Japanese was always the most popular purpose in the past years, as far as I remember. To my surprise, however, "becoming able to read in Japanese" was the top reason for taking the course in the most recent course, which I am currently teaching. This is perplexing to me after seeing students using online translation tools and screen capture translation apps. Why is reading the most popular reason for taking the course when many useful translation tools and apps are available? In second language teaching methodologies, a metaphor, "pendulum," can be used to describe changes in teaching methods (Mitchell & Vidal, 2001, p. 26). That is, the grammar-translation method with a focus on reading was popular at one time, but the direct method focusing on communication emerged in reaction to grammar-translation (Larsen-Freeman & Anderson, 2011; Richards & Rodgers, 2014). With the rise of structural linguistics, the audio-lingual method with repetitive pattern practice became popular, which will later be replaced by communicative language teaching (Larsen-Freeman & Anderson, 2011; Richards & Rodgers, 2014). As can be seen in the historical changes in teaching methodologies, the focus seems to shift between reading/grammar and communication over time. The shift from oral communication to reading in my students' interest reminded me of this "pendulum" metaphor. Do learners also follow this "pendulum" movement? Are they moving back to grammar-translation for reading again in this digitally advanced era?

This chapter discusses (i) why we want to learn languages when we are surrounded by useful digital technologies for plurilingual and multilingual communication and (ii) what we (i.e., learners) expect from taking language courses in this digitally advanced milieu. In other words, I will re-examine the meaning of learning languages in this digitally advanced environment by shedding light on how digital technology has changed our ways of communication in plurilingual or multilingual contexts and how it has affected our needs and expectations from learning languages, particularly in classroom contexts. As a language instructor, these are rather urgent questions for me to meet students' expectations from taking language courses. I hope this chapter will help teachers and researchers explore effective teaching that supports learners' language development in this digitally advanced environment. In the following sections, I introduce theoretical frameworks used in this chapter, review the literature on digital technology in everyday communication and language education, discuss the meaning of learning languages in this technologically advanced society and learners' expectations from taking language courses in relation to the theories and literature reviewed, and conclude this chapter with theoretical and pedagogical implications and future research.

I would like to add a few notes on the use of certain terms and the use of my personal anecdotal experiences as a language instructor in this chapter. First, since technologically related words will likely become quickly outdated, it may not be recommended to use them in a paper. However, I will use specific words and terms in this chapter to present current situations and relevant concerns, as well as to record changes and progress in technology in relation to everyday communication and classroom language learning/teaching. Second, I will use the terms "plurilingualism" and "multilingualism" interchangeably in this chapter, while acknowledging the differences between them; multilingualism is a competence of "a number of languages" or the "co-existence of different languages in a given society" (Council of Europe, 2001, p. 4), while plurilingualism is a "dynamically developing, unbalanced, partial competence" (Piccardo & North, 2019, p. 214) of an individual person (Council of Europe, 2020). I will use these terms interchangeably to target a wider audience inclusively, focusing on their common, shared concepts of competences in more than one language. Lastly, I use my personal anecdotal experiences as a Japanese language instructor in this chapter for the following two reasons. One reason is that this chapter was motivated by my own teaching experiences and observations of a drastic change in students' use of technology in classrooms after the COVID-19 pandemic. Additionally, as far as I know, such personal, unique, and autonomous use of technology by students after the COVID-19 pandemic has not yet been documented in published research, although there is research documenting teachers' use of technology for their students' language learning, which I will discuss later in this chapter. This lack of focus on student-driven use of digital technologies might be due to the gap in the interest in classroom ecological validity between researchers and teachers, although both share a common goal to pursue effective teaching for learners (Sato & Loewen, 2022; Spada & Lightbown, 2022). As a practitioner, I noticed the change in students' use of technology first and foremost after the COVID-19 pandemic, which urged me to consider the meaning of learning languages in this digitally advanced era.

LITERATURE REVIEW

Theoretical Frameworks

To examine the meaning of learning languages in this digitally advanced milieu, I will use several theoretical concepts: they are ecology (van Lier, 2007, 2010), digital nature (Ochiai, 2015, 2018), the action-oriented approach (North, 2023; Piccardo, 2010; Piccardo & North, 2019), and instructed second language acquisition (SLA) (Loewen, 2020; Spada, 2022; Spada & Lightbown, 2013). I will review each theoretical concept in the following paragraphs.

I will use *ecology* (van Lier, 2007, 2010) and *digital nature* (Ochiai, 2015, 2018) as conceptual frameworks to examine how digital technology has changed the ways of everyday communication in plurilingual or multilingual contexts, as well as the ways of learning languages. The concept of ecology in language education examines the interdependencies among social, physical, and symbolic worlds (van Lier, 2007, 2010). When a change in learning emerges with affordances or opportunities, it will, in turn, trigger changes in learning in dynamic and complex ways. The concept of ecology has further been expanded to digital technology, or more specifically *digital nature*. According to Ochiai's (2015, 2018) theoretical concept of digital nature, all living things, physical items, and virtual objects coexist without boundaries among them as part of the ecological system. He continues to say that people in this digitally advanced era often take all "magic" - or useful tools created by technology - for granted and do not even question whether what they see and hear is virtual or a physically existing object. For example, we tend to forget that the person we see through a video on a smartphone (e.g., FaceTime, LINE) is the product of digital technology and do not even think if the person is virtual or not. Instead, we tend to accept them and consider them as physically existing human beings or part of nature rather than virtual. Consequently, the difference between virtual (or products of digital technology) and physically existing objects is becoming fuzzy and even meaningless. That is, both virtual and physical objects exist in the ecological system or digital nature. This logic leads to the idea that all knowledge searchable on the Internet can be considered "our" knowledge that is externally available (Ochiai, 2015, 2018). Although the concept of digital nature has been developed in the field of digital art (Ochiai, 2015, 2018), it explains why students in this digitally advanced environment use technology as if it is part of nature or part of themselves. For example, students capture texts in another language as if it is what they see through their eyes; they accept automated suggestions in typing (as if it is what they are about to type with their fingers); and they use translated sentences (as if it is what they have produced). Thus, such digitally existing codes or language are affordances and resources available for them as part of the "nature" in their ecological systems.

The *action-oriented approach,* that entails learner agency, emotions, and competence (North, 2023; Piccardo, 2010; Piccardo & North, 2019), will be exploited to discuss the meaning of language learning in this digitally advanced environment and learners' needs in language learning. The action-oriented approach is not only task-based language learning but also includes perspectives of complexity theory (Larsen-Freeman, 2011) and sociocultural theory (Swain et al., 2015). In the action-oriented approach, active participation in problem-solving actions with emotionally engaged attitudes and agency is the key to learning, which is non-linear, unpredictable, and dynamic. Learners are encouraged to take risks and co-create learning processes with their peers and teachers, utilizing all linguistic and non-linguistic resources available in plurilingual contexts. Such resources are mediational tools to stretch their competences and to use language creatively (North, 2023; Piccardo, 2010; Piccardo & North, 2019). Empirical classroom studies that used the action-oriented approach, specifically action-oriented scenarios, show how learner agency and emotions were well integrated into actions through scenario-based teaching, which influenced learners' language competences (Scholze et al., 2022; Townend et al., 2022).

I will draw on, once again, the action-oriented approach (North, 2023; Piccardo, 2010; Piccardo & North, 2019) within the context of *instructed second language acquisition (SLA)* (Loewen, 2020; Spada, 2022; Spada & Lightbown, 2013) to discuss what language learners expect from language classes and what language teachers can do to respond to learners' needs and expectations. Instructed SLA examines the relationship between types of instruction and language learning, as well as learners' and teachers' beliefs and preferences about language learning/teaching. Thus, the effects of instruction are discussed in relation to instructional conditions, such as teaching techniques (e.g., corrective feedback) (Goo, 2020; Li, 2010; Lyster & Saito, 2010), types of instruction (e.g., implicit and explicit instruction) (Karimi & Abdollahi, 2022; Norris & Ortega, 2000; Spada & Tomita, 2010), timing of instruction (Spada et al., 2014), task characteristics (Ellis, 2003; Ellis et al., 2020; Robinson, 2001) and learner characteristics (Li, 2015; Sheen, 2008). In the next two sections, we will see how digital technology has changed the way of communication in plurilingual or multilingual contexts and how it has been used in language education.

Digital Technology and Communication

Digital technology is used for everyday communication. This includes synchronous computer-mediated communication (e.g., Microsoft Teams, Zoom), computer-mediated communication (e.g., FaceTime, LINE), social networking sites (e.g., Facebook, Twitter), and video-sharing services such as YouTube (Mensah et al., 2023; NHK, 2022; Yeung et al., 2023). Using these technologies, communication without language is also possible. For example, we can share pictures and videos, instead of describing scenery. Also, we can look at Google Maps, instead of asking for directions. As I presented at the beginning of this chapter, digital technology is also used for public services in plurilingual or multilingual contexts. Here, I would like to compare two conversational situations at a station in Japan, using two YouTube videos as shown in Excerpts 1 and 2. Both videos show a similar situation, where a tourist communicates with station staff to purchase a train ticket at a station. However, these two videos are different in terms of the use of digital technology; one (Excerpt 1) shows communication without digital technology, and the other (Excerpt 2) shows communication with digital technology (translation monitors). I use Ten Have's (2007) conversation analysis conventions to present how a tourist and station staff engage in the conversation or discursive practice (Young, 2008, 2009) in each video.

Excerpt One: Conversation Without Digital Technology

Tourist: *I just pressed the assistance button. ((Looking at the ticket vending machine.))*

It says, please wait a moment.

[The door opens.]

Station Staff: *Hai omatase shimashita. ("Hello. Thank you for waiting.") ((The station assistant appears from the small door next to the vending machine.))*

Tourist: *Hai. I want to select the…Hibiyu? Hibiyu line? ((pointing at the train map above the vending machine.))*

Station staff: *Hibiya line? Haha. ((Smiling))*

Tourist: *((Smiling))*

((The station staff's body comes out from the door but goes back into the door again, waving his hand. The tourist is looking at the station staff with a smile with his hand under his chin. The station staff appears again, changing his body's direction and pointing at the map.))

Station staff: *Two-sixty.*

((The station staff presses the button, looking at the vending machine screen. The tourist is looking at the vending machine screen.))

Tourist: *The tsuri…("change…")*

Station staff: *Oh, sorry.*

Tourist: *That's okay. ((Nodding))*

Arigato. Arigato gozaimasu. ("Thank you. Thank you very much.") ((picking up the change))

Station staff: *((Smiles at the camera, nodding.))*

Tourist's friend: *Did he come out of the machine?*

Tourist: *Yeah. ((Smiling))*

(https://youtu.be/R-fP_xJDIYg)

Excerpt Two: Conversation With Digital Technology

Tourist: *Hello. I want to go to Fukuoka airport. ((Talking to the microphone.))*

[On the monitor, it says, "Konnichiwa. Fukuoka kukoni ikitaindesu." ("Hello. I want to go to Fukuoka Airport.")]

((The station staff is looking at the monitor.))

Station staff: *Chikatetsu to basu ga gozaimasu. ("There is a subway and a bus.") ((Talking to the microphone and looking down. After speaking, looking at the tourist.))*

(https://youtu.be/8Jjlv8VRBLk)

Some readers may have noticed that the dialogue at the beginning of this chapter is from Excerpt 2. I used this excerpt as an introduction to this chapter because it clearly shows how technology – real-time automatic translation in case of Excerpt 2 – has made it possible for people who speak different languages to communicate without understanding or producing the other person's language. Here, Excerpt 2 (i.e., conversation with digital technology) is used for further examination in comparison with Excerpt 1 (i.e., conversation without digital technology). As these two excerpts show, the tourists in both situations will probably complete their tasks successfully: getting to where they want to go. However, the difference in language use between these two scenarios is rather clear: the conversation was extremely efficient with digital technology in Excerpt 2. That is, the mission was completed in minimum sentences without any errors, miscommunication, or unexpected, unwanted, unnecessary difficulties, which might be called "noise" (Mogi, 2008; Yoro, 2014) because everything was instantly and accurately translated into the languages they used. With such smooth communication, the tourist in Excerpt 2 must have been happy to find a way to the airport efficiently and quickly. This reinforces my question: Why is it necessary to learn another language when surrounded by various useful digital tools? This section presented how digital technology has been used for efficient communication between speakers/users of different languages. In the next section, I look at how digital technology has changed the way people learn languages.

Digital Technology and Language Learning

In this section, I will review recent empirical studies published in the past three years (i.e., during and after the COVID-19 pandemic) on the influence of digital technology on language learning. The reason for selecting these publication years – 2021, 2022, and 2023 – is based on my personal experience as a Japanese language instructor. As I mentioned above, when I returned to in-person teaching after the pandemic, I noticed a significant change in students' use of digital technology in Japanese language classes at a Canadian university. Seeing students use screen capture translation apps and type with automated suggested phrases, I have become interested in finding out how learners use technology for language learning in this technologically advanced environment, particularly after the COVID-19 pandemic. However, as I mentioned in the introduction section, there is yet little research documenting learners' autonomous use of technology outside of instructional plans (e.g., teachers' lesson plans) and designs (e.g., computer-assisted language learning) after the pandemic, while the use of technology for language learning has been extensively researched. Therefore, in this section, I review studies on the use of digital technology in language education and language learning in general.

Although digital technology was used in language learning and teaching before the COVID-19 pandemic, the pandemic did accelerate the spread and advancement of digital technology in our lives, including educational, work-related, and daily-life contexts (Hirai & Kovalyova, 2023; Suarez & El-Heawy, 2023). Examples include automatic speech recognition, real-time translation, word lens, and grammar checker, to name a few (Hirai & Kokvalyova, 2023; John & Woll, 2020). In language education, online learning – be it synchronous, asynchronous, or hybrid – has become accepted as one of the curriculum platforms (Zhang & Zou, 2022) and its positive impact on students' learning and satisfaction has been reported (Almusharraf & Bailey, 2021; Bailey et al., 2021; Choi et al., 2022). Even outside of the classroom, a variety of self-study technology has gained popularity. Within the language education field, this includes app-based mobile learning or mobile-assisted language learning (MALL), such as Anki (Hanson & Brown, 2020), Babel (Loewe, Isbell, & Sporn, 2020), Duolingo (Shortt et al., 2021), and Memrise (He & Loewen, 2022).

Many of the aforementioned app-based platforms make use of game-style tasks for language learning. For example, with the advancement in technology, augmented reality games have also been found to be beneficial for learners' satisfaction and language learning (Wu, 2021). In a study of augmented reality games, Hellerman and Thorne (2022) examined three learners' interactional dynamics while engaging in an augmented reality game developed by one of the authors. The findings showed that learners collaboratively produced and used language and engaged in cooperative practices, such as gazing at the same items and mirroring each other's gestures.

Many of these app-based mobile learning platforms and augmented reality games, in addition to translation apps, have recently been used in instructional settings (Luque-Anullo & Almazan-Ruiz, 2023) either as a part of classroom activities (Wu, 2021), assignments (He & Loewen, 2022), or supplemental materials (Hanson & Brown, 2020). Digital technologies not originally developed for education can also be used for language learning and teaching. For example, Hirai and Kovalyova (2023) suggested that automatic speech-to-text recognition technology that displays spoken texts in real time can be beneficial for pronunciation learning. Overall, the positive impact of using these digital technologies on learning has been reported (Zhang & Zou, 2022).

In addition to more general fields of language teaching and learning, the positive impact of digital technology has also been examined in instructed second language acquisition (SLA), where the relationship between types and timing of instruction (i.e., second language teaching) and learning is investigated (Loewen, 2020; Spada, 2022; Spada & Lightbown, 2013). Positive effects of technology-based corrective feedback on second language development have been reported in empirical studies in various areas, such as writing (Brudermann et al., 2021; Gonzalez-Cruz et al., 2022), speaking (Kataoka et al., 2023), tones (Bryfonski & Ma, 2020), and vocabulary learning (Henderson, 2021). For example, learners receive pre-programmed feedback comments on their errors in online writing tasks along with follow-up online exercises related to the error. Another example is providing pre-recorded recasts (or correct utterances) on errors in speech submitted to online language learning management systems. However, some studies report trade-offs between accuracy through corrective feedback and fluency (Criado et al., 2022) and larger effects of instructor corrective feedback on free writing than computer-based automated corrective feedback on drills (Gao & Ma, 2022). Nonetheless, positive effects of technology-based corrective feedback could be because technology-based corrective feedback raises learners' awareness toward the target forms and promotes noticing (Barrot, 2023; Reynolds & Kao, 2021). Learners' proficiency and education levels have also been reported as mediating factors on the effects of technology-based corrective feedback (Ko, 2022; Penning de Vries et al., 2020). Overall, corrective feedback in technology-based learning environments has been found to be effective (Cerezo, 2021).

Thus far in this section, we have seen how widely technology has spread in our lives and how it supports language learning in and outside the classroom. Thus, studies show that both instruction with technology and self-study with technology facilitate language learning. Although I understand the positive effect of technology on language learning, I am even more amazed that there are language users who become plurilingual or multilingual through multimedia entertainment without systematic self-studying or taking language courses. In the "ecology of [plurilingual/multilingual] environments" (Sauro & Thorne, 2021, p. 228), some language users become plurilingual/multilingual through multimedia entertainment – particularly popular culture – including anime, comics, movies, music, TV dramas, and video games (Sauro & Thorne, 2021; Zhang & Vazquez-Calvo, 2022). They enjoy and often immerse themselves in plurilingual/multilingual culture and language through various multimedia delivery systems, such as Netflix, Tik Tok, and YouTube (Shafirova & Araújo e Sá, 2023). Not only do they enjoy watching, reading, and listening to multimedia entertainment content, but some even create and produce their own content in multiple languages they have acquired through multimedia (Zhang & Vazquez-Calvo, 2022). This makes me think again about the meaning of "learning" another language and, furthermore, taking a language course in this current world of digital nature with abundant digital resources, affordances, and opportunities. I myself have a strong interest in learning other languages and have always been fascinated by the idea of taking various language courses, even though I should be able to communicate in plurilingual contexts without using any common language due to all the useful digital technologies (e.g., automatic real-time speech recognition). This, in turn, leaves me curious: What motivates me, or anyone, to learn a new language or take a language course?

While existing studies discuss language learning motivation and digital technologies these studies often illustrate either (i) how motivation affects learning outcomes, satisfaction, or confidence in the technology-mediated language learning contexts (Hsu & Lin, 2021; Sun & Gao, 2020) or (ii) how technology-mediated language learning affects learner motivation (Chen, 202; Chen, Huang, & Yeh, 2021; Guanuche et al., 2020; Parsazadeh et al., 2021; Vonkova et al., 2021). That is, it seems there is little research on the meaning of learning another language or taking a language course in this digitally advanced world or "digital nature." It seems there is an unquestioned assumption that people are (or will continue to be) interested in learning another language and taking a language course. Yes, it might have been true before that learning another language was the only way to communicate with others who speak different languages or to enjoy other cultures. Today, however, we are surrounded by plenty of *magic* (Ochiai, 2015; 2018) that makes it possible for us to communicate in plurilingual contexts and enjoy plurilingual cultures. Despite the magical tools, it is also still true that there are a great number of language learners, and many of them have decided to take language courses.

Therefore, as a language teacher and researcher, I believe it is important to think about the reasons for learning languages and learners' expectations from taking language courses, despite the fact that we can communicate in plurilingual or multilingual contexts using digital technology and even without using an L2. In the following sections, I discuss, in relation to empirical studies and theories, (i) reasons for learning languages and (ii) learners' expectations from taking language courses. First, I discuss how digital technologies have changed our ways of communication, which will reveal one of the key factors for learning languages: noise. Second, I discuss why we are interested in learning languages in this technologically advanced society, which will reveal another important factor playing in learning languages: freedom. Third, I discuss why we want to take language courses when free, useful apps are

Digital Technology and Language Learning

available, which will uncover another factor in language learning: risks. Fourth, I discuss what learners expect from taking language courses, which integrates all the key factors (i.e., noise, freedom, and risks) and one last factor—teachers.

DISCUSSION

Digital Nature and the Role of Noise in Plurilingual or Multilingual Communication

I would like to start by discussing how digital technology has changed our ways of communication in plurilingual or multilingual contexts from the perspectives of ecology and digital nature, which will shed light on the reasons for language learning. As the literature shows, human beings and language are considered to be part of an ecological system, where all resources, affordances, agencies, and emotions interact in a complex and dynamic way (van Lier, 2007, 2010; Piccardo & North, 2019). In the ecological system with digital technology, the boundary between the natural and the digital has become ambiguous. Thus, it is no longer crucial whether what we see exists in nature or in the virtual world. Some do not even care or are unaware of the boundaries or differences (e.g., Does the person we see through the LINE video chat exist in nature physically or as an image in the virtual world?). Instead, they often accept what they see as part of nature or "digital nature" (Ochiai, 2015, 2018). In digital nature, what is important for us is the philosophy that values delicate art and experience that arouses physical, sensory, and emotional reactions through encountering fine-tuned delicate work (Ochiai, 2018). In other words, based on my interpretation of this philosophy, we are encouraged to nurture our appreciation toward culture and art, including empathy, hospitality, beliefs, behaviours, and creation (i.e., delicate art), while practicing them (i.e., fine-tuned delicate work). Fine-tuned delicate work may include, for example, interacting with others appropriately in a given context, designing tools considering specific needs, and even completing tasks with care and dedication. Both "delicate art" and "fine-tuned delicate work" can be applied to our everyday life, including education, such as language learning and teaching. These features of delicate art and fine-tuned delicate work can also bring unexpected serendipity, which might also be considered to be noise in some situations or from different viewpoints (Mogi, 2008).

When looking at the YouTube videos at the stations in Japan (i.e., Excerpts 1 and 2), we see two types of "fine-tuned delicate work": work done by a person (i.e., station staff trying to assist the tourist) as in Excerpt 1 and by technology (i.e., automatic real-time translation) as shown in Excerpt 2. Even though both reflect fine-tuned delicate work to assist the tourists with plurilingual or multilingual communication, the differences are rather clear: the efficiency of the work. That is, the task was done efficiently in a much shorter time with technology through the automatic real-time translation, where necessary information was provided instantly (see Excerpt 2). On the other hand, the situation without technology was full of *noise* (Mogi, 2008; Yoro, 2014), including gestures, eye contact, smiles, waiting time, communication breakdowns, and mistakes, all of which are not necessary to accomplish the task of purchasing a ticket (see Excerpt 1). As Mogi (2008) states, however, it is noise that arouses emotional feelings, stimulates curiosity, and fosters creativity. Without any noise, processing is efficient, which is also vital in this technologically advanced modern life. However, such an efficient process of work without any noise may lack an emotional impact that is essential for creative and innovative activities. Emotion and cognition are closely interconnected (Piccardo & North, 2019; Poehner & Swain, 2016), and the interconnection (or lack thereof) between emotion and cognition seems to be reflected in the formats of the videos. That is, the conversation without digital technology (i.e., Excerpt 1) led to the tourist's own creation of a video clip — probably with joy — to share his unexpected surprise, while the efficient conversation with technology (i.e., Excerpt 2) was for public news to report on up-to-date factual information. Thus, we can also see how interactions with the station staff (see Excerpt 1), despite a great deal of noise, aroused emotional and physical reactions, which might have driven the tourist to create the video clip. In sum, digital technology has made communication efficient by removing noise, but it is noise that arouses various emotional feelings, cultivates our curiosity, and nurtures creativity. It seems that we miss and long for noise as emotional, curious, and creative beings and look for opportunities to experience "noise," particularly in this technologically advanced society.

Freedom in Language Learning

In this section, I discuss how digital technology has affected the ways we learn languages and the meaning of learning languages. First, I would like to remind readers that reading (i.e., becoming able to read in Japanese) is the most popular reason for learning Japanese among the most recent students in the Japanese course I am currently teaching. What motivates them to read in Japanese when surrounded by convenient tools, such as automatic real-time translation?

In this digital nature environment, searchable information on the Internet is considered to be "our" knowledge that happens to exist externally (Ochiai, 2015, 2018). With such useful technology providing external knowledge, we should have no obstacle or challenge regarding reading in L2 or even learning another language. According to Ochiai (2018), once our challenges are solved, we are likely to go back to the previous state of mind and practice, where the challenges had not been recognized, while keeping and further developing the diversity in agency cultivated through the periods with the challenges. Ochiai (2018) provides an example of this. There was little waste or garbage during the Edo period (1603-1868) in Japan because all parts of nature were fully used and recycled for various purposes. However, as society was modernized, the concept of waste was recognized as a challenge to overcome until society became equipped with methods of processing waste efficiently. After the challenge was solved, we became "free" from the challenge, and now it seems we are back to the Edo period again, where we see a meaning in all parts of nature and value recycling. However, it is not merely going back to the old times like a "pendulum" (Mitchell & Vidal, 2001, p. 26). Instead, we continue fostering diversity in agency cultivated through facing the challenge for creativity and innovation, which can be represented with another metaphor Mitchell and Vidal (2001) provided: "a river flowing" (p. 26). Here, the challenge plays a similar role as Mogi's (2008) *noise*. That is, it is an obstacle for immediate concern, but it triggers emotions and actions, leading to creativity and innovation.

This cycle seems to explain the reason for *reading* to be the most popular goal among the students in the Japanese course I am teaching currently, despite the availability of "our knowledge" existing externally (e.g., information on the Internet) and useful digital technologies, such as automatic real-time translation. That is, in this world of digital nature, we have become free from the pressure or challenge to memorize all the vocabulary words to understand both written texts and spoken language, as well as the pressure to develop proficiency in order to communicate successfully in an additional language as promoted in the communicative language teaching approach (see Larsen-Freeman & Anderson, 2011, for teaching methodologies). Excerpt 2 shows an example of communication between two people who have chosen to enjoy freedom in the moment. Following Ochiai (2018), this freedom from the pressure/

challenge allows learners to go back to the old times – where communication in an additional language is not required or demanded – while fostering diversity in the agency and further cultivating creativity. That is, by becoming free from such burdens as mentioned above owing to our external knowledge and digital technologies, learners can pursue whatever interests they have by exerting their agency and can appreciate exercising their creativity and engaging in innovative work. Therefore, some may choose to read in another language and enjoy different interpretations from various perspectives; some may choose to translate newly released videos into another language with their own creative expressions; some may be fascinated by analyzing languages to develop an innovative linguistic theory; and some may be interested in expanding their oral communication skills in an additional language to conduct a pioneering collaborative project. Thus, the freedom from burdens thanks to digital technology and affordances in the ecological system of digital nature have given us opportunities to exercise our agency and to foster diversity in learning purposes, goals, styles, and strategies, as well as in the creative use of resources.

Risks and Language Learning

The previous section shows how digital technology has reduced our burdens (e.g., memorizing many vocabulary words) and provided us with opportunities to pursue whatever we are interested in, be it reading, grammar, or translation. However, this might not fully explain why one decides to "start" learning another language in this technologically advanced era. I discuss this question in this section. According to the concept of digital nature (Ochiai, 2018) and the educational concept of the action-oriented approach (Piccardo & North, 2019), people (or learners) tend to choose to take a risk. For example, in a language classroom context, a learner may take a risk in talking to their classmates without any guarantee of successful attempts; that learner does not know whether their classmates will understand or even listen to them. Another example of a risk would be trying out newly learned expressions in a conversation with classmates, wondering whether it would be accepted, rejected as a show-off, or cause a communication breakdown due to their erroneous use of a particular expression. However, taking a risk often leads to innovation and creativity. It seems that risks play a similar role as noise – an essential trigger for creative and innovative work – as we saw in the YouTube video (Excerpt 1). Moreover, Ochiai (2018) states that there are positive correlations between degrees of risks and degrees of motivation. Since computers or digital technologies aim to perfectly control risks and avoid them for guaranteed success by statistical calculations, taking a risk is, paradoxically, highly valued in digital nature; it is what only people want to do, and it is what leads to creativity and innovation in digital nature.

Considering the human tendency to take a risk, it seems that *learning* can also be a risk that people choose to take. Learning is a risky commitment since nothing is guaranteed after spending valuable time and energy. However, only such a risky commitment can lead to creative and innovative work, which is supported by motivation correlated to the degrees of risks; the more risks one takes, the more motivated one tends to be (Ochiai, 2018). Furthermore, learning entails *fine-tuned work* highly valued in digital nature, as discussed above. It requires delicate physical and mental work that arouses sensory and emotional reactions, such as joy and a sense of accomplishment. Therefore, as I mentioned before, since being offered our external knowledge (i.e., the Internet resources) and convenient digital technologies (e.g., automatic real-time translation), we have become free from the pressure to memorize vocabulary words and to develop communicative competence for successful interactions. This makes learning a valuable risk that we take to exert our agency beyond processing information, through engaging in fine-tuned work and appreciating diversity in motivation, values, and experiences.

Learners' Expectations From Taking Language Courses in the World of Digital Nature

Thus far, I have argued that noise, freedom from pressure, and taking risks in this digital nature can all intertwiningly explain the reasons for learning languages. Building on the concepts of noise, freedom, and risks, this last discussion section explores what learners may expect from taking language courses in this technologically advanced environment with plenty of effective self-study language learning apps. What is more, as reviewed above, becoming plurilingual language users through popular culture multimedia without taking courses has also been reported. Therefore, I discuss the purpose of taking language courses and what learners might expect from taking language courses.

According to the action-oriented approach, an educational concept for language learning and teaching (Piccardo & North, 2019), emotions, agency, and creativity play important roles in language learning. They seem to be well integrated with the aforementioned features in digital nature: noise, freedom from pressure, and taking risks. Furthermore, these features are available in classroom contexts, simultaneously arousing emotions, evoking agency, and cultivating creativity. We will look at each below.

First, classrooms are often full of unexpected and unnecessary noise rather than simply passing information or knowledge. That is, instead of just receiving information from the teacher, we are constantly in a state of uncertainty without knowing what other classmates would say or how they would react during interactions, which can be "noise" because they may interfere with our flow of thoughts and may force us to change plans of rehearsed sentences. However, such unpredictable utterances can bring creative and innovative conversations and ideas with vivid emotions such as joy (Mogi, 2011; Ochiai, 2018). According to the action-oriented approach, while emotions were traditionally considered to emerge internally, it has recently been argued that emotions are, in fact, "generated in social interaction" (Piccardo & North, 2019, p. 79). As discussed above, learners may miss and long for noise that they can experience through interacting with others in class, particularly in this technologically advanced environment, where noise is supposed to be perfectly controlled. Therefore, learners may be expecting to have more "noise" or unpredictable interactions through taking language courses, where they can experience various emotions and creative moments.

Second, in this technologically advanced environment, we have become free from the pressure to memorize numerous vocabulary words and to develop communicative competence for successful communication thanks to our externally available knowledge (e.g., the Internet) and useful technologies (e.g., automatic real-time translation). Therefore, we can pursue our own interests by exercising our agency and freely utilizing all linguistic and non-linguistic resources to fully exert our creativity. However, creativity does not exist without an audience. Creativity needs to be recognized, and its novelty needs to be validated by a group of experts in the field, who appreciate its value (Csikszentmihalyi, 2014; Piccardo & North, 2019). Thus, a classroom constitutes an ideal place, where learners can meet experts (e.g., classmates and teachers) who recognize their creative use of resources and affordances available to all members in the classroom. Those resources and affordances include content covered in the class (e.g., vocabulary, grammar, topics discussed in class), shared experiences (e.g., episodes in the classroom), classmates' utterances during class, and their "external knowledge" (i.e., information on the Internet). Therefore, after obtaining freedom thanks to digital technology and being granted opportunities to pursue their interests to enjoy creative activity, learners may want an appropriate audience or experts who can recognize their creativity or their creative use of resources. This can be another reason for learners to take language courses: meeting experts (e.g., classmates and teachers) who recognize their creativity.

Digital Technology and Language Learning

Third, it might be the *risk* that brings students to language courses. As mentioned above, digital technology is not intended to take risks; it is supposed to be perfectly controlled to avoid risks. Thus, these risks, which are so highly valued in digital nature, are appealing only to human beings. It is risky to take a course; we do not know whether we will have positive learning experiences or not after expending time and energy. It is risky to interact and perform tasks with classmates in another language without knowing how they would react to what we said, whether we could understand what they said, and what we should do if we could not make ourselves understood (Piccardo & North, 2019). Finally, it is risky to share our personal motivations for language learning with our classmates; not everybody will share the same passions. In sum, taking a language course is simply full of risks. However, as discussed before, the more risks we have, the more motivated we tend to become (Ochiai, 2018). Therefore, although taking a language course is risky, knowing how risky it is can motivate learners to enroll in a course, interact with others, and solve problems collaboratively (e.g., in tasks and group projects). Such social interactions in class, despite constant possible risks, provide learners with rich emotions, leading to creative work and innovative thoughts. Therefore, taking a risk might be another reason for some learners to take courses.

Lastly, learners may take courses to meet teachers who are motivated to take risks. As Ochiai (2018) discussed, taking risks and having motivation are unique to human beings; computers do not take risks, nor are they meant to take risks. Thus, learners may expect to meet teachers who are motivated to take risks in teaching, such as utilizing new ways of teaching and testing, adopting new materials, and reflecting on their teaching philosophy from new perspectives, as well as risks in their professional life outside the classroom, such as continuing learning and researching despite their limited time. Learners may also expect to meet teachers who take risks in encouraging learners to express their opinions from various perspectives, actively interacting with learners, who may ask unpredictable questions and share unexpected thoughts in class, and in providing (or not providing) corrective feedback at the appropriate timing. These are risky actions because teachers cannot predict their outcomes. However, it is not only learners, but also teachers, who need to be motivated (Dornyei, 2001), particularly to take risks in this technologically advanced environment.

CONCLUSION

This chapter explored the meaning of learning languages and taking language courses in the technologically advanced era, surrounded by various useful technologies or "magical" (Ochiai, 2015) tools for communication (e.g., automatic real-time translation), self-study apps, and plurilingual/multilingual multimedia. Theoretical concepts in (a) language education, such as ecological systems (van Lier, 2007, 2010) and the action-oriented approach (Piccardo & North, 2019), (b) instructed second language acquisition (Loewen, 2020; Spada, 2022; Spada & Lightbown, 2013), and (c) digital nature (Ochiai, 2015, 2018) revealed key factors in language learning in this technologically advanced society: noise, freedom from pressure, and risks. These concepts uncover the reasons for learning languages and particularly for taking language courses in the world of digital nature.

In summary, first, learners may expect to experience more unpredictable and unnecessary "noise" through learning languages in the classroom context; noise triggers abundant emotional reactions, leading to creativity and innovation. Paradoxically, noise has become valued even more in the current technologically advanced society. Second, by taking language courses, learners may expect to meet experts, or appropriate audiences, who can recognize their creative use of resources and affordances. Being granted freedom from the intense pressure, for example, to memorize countless vocabulary words, learners can exert their agency to unleash their creativity by pursuing what they have a strong desire for. Classrooms serve as an ideal place for this, where the novelty of learners' creativity is recognized and appreciated by an audience who shares the same resources, experiences, and goals. Third, learners may learn language through taking courses because both learning and taking a course are risky commitments, further motivating them to engage in learning activities. Lastly, learners may expect to meet teachers who are motivated to take risks in implementing new teaching and assessment methods, reflecting on their teaching philosophy from various perspectives, interacting with their learners, and continuing their learning.

This chapter has shed light on the reasons and purposes for learning languages, particularly in the classroom contexts in this digitally advanced environment, hoping this will help learners, teachers, and researchers become aware of what learners expect from taking language courses. Although teachers and researchers are often considered to have a gap in their interests in classroom ecological validity, they do share a common passion for seeking better, more effective instruction for learners (Sato & Loewen, 2022; Spada & Lightbown, 2022). I hope the concepts of noise, freedom, and risks will help teachers and researchers to co-create better learning environments for learners. I would like to conclude this chapter with theoretical, pedagogical, and future research implications.

Even though the theoretical concept of digital nature (Ochiai, 2015, 2018) has been developed in the digital art field, I have found it very helpful to see language learning and digital technology in multilayered ecological systems, with technology being a mediator between learners and external environments, making the boundaries between them blurred or even meaningless. The key concept of ambiguous boundaries between natural – including our body – and digital objects in digital nature uncovers what language learners need to do using languages in the world of digital nature in order to live a life with joy, exercising their agency and unleashing their creativity through social interactions. This will open up new perspectives on teaching methodologies, instructional techniques, types of tasks, assessment, learner knowledge, individual differences, and learner identity in the field of language education. First things first, we may need to think about what we mean by a "user of a language" in digital nature.

Pedagogical implications include the importance of awareness towards diversity and teachers' passion for learning to become a better "audience" for their learners. First, by being granted affordances and freedom from memorization thanks to digital technology, learners can pursue their interests. In such contexts, it is important for both learners and teachers to appreciate diversity; not everyone has the same interests. Therefore, both learners and teachers need to be reminded and encouraged "to be naturally curious about diversity and to consider it as an ordinary characteristic of human nature and everyday life" (Piccardo & North, 2019, p. 84). Second, one of the reasons for taking language courses in spite of being surrounded by useful technological tools for plurilingual/multilingual communication and culture is to seek opportunities to share their creative ideas and work with experts and appropriate audiences who can recognize its novelty (Csikszentmihalyi, 2014; Piccardo & North, 2019). Thus, teachers need to be a "good audience" by creating a supportive and non-judgemental atmosphere for their learners and their future possibilities, considering that learners are taking a risk to take a course, to use available resources creatively, and to share their creative work with others. Of course, it is impossible to know everything. However, teachers can at least show their interest in the fields that learners have a passion for. If possible and if time permits, teachers can learn about their learners' fields of interest – be it literature, linguistics, history, music, philosophy, agriculture, or astronomy – in order to be able to better appreciate learners' creative work. Teachers' appreciation can be expressed through feedback (including corrective feedback), interactions with their learners, and teaching materials (e.g., tasks and scenarios).

Building on this chapter, I hope to conduct an experimental study that further examines the reasons for learning languages in the classroom context in this technologically advanced era through, for example, interviews, observations, and questionnaires, as well as the effect of teaching that reflects the concepts of noise, freedom, and risks. With this in mind, there may be a need to explore novel research methods to investigate language learning in the field of digital nature.

REFERENCES

Almusharraf, N. M., & Bailey, D. (2021). Online engagement during COVID-19: Role of agency on collaborative learning orientation and learning expectations. *Journal of Computer Assisted Learning*, *37*(5), 1285–1295. doi:10.1111/jcal.12569 PMID:34226784

Andrei, E. (2019). Adolescent English learners' use of digital technology in the classroom. *The Educational Forum (West Lafayette, Ind.)*, *83*(1), 102–120. 10.1080/00131725.2018.1478474

Bahari, A. (2022). Affordances and challenges of technology-assisted language learning for motivation: A systematic review. *Interactive Learning Environments*, 1–21. doi:10.1080/10494820.2021.2021246

Bailey, D., Almusharraf, N., & Hatcher, R. (2021). Finding satisfaction: Intrinsic motivation for synchronous and asynchronous communication in the online language learning context. *Education and Information Technologies*, *26*(3), 2563–2583. doi:10.100710639-020-10369-z PMID:33169066

Barrette, C. (2001). Students' preparedness and training for call. *CALICO Journal*, *19*(1), 5–36. doi:10.1558/cj.v19i1.5-36

Barrot, J. S. (2023). Using automated written corrective feedback in the writing classrooms: Effects on L2 writing accuracy. *Computer Assisted Language Learning*, *36*(4), 584–607. doi:10.1080/09588221.2021.1936071

Brudermann, C., Grosbois, M., & Sarré, C. (2021). Accuracy development in L2 writing: Exploring the potential of computer-assisted unfocused indirect corrective feedback in an online EFL course. *ReCALL*, *33*(3), 248–264. doi:10.1017/S095834402100015X

Bryfonski, L., & Ma, X. (2020). Effects of implicit versus explicit corrective feedback on mandarin tone acquisition in a SCMC learning environment. *Studies in Second Language Acquisition*, *42*(1), 61–88. doi:10.1017/S0272263119000317

Cai, Y., Pan, Z., & Liu, M. (2022). Augmented reality technology in language learning: A meta-analysis. *Journal of Computer Assisted Learning*, *38*(4), 929–945. doi:10.1111/jcal.12661

Cerezo, L. (2021). Corrective feedback in computer-mediated versus face-to-face environments. In H. Nassaji & E. Kartchava (Eds.), *The Cambridge Handbook of Corrective Feedback in Second Language Learning and Teaching* (pp. 494–519). Cambridge University Press., doi:10.1017/9781108589789.024

Chapelle, C. (2003). *English language learning and technology*. John Benjamins. doi:10.1075/lllt.7

Chen, C. (2020). AR videos as scaffolding to foster students' learning achievements and motivation in EFL learning. *British Journal of Educational Technology*, *51*(3), 657–672. doi:10.1111/bjet.12902

Chen, C., Hung, H., & Yeh, H. (2021). Virtual reality in problem-based learning contexts: Effects on the problem-solving performance, vocabulary acquisition and motivation of English language learners. *Journal of Computer Assisted Learning, 37*(3), 851–860. doi:10.1111/jcal.12528

Choi, Y., Tomita, Y., Ko, K., & Komuro-Lee, I. (2022, May). *Understanding students' perception of online language learning*. Paper presented at the annual meeting of Canadian Association of Applied Linguistics, (online).

Council of Europe. (2001). *Common European Framework of Reference for Languages: Learning, Teaching, Assessment*. Cambridge University Press.

Council of Europe. (2020). *CEFR Companion Volume*. Council of Europe Publishing.

Criado, R., Garcés-Manzanera, A., & Plonsky, L. (2022). Models as written corrective feedback: Effects on young L2 learners' fluency in digital writing from product and process perspectives. *Studies in Second Language Learning and Teaching, 12*(4), 697–719. doi:10.14746sllt.2022.12.4.8

Csikszentmihalyi, M. (2014). *The systems model of creativity: The collected works of Mihaly Csikszentmihalyi*. Springer Netherlands., doi:10.1007/978-94-017-9085-7

Dörnyei, Z. (2001). *Motivational strategies in the language classroom*. Cambridge University Press. doi:10.1017/CBO9780511667343

ElevenLabs. (2023). High quality AI voice cloning. https://elevenlabs.io/voice-cloning

Ellis, R. (2003). *Task-based language learning and teaching*. Oxford University Press.

Ellis, R., Skehan, P., Li, S., Shintani, N., & Lambert, C. (2020). *Task-based language teaching: Theory and practice*. Cambridge University Press.

Gao, J., & Ma, S. (2022). Instructor feedback on free writing and automated corrective feedback in drills: Intensity and efficacy. *Language Teaching Research, 26*(5), 986–1009. doi:10.1177/1362168820915337

González-Cruz, B., Cerezo, L., & Nicolás-Conesa, F. (2022). A classroom-based study on the effects of WCF on accuracy in pen-and-paper versus computer-mediated collaborative writing. *Studies in Second Language Learning and Teaching, 12*(4), 623–650. doi:10.14746sllt.2022.12.4.5

Goo, J. (2020). Research on the role of recasts in L2 learning. *Language Teaching, 53*(3), 289–315. doi:10.1017/S026144482000004X

Grgurović, M., Chapelle, C. A., & Shelley, M. C. (2013). A meta-analysis of effectiveness studies on computer technology-supported language learning. *ReCALL, 25*(2), 165–198. doi:10.1017/S0958344013000013

Hellerman, J., & Thorne, S. L. (2022). Collaborative mobilizations of interbodied communication for cooperative action. *Modern Language Journal, 106*(S1), 89–112. doi:10.1111/modl.12754

Henderson, C. (2021). The effect of feedback timing on L2 Spanish vocabulary acquisition in synchronous computer-mediated communication. *Language Teaching Research, 25*(2), 185–208. doi:10.1177/1362168819832907

Hockly, N. (2023). Artificial intelligence in English language teaching: The good, the bad and the ugly. *RELC Journal*, 3368822311685. doi:10.1177/00336882231168504

Hsu, H., & Lin, C. (2022). Extending the technology acceptance model of college learners' mobile-assisted language learning by incorporating psychological constructs. *British Journal of Educational Technology*, *53*(2), 286–306. doi:10.1111/bjet.13165

Hsu, L. (2013). English as a foreign language learners' perception of mobile assisted language learning: A cross-national study. *Computer Assisted Language Learning*, *26*(3), 197–213. doi:10.1080/09588221.2011.649485

Japan Foundation. (2021). *Nendo kaigai nihongo kyoiku kikan chosa kekka gaiyou [Results of the survey on fiscal year 2021 Japanese language education]*. Japan Foundation. https://www.jpf.go.jp/j/about/press/2022/dl/2022-023-02_1228.pdf

Japan Foundation. (December 15, 2022). *JF special stories: Language*. Japan Foundation. https://jf50.jpf.go.jp/en/story/learning_japanese_changed_my_life/

John, P., & Wolf, N. (2020). Using grammar checkers in an ESL context: An investigation of automatic corrective feedback. *CALICO Journal*, *37*(2), 169–196. doi:10.1558/cj.36523

Karakaya, K., & Bozkurt, A. (2022). Mobile-assisted language learning (MALL) research trends and patterns through bibliometric analysis: Empowering language learners through ubiquitous educational technologies. *System (Linköping)*, *110*, 102925–. doi:10.1016/j.system.2022.102925

Karimi, M. N., & Abdollahi, S. (2022). L2 learners' acquisition of simple vs. complex linguistic features across explicit vs. implicit instructional approaches: The mediating role of beliefs. *Language Teaching Research*, *26*(6), 1179–1201. doi:10.1177/1362168820921908

Kataoka, Y., Thamrin, A. H., Van Meter, R., Murai, J., & Kataoka, K. (2023). Investigating the effect of computer-mediated feedback via an LMS integration in a large-scale Japanese speaking class. *Education and Information Technologies*, *28*(2), 1957–1986. doi:10.100710639-022-11262-7 PMID:35967830

Ko, C.-J. (2022). Online individualized corrective feedback on EFL learners' grammatical error correction. *Computer Assisted Language Learning*, 1–29. doi:10.1080/09588221.2022.2118783

Kohnke, L., Moorhouse, B. L., & Zou, D. (2023). ChatGPT for Language Teaching and Learning. *RELC Journal*, 3368822311628–. doi:10.1177/00336882231162868

Larsen-Freeman, D. (2011). A complexity theory approach to second language development/acquisition. In D. Atkinson (Ed.), *Alternative approaches to second language acquisition* (pp. 48–72). Routledge.

Larsen-Freeman, D., & Anderson, M. (2011). *Techniques and principles in language teaching* (3rd ed.). Oxford University Press.

Lee, S.-M., & Park, M. (2020). Reconceptualization of the context in language learning with a location-based AR app. *Computer Assisted Language Learning*, *33*(8), 936–959. doi:10.1080/09588221.2019.1602545

Li, S. (2010). The effectiveness of corrective feedback in SLA: A meta-analysis. *Language Learning*, *60*(2), 309–365. doi:10.1111/j.1467-9922.2010.00561.x

Li, S. (2015). The association between language aptitude and second language grammar acquisition: A meta-analytic review of five decades of research. *Applied Linguistics*, *36*(3), 385–408. doi:10.1093/applin/amu054

Loewen, S. (2020). *Introduction to instructed second language acquisition* (2nd ed.). Routledge. doi:10.4324/9781315616797

Loewen, S., Crowther, D., Isbell, D. R., Kim, K. M., Maloney, J., Miller, Z. F., & Rawal, H. (2019). Mobile-assisted language learning: A Duolingo case study. *ReCALL*, *31*(3), 293–311. doi:10.1017/S0958344019000065

Loewen, S., Isbell, D. R., & Sporn, Z. (2020). The effectiveness of app-based language instruction for developing receptive linguistic knowledge and oral communicative ability. *Foreign Language Annals*, *53*(2), 209–233. doi:10.1111/flan.12454

Luque-Agulló, & Almazán-Ruiz, E. (2023). A checklist proposal for assessing the potential of language teaching apps. In Suárez, M.-M., & El-Henawy, W. M. *Optimizing Online English Language Learning and Teaching* (pp. 357-382). Springer International Publishing. doi:10.1007/978-3-031-27825-9

Lyster, R., & Saito, K. (2010). Oral feedback in classroom SLA: A meta-analysis. *Studies in Second Language Acquisition*, *32*(2), 265–302. doi:10.1017/S0272263109990520

Mensah, R. O., Quansah, C., Oteng, B., & Nii Akai Nettey, J. (2023). Assessing the effect of information and communication technology usage on high school student's academic performance in a developing country. *Cogent Education*, *10*(1), 2188809. doi:10.1080/2331186X.2023.2188809

Mitchell, C. B., & Vidal, K. E. (2001). Weighing the ways of the flow: Twentieth century language instruction. *Modern Language Journal*, *85*(1), 26–38. doi:10.1111/0026-7902.00095

Mogi, K. (2008). *Nou to souzousei* [Brain and creativity]. PHP.

Narváez, F. R., Vallejo, D. F., Morillo, P. A., & Proaño, J. R. (2020). Corrective feedback through mobile apps for English learning: A review. In Smart Technologies, Systems and Applications (Vol. 1154, pp. 229–242). Springer International Publishing AG. doi:10.1007/978-3-030-46785-2_19

NHK. (2022, March 17). *Kurozu appu gendai [A close-up view of today]*. NHK. https://www.nhk.or.jp/gendai/articles/4646/

Norris, J. M., & Ortega, L. (2000). Effectiveness of L2 instruction: A research synthesis and quantitative meta-analysis. *Language Learning*, *50*(3), 417–528. doi:10.1111/0023-8333.00136

North, B. (2023). The CEFR companion volume and the action-oriented approach. *Italiano LinguaDue*, 1-23.

Ochiai, Y. (2015). *Mahoo no seiki* [*Century of Magic*]. Planets.

Ochiai, Y. (2018). *Dejitaru neicha: seitaikei wo nasu hanshinkashita keisanki ni yoru wabi to sabi* [*Digital nature: wabi and sabi of ecological digital technology*]. Planets.

Open A.I. (2023). ChatGPT. *OpenAI.* https://openai.com/blog/chatgpt/

Parsazadeh, N., Cheng, P.-Y., Wu, T.-T., & Huang, Y.-M. (2021). Integrating computational thinking concept into digital storytelling to improve learners' motivation and performance. *Journal of Educational Computing Research, 59*(3), 470–495. doi:10.1177/0735633120967315

Penning de Vries, B. W., Cucchiarini, C., Strik, H., & van Hout, R. (2020). Spoken grammar practice in CALL: The effect of corrective feedback and education level in adult L2 learning. *Language Teaching Research, 24*(5), 714–735. doi:10.1177/1362168818819027

Piccardo, E. (2010). From communicative to action-oriented: New perspectives for a new millennium. *CONTACT TESL Ontario, 36*(2), 20–35.

Piccardo, E., & North, B. (2019). *The action-oriented approach: a dynamic vision of language education.* Multilingual Matters.

Plonsky, L., & Ziegler, N. (2016). The CALL–SLA interface: Insights from a second-order synthesis. *Language Learning & Technology, 2*(20), 17–37.

Poehner, M. E., & Swain, M. (2017). L2 development as cognitive-emotive process. *Language and Sociocultural Theory, 3*(2), 219–241. doi:10.1558/lst.v3i2.32922

Reager, S. E. (2022, November 30). Voice cloning: A breakthrough with boundless potential. *Speech Technology.* https://www.speechtechmag.com/Articles/ReadArticle.aspx?ArticleID=156129

Reynolds, B. L., & Kao, C.-W. (2021). The effects of digital game-based instruction, teacher instruction, and direct focused written corrective feedback on the grammatical accuracy of English articles. *Computer Assisted Language Learning, 34*(4), 462–482. doi:10.1080/09588221.2019.1617747

Richards, J. C., & Rodgers, T. S. (2014). *Approaches and methods in language teaching* (3rd ed.). Cambridge University Press. doi:10.1017/9781009024532

Rienties, B., McFarlane, R., Nguyen, Q., Lewis, T., & Toetenel, L. (2018). Analytics in Online and Offline Language Learning Environments: The Role of Learning Design to Understand Student Online Engagement. *Computer Assisted Language Learning, 31*(3), 273–293. doi:10.1080/09588221.2017.1401548

Robinson, P. (2001). Task complexity, cognitive resources, and syllabus design: A triadic framework for examining task influences on SLA. In P. Robinson (Ed.), *Cognition and Second Language Instruction* (pp. 287–318). Cambridge University Press. doi:10.1017/CBO9781139524780.012

Sadeghi, K. (2023). *Technology-assisted language assessment in diverse contexts : lessons from the transition to online testing during COVID-19* (K. Sadeghi, Ed.). Routledge.

Sato, M., & Loewen, S. (2022). The research–practice dialogue in second language learning and teaching: Past, present, and future. *Modern Language Journal, 106*(3), 509–527. doi:10.1111/modl.12791

Sauro, S., & Thorne, S. L. (2020). Pedagogically mediating engagement in the wild: Trajectories of fandom-based curricular innovation. In V. Werner & F. Tegge (Eds.), *Pop culture in language education* (pp. 228–239). Routledge.

Scholze, A., Potkonjak, S., Marcel, F., Folinazzo, G., & Townend, N. (2022). Scenarios for learning – scenarios as learning: A design-based research process. In E. Piccardo, G. Lawrence, A. Germain-Rutherford, & A. Galante *Activating Linguistic and Cultural Diversity in the Language Classroom* (pp. 113–140). Springer. doi:10.1007/978-3-030-87124-6_6

Shafirova, L., & Araújo e Sá, M. H. (2023). Multilingual encounters in online video practices: the case of Portuguese university students. *International Journal of Multilingualism*. doi:10.1080/14790718.2023.2205142

Sheen, Y. (2008). Recasts, language anxiety, modified output, and L2 learning. *Language Learning*, *58*(4), 835–874. doi:10.1111/j.1467-9922.2008.00480.x

Shortt, M., Tilak, S., Kuznetcova, I., Martens, B., & Akinkuolie, B. (2021). Gamification in mobile-assisted language learning: A systematic review of Duolingo literature from public release of 2012 to early 2020. *Computer Assisted Language Learning*, 1–38.

Spada, N. (2022). Reflecting on task-based language teaching from an instructed SLA perspective. *Language Teaching*, *55*(1), 74–86. doi:10.1017/S0261444821000161

Spada, N., Jessop, L., Suzuki, W., Tomita, Y., & Valeo, A. (2014). Isolated and integrated form-focused instruction: Effects on different types of L2 knowledge. *Language Teaching Research*, *18*(4), 453–473. doi:10.1177/1362168813519883

Spada, N., & Lightbown, P. (2022). In it together: Teachers, researchers, and classroom SLA. *Modern Language Journal*, *106*(3), 635–650. doi:10.1111/modl.12792

Spada, N., & Lightbown, P. M. (2013). Instructed SLA. In P. Robinson (Ed.), *The Routledge encyclopedia of SLA* (pp. 319–327). Routledge. doi:10.4324/9780203135945

Spada, N., & Tomita, Y. (2010). Interactions between type of instruction and type of language feature: A meta-analysis. *Language Learning*, *60*(2), 263–308. doi:10.1111/j.1467-9922.2010.00562.x

Speechify. (2023). *AI voice cloning: Clone your voice instantly*. Speechify. https://speechify.com/voice-cloning/?landing_url=https%3A%2F%2Fspeechify.com%2Fblog%2Fchat-gpt-4-text-to-speech%2F

Sun, Y., & Gao, F. (2020). An investigation of the influence of intrinsic motivation on students' intention to use mobile devices in language learning. *Educational Technology Research and Development*, *68*(3), 1181–1198. doi:10.100711423-019-09733-9

Swain, M., Kinnear, P., & Steinmann, L. (2015). *Sociocultural theory in second language education: An introduction through narrative* (2nd ed.). Multilingual Matters. doi:10.21832/9781783093182

ten Have, P. (2007). *Doing conversation analysis: A practical guide* (2nd ed.). SAGE. doi:10.4135/9781849208895

Teo, T., Hoi, C. K. W., Gao, X., & Lv, L. (2019). What Motivates Chinese University Students to Learn Japanese? Understanding Their Motivation in Terms of "Posture.". *Modern Language Journal*, *103*(1), 327–342. doi:10.1111/modl.12546

Townend, N., Bartosik, A., Folinazzo, G., & Kelly, J. (2022). Teachers implementing action-oriented scenarios: realities of the twenty-first century classroom. In *E. Piccardo, G. Lawrence, A. Germain-Rutherford, & A. Galante Activating Linguistic and Cultural Diversity in the Language Classroom* (pp. 179–234). Springer. doi:10.1007/978-3-030-87124-6_8

Ushida, E. (2005). Role of students' attitudes and motivation in Second language learning in online language courses. *CALICO Journal, 23*(1), 49–78. doi:10.1558/cj.v23i1.49-78

van Lier, L. (2007). Action-based teaching, autonomy and identity. *Innovation in Language Teaching and Learning, 1*(1), 1–19.

van Lier, L. (2010). The ecology of language learning: Practice to theory, theory to practice. *Procedia: Social and Behavioral Sciences, 3*, 2–6. doi:10.1016/j.sbspro.2010.07.005

Vonkova, H., Jones, J., Moore, A., Altinkalp, I., & Selcuk, H. (2021). A review of recent research in EFL motivation: Research trends, emerging methodologies, and diversity of researched populations. *System (Linköping), 103*, 102622–. doi:10.1016/j.system.2021.102622

Werner, V., & Tegge, F. (2020). *Pop culture in language education theory, research, practice* (V. Werner & F. Tegge, Eds.). Routledge. doi:10.4324/9780367808334

Winke, P., & Goertler, S. (2008). Did we forget someone? students' computer access and literacy for CALL. *CALICO Journal, 25*(3), 482–509. doi:10.1558/cj.v25i3.482-509

Yeung, M. Y., Cheng, H. H., Chan, P. T., & Kwok, D. W. (2023). Communication technology and teacher–student relationship in the tertiary ESL classroom during the pandemic: A case study. *SN Computer Science, 4*(2), 202–202. doi:10.100742979-023-01667-7 PMID:36789247

Yoro, T. (2014). *Jibun no kabe* [*The wall of oneself*]. Shinchosha.

Young, R. F. (2008). *Language and interaction: An advanced resource book*. Routledge.

Young, R. F. (2009). *Discursive practice in language learning and teaching*. Wiley Blackwell.

Zhang, R., & Zou, D. (2022). Types, purposes, and effectiveness of state-of-the-art technologies for second and foreign language learning. *Computer Assisted Language Learning, 35*(4), 696–742. doi:10.1080/09588221.2020.1744666

Zhang, T. (2021). The effect of highly focused versus mid-focused written corrective feedback on EFL learners' explicit and implicit knowledge development. *System (Linköping), 99*, 102493–. doi:10.1016/j.system.2021.102493

Section 4
Teacher Practices

Chapter 7
Reconceptualizing Language Education With Mediation:
Perspectives From Israel

Leor Cohen
https://orcid.org/0000-0002-3286-7616
The Open University, Israel

Ingrid Barth
The Open University, Israel

ABSTRACT

The central argument in this chapter is that mediation is not simply a fourth mode of communication sitting alongside the other three modes of communication in the CEFR-CV, but should continue to evolve to become a core principle of the framework and a powerful engine for reconceptualizing language education. The central goal of this chapter is to support wide-scale implementation of mediation by putting forward possible paths for helping practitioners overcome some prevalent misunderstandings regarding mediation. To provide language educators with a deeper understanding of the entangled relationship between language and context, the authors borrow the concept of context from linguistic anthropology, as well as concepts such as positioning, roles and relationships. The overlapping, yet widely differing mediation activities described in the CEFR-CV are distilled down to just two groups - single context and double context - each with its own set of student-centered competences. Practitioner-friendly recommendations are provided for classroom use.

INTRODUCTION

This book's call for reconceptualizing language norms in multilingual contexts comes at a time of division and disorder within and between societies: Everywhere we see battle lines drawn, with increasingly complex challenges facing societies on multiple fronts. These 21st century challenges – international conflicts, immigration issues, threats to freedom and democracy – have dramatically increased the need

DOI: 10.4018/978-1-6684-8761-7.ch007

for people to communicate appropriately and effectively, in a way that facilitates communication across gaps and barriers and creates conditions in which people can move forward together. On top of all this, generative AI-based technologies are disrupting language programs worldwide and creating an unprecedented demand for rethinking the way we learn and teach languages.

In this light, we argue for a reconceptualization of language education by drawing on an expanded understanding of mediation. An expanded conceptualization of mediation is already presented in the 2020 Companion Volume (CV) of the Common European Framework of Reference (CEFR), and it provides a blueprint for helping language students to develop this potentially powerful mode of communication that could move us forward towards addressing 21st century challenges. Since its 2001 publication by the Council of Europe, the CEFR has become an internationally accepted framework for learning, teaching and assessing languages worldwide, adopted in many countries, across Europe and beyond (see Byram & Parmenter, 2012). According to Figueras, by 2012 (p.477), the document had been translated into many European languages, and its scales were available in more than 40 languages, including in sign language. As we describe below, the CEFR-CV, which updated and extended the earlier, 2001, version of the CEFR, puts forward a number of ground-breaking innovations including a new vision for mediation that has the potential to reconceptualize language education programs worldwide. This new vision goes beyond the vision of a language user as just an intermediary between two interlocutors who cannot communicate independently due to a communicative gap between them. This new vision retains this deficit concept but extends it to now include the potential power of the language user as a constructor of meaning and a facilitator of collaboration.

The central argument in this chapter is that mediation should continue to evolve in order to become a core principle of the CEFR-CV – and not simply a fourth mode of communication sitting alongside other modes of communication. In order to make this case, we first briefly review the history of CEFR and CEFR-CV and then position mediation therein. Next, we take a deeper look at mediation in its current form to draw insights about mediation's full potential. We illustrate why mediation requires additional clarification to allow this concept to unfurl and take up its position as a key aspect of the CEFR-CV, instead of being one of its least-visited corners. Third, we discuss potential sources of confusion that we have found working within the Israeli context, as well as potential sources of confusion that result from overlapping and disparate competences that emerge from mediation descriptors in the CEFR-CV. Fourth, we draw on understandings of language and communication from the literature in linguistic anthropology to relate core conceptualizations of the way language works with context as a fruitful way to move mediation forward. Lastly, we operationalize the conception of mediation put forward in this paper for practical use by practitioners. Our hope is that this chapter will contribute towards more effective pedagogies and professional development on mediation, enabling this mode of communication to serve as a potential engine for changing the way we learn and teach languages.

THE CEFR AND THE CEFR-CV

During the past two decades since its publication in 2001, much has been written on the CEFR and the Council of Europe's website offers a wealth of support materials on the framework (n.d.). Though they began as separate processes, the CEFR coincided with the Bologna Process, in that it introduced a set of descriptors of linguistic and communicative abilities set at a range of levels, providing standards for language education programs. And thus, language education programs at the tertiary level, in many countries throughout Europe and beyond, are now expected to align to this framework. The CEFR in 2001 organized communicative language activities into four modes of communication: Reception which includes reading and listening), production (which includes writing and speaking), interaction and mediation, even though the term "mode" itself did not appear in the English version. Most users of the CEFR did not notice this and referred to interaction as a fifth skill. The framework was immediately interpreted as a set of standards that testing companies could adopt to produce assessment devices to serve academic, governmental, and industry-based needs. However, the initial purpose for which the descriptors were designed was to aid practitioners in creating curricula/lesson plans and then implementing these ideas in classroom practices. In addition to goal setting, the descriptors are also meant to facilitate creativity and generate new ideas for creating more engaging and dynamic language classroom environments (E. Piccardo, personal communication, October 24, 2022).

The 2001 version of the CEFR was updated and replaced in 2020 by CEFR-CV, after first appearing in provisional form in 2018. In the CEFR-CV, the move from what was perceived by many users as four skills to four modes of communication are more explicitly presented. This move from skills to modes of communication is not a simple reorganization, but a fundamental and highly significant change in mindset: Skills connote applying technical know-how to particular sets of tasks, whereas entering into a mode of communication, in contrast, encompasses the whole person and connotes a "way-of-being" when engaged in the doings of a social agent. For instance, in reception, when one listens or reads, one is actively engaged in integrating information, constructing meaning, and understanding content in such a way as to be able to apply it going forward for the real-world task at hand. Communicating in a particular *mode* connotes a posture of engagement and a reaching out toward another person, with the whole of the person's being involved in the communicative act; a mode is a wider, more comprehensive notion than is the just the technical act of applying a skill. One enters into a mode, which is constituted by what one does.

In line with this shift in mindset, the CEFR-CV expands the two modes of communication that were not fully developed in the 2001 CEFR, namely interaction and mediation. Interaction in the language classroom emphasizes the co-construction of meaning and learning. Interaction fits in with the new change in mindset since conversational interaction is said to be the primordial genre (Schegloff, 1987; 2005) from which all other genres are descendant – showing this to students provides them with a lens through which to view communication across many genres. Mediation also fits in with this shift in mindset, but as we argue here, it lies at the base of this shift and can be a powerful engine for change. Currently, in the CEFR-CV, mediation is the fourth mode of communication, but the authors of the CEFR-CV positioned mediation fourth not because it is fourth in importance. Rather, it just happens to be the most complex mode to explain, as it encompasses the other three modes, which is part of the central argument of our chapter. Without mediation, the other modes of communication – reception, production, interaction – are reified idealizations. Without mediation, student performance tends to operate at a technical level, going through the motions without monitoring performance and without adapting messages to a particular real-world context. For a description of additional innovations in the CEFR-CV, see *Enriching 21st Century Language Education* (Council of Europe, 2022, p.29).

The status and position of mediation in relation to the other three modes of communication become much clearer when we examine what happens if mediation does not permeate and weave through these other modes. Without mediation, reception would lack comprehension monitoring and recovery strategies. Without mediation, production would lack audience design (Androutsopoulos, 2014; Bell, 1984), i.e., the adaptations necessary to package a message so that it is relevant to a particular target audience. Without mediation, interaction would lack competences to overcome and bridge the naturally occurring barriers and gaps found all too often in real-world interactions. Mediation, therefore, is the mode of communication that enables the other three modes to face up to the messiness of communicating in the real-world. As the authors of the CEFR-CV observe, mediation involves "enhancing communication and reciprocal comprehension, bridging gaps and solving conflicts" (North & Piccardo, 2016, p.11). In view of the key role played by mediation in potentially enriching the other three modes of communication instead of simply sitting alongside them, we suggest taking this notion one step further by viewing mediation as operating on a higher level, cutting across the whole of the CEFR-CV, similar to key concepts such as "plurilingualism" and "action-oriented".

The entire CEFR-CV is based on the action-oriented approach which instructs practitioners to create learning experiences for their students that have them work towards accomplishing communicative tasks. To illustrate further, the CEFR-CV states:

The CEFR's action-oriented approach represents a shift away from syllabuses based on a linear progression through language structures, or a predetermined set of notions and functions, towards syllabuses based on needs analysis, oriented towards real-life tasks and constructed around purposefully selected notions and functions. (Piccardo & North, 2019, p. 28)

Real-life tasks take place and resolve the needs that arise in real-life situations. Those situations are made up of the various contextual variables, which provide a set of conditions that make a particular way of communicating appropriately and effectively. In envisioning the kinds of real-life situations that are relevant to our students, we begin to form an image of the kind of graduates equipped with a professional identity that can competently handle themselves in such situations.

(Re)Positioning Mediation Within the CEFR-CV

Our argument in this chapter aims at maximizing mediation's potential contribution to reconceptualizing language education programs by attempting to push it along the evolutionary trajectory that it is already on. What started out in 1991 in Rüschlikon, Switzerland (North, 1992) as *processing* is currently a fourth mode of communication (that is mediation) sitting alongside the other three modes of communication in the CEFR-CV, namely reception, production and interaction (North & Piccardo, 2016, p. 7). In the current chapter, we argue that mediation should be understood not just as an additional mode of communication alongside the other three modes – but as a much wider set of competences that closely interweave with and permeate through the other three modes of communication. The need for such argumentation is in keeping with the observation that the CEFR should be "open," "capable of further extension and refinement," and "dynamic - in continuous evolution in response to experience in its use" (Council of Europe, 2001, p. 8).

At the heart of this wider set of competences lies the knowledge, skills and attitudes required to overcome obstacles to communication often found in the messy hurly-burly of the real world, aiding language learners on the path towards appropriate and effective communicative competences. Appropriate communication, as will be further expanded upon below, has a past orientation and is contingent on relevant presuppositions at any moment of communication; every situation comes with its set of expectations and deontic forces – perceived moral obligations and entitlements – as studied in conversation analysis (Antaki 2012; Antaki & Webb, 2019; Stevanovic & Peräkylä, 2012), philosophy (Darwall,

2009; Korsgaard, 2007), and social psychology (Davies & Harré, 1990; Harré & Moghaddam 2015). In contrast, effective communication has a future orientation, and is constituted by entailments, implicatures and any other effects brought about by communication – as studied in pragmatics (Austin 1962, 1975; Levison 1983), linguistic anthropology/sociolinguistics (Silverstein 1976, 1993), and social construction (Shotter & Gergen, 1994).

In this chapter, we will recommend that continuing mediation's evolutionary trajectory will help to clarify its role as sitting more appropriately alongside other key aspects central to the CEFR-CV, such as "action-oriented", "real world", "social agent" and "integrating modes of communication". For us, this means that, unless mediation competences are applied in the other three modes to adapt messages making them appropriate and effective, communication is likely to break down in confronting the "messiness" of the real world.

The Israeli Context

As we will argue, mediation is a potentially powerful resource for reconceptualizing language education – however, our experience as teacher educators in the Israeli context indicates that this fourth mode of communication often seems to be the least-visited, least-understood corner of the CEFR-CV. In Israel, as in many European countries, English is the first foreign language studied in school (EACEA/Eurydice, 2012). In addition, the study of academic English is mandatory in higher education (Aronin & Yelenevskaya, 2022), and in December of 2019, Israel's Council of Higher Education mandated that all English for Academic Purposes programs at the tertiary level align to the CEFR. This created an unprecedented demand for CEFR professional development at a national level, with which the authors of the current chapter were intensively involved. With this, from our experience and collaboration on EU-funded projects (such as TEMPUS and Horizons 2020), language educators at the tertiary level in Israel should not be viewed as unique to Israel, but struggle with much of the same issues as their counterparts abroad.

Our central aim in this section of the chapter is to outline some frequent misunderstandings that we have encountered, in order to enable teacher educators and professional development (PD) designers to pre-empt possible misconceptions that could hinder teachers from incorporating mediation in their lesson plans and classroom teaching. This approach is based on research by Borg (2011), who observes that teacher education is more likely to impact what teachers do in class if PD enables teachers to "surface" their partial understandings, misconceptions and impeding beliefs. By raising awareness of these sources of confusion, the chapter aims to contribute towards more effective PD on mediation, which will enable it to potentially reconceptualize the way we learn and teach languages.

The misunderstandings outlined below have emerged across a number of contexts. These include conference roundtable discussions, think tank sessions, and participation in national-level PD and PD-participant feedback among language professionals from a wide range of tertiary level institutions. In the second part of the chapter, we describe a number of ways that can help language professionals across the entire continuum "get a handle" on what may otherwise seem like an abstract and multi-layered concept. The misunderstandings that we encounter most often among language professionals in our context are powerfully captured in the following utterances that we have heard among our cohort of language educators in working with mediation:

"Mediation is a type of bridging that professionals require in fields such as law, family counseling and negotiations. It requires context-specific professional training and is therefore beyond the scope and mandate of my language classroom."

"Mediation requires too much emotional intelligence which my students - and I myself - may not have."

"This is beyond my pay grade - I don't have the skill set required for teaching mediation - what if things get out of hand and students get really angry or upset?"

"I would need extensive specialized PD before I have the confidence to try this in class."

"My students couldn't engage in mediation activities in their L1 - never mind in L2."

"Only students who already have high levels of L2 can engage in mediation."

These sentiments highlight the need to put more focus on mediation to help practitioners see its usefulness and make the most of its creative potential. The first four misconceptions relate to language educator perceptions of the competences required for teaching mediation. The last two misconceptions relate to language educator perceptions of students' language proficiency levels required before they begin acquiring mediation competences. All of the above sentiments miss the mark because, as will be shown below, mediation is part and parcel of any language use and therefore cannot be isolated from language instruction.

Overlapping and Disparate Mediation Competences

This section provides a deep dive into mediation to understand how it is conceptualized in its current form and where it could go. Figure 1 below can be found in the CEFR-CV (Council of Europe, 2020, p. 90), and it illustrates the various types of mediation in its current manifestation. In this figure, the mediation categories are arranged in a tree diagram that splits activities from strategies. It is outside the scope of this chapter to get into the distinctions between these two major branches, as the focus of this analysis will be on the end-nodes and relating the end-nodes to one another and to the other three modes of communication.

Reconceptualizing Language Education With Mediation

Figure 1. CEFR-CV graphic organization

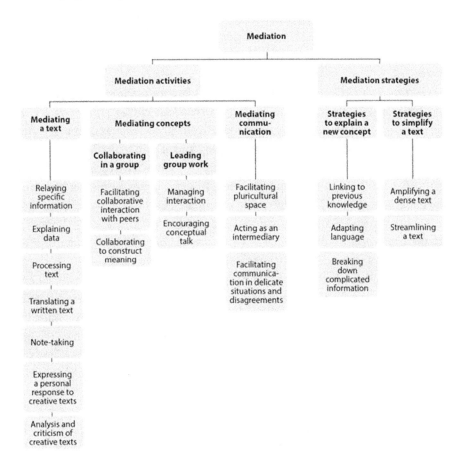

Figure 1 is taken from the CEFR-CV; it graphically organizes the various mediation categories and the descriptors therein.

Let us begin with relating the end-nodes to the other three modes of communication starting with the first branch, *Mediating a text*, and then the first end-node *Relaying specific information.*

At the C1 level, the CEFR's highest level of language competence for the set of descriptors in this category, the descriptor reads as follows, "Can explain (in Language B) the relevance of specific information found in a particular section of a long, complex text (in Language A)." This descriptor includes production (speaking or writing), the mode of communication in which "explaining" is to be accomplished, as well as reception (reading or listening) by which the "specific information" is to be elicited from "a particular section of a long, complex text". This category integrates and overlaps with activities in two other modes of communication, namely reception and production. The argument has been made by participants engaged in our PD programs that if mediation incorporates the other modes, then is it necessary?

A deeper look into the type of overlap illustrated above would find it reminiscent of a Rylean supra-act (Ryle, 2000), where the action of interest, for example, training a dog (which is the particular example Ryle uses in his paper), is a collection of smaller infra-acts – e.g., throwing a stick, petting, and giving a treat – organized into a larger course of action leading up to the supra-act. Ryle's point is that a supra-act cannot be captured in any single instance, as any single instance will be of an infra-act within a larger course of action. From our experience as teacher educators tasked with introducing teachers to the CEFR-CV's (Council of Europe, 2020) view of mediation, this feature of mediation, namely that each mediation category is a larger course of action composed of smaller infra-acts, may be a significant source of confusion.

In comparing end-nodes to end-nodes, overlap results when we juxtapose *Relaying specific information* with the first category in mediation strategies, namely '*Strategies to explain a new concept*' and its first node *Linking to previous knowledge*. Linking to previous knowledge is a strategy that will likely be part of accomplishing the explaining specified in relaying specific information; when explaining a new concept, do we not relay specific information? And so, many more such overlaps can be found across the mediation descriptors with those in other modes, and similarly, many more overlaps can also be found across descriptors *within* mediation. And thus, when compared to the other three modes of communication, mediation is more difficult for practitioners to conceptualize.

In contrast to the overlapping competences of various types of mediation in the CEFR-CV, there are also disparate competences across different types of mediation, i.e. end-nodes. For practitioners, the CEFR-CV's grouping together of so many essentially different activities under the category of mediation can make this an extremely difficult concept for practitioners to "wrap their heads around". For example, why are the following activities grouped under the same mode: "note-taking", "encouraging conceptual talk" and "defusing a potentially delicate situation and disagreements"? What single mode would one need to be in throughout the performance of these quite disparate tasks? This source of confusion can result in responses such as "if mediation is everything, then it is nothing", as reflected in prior conceptualizations of mediation as a "nomadic concept" (captured by Lenoir, 1996, as cited in North & Piccardo (2016, p. 11).

This ubiquity of mediation, as seen in both its overlapping and in its wide-ranging coverage of different types of tasks, clued us into what may be going on with this particular mode of communication. Teaching mediation is a bit like convincing a fish that it is wet; language does not work separate from context. In mediation, the authors of the CEFR-CV are capturing the way language must be tied to context when communication is judged to be appropriate and effective (or inappropriate and ineffective if language is not well tied to context). In the section below, we unpack the connection between language and context

To wrap up this section, the combination of overlaps, differences and misunderstandings described above may impact practitioners' implementation of mediation activities in two ways: Firstly, these potential puzzlements tend to make the learning curve comparatively steep: Many of our PD participants, when introduced to this concept, often see mediation as a complex, rather overwhelming concept that takes a considerable amount of time to "wrap their heads around". Secondly, when tasked with planning a mediation activity, practitioners who have not yet grasped the full richness and potential power of this concept, may stay within their comfort zones by focusing only on activities that have relatively small, easier-to-resolve gaps and distances, such as translating and summarizing. The problem with focusing on such mediation activities that can now be done by generative AI-based technologies is two-fold: Firstly, as mentioned below, these types of activities can now be allocated to chatbots, so the need for students to learn them is called into question. Secondly, classroom time tends to be a zero-sum equation: Resources spent on types of mediation activities that have gaps and distances easily bridged by generative AI-based technologies will leave less time and resources available for practicing 21st-century skills such as defusing delicate situations, collaborating in a group and managing interactions (leading groupwork) that are necessary for today's students.

Towards Solutions: What Language Practitioners Can Take From Linguistic Anthropology

The chapter now turns to reviewing literature from linguistic anthropology to deepen the kind of understanding of the relationship between language and context that can serve language educators in reconceptualizing language education.

Back in 1992, Duranti and Goodwin (following Schieffelin & Ochs, 1986) in their edited volume entitled *Rethinking Context*, wrote that the notion of language acquisition cannot encompass all that is entailed in actual processes of language socialization. What this means is that learners of a language do not simply retain lexical items and grammatical structures; they internalize forms of different ways of being and different ways of seeing the world. We will show how this notion is in line with the CEFR-CV's notion of the social agent, which will ultimately allow for mediation to unfurl out in becoming a powerful resource that can move us from acquisition to socialization. Kramsch's (1993) book *Context and Culture in Language Teaching* is rather prescient in the way it incorporates mediation competences (if just not termed as such) against the backdrop of previous work done in linguistic anthropology that informs her pedagogy.

The starting point for this scholarship is usually recognized as Silverstein's seminal work, entitled *Shifters, Linguistic Categories, and Cultural Description* (1976), which launched what is an ongoing project among linguistic anthropologists to spell out the symbiotic and enmeshed relationship between language and context. This relationship provides the added value for language educators in thinking about their work as a process of socialization rather than more simply acquisition; in learning to use a language, there is more to learn than just the language. There is a whole slew of aspects of context that are key to any language program. Silverstein adapted a mapping of context from his mentor Roman Jakobson (1976), which Hymes also adapted to derive his SPEAKING acronym/heuristic (1974a). Silverstein's mapping of context, seen in Figure 2 below, is to date one of the most useful for language practitioners as well as a clear and comprehensive laying out of contextual variables relevant to communication (1985, 2022).

Figure 2. Silverstein's map of factors

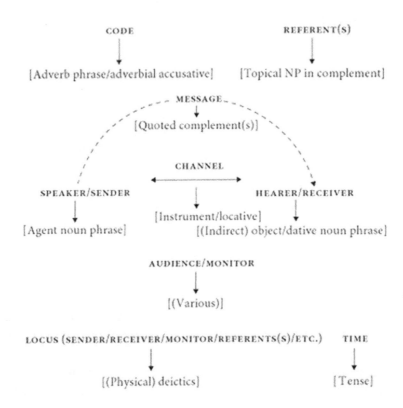

Figure 2 depicts Silverstein's mapping of the factors constituting a communication event, which he adapted from his mentor Jakobson.

For each one of the contextual components in Figure 2, language marks the particularities of given situations sometimes explicitly (by way of denotational meaning/reference, e.g., determiners and demonstratives) and sometimes implicitly (grammatically, e.g., infixes and adpositions). The central point here is that any one change in one component of context results in changes that need to be made to the message, i.e., the language.

Silverstein (1985) has gone on to further theorize much of pragmatics (entailments, presuppositions and implicatures) by understanding any bit of communication as being set on the dual scales of appropriate-inappropriate and effective-ineffective. Judging communication to be appropriate or not takes a past-oriented focus, and it has to do with the degree by which an act of communication regiments/aligns to a set of conventional and generic expectations. Judging communication to be effective or not takes a future-oriented focus, and it has to do with the degree by which an act of communication reshapes or creates a set of conditions and is constitutive of those conditions. To communicate both appropriately and effectively, social agents need to be able to apply their knowledge of the situationally relevant contextual variables in order to adjust their messages accordingly – to meet expectations and create conditions favorable to them.

Silverstein's work has contributed to an understanding of context as ever dynamic and evolving over time, at such degrees of sensitivity that utterances spoken at any one moment are constitutive of the context of the very next moment and the utterances therein, i.e., cotext. On the other hand, there are

Reconceptualizing Language Education With Mediation

elements of context that are more stable, operating at the level of an entire culture or society that play an explicit role in micro-interactions (see Goffman (1981) and Levinson (1988) on participation roles; see Bauman and Sherzer (1975) on group/community communicative conventions or ways of speaking; see Drew and Heritage (1992) on institutional ways of speaking).

And thus, context is a notion that needs to be unpacked, and research in linguistic anthropology (and related fields) has contributed to a comprehensive, yet nuanced, understanding of context and how it relates to language as briefly reviewed above. The core principle arising out of the discussion above is that at the center of the close relationship between context and language are these dual notions of appropriate and effective ways of communicating. These two notions will help us understand how language aligns to and is calibrated along various dimensions of context.

Operationalizing Context for Practitioners

In making mediation more accessible for practitioners, we have identified a set of contextual variables that we have implemented in an online PD program on a national scale in Israel to introduce tertiary-level practitioners to the CEFR-CV. These contextual dimensions are: platform/channel, language/register, author/speaker, genre/activity type, purpose, audience, time and place/location (this list is very similar to Hymes' SPEAKING heuristic). To get this idea across more effectively, we use the image of a soundboard with buttons representing eight different contextual dimensions that curriculum developers and instructors can adjust in order to shape the action-oriented scenarios they bring into the classrooms to immerse their students in, and thereby target one or another set of CEFR-CV descriptors.

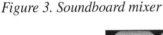

Figure 3. Soundboard mixer

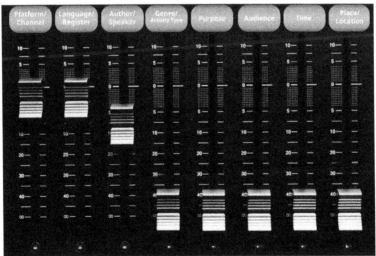

Figure 3 is an image of a soundboard mixer with eight dimensions of context listed above each slider (volume control). The image conveys the potential creativity practitioners have in working with configuring contexts for the purposes of their lessons. As this image illustrates, these contextual dimensions create specific configurations that can call attention to one or another contextual dimensionThe image of the soundboard illustrates the creative potential that curriculum developers and instructors can tap into by allowing them to shape the various contexts (scenarios) they build into their curricula according to the needs of their students. In this way, mediation becomes a powerful resource for any language program.

When practitioners understand context in this dynamic and comprehensive way, they can use it as a resource for instructional design and in-class teaching. Context, as a multi-dimensional concept, can be used to prepare students to communicate in the scholarly contexts of their disciplines or in the industry-based contexts of their fields. The particular and relevant target context can be unpacked for students in providing an engaging didactic experience in which students can learn and practice. This understanding would enable practitioners to create materials and learning experiences where students accomplish tasks in different contexts, varying learning experiences. Class instruction and reflection would highlight the way changes in context result in adaptations needed in crafting messages and accomplishing tasks. This is the point Kramsch is driving at in her analyses of the five cases of language teaching described in her above-mentioned book (1993, pp. 70-103).

Fascinating examples of the adaptations needed to be made when changing audience, for instance, is produced by WIRED in their *5 Levels* series on Youtube (Gershon, 2018). In each episode, an expert explains a difficult concept at five different levels starting from explaining the concept to a child and working up to discussing the concept with a fellow expert. This type of activity can facilitate tasks in reception, production and interaction. Surfacing and reflecting on the adaptations and adjustments needed in different contexts can help students develop the key sociolinguistic and pragmatic competences they need in order to communicate appropriately and effectively in a specific context.

This way of operationalizing context focuses on the changes and adaptations needed when trying to convey a message in a particular context or in carrying a message across from one context to another, and we have seen this approach resonate with practitioners that we have worked with.

A More Familiar Type of Context: An Alternative Route

For some practitioners, the above conceptualization was sufficient for them to begin designing and teaching content generated within the framework provided by the CEFR-CV. However, for others, an alternative route has been more helpful. For some, emphasizing the professional and (inter)personal aspect of context is more salient, and it also provides a useful starting point to begin working with mediation. The constructs relevant in this approach are roles/professional identities and the relations between people in real-world situations.

Roles refers to the professional roles in professional, real world contexts. Roles are professional identities, which our students can inhabit to practice what it would be like to communicate from such a position in the workplace. Consider students in health-related programs at the tertiary-level, such as nursing, clinical psychology, and medicine. These programs do not simply transmit knowledge to students, but they socialize them to becoming healthcare professionals, on whom many lives will depend. The same is true of engineering, law, and education students. In short, for all students, becoming a professional takes work. This aspect of mediation provides students with the opportunity to try on professional roles and the kind of talk (or any mode of communication) that the relevant roles engage in. As teacher educators, we recommend using scenarios that include the types of professional roles that students will play in their future careers. Lessons with scenarios can also include debriefing sessions that provide students with opportunities to think about the kinds of interactions and communications they expect those professionals to have.

However, roles can engender a more static understanding of constantly fluctuating positionings that occur in communication. In their seminal paper, Davies and Harré worked up a conception of positioning to replace and improve upon the use of "roles" (1990). Positioning is about the rights and responsibilities asserted, demanded, negotiated, inherited, earned, lost, etc. that shape an individual's normative behaviour guiding communication. In Harré's own words:

Positioning Theory is the study of the nature, formation, influence and ways of change of local systems of rights and duties as shared assumptions about them influence small scale interactions. Positioning Theory is to be seen in contrast to the older framework of Role Theory. Roles are relatively fixed, often formally defined and long lasting. Even such phenomena as "role distance" and "role strain" presuppose the stability of the roles to which they are related. Positioning Theory concerns conventions of speech and action that are labile, contestable and ephemeral. (Harré & Moghaddam, 2015)

Critical here are the moral and practical (ethical) considerations within the "second-person mode" elementary to all communications (Darwall 2009; Korsgaard 2007; Stevanovic & Peräkylä 2012). In other words, roles always operate in relation to others (as they occupy other roles). Relationships are about what happens between or among people, i.e., interpersonal relationships, who occupy particular positions and take up particular roles. Roles/identities are usually positioned within their particular institutional setting (context) in particular ways, in relationship to others in that setting. In any situation, every person involved has certain rights and certain responsibilities, things they are owed and things they owe to others.

This is where students can practice viewing a situation from the various perspectives of the participants that are part of a professional scenario. This is where the students can think, "Well, she would say this to him, and he would say that to her." They are engaged in this type of thinking, which is focused on the ethical dimensions of communication. But, it also gets them thinking about the practical dimension of communication: How do we move forward? How do we create the conditions to move forward together? In these types of mediation activities, students have the opportunity to learn to what extent finding the right words at the right time can make a difference, as well as learning when just listening is required.

Fundamentally, relationships that enhance communication and reciprocal comprehension are about honoring the other person and giving them the respect they deserve as a person and as a professional in any delicate or difficult situation. This is what Goffman was theorizing in his concept of *face* and *interaction rituals*; interaction rituals are designed to guard the sacredness of the self and that of others (1967). Thinking about relationships and drawing on widely used cultural conceptions of the types of roles/positions in society is one way of operationalizing context that resonates with many of the practitioners we have worked with. This way of operationalizing context focuses on the adjustments needed when trying to convey a message to particular images of professional persons, where relationships among those persons can be depicted as having become strained for real-world reasons.

And so, this way into mediation, by way of roles and relationships, has at its center appropriate and effective communication. For communication to be judged as role-appropriate, it must be expected, in that the role of the person communicating is in line with societal expectations of that role. Regarding relationships, these are often built on histories of interactions that are built on routines and stable behavior patterns, which contribute to the durability of these relationships. As with Bauman's definition of genres as "sets of expectations" (1999), roles and relationships too are built on expectations, and it is to these expectations that communication must calibrate itself in order to be judged as appropriate.

And with effective communication, there are at least two aspects that are relevant here. Firstly, effective communication reconstructs and maintains roles and relationships contributing to their durability across interactions (or, with slight innovations and shifts, thereby contributing to their evolution). Secondly, effective communication brings felicitous results by enabling people to achieve their goals.

The following section further operationalizes mediation, as unpacked above, by applying it to concrete classroom practices.

Mediation in Single and Double Contexts

The above discussion of context forms the base for a practitioner-friendly solution to the puzzlements and misunderstandings also outlined above. Our approach consists of introducing the concepts of single and double contexts as an organizing principle or resource to help practitioners sort the various (and seemingly unconnected) types of mediation into just two groups, making it easier for practitioners to understand and work with mediation. The use of just two groups enables teachers to make sure that they provide students with adequate opportunities to practice two sets of competences.

And so, rather than focusing on the *object of mediation* – as in mediating a text, concept or idea – we suggest focusing on the *method of mediation*. Within each type of mediation – single and double context – we distinguish two major methods of mediating, i.e., two different sets of competences, covering all of the various types of mediation as found in the CEFR-CV. The first set of competences focuses on mediation as it occurs in a single, particular situation or context – single context mediation. The second set of competences focus on mediation as it occurs when a message needs to cross from one situation/context to another – double context mediation. Common to both types of mediation is the focus on appropriate and effective communication as set out above.

In single context mediation, the social agent is confronted by some gap or barrier in a professional setting. A classic type of mediation in the CEFR-CV that illustrates this type of mediation is defusing a delicate situation, where the social agent must be aware of the ever-shifting epistemic and affective conditions of the situation in order to get the job done (Antaki & Webb, 2019; Heritage, 2012; Ruusuvuori, 2012; Stevanovic & Peräkylä, 2012). One example of this is to have students confront one another in typical workplace scenarios, such as a disruptive colleague, student groupwork gone bad, or helping a fellow student cope with a low grade or bad news. A less obvious illustration of single context mediation can be found in the case of notetaking (a node on the mediation tree as depicted above), where the social agent actively takes notes to monitor her own comprehension, integrate information, and construct meaning of a difficult text when reading on her own. The method of mediation in single context mediation is in thinking how to overcome the obstacles on the path towards reciprocal understanding (between author and reader, in the notetaking instance).

In double context mediation, the social agent is tasked with taking a message from one context and adjusting it to fit another, significantly different, context. The type of know-how involved here is of the ways of communicating in both contexts. The term "ways of communicating" is derived from Hymes' "ways of speaking" (1974b), where the contextual dimensions explicated above can configure in almost infinite sets so as to help account for many appropriate and effective linguistic phenomena. How communication is done in one context, within one group/speech community, is not how it gets done in another. Teaching students to make the necessary adjustments to their messages when those messages "travel" from one context to another taps into their sociolinguistic competences and builds on them – making them more familiar and aware of different ways of communicating in different groups and settings. This

Reconceptualizing Language Education With Mediation

is a potentially empowering act that can enable students to be more versatile in a wider-ranging set of circumstances and more ready for an ever-globalizing world. And when practitioners become aware of how they can more effectively use context to construct their action-oriented scenarios, they have a far richer set of resources they can use to provide opportunities to practice more meaningful mediation activities.

Scaffolding mediation in either single or double context activities consists of providing students with the discursive moves and their concomitant/constitutive language chunks (multi-word expressions) that enable students to bridge gaps and move past the messiness. This "moves and chunks" scaffolding enables students to identify what needs to be said and why, i.e. the sequence of appropriate and effective communication acts, that meet the needs of any real-world scenario. For example, when student groupwork goes wrong because a group member presents sub-par work, students need to defuse the situation in a way that creates conditions for getting over this obstacle and moving forward together. In order to progress through these moves, practitioners can provide students with the language chunks they need to enact the set of discursive moves. Enabling students to fine-tune moves and chunks introduces a dynamic, highly engaging element and highly relevant mediation activity into the language classroom.

CONCLUSION

The primary argument in this chapter is that mediation is not simply a fourth mode of communication sitting alongside the other three modes, but that it permeates throughout all of the other modes of communication and is a powerful engine for reconceptualizing language education. Mediation is a core principle of the CEFR-CV interwoven throughout, helping practitioners to interpret the other modes of communication and enrich their understandings of them. In making this argument, the chapter had two central foci: In the first part of the chapter, our objective was to identify misunderstandings and puzzlements that still need to be clarified to make mediation more accessible and practitioner-friendly in order to reach wider-scale implementation of mediation in language classrooms. In the second part of the chapter, our objective was to outline a path towards solutions that we developed and successfully field-tested in our national level PD program to help practitioners "wrap their heads around" and implement mediation.

This path towards possible solutions included (1) borrowing concepts from linguistic anthropology such as context, positioning, roles and relationships to provide language educators with a deeper understanding of the entangled relationship between language and context. This step emphasizes the common threads that weave through the wide variety of activities included under mediation; (2) distilling the multiple, widely differing mediation activities described in the CEFR-CV to just two groups – single context and double context – each with its own set of competences; and (3) scaffolding mediation activities by identifying in advance the discursive moves and their concomitant/constitutive language chunks that will equip students with the language and know-how necessary to bridge gaps and move past real-world messiness. By delineating this path towards solutions, this chapter aims not only to support practitioners' engagement with mediation, but also to help mediation along its evolutionary trajectory and towards its full potential.

Looking Ahead

Against the current backdrop of increasing global tensions and disruptive AI-based technologies, the call for reconceptualizing language education has never felt more urgent. The tectonic shifts in the language landscape require us to now rethink the way we learn and teach languages by mapping out which mediation competences we should focus on and which ones can already be allocated to the AI-generative machines (saving valuable classroom time). As the new challenges presented by such disruptive technologies become clearer, mediation will become even more necessary to help students rise to these challenges. And yet, generative AI-based technologies will present new opportunities for mediation, such as accurately specifying contextual dimensions for optimal prompt engineering. Furthermore, the outputs of the machine have introduced an unprecedented need for critical evaluation of information (note how deeply mediation competences are involved here). These challenges and opportunities will help mediation move forward from the least-visited, least-understood corner to a key aspect of the CEFR-CV.

REFERENCES

Androutsopoulos, J. (2014). Languaging when contexts collapse: Audience design in social networking. *Discourse, Context & Media*, *4*, 62–73. doi:10.1016/j.dcm.2014.08.006

Antaki, C. (2012). Affiliative and disaffiliative candidate understandings. *Discourse Studies*, *14*(5), 531–547. doi:10.1177/1461445612454074

Antaki, C., & Webb, J. (2019). When the larger objective matters more: Support workers' epistemic and deontic authority over adult service-users. *Sociology of Health & Illness*, *41*(8), 1549–1567. doi:10.1111/1467-9566.12964 PMID:31215067

Aronin, L., & Yelenevskaya, M. (2022). Teaching English in multilingual Israel: Who teaches whom and how. A review of recent research 2014–2020. *Language Teaching*, *55*(1), 24–45. doi:10.1017/S0261444821000215

Austin, J. L. (1975). *How to do things with words: The William James lectures delivered at Harvard University in 1955* (2nd ed.). Harvard University Press. doi:10.1093/acprof:oso/9780198245537.001.0001

Bauman, R. (1999). Genre. *Journal of Linguistic Anthropology*, *9*(1/2), 84–87. doi:10.1525/jlin.1999.9.1-2.84

Bauman, R., & Sherzer, J. (1975). The ethnography of speaking. *Annual Review of Anthropology*, *4*(1), 95–119. doi:10.1146/annurev.an.04.100175.000523

Bell, A. (1984). Language style as audience design. *Language in Society*, *13*(2), 145–204. doi:10.1017/S004740450001037X

Borg, S. (2011). The impact of in-service teacher education on language teachers' beliefs. *System*, *39*(3), 370–380. doi:10.1016/j.system.2011.07.009

Byram, M., & Parmenter, L. (Eds.), *The Common European Framework of Reference: The Globalization of Language Education Policy*. Multilingual matters.

Council of Europe. (2001). *Common European Framework of Reference for Languages: Learning, teaching, assessment*. Cambridge University Press.

Council of Europe. (2020). *Common European Framework of Reference for Languages: Learning, teaching, assessment – Companion volume*. Council of Europe.

Council of Europe. (2022). *Enriching 21st-century language education: The CEFR Companion volume in practice*. Council of Europe.

Council of Europe. (n.d.). *Common European Framework of Reference for Languages (CEFR)*. The Council of Europe. https://www.coe.int/en/web/common-european-framework-reference-languages

Darwall, S. (2009). *The second-person standpoint: Morality, respect, and accountability*. Harvard University Press. doi:10.2307/j.ctv1bzfp0f

Davies, B., & Harré, R. (1990). Positioning: The discursive production of selves. *Journal for the Theory of Social Behaviour, 20*(1), 43–63. doi:10.1111/j.1468-5914.1990.tb00174.x

Drew, P., & Heritage, J. (1992). *Talk at work: Interaction in institutional settings*. Cambridge University Press.

Duranti, A., & Goodwin, C. (Eds.). (1992). *Rethinking context: Language as an interactive phenomenon (No. 11)*. Cambridge University Press.

EACEA/Eurydice. (2012). Key Data on Teaching Languages at School in Europe 2012. *The Education, Audiovisual and Culture Executive Agency* (EACEA P9 Eurydice and Policy Support). Brussels: EACEA P9 Eurydice. doi:. doi:10.2797/83967

Figueras, N. The impact of the CEFR. *ELT Journal, 66(4)*, 477-85

Gershon, T. (2018, June 25). *Quantum Computing Expert Explains One Concept in 5 Levels of Difficulty*. [Video]. YouTube. https://www.youtube.com/watch?v=OWJCfOvochA

Goffman, E. (1967). *Interaction ritual: Essays on face behavior*. Pantheon Books.

Goffman, E. (1981). *Forms of talk*. University of Pennsylvania Press.

Harré, R., & Moghaddam, F. M. (2015). Positioning theory. The Wiley handbook of theoretical and philosophical psychology: Methods, approaches, and new directions for social sciences, 263-276. Wiley.

Heritage, J. (2012). The epistemic engine: Sequence organization and territories of knowledge. *Research on Language and Social Interaction, 45*(1), 30–52. doi:10.1080/08351813.2012.646685

Hymes, D. (1974a). *Foundations in sociolinguistics: An ethnographic approach*. University of Pennsylvania Press.

Hymes, D. (1974b). Ways of Speaking. In R. Bauman & J. Sherzer (Eds.), *Explorations in the Ethnography of Speaking* (pp. 433–451). Cambridge University Press.

Jakobson, R. (Ed.). (1976). *Metalanguage as a linguistic problem* (pp. 113–121). Akadémiai Nyomda.

Korsgaard, C. M. (2007). Autonomy and the second person within: A commentary on Stephen Darwall's the second-person standpoint. *Ethics, 118*(1), 8–23. doi:10.1086/522019

Kramsch, C. (1993). *Context and culture in language teaching*. Oxford University Press.

Lenoir, Y. (1996). Médiation cognitive et médiation didactique. In C. Raisky & M. Caillot (Eds.), Le didactique au delà des didactiques. Débats autour de concepts fédérateurs (pp. 223–251). Bruxelles: De Boeck Université.

Levinson, S. C. (1988). Putting linguistics on a proper footing: Explorations in Goffman's participation framework. In *Goffman: Exploring the interaction order* (pp. 161–227). Polity Press.

North, B. (1992). European Language Portfolio: Some options for a working approach to design scales for proficiency. In Council of Europe *Transparency and coherence in language learning in Europe: Objectives, assessment and certification.* (pp. 158–174). Strasbourg: Council for Cultural Co-operation.

North, B., & Piccardo, E. (2016). Developing illustrative descriptors of aspects of mediation for the Common European Framework of Reference (CEFR): A Council of Europe project. *Language Teaching*, *49*(3), 455–459. doi:10.1017/S0261444816000100

Piccardo, E., & North, B. (2019). *The action-oriented approach: A dynamic vision of language education* (Vol. 72). Multilingual matters.

Ruusuvuori, J. (2012). *Emotion, affect and conversation. The handbook of conversation analysis.* Wiley-Blackwell.

Ryle, G. (2000). Courses of action or the uncatchableness of mental acts. *Philosophy (London, England)*, *75*(3), 331–344. doi:10.1017/S0031819100000437

Schegloff, E. A. (1987). Analyzing single episodes of interaction: An exercise in conversation analysis. *Social Psychology Quarterly*, *50*(2), 101–114. doi:10.2307/2786745

Schegloff, E. A. (2005). Discourse as an interactional achievement III: The omnirelevance of action. In D. Schiffrin, D. Tannen, & H. E. Hamilton (Eds.), *The handbook of discourse analysis* (pp. 229–249). Blackwell Publishing Ltd. doi:10.1002/9780470753460.ch13

Schieffelin, B. B., & Ochs, E. (1986). Language socialization. *Annual Review of Anthropology*, *15*(1), 163–191. doi:10.1146/annurev.an.15.100186.001115

Shotter, J., & Gergen, K. J. (1994). Social Construction: Knowledge, Self, Others, and Continuing the Conversation. *Annals of the International Communication Association*, *17*(1), 1, 3–33. doi:10.1080/23808985.1994.11678873

Silverstein, M. (1976). *Shifters, linguistic categories, and cultural description. Meaning in anthropology.* University of New Mexico Press.

Silverstein, M. (1985). The functional stratification of language and ontogenesis. In J. V. Wertsch (Ed.), *Culture, communication, and cognition: Vygotskian perspectives* (pp. 205–235). Cambridge University Press.

Silverstein, M. (1993). Reflexive language: Reported speech and metapragmatics. In J. Lucy (Ed.), *Metapragmatic Discourse and Metapragmatic Function*. Cambridge University Press Cambridge.

Silverstein, M. (2022). *Language in Culture: Lectures on the Social Semiotics of Language.* Cambridge University Press., doi:10.1017/9781009198813

Stevanovic, M., & Peräkylä, A. (2012). Deontic Authority in Interaction: The Right to Announce, Propose, and Decide. *Research on Language and Social Interaction*, *45*(3), 297–321. doi:10.1080/08351813.2012.699260

Chapter 8
Bilingualism in Cuba:
Social and Economic Impact of English Among Teachers

Ali Borjian
San Francisco State University, USA

ABSTRACT

This chapter considers the impact of English in a context where it is not a predominant language. For decades, the post-revolutionary Cuban government has recognized the importance of English in the economic advancement of the country. Although other world languages, especially Russian, have been promoted in Cuba, English has remained the most popular second language for the Cuban population. How Cuban teachers of English became interested in learning English and factors that contributed to their high level of proficiency in English is examined, and the social and economic impact of this language in their lives is investigated. Obstacles teachers face and their recommendations for ways to enhance English language development in Cuba are presented. Factors that keep them in the teaching profession or could force them to leave are also revealed.

INTRODUCTION

Socio-political ideologies and national educational agendas are directly impacted by the immense power of global English (Ushioda, 2017). Globalization has forced many countries in the Global South to train their workforces to respond to the demands of businesses that use English to communicate. Many countries emphasize English language teaching to equip their citizens with the language skills necessary to understand and respond to the language's growing presence and importance in the global economy. By doing so, countries can ensure that their workforces are better able to communicate in English and can gain access to better employment opportunities in the global marketplace. Delgado Hellester (2013) reports that Mexican workers who are proficient in English earn 28% more than their monolingual co-workers. Guo and Sun (2014) present similar findings from China where college graduates with English proficiency have higher starting salaries and enjoy higher future earning potential. The growing pressures for English language learning calls for many more teachers around the world. Hence, many countries

DOI: 10.4018/978-1-6684-8761-7.ch008

have mandated the teaching of English in their schools and universities (Crystal, 2003). In spite of much efforts to improve English language learning in many countries in Latin America, schooling systems are not fully capable of developing sufficient number of qualitied teachers of English (Ministerio de Educación Nacional de Colombia, 2014; Ministerio de Educación Ecuador, 2016).

Realizing that monolingualism is not a viable stance in a diverse and highly competitive global market, many nations have prioritized the development of multilingualism by creating opportunities for their workforces to learn different languages, in particular, English. Some countries emphasize the development of English language proficiency through investing a great amount of resources including inviting native speakers of English to fill the gap (e.g. China, Japan, South Korea). This response may seem feasible as a short-term solution, but is not pedagogically sound and not realistic for long-term language planning. Furthermore, it is not economically viable for many countries. In contrast, some countries have relied upon their own educational system to develop a teaching force that can respond to the growing demand of English language instruction (e.g., Cuba). Since Cuba has enjoyed much success in educating its population, including teachers of English, it is valuable to explore factors that have led to such accomplishment.

Cuba has experienced much success in providing quality education to its population since the 1959 revolution, including the development of bilingualism among school-aged children and university students (UNESCO, 2008). Many factors are associated with individuals' motivations to learn English as a second language and become bilingual. Among these factors are utility, social capital, economic advancement, and job security (Ushioda, 2017). These pragmatic reasons for learning English significantly impact one's reason to enhance their overall proficiency in this language. Furthermore, individuals who are motivated to learn, and eventually teach, a second language must have opportunities to acquire mastery in different domains of that language, including grammatical and pragmatics. Their perseverance plays an important role in becoming highly fluent bilinguals.

Although the literature on the teaching of English as a world language is extensive, the voices of bilingual teachers from the Global South are often missing. Investigations in the field of teaching world languages are not complete by solely looking at the reasons individuals decide to become bilingual. It is important to learn why they become teachers and to better appreciate the social and economic impact of this language on their lives. We must also learn about the obstacles they confront when teaching English as a world language.

Bilingual teachers are uniquely positioned to bridge the gap between cultures and foster global understanding. They are able to provide students with a deeper understanding of the world and its many cultures, while also helping to develop their language skills. This can help to foster a sense of identity and belonging in students, as well as a greater appreciation for diversity. Bilingual teachers can also help to motivate students to learn and explore new cultures, as well as to develop their own sense of identity and global citizenship.

This chapter considers the impact of English in the context of Cuba where it is not a dominant language. I examine how a group of Cuban teachers of English became interested in learning English, factors that contributed to their high level of proficiency in English, and the social and economic impact of this language in their lives. I present the obstacles teachers face and their recommendations for ways to enhance English language development in Cuba. Factors that keep them in the teaching profession or could force them to leave are also presented. Learning about the preparation of teachers of English in Cuba, their motivation to teach this language, and pressures that negatively impact their teaching effectiveness can provide insightful lessons to bilingual teachers and teacher educators around the world.

History of English in Cuba

Since the dramatic fall of the Spanish Empire and the occupation of Cuba by the U.S. in 1898, English has played an important role in the educational system of this country (Pérez, 1982). Since Cuba is experiencing cultural and political transformations after the death of Fidel Castro, it is important to briefly discuss the history of English language teaching in this island nation. As Martin (2007) describes in detail, from the 1960s, the post-revolutionary Cuban government recognized the importance of English in the economic advancement of the country. Although other world languages, especially Russian, have been promoted in Cuba, English has remained the most popular second language for the Cuban population. Since 1985, English has been regarded as the language of international communication and scientific activity. Cuba is highly interested in enhancing English proficiency among its population and language policies have made English mandatory from junior high school to the university level. English is vital for the Cuban scientific community and technology professionals. Furthermore, increased tourism to Cuba and international commercial ventures requires many more Cubans to be proficient in English (Martin, 2007). In general, multilingualism is viewed by Cuba as one approach to achieve economic independence.

Smith (2016) describes the various transformations in the pedagogy of English language instruction and notes that the Communicative Approach is highly emphasized in the teaching of English in Cuba. Furthermore, Carnoy and Marshall (2005) emphasize that the Cuban model of pedagogy places much emphasis on collectivism and collaboration rather than individualism and competition. Turner, Martí and Pita Cespedes (2001) describe this model as "pedagogy of tenderness" where learning necessitates engagement of family and community in every student's schooling.

All Cuban teachers have university degrees and are offered frequent professional development opportunities (Hickling-Hudson, 2004). Individuals wishing to become teachers of English in Cuba must demonstrate an advanced level of proficiency through a series of written and oral examinations. Candidates are interviewed by a selection panel and must demonstrate a high degree of motivation to develop their English language proficiency. A minimum of five years of university course work and field experience are necessary to obtain a certificate for teaching English. In short, becoming a teacher of English requires much personal dedication and significant resources from the government of Cuba.

Although over the past several decades the U.S. has had a small role in promoting English in Cuba and this task has been mostly delegated to Canada, Great Britain, and Anglophone Caribbean nations, Cubans are more interested to learn the American version of English (Personal Communications with Cuban teacher educators, July-November, 2022). This may be due to the significant historical ties between the two countries as well as the aspirations of some Cubans to emigrate to this neighboring country. The United States remains the top destination for Cuban immigrants (Blizzad & Batalova, 2020).

Motivation and Second Language Development

The educators I had the opportunity to learn from are elective bilinguals who chose to learn English in an environment in which Spanish is used in virtually all areas of their lives. The importance of motivation in the context of learning a second language has been extensively studied (Gardner, 1985; Oxford & Shearin, 1994; Wigfield & Eccles, 2000; Williams & Burden, 1997). Yet, few have investigated teachers' own motivation and attitude toward learning English. Below I review the literature on motivation, self-determination, commitment, and self-efficacy.

As individuals pursue a goal of achieving high proficiency in a second language, they are also mindful of potential benefits of that achievement. Beliefs and identity of teachers of English are mediated by how and why they learned English. Furthermore, the methods they employ to teach English can be linked to their level of proficiency in various domains of this language. Many factors are associated with individuals' motivations to learn English as a second language. Among these factors are utility, social capital, economic advancement, and job security.

Motivation underlies learning because it addresses the goals and expectations of the learner (Ryan & Deci, 2000). Gardner (1985) argues that anyone who seeks to learn a second language recognizes the potential value of speaking a new language and must be motivated to learn the language for either instrumental purposes (e.g., to get a job or to meet a school graduation requirement) or for integrative purposes (e.g., to better understand how local users of the language think and behave). If a person is only interested in basic conversational skills in a new language then the level of attainment will be different from learners who want to read and discuss the important literature of another culture.

In addition to motivation, time is an important factor to consider for second language acquisition. The time needed to obtain a high level of proficiency for interpersonal communication is considerably less than the time required to master second language oral and literacy skills in order to do academic level coursework in the second language (Padilla & Borjian, 2009). This includes being able to use the new language with increasing grammatical accuracy in ways that are contextually and culturally authentic. Proficient users in a second language are able to exhibit a high level of accuracy in the second language. Accuracy pertains to the precision of the message in terms of fluency, grammar, vocabulary, pronunciation, and cultural appropriateness. When language practice reflects real-world use, it forms the foundation for developing proficiency. This is true regardless of age, grade level, and type of language instruction offered the student.

Bilingual teachers can help facilitate language learning by creating an engaging teaching environment. By providing learners with a safe space to express their language abilities and cultural identity, teachers can help foster a sense of acceptance and belonging. Furthermore, teachers can use both language and culture to provide students with meaningful learning experiences that can result in increased motivation and improved language learning outcomes.

Self-Determination, Commitment, Self-Efficacy

Williams and Burden (1997) learned that language acquisition is significantly enhanced when the learner is motivated to learn and is self-confident. Kormos and Csizér (2014) emphasize that achievement of high level of language competence is attainable through self-learning initiatives by learners themselves. Furthermore, Oxford and Shearin (1994) emphasize that the learners' ability to provide self-reward and self-evaluation can significantly influence language learning. Similarly, Williams and Burden (1997) maintain that learners are more motivated when they are convinced that their learning experiences are meaningful. In addition, when learners are working on a task or learning that is new to them, they require a sense of autonomy or self-determination (Denney & Daviso, 2015; Gagné & Deci, 2005; Wigfield & Eccles, 2000). We also know that students need to feel connected with their peers and teachers in order to have a positive perspective on a topic or task (Anderman & Freeman, 2004). Equally important as self-determination and connectedness is the necessity to feel capable in responding to a new learning task (Pintrich, 2003).

Studies investigating teachers' values and ways of living have contributed to our deeper awareness of teachers' practices. Moodie and Feryok (2015) maintain that understanding teachers' beliefs and perspectives about language teaching and learning can help to uncover why people commit to language teaching in the first place. Commitment diverges from motivation since it is persistent over time and connects a person to actions toward that goal (Meyer & Herscovitch, 2001).

Learning English as a second language can be a long and difficult process. Lasagabaster (2017) maintains that learning a new language is not only demanding but at times it is quite frustrating. It is only through sustained effort and dedication that students can master the language and achieve fluency. Additionally, having access to a supportive and encouraging learning environment is also beneficial, as it can help learners stay motivated and on track in their studies (Gardner, 1985). Bilingual teachers are well-placed to help sustain this learning environment, as they can provide learners with both supportive feedback and guidance as well as their own experiences in learning English (Holliday, 2005). This helps to provide a safe and encouraging space where learners can practice their English skills and grow in confidence. Additionally, offering assessments throughout the learning process can help to measure improvement and keep language learners on track with their goals (Cummins, 1984).

It has been argued that personal efficacy beliefs impact people's effectiveness (Bandura, 1997). As proficient users of English, bilingual teachers of English may develop a higher sense of self-efficacy. Furthermore, since individuals normally work within a social unit they are influenced by the collective perspective of that group (Bandura, 1997). Bandura asserts that, just like self-efficacy beliefs, collective efficacy beliefs can modify group performance in various fields of functioning including education. Similarly, Mockler (2011) maintains that professional identity is influenced by a complex interplay between individuals' personal experiences, professional contexts, and external political ideologies. Ultimately, having both a sense of confidence to teach and a supportive teaching environment are essential for becoming effective teachers.

Study Context

To further understand teachers' motivation and commitment to teaching English, their expectations of how and what students should learn, and teachers' understanding of their students' realities and possible obstacles that they face, a group of Cuban teachers of English were asked to participate in this study.

The role of perceived social status among teachers of English in the Global South has received little attention. Therefore, I aimed to examine factors that contributed to respondents' bilingualism, impact of English in their lives, description of obstacles they face as teachers of English, and their recommendations for improving English language proficiency of students in Cuba.

Specifically, I aimed to address the following questions:

1) What factors contributed to the respondents' motivation to learn English?
2) What has been the impact of English in the lives of respondents?
3) What suggestions do respondents provide for enhancing students' proficiency in English?
4) What obstacles do they view as significant for learning English in Cuba?
5) What teaching practices do they employ to respond to such obstacles?
6) What keeps them in the teaching profession and what could cause them to quit?

Faculty members in the Department of Languages at the University of Havana and secondary school teacher educators from Santiago de Cuba referred participants to this study. I presented the study to prospective participants and requested their participation. From those who agreed to participate, I selected a sub-group based on the criteria that they were Cuban nationals and were currently teaching English to Cuban students attending schools and universities.

Methods

With the understanding that teachers' own trajectories in learning English and their fluency in this language impact the way they teach, two comprehensive questionnaires were developed. I asked participants to describe: 1) their own English language development, 2) social and economic impact of English on their lives, 3) the obstacles they face as teachers, and 4) pedagogical approaches to overcome such obstacles.

The first questionnaire consisted of four sections: 1) teacher's English language acquisition, 2) the economic and social impact of English in their lives, 3) their opinion regarding major obstacles facing Cuban students in learning English in Cuba, and 4) suggestions for students who are interested in learning English. Participants also provided demographic information such as age, gender, and years of teaching experience.

To gain a deeper understanding of the experiences of our respondents, I developed a second questionnaire and asked participants to describe their instructional practices and ways in which they make English accessible to their students. They were also asked to rate their own English language proficiency. Using the European Language Passport Self-Assessment Grid (Council of Europe, 2011), respondents self-rated their listening, reading, spoken interaction, spoken production, and writing skills. Cuban teachers and teacher educators were consulted for clarifications regarding data coding throughout the data gathering and analysis of this investigation.

Participants

Fourteen bilingual educators participated in this study. Participants taught at two different institutions in two major Cuban cities, Havana and Santiago de Cuba. Respondents had an average of nine years of teaching experience. Eleven out of 14 (78%) respondents were female and their average age was 33 with a range from 23 to 65 years old. Twelve respondents taught English at the high school level and two were university professors.

All respondents were nonnative speakers of English and had become bilingual in Cuba. They overwhelmingly and collectively expressed that they were highly proficient users of English. In the Language Passport Self-Assessment Grid, a rating of A1 or A2 indicates basic user, B1 or B2 indicates independent user, and C1 or C2 denotes a proficient user. Teachers averaged C2 on listening and reading, indicating that they have no difficulty understanding any kind of spoken English language, given some time to become familiar with the accent of the speaker. Respondents expressed that they were equally capable in reading all forms of the written English language including literary works. Many respondents conveyed that they considered themselves as independent users of English (B2 category) for spoken interaction, spoken production, and writing. They noted that they can easily converse with native speakers of English and are able to take an active part in discussions. Participants emphasized that they could write detailed texts on a wide range of subjects related to their interests.

Data Analysis

A coding system was developed to obtain an initial understanding of the data (Miles, Huberman, & Saldaña, 2014). I analyzed data using an inductive analytical approach that involved multiple readings of each questionnaire's transcript and organizing themes into categories within and across responses (Merriam, 1998). For instance, when a respondent repeated a point several times, or multiple respondents presented the same theme, this constituted a pattern. As I identified themes, I compared them with other themes and further analyzed them to find concepts related to research questions and the theoretical framework. This process helped to identify issues requiring further attention or alternative accounts of teachers' motivation to learn English (Miles & Huberman, 1994). In the process of data reduction I focused on the most salient portions of the corpus related to the study and carefully examined the remaining components for future review (Saldaña, 2016). The coding process continued, and the remaining corpus was reviewed once again. Overlapping or redundant codes were collapsed into themes, which eventually became the headings in the findings of this study (Creswell, 2015). Throughout the data analysis process transcripts were reread and examined for applicability to each research question. Personal communications via email with key informants provided clarification and enhanced the understanding of developed themes. This process enhanced the degree of consistency of the analyzed data (Merriam, 1998).

RESULTS

Motivation to Learn English

While some of the bilingual teachers may be driven and inspired by the potential for helping to increase literacy skills among their students, other teachers may find motivation simply from their love of teaching and providing students with the tools and guidance to help them learn. Regardless of their individual motivations, both groups of teachers can be integral in providing students with a high-quality language learning experience that can help to equip students with the necessary skills to become bilingual.

Teachers were asked to describe their own motivation to learn English. All teachers expressed that both integrative (i.e., feeling connected to English) and instrumental (i.e., higher paying jobs) motivations played important roles in their journeys in becoming fluent users of English. Respondents indicated that awareness of the economic opportunities that English provides played an important role in their decision to become bilingual. Nevertheless, they added that they were intrigued with the various cultures of people who speak English. Several respondents maintained that their positive views regarding English speakers and the joy they experienced as they learned English highly motivated them to continue their second language acquisition journeys. Nine respondents explained that due to cultural and historical connections with the U.S., American English was the most preferred variety of English among Cubans.

Multiple factors contributed to respondents' positive views on learning English and ultimately to their achievement of becoming highly proficient Bilinguals. One respondent stated: "First because I liked it; second, I wanted to be a teacher of English". Another respondent noted:

The most important reason [to learn English] for me was to share with people who spoke English, most of them Jamaican families that lived in Guantanamo. Also, I enjoyed listening to songs and understand broadcasts. Many people in my hometown (Caribbean descendants) used English in their houses and it sounded nice to me.

A different teacher explained: "I just liked it [English]. Its melody, intonation, the way it sounds." Another respondent indicated that learning English was enjoyable and became a pastime. A different respondent expressed: "I have always loved the [English] language. I wanted to be a teacher of English since I was 7 years old." Several teachers emphasized the utility as well as power of English. Being able to have access to international news in English as well as searching for digital information not easily obtainable in Cuba was seen as valuable to this group of teachers. For example, one respondent noted:

I have looked for updated information online and the most suitable ones appear in English. Besides, on the web, the amount of projects, papers, thesis, books, and articles written in English is higher than the amount of those written in Spanish.

Four respondents pointed out that they were aware of career opportunities for people who are bilingual. Among this group, three respondents noted that English is "the universal language" and expressed that learning English has brought them more job opportunities.

Four participants first became interested in learning English due to parents' influence and schooling. The following quote represents this group of teachers: "My father knew English and I used to play with an illustrated dictionary he had." Similarly, three respondents emphasized the influence of their teachers in motivating them to learn English. They mentioned: "I got interested in learning English from high school because of an English teacher I had. He told me and taught me the importance of this language."

Impact of English

Social mobility is an important factor that can influence an individual's motivation to become bilingual. Teachers in this study felt that English was highly important in their profession and had a very positive impact in their lives. The influence of English on respondents' students and others they know personally was viewed favorably, but not as strongly as this language's impact on their own lives. Learning English helped these educators to open opportunities for better employment and improved economic prospects, which in turn fostered their social mobility. Most respondents indicated that knowledge of English facilitated the attainment of their current positions as bilingual educators in Cuban high schools and universities.

Additionally, a high level of English proficiency improved some teachers' economic prospects, allowing them to seek better wages and to have greater earning potentials. Thirteen educators remarked that their bilingual status had helped them in elevating their social and economic status. One teacher expressed: "I think that in my country English teachers are more stable than those of other specialties or subjects." Two respondents expressed that knowing English allowed them to receive slightly higher salaries. They further noted that their high level of English proficiency helped them to expand their social circles both personally and professionally. This group of educators noted that the overall influence of English in their lives was positive. The following quote represents the sentiments of most of the respondents' gratification from their role as educators:

Being a teacher is a very important profession giving knowledge to students who in the future will be grateful for having learned a [second] language. It is also exciting to see how they learn by studying in class by communicating with each other preparing dialogues and writing texts, etc.

In contrast, one respondent explained that although knowing English was instrumental in obtaining her current position in a high school, the knowledge of this language has not afforded her significant economic advantages as her current salary is comparable to other teachers who are Spanish monolinguals.

Obstacles for Learning English for Students

Cuban teachers acknowledged that Cuban students face various obstacles in becoming bilingual English speakers. These obstacles include lack of resources, limited access to qualified teachers, and time constraints. Teachers expressed that the Cuban educational system has traditionally had limited resources and access to educational materials is challenging, which makes it more difficult for students to learn English. Additionally, teachers noted that many students do not have the chance to interact with English speakers, meaning they have limited opportunities to practice their English-speaking skills.

Eight teachers commented that limited quality of teaching materials and less than adequate teaching practices were impediments for the development of English in Cuba. One teacher expressed:

The fundamental obstacles facing English teachers may be the updating of the methods they use, which are almost always old, due to the lack of manuals and audiovisual materials. I also think that there is a lack of unification in the English variant they teach, because although most prefer the American variant, others opt for the British form they consider most correct, and this can bring concerns to students if they change from one form to another.

Six respondents maintained that their students do not have sufficient access to online resources that can help them to improve their English proficiency. The following statement from one teacher expresses this group's overall perspective: "The biggest obstacle in teaching English in Cuba is the absence of equipment for using websites." This group of teachers emphasized that curricular priorities prevent schools from allocating sufficient time and resources for English. For example, one teacher noted: "Sometimes students are so involved in their content subjects of their major that they do not dedicate much time to English."

Suggestions for Students

By far the most common recommendations participants provided in support of bilingualism focused on motivation and attitude toward learning English. They stressed that learners need to be self-driven and enthusiastic about learning English but called attention on the role of teachers in providing practical tools that make learning English more accessible to their students.

Teachers maintained that in addition to finding opportunities to communicate with native speakers of English, Cuban students should use online resources to improve their English proficiency. They added that technology-based learning tools are not only effective for reviewing concepts introduced in the classroom but also can greatly enhance language development by providing new learning opportunities.

Instructional Practices

Respondents indicated that teachers must provide clear goals and objectives to their students and should give engaging materials that can motivate students to continue to learn English. They further argued that giving additional practice and time for discussion of key concepts supports students' English language proficiency. Teachers emphasized that modeling language learning strategies (i.e., vocabulary repetition, scaffolding) are highly important and are linked to increasing student participation in classroom activities. Six teachers discussed teacher practices that they deemed effective and emphasized that audio-visuals that support teaching are very motivating and support students in developing positive attitudes about learning English. For example, one teacher noted: "Usually I start my class with listening to a song. Those are the famous and modern songs to motivate them [students]." Another teacher articulated that she uses pictures and real objects for teaching of vocabulary or complex concepts.

Eleven respondents maintained that at times they use Spanish in the classroom to provide brief explanations to enhance student comprehension and noted that this practice positively influences development of English proficiency. One teacher provided specific recommendations for future teachers and noted:

Well, for those who want to become a teacher, I may advise them to study a lot because to learn a foreign language is like a child who is learning to talk and also, should be patient because in every school there are a lot of students who don't like the English language and that's why they [teachers] should be ready to prepare their lessons with images, games, etc. to call the attention of the students.

Five teachers expressed that lesson previews and reviews in Spanish helps them to enhance students' understanding of key concepts. Another five participants mentioned that teacher feedback to students is essential and helps teachers assess their own teaching effectiveness and offers teachers relevant information regarding re-teaching of topics as needed. They also expressed that occasionally they discuss their own experiences in learning English and noted that their students are largely interested in learning about their teachers' bilingual development.

Remaining in the Profession and Reasons for Leaving

Teachers noted that several factors have kept them in the teaching profession. For some, it was the passion for teaching and the reward they get from seeing their students' progress. Teaching was seen as a highly rewarding profession, and it brought great satisfaction for some teachers as they observed their students learning and growing. Additionally, some teachers found fulfillment in contributing to their communities by helping to bridge cultural divides and foster global understanding. For others, teaching was also a convenient job, offering stability and flexibility that allows them to pursue other opportunities at the same time. Ultimately, it was the combination of these factors that helped them to remain in the teaching profession.

Conversely, educators presented several factors that could cause them to quit the teaching profession. They noted that low wages (as compared to other sectors) and limited professional opportunities are considerations in driving teachers away from the field of education. Additionally, they expressed that Cuban teachers could be motivated to quit teaching if they are unable to provide their students with the sufficient resources to learn English effectively, such as adequate materials and guidance. Others expressed that they may be driven away from teaching due to feelings of frustration and exhaustion from long working hours and students' negative attitudes towards learning. Seeking better opportunities in other sectors was indeed the largest motivating factor for respondents in this study to leave the teaching profession. According to seven teachers, seeking better economic opportunities plays the most important role regarding teacher attrition in the Cuban context. These educators noted that some of their colleagues chose to leave teaching to become translators or tour guides, professions that offer significantly higher salaries.

With increased globalization, English language proficiency has become a valuable skill in many sectors in Cuba, allowing bilingual teachers to access higher wages and employment opportunities in a variety of industries. As such, some Cuban teachers expressed their desire to seek better opportunities in areas where they can utilize their English language skills to advance their economic and professional prospects. Tourism and translation/interpreting are two popular industries among Cuban teachers who are looking for better opportunities. By working as a tour guide, Cuban teachers can apply their bilingualism to help visitors explore the country in a more meaningful way. Additionally, some teachers noted that translation and interpreting opportunities enable them to use their English language skills to promote cultural appreciation and understanding between Cubans and international visitors.

RECOMMENDATIONS FOR FUTURE RESEARCH

The results of this preliminary investigation cannot be generalizable. More in-depth approaches as well as larger sample sizes will provide valuable information for language planners. For example, examining teachers' approaches to teaching a second language can offer useful data for teacher educators. Furthermore, since low salaries compared to other professions requiring English proficiency (e.g., tour guides, translators) can contribute to teachers' desire to leave their teaching careers, future research should further examine factors associated with retention in the teaching profession.

I did not examine Cuban students' educational and career paths. Future research can examine how teachers' approaches may shape students' career goals. Furthermore, examining the social, cultural, and historical influences between the United States and Cuba was beyond the scope of this study. Cross-cultural research on students' motivation to become bilingual and exploring how policy between nations plays at the local level is a promising area for research on multicultural and multilingual development. We need to learn more about the development of practices and attitudes that make students lifelong multilingual learners.

Significance

Cuban teachers of English possess a range of valuable skills that can enhance their teaching practices. By code-switching, translating from one language to another, and sharing their own journeys to bilingualism, they can better support the bilingual development of their students (Belz, 2002). Furthermore, these educators are culturally competent and have a deep appreciation of the important link that exists between language and culture.

Understanding the perspectives of Cuban teachers of English can be valuable for language policy makers to gain insight into teachers' own language learning experiences and to better appreciate their role in further developing multilingualism in Cuba. Such understanding includes looking at their motivations for learning English, the challenges they face, the strategies they use to overcome them, the awareness they provide regarding language teaching, and factors that keep them in the teaching profession or motivate them to leave. Learning about teachers' attitude towards the teaching of English, as well as their perception of their role in the Cuban educational system provided a better understanding of English language education in Cuba and is important for developing more effective language policies that enrich multilingualism in other countries.

In the field of world language teaching, little research exists on second language development trajectories of teachers and their reflections upon their motivation to become highly proficient bilinguals. I found that initial motivation of Cuban teachers to learn English was influenced by a variety of factors. The acquisition of English enabled respondents to develop more complex and diverse perspectives regarding human communication and eventually lead them to become promoters of bilingualism. Educators in this study overwhelmingly communicated that English had a positive impact in their lives, both professionally (i.e., social networks) and economically (i.e., social mobility). Teachers discussed instructional practices that are consistent with the recommendation of language teaching experts (Padilla & Borjian, 2009). Teachers in this study are aware of many obstacles their students face in learning English and becoming highly proficient bilinguals but noted that employing pedagogical practices that support language development is not sufficient as limited access to quality materials and technology impairs their efforts.

Developing successful intercultural communication cannot be achieved through only individual efforts. Schools, as institutions that promote equity and fairness, must also play a significant role in promoting ongoing learning opportunities that motivate and support students in becoming bilinguals so that they can better navigate our multilingual world. By establishing curricula and activities geared towards global citizenship and cultural understanding schools can enhance students' motivation to continue their bilingual journeys. These experiences will also help students to develop a deeper appreciation for cultural diversity as well as seeking economic advancement for themselves and their communities.

Finally, increasingly dire economic conditions in Cuba, caused by multiple factors including a crushing U.S. economic embargo, has had a significant negative impact upon the lives of most Cubans, including teachers. Some bilingual teachers reluctantly have left the profession and their absence in the field could have a significant negative impact in the educational development of the country. Educational policy makers must acknowledge that multilingualism contributes to economic independence and that teacher attrition is a national challenge. To mitigate this collective loss of human capital resources are needed to support and motivate teachers to continue to use their linguistic talents to respond to current extreme economic challenges that Cuba faces.

REFERENCES

Anderman, L. H., & Freeman, T. (2004). Students' sense of belonging in school. In M. L. Maehr and P. R. Pintrich, (Eds.) Advances in motivation and achievement, volume 13: Motivating students, improving schools; The legacy of Carol Midgley, (pp. 27-63). Greenwich, CT: JAI.

Bandura, A. (1997). *Self-efficacy: The exercise of control.* Freeman.

Belz, J. (2002). The myth of the deficient communicator. *Language Teaching Research*, 6(1), 59–82. doi:10.1191/1362168802lr097oa

Blizzad, B., & Batalova, J. (2020). *Cuban immigrants in the United States.* Migration Policy Institute, Washigton D.C. https://www.migrationpolicy.org/article/cuban-immigrants-united-states

Borjian, A., & Padilla, A. (2010). Voices from Mexico: How U.S. teachers can meet the needs of immigrant students. *The Urban Review*, *42*(4), 316–328. doi:10.100711256-009-0135-0

Choi, P. L., & Tang, S. Y. F. (2009). Teacher commitment trends: Cases of Hong Kong teachers from 1997 to 2007. *Teaching and Teacher Education*, *25*(5), 767–777. doi:10.1016/j.tate.2009.01.005

Council of Europe. (2011). *European Language Portfolio*. Council of Europe. www.coe.int

Creswell, J. (2015). *30 essential skills for the qualitative researcher*. SAGE.

Crystal, D. (2003). *English as a global language* (2nd ed.). Cambridge University Press. doi:10.1017/CBO9780511486999

Cummins, J. (1984). *Bilingualism and special education: Issues in assessment and pedagogy*. Multilingual Matters.

Delgado Hellester, M. (2013). *English skills and wages in a non-English speaking country: Findings from online advertisements in Mexico*. Cite Seer. https://citeseerx.ist.psu.edu/viewdoc/ download?doi=10.1.1.406.6883&rep=rep1&type=pdf.

Denney, S. C., & Daviso, A. W. (2012). Self-determination: A critical component of education. *American Secondary Education*, *40*(2), 43–51. http://www.jstor.org/stable/43694129

Gagné, M., & Deci, E. L. (2005). Self-determination theory and work motivation. *Journal of Organizational Behavior*, *26*(4), 331–362. http://www.jstor.org/stable/4093832. doi:10.1002/job.322

Gardner, R. C. (1985). *Social psychology and second language learning: The role of attitudes and motivation*. Edward Arnold.

Hickling-Hudson, A. (2004). South-south collaboration: Cuban teachers in Jamaica and Namibia. *Comparative Education*, *40*(2), 289–311. http://www.jstor.org/stable/4134653. doi:10.1080/0305006042000231392

Holliday, A. (2005). *The struggle to teach English as an international language*. Oxford University Press.

Hong, J. Y. (2010). Pre-service and beginning teachers' professional identity and its relation to dropping out of the profession. *Teaching and Teacher Education*, *26*(8), 1530–1543. doi:10.1016/j.tate.2010.06.003

Irizar, T. (2001). English language education in Cuba. *ESL Magazine*, *4*(1), 26–28.

Kormos, J., & Csiér, K. (2014). The interaction of motivation, self-regulatory strategies, and autonomous learning behavior in different learner groups. *TESOL Quarterly*, *48*(2), 275–299. http://www.jstor.org/stable/43268052. doi:10.1002/tesq.129

Ladson-Billings, G. (2006). Yes, but how do we do it? Practicing culturally relevant pedagogy. In J. Landsman & C. W. Lewis (Eds.), White teachers/diverse classrooms: A guide to building inclusive schools, promoting high expectations and eliminating racism (pp. 29–42). Sterling, VA: Stylus Publishers.

Lasagabaster, D. (2017). Language learning motivation and language attitudes in multilingual Spain from an international perspective. *Modern Language Journal*, *101*(3), 583–596. http://www.jstor.org/stable/44981007. doi:10.1111/modl.12414

Martin, I. (2007). Some remarks on post-1990 English language teaching policy in Cuba, language policies and TESOL: perspectives from practice. *TESOL Quarterly*, *41*(3), 551–557. doi:10.1002/j.1545-7249.2007.tb00085.x

Merriam, S. B. (1998). *Case study research in education: A qualitative approach*. Jossey-Bass.

Meyer, J. P., & Herscovitch, L. (2001). Commitment in the workplace: Toward a general model. *Human Resource Management Review*, *1*, 61–89. doi:10.1016/1053-4822(91)90011-Z

Miles, M. B., & Huberman, A. M. (1994). *Qualitative data analysis*. Sage.

Miles, M. B., Huberman, A. M., & Saldaña, J. (2014). *Qualitative data analysis: A methods sourcebook* (3rd ed.). SAGE.

Ministerio de Educación Nacional de Colombia. (2014). *Colombia, Very Well!: Programa Nacional de Inglés, July, 2015–2025*. Colombia Aprende. http://www.colombiaaprende.edu.co/html/micrositios/1752/articles-343287_recurso_1.pdf

Ministerio de Educación Perú. (2016). *Inglés, puertas al mundo*. Ministry of Education, Peru. http://www.minedu.gob.pe/inglés-puertas-al-mundo/pdf/infografia.pdf.

Mockler, N. (2011). Beyond "what works": Understanding teacher identity as a practical and political tool. *Teachers and Teaching*, *17*(5), 517–528. doi:10.1080/13540602.2011.602059

Moodie, I., & Feryok, A. (2015). Beyond cognition to commitment: English language teaching in South Korean primary schools. *Modern Language Journal*, *99*(3), 450–469. http://www.jstor.org.jpllnet.sfsu.edu/stable/43651977. doi:10.1111/modl.12238

Oxford, R. L., & Shearin, J. (1994). Language learning motivation: Expanding the theoretical framework. *Modern Language Journal*, *78*(1), 12–28. doi:10.1111/j.1540-4781.1994.tb02011.x

Padilla, A. M., & Borjian, A. (2009). Learning and teaching foreign languages (pp. 541-544). Psychology of Classroom Learning: An Encyclopedia. Macmillan Reference USA.

Pérez, L. (1982). The imperial design: Politics and pedagogy in occupied Cuba, 1899- 1902. Cuban Studies/Estudios Cubanos, 12, (pp.1-18).

Pintrich, P. (2003). A motivational science perspective on the role of student motivation in learning and teaching contexts. *Journal of Educational Psychology*, *95*(4), 667–686. doi:10.1037/0022-0663.95.4.667

Ryan, R. M., & Deci, E. L. (2000). When rewards compete with nature: The undermining of intrinsic motivation and self-regulation. In C. Sansone & J. M. Harackiewicz (Eds.), *Intrinsic and extrinsic motivation: The search for optimal motivation and performance* (pp. 13–55). Academic Press. doi:10.1016/B978-012619070-0/50024-6

Saldaña, J. (2016). *The coding manual for qualitative researchers*. SAGE.

Smith, J. S. (2016). Cuban voices: A case study of English language teacher education. *The International Education Journal: Comparative Perspectives*, *15*(4), (pp. 100-111). http://openjournals.library.usyd.edu.au/index.php/IEJ.index

Turner Martí, L., & Pita Cespedes, B. (2001). *A pedagogy of tenderness*. Asociación de Educadores de Latinoamerica y el Caribe.

UNESCO. (2008). Student achievement in Latin America and the Caribbean, Santiago, Chile. OREALC, UNESCO.

Ushida, E. (2017). The impact of global English on motivation to learn other languages: Toward an ideal multilingual self. *Modern Language Journal*, *101*(3), 469–482. http://www.jstor.org/stable/44981000. doi:10.1111/modl.12413

Wigfield, A., & Eccles, J. S. (2000). Expectancy-value theory of achievement motivation. *Contemporary Educational Psychology*, *25*(1), 68–81. doi:10.1006/ceps.1999.1015 PMID:10620382

Williams, M., & Burden, R. (1997). *Psychology for language teachers*. Cambridge University Press.

Section 5
International Migration

Chapter 9
Teachers' Mindsets About Their Role in Shaping the Norms of Students' L1 Use in Greek Classrooms

Eftychia Damaskou
University of Thessaly, Greece

ABSTRACT

In Greece, mainstream classes consist of linguistic and cultural mosaics, where pupils face problems related to the absence of their L1. Teachers play a significant part in this, as when L1 is welcome, the sense of belonging increases, being highly influenced by their mindsets, in terms of values, teaching attitudes and methods. The chapter explores teachers' mindsets about their role in handling the presence and set the norms of different L1 use in class, presenting the findings of a qualitative research conducted as part of a doctoral thesis on the production of multilingual teaching material for the awakening of first-schoolers to linguistic diversity. The data was collected through semi-structured interviews, exploring 60 teachers' mindsets about their role in promoting the use of L1 in class. All interviews were recorded, transcribed, and processed through thematic analysis. Encouraging the L1 use, adopting integrative routines, creating conditions of cooperation, and cultivating values among pupils are the main axes that set the norms of students' L1 use in class.

INTRODUCTION

Modern societies are shaped through intense mobility of populations, with multilingualism being more of the rule than the exception (Cummins, 2008; Lasagabaster, 2015). Within these societies, school contributes significantly to the smooth settlement of children who are forcibly or voluntarily displaced, by meeting their emotional, educational and social needs (Nakeyar et al., 2018). Indeed, the interaction of these children with their teachers and classmates, whether during lessons, breaks, or other activities

DOI: 10.4018/978-1-6684-8761-7.ch009

and events of the school, cultivates and encourages their social inclusion (Farmer et al., 2019; Juvonen et al., 2019).

First-school age is a particularly important phase in a child's school life in terms of language, because all students are in a literacy development phase in their L1. In fact, different cultural and linguistic background constitutes the "luggage" that young students carry with them as a crucial part of their identity. It is, therefore, very important to ensure the well-being of all students at school, through the reinforcement of their emotional security provided by their L1 (Coelho, 1998), but also within an inclusive environment open to diversity, and through making use of all children's abilities and knowledge (Stergiou, 2019). Yet, banning the use of their L1, through an implicit linguistic assimilation, according to Cummins (2008), is likely to deprive them of access to their basic cognitive tool, forcing them to acquire the stigma of belonging to an "inferior" group. In addition, according to Tseng (2020, 112), "hybridity and translanguaging are inherent parts of heritage speakers' repertoires", however, this hybridity is often stigmatised as being a sort of deficient language (Zentella, 2014). This language delegitimisation within monolingual-normed contexts has also consequences for heritage speakers' acceptance and self-esteem (Tseng, 2020). However, especially for the refugee children, stigmatisation is synonym to social instability, or even exclusion (Hart 2009), while their placement is specific accommodation structures encourages social exclusion and "territorial stigmatization" and school segregation, making it difficult for children to build relationships with their classmates outside of the few hours of school (Vergou, 2019).

In Greece, an institutionally monolingual country, the continuous flow of refugees and immigrants from countries of the Balkans, Africa and Asia (Greek Ministry of Migration Policy, 2019), form a linguistic and cultural mosaic in the school classrooms, since the schooling of these children from 5 to 14 years in Greek school is compulsory (Law 4636/2019). Within the Greek educational context, teachers involved in the education of young students report facing important issues with students of immigrant origin, because most of the time they do not speak or understand Greek well and are thus marginalized (Avramidou, 2014; Diakogeorgiou, 2016). In addition, according to Gkaitartzi et al. (2015), many teachers seem to be positive towards promoting pupils' heritage language but they do not relate them to children's school language learning and their own role as educators. Furthermore, other research within the Greek context reveals a discrepancy between teachers' positive views about integrating students' multilingualism in class and their teaching practice (Fotiadou et al., 2022; Simopoulos & Magos, 2021).

In this chapter, the author will first define the concept of teachers' mindsets and link it to that of teachers' identity, situating both of them in the context of teachers' willingness to promote their students' L1 in class. The author will then present the findings of a study on primary teachers' mindsets about their contribution to shaping the context of all students' L1 use in class. In fact, ever since the early 1980s, Bakhtin (1981, 346) had claimed that it is very important for mainstream teachers of multilingual learners to "recognize their ideological points of view, approaches and values" both on a professional and personal level and how they influence their teaching practices. Thus, exploring teachers' mindsets about their role in establishing a framework for handling the presence and delimiting the norms of use of the different L1 in their classroom, would be of important research interest, as teachers' attitudes and beliefs towards multilingual pupils' cultural background and languages are considered to exert an important influence not only on their professional practices (Llurda & Lasagabaster 2010; Xu 2012), but also all aspects of learning (Vázquez-Montilla et al., 2014).

LITERATURE REVIEW

According to Dweck (2006), mindsets are beliefs that individuals hold about their most basic qualities and abilities. Mindsets in language learning have become a considerable research topic (Lou & Noels, 2019), yet, there is very little research examining the mindsets of teachers (Calafato, 2021; Haukås & Mercer, 2022; Irie et al., 2018). Specifically, teachers' beliefs towards multilingual students' background are considered to exert a crucial role in assuring a pleasant atmosphere in the classroom (Whitebread, 1996). In addition, Xu (2012) claims that teachers are highly influenced by their mindsets, which in turn are closely linked to their values, to their views of the world, their consciousness, teaching attitude, teaching methods and teaching policy. Teachers who are willing to explore their mindsets, and how their beliefs relate to practice and the professional knowledge base, can capitalize on the beliefs they hold to promote students' intellectual growth, autonomy and reciprocity, and equity in their classrooms.

Research from multiple settings points to the significance of teachers' beliefs about their students' use of their L1 at school and in class. Within the Greek educational context, literature relevant to the teacher's role towards the presence and use of other than Greek languages in the classroom, mainly focuses on beliefs, perceptions and attitudes towards the students' L1s (Gkaravelas & Koutousi, 2018; Gorter & Arocena, 2020; Magos & Simopoulos, 2020; Maligkoudi et al., 2018), the teachers' difficulty in dealing with students with different linguistic backgrounds (Galani & Stavrinidis, 2020) and their training needs (Magos & Margaroni, 2018; Zachos et al., 2020) as well. Maligkoudi et al. (2018) indicated that even if teachers' participating in their study claim supporting their refugee students, few of them implement teaching practices that involve their students' language and cultural backgrounds. These findings are in accordance with those presented by Koukoula (2017), who suggests that teaching students of immigrant/refugee backgrounds should rely on the fundamental principles of intercultural education, which in practice is not very frequent, as teachers could not be characterized as interculturally competent. Vikøy and Haukås (2021) explain teachers' hesitance or unwillingness to focus on learners' multilingualism on the grounds of their limited knowledge of how a multilingual approach can be implemented in class.

The research of Tsaliki (2017) is of interest at this point, concluding that for teachers, the social integration of children is much more important than, for example, their school performance. In fact, the importance of the social integration of these children is also confirmed by the study of Sgoura et al. (2018), according to which, it appears that teachers do not consider the presence of these children in schools particularly positive. When talking about the interaction of young children who have just joined a new and possibly different linguistic, cultural and social environment, it is important to keep in mind that these are children who, while in the phase of literacy development in L1, are called upon to coexist and cooperate with peers who use unfamiliar and different linguistic codes. Of course, the simple coexistence of these children with the students of the "dominant" group is not enough by itself, and any intervention by the teacher should aim at cultivating values such as acceptance, respect for diversity, solidarity, empathy and cooperativeness (Farmer et al., 2019; Hymel & Katz, 2019). In addition, Alstad and Tkachenko (2018) present how multilingualism is expressed through teachers' language teaching practices, concluding that exposure to a new language encourages children's interest in linguistic diversity, while discussions between teachers and children lead to a deeper exploration of the differences between languages, promoting linguistic diversity and fostering metalinguistic awareness of young students. At the same time, teachers can make use of the language resources available to them in children's L1 and enhance early literacy development.

Cohen (2008) argues that teachers' beliefs are a central part of their identity which not only defines the value and implementation of their teaching but also has an impact on the level of their devotion, participation and behaviors. Indeed, Pennington and Richards (2016) explain that one's self-image and sense of identity is based on values and beliefs about how one should behave, relating identity to "good" and "proper" or "appropriate" behavior guiding actions. Within the school context, this means that teachers' projected identity in class is directly dependent on teachers' view of themselves as an institutional factor that holds a unique identity, based on a personal biography, but also on the specific learners' profile and teaching context.

Reeves (2018) falls in line with Rennington and Richards (2016) explaining that teachers' identity is closely connected with their teaching methods, but also their relations with their students. Varghese et al. (2005) introduce the concept of critical reflexivity regarding teachers' identity, which consists of the teachers' ability to reflect on how social, cultural and political forces shape them within their professional framework, but also how their own role shapes others' context and identity.

METHODOLOGY

This chapter draws on a part of an ongoing doctoral thesis that investigates the parameters of creating teacher-generated multilingual materials for the awakening of first-schoolers to linguistic diversity. One of the research questions concerns how could a teacher contribute to the awareness and negotiation of negative stereotypes and prejudices against other L1s in the class. The research design consists of a qualitative research, which in a first stage included teacher survey interviews about first-schoolers' coming into contact with their peers' L1 within their classroom, with specific focus on the formers' reactions, motives, interest and attitudes. The data presented in the current chapter emerged during this first stage of the research, where, through interviews with teachers, a wide range of the participants' beliefs emerged about their role in fostering and promoting the use of all students' L1 in class.

Sixty semi-structured interviews were conducted individually with general and special education teachers and teachers of other subjects such as drama, arts, music, sports, ICT and English as a Foreign Language. The selection of the sample consisted of multiple purposive techniques (Teddie & Yu, 2007): A convenience sample frame was initially employed for the first 15 interviews, and then, in order to gain access to more data the snowball method was applied, increasing the chain of participants through networking and referrals (Parker et al., 2019). The sample involves a wide range of participants, aged from 25 to 55 years old, all involved in the first two years of primary education, with 25% of them being males. These teachers were selected on the basis of their at least 3-year teaching experience in the first two grades of primary school, and also with consideration to their service in state schools of the Greek territory (big cities, villages, islands, peripheral cities). Oral recorded consent of participation in the survey was obtained from all participants.

In order to collect the data, we chose the technique of semi-structured interviews, as an interview enables the researcher to collect "descriptive and explanatory information in a people-oriented manner" (Eyles, 1988, 12), but also a set of rich, detailed and multi-layered responses (Burgess, 1984). In particular, during the interviews they were asked the following questions: "How do the students of these classes treat foreign language students?". "What do you think is the most appropriate teaching method for these classes?", "In your opinion, what should be the role of the teacher in the context of a multilingual classroom?".The open-ended questions used during the interview sought to give prominence to teachers' mindsets about first-schoolers' behavior towards their classmates' linguistic repertoire, but also the teachers' role in the promotion and use of the L1 of all students in the class. All interviews were conducted in Greek, recorded, transcribed and analyzed using the 6-phased thematic analysis technique (Terry et al., 2017). The excerpts presented in this paper were translated into English by the author, while the participants' names have been anonymized for protection of privacy, using the initials of their specialty (GT for general teacher, AT for art teacher, ET for English teacher, etc.) and a reference number.

FINDINGS

The thematic codes extracted from the interviews produced the following key themes concerning teachers' role in shaping the norms of diverse students' L1 in class: creating a framework for communication and interaction among students, integrating L1s other than Greek in class, presenting linguistic diversity as an asset, cultivating positive language attitudes, building intercultural projects, cultivating values of respect to diversity, creating positive classroom atmosphere, and respecting diverse students' background.

Interaction Between Greek and Non-Greek Speaking Students

According to Prajapati and Gupta (2023), mastery over the teaching subject or the material used was only one of the criteria of being a "good teacher" (Hoyle & John, 1995). However, nowadays, a good teacher is beyond a simple knowledge transmitter, as they assume the role of learning facilitator, through creating effective activities, communication bridges, and favoring all students' engagement in class (Hanna et al., 2020; Trent, 2010). These are some aspects of the teacher's identity and have an influence not only on their development (De Costa & Norton, 2017; Varghese et al., 2016), but also on their teaching and learning decisions or classroom management (Duff & Uchida, 1997).

In this study, several teachers mentioned the necessity of creating communication conditions in the classroom, explaining that this ensures the children's expression in their language and their participation in the lesson in general. At the same time, according to the participants in our study, children like interactive teaching approaches, and especially approaches which involve them in communicating and working together with their classmates. One general teacher (GT15) recalls a conversation she had with a student's mother, who saw her son's enthusiasm for how she was teaching in class:

You know what one of my students' mothers told me once? You see, from the first day I get them to work in groups, so the next day, here comes one mother and tells me that A. [her son] was very excited. I asked her why, and she answered that her son had told her that this teacher does very different things with us!

GT05 extends this thought, explaining that it is very important for a young child who has just joined Greek school and does not speak Greek, to have eye contact with the other children within a group context, in order not to feel isolated. In particular, she states:

Teamwork is needed even at these ages, as long as we (the teachers) cultivate this. It is difficult for a child to open up, you have to work a little on the feeling to establish a foundation of respect and trust, let alone when they come from another country. And of course, the arrangement of the desks also plays a role; the child should not see the other's back, but one should see the other, there should be eye contact.

In addition, for another general teacher (GT07), within a classroom setting with students who speak languages other than Greek, the teacher should adopt practices such as mutual teaching, but also create two-way exchange relationships. In specific, he reported:

Usually, in order for non-Greek speaking children to join in, it was our tactic in the classroom to assign our children to teach Greek during break time, during activities, group activities, and, at the same time, to be taught from the others their L1. So, there was a two-way relationship and an exchange between Greek and Albanian terms. Thus, it was like a game, some kind of approach that facilitated their inclusion which interested us.

Another interesting point of view that emerged from the analysis of the interviews comes from an art teacher, who apart from the importance of mutual learning focuses on the importance of the nature of her own lesson for the children in order to cooperate and communicate, in case the main classroom teacher has not set the diverse children's cooperation and inclusion in the classroom. In specific, she reports:

I had, let's say, classes which were divided into groups, Greeks and non-Greeks, because the main teacher had never gone through the process of bringing all these kids together. Of course, that's why there is also music, arts and theater (in the curriculum), because if a teacher can't do it, let us be the ones to make the groups cooperate and children express themselves through group bonding, make them feel they are all equal and all do the same tasks, whether it is a child who speaks a foreign language or a child who may have a disability, and one learns from the other. Each child gains things from the other, and that's why I tell the children who come from other countries that we should also learn from them and learn the languages at home so that we don't forget them. (AT01)

GT52 shares a similar perspective of exchanging elements in different languages, but in a creative way. Particularly, she states that:

I think it is good to highlight the importance of each language, and we must respect each language, because each language has its own elements, its own culture behind, so we have to use them creatively in the classroom, so that every child from another country who speaks another language can bring to the classroom cultural elements, cultural elements and share them with their classmates through activities. There should be an exchange of knowledge, getting to know other cultures and other languages and even listening to their sounds, but it can also go to another level, that is to share other elements not only in relation to the language, that is, let's say that language is an occasion to come closer to a different culture.

Inclusive Approaches to Languages Other than Greek in Class

The research of Bohr & Acar (2021), focuses on the importance of the L1 of young children, highlighting the significance of teachers' support through the integration of the child's L1, teaching the other children words and phrases, such as how to say hello in the languages spoken in their class, establishing, thus, multilingual routines. The following excerpt underlines the importance of including the first languages of students who do not speak Greek in the classroom in order to ensure the emotional well-being of these children:

Teachers' Mindsets About Their Role in Shaping Students' L1 Use

Teachers should and are able to make use of the languages of non-speaking children, and try to bring it out of the children, that is to say, be encouraging and make them feel much better, many do not feel good about speaking, they may be embarrassed to use their mother tongue. (ET03)

Baker (2018) at this point argues that when children feel that their L1 is welcome, the sense of belonging increases, stressing, however, that in order to cultivate a positive emotional environment, teachers should know things about the linguistic and cultural background of the children so that they can adapt their interactions appropriately.

In the context of a multilingual and multicultural classroom, the language lesson should expand towards children's interests, involving them in creative collaborative activities, and incorporating the exploration of aspects of L1s with the help of the speakers of Greek. Thus, these children acquire a resounding presence and identity even if they do not yet possess the language of the dominant group (Ohta, 2017; Stergiou & Simopoulos, 2019). This is in line with our findings, as according to the following excerpt, a general teacher (GT23) states that teachers should present other languages spoken by the students in an attractive way, taking into account students' interests:

[Researcher: Do you think if you talk to them about another country, would it catch their interest? Or let's say about the fairy tales or songs of another country, do you think they would like that?]

GT23: Of another country? Uhh it depends on the student, there are students who might be bored... um, I think that they are divided, or it depends on how you present it. The way you present something to your students, it may arouse their interest.

Another teacher (GT31) argues that first-schoolers are cognitively able to assimilate linguistic elements in languages other than their mother tongue or those taught at school, as long as it is done through the appropriate approach, and in particular through play. She refers to an example from a class in which she taught where there were also Roma children, describing the following experience:

This year at school we have Roma children and they explained a song to me in the romani language and told me some words that corresponded to Greek and in fact some of the other children they could retain those words more than I could! Through this specific experience also emerges the teacher's willingness to open or extend the traditional lesson through the integration of elements from the students' L1s.

Similarly, according to GT14, the teacher's prompting is very important in cultivating children's curiosity to learn some words in the other languages of their classmates. Particularly, she reports:

The approach that children have to non-native speakers is negative, at least in the first place, ok? However, I believe that within the class and the teacher's push in this matter, at some point they could have the curiosity to learn some words. At first, they make fun of them, yet through the lesson they become interested in learning some words.

Routines for the integration of these languages in the lesson seem to be a very effective and attractive way to introduce other languages, in order to foster linguistic diversity in class.

The following excerpt indicates how routines could work within a multilingual first or second grade of primary school:

Every day we start the lesson by saying "good morning" and what we had learned in different languages, it was not very obvious to them which language it was. They understood that this is how some of their classmates speak. [Should it be done through a game, for example?] Systematically, though. And through routines, meaning that we greet each other in all languages, we say "Happy Birthday" in all languages. Everything, every day. We just speak our languages freely, we write on a board "good morning" in all languages, so that we know what they are like, how they look, so we can edit them, etc. in the logic that there are other languages. (GT59)

GT59 claims that a teacher could familiarize their students with linguistic diversity, through the systematic use of routines. However, she emphasizes that children at this age cannot name languages, for example know that one classmate speaks Turkish, Albanian or Bulgarian, but that they speak a different language. Of course, this does not mean that similarities and differences cannot be worked out through interesting activities.

Multilingual Projects

In the context of a previous educational project, the author had the opportunity to collaborate with one of the participants (GT48), in order to implement awakening to linguistic diversity activities in her classroom. The project was about numbers and was created in order to familiarize the children through experiential activities with the vocabulary of numbers in the languages spoken by the students in this class. The teacher used this particular experience to explain the importance of such a project in that the local students put themselves in the shoes of their newly-arrived classmates and realize how difficult it is for them to learn a different language. GT48 emphasizes the importance of teamwork, cooperation and mutual help in the context of a multi-language class, however she focuses on the advantages that the experiential nature of a multilingual project can have. Specifically, during the interview, she stated the following:

For me, you have to bring children together and not make them feel different. My goal is to play in groups, cooperate, communicate, and help each other. I am very happy when I see a Greek speaking child playing with or helping a child from India, even showing him the toilets for example. And especially when we did the project together (the awakening to languages activities), I found out the concern of the children at the age of 7, as they felt how difficult it is for children who come from another country to learn Greek. Because when we did the numbers in the project, they realized how difficult it is for them, and I'm talking about the excellent students, I saw them very troubled. They literally fell into their place. [Have you noticed any improvement?] Yes, yes, yes, a very obvious one, and even within some students who at the beginning were making fun of the non-Greek speaking ones, and I believe that these students finally became very good friends with them.

Another interesting project example comes from the music class. As already mentioned, the use of the arts for the fostering of multiculturalism and multilingualism in the classroom is of high significance, as they favor the effortless and free expression of all children within a pleasant and not strictly academic atmosphere. MT01 proposes the creation of a small orchestra in the context of a multi-language classroom, and with this idea in essence sums up the previously mentioned cooperative and playful learning. More specifically, the activity she proposes is described in detail in the following excerpt:

We could do a small orchestra, or a small choir, and learn let's say a little song where they don't understand the language. You can give a tempo, a rhythm, and start a game with, let's say "what's your name?" in many languages (the teacher gives an example of such an activity by clapping her hand as many times as the syllables of the researcher's name) and this is how the syllables are divided and in this way we make into syllable words that the children do not understand from foreign songs, in order to learn exactly where the word clicks. Usually children really like fast and traditional rhythms.

Presenting the Speaking of Other Languages as an Asset

Gonzalez (2009) presents an interesting view, according to which teachers involved in the education of young students build bridges between students' home culture and language and those of the rest of the classroom, as they should adapt their educational techniques and teaching according to the cultural and linguistic educational needs of diverse children. As well as focusing on teachers' pedagogical approaches, many teachers interviewed in our sample also spoke of teachers' prompting of the L1 use in class, as well as presenting plurilingualism as an asset. Encouragement, initiative taking and addressing the knowledge of multiple languages as a privilege are some of the aspects of teachers' practice, in order to promote their class's linguistic plurality.

In fact, according to GT11, "the teacher should support all the children, not snub them, but help them a lot to learn about their own culture and not be ashamed to speak their language if they can, even among peers with the same L1." In addition, SET01, a special education teacher, admits that:

The teacher has a crucial role, mainly during the first years of schooling, and even more concerning the education of diverse pupils. They must pay particular attention to emphasize their particularities by asking them about the countries of their origin, and certainly, not to behave as if they do not come from somewhere else, not to differentiate them.

Another participant, GT20, focuses on the positive feelings that young students with a different background can experience when the teacher gives them opportunities to present in the class elements from their own language, as well as elements of their cultural identity. Specifically, she states:

I believe that it is decisive that teachers help and integrate the non-native children in the classroom, try to give stimuli to the other children to learn the language of the non-native children so that they too feel proud. Because they are very happy when you pay attention to their language and ask them what something is called in their language or about some customs they have. They are very happy if you treat them in the same way as others.

Some other participants focus on how the teacher should present the fact that some students speak more than one language, arguing that a person knowing several languages is an asset, it is something very positive. Two such excerpts from the interviews are as follows:

Teachers should highlight the fact that some children speak other languages as a great privilege and take advantage of it as much as they can in their teaching. I mean, there are a lot of things you can do within cross-curricular activities. (GT16)

The teacher in a multilingual class should be, of course, on the side of all the children, they should not discriminate against diverse students, so as not to bring out that this language is a peculiarity. On the contrary, they should emphasize it as something positive. (GT19)

It is worth noting the inclusive perspective of the teacher's identity, expressed by one participant through the term "citizen of the world". This particular perspective gives a wider dimension to the teacher's identity with direct reference to the openness of their thoughts and teaching practices in the classroom. In the following excerpt, the teacher is seen as a citizen of the world and is emphasized as someone who within the classroom struggles to preserve the culture of the students, and improve the feeling the latter have for their culture, in order to combine cultures and languages as a painter would combine colors. Specifically, GT41 states:

I think today's teacher should be a citizen of the world. They think globally and don't stick to their narrow beliefs, because public school is full of every case of children. Anyone who takes the first grade must be prepared and have a "citizen of the world" philosophy to accept that they have to deal with a group of children who come from different environments, and have to understand that they are not there to change the cultures but to improve them all together in this colorful group. There are many colors that come to you. Well, you have to combine them. It's not easy at all. It takes effort.

Culture of Language Attitudes

In addition, there are studies (Bensekhar et al. 2015; Di Meo et al. 2015) which focus on the strong effect that teachers' negative attitudes towards children's first languages have on these children's willingness to speak these languages at school. In Moon's research (2010, as cited by Mary & Young, 2022), the inextricable relationship between negative and positive attitudes of teachers and students is shown with students demonstrating empathy and understanding of the emergent literacy of their peers with different language backgrounds when the classroom climate was open to the different languages from that of the school on the part of the teacher, on the contrary, in cases where the children's first languages were considered socially inappropriate and had to be excluded from the classroom, the children followed the teacher's example and rejected the children's attempts to use their own language repertoires.

According to Mogli et al. (2020), teachers' helping students from diverse backgrounds adjust in their new school and social environment is crucial, while providing refugee students with a welcoming environment has a key role to play in achieving school success, depending largely on teachers' knowledge, values, practices, and attitudes (Kovinthan, 2016).

In this study, according to some participants, the teacher should cultivate a positive attitude towards languages other than Greek by all the students. GT14 claims that "the teacher must eliminate some prejudices and stereotypes, because I believe they are the ones who handle some situations. They must eliminate the stigma given by society because these children must first be accepted by the teacher and then transmit the acceptance to the other children and if they act like this, I think that the rest of the students will embrace and accept these children and may critically learn some words in their language."

In addition, GT16, insists on the importance of implementing multicultural projects, through which the teacher has the opportunity to highlight the advantages of speaking several languages, and to avoid any negative attitudes towards the L1 of students with different backgrounds. Particularly, she reports:

I believe that the teacher plays a very important role in this, that is, if you do some... because I usually do multicultural programs and so cross-curricular, always those who speak another language, we have it as a great advantage, we put it in the classroom, so it is not in any a case of mockery, equal parts admiration of how difficult it is. That is, it's how the teacher will put it, if he engages, how he will cultivate it, because I always engage and say how lucky they are and we can benefit and learn. We see it as a positive always.

Teachers should be aware of the fact that young students coming from different cultural and linguistic backgrounds seem to feel isolated and confused by the norms and expectations of the mainstream school, such as achieving high academic scores, or adopting to the way things are traditionally done at school (Gonzalez, 2009). According to Juvonen and Bell (2018), teachers and school environments play an important role not only in the socialization and the integration of children with a refugee or immigrant background, but the development of their resilience as well (OECD, 2018), on condition that it encourages inclusion and empowerment (Hayward, 2017).

Cultivation of Values

In the literature review section, several studies were presented focusing on the role of personal values in the formation of the teacher's identity. In addition, in order to ensure a prosperous coexistence of all these children in the classroom, the teacher should cultivate fundamental values such as acceptance, respect for diversity and cooperation (Farmel et al., 2019; Hymel & Katz, 2019). In the present research, the cultivation of values such as respect, equality and cooperation are found in several participant responses, each one of which focusing on the necessity of their existence in the context of a multilingual classroom, mainly due to some fixed perceptions, which make it difficult for students with different backgrounds to become part of and engage actively in their class. For GT05, "there should be respect for the difference. You know, many times we Greeks are frightened by what is different. There must be respect for multilingualism in diversity and children should be proud of their origins." In addition, GT23 claims that:

At this age, children cannot work together in groups, as there are always issues that come up and they will definitely argue. Yet, second graders can work together, I've seen it, either in pairs or in groups of four. It depends on what kind of instruction your are going to give them. If, let's say, I assign a task and tell children that the one who completes it first, he/she will be the best, etc., children won't cooperate.

GT01 shares the same perspective of a teacher cultivating values within a multilingual classroom, focusing on the values of equality and respect. According to her:

The teacher should make it clear through the appropriate discussions that regardless of which country everyone comes from, we are all the same. There should be no racist predispositions. They should bring out the good aspects of the diverse children's character, and encourage them because it is difficult for them to live in a foreign city and deal with a language that is not their mother tongue.

For GT38, cultivation of values of equality is more important than the implementation of the course itself. His statement is in line with GT41 as regards the fact that trying to impart values is a difficult task, reporting that:

Having to deal with children who come from different cultural groups, different societies, different beliefs, different habits, we have to convey the message that everyone is equal to us, regardless of whether he/she is performing good or not performing well, having problems, or not having problems, being from this country, or not from this country. But that's the hard part. (GT38)

Creating a Positive Classroom Atmosphere

According to Pinter (2017), young learners' motivation is influenced by the classroom climate, while Whitebread (1996) refers to the importance of creating an atmosphere of emotional warmth where all students feel they have individual worth. Recognizing and utilizing children's home languages in the school context seem, according to Mary and Young (2017), to create a climate of trust and well-being in the classroom, and promote positive relationships between home and school. Thus, the cultivation of the value of students' languages and cultures, through the promotion of their interlinguistic abilities, undoubtedly plays a facilitating role, for their transition from home to school, cultivating, at the same time, positive relationships with their families. GT38 focuses on the importance of group bonding, and the quality of the group students are going to form, explaining that:

There are first graders who work in groups for the first time, although they come from kindergarten used to this kind of work in class, but there are also classes where you have to work with groups. At some point these kids have to sit down and have eye contact.

Furthermore, according to GT15, the playful use of students' L1s seems to be an effective way to attract students' interest and attention:

I once had a student who came from Albania and anyway he was very naughty in class, and once I told him "Look! Now you will sit down and... will sing us a song in Albanian!" He was really stunned! He kept looking me in the eyes, telling me that I was wacky! This was really fun!

However, ET04 refers to the importance of the family in the formation of the child's character. She explains, in particular, that it is up to the children themselves whether or not they will use their L1 in class. In the following excerpt she describes a similar experience from the classroom, where children having the same linguistic background were taking initiatives and helping each other to understand the lesson, confirming and emphasizing the importance of teachers cultivating a positive atmosphere in their class:

I have not come across natives ignoring non-native speakers, but they may either make fun of them or help them in lessons, or even become interested in learning words in their classmates' languages, depending, of course, on the family the child comes from, or on the classroom climate. This year, we had a child from Syria in the third grade. I was very impressed because when she came to class, all the children fell on her and tried to encourage her to participate in the activities, even though she was having a lot of difficulty. Yet, all the children were very positive towards her. However, I've also seen them making fun of other than Greek speaking children, or correcting them. Last year there was a little boy who also helped two Syrian brothers. During the lesson, he was keeping his mind back on those two little boys telling them go there, do this, do that, B., just by themselves, without any prompting from my side. [Researcher: So, do you think that this is cultivated by the family?] In some cases, yes. In some others, the atmosphere is cultivated by the teacher.

Empathy Towards Students Who Speak Other Languages

Block et al. (2014) consider schools as a critical point for promoting successful social inclusion, expressing however their concern about how they could effectively support refugee students who are challenged with unfamiliar education systems, recovering from trauma (mental and physical), facing social discrimination and dealing with a totally different linguistic reality. As Noddings (2013) asserts, empathy is necessary for gaining a deep understanding of the other person's needs, which results in taking responsibility and acting for the person in need. In terms of education, McAllister and Irvine (2002) claim that empathy consists of a very important relationship when teaching in diverse sociocultural settings, and particularly when the teachers are external to those sociocultural contexts.

The analysis of the interviews also revealed a more emotional side of the teachers' identity, as they not only empathize with the environment their students come from but also with how these students feel. What is interesting in the findings is that teachers do not dwell only on how they feel themselves but try to cultivate similar feelings in the rest of the class, and adapt their teaching according to diverse students' experience. In the following excerpts, the role of empathy towards the difficulties of these children and the cultivation of positive emotions is observed:

I have also tried to work within some groups on feelings, in order to talk about how they feel, because children at the beginning when they come to school need to know what environment they belong to. They do not easily talk about their families. They feel more comfortable talking about their friends and making friendships easily, but they are still in the stage of selfishness . There are more "Me" and then my friend at this age. (GT19)

During reception class, even when we work on spelling, dictating to them in order to write something in Greek, that would be related to a previous discussion. "What did you do yesterday?" "How is your sister?", for example. And then, I would take something from all this discussion and ask them to write "My brother.. this, that..". (GT59)

However, there were also several participants who expressed more reflective thoughts, focusing on the lack of understanding on behalf of teachers towards their students from diverse backgrounds. Specifically, GT23 admits:

The teacher must show understanding to those children because many times we do not show understanding, i.e. we take it for granted, we do not think that these children have another mother tongue, they have other stimuli. It is necessary for the teacher to insist on language and discuss with them, in order to try to cover their weaknesses, either in the spoken or written language. For instance, discuss the synonyms in their L1. There should be an interaction between Greek and their mother tongue. Of course, this is difficult and not always possible. Usually, we enter the classroom and have in our mind that for some reason these children may be struggling but many times we do nothing, and the teacher tells them to just learn these things without understanding that this child also has another background.

DISCUSSION AND CONCLUSION

The presence of students with different linguistic and cultural backgrounds in the primary school period forms a special context of communication, in which the teacher through their perceptions plays an important role. Specifically, the identity of the teachers emerges through thoughts, practices and behaviors in relation to the presence and utilization of the L1 of all students. These thoughts, practices and behaviors define a particular context of explicit and implicit linguistic contact, where language is a bridge of communication and a means of cultivating universal values such as respect, equality and cooperation. This chapter does not aspire to reach generalized conclusions, but to detect some trends in the beliefs of teachers in relation to the role they themselves play in their classrooms in terms of retrieving the invisible languages of students from different backgrounds, which remain silent because of their exclusion from the school curriculum, and due to the pervasive monolingual ideology (Gkaintartzi et al., 2015), in order to strengthen and integrate them in the educational framework in which they were found. The trends detected in the teachers' beliefs regarding their role in the formation of the rules for the use of all the languages of the class in the lesson, concern the adoption of appropriate inclusive pedagogical approaches of the L1s through routines and multicultural projects, the cultivation of a climate of cooperation, exchange and interaction between all the students, the cultivation of positive attitudes towards the languages of the class and finally the development of empathy in the students but also the utilization of it as a personal feeling to understand and respect the special characteristics of children with different backgrounds.

Comparing the current study with other previous ones on teachers' beliefs about the languages of children with different backgrounds in the Greek educational setting, I would say that this study focuses more on the participants' reflections on related experiences to handling the linguistic capital of the students in their class. However, this is not the case in the study of Mattheoudakis et al. (2017), who conclude that teachers' attitudes towards their students' use of their L1 are not particularly encouraging. This could be explained by Wang et al. (2022), who suggest that there seems to be an impact of teachers' thoughts and opinions about their diverse pupils' characteristics on the formers' attitudes. However, in practice, teachers appear to respond to teaching situations according to their beliefs about appropriate behavior and classroom relationships (ibid.). As regards Europe, in De Angelis' (2011) research, teachers are reported to encourage diverse students to use their L1 but not in class, for fear that it may be a hindrance to the acquisition of the majority language. In a similar study, Haukås (2015) confirmed that teachers may declare having positive beliefs about promoting multilingualism, however in practice they do not make use of their students' previews of linguistic knowledge. Within the Greek educational system, the study of Maligkoudi et al. (2018) converges with this discrepancy, concluding that teachers claim to be supportive towards the refugee students. Nevertheless, they show reluctance to engage their students in practices that promote linguistic and cultural diversity for fear of sacrificing the natives' progress. Lundberg's (2019) study aligns with this discrepancy between theory and practice, as in spite of language policies promoting more pluralistic teaching approaches, teachers' beliefs seem to remain rooted in monolingual and traditional ideologies. In their study, Coelho and Ortega (2020) sustain teachers' belief that promoting cultural and linguistic awareness in class is as crucial as formal language learning. Zarrinabadi and Afsharmeler (2022), in their study conclude that teachers mindsets can significantly influence their teaching styles, but also the way they treat diverse students. I will close this chapter referring to Young's (2014) statement that a better understanding of how teachers think is a prerequisite to rebuild their beliefs in favor of educating plurilingual children.

ACKNOWLEDGMENT

I gratefully acknowledge the contribution of all the participants to my research. I am grateful to them for their availability to share their knowledge and experiences and contribute to the conduct of this research.

REFERENCES

Alstad, G. T., & Tkachenko, E. (2018). Teachers' beliefs and practices in creating multilingual spaces: The case of English teaching in Norwegian early childhood education. In M. Schwartz (Ed.), *Preschool Bilingual Education* (pp. 245–282). Springer International Publishing. doi:10.1007/978-3-319-77228-8_9

Avramidou- Αβραμίδου, B. (2014). Diachirisi tis polipolitismikotitas sto scholio: Mia empiriki erevna. [Managing multiculturalism in school: An empirical study.] *Πολύδρομο, 7*, 18-25.

Baker, M. (2018). Playing, talking, co-constructing: Exemplary teaching for young dual language learners across program types. *Early Childhood Education Journal, 47*(1), 115–130. doi:10.100710643-018-0903-0

Bakhtin, M. M. (1981). Discourse in the novel. In M. Holquist (Ed.), *The dialogic imagination: For essays by M. M. Bakhtin* (pp. 259–422). University of Texas press.

Bensekhar Bennabi, M., Simon, A., Rezzoug, D., & Moro, M. R. (2015). Les pathologies du langage dans la pluralité linguistique. *La Psychiatrie de l'Enfant, 58*(1), 277–298. doi:10.3917/psye.581.0277

Block, K., Cross, S., Riggs, E., & Gibbs, L. (2014). Supporting schools to create an inclusive environment for refugee students. *International Journal of Inclusive Education, 18*(12), 1337–1355. doi:10.1080/13603116.2014.899636

Bohr, C., & Acar, S. (2021). Supporting language acquisition and peer interaction through guided play in a multilingual classroom. *Young Exceptional Children, XX*(X), 1–10.

Burgess, R. (1984). *In the field: An introduction to field research researching human geography*. George Allen and Unwin.

Calafato, R. (2021). "I feel like it's giving me a lot as a language teacher to be a learner myself": Factors affecting the implementation of a multilingual pedagogy as reported by teachers of diverse languages. *Studies in Second Language Learning and Teaching, 11*(4), 579–606. doi:10.14746sllt.2021.11.4.5

Coelho, D., & Ortega, Y. (2020). Pluralistic approaches in early language education: shifting paradigms in language didactics. In S. Lau & S. Van Viegen (Eds.), *Plurilingual Pedagogies. Critical and creative Endeavors for equitable language in education* (pp. 145–160). Springer. doi:10.1007/978-3-030-36983-5_7

Coelho, E. (1998). *Teaching and learning in multicultural schools: An integrated approach*. Multilingual Matters. doi:10.21832/9781800417953

Cohen, J. L. (2008). 'That's not treating you as a professional': Teachers constructing complex professional identities through talk. *Teachers and Teaching, 14*(2), 79–93. doi:10.1080/13540600801965861

Cummins, J. (2008). Total immersion or bilingual education? Findings of international research on promoting immigrant children's achievement in the primary school. In J. Ramseger & M. Wagener (Eds.), *Chancenungleichheit in der Grundschule* (pp. 45–55). VS Verlag für Sozialwissenschaften. doi:10.1007/978-3-531-91108-3_4

De Angelis, G. (2011). Teachers' beliefs about the role of prior language knowledge in learning and how these influence teaching practices. *International Journal of Multilingualism, 8*(3), 216–234. doi:10.1080/14790718.2011.560669

De Costa, P. I., & Norton, B. (2017). Introduction: Identity, transdisciplinarity, and the good language teacher. *Modern Language Journal, 101*(S1), 3–14. doi:10.1111/modl.12368

Di Meo, S., & van den Hove, C. Serre-Pradère, G., Simon, A. Moro, M., R. & Thierry Baubet, T. (2015). Le mutisme extra-familial chez les enfants de migrants. Le silence de Sandia. *L'Information Psychiatrique, 91*(3), 217–224.

Diakogeorgiou- Διακογεωργίου. A. (2016). Η ένταξη των αλλοδαπών και των παλιννοστούντων μαθητών στο Δημοτικό Σχολείο. [The inclusion of non-natives and repatriated students in the Primary School]. In the *Proceedings of the 8th Conference of the Greek Institute of Applied Pedagogy and Education*.

Duff, P. A., & Uchida, Y. (1997). The negotiation of teachers' sociocultural identities and practices in postsecondary EFL classrooms. *TESOL Quarterly, 31*(3), 451–486. doi:10.2307/3587834

Dweck, C. S. (2006). *Mindset: The new psychology of success*. Random House.

Eyles, J. (1988). *Research in human geography*. Basil Blackwell.

Farmer, T., Hamm, J., Dawes, M., Barko-Alva, K., & Cross, J. (2019). Promoting inclusive communities in diverse classrooms: Teacher attunement and social dynamics Management. *Educational Psychologist, 54*(4), 286–305. doi:10.1080/00461520.2019.1635020

Fotiadou, G., Prentza, A., Maligkoudi, C., Michalopoulou, S., & Mattheoudakis, M. (2022). Investigating teachers' beliefs, attitudes and practices regarding the inclusion of refugee and immigrant students in Greek state schools. *Journal of Applied Linguistics, 35*, 36–58.

Galani, M., & Stavrinidis, P.- Γαλάνη, M. & Σταυρινίδης, Π. (2022). Antilipsis ke praktikes ton ekpedeftikon protovathmias ekpedefsis schetika me ti diachirisi tis psychikis hygias pedion prosfigon pou fitoun stis domes ipodochis ke ekpedefsis prosfigon stin Ellada. [Perceptions and practices of primary school teachers regarding the management of the mental health of refugee children attending Refugee Reception and Education Facilities in Greece]. *Erevna stin Ekpedefsi, 11*(1), 197–216.

Garmon, M. (2004). Changing preservice teachers' attitudes/beliefs about diversity: What are the factors? J. *Journal of Teacher Education, 55*(3), 201–213. doi:10.1177/0022487104263080

Gkaitartzi, A., Kiliari, A., & Tsokalidou, R. (2015). 'Invisible' bilingualism – 'Invisible' language ideologies: Greek teachers' attitudes towards immigrant students' heritage languages. *International Journal of Bilingual Education and Bilingualism, 18*(1), 60–72. doi:10.1080/13670050.2013.877418

Gkaravelas, K. & Koutoussi, A. (2018). I stasis ton ekpedeftikon protovathmias ekpedefsis gia tin entaksi diglosson pedion sta dimosia scholia tis Atikis. [The attitudes of primary education teachers towards the inclusion of bilingual students in the Public Primary Schools of Attica]. *Theoria kai erevna stis epistimes tis agogis, 31*, 45-58,

Gonzalez, V. (2009). *Young learners, diverse children: Celebrating diversity in early childhood.* Corwin Press.

Gorter, D., & Arocena, E. (2020). Teachers' beliefs about multilingualism in a course on translanguaging. *System, 92*, 1–10. doi:10.1016/j.system.2020.102272

Hanna, F., Oostdam, R., Severiens, S. E., & Zijlstra, B. J. (2020). Assessing the professional identity of primary student teachers: Design and validation of the Teacher Identity Measurement Scale. *Studies in Educational Evaluation, 64*, 100822. doi:10.1016/j.stueduc.2019.100822

Hart, R. (2009). Child refugees, trauma and education: Interactionist considerations on social and emotional needs and development. *Educational Psychology in Practice, 25*(4), 351–368. doi:10.1080/02667360903315172

Haukås, Å. (2015). Teachers' beliefs about multilingualism and a multilingual pedagogical approach. *International Journal of Multilingualism, 13*(1), 1–18. doi:10.1080/14790718.2015.1041960

Haukås, Å., & Mercer, S. (2022). Exploring pre-service language teachers' mindsets using a sorting activity. *Innovation in Language Learning and Teaching, 16*(3), 221–233. doi:10.1080/17501229.2021.1923721

Hayward, M. (2017). Teaching as a primary therapeutic intervention for learners from refugee backgrounds. *Intercultural Education, 28*(2), 165–181. doi:10.1080/14675986.2017.1294391

Hoyle, E., & John, P. (1995). *Professional knowledge and professional practice.* Cassell.

Hymel, S., & Katz, J. (2019). Designing classrooms for diversity: Fostering social inclusion. *Educational Psychologist, 54*(4), 331–339. doi:10.1080/00461520.2019.1652098

Irie, K., Ryan, S., & Mercer, S. (2018). Using Q methodology to investigate pre-service EFL teachers' mindsets about teaching competences. *Studies in Second Language Learning and Teaching, 8*(3), 575–598. doi:10.14746sllt.2018.8.3.3

Juvonen, J., & Bell, A. N. (2018). Social integration of refugee youth in Europe: Lessons learnt about interethnic relations in U.S. schools. *Polish Psychological Bulletin, 49*(1), 23–30.

Juvonen, J., Lessard, L. M., Rastogi, R., Schacter, H. L., & Smith, D. S. (2019). Promoting social inclusion in educational settings: Challenges and opportunities. *Educational Psychologist, 54*(4), 250–270. doi:10.1080/00461520.2019.1655645

Kanno, Y., & Stuart, C. (2011). Learning to become a second language teacher: Identities-inpractice. *Modern Language Journal, 95*(2), 236–252. doi:10.1111/j.1540-4781.2011.01178.x

Koukoula, A. (2017). *Attitudes and opinions of teachers regarding refugee and immigrant integration in the Greek educational system. The case of the municipality of Lesvos and of Serres* [Dissertation, Hellenic Open University].

Kovinthan, T. (2016). Learning and teaching with loss: Meeting the needs of refugee children through narrative inquiry. *Diaspora, Indigenous, and Minority Education, 10*(3), 141–155. doi:10.1080/15595692.2015.1137282

Lasagabaster, D. (2015). Different educational approaches to bi- or multilingualism and their effect on language attitudes. In M. Juan-Garau & J. Salazar-Noguera (Eds.), *Content-based Language Learning in Multilingual Educational Environments. Educational Linguistics* (Vol. 23, pp. 13–30). Springer. doi:10.1007/978-3-319-11496-5_2

Liu, S., Volcic, Z., & Gallois, C. (2019). *Introducing intercultural communication: Global cultures and contexts* (3rd ed.). SAGE.

Llurda, E., & Lasagabaster, D. (2010). Factors affecting teachers" beliefs about interculturalism. *International Journal of Applied Linguistics, 20*(3), 327–353. doi:10.1111/j.1473-4192.2009.00250.x

Lou, N., & Noels, K. (2019). Promoting growth in foreign and second language education: A research agenda for mindsets in language learning and teaching. *System, 86*, 102–126. doi:10.1016/j.system.2019.102126

Lundberg, A. (2019). Teachers' beliefs about multilingualism: Findings from Q method research. *Current Issues in Language Planning, 20*(3), 266–283. doi:10.1080/14664208.2018.1495373

Magos, K., & Margaroni, M. (2018). The importance of educating refugees. [Editorial]. *Global Education Review, 5*(4), 1–6.

Magos, K., & Simopoulos, G. (2020). Teaching L2 for students with a refugee/migrant background in Greece: Teachers' perceptions about reception, integration and multicultural identities. *Global Education Review, 7*(4), 59–73.

Maligkoudi, C., Tolakidou, P., & Chiona, S. (2018). "It is not bilingualism. There is no communication". Examining Greek teachers' views towards refugee children's bilingualism: A case study. *Dialogoi, Theory &. Praxis Educativa (Santa Rosa), 4*, 95–107.

Mary, L., & Young, A. (2017). Engaging with emergent bilinguals and their families in the pre-primary classroom to foster well-being, learning and inclusion. *Language and Intercultural Communication, 17*(4), 455–473. doi:10.1080/14708477.2017.1368147

Mary, L., & Young, A. (2020). Teachers' beliefs and attitudes towards home languages maintenance and their effects. In A. C. Schalley & S. A. Eisenchlas (Eds.), *Handbook of Home Language Maintenance and Development: Social and Affective Factors* (pp. 444–463). De Gruyter Mouton. doi:10.1515/9781501510175-022

Mattheoudakis, M., Chatzidaki, A., & Maligkoudi, C., (2017). Greek teachers' views on linguistic and cultural diversity. *Selected papers on theoretical and applied linguistics, 22*, 358-371.

McAllister, G., & Irvine, J. J. (2002). The role of empathy in teaching culturally diverse students: A qualitative study of teachers' beliefs. *Journal of Teacher Education, 53*(5), 433–443. doi:10.1177/002248702237397

Ministry of Migration Policy. (2019). *National strategy for inclusion*. Ministry of Migration Policy.

Mogli, M., Kalbeni, S., & Stergiou, L. (2019). "The teacher is not a magician": Teacher training in Greek reception facilities for refugee education. *International e-Journal of Educational Studies. 4*, 42-55.

Moons, C. (2010). *Kindergarten teachers speak: Working with language diversity in the classroom*. MA thesis. McGill University

Nakeyar, C., Esses, V., & Reid, G. J. (2018). The psychosocial needs of refugee children and youth and best practices for filling these needs: A systematic review. *Clinical Child Psychology and Psychiatry, 23*(2), 186–208. doi:10.1177/1359104517742188 PMID:29207880

Noddings, N. (2013). *Caring: A relational approach to ethics and moral education*. University of California Press.

OECD. (2018). The *resilience of students with an immigrant background: factors that shape well-Being*. OECD. https://www.oecd-ilibrary.org/docserver/9789264292093en.pdf?expires=1556025290&id=id&accname=guest&checksum=13625606919D4245C468D06156AEB392

Ohta, A. S. (2017). Sociocultural theory and second/foreign language education. In N. Van Deusen-Scholl & S. May (Eds.), *Second and foreign language education, encyclopedia of language and education* (Vol. 4, pp. 57–68). Springer. doi:10.1007/978-3-319-02246-8_6

Parker, C., Scott, S., & Geddes, A. (2019). Snowball sampling. SAGE Research Methods Foundations., 10.4135.

Pennington, M. C., & Richards, J. C. (2016). Teacher identity in language teaching: Integrating personal, contextual, and professional factors. *RELC Journal, 47*(1), 5–23. doi:10.1177/0033688216631219

Pinter, A. (2017). *Teaching young language learners* (2nd ed.). Oxford University Press.

Prajapati, R., & Gupta, S. (2023). Engaging students: The assessment of professional identity and emotional intelligence of language teachers. In S. Karpava (Ed.), *Handbook of research on language teacher identity* (pp. 116–130). IGI Global. doi:10.4018/978-1-6684-7275-0.ch007

Reeves, J. (2018). Teacher Identity. Framing the Issue. In J. I. Liontas (Ed.), *The TESOL Encyclopedia of English Language Teaching* (pp. 1–7). Wiley-Blackwell. doi:10.1002/9781118784235.eelt0268

Sgoura et al.- Σγούρα, Α., Μάνεσης, Ν., & Μητροπούλου, Φ. (2018). Diapolitismiki ekpedefsi ke kinoniki entaksi ton pedion prosfigon. Antilipsis ekpedeftikon. [Intercultural education and social integration of refugee children: Teachers' perceptions.] *Dialogi! Theoria ke praksi stis epistimes tis agogis ke ekpedefsis, 4*, 108-129.

Simopoulos, G., & Magos, K. (2021). Approaching the education of young refugees. Teachers' perceptions and students' voices. In A. Chatzidaki & R. Tsokalidou (Eds.), *Challenges and Initiatives in Refugee Education: The Case of Greece* (pp. 37–56). Cambridge Scholars Publishing.

Singh, G., & Richards, J. C. (2006). Teaching and learning in the language teacher education course room: A critical sociocultural perspective. *RELC Journal, 37*(2), 149–175. doi:10.1177/0033688206067426

Stergiou, A. (2019). The contribution of the University of Ioannina to refugee education. In K. Plakitsi, E. Kolokouri, & A.-C. Kornelaki (Eds.), *ISCAR 2019 Crisis in Contexts, E-proceedings* (pp. 173–186). University of Ioannina.

Teddlie, C., & Yu, F. (2007). Mixed methods sampling: A typology with examples. *Journal of Mixed Methods Research, 1*(1), 77–100. doi:10.1177/1558689806292430

Terry, G., Hayfield, N., Clarke, V., & Braun, V. (2017). Thematic analysis. In C. Willig & W. Stainton (Eds.), *The SAGE Handbook of Qualitative Research in Psychology* (pp. 17–37). SAGE. doi:10.4135/9781526405555.n2

Trent, J. (2010). Teacher education as identity construction: Insights from action research. *Journal of Education for Teaching, 36*(2), 153–168. doi:10.1080/02607471003651672

Tsaliki, E. (2017). Teachers' views on implementing intercultural education in Greece: The case of 13 primary schools. *International Journal of Comparative Education and Development, 19*(2/3), 50–64. doi:10.1108/IJCED-07-2017-0013

Varghese, M., Morgan, B., Johnston, B., & Johnson, K. A. (2005). Theorizing language teacher identity. *Journal of Language, Identity, and Education, 4*(1), 21–44. doi:10.120715327701jlie0401_2

Varghese, M. M., Motha, S., Park, G., Reeves, J., & Trent, J. (2016). In This Issue. TESOL Quarterly on Language Teacher Identity, 50(3), 545-571.

Vázquez-Montilla, E., Just, M., & Triscari, R. (2014). Teachers' dispositions and beliefs about cultural and linguistic diversity. *Universal Journal of Educational Research, 2*(8), 577–587. doi:10.13189/ujer.2014.020806

Vergou, P. (2019). Living with difference: Refugee education and school segregation processes in Greece. *Urban Studies (Edinburgh, Scotland), 56*(15), 3162–3177. doi:10.1177/0042098019846448

Vikøy, A., & Haukås, Å. (2021). Norwegian L1 teachers' beliefs about a multilingual approach in increasingly diverse classrooms. *International Journal of Multilingualism*, 1–15.

Wang, J.-S., Lan, J. Y.-C., Khairutdinova, R., & Gromova, C. (2022). Teachers' attitudes to cultural diversity: Results from a qualitative study in Russia and Taiwan. *Frontiers in Psychology, 13*, 976659. doi:10.3389/fpsyg.2022.976659 PMID:36467240

Warren, C. A. (2014). Towards a pedagogy for the application of empathy in culturally diverse classrooms. *The Urban Review, 46*(3), 395–419. doi:10.100711256-013-0262-5

Whitebread, D. (Ed.). (1996). *Teaching and learning in the early years*. Routledge. doi:10.4324/9780203436493

Xu, L. (2012). The role of teachers beliefs in the language teaching-learning process. *Theory and Practice in Language Studies, 2*(7), 1397–1402. doi:10.4304/tpls.2.7.1397-1402

Young, A. S. (2014). Unpacking teachers' language ideologies: Attitudes, beliefs, and practiced language policies in schools in Alsace, France. *Language Awareness, 23*(1–2), 157–171. doi:10.1080/09658416.2013.863902

Zachos, D. T., Papadimitriou, N. T., & Sideri, E. (2020). Minority education in Greece: Thrace Muslim teachers' approaches and views. *Preschool and Primary Education, 8*(2), 144–157. doi:10.12681/ppej.21897

Zarrinabadi, N., & Afsharmehr, E. (2022). Teachers' mindsets about L2 learning: Exploring the influences on pedagogical practices. *RELC Journal*, 1–15. doi:10.1177/00336882211067049

Chapter 10
Challenging the Monoglossic Ideology in English–Medium Higher Education in Türkiye

Talip Gülle
https://orcid.org/0000-0002-7049-9885
Bartın University, Turkey

Yavuz Kurt
https://orcid.org/0000-0003-3301-5316
Marmara University, Turkey

ABSTRACT

Türkiye has witnessed exponential growth in the number of English-medium instruction (EMI) programs and an influx of international students — changes that are accompanied by challenges and opportunities. This chapter examines the discrepancy between the prevailing English-only policy and the increasing linguistic and cultural diversity in EMI higher education institutions in Türkiye. While the chapter focuses more on EMI programs, similar challenges in Turkish-medium (TMI) programs are also examined. The chapter argues for a shift in perspective that recognizes and embraces language diversity, and proposes the development of inclusive language policies to facilitate student interaction and involvement. It also calls for further research on multilingualism in EMI and TMI programs to inform policymaking, curriculum development, and teacher training. Overall, it argues for a comprehensive understanding of actual language needs and practices in linguistically diverse classrooms to develop policies that better serve the increasingly multilingual student body in Türkiye's universities.

INTRODUCTION

The exponential increase in the number of tertiary-level English-medium instruction (EMI) programs in Türkiye seems not to be accompanied by informed policies and practices that take account of the new linguistic realities and needs created by learning in the second language (L2) for L1-Turkish students

DOI: 10.4018/978-1-6684-8761-7.ch010

and increasing numbers of (international) students from other lingua-cultural backgrounds. The so-called English-only policy persists, despite being frequently challenged and breached by both students and instructors. A similar picture is emerging in Turkish-medium instruction (TMI) programs as well, with a large number of inbound international students, particularly Syrian nationals, arriving in Türkiye following the war in Syria. While Arabic-medium programs are also being offered, their number is only limited, and therefore most Syrian students are enrolled in EMI or TMI programs.

In this chapter, we problematize the discrepancy between policy statements that are aligned with a monoglossic perspective, on the one hand, and the increasing linguistic and cultural diversity of university classrooms, on the other, and we discuss the potential implications of such diversity for language policies and teaching/learning. Acknowledging that the multilingualism and multiculturalism in higher education institutions (HEIs) necessitates a shift from the monoglossic perspective is an important step towards developing appropriate policy responses to the evolving linguistic landscapes of universities. Next should follow the enactment of educational policies that better represent the realities of linguistically diverse classrooms, which could include, for example, encouraging "translanguaging spaces" for students to increase their involvement and interaction (Wei, 2011), in principled and pedagogically sound ways. Such an approach would involve avoiding the imposition of a one-language-only policy, which we know is not actually practiced in many classrooms and whose implementation, or lack thereof, is up to individual instructors, who are rarely provided with training on good practices regarding when and how the multilingualism of students can be invited to facilitate the learning process and to achieve deeper learning. With this chapter, we also aim to invite researchers to conduct further research in EMI and TMI higher education (HE) programs in Türkiye with a multilingual lens to help better understand the micro-level practices of instructors and students, to observe how multi- or translingual acts are manifested in and out of the classroom, and to understand their roles in the course of teaching and learning, as well as managing multicultural campuses, so that policy-making, curriculum-development, and in-service and pre-service teacher training can be informed by more empirical data.

To this end, we first provide a brief overview of the monoglossic ideology and how it is reflected in policy while at the same time being challenged on many occasions by students and instructors. To put matters into perspective within HE in Türkiye, we then present the changes that have been taking place in recent years in terms of the linguistic landscape of EMI and TMI HEIs in the country. These developments also underline the importance of coming to grips with the increasing urgency of better understanding, and creating (language) policy responses to, the needs of students from diverse lingua-cultural backgrounds. The need for more attention to the role of language in education cannot be overstated given that it is "perhaps the most important tool in education because language is needed to communicate ideas and negotiate understandings" (García & Torres-Guevara, 2010, p. 182). Lastly, we argue that the translanguaging perspective rather than the dominant monoglossic ideology is a better fit not only for approaching the teaching and learning of these students but also for increasing social justice for them.

The Monoglossic Ideology

The monoglossic ideology refers to the perspective that aims to restrain language diversity with restrictive linguistic policies (Thomas, 2017). Its origins lie in the nation-state ideology in Europe (Flores & Schissel, 2014). The monoglossic ideology "assumes that legitimate linguistic practices are only those enacted by monolinguals" (García, 2009, p. 115) and "treat[s] monolingualism as the norm" (Flores & Schissel, 2014, p. 455).

The consequences of this ideology extend to educational areas. Cummins (2007) refers to three interconnected monolingual instructional principles: conducting instruction solely in the target language, avoiding translation between L1 and L2 in language or literacy teaching, and maintaining strict separation of the two languages in immersion and bilingual programs. It could be argued that these instructional policies characterize EMI language policies in Türkiye, too. Despite the paucity of empirical studies documenting how the monoglossic ideology reveals itself and influences educational practices in Türkiye, it has been revealed that the English-only policy is pursued by the institutions and authorities (Karakaş & Bayyurt, 2019). Explanations regarding the medium of education on university websites, for instance, can give an idea about institutional expectations. The following statements were taken from the websites of two different universities in Türkiye:

The language of instruction is English, and 100% of the courses are conducted in English. Students, who cannot achieve their language proficiency, go to the English Preparatory School. (İstanbul Technical University, 2023)

The language of instruction at ABU is English. Therefore, all lectures, additional work, laboratory sessions and problem-solving meetings are conducted in English. [The authors' translation] (Antalya Bilim University, 2023)

Such statements, which can be found on the websites of other EMI programs as well, make it quite clear that from a policy perspective, languages other than English are not welcome once students start their programs. It is also possible to observe the monoglossic ideology among students who might perceive local languages as obstacles or contamination in the course of mastering English language skills (Kiramba, 2018). In the Turkish context, Akyay-Engin (2019) and Yıldız and Yeşilyurt (2016) revealed that university students training to become language teachers believe that students should not be allowed to use their L1 in English language classrooms. Karakaş (2023), on the other hand, reported how some instructors might follow individual linguistic policies in their EMI content lessons and not tolerate the use of languages other than English. Similarly, a large-scale study in 2015 across multiple universities around Türkiye revealed that the use of Turkish was generally highly limited in university-level language classrooms (British Council & TEPAV, 2015). However, as we show below, the monoglossic ideology is also being challenged in many other EMI classrooms in Türkiye.

Language of Higher Education in Türkiye

The Republic of Türkiye was founded as a nation-state after the collapse of the Ottoman Empire. Just like during the Ottoman era, multiple languages exist within the Republic of Türkiye as well. Yağmur (2001) identifies more than forty languages spoken in Türkiye. However, while "the Ottomans never interfered with religious and linguistic practices of nations that lived under the Ottoman Empire," (Yağmur, 2001, p. 408), when the Republic of Türkiye was founded, as in many other areas of life where nation-building policies were put into effect, linguistic policies were heavily centered on the ideology of a single national language, the Turkish language (Doğançay-Aktuna, 1998).

During the initial decades of the republic, the few universities established were state-owned and Turkish-medium. The Middle East Technical University, the first public university that offered education in a foreign language (English), has remained English-medium since its foundation in 1956. Foreign-owned schools had a longer history of foreign language medium education, such as Robert College, which dates back to 1863, but such schools were not many in number (British Council & TEPAV, 2015). The first private university offering EMI, Bilkent University, was founded in 1984.

Until the 2000s, only a few institutions offered EMI in Türkiye. However, in the last two decades, EMI has been a rapidly expanding phenomenon among universities, especially private institutions. Ege, Yüksel, and Curle (2022) divide EMI in Türkiye into two phases, first and second generation. The first phase broadly refers to EMI implementation before the 2000s, while the second phase refers to the period after this. During the second phase, institutions have become more active and willing in their internationalization and EMI implementation than they had been during the earlier period, growing a higher interest in attracting international students. Therefore, although multilingualism has always been a part of the history of the Republic of Türkiye (Yağmur, 2001; Kurt & Bayyurt, forthcoming), the current linguistic situation in Turkish HE marks a recent development.

Non-English foreign language medium programs, however, have always remained limited in prevalence and influence in Turkish HE. The first and only institution that offers French-medium education in Türkiye is Galatasaray University, which was founded in 1992, and the only institution that offers German-medium education is Turkish-German University, which was founded in 2010. Apart from these two, education in a foreign language is also observed at the program level, usually in language and/or literature and translation programs. Council of Higher Education (2023a) data shows that there is a huge gap between the number of English medium and other foreign language medium programs, with German being the second most common (55 fully German and 9 partially German bachelor's programs), and French being the third (34 bachelor's programs). Programs in other languages such as Arabic, Russian, Spanish, and Bulgarian also exist, but to a lesser degree (Council of Higher Education, 2023a).

The Current State of EMI in Türkiye

The growing interest of institutions in offering EMI is reflected in the number of EMI programs in 2022 (See Table 1). There are 208 HEIs in Türkiye and 75 of them are private (foundation) universities. In total, 3792 programs are offered at different levels either entirely or partially through English (Council of Higher Education, 2023a). The number of undergraduate EMI programs corresponds to almost one-fifth of all programs offered at the undergraduate level.

Table 1. Number of EMI programs in Türkiye

	Bachelor's	Master's	Doctorate
Full EMI	1512	1140	578
Partial EMI	408	97	57

Note: These numbers were taken from the Council of Higher Education website on 13 January 2023.

Full EMI programs offer all courses in English, while in Partial EMI programs, only 30% of courses are in English.

Implementation of EMI

EMI is implemented in several ways in Turkish HE. One important variation is observed in terms of the scope of implementation. EMI may be offered at the program level or at the institutional level. In institutions where full EMI is implemented, most of the courses, if not all, are offered in English. Some institutions offer the same program in both Turkish and English, with parallel programs in the two languages. Apart from parallel and full EMI programs, partial EMI programs are another option. Students who are enrolled in these programs are required to complete a certain percentage of courses offered in English. Although various versions of such programs were available in the past, such as 50% or 70% English, currently only 30% English programs are available. The motivation behind such programs has been to ensure that students acquire English language competence in their discipline to take place in global competition and at the same time to prevent Turkish from being pushed aside as an academic language (Reagan & Schreffler, 2005).

Another variation is in terms of language proficiency requirements at the time of entry into the program, and this variation may produce consequences that extend beyond the English preparatory programs and affect students' EMI experiences. Turkish HE regulations require universities that offer education in foreign languages to provide preparatory language support to students (Official Gazette, 2016), but universities have autonomy in terms of exemption requirements from the English preparatory program. For example, Özdemir-Yılmazer (2022) studied the English language proficiency requirements at 57 public universities with EMI programs in Türkiye. The study revealed considerable variation in terms of the minimum score requirements in different tests. For example, the minimum score required ranged between 55 and 90 in the YDS (Yabancı Dil Sınavı [Foreign Language Test]) given by the Centre for Assessment, Selection and Placement, which is the institution responsible for holding nationwide exams in Türkiye. In the TOEFL IBT, the range was found to be between 60 and 108, but the majority of programs required a TOEFL IBT score of 72 or 84. Additionally, Özdemir-Yılmazer (2022) found that the language requirements tended not to be based on empirical data. Dearden, Akincioglu, and Macaro (2016) state that proficiency tests in EMI HEIs in Türkiye are "often written in-house by individual universities with little standardisation" (p. 3) and report that teachers in their study believed most students' language proficiency was insufficient for EMI despite having obtained passing scores in language assessments. While inconclusive, research has revealed English proficiency to be a significant predictor of academic performance (e.g., Li, 2018), but the variance explained by L2 proficiency scores seems not to be substantial, e.g., 3% in Cho and Bridgeman (2012) and 6% in Bo, Fu, and Lim (2022), who examined TOEFL IBT scores and in-house proficiency test scores, respectively. With limited standardization in L2 requirements, it is possible that the language of instruction incurs learning costs for L2-English students. Research into student challenges in EMI indicates that this is indeed the case. For example, Aizawa and Rose (2019) report challenges such as difficulty understanding certain grammatical structures among lower proficiency students, and difficulty with academic literacy, such as essay writing, among higher proficiency students. Students in EMI programs in Türkiye were also found to be challenged in comprehending content due to limited knowledge of terminology in English (Yıldız et al., 2017). Issues with production skills have been reported, too. For instance, Arkın and Osam (2015) report student challenges in expressing their ideas in writing at a Turkish EMI university, with the consequence of hampered test performance according to student accounts.

Internationalization Discourses behind EMI

Before we present the numbers of and educational efforts directed towards international students, a clarification is in order. When the term "international student" is used in this chapter, it is based on the UNESCO (2023) definition, according to which it refers to "individuals who have physically crossed an international border between two countries with the objective to participate in educational activities in the country of destination, where the country of destination of a given student is different from their country of origin." However, it is also important to keep in mind Jones's (2007, p. 193) cautionary note that the traditional divide between "international" and "domestic" students may not hold as some so-called international students might already know the host country's culture and language due, for example, to prior education, and domestic students with diverse backgrounds might have similar needs to those categorized as international students.

The goal of increasing the number of international students in Türkiye has been set forth as a state policy. In 2017, the Council of Higher Education of Türkiye published its Internationalization Strategy Document, which particularly served to introduce policies to (a) increase Türkiye's competitiveness in attracting both students and instructors from other countries, (b) enhance the quality of HE, and (c) strengthen institutional structures to cater to a more international student and instructor body (Council of Higher Education, 2017). These policies included increasing the number of programs offering education in other languages, enhancing cooperation with international and multinational institutions, and providing more accommodation and scholarship opportunities to international students, among others. In 2021, the Council of Higher Education published another report, "The Target-oriented Internationalization Report", which presents the actions taken as part of the internationalization strategy and the outcomes achieved (Council of Higher Education, 2021). According to this report, the Council's internationalization strategy seems to have produced the desired effect. The domestic demand for EMI programs has been increasingly accompanied by international demand, with more international students arriving in Türkiye over the years. Recent statistics show that 260,289 students came to Türkiye for university education in 2022 (see Figure 1). This number is more than double when compared to five years ago, and almost tenfold what it was in 2011 (Council of Higher Education, 2023b).

Figure 1. The number of international students enrolled in universities in Türkiye across years
Note: Adapted from information on the website studyinturkiye.gov.tr, managed by the Council of Higher Education.

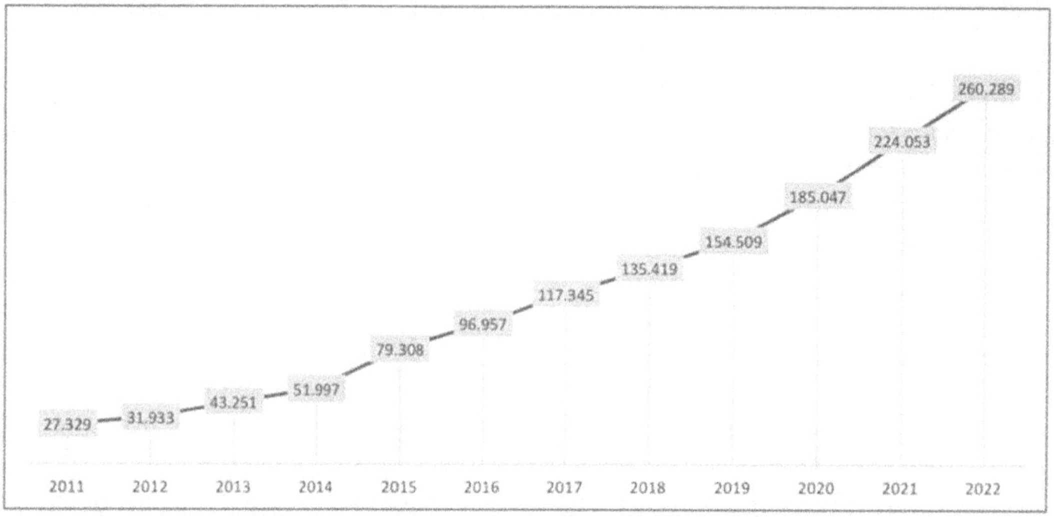

Increasing numbers of incoming international students seem to be a global trend; however, as for the scale of that increase, Türkiye is one of the leading countries. It was second only to the United Arab Emirates, with an astounding increase of 156% from 2015 to 2020 (Time Association, 2022). This increase placed Türkiye among the top 10 countries in terms of the number of inbound international students in 2020 (see Table 2). Considering that it was not even among the top 20 in 2014 (The Guardian, n.d.), Türkiye's progress in that regard is a notable case, which has also led to its ranking among the top 10 countries in terms of international education market share (OECD, 2022).

Table 2. Top countries that host the highest number of international students

Country	2015	2020	Change between 2015-2020	Ranking 2015	Ranking 2020
USA	907,251	957,475	6%	1	1
UK	430,833	550,877	28%	2	2
Australia	294,438	458,279	56%	3	3
Germany	228,756	368,717	61%	5	4
Canada	171,603	323,157	88%	6	5
France	239,409	252,444	5%	4	6
China	123,127	225,100	83%	7	7
U. Arab Emirates	73,445	215,975	194%	11	8
Türkiye	72,178	185,047	156%	13	9
Netherlands	86,189	124,876	45%	10	10

Note: Adapted from Time Association (2022)

Challenging the Monoglossic Ideology in English-Medium Higher Education

Governmental and institutional policies highlight the instrumental motivation behind EMI, which seems to interact with the supply and demand equilibrium, a process that continuously maintains EMI's growth. However, the growth of EMI does not go without opposition. Selvi (2020) reports that some challenge it with nationalistic concerns of the Turkish language being corroded by English. Others point to concerns about the gradual fading of Turkish as a scientific language (Doğançay-Aktuna, 1998; Reagan & Schreffler, 2005). The opposition is, however, negligible compared to upholders, and quite far from posing any hindrance to EMI's growth. For the time being, the increasing demand and the educational policies that aim to respond to this demand continuously expand and secure the place of EMI in Turkish HE.

Students Under Temporary Protection in Türkiye

The demographic composition of classrooms at all levels of education in Türkiye has been changing due to the unprecedented number of refugees arriving in the country following the war in Syria that broke out in 2011. The total number of Syrians under temporary protection in Türkiye, the total number of foreigners who have obtained a residence permit in Türkiye, and the number of foreigners according to the type of permit obtained are shown in Figure 2, Figure 3, and Table 3, respectively.

Figure 2. Number of Syrians under temporary protection in Türkiye across years
Note: Adapted from Directorate General of Migration Management (2023a) of Republic of Türkiye Ministry of Interior.

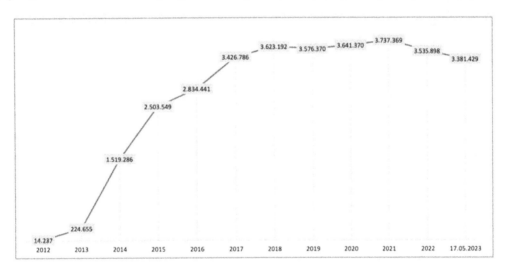

Figure 3. Number of foreigners with Turkish residence permit across years
Note: Adapted from Directorate General of Migration Management (2023b) of Republic of Türkiye Ministry of Interior.

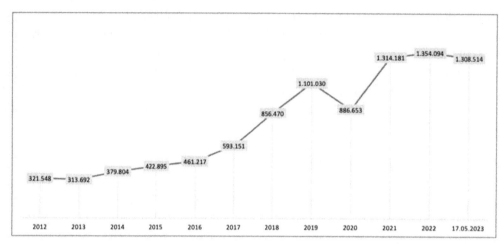

Table 3. Numbers of resident permit types given by 17.05.2023

Short-term residence permit	853,079
Student residence permit	161,012
Family residence permit	106,588
Others	187,835

Source: Presidency of Migration Management (2023b) of Republic of Türkiye Ministry of Interior.

According to Council of Higher Education data, in the 2022-23 academic year, there were 301,549 students from other nationalities enrolled in Turkish HEIs, of whom 58,213 were from the Syrian Arab Republic (Council of Higher Education, 2023c). The global average for refugees' enrollment in HE was 6% in 2023, compared to a mere 1% in 2019 (UNHCR, 2023). Given that the HE enrollment rate for Syrian students in Türkiye was 9.5% in 2021 (Esen, 2022), it may be argued that Türkiye has been relatively successful in providing educational opportunities to Syrians at the HE level, which is critical since access to HE allows for access to a better life (Erdoğan & Erdoğan, 2020). As Yıldız (2019a) suggests, Türkiye has embraced "a constructive approach to ensure all refugees' and refugee like populations' access and engagement in the Turkish higher education system" (p. 77). The facilitative factors in this process include the positive discrimination afforded to Syrian students in terms of university entrance exams, exemption from tuition fees and provision of "special student" status, scholarships and financial support (Arar et al., 2020).

While the acceptance and registration of Syrian students in Turkish universities is facilitated by the policies of the Turkish government, their integration into the education system seems to suffer from a variety of issues. Language-related challenges are among the most important issues these students face (Cennetkuşu & Ölmez, 2022; Dereli, 2018). Since both Turkish and English are second languages for many Syrian students, the challenges experienced in TMI and EMI programs overlap in several ways, yet since Turkish is the language used in social life, lack of L2-Turkish skills creates a broader range of challenges.

Drawing Parallels Between EMI and TMI Programs

While the main focus in this chapter is on EMI, we also present the experiences of international students in TMI programs to highlight the commonality of language-related issues in L2-medium educational settings.

International students registered in TMI programs are required to certify their language proficiency or are offered L2-Turkish courses by Turkish and Foreign Language Teaching, Application and Research Centers (TÖMER) of universities. Variations exist across universities as to the minimum proficiency required, and the quality of instruction offered by TÖMER is argued to be controversial (e.g., Güngör & Soysal, 2021). Even those who have successfully completed TÖMER courses were found to lack sufficient levels of Turkish proficiency for their academic studies, needing further language support in terms of writing and speaking skills in particular, during both lessons and exams (Yıldız, 2019b). The same is reported by Dereli (2018), who implicitly points to limited disciplinary literacy skills in the L2 by stating that the level of proficiency reached even after advanced L2-Turkish language courses "is not enough to understand Turkish in an academic environment due to the specialised vocabulary required that is not learned in a standard language course" (p. 15). However, while TÖMER courses have room for further improvement, this is not meant to devalue the importance and contributions of TÖMER courses to students' adaptation and future success (Güngör & Soysal, 2021).

Arar et al. (2020) provide a picture of HE policies towards Syrian refugees in Türkiye and report on the challenges encountered by Syrian students and the policy implications and consequences of these challenges. They point to the language of instruction as a leading challenge, with most universities offering TMI, while a "limited number" (p. 272) of universities offer EMI (We should note that the number of EMI universities is limited only relative to the number of TMI universities; otherwise, there are a considerable number of EMI programs in Türkiye and their number has increased substantially in recent years). The policies developed in response to language challenges involve the provision of support in L2-Turkish and the establishment of Arabic-medium programs (Arar et al., 2020). Arar et al. (2020) also report the findings of interviews with Syrian students, which include the following:

- Syrian students' academic performance and social integration were hindered by lack of proficiency in Turkish.
- They faced higher time costs in their studies relative to L1-Turkish students as they were challenged in comprehending academic content.
- While they were able, over time, to use Turkish sufficiently well for social purposes, they needed support in terms of academic literacy such as academic writing.
- They suggested the use of their L1, communication tools and additional materials in Arabic to facilitate their academic performance, and argued that the libraries lacked sufficient Arabic resources.

Challenges in comprehension of lessons and exam questions were reported in a more recent study by Cennetkuşu and Ölmez (2022) as well, which signals that there is work to be done in terms of alleviating language-related challenges experienced by Syrian students. In that regard, one micro-level accommodation that can improve academic outcomes for international students comes from Yıldız (2019b), who suggests that international students, who are in the process of further developing their Turkish language skills, be given extra time in exams.

While there is a paucity of studies into the experiences of international students at EMI programs in Türkiye, the existing research points to similar issues to those in TMI programs. For example, Dereli (2018) states that Syrian students who are enrolled in English- or Arabic-medium programs have less opportunity to learn Turkish, which has implications for their lives on and off campus. L1-Arabic students in EMI programs interviewed by Gülle (2023) reported that experiencing challenges with comprehension and production in English formed a hindrance in terms of their academic outcomes, which confirms that, just like L1-Turkish students, international students in EMI programs in Türkiye also grapple with "the difficulty of studying intellectually demanding courses through English" (Karakaş & Bayyurt, 2019, p. 112).

Language Practices Inside and Outside of the Classroom

The official documents of most EMI universities simply state that the language of education in their institution is English, with no further explanation that would acknowledge the existence or use of other languages for any kind of communicative purposes in the classroom or around the campus. As Shohamy (2006) states, linguistic policies are practiced through various channels such as rules, regulations, educational policies, and language tests. Although it may look quite straightforward and accurate on the surface, such a statement as "the language of education in this institution is English" is too simplistic, and prescriptive in nature. It certainly does not describe the existing situation in EMI programs because neither all students nor staff in the institution use English only.

Use of other languages is motivated by various factors, but proficiency in English obviously plays an important role. Indeed, proficiency in English has been reported to be important for success in EMI (Costa & Coleman, 2013; Moore-Jones, 2015). Studies in several countries have shown challenges related to L2 proficiency in EMI programs (e.g., Tatzl, 2011; Lasagabaster, 2015), and Türkiye is no exception (Kamaşak et al., 2021). Linguistic challenges in English can be observed among students and instructors (Gürtler & Kronewald, 2015), which in turn results in difficulty with comprehension (Aizawa & Rose, 2019) and production (Kamaşak et al., 2021), as well as bias in content assessments, as students reported "limited test performance due to inability to express ideas in written English" (Arkın & Osam, 2015, p. 190). In Arkın and Osam's (2015) study, another challenge was less effective use of time in English-medium content lessons (e.g., fewer examples provided by the instructor and fewer questions asked by the students) when compared to the parallel content lessons where the medium was L1-Turkish. One strategy that instructors have been found to occasionally employ to alleviate such challenges is using the L1 in the classroom (e.g., Hu et al., 2014), and allowing the use of the L1 to varying extents in content assessments (Karakaş & Bayyurt, 2019; Sahan & Şahan, 2022).

Another step towards addressing the linguistic needs of students in EMI programs may be to shift the overall approach in HEIs from EMI to Content and Language Integrated Learning (CLIL). The distinctive characteristic of CLIL is its binary focus on language and content learning (Coyle, Hood, & Marsh, 2010), while EMI is usually associated with content learning only (Smit & Dafouz, 2012). While implicit acquisition of relevant linguistic features and items may be expected as a by-product of EMI, the extent of the development of subject-specific language repertoire would benefit from an explicit focus on how knowledge is communicated in specific subjects. The lack of attention to language in EMI poses costs in terms of deeper learning. As Meyer and Coyle (2017) argue, "deeper learning will not be the automatic by-product of subject teaching and learning. Students will only successfully master subject specific literacies in an environment that focuses on building learners' meaning-making potential by enabling them to actively demonstrate their understanding, primarily through the adequate use of appropriate language" (p. 202). Additionally, many students in EMI programs fail to meet the institutional minimum proficiency requirements after one year of English preparatory lessons and have to invest more time and money for another year; and those who fail after the second year are dismissed from their EMI programs. Students who meet the minimum proficiency requirements face another disadvantage in the absence of further (subject-specific) language support once they are in EMI programs, given that English preparatory programs tend to target general academic language competence. Therefore, CLIL may serve to remove a lot of stress on students during their initial years, and can also contribute to students' academic outcomes. This, of course, is a process that requires time, effort, and resources. It will require, among other things, a great deal of preparation and time to lay the groundwork, and prepare qualified staff to respond to both the linguistic and content-related needs of learners.

Translanguaging in EMI classrooms

The co-occurrence of different named languages has been referred to as *code-mixing* or *code-switching* conventionally. The former can be defined as "intra-clausal/sentential alternation" of languages, and the latter as "alternation at the inter-clausal/sentential level" (Lin, 2013, p. 195). However, as pointed out by García and Lin (2017), the concept of code-switching rests upon the conception of the language repertoire of bilinguals as being composed of separate, homogeneous linguistic systems. They argue that *translanguaging*, which involves viewing the language use of bilinguals as reliant on a unified and integrated linguistic system, is a more useful theory (than code-switching) for bilingual education. The translanguaging perspective does not consider the language practice conventionally captured by the term *code-switching* as the simultaneous use of separate, distinct and homogeneous codes. Instead, it acknowledges that bilingual individuals have "one linguistic repertoire with features that have been socially assigned to constructions that are considered "languages," including academic ones" (Velasco & García, 2014, p. 8) and they draw upon their linguistic resources in complex and integrated ways (García, 2009), depending on the social context and communicative demands of a given situation. Given that classroom interactions in EMI settings are characterized by the moment-by-moment unfolding of fluid use of language resources, we also adopt the term translanguaging.

Translanguaging is not unusual in EMI classrooms in Türkiye (Sahan, 2020). Several studies have revealed that both instructors and students use the different named languages in their repertoire within the same classroom, thereby "violating" the officially monolingual policy of their institutions (e.g., Cosgun, 2020; Karakaş, 2019). Based on their observations in seven EMI universities in Türkiye, which revealed the presence of L1 in EMI classrooms, Sahan et al. (2021) suggest that these EMI programs can be described as bilingual educational settings despite being envisioned as monolingual spaces where English is the one and only working language. Indeed, research in other settings has shown that the use of L1 in EMI classrooms serves various functions such as providing scaffolding (Lasagabaster, 2013); building rapport with students (Tien & Li, 2014), explaining complex content (Kim, Kweon, & Kim, 2017), and clarifying grammar or vocabulary (Macaro, Tian, & Chu, 2020). Recent research in EMI universities in Türkiye has also revealed that the L1 is deployed to create "a space for deeper content learning" (Sahan & Rose, 2021, p. 31). Indeed, in their study in various EMI departments in two public universities in

Türkiye, Kırkgöz et al. (2021) conclude that "knowledge acquisition becomes much quicker and more effective for most students when they are instructed through translanguaging since they can compensate for the knowledge gap caused by one of the media with the help of the other(s)." (p. 115).

Although most of the time the languages involved are English and Turkish, other languages have started to play an increasingly larger role. Incoming students most commonly come from Turkic countries such as Turkmenistan, Azerbaijan, and Kyrgyzstan, or Middle Eastern countries such as Iraq, Iran, and Syria. According to the statistics provided by the Council of Higher Education (Table 4), of the top ten countries from where international students arrive in Türkiye, seven have Arabic as their official language.

Table 4. Origin countries of international students coming to Türkiye (2022)

Country	Number of Students
Syria	53097
Azerbaijan	28922
Iraq	17010
Turkmenistan	15578
Iran	14886
Somalia	11074
Afghanistan	9002
Egypt	7847
Yemen	7714
Jordan	6518

Source: Council of Higher Education website: https://istatistik.yok.gov.tr/

One consequence of this is that while English functions as the main common language between local and international students and staff, the transiency of contexts also creates situations where the linguistic ambiance orients towards other languages, which may be realized through the use of another named language or flexible use of multiple named languages. Kırkgöz et al. (2021) has shown this to be the case with L1-Arabic students. They report that L1-Arabic students engage in translanguaging through the use of features from English and Arabic, and at times also from Turkish (as they are exposed to and learn Turkish words in their interactions with their Turkish friends), thereby creating a linguistically richer environment with fluid use of three named languages.

Two recent Ph.D. dissertations have revealed how translanguaging is ingrained in the everyday lives of both local and international students in EMI programs in Türkiye, with various functions and benefits. In Bak (2023), EMI students reported experiencing difficulty and a decrease in comprehension, which required the devotion of extra time to make sense of the content. To increase their comprehension, students used various strategies, which included referring to L1-Turkish sources, using translation software and online dictionaries, or taking notes in the L1, among others. In terms of production, some students reported expressing themselves in Turkish if they were unable to do so in English. Gülle (2023) investigated the potential of integrating translanguaging in content assessments in EMI programs and interviewed students about their EMI experiences at a private EMI university. Student reports showed that translanguaging emerged in various forms both within the classroom setting and in out-of-class learning activities. L1-Turkish and L1-Arabic students were found to take advantage of their L1s in their learning activities in several ways. Instructors were also reported to use or allow students to use their L1 when students were challenged in understanding content in English, and students used their L1 to express themselves in cases when they felt they were unable to fully express their ideas in English. Outside of the classroom, the L1 came into play when students read resources in Turkish or Arabic to support their understanding of the content, took notes in the L1 or in both their languages, discussed topics in group work by utilizing features associated with different languages within the same conversation, or deployed two-way translation when trying to make sense of the textbooks they read. The everyday reality of the EMI programs investigated was presented to be characterized by linguistic diversity and translanguaging. The same study also revealed that students were at times unable (according to their reports) to understand exam questions or to put their content knowledge into words in English during exams, which potentially resulted in lower test performance. When given the opportunity to respond using their full language repertoire, while some students replied exclusively in their L2 or L1, others used both their languages within the same response. The study points to a need to reconsider language support provided to L2-English students, to research the potential (roles) of multi- or translingual assessment, and to conduct needs analyses to understand L1 and L2 disciplinary literacy needs of EMI students in Türkiye (Gülle, 2023).

On a promising note, change is actually taking place, albeit in a gradual manner. Initial insights from a study in which we interviewed instructors from a private (foundation) university in Istanbul, which offers EMI, have revealed that the changing linguistic composition of the student body has triggered changes in material design and teaching practices, and urged instructors to devise strategies to integrate international students' L1s into their classes to foster the comprehension and active participation of these students (Kurt & Gülle, 2023). In terms of material design, for example, a translation exercise that was initially titled "Translate into Turkish" was changed into "In Your Own Language", allowing students to use dictionaries to translate content into their L1, following the diversification of the student population. As for in-class practices, teachers used online English-to-Arabic or English-to-Persian dictionaries on the board when explaining content that was challenging for L1-Arabic or L1-Persian students to understand, or allowed students to use their L1 to explain content to each other. Similar accommodations were made in an EMI university where the first author previously worked. For example, the instructions in the initial English placement test were provided in several languages. The L1s of the incoming students were obtained from the registrar's office and the instructions were translated into as many languages as was needed. Another instance is when instructions on how to use the scantron sheet were added to the test administration upon the realization that, unlike Turkish students, students from some other educational cultures were unfamiliar with the scantron sheet, e.g., a pencil must be used, not a pen.

The studies presented so far make it clear that EMI settings with students from diverse lingua-cultural backgrounds are de-facto translanguaging spaces. In that regard, Jenkins' (2020) suggestion to rename EMI as Translanguaging as Medium of Instruction due to the multilingual environment in EMI settings is an important call. Dafouz and Smit (2016) propose the term EMEMUS, i.e., English-Medium Education in Multilingual University Settings, as a "semantically wider" (p. 3) alternative to EMI – a proposition which captures not only the multilingual nature of universities with an ever-increasing international student makeup, but also the wider learning and teaching experiences outside the classroom by replacing "instruction" with "education". Given the fluid use of language that transcends socio-politically delineated boundaries between named languages, the term "translanguaging" captures the totality of linguistic practices on and beyond university campuses and involves, but is not limited to, English.

"Education" better captures the totality of learning and teaching practices because it involves, but is not limited to, instruction. For these reasons, we argue that the term Translanguaging as a Medium of Education can better capture the learning/teaching and languaging practices in and beyond university classrooms characterized by linguistic variation.

Translanguaging as a Medium of Education

Since students are already using their full repertoire of linguistic resources in the course of individual learning, giving them more space to use the same resources in and out of the classroom might create new opportunities for education. This, of course, does not mean abandoning EMI policies, but rather reconsidering the role of languages and the fluid use of communicative resources. Given that most international and local students struggle with English in EMI, and given that Turkish is an additional challenge for international students in both TMI and EMI, one-language-only policies fail to capture the realities of L2 students' academic lives. Especially during the initial years of HE, the involvement of students' other languages should be regarded as only natural and welcomed by both the lecturers in the classroom and the institutional regulations in the larger context.

Flores and Schissel (2014) point out that rather than waiting for policy shifts an immediate approach would be to work with students and teachers for the move away from a monoglossic perspective. It appears from research results that students and teachers in EMI programs in Türkiye are already taking advantage of the wider language resources rather than strictly following what would be expected in an English-only classroom, although this may not always be done in planned ways. Simply put, the linguistic ideologies of "English only" and "standard English" do not comply with the reality in EMI universities. Research has consistently revealed that students in EMI settings in Türkiye use a mix of named languages in the classroom (Genç, Yüksel & Curle, 2023; Sahan, 2020), lecturers benefit from different linguistic resources (Kırkgöz et al., 2023), and multiple named languages exist in other areas in EMI-university campuses (Karakaş & Bayyurt, 2019). Therefore, existing language policies are breached at multiple levels and in many areas.

While translanguaging practices are evident in EMI HE classrooms in Türkiye as reported in the studies reviewed above, they seem to occur as a result of the fluid, unplanned, moment-by-moment practices of bi/multilingual students and teachers within the classroom; their going beyond what is termed "language-specific performance" by García et al. (2017), which refers to the deployment of features associated with one named-language to express knowledge, at their own initiative; or students' making use of resources in other languages than the language of instruction to construct and further develop their knowledge of the topic at hand. Since these practices occur unplanned, the caution by Meier (2017) is rather relevant for what is happening in many EMI classrooms in HEIs in Türkiye: "a multilingual approach to learning and teaching does not advocate a laissez-faire attitude, where learners and teachers use any languages they like" (p. 156).

While the contexts and participants explored in García et al. (2017) differ from those targeted in the current chapter, we argue that the evolving linguistic landscapes in EMI (and TMI) HE programs in Türkiye make the following description of a translanguaging classroom a model that can be implemented in, and can offer valuable contributions to, these programs:

Teachers in translanguaging classrooms design their instructional units and their assessment systems purposefully and strategically to mobilize all features of their bilingual students' linguistic repertoires, accelerate their content learning and language development, encourage their bilingualism and ways of knowing, strengthen their socioemotional development and bilingual identities, and advance social justice. (García et al., 2017, p. 78)

García et al. (2017) point out that translanguaging pedagogy has three strands: a translanguaging stance, a translanguaging design, and translanguaging shifts. The translanguaging stance is about beliefs, and relates to teachers' understanding of bi/multilinguals as having one language repertoire that includes features that are attributed, from an external perspective, to different named languages. The translanguaging design involves making instructional choices that connect students' home language and language of schooling. Translanguaging shifts are about flexibility and moment-by-moment decisions that incorporate translanguaging even when these are not part of the translanguaging design. García et al.'s (2017) book-length treatment of pedagogical translanguaging is a valuable resource that teachers can greatly benefit from in understanding how the translanguaging perspective can inform and shape their teaching. In this regard, student voices from universities in Türkiye provide similar insights into in what ways translanguaging may become a purposeful pedagogy. L1-Arabic students in Arar et al. (2020), for example, express the need for the use of additional materials in Arabic, communication tools such as translation software that can facilitate interaction, and increasing the number of Arabic resources in the libraries.

In relation to such shifts, a concern is raised by Flores (2013), who argues that the advocates of a shift away from monolingual pedagogical approaches should be wary of the potential of their arguments to support the neoliberal project, which "consists of both a desire to reinforce English hegemony and to mold multilingualism into a commodity that serves the interests of transnational corporations" by creating "dynamic subjects who engage in fluid language practices that fit the needs of global capitalism" (p. 504). Flores (2013) adds that one way of "becom[ing] part of a larger institutional critique of neoliberalism" is through "providing a space for students to experiment with language practices and identities that challenge the universalizing narrative of neoliberalism" (p. 518). In the case of EMI and TMI programs in Turkish HE, the shift towards a translanguaging perspective would challenge the hegemony of English in various ways. It would mean integrating materials written in students' other languages so that students construct and develop knowledge in multiple named languages, which can also serve to increase awareness that English is not "the" language of science. It would also mean creating space for students to take more advantage of their prior learning given that "if students' prior knowledge is encoded in their L1, then their L1 is clearly relevant to their learning even when instruction is through the medium of L2" (Cummins, 2007, p. 231). Additionally, it would mean offering students space to utilize their language resources for conceptualizing and communicating knowledge rather than, for example, keeping students silent only because they cannot yet express their knowledge in English at that particular time, by saying "Please say it in English" or "Ask your questions in English", which is a familiar scene in some EMI courses. The unequal power hierarchies established within English-medium institutions through the exclusion of students' other languages from the classroom and the restriction of their educational and scientific endeavors to English-only can be brought under critical questioning through a translanguaging perspective. Translanguaging creates a space where bilingual students can engage in active participation in the classroom and where their linguistic and cultural identities are valued. In such spaces, the socially constructed hierarchies between languages and cultures are deconstructed, and a more just society is aimed (García et al., 2017).

CONCLUSION

In EMI HEIs in Türkiye, when they arrive at the university, many students begin from CEFR A1 English courses. Kerestecioğlu and Bayyurt (2018) emphasize that offering language support throughout the duration of undergraduate studies is essential due to the inadequacy of a single year of English preparatory classes for students arriving at HEIs with little or no prior language proficiency in English. However, EMI programs tend to be planned with the assumption that after one year of English preparatory classes, students can perform the academic functions expected of them in one of the named languages in their repertoire, English, (a) without any further language support and (b) without utilizing their linguistic resources associated with the other languages in their repertoire. We argue that, to address (a), programs can benefit from, and serve their students better, with a shift from EMI to CLIL, and to address (b), they can take advantage of translanguaging pedagogy, which involves creating opportunities for mobilizing the whole of students' language resources for deeper learning. Students in EMI programs interviewed by Gülle (2023) were found to hold the belief that when they did not limit themselves to only one of the named languages in their repertoire in their learning practices, their mastery of content was both faster (taking less time) and deeper (developing more robust conceptualizations). Similarly, a recent study by Karakaş (2023) revealed that university students in EMI contexts tend to acknowledge the benefits of translanguaging in the classroom for the sake of better content learning even if such practices do not align with institutional or teachers' individual English-only policies. The break of the English-only policy in the classroom was associated by the students not only with deeper learning but also establishing rapport (e.g., use of humor) and building confidence. Karakaş (2023, p. 8) comments "the positive orientations of most students towards these [translanguaging] practices suggest that translanguaging serves valuable functions including pedagogical, managerial and socio-cultural/emotional ones in EMI teaching and learning".

We should also note that what we are proposing is not a one-size-fits-all approach that is blind to contextual variations or students' identifications and aspirations, nor do we remain oblivious to potential challenges and tensions such a shift from the monoglossic ideology to a translanguaging perspective may create. The inclinations and viewpoints of students and teachers might coincide with adherence to English-only regulations (Lasagabaster, 2016), or as Gevers (2018) emphasizes in relation to writing instruction, implementing an expressly translingual pedagogy can face challenges due to required institutional changes, potential lack of teacher knowledge or support, the varying suitability of translingual practices for different proficiency levels, and lack of desire on the part of students to engage in translingual practices. What we are proposing is that the monoglossic ideology that is so entrenched in educational policy is already being challenged at the level of in-class and out-of-class learning practices, but usually in an unplanned manner; therefore, there is a need at the policy level to make decisions that better reflect and better cater to the needs and practices of lingua-culturally diverse student (and instructor) bodies at EMI HEIs in Türkiye, and there is a need at the practice level to conduct research, with a multilingual lens, on the potential of and ways of utilizing the wider language repertoires of multilingual students and to develop classroom pedagogies that take advantage of this repertoire in planned and principled ways. In those respects, EMI classrooms can turn into settings that enact translanguaging spaces – spaces that challenge and transform the monolingual classroom environment, and thus EMI can be reconceptualized as Translanguaging as a Medium of Instruction. This has the potential not only to allow for deeper learning but also to increase social justice as this new orientation "creates the space for fair educational and assessment practices for bilingual students – without the linguistic prejudice that accompanies accepting only the linguistic features of standard English – the language of power." (García et al., 2017, p. 53).

In a multilingual setting where most students and staff speak multiple named languages, any regulation or rule that implicitly or explicitly discourages individuals from using their whole linguistic repertoire goes against reality and is a road to nowhere. A failure to acknowledge linguistic diversity not only constrains us from understanding the educational potential of multilingualism in HE but also hurts social justice (Jenkins, 2019), by perpetuating imperialism in native linguistic norms (Phillipson, 1992). The face of EMI is changing in Türkiye due to socio-political reasons such as migration, and also economic reasons that commercialize HE. As a result, the country and HEIs are becoming more multicultural and hosting more diversity. Linguistic and cultural norms are more fluid than ever before. For these reasons, translanguaging as the medium of education can be promising for the academic development and empowering of students in Turkish HEIs. A translanguaging approach in EMI can also help us avoid the pitfalls of the monoglossic ideology that does not reflect reality in the classrooms, and expects students and teachers to align with unrealistic ideals. The regulatory insistence on an English-only policy does not do justice to the actual language practices within EMI settings. Therefore, instead of simplistic top-down regulations, the complexity of the situation should be researched in its context to understand how cultural and linguistic diversity unfolds in and out of the classroom. Such research can focus on how one-language-only policies are breached in the classroom by students and teachers, what kind of academic and social purposes these breaches serve, and what kind of influences they have on students in terms of content learning, linguistic repertoire building, and identity construction, among others. EMI (and TMI) programs can better determine how to cater to their (international) student body through a more complete understanding of how students create meaning through their whole linguistic and semiotic resources.

REFERENCES

Aizawa, I., & Rose, H. (2019). An analysis of Japan's English as medium of instruction initiatives within higher education: The gap between meso-level policy and micro-level practice. *Higher Education*, *77*(6), 1125–1142. doi:10.100710734-018-0323-5

Akyay-Engin, E. (2019). Effective foreign language teaching: ELT students' and teachers' beliefs. *International Language Teacher Education Research Group (ILTERG) Conference Proceedings* (pp. 75-85). Antalya, Turkey. www.iltergconference.org

Antalya Bilim University. (2023, August 12). *Language of education*. Antalya. https://antalya.edu.tr/tr/fakulte-ve-enstituler/bolumler/elektrik-ve-bilgisayar-muhendisligi-tezli-ingilizce/icerik/hakkimizda-1/egitim-dili

Arar, K., Kondakci, Y., Kaya Kasikci, S., & Erberk, E. (2020). Higher education policy for displaced people: Implications of Turkey's higher education policy for Syrian migrants. *Higher Education Policy*, *33*(2), 265–285. doi:10.105741307-020-00181-2

Arkın, E., & Osam, N. (2015). English-medium higher education. A case study in a Turkish university context. In S. Dimova, A. K. Hultgren, & C. Jensen (Eds.), *English-medium instruction in higher education in Europe* (pp. 177–199). Mouton de Gruyter. doi:10.1515/9781614515272-010

Bak, Ç. (2023). *Effects of foreign language-medium instruction on content courses in higher education.* [Unpublished doctoral dissertation, Boğaziçi University].

Baynham, M. (2020). Comment on Part 1: Collaborative Relationships. In E. Moore, J. Bradley, & J. Simpson (Eds.), *Translanguaging as Transformation* (pp. 15–22). Multilingual Matters.

Bo, W. V., Fu, M., & Lim, W. Y. (2022). Revisiting English language proficiency and its impact on the academic performance of domestic university students in Singapore. *Language Testing*, 1–20. doi:10.1177/02655322221106462

British Council & TEPAV. (2015, November). *The state of English in higher education in Turkey: A baseline study.* British Council. https://www.britishcouncil.org.tr/sites/default/files/he_baseline_study_book_web_-_son.pdf

Cennetkuşu, N. G., & Ölmez, M. (2022). Transition and adaptation to higher education: Syrian immigrant students in Turkey within cultural, social, and linguistic context. *Socrates Journal of Interdisciplinary Social Studies*, 20, 1–19.

Cho, Y., & Bridgeman, B. (2012). Relationship of TOEFL iBT scores to academic performance: Some evidence from American universities. *Language Testing*, 29(3), 421–442. doi:10.1177/0265532211430368

Cosgun, G. (2020). Investigating the perceptions of students on the use of L1 in departmental courses in a Turkish EMI university. *The Journal of Language Teaching and Learning*, 10(2), 30–40.

Costa, F., & Coleman, J. A. (2013). A survey of English-medium instruction in Italian higher education. *International Journal of Bilingual Education and Bilingualism*, 16(1), 3–19. doi:10.1080/13670050.2012.676621

Council of Higher Education. (2017). *Yükseköğretimde uluslararasılaşma strateji belgesi 2018-2022 [Internationalization strategy document in higher education 2018-2022].* Council of Higher Education. https://www.yok.gov.tr/Documents/AnaSayfa/Yuksekogretimde_Uluslararasilasma_Strateji_Belgesi_2018_2022.pdf

Council of Higher Education. (2021). *Yükseköğretimde hedef odaklı uluslararasılaşma [Target-oriented internationalization policy in higher education].* Council of Higher Education. https://www.yok.gov.tr/Documents/Yayinlar/Yayinlarimiz/2021/yuksekogretimde-hedef-odakli-uluslararasilasma.pdf

Council of Higher Education. (2023a). *Study finder.* Council of Higher Education. https://www.studyinturkiye.gov.tr/StudySearch/List

Council of Higher Education. (2023c). *Uyruğa göre öğrenci sayıları raporu [Student numbers report by nationality].* Council of Higher Education. https://istatistik.yok.gov.tr/

Coyle, D., Hood, P., & Marsh, D. (2010). *CLIL: Content and language integrated learning.* Cambridge University Press. doi:10.1017/9781009024549

Cummins, J. (2007). Rethinking monolingual instructional strategies in multilingual classrooms. *Canadian Journal of Applied Linguistics*, 10(2), 221–240.

Dafouz, E., & Smit, U. (2016). Towards a dynamic conceptual framework for English-medium education in multilingual university settings. *Applied Linguistics*, *37*(3), 397–415. doi:10.1093/applin/amu034

DeardenJ.AkincioglaM.MacaroE. (2016). *EMI in Turkish universities: Collaborative planning and student voices*. Oxford: Oxford University Press. doi:10.13140/RG.2.2.15435.39204

Dereli, B. (2018). *Refugee integration through higher education: Syrian refugees in Turkey. Policy Report, UNU Institute on Globalization, Culture and Mobility*. UNU-GCM.

Directorate General of Migration Management. (2023a). *Temporary protection. General of Migration Management. (2023b). Residence permits*. Directorate General of Migration Management. https://en.goc.gov.tr/residence-permits

Dogancay-Aktuna, S. (1998). The spread of English in Turkey and its current sociolinguistic profile. *Journal of Multilingual and Multicultural Development*, *19*(1), 24–39. doi:10.1080/01434639808666340

Ege, F., Yuksel, D., & Curle, S. (2022). A corpus-based analysis of discourse strategy use by English-Medium Instruction university lecturers in Turkey. *Journal of English for Academic Purposes*, *58*, 58. doi:10.1016/j.jeap.2022.101125

Erdoğan, A., & Erdoğan, M. M. (2020). Syrian university students in Turkish higher education: Immediate vulnerabilities, future challenges for the European higher education area. In A. Curaj, L. Deca, & R. Pricopie (Eds.), *European higher education area: Challenges for a new decade*. Springer. doi:10.1007/978-3-030-56316-5_16

Esen, O. (2022, February 5). University study offers way to integrate Syrian refugees. *University World News*. https://www.universityworldnews.com/post.php?story=20220203061816422

Flores, N. (2013). The unexamined relationship between neoliberalism and plurilingualism: A cautionary tale. *TESOL Quarterly*, *47*(3), 500–520. doi:10.1002/tesq.114

Flores, N., & Schissel, J. L. (2014). Dynamic bilingualism as the norm: Envisioning a heteroglossic approach to standards-based reform. *TESOL Quarterly*, *48*(3), 454–479. doi:10.1002/tesq.182

García, O. (2009). *Bilingual education in the 21st century: A global perspective*. Blackwell/Wiley.

García, O., Johnson, S. I., & Seltzer, K. (2017). *The translanguaging classroom: Leveraging student bilingualism for learning*. Caslon.

García, O., & Lin, A. M. Y. (2017). Translanguaging in bilingual education. In O. García & A. M. Y. Lin (Eds.), *Bilingual and multilingual education* (pp. 1–14). Springer. doi:10.1007/978-3-319-02258-1_9

García, O., & Torres-Guevara, R. (2010). Monoglossic ideologies and language policies in the education of U.S. Latinas/os. In E. G. Murillo Jr, S. A. Villenas, R. T. Galván, J. S. Muñoz, C. Martínez, & M. Machado-Casas (Eds.), *Handbook of Latinos and education: Theory, research, and practice* (pp. 182–193). Routledge.

Genc, E., Yuksel, D., & Curle, S. (2023). Lecturers' translanguaging practices in English-taught lectures in Turkey. *Journal of Multilingual Theories and Practices*, *4*(1), 8–31. doi:10.1558/jmtp.23945

Gevers, J. (2018). Translingualism revisited: Language difference and hybridity in L2 writing. *Journal of Second Language Writing*, *40*, 73–83. doi:10.1016/j.jslw.2018.04.003

Gülle, T. (2023). Language challenges in English medium higher education and translingual assessment as an alternative tool. [Unpublished doctoral dissertation]. Boğaziçi University.

Güngör, H., & Soysal, T. (2021). Türk yükseköğretiminde Suriyeli mülteciler [Syrian refugees in Turkish higher education]. *Milli Eğitim Dergisi, 50*(1), 1245–1264.

Gürtler, K., & Kronewald, E. (2015). Internationalization and English-medium instruction in German higher education. In S. Dimova, A. K. Hultgren, & C. Jensen (Eds.), *English-medium instruction in higher education in Europe* (pp. 89–114). Mouton de Gruyter. doi:10.1515/9781614515272-006

Hu, G., Li, L., & Lei, J. (2014). English-medium instruction at a Chinese University: Rhetoric and reality. *Language Policy, 13*(1), 21–40. doi:10.100710993-013-9298-3

Istanbul Technical University. (2023, August 12). *Management Engineering (100% English)*. Istanbul Technical University. https://islmuh.itu.edu.tr/en/academic/education/undergraduate-programs/management-engineering

Jenkins, J. (2019). English medium instruction in higher education: The role of English as a lingua franca. In X. Gao (Ed.), *Second handbook of English teaching* (pp. 91–108). Springer.

Jenkins, J. (2020). Red herrings and the case of language in UK higher education. *Nordic Journal of English Studies, 19*(3), 59–67. doi:10.35360/njes.577

Jones, E. (2017). Problematising and reimagining the notion of 'international student experience'. *Studies in Higher Education, 42*(5), 933–943. doi:10.1080/03075079.2017.1293880

Kamaşak, R., Rose, H., & Sahan, K. (2021). Quality of instruction and student outcomes in English-medium programs in Turkey. New Connections in EMI Turkey Research Partnership Fund 2020. Turkey: British Council.

Karakaş, A. (2019). A critical look at the phenomenon of 'a mixed-up use of Turkish and English' in English-medium instruction universities in Turkey. *Journal of Higher Education and Science, 9*(2), 205–215. doi:10.5961/jhes.2019.322

Karakaş, A. (2023). Translanguaging in content-based EMI classes through the lens of Turkish students: Self-reported practices, functions and orientations. *Linguistics and Education, 77*, 101221. doi:10.1016/j.linged.2023.101221

Karakaş, A., & Bayyurt, Y. (2019). The scope of linguistic diversity in the language policies, practices, and linguistic landscape of a Turkish EMI university. In J. Jenkins & A. Mauranen (Eds.), *Linguistic diversity on the EMI campus: Insider accounts of the use of English and other languages in universities within Asia, Australasia, and Europe* (pp. 96–122). Routledge. doi:10.4324/9780429020865-5

Kerestecioğlu, F., & Bayyurt, Y. (2018). *English as the medium of instruction in universities: A holistic approach*. Symposium conducted at the meeting of Kadir Has University, Istanbul.

Kim, E. G., Kweon, S. O., & Kim, J. (2017). Korean engineering students' perceptions of English-medium instruction (EMI) and L1 use in EMI classes. *Journal of Multilingual and Multicultural Development, 38*(2), 130–145. doi:10.1080/01434632.2016.1177061

Kırkgöz, Y., İnci-Kavak, V., Karakaş, A., & Panero, S. M. (2023). Translanguaging practices in Turkish EMI classrooms: Commonalities and differences across two academic disciplines. *System*, *113*, 102982. doi:10.1016/j.system.2023.102982

Kırkgoz, Y., Moran Panero, S., Karakas, A., & Inci Kavak, V. (2021). *Classroom discourse in EMI courses in Turkey: On the dynamics of translanguaging practices*. British Council.

Kurt, Y. & Bayyurt, Y. (forthcoming). English Medium Instruction in Higher Education in Turkey. In K. Bolton, W. Botha and B. Lin (Eds.), The Routledge Handbook of English-medium instruction (EMI) in higher education. Routledge.

Lasagabaster, D. (2013). The use of the L1 in CLIL classes: The teachers' perspective. *Latin American Journal of Content & Language Integrated Learning*, *6*(2), 1–21. doi:10.5294/laclil.2013.6.2.1

Lasagabaster, D. (2015). Multilingual language policy: Is it becoming a misnomer at university level. In S. Dimova, A. K. Hultgren, & C. Jensen (Eds.), *English-medium instruction in higher education in Europe* (pp. 115–136). Mouton de Gruyter. doi:10.1515/9781614515272-007

Lasagabaster, D. (2016). Translanguaging in ESL and content-based teaching: Is it valued? In D. Lasagabaster & A. Doiz (Eds.), *CLIL experiences in secondary and tertiary education: In search of good practices* (pp. 233–258). Peter Lang. doi:10.3726/978-3-0351-0929-0/13

Li, M. (2018). The effectiveness of a bilingual education program at a Chinese university: A case study of social science majors. *International Journal of Bilingual Education and Bilingualism*, *21*(8), 897–912. doi:10.1080/13670050.2016.1231164

Lin, A. (2013). Classroom code-switching: Three decades of research. *Applied Linguistics Review*, *4*(1), 195–218. doi:10.1515/applirev-2013-0009

Macaro, E., Tian, L., & Chu, L. (2020). First and second language use in English medium instruction contexts. *Language Teaching Research*, *24*(3), 382–402. doi:10.1177/1362168818783231

Meier, G. S. (2017). The multilingual turn as a critical movement in education: Assumptions, challenges and a need for reflection. *Applied Linguistics Review*, *8*(1), 131–161. doi:10.1515/applirev-2016-2010

Meyer, O., & Coyle, D. (2017). Pluriliteracies teaching for learning: Conceptualizing progression for deeper learning in literacies development. *European Journal of Applied Linguistics*, *5*(2), 199–222. doi:10.1515/eujal-2017-0006

Moore-Jones, P. J. (2015). Linguistic imposition: The policies and perils of English as a medium of instruction in the United Arab Emirates. [JELTAL]. *Journal of ELT and Applied Linguistics*, *3*(1), 63–72.

OECD. (2022). International and foreign student mobility in tertiary education (2015 and 2020): International or foreign student enrolment as a percentage of total tertiary enrolment. In *Education at a Glance 2022: OECD Indicators*. OECD Publishing. doi:10.1787/b6a69272-

Özdemir-Yılmazer, M. (2022). Direct access to English-medium higher education in Turkey: Variations in entry language scores. *Dil Eğitimi ve Araştırmaları Dergisi*, *8*(2), 325–345. doi:10.31464/jlere.1105651

Phillipson, R. (1992). *Linguistic imperialism*. Oxford University Press.

Reagan, T., & Schreffler, S. (2005). Higher education language policy and the challenge of linguistic imperialism: A Turkish case study. In A. Lin & P. Martin (Eds.), *Decolonisation, globalisation: Language-in-education policy and practice* (pp. 115–130). Multilingual Matters. doi:10.21832/9781853598265-009

Sahan, K. (2020). ELF interactions in English-medium engineering classrooms. *ELT Journal, 74*(4), 418–427. doi:10.1093/elt/ccaa033

Sahan, K., & Rose, H. (2021). Problematising the E in EMI: Translanguaging as a pedagogic alternative to English-only hegemony in university contexts. In B. Paulsrud, Z. Tian, & J. Toth (Eds.), *English-medium instruction and translanguaging* (pp. 22–33). Multilingual Matters. doi:10.21832/9781788927338-005

Sahan, K., Rose, H., & Macaro, E. (2021). Models of EMI pedagogies: At the interface of language use and interaction. *System, 101*, 102616. doi:10.1016/j.system.2021.102616

Sahan, K., & Şahan, Ö. (2022). Content and language in EMI assessment practices: Challenges and beliefs at an engineering faculty in Turkey. In Y. Kırkgöz & A. Karakaş (Eds.), *English as the medium of instruction in Turkish higher education* (pp. 155–174). Springer. doi:10.1007/978-3-030-88597-7_8

Selvi, A. F. (2022). Resisting English medium instruction through digital grassroots activism. *Journal of Multilingual and Multicultural Development, 43*(2), 81–97. doi:10.1080/01434632.2020.1724120

Shohamy, E. (2006). *Language policy: Hidden agendas and new approaches*. Routledge. doi:10.4324/9780203387962

Smit, U., & Dafouz, E. (2012). Integrating content and language in higher education: An introduction to English-medium policies, conceptual issues and research practices across Europe. *AILA Review, 25*, 1–12. doi:10.1075/aila.25.01smi

Taquini, R., Finardi, K. R., & Amorim, G. B. (2017). English as a medium of instruction at Turkish state universities. *Education and Linguistics Research, 3*(2), 35–53. doi:10.5296/elr.v3i2.11438

Tatzl, D. (2011). English-medium masters' programmes at an Austrian university of applied sciences: Attitudes, experiences and challenges. *Journal of English for Academic Purposes, 10*(4), 252–270. doi:10.1016/j.jeap.2011.08.003

The Guardian. (n.d). Top 20 countries for international students. *The Gurardian.* https://www.theguardian.com/higher-education-network/blog/2014/jul/17/top-20-countries-international-students

Tien, C. Y., & Li, C. S. D. (2014). Codeswitching in a university in Taiwan. In R. Barnard, R., & J. McLellan (Eds), Codeswitching in university English-medium classes: Asian perspectives (pp. 24-42). Bristol: Multilingual Matters.

Time Association. (2022, November 28). *International student mobility at a Glance 2022*. Top International Managers in Engineering. https://timeassociation.org/2022/11/28/international-student-mobility-key-numbers-2022/

UNESCO. (2023, August 12). *Definition of "International (or internationally mobile) students"*. UNESCO. https://uis.unesco.org/glossary

UNHCR. (2023). *Tertiary Education.* UNHCR. https://www.unhcr.org/tertiary-education.html.

Velasco, P., & García, O. (2014). Translanguaging and the writing of bilingual learners. *Bilingual Research Journal*, *37*(1), 6–23. doi:10.1080/15235882.2014.893270

Wei, L. (2011). Moment analysis and translanguaging space: Discursive construction of identities by multilingual Chinese youth in Britain. *Journal of Pragmatics*, *43*(5), 1222–1235. doi:10.1016/j.pragma.2010.07.035

Yağmur, K. (2001). Turkish and other languages in Turkey. In G. Extra & D. Gorter (Eds.), *The other languages of Europe* (pp. 407–428). European Cultural Foundation.

Yıldız, A. (Ed.). (2019a). *Integration of refugee students in European higher education: Comparative country cases*. Yaşar University Publications.

Yıldız, A. (2019b). *Suriye uyruklu öğrencilerin Türkiye'de yükseköğretime katılımları* [*Participation of Syrian students in higher education in Türkiye*]. Yaşar Üniversitesi Yayınları.

Yıldız, M., Soruç, A., & Griffiths, C. (2017). Challenges and needs of students in the EMI (English as a medium of instruction) classroom. *Konin Language Studies*, *5*(4), 387–402.

Yıldız, M., & Yeşilyurt, S. (2017). Use or Avoid? The Perceptions of Prospective English Teachers in Turkey about L1 Use in English Classes. *English Language Teaching*, *10*(1), 84–96. doi:10.5539/elt.v10n1p84

Zhu, H., & Li, W. (2020). Translanguaging, identity, and migration. In J. Jackson (Eds.), The Routledge handbook of language and intercultural communication (2nd ed.) (pp. 234–248). Routledge.

KEY TERMS AND DEFINITIONS

English-Medium Instruction: The use of English to teach academic content to students for whom English is a second language.

International Student: A student who is not a citizen or permanent resident of the country where they are receiving formal education.

Monoglossic Perspective: The assumption that takes monolingualism as the norm and follows a strict separation of named languages.

Multicultural: Involving or equipped with cultural features and practices that are associated with different communities of practice

Multilingual: (It can refer to people or settings) A person who uses, or can use, more than one named language for discursive/communicative purposes, or a setting where more than one language is used/being used.

Named Language: Language features and practices that are socio-politically associated with particular (a) group(s) of speakers and are given a specific name, e.g., English, Turkish, Arabic.

Translanguaging: Flexible and dynamic use of language and other semiotic resources for meaning making, communication and interaction that transcend boundaries between socially constructed named languages and modalities.

Section 6
Intranational Migration

Chapter 11
Migration and Language Dynamics:
Reflections From the University of Education Community, Ghana

Esther Yeboah Danso-Wiredu
https://orcid.org/0000-0003-0310-9741
University of Education, Winneba, Ghana

Emma Sarah Eshun
University of Education, Winneba, Ghana

ABSTRACT

Many different cultural traits are assimilated through migration; one such trait is language. In the processes of migration, many languages are moved from their ecological domain to new ecologies. About 60 known languages are spoken in the country of Ghana, and language experts argue that at the initial stages of migration, migrants might keep their indigenous languages. However, with time, the intents of maintaining the original language become wobbly. This study examines language dynamics in migration at University of Education, a multilinguistic community with diverse migrants. This case study uses a mixed methods approach. Findings indicate evidence of code-switching, code-mixing, dilution of original language, language shift, and total loss of original language and development of a new language. Negotiation of language use among migrants is paramount in or during migration so that existing indigenous languages will be saved from extinction as well as to maintain their vitality and the identity of the people who owns it.

DOI: 10.4018/978-1-6684-8761-7.ch011

INTRODUCTION

Migration is defined as movement across the boundary of an aerial unit; this could be within or outside a country (Castles, 2000; Geremia et al., 2014). Migration has become a frequent occurrence in human society, with hundreds of millions of people having migrated or planning to migrate in the course of their lifetimes. National populations have not only expanded but continue to maintain an accelerated rate of growth (Lewis, 1971; White, 2016). Migration then becomes a major cause of demographic distribution within and beyond country borders. There are numerous reasons why people migrate; some with the intention of eventually returning to their original places of residence, whilst others vouch never to return because of the conditions that pushed them out. In Ghana, many people migrate from their places of origin to other places in the country for economic reasons (Czaika & Reinprecht, 2022; Kwankye et al, 2009; Sabates-Wheeler et al, 2008; Wong, 2014). However, studies have revealed other motivations for migration: Women, especially, have been found to migrate mostly on marital grounds (Awumbila, 2015).

It has also been suggested that migration is a key extra-linguistic factor leading to contact-induced language change (Czaika & Reinprecht, 2022; Kerswill, 2006). That is, in every case of migration, except where a homogeneous group of people moves to an isolated location, language or dialect contact ensues (Kerswill, 2006; Regan, 2017; Thomason & Kaufman 1988; Trudgill 1994). It follows, therefore, that migration has profound sociolinguistic consequences, as the demographic balance of the outgoing and incoming populations is altered. Sociolinguistically, the critical directional parameter is that of an in-out migration, which typically brings with it demographic changes in terms of age, socio-economic class, ethnicity, language, and politics. At the same time, social network densities will change both for the migrants and the destination societies, with the result being that both language change and language shifts (i.e., from one language to another) may increase (Kerswill, 2006; Waldinger, 2015).

Another noticeable effect of migration is the gradual eradication of ethnicity, language differentials and traditions (European Union, 2018; Lewis, 1971). Other effects include inter-marriage and assimilation of cultures. For instance, emigrants may adopt some of the cultural traits of their new place of abode and also abandon some of their existing cultural traits. Of the many different cultural traits that are assimilated, one key trait is language. This is the primary reason why, on a global scale, people are encouraged to learn other languages: to enhance their possible modes of communication as they move out of their immediate environment (Gong et. al, 2020; Hampel & Stickler, 2005). However, in the process of learning other languages, people can dilute their own original languages. Many African countries have diluted their rich African native languages because of the contact they have had with the colonial masters. This process continues today due to migration (Danso-Wiredu & Brako, 2021; Okafor et al, 2022).

There are more than sixty indigenous Ghanaian languages spoken across the country (Lentz & Nugent, 2000; Owu-Ewie, 2017), of which only fifteen - Akuapem Twi, Asante Twi, Dagaare, Dagbani, Dangme, Ewe, Mfantse, Ga, Gonja, Gurune, Kasem, Nzema, Kusaal, Sisaali, Buli - are studied in schools (Lentz & Nugent, 2000; Owu-Ewie, 2017). Language experts (Bhugra & Becker, 2005; Olwig, 2013; Rumbaut, 2004) explain that individuals in the initial stages of migration maintain their indigenous languages, especially if the migration was carried out by the entire family. However, with time, the original languages are diluted and even become extinct when the generations that follow refuse to speak their original languages to embrace those of their new destinations. For example, such is usually the case because local languages are geographically based and, as individuals and communities move away from their hometown, they are usually obligated to learn other languages, especially those who speak minority languages.

Migration and Language Dynamics

Children of migrant families are required to learn languages other than their original languages in schools because of institutional limitations. For example, school-going children from most parts of the Central Region of Ghana who speak other languages (such as Effutu and Guan) must learn Mfantse in school. The Mo, Ligbi and Nafaana people from the then Brong Ahafo Region are made to learn Asante Twi. The speakers of Guan dialects like Sele, Siwu, Avatime in the Volta region have to learn Ewe while the Sisaala and Lobi in Upper West are forced to learn Dagaare (Lentz & Nugent, 2000; Owu-Ewie, 2017). Apart from this, inter-ethnic marriages also minimize the ability for migrants to keep speaking their indigenous languages, especially when there are children involved in the marriage. Most couples speak one Ghanaian language (usually from one of the spouses) at home or totally forfeit the speaking of any Ghanaian language to the speaking of English.

Given the above, this chapter examines the issue of language in migration on the basis that, in cases of cross-linguistic migration, there is a reduced likelihood of maintaining the original language. In this empirical study, there is evidence among participants of both dilution of the original language and total loss of the original language. These occurrences are also represented in relevant literature, such as in the multilingual repertoires of young adult Xhosa mother tongue speakers (George, 2006); in the language and identity formation of students in Zambia (Kasonde, 2015); and in the immigrant dialects and language maintenance practices of Limburg and Swabian speakers in Australia (Pauwels, 2010). This study contributes to the existing literature on language dynamics in intranational migration, by investigating it from a different geographical perspective.

This chapter discusses findings from a case study that focused on staff of the University of Education, Winneba (UEW). UEW was selected because, like many formal institutions in Ghana, most of the staff migrated from other parts of the country to settle in Winneba. This provided a fruitful context for the researchers to delve into migration, by investigating UEW staff's usage of indigenous languages in a new geographical area which does not require their practical use. The chapter is organized into four sections, as follows: Section One, which is the introduction, examines the language situation in Ghana; Section Two discusses the theory, study setting, and methodology; Section Three presents the study's findings; and Section Four summarises and concludes the paper.

Conceptual Framework

Migration speeds the process of diffusion of innovative ideas, intensifies spatial interaction and transforms regions (Boyle, 2014; Lee, 2015). This chapter conceptualizes migration as a cause of both the diffusion as well as the total transformation of languages. We refer to these processes as social transformation and as a convenient label to facilitate discussion of the complexity, interconnectedness, variability, contextuality and multi-level mediation of the transformations that languages go through in the migration process, which invariably leads to code switching, code mixing, language shifting or language loss (George, 2006; Kasonde, 2015). Further, we recognize that the reality of today's globalisation processes leads to higher and more pervasive levels of economic, political, social and cultural integration than ever before (Castles, 2016; Lechner & Boli, 2020).

In migration, a plethora of interactions occur as migrants come into contact with other cultures. The languages of the migrants go through different forms of transformation as users of the languages pass them on from one person to the other. Interlinguistic contact in migration may lead to code switching[1]; code mixing[2], and language shift[3], especially in either diglossic[4] or triglossic[5] situations. Other factors that may occur in migration include total loss or death of original languages and development of new language varieties such as creoles. Language death occurs where a particular language is no longer used. If a language is not transferred intergenerationally, when the last speaker dies, so does the language. Language extinction is particularly worrisome due to the intimate relationship between people, their language and culture. Ghanaians who cannot speak their local languages are seen as culturally "lost" to their ethnic groups. Language preservation therefore implies cultural preservation. This chapter draws on the aforementioned concepts in relation to responses from the study respondents.

Study Setting and Methodology

Like most African countries, Ghana is ethnically diverse, and the basis of this diversity is largely seen in the different languages spoken and other cultural traits depicted by different ethnic groups. According to Anyidoho and Dakubu (2008) and Godefroidt et al. (2016), for the people of Ghana, language appears to be the main marker of sub-national ethnic identity. According to the 2010 and 2021 National Population and Housing Census, Ghana boasts a high degree of linguistic and cultural heterogeneity, as depicted in Table 1.

Table 1. Major ethnic groups in Ghana

Ethnic Group	2010 (%)	2021 (%)
Akan	47.5	45.7
Mole-Dagbani	16.6	18.5
Ewe	13.9	12.8
Ga-Adangbe	7.4	7.1
Mande	1.1	2.0
Grusi	N/A	2.7
Guan	N/A	3.2
Gurma	N/A	6.4
Other	13.4	1.6

The locus of this study, Winneba, contributes to this national diversity, and is found in the Central Region of Ghana. Winneba town is the capital of the Effutu Municipal Assembly. According to community leaders, the town was traditionally known as Simpa, named after one (Osimpam) who led the Effutu people from Northern Ghana to their present location (Effutu Municipal, 2011). Centuries later, the Europeans who visited the land constantly referred to it as the "windy bay" owing to its serene and breezy sandy beaches and gentle rolling landscape. From this appellation, the name Simpa gradually gave way to the more popular name, Winneba. The people of Winneba speak the Effutu language. Historically, Winneba was a fishing port and was once a harbour town important in the past to the economy of Ghana (Danso-Wiredu, 2016; Dickson, 1965).

Winneba, like many other cities and towns in Ghana, has gradually evolved from a fishing community to an educational town. The main economic activity among the indigenous population remains fishing. Other economic activities in the town include commerce, service and manufacturing (Danso-Wiredu, 2016; Effutu Municipal, 2011). The service sector employs a large number of migrants. Winneba has a total population of 56,356, according to the 2010 population census. The population of the municipality stands at 107,798.

In investigating the migration and language practices of staff members at the University of Education, Winneba, this study draws on a primarily qualitative data collection process. However, due to the large size of the dataset, the data was partially analysed using quantitative tools such as descriptive analysis. As such, the study can be described as qualitative-quantitative (Richards, 2006), ensuring rigour in the analysis and interpretation of the large qualitative data set (White et al., 2012). With this approach, the qualitative data collection allowed the authors to access more detailed information whilst the quantitative data analysis enabled the views of large quantities of participants to be considered. The study employed a purposive sampling technique to recruit migrants working at UEW.

The researchers designed a semi-structured interview protocol and distributed it through a Google Form link which allowed respondents to provide open-ended reasons for their selected answers. The link was sent to UEW WhatsApp group platforms with over 600 members, purposively requesting staff from the university who are migrants to complete the form. 141 people completed and returned the interview guide. The collected data were then analyzed using a thematic inductive qualitative analysis and descriptive statistics to analyze the demographic characteristics and specific issues related to respondents' demographics.

Findings and Discussion

The 141 participants primarily represented a middle-class income group with high educational levels, with about 65% of the sample being male. This is consistent with studies in the literature (Adu, 2020; Christel, 2020) which indicate that there are more men than women with higher education degrees and, consequently, working in university settings in Ghana. Respondents included individuals from various ethnic backgrounds, as illustrated in Table 2 below.

Table 2. Demographic features of respondents

Variable	Frequency (n)	Percentage (%)
Gender		
Male	92	65.2
Female	49	34.8
Age Range		
21-30	4	2.8
31-40	57	40.4
41-50	35	24.8
51+	45	31.9
Level of Education Achieved		
PhD	66	46.8
MPhil	59	41.8
MA/MEd	14	9.9
Bachelor's	2	1.4
Ethnic Background		
Akan	78	55.3
Ewe	25	17.7
Ga-Adangbe	15	10.6
Guan	12	8.5
Other	11	7.8
Primary Occupation		
Accountant	3	2.1
Administrator	11	7.7
Auditor	2	1.4
Estate Officer	3	2.1
Lecturer	119	84.3
Research Fellow	3	2.1

Note. N=141

The majority of participants have lived in multiple parts of the country, and some even lived outside Ghana before migrating to Winneba and working at UEW. Participants in the study sample have lived in Winneba from a year to over 45 years, as shown in Table 3.

Migration and Language Dynamics

Table 3. Number of years respondents have lived in Winneba

Length of Residency (years)	Frequency (n)	Percentage (%)
1-9	53	37.6
10-19	35	24.8
20-29	29	20.6
30-39	14	9.9
40+	10	7.1

Note. N=141

As Table 4 indicates, some respondents can speak up to three and four Ghanaian languages.

Table 4. Ghanaian languages spoken by respondents

Language(s) Spoken	Frequency (n)	Percentage (%)
Effutu only	12	8.5
Mfantse only	34	24.1
Mfantse & Effutu	15	10.6
Mfantseante, Effutu, & Ahanta	4	2.8
Mfantse, Effutu, Ahanta, & Gomoa	3	2.1
Ga only	3	2.1
Ga & Effutu	10	7.1
Ga, Mfantse, & Twi	3	2.1
Twi only	27	19.1
Twi & Ga	7	5.0
Twi, Ga, & Hausa	1	0.7
Twi, Mfantse, & Effutu	10	7.1
Twi, Mfantse, & Ewe	6	4.3
Twi, Ga, & Ewe	5	3.5
Twi, Ga, Ewe, & Dangbe	1	0.7

Note. N=141

The Impact of Early Life Experiences on Local Language Use

Part of the interview protocol inquired about the experiences of respondents in relation to their initial opportunities to acquire their local languages in their hometowns. Findings revealed that 53.9% of the respondents spent their early lives outside of their hometowns. This means that, right from infancy, these respondents were exposed to different languages. As children, they learned up to three languages as, usually, the parents (if they speak the same or similar languages) continue to speak a local language at home and the children study a Ghanaian language at school in addition to the community's language (if different from the one learned at school).

When respondents were asked if they spoke their local languages in their childhood, 78.6% of them responded that they did. However, as soon as children start going to school, playing outside the home, or participating in community activities, they are exposed to different local languages as well as the English language introduced to them at school. This explains why the remaining 21.4% of respondents reported that they did not speak their local languages in their early lives. These responses represent cases in which parents do not speak the same local languages and/or do not pass their local languages on to their children. The following excerpts juxtapose the perspectives of children and parents in relation to this phenomenon:

I feel bad that I cannot speak my parents' language, I feel lost and I pray I can visit and get in touch with my family members but my work and the distance make it difficult. My daddy speaks Twi and my mummy speaks Ewe. I cannot speak any of them. I actually cannot blame my parents much because they speak different languages. [27-year-old assistant lecturer]

The children blame me for not being able to speak my local language, but it is not my fault, we have lived in many places and unfortunately, my husband and I speak different local languages. I try sometimes, my husband doesn't care about them speaking his language, but he speaks it with his family when they come around. [55-year-old administrator]

In such situations, the parents (if well-educated) speak English or, in other cases, even the parents speak a neutral language at home (usually, the language of their new location). Those who did not grow up in their hometowns cited migration as the main reason why they no longer speak their home languages, as exemplified in the interview excerpt below:

I left my hometown which is Naandom, Northern region at the age of 12 for Damango. I was speaking Dagaare, then and when I got to Damango I continued speaking Dagaare and learnt Gonja. Then I went to Tamale to attend Polytechnic where I learned Dagbani as well. I met my husband there. Then I got married and moved to Apam. My husband speaks Dakomba so I speak English with my husband. At Apam I learnt the Fante and lost the Gonja, but still speak the Dagaree. Then we moved to Komenda from Apam. We then moved to Bechem where my husband worked as a tutor and I as an administrator. I learnt Twi from there. My husband moved to Winneba and I returned to Apam Senior High School. In 2007, I joined my husband in Winneba where I was employed as an administrator here. [52-year-old lecturer]

Language Shift and Language Loss

To further investigate the use of local languages by migrants at UEW, the interview protocol inquired about respondents' knowledge of the other Ghanaian languages spoken in Winneba. In Winneba, indigenous people along the coast speak the Effutu language, while people in the town largely speak the Mfantse language. When asked if they speak either the Mfantse or the Effutu language, 34 of the respondents reported knowledge of only the Mfantse language, followed in frequency by knowledge of Twi only, and the Mfantse and Effutu languages (see Table 4).

Migration and Language Dynamics

Research has shown that indigenous languages survive if they are spoken and are passed on from generation to generation. This process is possible if migrants move in groups or if people from the same origins find each other in their new environment. In light of this, the study investigated whether respondents had migrated to Winneba alone, with responses indicating that 61.2% moved to Winneba alone, while the remaining 38.8% moved with their families. These results give room for the possibility of language shift and language loss. The responses from Table 4 show that migrants in Winneba can speak at least multiple different Ghanaian languages. This is so because many of those who migrated to Winneba alone are most likely to marry in the town during their period of stay. The possibility of people marrying outside their main ethnic groups is high in fluid migrant communities such as a university workplace.

Given this, the study asked the respondents who are married whether they speak the same local language with their spouses. 65% reported that their spouses cannot speak their local languages, so they tend to speak English together. There were also instances in which one spouse compromised to speak the local language of the other; in such instances, one language was sustained in the family at the expense of the other, as depicted in the following interview excerpt:

My mum is a Fante and my father an Akuapim so the family speaks both Fante and Akuapim which are different dialects of the Akan language. The family moved to Accra when I was a child so I learned the Ga language as well. My husband is a Frafra and since I cannot speak the Frafra, I speak Twi with him because he has been travelling to the south a lot so he can speak the Twi. I speak Twi and English with the children and my husband speaks English and Frafra with them. The children can speak Twi and English, they understand some Frafra but cannot speak it. Among the children, they mostly speak English but once a while they speak Twi. Hardly do they speak the Frafra among themselves. [45-year-old lecturer]

All 38.8% of respondents who did not move to Winneba alone indicated that they migrated to Winneba with their spouses and children. When they were asked which language they spoke with their spouses, 24 of them said they spoke Twi and English. This is not surprising because the most common Ghanaian language spoken in the country is Akan (of which Twi is a variety), and English is the official and most commonly spoken language among educated Ghanaians.

Of the 141 respondents, 119 said they have children, and of these, 47 of them said they have three or more children. This question is very important to the study because language sustainability depends on the ability to pass the language from one generation to another. The study therefore inquired whether respondents spoke their local languages with their children and, more importantly, if the children spoke the languages among themselves. Of these 119 respondents with children, 82.1% spoke their local languages with their children at home, while 17.9% did not due to inter-marriage relations to migration.

When respondents were asked if their children spoke their local languages among themselves, 53.1% responded "yes"; 43% said "no"; and the remainder replied "sometimes". Meanwhile, 74.5% explained that their children could neither read nor write fluently in their local languages. The following excerpt illustrates this situation:

I married in Cape coast till 2014 when we moved to Winneba, the two of us speak different Akan dialects. I have four children. The children understand the Twi but struggle to speak the Twi among themselves. Between them, they speak English. The children are now learning Fante at school, whilst we speak the Kwahu and Asante Twi. So very confusing, you see. [38-year-old senior lecturer]

Finally, respondents were also asked if they still spoke their mother tongue: 7% responded that they do not. These respondents were individuals who migrated to Winneba alone and married into a different ethnic groups, shifting to the use of English, or of English and another Ghanaian dialect – usually one of the Akan dialects. These individuals were either born in Winneba or were brought to Winneba at very young ages by parents of different ethnic groups, or have gone through a series of migrations as a result of their parents' occupation; hence, they have picked up the dominant languages from where their parents have lived. The potential outcome of these experiences – eventual language loss – is reflected in the comment of one 40-year-old administrator, who noted that "My spouse doesn't speak the same language as me, my children and spouse cannot speak my language, I am the only one who can speak the language among my friends".

The Future of Local Ghanaian Languages

The study findings show that, among this group of 141 Ghanaian migrants, there is evidence of language switching, shifting, and loss. The latter raises concerns for the preservation and vitality of Ghanaian languages, especially minority languages. With this in mind, the study collected participant perspectives on how to reduce the possibility of language loss and, indeed, whether such a move is considered feasible. The responses below represent some of the perceived logistical challenges involved in achieving this goal:

I don't know where we can start from, women are now working mothers and so children are sent to school at early ages. They go to school early and when they are in school, they are introduced to English from that early stage, which makes it difficult for them to speak the local language. These children usually spend about two-thirds of their daily time with the teachers where they speak the English language. For the home, parents try to speak the local language with the children. I know parents are doing their best but it's difficult, me for instance, I keep telling my children to speak the Twi, but they only smile and easily go back to the speaking of the English language. Learning other dialects seems confusing but it's not a problem because at least some of the dialects are left to keep going so it's ok. The speaking of the L1 at early levels of school, as it's the policy in this country, should be insisted on at the schools. [38-year-old senior lecturer]

When I marry, I will often send my children to the village. I think if we want to sustain our languages we have to travel often to our villages. I am told if I go and live there for three months, I can speak it. But now I am working and because of the distance, it seems almost impossible. [28-year-old assistant lecturer]

These discussions suggest that there is a need to maintain and revitalize Ghanaian language usage among generations in order to maintain and keep them from going extinct since indigenous language preservation is directly linked to the preservation of the Ghanaian culture. However, it is clear that many homes and users of Ghanaian languages are still struggling to maintain their native languages since there is competition with other languages due to instances of contact in contexts of migration. The most startling concern in this regard is the inoperative use of the Ghanaian languages by younger generations, which is an indicator for future language loss of most Ghanaian languages. This calls for critical attention to and conscious use of indigenous languages among all users, especially the younger generations. One way to enable this is through the flexibility of students to select any Ghanaian language they want to study across the country without existing geographical restrictions. The need to preserve indigenous languages and pass them on to the younger generation must also be explicitly promoted across educational and societal communities.

CONCLUSION

The purpose of this chapter has been to analyse migration and language dynamics focusing on reflections from the staff community at the University of Education, Winneba. It also discussed the implications of migration experiences on the vitality of indigenous languages in Ghana. It was found that, as people migrate, there is an indication of the acquisition of new languages as well as an assimilation of new cultures, while the likelihood of people exterminating their own cultures and languages becomes viable.

Again, it was indicative in this study that most migrants adopt at least one of the Ghanaian languages of their new community or forfeit entirely one of their own Ghanaian languages in favour of the English language. This clearly shows that, if migrants become incurious about speaking their own indigenous languages to their future generations as they migrate, it is likely that most indigenous Ghanaian languages will gradually lose their vitality. This has serious consequences for the maintenance of cultural and linguistic identity.

Maintenance of local languages must be considered paramount during migration for existing languages to be saved from extinction. The issue of language maintenance is key as it is directly linked to the preservation of Ghanaian culture. It is also recommended that Ghana propose at least one official Ghanaian language so that a person can be fluent in a National Ghanaian language; a means of revitalising our indigeneity.

REFERENCES

Adu, O. O. (2020). Women in higher education institutions in Ghana: Discourse on colonial legacies and cultural norms. *Brock Journal of Education*, 8(6), 18–26. doi:10.37745/bje/vol8.no6.p18-26.2020

Anarfi, J., Kwankye, S., Ababio, O. M., & Tiemoko, R. (2003). *Migration from and to Ghana: A background paper.* University of Sussex: DRC on Migration, Globalisation and Poverty. http://www.sussex.ac.uk/Units/SCMR/drc/publications/working_papers/WP-C4.pdf

Anyidoho, A., & Dakubu, M. E. K. (2008). Ghana: Indigenous languages, English, and an emerging national identity. In A. Simpson (Ed.) Language and National Identity in Africa (pp. 141 – 157). Oxford University Press

Awumbila, M. (2015). Women moving within borders: Gender and internal migration dynamics in Ghana. *Ghana Journal of Geography*, 7(2), 132–145.

Ayentimi, D. T. (2023, March 23). Women occupy very few academic jobs in Ghana. Culture and society's expectations are to blame. *The Conversation.* https://theconversation.com/women-occupy-very-few-academic-jobs-in-ghana-culture-and-societys-expectations-are-to-blame-200307

Bhugra, D., & Becker, M. A. (2005). Migration, cultural bereavement and cultural identity. *World Psychiatry; Official Journal of the World Psychiatric Association (WPA)*, 4(1), 18–24. PMID:16633496

Boyle, P., Halfacree, K., & Robinson, V. (2014). *Exploring contemporary migration*. Routledge. doi:10.4324/9781315843100

Castles, S. (2016). Understanding global migration: A social transformation perspective. In A. Amelina, K. Horvath. & B. Meeus (Eds.), An anthology of migration and social transformation: European perspectives (pp. 19-41). Springer. doi:10.1007/978-3-319-23666-7_2

Chachu, S. (2022). Implications of language barriers for access to healthcare: The case of francophone migrants in Ghana. *Legon Journal of the Humanities*, *32*(2), 1–36. doi:10.4314/ljh.v32i2.1

Christel, K. (2020). Gender disparities in Ghana's tertiary education system. *Journal of Student Affairs, New York University*, *16*, 34–39.

Czaika, M., & Reinprecht, C. (2022). Migration drivers: Why do people migrate. In P. Scholten (Ed.), *Introduction to migration studies: An interactive guide to the literatures on migration and diversity* (pp. 49–82). Springer. doi:10.1007/978-3-030-92377-8_3

Danso-Wiredu, E. Y., & Brako, I. (2021). Regionalism, ethnicity, and politics in Ghana. *Ghana Journal of Geography*, *13*(3), 278–303.

Danso-Wiredu, E. Y., Dadson, Y. I., & Amoako-Andoh, F. O. (2016). Social, economic and environmental impacts of the recent electricity crisis in Ghana: A study of Winneba. *Journal of Social Sciences*, *49*(3-1), 277-288.

George, E. B. (2006). *A profile of multilingual skills of young adult Xhosa mother tongue speakers* [M.Phil Thesis, University of the Western Cape].

Geremia, C., White, P. J., Hoeting, J. A., Wallen, R. L., Watson, F. G., Blanton, D., & Hobbs, N. T. (2014). Integrating population-and individual-level information in a movement model of Yellowstone bison. *Ecological Applications*, *24*(2), 346–362. doi:10.1890/13-0137.1 PMID:24689146

Godefroidt, A., Langer, A., & Meuleman, B. (2016). *Towards post-modern identities in Africa? An analysis of citizenship conceptualizations in Ghana*. Centre for Research on Peace and Development. https://soc.kuleuven.be/crpd/files/working-papers/WP%2051%20Towards%20post-modern%20identities%20in%20Africa.pdf

Gong, Y., Ma, M., Hsiang, T. P., & Wang, C. (2020). Sustaining international students' learning of Chinese in China: Shifting motivations among New Zealand students during study abroad. *Sustainability (Basel)*, *12*(15), 6289. doi:10.3390u12156289

Hampel, R., & Stickler, U. (2005). New skills for new classrooms: Training tutors to teach languages online. *Computer Assisted Language Learning*, *18*(4), 311–326. doi:10.1080/09588220500335455

Kasonde, A. (2015). Language and identity in general education in Zambia. In E. Khachaturyan (Ed.), *Language-Nation-Identity: The" Questione della Lingua" in an Italian and Non-Italian Context* (pp. 96–119). Cambridge Scholars Publishing.

Kwankye, S. O., Anarfi, J. K., Tagoe, C. A., & Castaldo, A. (2009). Independent North-South child migration in Ghana: The decision-making process. *University of Sussex: DRC on Migration, Globalisation and Poverty*. http://www.sussex.ac.uk/Units/SCMR/drc/publications/working_papers/WP-T29.pdf

Lechner, F. J., & Boli, J. (Eds.). (2020). *The globalization reader*. John Wiley & Sons.

Lee, N. (2015). Migrant and ethnic diversity, cities and innovation: Firm effects or city effects? *Journal of Economic Geography*, *15*(4), 769–796. doi:10.1093/jeg/lbu032

Lentz, C., & Nugent, P. (2000). *Ethnicity in Ghana: A comparative perspective*. doi:10.1007/978-1-349-62337-2

Lewis, E. G. (1971). Migration and language in the USSR. *The International Migration Review*, *5*(2), 147–179.

Okafor, L. E., Khalid, U., & Burzynska, K. (2022). The effect of migration on international tourism flows: The role of linguistic networks and common languages. *Journal of Travel Research*, *61*(4), 818–836. doi:10.1177/00472875211008250

Olwig, K. F. (2013). 'Integration': Migrants and refugees between Scandinavian welfare societies and family relations. In O. Abingdon (Ed.), Migration, family and the welfare state (pp. 1-16). Routledge.

Owu-Ewie, C. (2017). Language, education and linguistic human rights in Ghana. *Legon Journal of the Humanities*, *28*(2), 151–172.

Pauwels, A. (2010). *Immigrant dialects and language maintenance in Australia: The case of the Limburg and Swabian dialects* (Vol. 2). Walter de Gruyter.

Pieterse, J. N. (2003). Social capital and migration: Beyond ethnic economies. *Ethnicities*, *3*(1), 29–58. doi:10.1177/1468796803003001785

ReganB. P. (2017). *The effect of dialect contact and social identity on fricative demerger*. University of Texas at Austin. https://doi.org/ doi:10.15781/t2rf5kx7s

Richards, L. (2006). Thinking research. *Sage (Atlanta, Ga.)*.

Rumbaut, R. G. (2004). Ages, life stages, and generational cohorts: Decomposing the immigrant first and second generations in the United States. *The International Migration Review*, *38*(3), 1160–1205. doi:10.1111/j.1747-7379.2004.tb00232.x

Sabates-Wheeler, R., Sabates, R., & Castaldo, A. (2008). Tackling poverty-migration linkages: Evidence from Ghana and Egypt. *Social Indicators Research*, *87*(2), 307–328. doi:10.100711205-007-9154-y

Schildkrout, E. (2007). *People of the Zongo: The transformation of ethnic identities in Ghana*. Cambridge University Press.

Waldinger, R. (2015). *The cross-border connection: Immigrants, emigrants, and their homelands*. Harvard University Press. doi:10.4159/harvard.9780674736283

White, D. E., Oelke, N. D., & Friesen, S. (2012). Management of a large qualitative data set: Establishing trustworthiness of the data. *International Journal of Qualitative Methods*, *11*(3), 244–258. doi:10.1177/160940691201100305

White, M. J. (Ed.). (2016). *International handbook of migration and population distribution* (Vol. 6). Springer. doi:10.1007/978-94-017-7282-2

Wong, M. (2014). Navigating return: The gendered geographies of skilled return migration to Ghana. *Global Networks*, *14*(4), 438–457. doi:10.1111/glob.12041

ENDNOTES

[1] When speakers alternate between two or more languages in conversation.
[2] Using a word or phrase from one language while using another.
[3] Where speakers of a community abandon their original vernacular language in favour of another.
[4] Where two language varieties are spoken in the same speech community.
[5] Where a community has three levels of languages used in the community.

Chapter 12
Leaving Out No One:
Multilingualism and Inclusiveness in Public Health Awareness Campaign Messages in Nigeria

Saheed Omotayo Okesola
University of Freiburg, Germany

ABSTRACT

The COVID-19 pandemic altered human activities in several ways. It affected how people communicate and use language. Nigeria, with over 500 languages and just one official language, exploited multilingual resources to fight the COVID-19 pandemic. This chapter examines multilingualism and linguistic diversity in the discourse of COVID-19 public health awareness campaign messages in Nigeria. Thirty COVID-19 campaign messages in form of posters, audio jingles, videos, brochures, and sociolinguistic field interviews (30 unstructured one-on-one interviews) with some selected members of rural communities were analyzed. The study found that indigenous languages, multimodality, and translations were utilized as mass mobilization tools to promote inclusion. The study concludes that multilingualism and multimodality deliver COVID-19 sensitization messages effectively, increase access, and promote inclusiveness. It further suggests the localization of public health crisis in line with the sociolinguistic dynamics in multilingual settings.

INTRODUCTION

Language is an important tool in any human society, and it constitutes an integral part of human existence. In its various forms and manners, it is the tool for conducting human affairs in all contexts of the society. It is through language that humans communicate and manage personal and societal aspirations. These crucial roles that language plays in the socio-political, education, economy, health, and the overall development of nations have been stressed by several African scholars (Adegbija, 1994; Alamu & Iloene, 2003; Djite, 2008; Adedimeji, 2010). Thus, the choice of language for pursuing all human developmental goals and aspirations in multilingual contexts usually leads to serious debates as a result

DOI: 10.4018/978-1-6684-8761-7.ch012

of the multilingual profiles of these countries. Also important is the desire for equity, quest for inclusiveness, and the need to observe the linguistics rights of citizens. This becomes crucial, particularly in the midst of a global pandemic. The outbreak of COVID-19 in late 2019 took the whole world by surprise and the virus has been described as one of the greatest challenges of the human race in the 21st Century. With the outbreak of COVID-19, the world has continued to modify how people live and conduct their affairs. Nigeria, the most populous African country with a population of 210, 852, 900 (*World Population Review*, 2022), did not have enough medical facilities that could be deployed to fight the COVID-19 pandemic. Consequently, emphasis was placed on mass awareness and sensitization about the virus and how people could avoid being infected. Invariably, language becomes the main weapon for mobilization on the different media platforms.

Not only is Nigeria a multilingual country; it is one of the countries of the world with very complex linguistic diversity. Nigeria is one of the three countries in the world with more than 500 languages within their borders. Nigeria (with 517 languages) comes after Papua New Guinea (840 languages) and Indonesia (711 languages) to emerge as the third most linguistically diverse country in the world (*Ethnologue*, 2019). However, in spite of this huge linguistic complexity, as reflected in the presence of hundreds of languages, there are millions of indigenous people with little or no formal education, and consequently not proficient in the official language (English), and who do not speak any of the "major languages" (Hausa, Igbo and Yoruba). Further, no other language, including the most widely used Nigerian Pidgin (henceforth NP) is accorded official status. Apart from the official language (English), mostly spoken by educated people and less commonly used by people with no formal education, there are hundreds of languages spoken by the people and dominant in different regions of the country. Prominent among these indigenous languages are Hausa, Igbo, and Yoruba. These three languages are often described in the literature as "major languages" probably because of the regional presence they each seems to have in different parts of the country or their numerical strength and dominance in the three major segments of the country, even though none of them can boast of actual national spread. Other indigenous languages apart from these three "major languages" widely used by Nigerians in various locations of the country abound. Without any basis for their mention other than for just this academic purpose of illustration, some of these languages include Fulfulde, Isoko, Edo, Efik, Ibibio, Idoma, Kanuri, Ikwerre, Tiv, Kalabari, etc.

Furthermore, the list of languages and the discourse of multilingualism and linguistic diversity in Nigeria cannot be completed without talking about the Nigerian Pidgin (NP), a language that many scholars (Egbokhare, 2021; Faraclas, 2008; 2021; Akande & Okesola, 2021) have described as the "real" lingua franca of the country because of the roles it plays in inter-ethnic interaction across and among various distinct groups in the Nigerian sociolinguistic space. NP is a hybrid language that combines English and indigenous languages of the people of Nigeria. It is the most prominent language in Nigeria in terms of numerical strength, accessibility, and spread across all social classes in the country. Even when some educated people do not want to use NP due to issues of prestige and attitudes, they understand and can decode messages in it and respond accordingly. It is for these reasons that many people believe that it is the lingual franca in spite of the lack of recognition or assignment of roles to the language. Although, with no functions assigned to it or any official recognition, NP does not carry the limitations that other languages in Nigeria carry, in that, it accommodates speakers across social and geographical boundaries. For instance, English, the official language, is limited to mostly people with at least some level of formal education, and consequently comes with a social demand on speakers. The three "major languages" (Hausa, Igbo, and Yoruba) also have geographical limitations, in that they are all dominant in specific regions and largely confined in use to these different regions of the country with no national spread.

So, to a very great extent, it is Hausa in the North, Igbo in the East, and Yoruba in the West, even though it is not strange to see some speakers of any of these three languages outside of their regions of dominance. Thus, none of these "major languages" can be truly said to be a lingua franca, as the use of any of them usually leaves out a significant number of Nigerians. The official language (English) also fails to meet the lingua franca requirement as millions of Nigerians (about 38% of the population) with no formal education cannot function in the language. It is this lack of geographical limitation in spread and social status barriers that places NP in an unassailable position and as the most qualified of all the languages as the lingua franca in Nigeria. Even though English and these three regionally dominant languages (Hausa, Igbo, and Yoruba) are the only languages recognized and assigned functions in the constitution, the desire to carry along all and sundry in the face of COVID-19 changed the pattern of communication and linguistic practices in almost all parts of the country during the pandemic. The monolingual communicative posture of government agencies, non-state actors, and other stakeholders changed in different conventional print and electronic media as well as social media and other emerging media platforms.

It is against this background that this chapter examines multilingualism and its roles in the mass mobilization and dissemination of public health awareness campaign messages in Nigeria, focusing on the COVID-19 pandemic. The complexity of Nigeria's multilingual situation, and the huge linguistic diversity of the groups therein, calls for a detailed examination of linguistic practices in the discourse of COVID-19 public health awareness campaigns, particularly, how these messages reflect the sociolinguistic realities of the Nigerian society. Essentially, the chapter attempts a reconceptualization of language norms in this postcolonial multilingual setting in the context of the management of a global pandemic. This is with a view to interrogating linguistic practices during this critical period and recommending pragmatic suggestions in the design and dissemination of future public health communication for the well-being of the greatest number of people.

Multilingualism and Linguistic Diversity in Nigeria

Multilingualism as a concept in the African context is the norm and not an exception, and is to be seen as a product of so many sociolinguistic factors and experiences of the people of Africa, particularly people´s experiences with colonialization in different places and at different times. This is why some scholars believe that discourses about multilingualism and its consequences should be contextualized and situated within the context of the sociolinguistic realities and the particularities of the people in question. In the words of Anchimbe (2018, p. 6), "any comprehensive investigation of social interaction in postcolonial societies must take into account the complex constitution of these societies marked by contact, hybridism and the emergence of linguistic and social behavioral patterns during and after colonialism." During colonial rule in Nigeria, the official language used for administration and other duties of government was English in the different regions of the country. Today's dominance of English in the country is, thus, a reflection of this sociopolitical experience, and of course, the country's failure to revisit and address with a clear indigenous ideological vigor the important question of language use/choice at independence. For instance, even though the government has recognized three other "major languages" (Hausa, Igbo and Yoruba) alongside English as official languages in the legislature, the reality is such that these three "major languages" are rarely used to conduct official duties or legislative business on the floor of the national assembly. The sole or dominant language for administration and official functions has remained English in almost all domains and contexts of language use, including domains where there are constitutional provisions backing the use of these indigenous languages (such as in the legislature).

The concept of multilingualism in Nigeria has been studied from different perspectives by several people, many of whom have not only argued for its deployment in important domains of language use but have also given pragmatic suggestions on how it can be exploited for mass mobilization, inclusion, and ultimately for national development. Scholars (e.g., Adegbija, 1994; Alamu & Iloene, 2003; Akinnaso, 1991; Adedimeji, 2010; Akande, 2016) have examined the concept of linguistic diversity as the norm in Nigeria and have stressed the importance of indigenous languages in sustainable national development in various contexts of language use. Some Nigerian linguists (e.g., Bamgbose, 1999; Oyetade, 2003, Adegbite, 2010), have also examined multilingualism and the challenges arising from linguistic diversity, language planning, and implementation in Nigeria extensively. Some other studies on linguistic diversity in Nigeria have also observed the failure of Nigeria to recognize, develop, and utilize the country's huge multilingual resources to promote the well-being of the people in important sectors like education, health, economic, governance, etc., (see Essien, 2006; Adegbite, 2010; Bamgbose, 2014). Multilingualism and linguistic diversity are important to the discourse of development in Nigeria, and indeed Africa, because they are central concepts in the initiation and implementation of policies and programs in different contexts, as the success or failure of these programs are also usually measured through the instrument of language. In the case of Nigeria, for instance, given the number of people and volume of activities in the informal sector of the country, one can safely predict the unsuccessful outcome of a communication, policy, or program conceived and executed using a monolingual approach.

It is this multilingual complexity that attracts debates and different perspectives on language use and assignment of roles to languages in some multilingual contexts. The complex linguistic situation and the adoption/recognition of a sole language in Nigeria compounds the problems, as many citizens frequently question the rationale behind such recognition of a sole language as the official language for all activities in spite of the obvious limitations of this action. This leads to inaccessibility of the official language (English) by millions of citizens who cannot function in the language. Beyond linguistic diversity, which is the norm in most Nigerian communities, there is also the challenge of low literacy rates among indigenous people. There are communities in Nigeria where apart from the official language (English) and the three "major languages" (Hausa, Igbo and Yoruba), there are as many as eight languages available to the people for their everyday activities. This linguistic complexity becomes more worrisome in the face of a virus that spares no social class or group, making the issue of access to public health information by the indigenous people rights issues. To safeguard the linguistic rights of these people, especially in the communication of risk and preventive strategies during the pandemic, there was the need to recontextualize communication as well as the design and packaging of public health information especially during this COVID-19 public health emergency.

Some scholars (Piller, 2016; Ahmad, 2020) posit that in multilingual contexts, particularly in Africa, where millions of people speak different languages, there is the need to deploy multilingual resources in winning the war against public health emergencies. In one study, Igboanusi, Odoje, and Ibrahim, (2017) explore how Nigerian linguistic resources can be put to use in information and awareness campaigns about HIV and AIDS. The authors in that study on how to stop the troubling increase in these diseases attempt "lexical modernization" of HIV and AIDS nomenclatures in Nigeria's three major languages. As pointed out by these scholars, enlightenment campaigns messages about HIV and AIDS have not achieved the desired impact due to the non-use of appropriate nomenclatures in this important communication with the people. The study advocates the deployment of multiple African languages if medical practitioners want to get messages about HIV and AIDS across to the people, and consequently win the war against these two killer diseases. The position of these scholars and some other Nigerian scholars is that in view of the low literacy rate and sociolinguistic profile of Nigeria and the need to carry along everyone in the fight against any public health crisis, there is the need to design inclusive messages that would be accessible to all.

Also, in a study in another African context with similar a sociolinguistic reality, Rudwick, Sijadu, and Turner (2021), focusing on COVID-19, examine linguistic choices of government officials in South Africa during the pandemic. The study reveals how South African public office holders switch to indigenous languages at various times in their communication with the people in order to effectively convey their messages to the largest number of the citizens. According to (Rudwick, Sijadu, & Turner 2021, p. 244), "These switches into African languages provided crucial information regarding lockdown rules and, hence, sought effective and interactive communicative strategies that would work during the pandemic". They argued that this switch to African languages is also capable of minimizing the misinformation that is likely to arise as a result of faulty translations of crucial information. Furthermore, Oyebode and Okesola (2020) explore the social semiotic significance of non-verbal communication modes deployed by agencies and international brands to communicate specific COVID-19 awareness and sensitization messages in order to flatten the alarming and rising curve of the coronavirus in different cities in Nigeria during the pandemic. Also, Amzat et al. (2020) examine the burden as well as the socio-medical responses to COVID-19 in the first one hundred days after the index case in Nigeria was reported. In the study, the authors focus on the sociological and medical responses in the management of coronavirus and their implications on the lives of the people.

In many African contexts, multilingualism and linguistic diversity have been examined and there are success reports of how stakeholders are exploiting multiple languages and deploying the enormous linguistics resources of the people in different domains and how this is yielding positive results and changing the narratives. For example, Benson (2010), in a study that focusses on three African countries, Guinea Bissau, Mozambique and Ethiopia, reports how the strategic utilization of multiple languages in educational instruction suggested new positive possibilities in terms of results. While advocating the use of home-grown and context-specific teaching methodologies and a redefinition of the needs of learners in each multilingual context, the scholar suggests a careful blend of Western research findings and the actual situation in these African contexts. As Benson (2010) opines, "This involves a reconstruction of multilingual pedagogy to capitalise on the strengths of learners, teachers and linguistic communities. The implications are that language-in-education policy should be based on what is possible in each sociolinguistic situation and should be flexible enough to offer equitable opportunities for all" (p. 323). This inclusive orientation appears to be one of the effective ways of bridging the gap between different groups of people in many African contexts. All the above studies show the multilingual peculiarity of Africa, particularly Nigeria, and posit that such peculiarity should be taken into consideration in policy formulation. Even though some of these earlier works have focused on other public health crisis such as HIV/AIDS, this chapter attempts to interrogate linguistic diversity, indigenous people's linguistic rights and access to COVID-19 public health information.

Significance and Aim of the Study

The sociolinguistic reality in multilingual contexts with the emergence of COVID-19 has not just brought up new challenges to public health discourse, but has imposed different dynamics in the deployment of linguistic resources for both preventive and combative strategies against the pandemic.

This chapter as conceived is significant because the negative impacts of COVID-19 cut across all social boundaries in any society and in a heterogeneous and linguistically complex country such as Nigeria, its management demands inclusiveness in the design and dissemination of public health awareness and sensitization messages. The first issue is that of linguistic rights among disadvantaged populations using languages different from the official or dominant languages. There is also the question of access to important preventive and life-saving information on COVID-19 in multilingual settings during the pandemic. Given the way people hitherto take for granted the use of dominant, official, or state languages, the pandemic compels stakeholders to examine closely the plight of indigenous people with respect to access to information in multilingual and multicultural contexts. Thus, this chapter, which focuses on linguistic diversity and COVID-19 awareness campaign messages and public health discourse in a post-colonial African country is significant and a timely intervention in understanding the nature of the communication of emergencies in the public health sector in a developing setting. One of the important pillars of development in any country is a healthy and productive population capable of bringing about sustainable development in the different critical areas of economy, health, education, governance/politics, etc. Hence, effectively managing linguistic diversity and promoting equity in terms of access to public health information remains one of the major obstacles facing multilingual African countries in their responses to and management of COVID-19 and indeed other public health emergencies. Under public health crisis such as the COVID-19 global pandemic, best known safety strategies, public health policies, and public well-being protocols are all unlikely to yield the desired results if the design and dissemination of such efforts and information are not packaged in ways that the generality of the public would be able to understand the important messages.

This chapter focuses on how human communication was redefined and reconceptualized during COVID-19 in a multilingual African context. It examines multilingualism and linguistic diversity in the design and dissemination of public health awareness and sensitization campaign messages in this developing setting with complex linguistic diversity, with particular focus on the management of the COVID-19 pandemic. In order to achieve this broad aim, the chapter addresses the following specific objectives: (i) review and identify the linguistic patterns in the discourse of COVID-19 awareness messages with regard to how they reflect linguistic diversity and inclusiveness; (ii) discuss how government agencies and stakeholders reconceptualize language norms to reflect multilingualism and linguistic diversity in COVID-19 public health awareness and sensitization messages; (iii) evaluate citizens' perception of language use for COVID-19 public health awareness and sensitization campaign messages in the management of the public health crisis.

Data Sources and Methods

The data for this study are COVID-19 public awareness and sensitization campaign messages by the National Centre for Disease Control (NCDC), National Orientation Agency (NOA), the Presidential Task Force on COVID-19 (PTF) and some national and international non-state actors in the fight against the pandemic. The purposively selected data are in a variety of forms such as jingles, posters, videos, and audio messages from different conventional print and electronic media, official websites, and social media handles of these agencies and non-state actors actively involved in the management of COVID-19. Supplementary data were also drawn from sociolinguistic interviews with respondents from selected rural communities in the three States with the highest number of reported cases of COVID-19 in Nigeria (Lagos, Abuja, and Kaduna). 120 interviewees with little or no formal education (artisans, traders, farmers & herdsmen) were interviewed on access to public health information and, language preferences and attitudes towards language choice in the design of COVID-19 public health awareness messages. The study draws insights from critical multimodal discourse analysis, using qualitative qualitative Critical Discourse Analysis (CDA) approach and supplemented by quantitative analysis where appropriate. Content analysis of the interviews and ethnographic analysis of language attitudes and ideologies articulated by interviewees were also carried out.

Profile of the Respondents

As earlier stated, 120 respondents were interviewed in unstructured sociolinguistic field interviews in selected rural communities in Lagos, Kaduna, and Abuja (40 each from different rural communities in the three states). The selection of the respondents was purposive in nature given that the focus was the issues of access or inaccessibility as a result of their inability to use the language deployed in COVID-19 awareness messages. The occupations of the respondents covered a wide range of professions. These include artisans, traders, farmers, herdsmen, local motorcycle riders, market women, and farm produce marketers. Although the ages of the respondents vary, they are made up of old and young, and there was a fair balance in the samples with respect to gender (20 male respondents and 20 female respondents from each of the states covered).

DATA ANALYSIS AND DISCUSSION

This section presents the data analysis and discussion of the findings of the study. The presentation of the analysis and discussion is guided by the identified multilingual practices in COVID-19 public awareness and sensitization messages in Nigeria during the pandemic. Specifically, I focus on communicative strategies and practices that seek to promote inclusion and access to this public health information to the people irrespective of their level of formal education, language, gender, or other social factors. The identified multilingual practices are presented and discussed:

Multilingualism and Linguistic Diversity for Mass Mobilization

Contrary to the practice in most of the communication in the public health sector in Nigeria before the COVID-19 public health crisis, the data show that multilingual communication and practices were adopted massively in COVID-19 awareness and sensitization campaign messages by government agencies and stakeholders in the management of the pandemic. Undoubtedly, communication in every human context, particularly multilingual settings, is influenced by certain sociolinguistic as well as culture-specific factors and considerations which members of the community are all familiar with and share. These shared socio-cultural values and nuances are sometimes not known by people outside of the culture, who are often too distant to appreciate the influence or meaning of these though subtle but important factors.

Thus, the considerations and issues before people in multilingual and multicultural communication become more complex. This is because, beyond the question of the right mode of communication (whether written or spoken), the encoder/sender also has to contend with the appropriate choice of language, and pay attention to these socio-cultural sensibilities. In multilingual communication, therefore, emphasis is often on how to get information to members of diverse social and linguistic groups. One thing that the COVID-19 pandemic did to people around the world was remove borders between nations, regions, and societies, infecting people in almost all regions. Soon it became obvious to everyone that people of the world had a collective battle to fight and win. The World Health Organization's (WHO) declaration of COVID-19 as a global pandemic confirmed the seriousness of the crisis and suggested to world leaders and stakeholders that the fight required collective and deliberate strategies to combat the virus in an all-inclusive manner.

In Figure 1, a four-minute COVID-19 awareness and sensitization message video designed by the Nigeria Centre for Disease Control (henceforth NCDC) is used to sensitize Nigerians on the outbreak of the coronavirus and the need for people to jettison common social behavioral practices (such as shaking hands, hugging, and joining large gatherings), which are capable of spreading the infections and increasing the number of infected persons, and to imbibe new preventive practices and safety protocols in order to stop the spread of the deadly virus. To achieve this in the Nigerian context, it was clear to the NCDC and stakeholders in the health sector that designing such important messages in just the official language (English) would not yield the intended result, which was to get the message across to every member of the society. Hence, in this single public health awareness and sensitization campaign message, the NCDC, in recognition of, and in coming to terms with, the multilingual and complex linguistic diversity nature of the country, through medical practitioners who are proficient in Nigerian languages, deployed twelve different languages to disseminate this important public health awareness campaign to members of the general public. It is noteworthy that essentially it is the same thing said in twelve different languages. This action of delivering the message in multiple languages increases people's access to the information being passed across and takes along more members of the public who are not proficient in English and the three "major languages" of the country. What follows immediately are transcripts of this important COVID-19 public awareness and sensitization message. Due to space constraints, only six randomly selected languages from the twelve languages used in this message from the NCDC have been transcribed and presented. The selected languages from the text are English, Hausa, Igbo, Yoruba, Nigerian Pidgin, and Tiv.

Leaving Out No One

Figure 1. COVID-19 awareness campaign by the Nigeria Centre for Disease Control

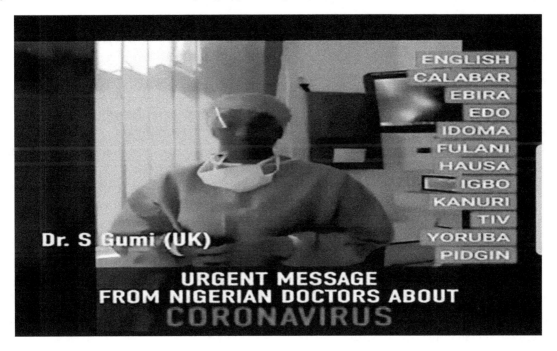

Excerpt of Text 1

> **English:** Please, help us to stop the spread of the coronavirus. Please, follow these three steps (i) wash your hands with soap and water (ii) avoid contacts with people (iii) keep your distance from others.
>
> **Nigerian Pidgin:** To stop dis disease, you go wash your hand well well with plenty water and soap. And if you wan sneeze, no sneeze enter your hand, sneeze for your elbow so that you no go spread the disease. Dis no be time wey dem they take dey shake or hug. If you wan greet person, you fit do elbow or leg greeting wey dem dey do now. We fit stop the disease.
>
> **Hausa:** Yaku jama'a, a wanke hanaye da sabulu a ruwa, a guje ku santan juma na kwot da kwot, taka tan kuwunchin yo mu saba, a bada tasara, tsakayin mutane na a kala taku uku.
>
> **Igbo:** Biko geenu nti. Ofu by na anyi ga-ejisi ike n'akroo aka anyi ofuma were ncha kroosie aka anyi ike na mnriri kroo ya ofuma. Nke abuo anyi ga-akronsi ikroe ndi mmadu n'aka maa na oria nwere ike ifere ndi ozo. Nke ato bun a ebe ndi mmndu gbakoro pgbako anyi ghara I no aga ebe ahu ma o bu ebe a na-eme ine omurue. Biko ihe nto a di nikpa.
>
> **Yoruba:** E maa foo owo yin pelu omi ati ose fun aabo iseju. E jina si ara yin, ki e si maa bowo pelu enikeni. E fi aye sile laarin yin ati enikeji ki o too bi ese bata meta.
>
> **Tiv:** Ityo yam oon ne ave fele fele sha ichahul man mngeren ma tsembelee. Pande nen ukuven man zuan ave. Tilen paleaa a ior ikuma er angahar atar nahan.

This multilingual message from the NCDC clearly underscores the multilingual profile of Nigeria and tacitly declares linguistic diversity as the norm. It also stresses the place of Nigerian Pidgin (NP) and indigenous languages as tools for mass mobilization in the country. As the third most linguistically diverse country in the world and one of the three countries where over 500 indigenous languages are spoken by the people, only the deployment of multiple languages can help communicate important public health information to all and sundry. Thus, any crucial message that targets the entire people of the country, particularly public health information, such as COVID-19 sensitization and preventive messages, should be designed in a way that will recognize heterogeneity, linguistic diversity, and promote inclusiveness of the different categories of the people in the country. It is for this reason that the NCDC, the leading agency of government in the management of COVID-19, deliberately adopted multiple languages in this public awareness and sensitization message at the crucial period. It is worthy of note that of all the twelve languages used in the message from the NCDC, only four of them have any official recognition or have roles assigned to them in the Nigerian constitution. These four languages are English, Hausa, Igbo, and Yoruba. All the other eight languages used in this video (Calabar, Ebira, Edo, Idoma, Fulani, Kanuri, Tiv, and Nigerian Pidgin) have no official recognition in the country. Although hardly ever used in the legislature, the three "major" languages (Hausa, Igbo, and Yoruba) are assigned functions in the constitution as the languages to be used alongside the official language (English) for conducting legislative businesses on the floor of the national assembly. Even though the other languages are not recognized or assigned functions, to get this important COVID-19 awareness and preventive information to the people, the NCDC deployed the official language (English) and eleven other indigenous languages to effectively reach out to the people. Since the intent of the NCDC was not just speakers of the official or the three so called "major" languages alone but the general public, the center goes beyond the official language to incorporate these other indigenous languages of the people in order to reach more citizens and curb the spread of the deadly virus.

Nigerian Pidgin and Access to COVID-19 Sensitization Messages

During the pandemic, Nigerian Pidgin (NP), a language generated by combining linguistic resources from English and indigenous languages, emerged as a very prominent tool for promoting inclusion and achieving mass mobilization of the people, especially the rural dwellers and ordinary citizens of the country. Although understood to a certain extent by most Nigerians, due to prestige and attitudes to the language, NP is rarely used in formal settings or by educated people. They see the use of the language as closely associated with people belonging to lower social classes in the society. One of the reasons for this thinking is the fact that there is no social requirement for anyone to use NP, and that is why it is widely spoken by people with little or no education. NP is the tool for establishing some form of common grounds among Nigerians of different social divides in their interactions. Most of the people in the rural communities in Nigeria have their professions and activities classified as belonging to the informal sector. The activities of these rural people are usually largely unrecorded and unreported in formal reckoning by the government. They are herdsmen, peasant farmers, farm producers and petty traders, as well as artisans in rural communities.

Apart from the argument of some scholars (such as Deuber, 2005; Egbokhare, 2021; Igboanusi, 2008; Olatunji, 2007; Osoba, 2014) about NP as Nigeria's "actual" lingua franca in terms of spread, population of speakers, and presence among members of different social groups in the country, its adoption and use in this message could also be seen as an acknowledgement of the language as not only the "lingua franca" in the actual sense of the word, but also one with the potential to reach the largest number of people in the country without hinderances. For some of the reasons already stated, no important COVID-19 public health awareness communication in Nigeria is likely to be effective and reach all and sundry, if in its conception and design this important language of unity (NP) is excluded. The exclusion of NP would mean the exclusion of millions of Nigerians, who due to lack of competence in English and the three "major" languages would be excluded from such communication. Even when it may sometimes appear on the surface that the selection and use of the official language (English) and these three "major" languages are appropriate and adequate to solve the communicative needs of the people in Nigeria, in reality there are several millions of Nigerians who do not speak any of these languages, and are consequently excluded from activities in them. Also, these "major" languages (Hausa, Igbo, Yoruba) are to a large extent limited to specific regions of the country, while the same cannot be said of NP, as it is usually the language most Nigerians can connect with to bridge the linguistic divide created by lack of proficiency in English and these three "major" languages. Figure 2 is a Nigerian Pidgin (NP) public awareness and sensitization message in the fight against COVID-19.

Figure 2. Nigerian Pidgin COVID-19 awareness message

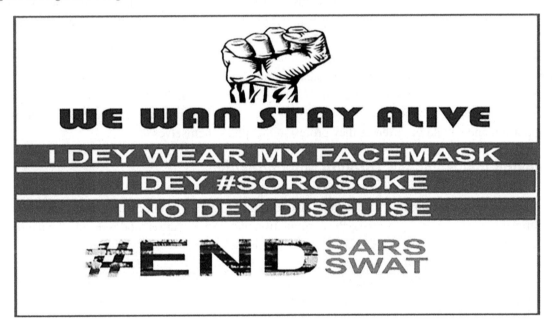

Figure 2 shows the potence of NP in the dissemination of COVID-19 awareness campaign information to the public during the pandemic. Unlike the official language (English) and the three "major" languages which are limiting one way or the other, the NP is a more inclusive language for mass mobilization. In this public awareness and sensitization campaign message to the public in NP, there was a contextual reference to one of the social happenings in Nigeria during the COVID-19 pandemic. It was the #Endsars civil demonstration by Nigerian youths, which was to kick against frequent harassment and intimidation of young people by officers of the Special Anti-robbery Squad (SARS) of the Nigeria Police during the pandemic, hence the mention of the protest in the awareness campaign message. In spite of the rising number of reported cases of COVID-19 and movement restrictions orders and lockdowns in some places, Nigerian youths could not wait or further tolerate the excesses and recklessness of this unit of the Nigeria Police force. The protests were in various notable cities and strategic locations across the country at the time. Young people in their thousands neglected official movement restriction orders and gathered to express their displeasure about constant harassment and intimidation. They called for the abolition of SARS and demanded responsible policing devoid of abuse of state power.

The NP awareness and sensitization message when translated to English means *"We want to stay alive"*, *"I am putting on my facemask"*, *"I am speaking up"*, *"I am not disguising"*. The NP text, through its words, supports the fight against police harassment and intimidation of young people which was the intention of the protesters, but in addition to this support, also cautioned people on the need to stay alive by protecting themselves from being infected with COVID-19 during the public demonstrations involving a lot of people. In what was a solidarity declaration of the thinking of the protesters, the text displayed a hand sign identifying with the protesters and symbolizing empathy. It communicated a sense of shared commitment to the demands of these young people, but in doing so, there was a genuine counsel to these young people to be safe. According to the text, to demand and seek redress of a perceived violation of one's fundamental human rights, one has to protect one's self from the virus and be alive to do so. As admonished by the text in NP, it is good to "speak up" and "not disguise" but in doing all this, people are reminded of the need to always "wear their facemask" in order to stay alive. The use of NP for this text is apt because, as typical of most gatherings of young people in Nigeria, there is usually a combination of people from different social backgrounds, and the issue of language choice in such mixed gatherings is often addressed with the use of NP. In order not to exclude any one of these young people from the message being passed across, the COVID-19 awareness campaign message listed actions that are important and should be taken as they protest and express themselves.

Achieving Inclusiveness Through Multimodality

One other strategy for promoting inclusion in the design of COVID-19 public awareness and sensitization campaign messages in Nigeria was the combination of communication modes during the pandemic. Agencies of government and stakeholders, in recognition of the universality of communication packaged in multiple modes combined different communication modes to educate and sensitize the people. Blending different communication modes into coronavirus awareness and sensitization messages appeals to more people irrespective of their social background. One reason for the attention that combination of modes attracted during the COVID-19 crisis was the nature and magnitude of the outbreak, and the number of people and groups to be reached. The NCDC and other agencies recognized the limitations of the verbal modes (spoken and written) in terms of reach in Nigeria because of various sociolinguistic factors, especially the issue of access to these awareness messages by some segments of the country. Figure 3, designed by the Federal Ministry of Health and the NCDC is an awareness and sensitization campaign message using a combination of modes.

Leaving Out No One

Figure 3. Verbal and nonverbal communication of COVID-19 symptoms

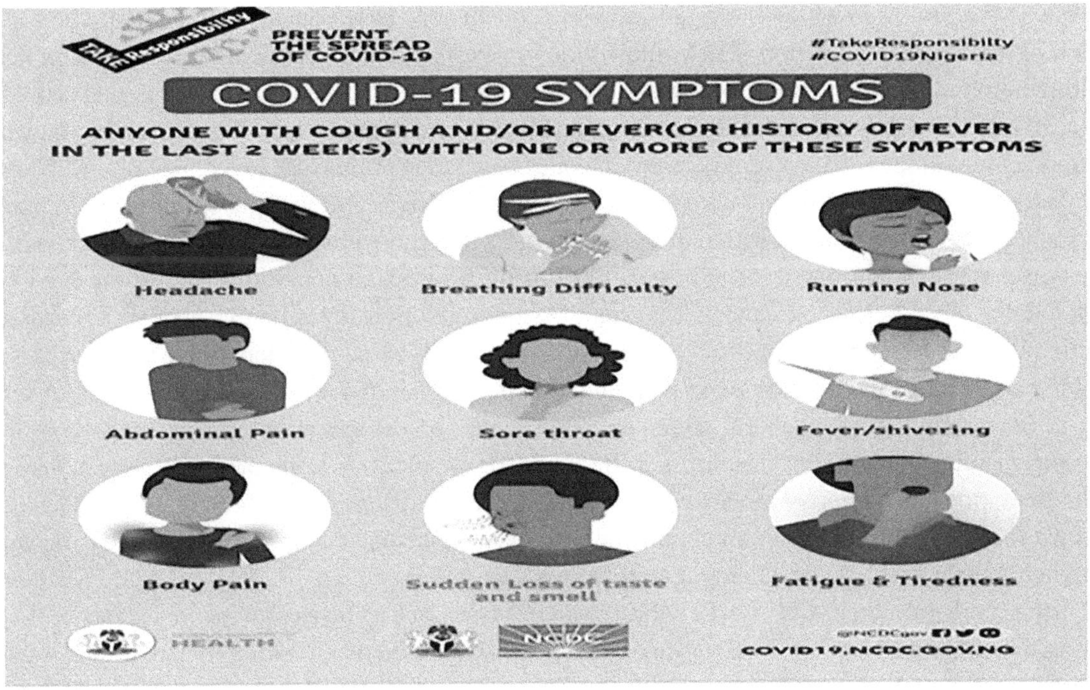

Verbal communication through a particular language is limited in a way to only people who are proficient in that language alone. To be reached by any verbal communication, one has to be able to use the language in which the message is encoded, and given that there are millions of people around the country with little or no formal education, verbal mode could therefore be discriminatory. During the COVID-19 pandemic, when actions or inactions of one person could be the determining factor of the fate of other people around the individual, the NCDC and other stakeholders could not afford to package messages in a single mode that would leave out anyone, hence, the massive use of multimodal communication as one of the preferred modes during the COVID-19 pandemic in order to increase the number of people in the communication net of these agencies. Figure 3 is an instance of a sensitization message in a combination of communication modes during the pandemic. While many of these COVID-19 public awareness messages are just images alone conveying meaningful messages, sometimes, these images are accompanied by verbal resources reinforcing the messages conveyed by the images. The present example is in this latter case where verbal resources are used to reinforce the message being passed across by the non-verbal resource such as the images and symbols in Figure 3. Using a combination of verbal and nonverbal modes and expanding its targeted audience, the text conveyed important information about the major symptoms of COVID-19 to the people. The text conscientized the public on the outbreak of the coronavirus and informed the people of the early signs in infected persons. The text, apart from just writing out the symptoms in words, also used different visuals to communicate the symptoms and the things to watch out for and pay attention to when someone is infected by COVID-19. So, beyond just verbal resources that educated people can read and respond to accordingly, the visuals further extend the campaign to uneducated people in the society, thereby helping the agencies, and by implication the government to sensitize everyone.

Specifically, the text could be seen and read by people without formal education or proficiency in English as long as they can see the signs and draw conclusions based on other contextual clues about COVID-19 at this crucial period. This combination of modes particularly becomes important in public health communication in Nigeria because of the low literacy rate in the country. It is on record that about 38% of the population are illiterate as at the 2022 World Literacy Day. Hence, relying on verbal communication alone, be it spoken or written, could be counterproductive in a pandemic, as it would leave out many people in different nooks and crannies of the Nigerian society. Combining communication modes makes the communication of important messages more universal across social strata of the society. Whereas similar feelings can be generated using a particular non-verbal image, the use of one word can lead to different conclusions and multiple interpretations by different people. For instance, nodding of head for approval or disapproval, waving of hands as sign of departure, facial expression showing anger, fear, and happiness are all commonly done in similar ways in many cultures. A closer look at intergroup and intercultural communication would reveal that people in recognition of these universal features of non-verbal resources shift to them or use them as supplements in order to take care of the limitations of the verbal mode and the nature of the participants in such interactions. The use of multiple modes in multilingual communication promotes inclusion and effectiveness in passing across important messages to people belonging to diverse social groups.

Furthermore, in another COVID-19 public awareness message using a combination of modes, Coalition Against COVID-19 (CACOVID), a private sector-driven initiative working in partnership with the Federal Ministry of Health, the Nigeria Centre for Disease Control (NCDC), the Presidential Task Force on coronavirus (PTF), as well as the World Health Organization (WHO) with the sole aim of combating COVID-19 in Nigeria, uses a combination of both verbal and nonverbal modes to appeal to the public to always wear their facemasks, as seen in Figure 4.

Figure 4. Verbal and nonverbal communication of COVID-19 symptoms

Leaving Out No One

The outbreak of the COVID-19 pandemic shortly before the end of the year 2019 redefined public health communication in Nigeria. Nonverbal communication gained prominence as one of the preferred modes of communication in different contexts. Figure 4 shows various categories of the people (old, young, male, female) in the society and enjoined them to wear a facemask as a way of curtailing the spread of the dreaded virus. This public awareness campaign message is telling everyone what people should do as one of the preventive strategies in the fight against COVID-19 so as to flatten the rising curve of reported cases at the time.

The main concern for most people in any multilingual communicative task is usually how to balance a lot of things. These include the intention of the sender, the choice of language, the choice of the medium (spoken or written), word choice, the target audience (known or unknown), etc. Combining communication modes in a single communication can to a large extent address some of these concerns, hence, the prevalence of this style of during the COVID-19 pandemic in Nigeria. There was a surge in the use of non-verbal modes and communication with multimodal resources in order to reach more people during the pandemic. This is because the aim of the agencies and stakeholders during this public health crisis was to pass information and message(s) intended to influence people's actions and make them behave in a particular manner. Important messages about the coronavirus pandemic are deliberately packaged in ways that will not leave out any segment of the society through this type of text using a combination of verbal and nonverbal modes. This strategic step was to increase accessibility due to the fact that the country was contending with a virus that does not respect class or any other social consideration. The messages target the generality of the people (old and young, rich and poor, educated and uneducated), hence the need to use a combination of modes that capture everyone. These essential pieces of information as regards how to stay safe and halt the spread of the virus during the COVID-19 pandemic are passed across through the use of images, pictures, signs, symbols, etc., as opposed to the usual single mode of verbal communication in the public health sector in Nigeria.

Attitudes to Language Use in COVID-19 Sensitization Messages

In this section, I present the analysis of the sociolinguistic interviews with selected members of some rural communities in the three states with the highest reported cases of COVID-19 in Nigeria. One of the things that makes the multilingual situation in Nigeria more complex than some other contexts, apart from the number of languages, is the social barrier imposed on many people by lack of proficiency in the official language (English), which is usually the dominant language of most communication from agencies of government. There are millions of Nigerians with no proficiency in English in different rural communities in the various states and regions of the country, and who are consequently cut off from any communication or discourse in the language, no matter how important the message is to the public. While the situation in most Nigerian cities may not be as serious as it is in the rural areas, there are also a lot of people in this category in the cities too. The randomly selected respondents, all from rural communities, were interviewed on their perception of language choice for COVID-19 public awareness and sensitization campaign messages during the pandemic. The restriction to this segment of the society was informed by the fact that the central concern here was the issue of access to important public health information and the need to gauge inclusiveness in these public awareness messages.

Most of the respondents in these rural communities believe that if truly the intention of COVID-19 public awareness and sensitization messages was to get across the information to everyone and not just some segments of the country, then the language used for the messages should be one that should manifest inclusion and carry along all Nigerians irrespective of their social status or educational background. In all, 58.1% of the respondents preferred the use of Nigerian Pidgin for the design and dissemination of COVID-19 public awareness and sensitization messages in order to reach everyone. Another 25% of the respondents opted for their different indigenous languages in the design and dissemination of these important messages in order to reach the greatest number of the people, while 16.9% opted for the official language (English). Given their backgrounds, although is it not surprising that the majority of these respondents preferred either Nigerian Pidgin (NP) or their indigenous languages in the design and dissemination of COVID-19 messages, what is foregrounded, and which calls for urgent attention is the legitimate concern about their rights to important public health information in a language that they understand. In an interview with one of them, a very expressive respondent reacting to the question of language choice for COVID-19 public awareness messages, said:

Box 1. Sociolinguistic interview excerpt

Na my language nah.
[*It should be my language, of course*]
Na only wetin dem talk for our language or talk for Pidgin
[*It's only whatever information given in our native language or Pidgin*]
The problem be say how person wey no dey speak oyinbo language go get dem message?
[*The problem is that how do people who do not speak English get the messages in that language*]
I no understand how e go take happen.
[*I don't understand how that would happen*]
We get old people wey old well well and no go school for this community, wey be say dem no dey speak any other language pass their native language and maybe small pidgin
[*There old really old people in this community who don't have formal education and can't speak any other language apart from their native language and maybe some little Pidgin*]
Na so e be
[*That's just the way it is*]

This respondent did not only lay bare his mind on language choice in the dissemination of COVID-19 public awareness and sensitization messages, but stressed that if the intention is to target people, then their languages should matter. To him, any form of communication that intends to deliver information to people in the rural areas of the country should be designed in the language that the people speak and understand, which according to him is either a native language or the Nigerian Pidgin. These rural dwellers sometimes feel that government agencies do not even think that they exist or see them as Nigerians who also deserve to get the information that they are trying to pass across to the people. It is this feeling of neglect and exclusion that permeates responses of most of the respondents. As expressed by this respondent, they see the dominant use of English as discriminatory, and that the action reflects the way rural residents are seen as people who do not really matter in the scheme of things. According to this respondent, the dominant use of English by agencies of government, especially in public health discourse, is discriminatory and does not serve the interest of many disadvantaged groups and individuals in the country.

Also, lending credence to the reaction of this respondent on the question of language choice for COVID-19 messages in order to reach everyone, another respondent lamented the plight of old and uneducated people in different parts of the country who do not use the official language (English). The excerpt in Box 2 is from the reactions of the respondent:

Leaving Out No One

Box 2. Sociolinguistic interview excerpt

> For me, na the language of the people wey go give them the message well.
>   [For me, I support the language of the people that would give them the actual message]
> If government people no wan waste time na native language dem suppose use for corona message.
>   [If government officials don't want to waste their time it's our native language that should be used for COVID-19 messages]
> Dem fit add pidgin join.
>   [Pidgin could be an additional language]
> Me no dey speak oyinbo language because I no be city people, na farmer be my work.
>   [I don't speak English because I am not in the city, I am a farmer]
> Ehmm . . . [pause]
> Person go know wetin dey happen if dem talk am for radio for the person language wey him hear.
>   [People would know what is happening if they announce on radio in a native language that they understand]
> The katakata wey dey government and this country too plenty, we all be oyinbo?
>   [There are too many problems and confusion in this country, are we all English?]
> If dem wan help us make dem give us the message for the language wey we dey use . . .
>   [If they really want to help us, they should give us the message in the language that we use]

To the present respondent, for government agencies not to end up wasting their time, it is the native language of the people that should be used in giving COVID-19 messages to the people in the rural areas. He argues that to ensure that this crucial information really get to the target audience and elicit the desired behavioral change among them, only a language they understand can play that role. Apart from the native languages of the people, this respondent added Nigerian Pidgin (NP) as another language that could also be used to give people access and increase reach, especially among the largely uneducated population of these rural communities. In addition, it was observed that many of these rural people displayed existing distrust towards government agencies and their actions, probably due to long history of failed promises and the government's inability to deliver on their mandates in various things that matter to the people. With this underlying lack of trust, it was easy for several conspiracy theories and myths to flourish among the rural dwellers. Some of them see COVID-19 as a creation of the West or white man and were skeptical to yield to public health safety advisories and protocols from professionals. In his reactions, this respondent also touched on a very vital issue in relation to access. According to him, important COVID-19 information in rural communities should only be given in indigenous languages or NP in order to guarantee effective delivery. Such messages should be disseminated through radio, which is the preferred mode of receiving information by peasants and most rural dwellers, he stated. This is important because there are a lot of rural communities in Nigeria with no electricity and some other social amenities available in the cities. To such communities, radio appears to be more effective to the people because even without electricity, radio can be powered by batteries and give people access to important public health information. Figure 5 is a graphical representation of the attitudes of the respondents to language use for COVID-19 public awareness and sensitization messages.

Figure 5. People's preference of language use for COVID-19 messages

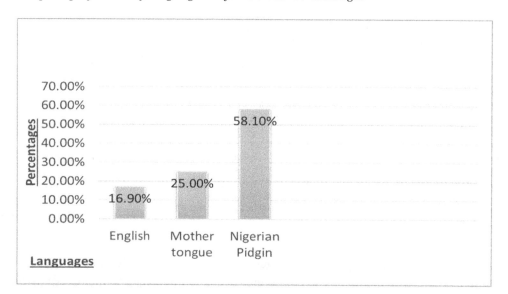

It is not surprising that most of the respondents unequivocally stated their preference for native languages of the people and in addition to these numerous indigenous languages, also opted for the Nigerian Pidgin (NP) as the most appropriate languages in the design and dissemination of COVID-19 public awareness and sensitization messages to rural people. These are people who were specifically targeted to evaluate their access to public health information due to their inability to function in the official language (English). What is significant to note is the language preference pattern among the people in these rural communities, and their indifference to the efforts of government agencies in the fight against the virus. To many of the respondents, any message aimed at educating them should come in a language that they can understand. This lack of interest in the discourse of COVID-19 or its awareness messages from the government could be responsible for the low compliance rate or outright rejection of the claim of threats in COVID-19 infections in some rural communities. While some did not believe the news of the outbreak at all, others were reluctant in their responses to the global crisis. This lack of awareness and distrust among rural and indigenous people could also be responsible for the huge misinformation that happened in some of these rural communities during the pandemic. Due to sheer ignorance, many people were spreading false information and narratives about the virus. On a lot of occasions there was misleading, false, and unsubstantiated information about the virus. Months into the pandemic and with feedbacks from some rural communities, it became incumbent on the government that, to avoid people being killed by ignorance and not even COVID-19 infections, the fight against misinformation should be as comprehensive and aggressive as the fight against COVID-19 itself in rural communities. It was this that led to the aggressive public awareness campaigns in indigenous languages and NP on radio and other media platforms about what people really need to know about the virus. There were the institution of multi-layered interventions involving different stakeholders across the various tiers of government, community, and religious leaders in order to ensure that people got adequate information on how to stay safe.

CONCLUSION

This chapter has demonstrated how public health communication in a multilingual developing context during a global pandemic was redefined, recontextualized, and localized in order to achieve inclusiveness. The chapter has shown how multilingual practices redefined communication in a developing African context in order to promote inclusiveness in public health awareness campaigns. I argue that for equity in multilingual contexts, there is the need for strategic design of communication in multiple languages in order to safeguard the linguistic rights of the people and guarantee access to important public health information. Through the analysis of communicative practices in the design and dissemination of COVID-19 awareness and sensitization messages in this multilingual setting, the study has revealed how linguistic diversity was strategically weaponized to promote inclusion as evidenced in the use of multiple languages in the delivery of coronavirus messages to the generality of the people. The messages of the key agencies studied show that in spite of its lack of official recognition or assignment of roles, Nigerian Pidgin (NP), the country's lingua franca, played prominent roles in the communication of risk and preventive recommendations to the people during the pandemic. Furthermore, the study also identifies multimodality in COVID-19 awareness and sensitization messages as one of the deliberate strategies to increase people's access to important public health information during the crisis. The chapter contends that linguistic diversity is the norm in Nigeria, and that multilingualism could be an advantage if strategically managed, and its resources exploited by government and its agencies for mass mobilization and involvement, inclusion, and sustainable development. It concludes that given their nature, public health messages in multilingual settings should be deliberately contextualized to incorporate the peculiarities and sociolinguistic nuances of the people in order to achieve the communicative intents of communicators, especially during public health emergencies that respect no social differentiation.

ACKNOWLEDGMENT

The author acknowledges the funding support given to him by the Alexander von Humboldt Foundation, Germany. This study is part of a bigger postdoctoral research project on linguistic diversity and the discourse of COVID-19 public health awareness campaign in Nigeria, funded by the foundation. Even though I have enjoyed their support, the foundation did not have any role in the study design, data collection, data analysis, interpretation, or writing of the manuscript.

REFERENCES

Adedimeji, M. A. (2010). Language question and the constitutional challenges of development in a multilingual country. *Journal of Research in National Development*, *8*(2). Advance online publication. doi:10.4314/jorind.v8i2.66801

Adegbija, E. (1994). *Language attitudes in Sub-Saharan Africa: A sociolinguistic overview*. Multilingual Matters. doi:10.21832/9781800418141

Adegbite, A. B. (2010). English language usage, uses and misuse(s) in a non-host second language context, Nigeria. *Inaugural lecture series 231*. Obafemi Awolowo University Press.

Ahmad, R. (2020). Multilingual resources key to fighting COVID-19. *Language on the move.*. https://www.languageonthemove.com/multilingual-resources-key-to-fighting-COVID-19/

Akande, A. T. (2016). Multilingual practices in Nigerian Army barracks. *African Identities*, *2*(14), 38–58. doi:10.1080/14725843.2015.1100108

Akande, A. T., & Okesola, S. O. (2021). Morpho-syntactic features of Nigerian Pidgin on Radio programmes rendered in Naija. In A. T. Akande & O. Salami (Eds.), *Current trends in Nigerian Pidgin English: A sociolinguistic perspective* (pp. 201–220). De Gruter Muoton. doi:10.1515/9781501513541-008

Akinnaso, F. N. (1991). The development of a multilingual language policy in Nigeria. *Applied Linguistics*, *12*(1), 29–61. doi:10.1093/applin/12.1.29

Alamu, G., & Iloene, J. (2003). On multilingualism and the medium of construction. In O. Ndimele, (Ed.) The linguistic paradise for E. Nolue Emenanjo, Aba: NINLAN, 319-336.

Amzat, J., Aminu, K., Kolo, V. I., Akinyele, A. A., Ogundairo, J. A., & Danjibo, M. C. (2020). Coronavirus outbreak in Nigeria: Burden and socio-medical response during the first 100 days. *International Journal of Infectious Diseases*, *98*, 218–224. doi:10.1016/j.ijid.2020.06.067 PMID:32585282

Anchimbe, E. A. (2018). *Offers and offer refusals: A postcolonial pragmatics perspective on world Englishes*. John Benjamins. doi:10.1075/pbns.298

Bamgbose, A. (1999). African language development and language planning. *Social Dynamics. Journal of African Studies*, *25*(1), 13–30.

Bamgbose, A. (2014). The language factor in development goals. *Journal of Multilingual and Multicultural Development*, *35*(7), 646–657. doi:10.1080/01434632.2014.908888

Benson, C. (2010). How multilingual African contexts are pushing educational research and practice in new directions. *Language and Education*, *24*(4), 323–336. doi:10.1080/09500781003678704

Deuber, D. (2005). *Nigerian Pidgin in Lagos: Language contact, variation and change in an African urban setting*. Battlebridge.

Djite, P. G. (2008). *The sociolinguistics of development in Africa*. Multilingual Matters Limited. doi:10.21832/9781847690470

Egbokhare, F. O. (2021). The accidental lingua franca: The paradox of the ascendancy of Nigerian Pidgin in Nigeria. In A. T. Akande & O. Salami (Eds.), *Current trends in Nigerian Pidgin English: A sociolinguistic perspective* (pp. 67–114). De Gruter Muoton. doi:10.1515/9781501513541-004

Essien, O. (2003). National development, language and language policy in Nigeria. In Essien, O. & Okon, M. (Eds.) Topical issues in sociolinguistics: The Nigerian perspective. Aba: National Institute for Nigerian Languages, 21-42.

Essien, O. (2006). Language and the Nigerian reforms agenda. In O. Ndimele, C. Ikekeonwu, & B.M. Mbah, (Eds.) Language and economic reforms in Nigeria. Ethnologue: Languages of the World (22nd ed.), Dallas.

Faraclas, N. (2008). Nigerian Pidgin. In B. Kortmann, E. W. Schneider, K. Burridge, & R. Mesthrie (Eds.), *Varieties of English* (Vol. 3, pp. 340–367). Mouton.

Faraclas, N. (2021). Naija: A language of the future. In A. T. Akande & O. Salami (Eds.), *Current trends in Nigerian Pidgin English: A sociolinguistic perspective* (pp. 9–38). De Gruter Muoton. doi:10.1515/9781501513541-002

Igboanusi, H. (2008). Empowering Nigerian Pidgin: A challenge for status planning? *World Englishes*, *27*(1), 68–82. doi:10.1111/j.1467-971X.2008.00536.x

Igboanusi, H., Odoje, C., & Ibrahim, G. (2017). The modernization of HIV and AIDS' nomenclatures in Nigeria's major languages. *Terminology. International Journal of Theoretical and Applied Issues in Specialized Communication, Vol.*, *2*(23), 238–260.

Olatunji, M. (2007). Yabis: A phenomenon in the contemporary Nigerian music. *Africology*, *1*(9), 26–46.

Osoba, J. B. (2014). The use of Nigerian Pidgin in media adverts. *International Journal of English Linguistics*, *4*(2), 26–37. doi:10.5539/ijel.v4n2p26

Oyebode, O. O., & Okesola, S. O. (2020). #Take responsibility: Non-verbal modes as discursive strategies in managing COVID-19 public health crisis. *Language and Semiotic Studies*, *6*(4), 21–45. doi:10.1515/lass-2020-060401

Oyetade, S. O. (2003). Language planning in a multi-ethnic state: The majority-minority dichotomy in Nigeria. *Nordic Journal of African Studies*, *12*(1), 105–117.

Piller, I. (2016). *Linguistic diversity and social justice*. Oxford University Press. doi:10.1093/acprof:oso/9780199937240.001.0001

Rudwick, S., Sijadu, Z., & Turner, I. (2021). Politics of language in COVID-19: Multilingual perspectives from South Africa. *Politikon: South African Journal of Political Studies*, *48*(2), 2, 242–259. doi:10.1080/02589346.2021.1917206

World Population Review. (2022). *Countries*. World Population Review. https://worldpopulationreview.com/countries/ (accessed 5th October, 2022).

Section 7
Dialectical Language Use

Chapter 13
Promoting US-Based Pre-Service ESOL Teachers' Understanding of Language Variation in Multidialectical Settings

Brian Hibbs
https://orcid.org/0009-0005-0894-1555
Dalton State College, USA

ABSTRACT

This chapter outlines the elements of a course unit on language variation within a culture and education ESOL course intended to support the development of pre-service elementary education teacher candidates' awareness of language variation writ large and, more specifically, their knowledge concerning the nature of American English dialects, along with their understanding and appreciation of their future students' home dialects/languages. The chapter begins with a discussion of various theories that frame the course unit (challenging language norms, heteroglossia, critical applied linguistics, language-as-problem/right/resource, and language variation) and provides an overview of several prevailing attitudes concerning dialectical variation and how the course unit works to counter these narratives. The chapter then highlights the resources, activities, and assignments that constitute the course unit along with an examination of how and why they are included and utilized in the unit.

INTRODUCTION

Norms are behaviors that are often presumed to be conventional and seen as given because the majority of members of a given social community exhibit and demonstrate these behaviors. Chitadze (2022) defines norms as "generalized standards of behavior that once accepted shape collective expectations about appropriate conduct" (p. 40). Norms are used both explicitly and implicitly in regards to a variety

DOI: 10.4018/978-1-6684-8761-7.ch013

of phenomena, including language. People frequently hold specific assumptions about ways in which others use language depending on the contextual factors of the communities in which they live. One could logically claim, for example, that the standard language norm in the United States is monolingualism since the practice of learning languages other than English is not consistently valued or promoted. More specifically, in the case of English learners, a common misperception is that their multilingualism is a deficit that prevents them from learning English, an assumption which is commonly advanced more for political and social reasons than pedagogical ones. This also holds true for minority language students who come to school speaking a myriad of varieties of (American) English; these students are often expected to reject the linguistic norms of their home dialect(s) and instead embrace and adopt the linguistic norms of standard American English (SAE).

Due to a variety of educational and societal factors, many teachers in elementary and secondary classrooms exclusively teach their students SAE due to their misguided and misinformed perception that this dialect equates to "proper" English, and they frequently endeavor to eliminate non-SAE features from the linguistic output of their students. Doing so, however, may signal to students that they are expected to assimilate to mainstream (white, middle-class, etc.) culture and that their linguistic (and cultural) identities do not matter. Such an approach treats all students as if they are monolingual and monocultural and neither acknowledges nor capitalizes on their cultural or linguistic funds of knowledge (González, Moll, & Amanti, 2005). Many such teachers have not studied the linguistic features of other varieties of American English and, consequently, have not learned to understand or value the linguistic diversity currently existing in the United States and in their own classrooms. Additionally, in order for students to be empowered to find their voice through their linguistic repertoire, teacher candidates should be educated about such issues in their educational preparation programs so that they develop an understanding and appreciation of the complexities of this issue and are equipped with specific strategies and techniques to create and foster a classroom environment that both supports and teaches students about linguistic diversity. Consequently, the goal of the proposed chapter is to attempt to suggest a possible remedy to fills this curricular (and societal) gap.

The chapter provides an overview of the specific activities and resources included in a course unit on dialectical variation in order to provide other educators with one possible blueprint for incorporating linguistic variation into course and program curricula. One of the principal goals of this course unit is to educate pre-service teacher candidates regarding the linguistic and culture nature of dialectical variation in order to provide a possible and viable antidote to the dilemmas outlined above. The ultimate goal of this course unit, thus, is to develop teacher candidates' linguistic awareness concerning the nature and evolution of language variation more generally and dialectical variation more specifically. Fairclough (1992) defines language awareness as "conscious attention to properties of language and language use as an element of language education" (p. 1). Bolitho et al. (2003) characterize language awareness as "a mental attribute which develops through paying motivated attention to language in use, and which enables language learners to gradually gain insights into how languages work" (p. 251). These definitions highlight the notion that language awareness involves learners' appreciation for and understanding of the organic nature of language and the ways in which language is used in context to achieve personal and professional aims. Advancing such awareness is not only important for language learners but for language educators as well.

Numerous scholars agree that it is incumbent upon educator preparation programs to produce a cadre of teachers who are linguistically aware and are cognizant of the educational, political, and social ramifications of language use. For example, García (2017) contends that developing educators' language awareness advances their abilities in "promoting questioning about language to develop linguistic understandings and challenge linguistic prejudices" (p. 264). Statistics consistently show that elementary and secondary classrooms are becoming increasingly diverse and will likely continue to do so (National Center for Education Statistics, 2022), implying that pre-service teachers must be prepared for the cultural and linguistic diversity they are likely to encounter in their future classrooms. In regards to language teacher education, Wright (2002) maintains that "the linguistically aware teacher can spot opportunities to generate discussion and exploration of language" (p. 115), while Tüzela and Akcan (2009) argue that activities that promote teacher candidates' language awareness "lead teachers to new discoveries about language, enable them to explore language points for teaching purposes, to be more aware of the difficulties which learners encounter and gain confidence to satisfy the demands of teaching language for communication" (p. 282). These quotes point out the importance of not only advancing teacher candidates' understanding of linguistic diversity for their own sake but also of familiarizing elementary and secondary students with the inherently dynamic and evolving nature of language. Additionally, Bolitho et al. (2003) indicate that developing pre-service language teachers' language awareness is an essential component in educator preparation since "trainee teachers need to be able to analyse language, to apply different strategies for thinking about language…in order to be able to plan lessons, to predict learners' difficulties, to answer their questions, and to write and evaluate materials" (p. 255). Wright and Bolitho (1993) concur with this view and assert that "successful [language] teaching depends more than ever on a high level of language awareness in a teacher" (p. 292) since it consists of "a process that aims to create and develop links between linguistic knowledge and classroom activity" (Wright, 2002, p. 129). These scholars emphasize that, in addition to the benefits mentioned above, facilitating pre-service teachers' language awareness also helps them make connections between language teaching theories and classroom practice and can help guide them in designing and implementing activities that are aligned with their beliefs and perspectives concerning language learning.

THEORETICAL FRAMEWORK

This section outlines five epistemological premises that shaped the course unit outlined in this chapter: challenging language norms, heteroglossia, critical applied linguistics, language-as-problem/right/resource, and language variation. Each of these theories is reviewed individually along with a brief discussion of the implications of the theory for dialectical variation.

Challenging Language Norms

The first theoretical framework that shaped the course unit was the concept of language norms. Language norms can be understood as assumptions, behaviors, beliefs, expectations, etc. that people possess and collectively employ regarding the use of language in specific linguistic contexts. These norms are often dictated by political and social forces that are not necessarily linguistic in nature. Ellis (2008) asserts that "an individual is monolingual who does not have access to more than one linguistic code as a means of social communication" (p. 313), while Hamers and Blanc (2000) define bilinguality as "the psychological state of an individual who has access to more than one linguistic code as a means of social communication" (p. 6). Bailey (2012) contends that "being a monolingual English speaker is an ideological default against which difference or distinctiveness is constructed in the USA" (p. 504). In other words, monolingualism is often viewed in this country as the standardized norm to which language behaviors are compared/contrasted, with the monolingual usage of language as linguistically unmarked and the utilization of multiple languages as linguistically marked. Escobar (2016) asserts that the field of applied linguistics has historically adopted such a position in that it "has largely operated upon the premise that monolingualism is the default for human communication and that the learning of an additional language later in life is to be examined vis-à-vis monolingual speakers' language competence" (p. 250).

Such a view is not merely restricted to applied linguistics, however; numerous political and social leaders across the world have co-opted monolingualism as a vehicle for advancing nationalism and patriotism in an effort to promote linguistic and cultural uniformity (and unity) within the community. Escobar (2016) contends that "the monolingual bias that still today permeates second and foreign language programs must be problematized" (p. 253); multilingualism, thus, is one possibility for challenging this bias not only in the field of applied linguistics but in all aspects of society. Multilingualism often works to disrupt this bias by offering a counternarrative to such monolingual prescriptive behaviors. These views concerning language use often emerge from specific language ideologies, which Errington (2001) defines as "the situated, partial, and interested character[s] of conceptions and uses of language" (p. 110). This definition underscores the fact that such perspectives on language are context-specific, can provide incomplete and inaccurate perspectives concerning language, and are often appropriated by others to achieve certain extralinguistic objectives. Farr and Song (2011) argue that ideologies can be powerful forces in shaping the ways speech communities are perceived and understood since such ideologies "are not simply about language, but also involve social and cultural conceptions of personhood, citizenship, morality, quality and value, etc." (p. 651). Farr and Song (2011) maintain that these ideologies "connect the linguistic with the social, and…do so in the interest of a particular, usually powerful, social position" (p. 651). That is, ideology is not a neutral phenomenon but instead is often used to establish/maintain the privileged status of one language variety at the expense of others. Farr and Song (2011) also assert that such judgments are oftentimes culturally-based rather than linguistically-based: "particular linguistic forms become salient and stigmatized because of the social categories of people they index, not because of their own characteristics" (p. 653). Espinet et al. (2020) contend that, in the United States, "normalized language practices…are tied to dominant white middle-class standards" (p. 221). In other words, monolingualism is often used as a specific language ideology to explicitly communicate the expectation that all should conform to the language behaviors demonstrated by mainstream American culture. To combat this standpoint, Espinet et al. (2020) highlight the importance of counteracting the hegemonic nature of monolingualism by providing spaces for both students and educators to question these assumptions by asking questions such as "Why is English so ubiquitous? What structures make it that way? Who benefits, and who is left out by this choice?" (p. 230). Farr and Song (2011) also remind us that educators are resources which can be utilized to support/promote or challenge such views concerning language ideologies through their instruction: "teachers produce, affirm, and/or disconfirm language policies every day" (p. 660). Angay-Crowder et al. (2023) conjecture that this might be the case since, according to the findings of their study, "PSTs (pre-service teachers) separated languages as binary or dichotomous constructs, which reflect monolingual perspectives" (p. 455). In other words, teacher candidates often tend to either implicitly or explicitly respect the establishment and maintenance of the boundaries between named languages, which often ultimately leads to privileging one language (variety) over others. Consequently, including a course unit on dialectical variation is one avenue for challenging the monolingual norm prevalent in society today in order to introduce teacher candidates to the inherently multilingual/multidialectical nature of our world.

Heteroglossia

The second theoretical framework that structured the course unit was heteroglossia. Heteroglossia essentially views language as a social phenomenon and investigates language use in its social, political, and historical contexts. Bailey (2012) argues that, rather than seeing it as an abstract, decontextualized, and theoretical entity, language is instead "a medium through which one participates in a historical flow of social relationships, struggles, and meanings" (pp. 499-500) since "linguistic signs come with social and historical associations, and…gain new ones in their situated use" (p. 500). In other words, language cannot be divorced from the larger sociohistorical and sociopolitical contexts it inhabits. Blackledge and Creese (2014) take this position a step further by asserting that languages are "ideological constructions" (p. 2) that are often used to serve political and social ends, and they reinforce the interdependent nature of language and society by claiming that "linguistic diversity [is] constitutive of, and constituted by, social diversity" (p. 11). Bailey (2012) defines heteroglossia as "(1) the simultaneous use of different kinds of forms or signs; and (2) the tensions and conflicts among those signs, on the sociohistorical associations they carry with them" (p. 499). Heteroglossia explores the political and social essence of language by examining the "social tensions inherent in language" (Bailey, 2012, p. 499). Heteroglossia, thus, is the study of language use within the broader historical and political contexts which circumscribe it: "heteroglossia…explicitly joins the linguistic utterance in the present and the sociohistorical relationships that give meanings to those utterances" (p. 506). This is to say, language usage links past associations and relationships with specific utterances to the present time and subsequently establishes such connections with these utterances to their future use: "all utterances…have a history and an anticipated future" (Blackledge and Creese, 2014, p. 10).

A foundational principle undergirding the concept of heteroglossia is the concept of diglossia, which focuses on the idea that, within a given speech community, one language type (high variety) often holds more authority, prestige, status, etc. (high variety) than another (low variety). High varieties of a given language tend to be more formal in nature, are often learned in academic contexts, and are frequently viewed as superior in comparison with other varieties, while low varieties have a propensity to be utilized in more informal settings, are oftentimes acquired naturally, and are commonly seen as inferior to other varieties (Kyriakou, 2019). One of the central tenets of heteroglossia is that words are not objective or unbiased entities but instead are bound up with the social associations connected with them and that, when using language, meanings associated with and conveyed by words are inextricably intertwined with these political and historical contexts they are connected to, regardless of the intentionality of the speaker: "these social tensions are at work even if the speaker does not intend them and is not conscious of them" (Bailey, 2012, p. 499).

Another important tenet of heteroglossia is that an omnipresent tension exists between linguistic heterogeneity and linguistic homogeneity. Some people advocate for the conventional use of language towards a codified national standard within a given speech community (what Bakhtin (1981) refers to as "centripetal forces"), while others work against the establishment of such a standard by encouraging and promoting the use of nonstandard varieties in local contexts (what Bakhtin (1981) refers to as "centrifugal forces"). Consequently, rather than focusing their efforts on studying language behaviors in terms of convergence to and/or divergence from a standard variety of a language, scholars adopting a heteroglossic view of language instead explore the multimodal resources of language users in order to better understand how these users utilize their linguistic repertoire to achieve communicative and social ends. Although heteroglossia tends to focus on people's abilities to move beyond the boundaries of constituted named languages, many of the points highlighted above equally apply to dialectical variation. For instance, just as with codified languages, dialects are imbued with historical, social, and political associations, attitudes, impressions, etc. that are actualized when deployed in social interactions, regardless of whether or not interlocutors are necessarily aware of them. Additionally, the centripetal and centrifugal forces at play concerning national languages are also at play in regards to language varieties, with some endorsing adherence to the standard variety of a given language and others championing speakers' nonconformity to these conventions through the use of their own idiolect. One important note to make is that heteroglossia is one avenue that can be used to challenge the monolingual norm prevalent in many parts of the world by replacing monolingualism with bilinguality as the norm, thereby de-centered monolingualism as the standard benchmark for linguistic behavior as mentioned above. Thus, heteroglossia was incorporated as a theoretical framework in the course unit in order to challenge and reframe students' understandings concerning the commonly-accepted monolingual/monodialectical norms that govern our society.

Critical Language Awareness

The third theoretical framework that contributed to the design of the course unit was critical language awareness. Fairclough (1992) defines language awareness as "conscious attention to properties of language and language use as an element of language education" (p. 1). This definition implies that language learning involves the processes of linguistic competence (e.g., knowledge concerning the functionality of specific grammatical features of a given language) and linguistic performance (i.e., the application of such features within specific communicative events) in order to solidify learners' awareness of the form/function relationship concerning particular structures within the language. Hammersley-Fletcher and Hanley (2016) argue that criticality centers around the notion that "the nature of reasoning, the self and our relations with others, are open to challenge and debate" (p. 979), thereby suggesting that people should explore opportunities to candidly and frankly question commonly-held notions about reality. Pennycook (2021) takes this position one step further by defining the notion of criticality as "taking social inequality and social transformation as central to one's work" (p. 26). In other words, from this perspective, critical applied linguists should focus their scholarly production on the study of how language is co-opted to further specific conservative and neoliberal agendas in order to maintain the status quo and how language can also be used to fashion a more just and equal society. Pennycook (2021) emphasizes this point by contending that "the political challenge of critical applied linguistics" (p. 41) is to "make one's applied linguistic practice accountable to an agenda for positive social change" (p. 38). Fairclough (1992) also emphasizes the importance of adding the element of criticality to language awareness by stating that critical language awareness "highlights how language conventions and language practices are invested with power relations and ideological processes which people are often unaware of" (p. 7). Pennycook (2001) agrees with this notion by pointing out that one of the fundamental aims of critical applied linguistics is to develop an understanding of "how the classroom, text, or conversation is related to broader social cultural and political relations" (p. 5). In other words, critical applied linguistics as a field "is concerned not merely with relating language contexts to social contexts but rather does so from a point of view that views social relations as problematic" (Pennycook, 2021, p. 25). Hazen (2017) also concurs with these views by stating that critical language awareness "requires speakers to pay attention to the social and political underpinnings of their language ideologies" (p. 149). These scholars highlight the fact that critical language awareness involves the study of language in terms of power relations to determine which language varieties hold more (or less) prestige within a given speech community, why this is so, and what can/should be done to foster linguistic (and social) equality. In terms of dialectical variation, speakers of language varieties should be consciously aware of the historical, social, and political consequences of (not) adhering to conventional usage of the standard variety of a given language. Consequently, critical language awareness was selected as a theoretical framework that structured the course unit in order to sensitize students to the inherently political and social nature of language/dialect use and to guide them in considering the ingrained hegemonic dominance of standard varieties of languages and dialects in our current society.

Language-As-Problem/Right/Resource

The fourth theoretical framework that outlined the course unit was the concept of language-as-problem/right/resource. Within the field of language policy and planning, one of the early seminal works that strove to highlight the major debates and dilemmas in the field is Ruiz (1984), who identified three prevailing views concerning the nature of language: language-as problem, language-as right, and language-as-resource. The goal of these orientations was to provide a framework for understanding and subsequently articulating specific language policies and procedures while simultaneously combatting "the assumption of English monolingualism as the only acceptable social condition" (p. 28). This section provides an overview of the three orientations; readers are encouraged to consult Hult and Hornberger (2016), for a more concise summary of these orientations.

The language-as-problem orientation asserts that the use of multiple languages within a given speech community can be problematic and that these "problems" typically result from issues involving breakdowns in communication in multilingual contexts; as a result, language policymakers adopting this perspective typically work to resolve such issues in their respective settings. In such circumstances, the solution to these language problems can often result in policymakers advocating for the uniform use of language in a given speech community to the exclusion of other varieties of the language or other languages. For example, although many politicians highlight the diversity of the cultural makeup of the United States as an inherent strength of the country, they also argue that children coming to this country who do not speak English as a first language must learn to do so as quickly and efficiently as possible, even to the exclusion of their previous linguistic backgrounds if necessary (as evidenced by several English-only policies adopted in several states such as California's Proposition 58 and Arizona's Proposition 203). In other words, those adopting the language-as-problem position allege that all people should speak the same language in order to help everyone integrate into the American social fabric. One might imagine that such issues are never wholly centered on a given person's use of language but are usually intertwined with social dilemmas as well: "language problems are never merely language problems, but have a direct impact on all spheres of social life" (p. 21). Consequently, the language-as-problem view promotes and reinforces monolingual language norms.

The language-as-right orientation equates language rights with civil rights and argues that one's use of language is as innate and inherent as other human rights. As with the language-as-problem perspective, some advocates who support this position believe that monolingualism can conceivably be viewed as a discriminatory practice since multilingual citizens in certain countries around the world are routinely denied the opportunity to utilize their native language(s) to achieve educational, political, and/or social aims. One could also claim that such conduct is potentially assimilationist in nature since it invalidates and negates specific facets of their linguistic and cultural identity. Hiatt et al. (2019) understand discrimination as "overt and covert behavior directed to individuals and groups intending to exclude, demean, or impose upon them extra requirements or otherwise deny them access from resources" (p. 192). This definition underscores the fact that, in addition to the difficulties cited above, such behaviors on the part of those who promote monolingualism may ultimately deny multilingual speakers access to essential goods and services necessary for their survival. Consequently. such discrimination is not necessarily relegated solely to the realm of language use but also touches on multiple aspects of social existence: "any comprehensive statement about language rights cannot confine itself to merely linguistic considerations" (Ruiz, 1984, p. 22). For example, one could conjecture that linguistic inequity (privileging one language over others within a given speech community) not only leads to social inequality but is also symptomatic of the inequalities existing at the institutional/systemic level. As a result, supporters of this position contend that those who have experienced linguistic discrimination may redress their concerns in the legal arena, as evidenced by court cases such as *Lau v. Nichols* (1974) and *Castañeda v. Pickard* (1978/1981), which legally codified the rights of non-English-speaking children in the U.S. education system by declaring that not supplying these students with equal educational opportunities was a violation of their civil rights.

Finally, the language-as-resource orientation posits that language is a linguistic and cultural asset that can ultimately be utilized to benefit society as a whole. For instance, such linguistic diversity advances views concerning cultural diversity while also promoting and supporting the awareness, knowledge, and appreciation of other languages/cultures. This orientation can also highlight the issues linguistic minorities face within a monolingual speech community and can help majority-language speakers better understand these dilemmas and work to dismantle and eradicate these cultural/linguistic barriers. Ruiz (1984) contends that, in addition to the reasons cited above, this third orientation can also help to overcome the inherent debates and struggles resulting from the first two orientations: "A closer look at the idea of language-as resource could reveal some promise for alleviating some of the conflicts emerging out of the other two orientations" (p. 25).

Although Ruiz's (1984) arguments concerning language planning and policy dealt with issues surrounding language use in multilingual contexts, these same arguments conceivably hold for language use in multidialectical settings as well. For instance, just as with multilingual speakers, those who employ a minority dialectical variety within a majority speech community may be seen as a "problem", may be judged as deficient, inferior, etc., and may ultimately be persuaded/forced to adopt the dialectical norms of the majority group at the expense of their linguistic identity. Some multidialectical speakers may believe that usage of their language variety is an inalienable right and that denying them opportunities to engage in receptive and productive communication in their dialect is a discriminatory and unjust practice. Finally, developing one's awareness and knowledge of dialectical variation can help promote the understanding and appreciation of linguistic (and cultural) diversity and can acquaint others with the dilemmas and issues that multidialectical speakers face. Therefore, language as problem/right/resource was included as a theoretical framework that shaped the course unit in order to familiarize teacher candidates with various perspectives concerning the nature of dialectical variation in the hopes of guiding them to understand such variation not as a problem but instead as a right, a resource, and ultimately a linguistic and cultural asset.

Language Variation

Finally, several principles concerning language variation undergirded the course unit as well. Tzakosta (2022) defines dialectical variation as "differences reported on typologically adjacent language systems which belong to the same language" (p. 26); Hazen (2017) contends that such variation "includes language change as well as social and geographic variation at any one point in time" (p. 146). Although language variation is often understood in terms of differences among varieties of a given language based on geography, such variation can additionally focus on a variety of social variables, including but not limited to, race and ethnicity, class and socioeconomic status, gender, sexual orientation, and age; it is conceivable to study language variation with respect to the intersectionality of these geographical and social factors as well. Hazen (2017) explains that, although these perspectives are slowly changing, discrimination of speakers of stigmatized varieties of a given language still exists among educators who either implicitly or explicitly favor standard varieties of the language and that "the problem is overwhelmingly one of social attitudes, rather than of…linguistic characteristics" (p. 152). Reaser (2014) agrees with this view by stating that "any evaluation of dialects as inferior, broken, lazy, or slang is inappropriate and is really [more of] an evaluation of the group that speaks the dialect" (p. 104). These quotes suggest that, as we have seen previously, attitudes and beliefs commonly held in regards to speakers of these varieties of a particular language are frequently based on social factors more so than linguistic ones. Hazen (2017) additionally contends that "[a] teacher's reception of language variation is directly related to the teacher's linguistic awareness" (p. 153), meaning that, the more informed educators are concerning the nature of dialectical variation, the more open they conceivably will be to accepting and validating students' use of their home language varieties in the classroom. Charity Hudley and Mallinson (2011) concur with this view by affirming that "all educators need knowledge and tools to understand their students' language differences and variations, address the language-related challenges they may face, and support their educational development and academic progress" (p. 1). Charity Hudley and Mallinson's (2011) contention adds an additional dimension concerning the relationship between marginalized students' language varieties and their ultimate educational success by highlighting the imperative for educators to embrace students' cultural and linguistic identities in order to facilitate their ultimate academic achievement. Reaser (2014) underscores the relationship between linguistic equality and social equity in education by arguing that "to privilege some [students' linguistic production] over others is to privilege some students over others" (p. 96). In other words, educators should take care to not see minority language students as deficient, incapable, inferior, etc. simply because they may communicate using stigmatized varieties of the language.

Charity Hudley and Mallinson (2011) assert that, in addition to receiving instruction regarding standard English, students should also be educated about dialectical variation and the systematicity of the varieties utilized in their own communities and that such learning can contribute significantly to their academic and professional success: "it is necessary to teach students the conventions of standardized English, but it is also critical to teach students that nonstandardized varieties of English play important roles in society" (p. 19). In other words, rather than subscribing to a subtractive view of language education in which minority language students must learn to replace their home language varieties with standard English, educators should instead adopt an additive position in which students are encouraged "to add standardized English to their linguistic repertoire" (p. 20) in order to complement the language varieties with which these students are already familiar. Reaser (2014) supports this position and contends that "the goal of formal education – for students to master academic English in its written and spoken form – should not be seen as incompatible with the goal of investigating and celebrating language diversity" (p. 106). To further elucidate this point, Reaser (2014) provides a brief overview of the history of language education in the United States in the nineteenth and twentieth centuries and highlights the fact that, in recent decades, there has been a pedagogical shift from attempting to replace learners' native language with English to enhancing their knowledge and awareness of their home language(s) while also receiving instruction in English; Reaser (2014) contends that such "shifts in perspective and approach…reflect the same shift that schools must undergo with regard to nonstandard dialects" (p. 104). In summary, minority language students should not be expected to relinquish or renounce their linguistic (and cultural) identities in order to pursue their scholastic aims: "A goal of education in the United States is to prepare students to be successful in academic, professional, personal, and community spheres. Dialect eradication…is not consistent with this goal" (p. 106). The perspectives described above concerning language variation guided the design and implementation of the course unit outlined in this chapter in order to advance teacher candidates' emerging understanding of and appreciation for the linguistic/dialectical diversity currently existing in elementary and secondary classrooms in the hopes that they may ultimately educate their future students to do the same.

POSITIONALITY

Maher and Tetreault (2001) describe positionality as a phenomenon in which "people are defined not in terms of fixed identities, but by their location within shifting networks of relationships, which can be analyzed and changed" (p. 164). This definition highlights the importance of scholars expressly conveying their positionality in order to contextualize and situate their work within a wider frame. The objective of this section, thus, is to familiarize readers with the background of the author in order to help them better understand his knowledge and expertise concerning dialectical variation.

The author completed undergraduate studies in foreign languages (French and Spanish) and secondary education and also completed graduate studies in education and foreign languages along with doctoral studies in second language acquisition and teaching. During his graduate studies, he taught numerous courses in both French and Spanish at the elementary, intermediate, and advanced levels, including a course for Spanish undergraduate heritage speakers on Spanish phonetics. Additionally, the author worked a lecturer in English for the Centro de Idiomas of the Universidad de Valladolid in Valladolid, Spain and the Université de Paris VII in Paris, France. These experiences not only fostered the development of his linguistic and cultural proficiency but also advanced his preliminary understanding of the nature of linguistic diversity. These experiences were enhanced by his appointment as assistant professor of education/ESOL at his current institution, which further supported his competencies in this area by teaching numerous sections of the ESOL course that provided the context for the unit outlined in this chapter. The unit was included in the course when it was taught by the previous instructor, and so the author initially experienced a steep learning curve regarding his understanding of linguistic diversity specifically regarding the dialects of American English, but through his own research and investigation, the author has regularly broadened his expertise in this area and continues to do so.

INSTITUTIONAL CONTEXT

In the summer semester of 2023, a four-day unit on language variation was embedded within two sections of an undergraduate course on culture and education specifically designed for pre-service elementary education teacher candidates attending a four-year institution of higher education in the southwestern United States who were pursuing the English for Speakers of Other Languages (ESOL) endorsement. The overall goal of the unit was to expand students' understanding of the multidialectal nature of elementary and secondary classrooms and equip them with strategies and techniques to teach their future students about important aspects of standard American English while simultaneously learning to appreciate and value these students' home dialect(s). The course unit was seen as essential to teacher candidates' educational preparation since the majority of students enrolled in our educator preparation programs have had little exposure to speakers of other varieties of American English. Thus, the intended outcome of this course unit was to develop these teacher candidates' linguistic competence by advancing their knowledge and attitudes concerning dialectical variation in order to promote their understanding of and respect for the linguistic diversity of their future students while simultaneously teaching these students to do the same. Table 1 below indicates the focus of each class meeting within the course unit.

Table 1. Course unit on dialectical variation

Day	Description of the Module
1	Prescriptive versus Descriptive Views of Language
2	An Overview of Dialects of American English
3	Practical Analysis of Dialectical Variation
4	A Balanced Approach to Teaching Dialectical Variation

The section below further explains the activities that constituted each of the class meetings within the course unit.

Day One: Prescriptive vs. Descriptive Views of Language

In preparation for the first class meeting of the unit, students read Hinkel (2018) which outlines two prevailing views concerning language: prescriptive grammar and descriptive grammar. This article was selected as an introduction to the unit in order to familiarize students with these perspectives on language use in general and dialectical variation more specifically. In essence, those who subscribe to a prescriptive view of language typically make value judgments concerning a given person's use of language and employ the standard variety of the language as the yardstick to compare other varieties of the language, while those who align with a descriptive view of language (which is the standpoint adopted by most linguists) attempt to document and understand a given speech community's language use without evaluating the legitimacy of the community's use of language. With respect to dialectical variation, prescriptivists tend to view language as a fixed and static entity and thus perceive nonstandard varieties of a given language as incorrect, inferior, ungrammatical, etc. when compared with the standard variety of the language. Conversely, descriptivists typically believe that language is a changing, evolving, growing entity, value dialectical diversity, and consequently do not see any specific language variety as inherently superior or inferior to any other variety. In class, students were separated into groups and completed the T-chart below (see Table 2 below) to guide them in identifying the salient points concerning each view of language. A class discussion then ensued concerning the fundamental characteristics of each view of language, how each view envisioned the phenomenon of dialectical variation, and where teacher candidates themselves stood in regards to both views.

Table 2. Hinkel (2018) T-chart

Prescriptive Grammar	Descriptive Grammar
• • • • •	• • • • •

Day Two: An Overview of Dialects of American English

In preparation for the second class meeting of the unit, students watched a documentary which familiarized them with the nature of dialectical variation and provided them with a synopsis of important linguistic features of several dialects of American English. Before completing this homework assignment, students were separated into four groups with each group watching a different documentary. Group A watched *American Tongues*, while Groups B-D watched one of the episodes of *Do You Speak American?*. Table 3 below outlines the documentaries each group watched. In regards to *Do You Speak American?*, the first episode explores dialects of American English found in the northeastern United States and the mid-Atlantic region, the second episode examines dialects of American English found in the southeastern United States and the state of Texas, and the third episode considers dialects of American English found in the western United States and, more specifically, the state of California.

Table 3. American dialect documentaries watched by group

Group	Documentary
A	*American Tongues*
B	*Do You Speak American?* (Episode 1)
C	*Do You Speak American?* (Episode 2)
D	*Do You Speak American?* (Episode 3)

Class discussion of the documentaries was organized as a jigsaw activity. In the first part of the activity, students who watched the same documentary/episode grouped together and discussed their responses to the documentary/episode along with pertinent details they gleaned from the documentary/episode (i.e., S1, S5, S9, and S13 in Table 4 below) (vertical groups). In the second part of the activity, students reassembled themselves such that the groups now contained one member from each of the original groups (i.e., S1, S2, S3, and S4 in Table 4 below) (horizontal groups). During the second part of the activity, students shared their perspectives concerning the documentary/episode they watched with group members who had not watched that particular documentary/episode along with essential points contained in their respective documentary/episode. In the third and final part of the activity, students returned to their original seats and wrote down three to five points of information they learned from the discussions in both the vertical groups and horizontal groups on a blank index card; they then shared these points with their tablemates and the whole class.

Table 4. Jigsaw groups

Group A	Group B	Group C	Group D
S1	S2	S3	S4
S5	S6	S7	S8
S9	S10	S11	S12
S13	S14	S15	S16

* "S" = "Student"

Day Three: Practical Analysis of Dialectical Variation

Up to this point, students had learned specific content regarding dialectical variation that is more theoretical and abstract in nature. Thus, the objective of the activity that constituted the third class meeting of the unit was to guide teacher candidates in a deeper exploration of specific linguistic features of various dialects of American English.

In the first part of the activity, students were initially acquainted with multiple subareas of linguistics and studied examples of each subarea that occur in one or more dialects of American English. These subareas and examples are outlined in Table 5 below.

Table 5. Linguistic subareas and examples

- 1. Phonology: "The study of the sound system of a given language" (Curzan & Adams, 2012, 64) (e.g., pronouncing "white" as [wæʔ] in a Southern pronunciation instead of [waIʔ])
- 2. Morphology: "The study of the meaning units…within a word" (Molina, 2013, 35) (i.e., "We *was* going camping this weekend" instead of "We *were* going camping this weekend")
- 3. Syntax: "The study of the smaller components or units within phrases and sentences, and the rules that govern their placement" (Molina, 2013, 45) (e.g., "Sue gave it Ø me" instead of "Sue gave it *to* me")
- 4. Orthography: "The set of conventions for representing language in written form" (O'Grady, Archibald, Aronoff & Rees-Miller, 2017, 532) (i.e., "cent*re*" instead of "cent*er*")
- 5. Semantics: "The study of the meanings of individual words, phrases, and sentences" (Molina, 2013, 68) (e.g., "Bruce is *fixing* the car" versus "Bruce is *fixing* to go"
- 6. Pragmatics: "The study of the meaning that linguistic expressions receive in use" (Spenser-Oatey & Žegarac, 2019, 74) (i.e., "honey child", "brother", "dog" to refer to people)

The second part of the activity continues with an overview of six major dialects of American English along with their geographical locations identified by Jacewicz & Fox (2016). These major dialects are outlined in Figure 1 below.

Figure 1. Map of the six major dialects of American English
(Reproduced from Jacewicz & Fox (2016), with the permission of the Acoustical Society of America)

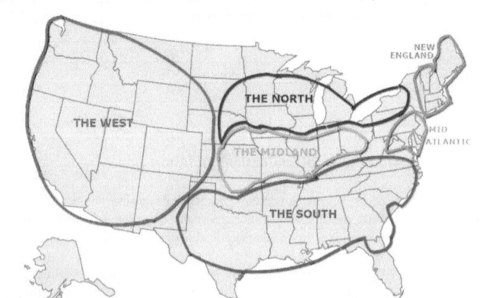

Students were then randomly assembled into six groups, one group per dialect. Table 6 below lists the groups which were organized according to dialect.

Table 6. Student groupings by dialect

Group	Dialect of American English
1	New England
2	Mid-Atlantic
3	The South
4	The Midland
5	The North
6	The West

The groups listened to one or more video clips containing speakers of their group's respective dialect and noted examples of each linguistic area that was represented in the speech patterns of the speakers represented in the video clip(s). Table 7 below provides sample video clips that might be used to exemplify speech patterns commonly associated with each of the American English dialects listed above.

Table 7. Sample video clips for the major dialects of American English

- 1. New England (e.g., Maine Video Canal, 2021)
- 2. The Mid Atlantic (i.e., People Like Us – The CNAM Channel, 2017)
- 3. The South (e.g., Chris Jones, 2012)
- 4. The Midland (i.e., Lavender Sky, 2014)
- 5. The North (e.g., Charlie Berens, 2019; 2021)
- 6. The West (i.e., Saturday Night Live, 2019)

Table 8 below illustrates a sample worksheet that was completed for Group 1 during the activity.

Table 8. Sample dialect worksheet for group 1

Group 1: New England

• Phonology
  o
  o
  o
• Morphology
  o
  o
  o
• Syntax
  o
  o
  o
• Semantics
  o
  o
  o
• Pragmatics
  o
  o
  o
• Other
  o
  o
  o

After having watched their respective video clip(s) and documenting particular linguistic features they noted in the video clips, the groups then individually shared their findings with the class, which subsequently lead to a class discussion concerning similarities and differences students noticed across the dialects along with linguistic and grammatical patterns they observed between dialects.

Day Four: A Balanced Approach to Teaching Dialectical Variation

In preparation for the fourth and final class meeting of the unit, students read one article in which the author(s) identified ways to teach elementary and secondary students about the nature of dialectical variation while also developing these students' understanding and appreciation of language variation. Table 9 below indicates the readings students completed in each group in preparation for the jigsaw reading activity that took place the next day.

Table 9. Articles on teaching dialectical variation separated by group

Group	Article
A	Christian (1997)
B	Delpit (2006)
C	Hazen (2001)
D	Wolfram (2013)

During the class meeting the next day, students participated in a jigsaw reading activity in which they first grouped themselves according to the vertical groups and discussed the same article that they had all read and then subsequently rearranged themselves based on the horizontal groups and shared important details from their respective article that their groupmates had not read. Finally, students returned to their original seats and, on an index card, identified several points of information they learned from both rounds of discussion, and shared these points with their tablemates and the entire class.

To conclude the unit, teacher candidates individually wrote an essay in which they reflected and commented on the most relevant and salient information they gained from the course unit and described how they might incorporate this knowledge in their future teaching. The intention of this assignment was to provide students with an opportunity to reflect on their emerging understandings concerning dialectical variation and consider how they could potentially include this knowledge in their own instructional contexts. The directions for the critical essay are listed in Table 10 below.

Table 10. Directions for the critical essay

A. Purpose
For this assignment, you will explore various concepts, ideas and theories you have learned in this course concerning language variation and linguistic features of several dialects of American English along with activities, strategies, and techniques for teaching minority language students standard English while also appreciating their home dialects/languages.

B. Task
The final product for this assignment is up to you (i.e., essay, PowerPoint, poster, video), so be as creative as possible! You should ensure that, regardless of the form of your assignment, the final product incorporates all of the requirements listed below.
- an overview of dialectical variation
   o a definition of the word "dialect"
   o a description of why dialects exist
   o an outline of various linguistic features of certain linguistic varieties of American English
   o an overview of cultural stereotypes people have regarding certain dialects, why these stereotypes exist, and why these stereotypes are (in)accurate
- a summary of prescriptive and descriptive linguistics
   o a definition and summary of prescriptivism
   o a definition and summary of descriptivism
   o a synopsis of how each perspective views dialects and why
   o a statement outlining which perspective you subscribe to and why
- an analysis of the pedagogical implications of dialectical variation
   o a rationale for why teachers should help minority language students learn standard English while also valuing their home dialects/languages
   o an explanation of specific strategies and techniques you will use in your future classroom to help minority language students learn standard English while also valuing their home dialects/languages

Reflections

Despite the fact that this chapter is not an empirical study and does not report on students' perceptions of the strengths and weaknesses of the course unit, it is nevertheless reasonable to include an overview of personal anecdotal observations on the part of the author concerning the activities and resources included in the unit. First, numerous students commented that the Hinkel (2018) article contributed positively to their developing understanding of various perspectives that are commonly held concerning language variation and support their reflections on their own attitudes and beliefs in regards to such variation. Second, a number of students remarked that the documentaries helped them better understand the nature of language variation in a general sense and dialectical variation in the United States particularly. Third, many teacher candidates observed that the dialect activity advanced their knowledge concerning specific linguistic features of the major dialects of American English and fostered their emerging metalinguistic awareness of dialectical variation generally but also of their own idiolects. Finally, a good number of the students enrolled in both sections additionally noted that the readings on teaching dialectical variation equipped them with concrete and specific strategies and techniques they could conceivably utilize with future students to foster their developing expertise regarding the natural and dynamic evolution of language. Additionally, in future iterations of the course, the author intends to collect and analyze data in regards to students' perspectives concerning the logistics of the course unit along with their suggestions for improving the unit moving forward.

Next Steps

Despite the fact that the course unit described in this chapter is intended to familiarize teacher candidates with the linguistic and cultural nature of dialectical variation and support them in reflecting on how they might incorporate this knowledge in their teaching, future iterations of the course unit might include the following components that were not included this semester which are outlined below. First, teacher candidates could examine the dialectical maps contained in Katz (2016) in order to ascertain where certain vocabulary words are used topographically within the United States along with possible variations of a given word (i.e., "buggy" versus "shopping cart"). This activity would better familiarize students with overall geographical trends in regards to the nature of semantic variation in the United States. Second, the unit could include a more specific exploration of particular grammatical and linguistic features of various dialects of American English as described in the appendix in Reaser et al. (2017). The aim of this activity would be to expand teacher candidates' knowledge in regards to how dialects of American English can vary grammatically along with the semantic meanings of these features. Finally, the course unit could also conceivably include information concerning the concept of World Englishes in order to acquaint students with linguistic variation beyond the dialectical level while also familiarizing them with the historical, political, and social implications and ramifications of this variation in other countries. Jenkins (2006) maintains that World Englishes consist of "all varieties of English worldwide and the different approaches used to describe and analyse them" (p. 159). Matsuda (2020) highlights the importance of teaching students (and teacher candidates) about the concept since "the lack of awareness of [World Englishes] may adversely affect [their] attitudes towards other varieties of English, their confidence in successful communication involving multiple varieties of English, and their actual ability to correctly interpret interactions in various Englishes" (p. 688). In other words, accustoming students about other varieties of English may promote their linguistic and cultural competencies by preparing them to negotiate future interactions with speakers of such varieties. Additionally, such work may educate pre-service teachers about the nature of dialectical variation concerning other varieties of English while also promoting their understanding and appreciation of other dialects of English.

CONCLUSION

Charity Hudley and Mallinson (2011) contend that many educators not only are largely unaware of the nature of language variation but that "educators are left with few tools to explain and work with the variations their students produce" (p. 17). Angay-Crowder et al. (2023) explain that this is likely the case since "Teaching English to Speakers of Other Languages (TESOL) courses remain non-inclusive of many languages spoken by multilingual learners. Instead, they focus mainly on the study of the English language system" (p. 445). In other words, such courses tend to explore the language system of standard English as a theoretical and abstract concept divorced from the reality of the linguistic and cultural implications of language use and often do not account for the multilingual/mutidialectical funds of knowledge (González et al., 2005) students possess. They also contend that, with regards to English learners, "all teachers are responsible for student's [multi]lingual development, not just English language proficiency" (p. 453). This contention also conceivably holds for multidialectical students in that educators should teach students about important features of standard English and also instruc them about the systematic nature of their home dialects while also familiarizing them with political and social nature of language use. This chapter, thus, outlines a variety of activities and resources that can hopefully be used in educator preparation courses and programs to remedy this curricular gap.

REFERENCES

Angay-Crowder, T., Choi, J., Khote, N., & Shin, J. H. (2023). Embedding multilingualism in undergraduate courses: A need for heteroglossia in US TESOL teacher preparation programs. In K. Raza, D. Reynolds, & C. Coombe (Eds.), *Handbook of multilingual TESOL in practice* (pp. 445–460). Springer. doi:10.1007/978-981-19-9350-3_29

Bailey, B. (2012). Heteroglossia. In M. Martin-Jones, A. Blackledge, & A. Creese (Eds.), *The Routledge handbook of multilingualism* (pp. 499–507). Routledge.

Berens, Charlie [Username]. (2019, October 22). *Midwest Voice Translator* [Video]. YouTube. https://www.youtube.com/watch?v=7OR7yPK4wEw

Blackledge, A., & Creese, A. (2014) Heteroglossia as practice and pedagogy. In A. Blackledge & A. Creese (Eds.), *Heteroglossia as practice and pedagogy* (pp. 1–20). Springer.

Bolitho, R., Carter, R., Hughes, R., Ivanic, R., Masuhara, H., & Tomlinson, B. (2003). Ten questions about language awareness. *ELT Journal, 57*(3), 251–259. doi:10.1093/elt/57.3.251

Center for New American Media (CNAM) (Producer), & Alvarez, L., & Kolker, A. (Directors) (1988). *American tongues* [Video file].

Charity Hudley, A. H., & Mallinson, C. (2011). *Understanding English language variation in U.S. schools*. Teachers College Press.

Chitadze, N. (2022). The main principles of democracy and its role in global development. In N. Chitadze (Ed.), *Global dimensions of democracy and human rights: Problems and perspectives* (pp. 1–40). IGI Global. doi:10.4018/978-1-6684-4543-3.ch001

Christian, D. (1997). *Vernacular dialects in US schools. ERIC Document Reproduction Services No. ED406846*. ERIC. https://files.eric.ed.gov/fulltext/ED406846.pdf

Curzan, A., & Adams, M. (2012). *How English works: A linguistic introduction* (3rd ed.). Longman.

Delpit, L. (2006). What should teachers do? Ebonics and culturally responsive instruction. In S. J. Nero (Ed.), *Dialects, Englishes, creoles, and education* (pp. 93–101). Routledge.

Ellis, E. M. (2008). Defining and investigating monolingualism. *Sociolinguistic Studies*, *2*(3), 311–330. doi:10.1558ols.v2i3.311

Errington, J. (2001). Ideology. In A. Duranti (Ed.), *Key Terms in language and culture* (pp. 110–112). Blackwell.

Escobar, C. F. (2016). Challenging the monolingual bias in EFL programs: Towards a bilingual approach to L2 learning. *Revista de Lenguas Modernas*, *24*, 249–266.

Espinet, I., Aponte, G. Y., Sánchez, M. T., Cardenas Figueroa, D., & Busone-Rodríguez, A. (2020). Interrogating language ideologies in the primary grades: A community language inquiry unit. In City University of New York-New York State Initiative on Emergent Bilinguals (Ed.), Translanguaging and transformative teaching for emergent bilingual students: Lessons from the CUNY-NYSIEB Project (pp. 219-237). Routledge.

Fairclough, N. (1992). Introduction. In N. Fairclough (Ed.), *Critical language awareness* (pp. 1–30). Routledge.

Farr, M., & Song, J. (2011). Language ideologies and policies: Multilingualism and education. *Language and Linguistics Compass*, *5*(9), 650–665. doi:10.1111/j.1749-818X.2011.00298.x

García, O. (2017). Critical multilingual language awareness and teacher education. In J. Cenoz, D. Gorter, & S. May (Eds.), *Language awareness and multilingualism* (3rd ed.) (pp. 263–280). Springer.

González, N., Moll, L. C., & Amanti, C. (2005). *Funds of knowledge: Theorizing practices in households, communities, and classrooms*. Routledge.

Hamers, J. F., & Blanc, M. H. A. (2000). *Bilinguality and bilingualism* (2nd ed.). Cambridge University Press. doi:10.1017/CBO9780511605796

Hammersley-Fletcher, L., & Hanley, C. (2016). The use of critical thinking in higher education in relation to the international student: Shifting policy and practice. *British Educational Research Journal*, *42*(6), 978–992. doi:10.1002/berj.3246

Hazen, K. (2001). Teaching about dialects. *ERIC Document Reproduction Services No. ED456674*. ERIC. https://files.eric.ed.gov/fulltext/ED456674.pdf

Hazen, K. (2002). Identity and language variation in a rural community. *Language*, *78*(2), 240–257. doi:10.1353/lan.2002.0089

Hazen, K. (2017). Variationist approaches to language and education. In K. A. King, Y.-J. Lai, & S. May (Eds.), *Research methods in language and education* (3rd ed.) (pp. 145–157). Springer International Publishing. doi:10.1007/978-3-319-02249-9_10

Hiatt, M. A., Mc Letchie, A., Bagasra, A. B., Laufersweiler-Dwye, D. L., & Mackinem, M. (2019). Perceptions of diversity, inclusion, and belongingness at an HBCU: Implications and applications for faculty. In R. Jeffries (Ed.), *Diversity, equity, and inclusivity in contemporary higher education* (pp. 175–193). IGI Global. doi:10.4018/978-1-5225-5724-1.ch011

Hinkel, E. (2018). Descriptive versus prescriptive grammar. In H. Nassaji (Ed.), *TESOL Encyclopedia of English Language Teaching*. Wiley. http://www.elihinkel.org/downloads/Descriptive%20v%20Prescriptive.pdf doi:10.1002/9781118784235.eelt0053

Hult, F. M., & Hornberger, N. H. (2016). Revisiting orientation in language planning: Problem, right, and resource as an analytical heuristic. *The Bilingual Review/La Revista Bilingüe, 33*(3), 30-49.

Jacewicz, E., & Fox, R. A. (2016). Acoustics of regionally accented speech. *Acoustics Today*, *12*(2), 31–38.

Jenkins, J. (2006). Current perspectives on teaching World Englishes and English as a lingua franca. *TESOL Quarterly*, *40*(1), 157–181. doi:10.2307/40264515

Jones, Chris [Username]. (2012, April 18). *Southern accent, North Carolina* [Video]. YouTube. https://www.youtube.com/watch?v=gAqm5ls8Ep8

Katz, J. (2016). *Speaking American: How y'all, youse, and you guys talk: A visual guide*. Houghton Mifflin Harcourt Publishing.

Kyriakou, M. (2019). A critical review of the theory of diglossia: A call to action. *International Journal of Linguistics. Literature and Translation*, *2*(5), 334–340.

Lavender Sky [Username]. (2014, September 23). *Accent challenge – Midwest – Iowa Minnesota Wisconsin USA – Mother & Daughter* [Video]. YouTube. https://www.youtube.com/watch?v=XUrpH0JedO0

Maher, F. A., & Tetreault, M. A. T. (2001). *The feminist classroom: Dynamics of gender, race, and privilege*. Rowman and Littlefield Publishers.

Maine Video Canal [Username]. (2021, November 9). *How to talk like a Maine-ah, 9 great words to mispronounce* [Video]. YouTube. https://www.youtube.com/watch?v=p3L5czFvyCc

Matsuda, A. (2020). World Englishes and pedagogy. In C. L. Nelson, Z. G. Proshina, & D. R. Davis (Eds.), *The handbook of World Englishes* (2nd ed.) (pp. 686–702). John Wiley & Sons, Inc.

Molina, S. G. (2013). *Linguistics for teaching English in multilingual classrooms*. CreateSpace Independent Publishing Platform.

National Center for Education Statistics. (2022). Racial/ethnic enrollment in public schools. *The condition of education*. NCES. https://nces.ed.gov/programs/coe/pdf/2022/cge_508.pdf

O'Grady, W., Archibald, J., Aronoff, M., & Rees-Miller, J. (2017). *Contemporary linguistics: An introduction* (7th ed.). Bedford/St. Martin's.

Pennycook, A. (2001). *Critical applied linguistics: A critical introduction.* Lawrence Erlbaum Associates, Inc. doi:10.4324/9781410600790

Pennycook, A. (2021). *Critical applied linguistics: A critical re-introduction.* Routledge. doi:10.4324/9781003090571

Reaser, J. (2014). Dialects and education in Appalachia. In A. D. Clark & N. M. Hayward (Eds.), *Talking Appalachian: Voice, identity, and community* (pp. 94–109). The University Press of Kentucky.

Reaser, J., Adger, C. T., Wolfram, W., & Christian, D. (2017). Appendix: An inventory of distinguishing dialect features. In *Dialects at school: Educating linguistically diverse students* (pp. 268–292). Routledge. doi:10.4324/9781315772622

Ruiz, R. (1984). Orientations in language planning. *Bilingual Research Journal, 8*(2), 15–34.

Saturday Night Live [Username]. (2019, October 18). *Every Californians ever (part 1 of 2)* [Video]. YouTube. https://www.youtube.com/watch?v=dCer2e0t8r8

Spenser-Oatey, H., & Žegarac, V. (2019). Pragmatics. In N. Schmitt & M. P. H. Rodgers (Eds.), *An introduction to applied linguistics* (3rd ed., pp. 72–90). Routledge. doi:10.4324/9780429424465-5

Thirteen / WNET, & MacNeil-Lehrer Productions (Producers), & Cran, W. (Director) (2005). *Do you speak American?* [Video file].

Tüzela, A. E. B., & Akcan, S. (2009). Raising the language awareness of pre-service English teachers in an EFL context. *European Journal of Teacher Education, 32*(3), 271–287. doi:10.1080/02619760802572659

Tzakosta, M. (2022). Language variation placed in the center of language teaching: The example of dialectical teaching in tertiary education. In S. Karpava (Ed.), *Handbook of research on multilingual and multicultural perspectives on higher education and implications for teaching* (pp. 1–41). IGI Global. doi:10.4018/978-1-7998-8888-8.ch001

Us, P.L. – The CNAM Channel [Username]. (2017, March 8). *#Real thick accent: Boston North End Italian* [Video]. YouTube. https://www.youtube.com/watch?v=omVFxtbZoyw

Wolfram, W. (2013). Sounds effects: Challenging language prejudice in the classroom. *Education Digest, 79*(1), 27–30.

Wolfram, W., & Schilling, N. (2015). Why dialects? In *American English: Dialects and variation* (3rd ed.) (pp. 27–58). Blackwell.

Wright, T. (2002). Doing language awareness: Issues for language study in language teacher education. In H. Trappes-Lomax & G. Ferguson (Eds.), *Language in language teacher education* (pp. 113–130). John Benjamins Publishing Company. doi:10.1075/lllt.4.09wri

Wright, T., & Bolitho, R. (1993). Language awareness: A missing link in language teacher education? *ELT Journal, 47*(4), 292–304. doi:10.1093/elt/47.4.292

KEY TERMS AND DEFINITIONS

Dialect: A variety of a given language that diverges linguistically from the standard variety of the language.

Dialectical Variation: An exploration of the linguistic similarities and differences that exist between varieties of a given language.

ESOL: English to Speakers of Other Languages

Language Norms: A set of behavioral expectations concerning a person's use of language within a certain speech community.

Language Variation: Differences that exist between varieties of a specific language.

Language: A shared system of symbols used within a given community to convey and interpret meaning

Multidialecticalism: A person's ability to utilize a range of varieties of a given language in specific contexts.

Norm: A socially-agreed-upon expectation for specific behaviors within a particular cultural community.

Teacher Candidate: A student enrolled in an educator preparation program who is also a prospective teacher at the elementary/secondary level.

Chapter 14
Construction of Dialogue:
The Language of an American Black Man Working in Higher Education

Lavon Davis
University of Maryland, Baltimore County, USA

ABSTRACT

The ways dialogue is constructed is influenced by a myriad of factors—institution, context, the multiple identities people hold. Based on these factors, people bring with them varied experiences that inform the way they communicate with one another, both consciously and subconsciously. This chapter takes an in-depth look at how dialogue is constructed in the higher education setting. Utilizing a discourse analysis lens, the author conducted a 45-minute-long interview to obtain information about the experience of one Black male professional in higher education. During this interview, the author sought to investigate his usage of multiple varieties of English that showcased how a professional in higher education employed racial linguistic practices as a bridge between faculty/staff norms and student dynamics and interactions. Through this process, the author takes a look at how language shifts and switches play a role to develop the legitimacy, connection, and sharing that takes place in a higher education environment for students and staff.

INTRODUCTION

Language is more than a construct. It shapes our understanding of the world around us, it gives us a means to communicate with others, and it aids in defining cultural significance that is distinct to who we are and our lived experiences. Language is a part of our being, which allows us to express ourselves, to challenge others, and to engage in learning environments. Unfortunately, power dynamics are also related to language, where, depending on a certain community's language variety, some speakers are viewed as unintelligent and illegitimate, a discriminatory view which poses harmful risks to those communities (Baugh 2005).

DOI: 10.4018/978-1-6684-8761-7.ch014

More specifically, Black English, which is also known as African American English (AAE) or African American Vernacular English (AAVE), has long been a stigmatized language. For the purpose of this paper, I will be using AAE and Black English throughout to denote the language of Black people in America. Baugh (2005) writes:

Unlike most white immigrants to urban centers, who eventually adopted local dialects, blacks generally remained isolated in impoverished ghettos and as a result, retained their dialect. This physical isolation contributed to linguistic isolation and the maintenance of AAE. The retention of unique misconceptions of this dialect, all of which amount to the opinion that speakers of this dialect lack intelligence. (p. 4)

Given this explanation, we find that the Black community has largely retained its language due to the environments in which they live. Because of this language retention of Black English, there continues to be a lack of understanding and meaningful interactions between those who employ this language variety and those who are not members of Black communities. While there is still growth needed in recognizing this language variety outside of the Black community, within the Black community, there tends to be a sense of togetherness that is built, along with culture and traditions revolving around language that are maintained. While others may view African American English/Black English as a deficit, most in the Black community have found value in it. Therefore, there must be a deeper conversation on how to raise awareness concerning this variety in order to prevent opportunities being denied based on language.

Baugh (2005) continues to say that the "personal and cultural identities [of AAVE speakers] are closely linked to the language of their friends, family, and forebears. And AAVE symbolizes racial solidarity" (p. 5). Because the network is built among the Black community based on the connection to culture and language, it helps to push against dominant narratives projected on language varieties like standard English, or — as I like to refer to it — White mainstream English, which perpetuates linguistic hegemony in both theory and practice.

The purpose of this chapter is to gain insight into the ways language is flexed in the higher education environment, specifically by a Black man in the United States of America. We recognize that the many linguistic repertoires a person may utilize, especially in higher education, is nuanced. More specifically, as it relates to race, the ways in which one communicates in higher education matters and could be a determining factor to grant or deny access based on what language variety is spoken and to whom it is spoken. Therefore, it is important to recognize that language is deeply connected to culture and should be valued in any given space, regardless of variety. This next section will help provide background into how race, culture, and language are intertwined.

Race, Culture, and Language

When we talk about language and how it links with the concept of linguistic hegemony, we must also consider race as a key element of discussion, recognizing a raciolinguistic approach. Rosa and Flores (2017) profess, "A raciolinguistic perspective seeks to understand the interplay of language and race within the historical production of nation-state/colonial governmentality, and the ways that colonial distinctions within and between nation-state borders continue to shape contemporary linguistic and racial formations" (p. 623). Through this understanding, we recognize that there is a longstanding, systemic issue at play that directly impacts societal views of how language is perceived. When we look at historically marginalized populations whose language varieties are often dismissed, there is a deeper need for

Construction of Dialogue

exploration in hopes of bringing light to the systems that continue to make small of the culture that is embedded within language.

When considering the impact language has on society and how it serves as a contributor to one's lived experiences, it is necessary to explore how race plays a critical role. Harper (2012) situates the concept of race in higher education, drawing upon a Critical Race Theory (CRT) perspective, by expressing, "Specifically in the higher education context, CRT has proven useful in examining the marginalization, stereotyping, and racial stress routinely experienced by students and faculty of color" (p. 21). Given this quote, it becomes clear that CRT is key in recognizing that race plays a pivotal role in all aspects of the lived experiences of the Black community. By recognizing the importance that race plays in a given society, especially one that has been built on the enslavement and appropriation of Black bodies and culture, there becomes a need to insert a critical understanding of the centering of race (Ladson-Billings & Tate, 1995). This framing is vital in understanding that, within the context and scope of this research, Black staff members already face disparities regarding race upon entering higher education environments, especially those at predominantly White institutions, or PWIs. PWIs are colleges and universities where over half of the student body are White. While these institutions serve as landing grounds for access to opportunities, they also present challenges to minoritized populations (Tomlin et al., 2023). Additionally, in these institutions, there is a, generally, unspoken way of being that is expected of Black men from dress, demeanor, and spoken language in such spaces that are primarily occupied by White people (McCluney et al., 2021). With that, it can be argued that Black men entering PWIs must maintain a deeper sense of awareness in relation to behavior and attitude in order to avoid overt gatekeeping that denies opportunities for advancement.

In order to further understand the intersections of race, language and professional status, it becomes vital to understand the staggering statistics surrounding Black male professionals working in higher education. Turner and Grauerholz (2017) write: "Data on Black male professionals in higher education outside faculty ranks are harder to obtain, but according to the Bureau of Labor Statistics (2015), just 13 percent of education administrators are Black or African American" (p. 212). Given these facts, it can be deduced that there is a larger issue that needs to be examined regarding Black male presence, and the lack thereof, in higher education. It is vital to unpack the various ways in which race and language are tied together and play a critical role in the experiences of Black men. Through this unpacking, it becomes clear that these are factors that limit opportunities for Black men in higher education.

Harper, Patton, and Wooden (2009) further this argument regarding opportunities of the Black community within higher education by noting that "in some ways, the recurrent struggle for racial equity is surprising, given the number of policies that have been enacted to close college opportunity gaps between African Americans and their White counterparts" (p. 1). Because there is still a divide in the ways Black folks are granted access to opportunities within higher education as compared to White folks, it can then also be concluded that Black male staff members who work in higher education face a more targeted scrutiny for their behaviors, norms, and customs than their White counterparts.

One of these scrutinized elements is the way in which Black male professionals utilize their linguistic repertoire. Smitherman (1973) expresses, "Being told to 'speak proper,' meaning that you become fluent with the jargon of power, is also a part of not 'speaking proper'" (p. 833). Even with the conception of this research by Smitherman dating back nearly 50 years, the phenomenon still permeates the higher education arena today and is often communicated to those within the Black community when they bring their own language to spaces where dominant linguistic ideologies exist; one of these spaces being higher education institutions — particularly PWIs. Being asked to "speak proper", or shift one's own language use to appease a more dominant discourse, is not proper because it begins to strip away a piece of culture and identity that is innately attached to Black English. As such, when we think of the disparities that Black communities face in society and tie that to PWIs, we must then consider how language in higher education is enacted by Black male professionals, and whether those language practices have the potential to snuff out access to opportunities.

Researcher Positionality

Because of my own connection to this body of research, it becomes necessary to share a foundational understanding of my own identities that inform my investment, passion, and interest in this scholarship. I am a Black, male, higher education professional who has been working in the field for 10 years. I have had the opportunity to work at multiple institution types, across multiple regions of the east coast of the United States, all of which are categorized as predominantly White institutions (PWIs). My own experiences around language construction and the ways it is depicted in academic spaces from PreK-12 to higher education have provided me with a lens to dissect this work; however, due to those experiences, I also carry with me biases that inform my view on the scholarship in many ways. Because of my own experience being denied opportunities based on the way I communicated or lacked language in a certain area, it is vital that I always approach this research with multiple viewpoints in order not to skew data, but also recognize that my experiences are equally valid and can help in making meaning for others who may be contesting similar issues (Tomlin & Davis, 2022).

Current Study

This chapter frames and shares findings from a study conducted in 2022 that explored how a Black male professional in higher education (HE) used their linguistic repertoire across different professional contexts. Investigating this topic will hopefully bring awareness to language inequities in institutions of higher education which, in turn, provide a deeper understanding to linguistic profiling and discrimination. This scholarship is particularly important to examine because it acknowledges that diversity in language is valued, and this research around linguistic diversity validates one's lived experiences. In understanding linguistic diversity, we begin to deconstruct and tear down racist ideologies revolving around language that permeate the academic and professional landscape in overt and covert ways. The conversation around linguistic diversity offers a deeper understanding of language and how the usage of different varieties and forms serves a greater population of learners, scholars, and constituents (Mallinson et al., 2017).

Podesva writes:

Scholars of language and race must attend to the ways that speakers employ linguistic features to take stances on issues that implicate race. Stance-based analyses of language enable a rich perspective on the raciolinguistic dynamics of communities in which such stances are taken. (Alim et al., 2016, p. 203)

Recognizing one's stance on various issues surrounding race can help to deepen the understanding of how language is connected to race, creating a stance-based approach to language. Knowing that various linguistic features can serve as a glimpse into identifying one's race, those linguistic features make evident that race is threaded within the concept of language, carrying with it the stigmas, stereotypes, and biases that society places on those identifying factors (Charity Hudley et al., 2022). Therefore, in order

Construction of Dialogue

to better display particular experiences of language varieties and illustrate the importance of linguistic diversity, I find it most useful to understand and examine the linguistic decisions made by a Black male professional in higher education more pointedly.

METHOD

The purpose of this project was to investigate language features of a Black male professional in higher education. I began with two research questions: 1) How does a Black, male, staff professional in higher education at a Predominantly White Institution (PWI) flex their linguistic repertoire utilizing one or more language varieties? 2) How might these depictions of language varieties and different styles reflect certain raciolinguistic concepts? To address these questions, I chose to utilize a single case study approach in order to gain a deeper understanding of language shifts at a four-year university in Alabama. Since research has not been done in this particular way of examining language varieties of Black, male, higher education professionals, I felt it important to focus in on one participant in order to work to begin creating themes that could shape future research in this area. Those themes found through investigating the data of this case study are as follows: *legitimacy*, *connection*, and *sharing*.

I elected to utilize a critical discourse analysis approach to examine how language is conveyed based on the conversations and how that language can be interpreted. Critical Discourse Analysis (CDA) is described as "how language and/or semiosis interconnect with other elements of social life, and especially a concern with how language and/or semiosis figure in unequal relations of power, in processes of exploitation and domination of some people by others" (Fairclough & Kress, 2001, p. 25). Given this understanding, CDA helps us to consider how language, in its many forms, is situated in power and privilege. Depending on the variety of language used, it could serve as a tool to grant access to certain spaces but could also deny access to opportunities. Recognizing that components of race, culture, and lived experiences all play a role in language formation and understanding, it becomes necessary to evaluate these tenants using a critical discourse lens. For this case study, I chose to draw from the experience of one Black male higher education professional, situated in the American South, in order to begin to develop and compile ways that this individual constructs dialogue within the workplace. My goal in this study was to break down, examine, and analyze how language plays a role for a single Black male professional when working with predominantly White counterparts and serving a predominantly marginalized and minoritized population of students.

I conducted a 45-minute semi-structured interview with a former classmate, Charlie. For the purpose of this project, I utilized a pseudonym to protect the anonymity of the participant. Charlie and I went to college together and served as resident assistants. We worked closely together and had a friendship outside of our professional roles as well. Through our time studying at the same university, we both developed a passion for teaching and working with students. We both served as education majors and facilitated conversations and tutoring on various subject areas, and so serving the student population both developmentally and academically became skills and talents of ours. Charlie went on to pursue his Master of Arts (MA) degree and then an Education Specialist (EdS) degree. Through these degrees, he was able to establish himself as a Dean of Student Affairs at a four-year university in Alabama where he works alongside other professionals who do not speak or (widely) acknowledge African American English (AAE) within the professional workplace. This four-year university is considered to be a diverse institution that is located within a racially diverse region.

When determining the reliability, validity, and trustworthiness of data, it becomes necessary to consider who your participants are and their relationship to the research. Clark and Creswell (2010) write, "Purposeful sampling means that researchers intentionally select sites and individuals to learn about or understand the central phenomenon" (p. 253). Based on this understanding, it is vital to consider where and who participants are in order to best determine if they fit the scale, scope, and dynamics of the research. As such, there is an element of intentionality in establishing a sense of reliability, validity, and trustworthiness. Because I personally knew the participant, I made sure not to provide any information about goals of the research: I refrained from providing questions or having conversations in advance of the interview, and I allowed the participant to answer questions in a way that they felt shaped their true authentic experiences. This participant was specifically chosen due to their grasp of multiple language varieties (AAE and White mainstream English), the type of work they do (higher education professionals), and their ethnicity (Black), which also informs culture and lived experiences.

Prior to the interview, I provided Charlie with a framework to guide our discussion, allowing for an organic and authentic flow. The framework I communicated prior to our conversational dialogue was centered around Charlie's understanding and experience utilizing Black language in higher education. The framework served as a tool to help situate my research and how Charlie connected to the concept. I then provided guiding questions to help fuel our conversation but made mention that these questions were only guides — not structured or mandated to be answered. The questions presented were as follows:

1. Do you feel like you have to code switch in higher education settings? If so, what does that look like?
2. As a native speaker of AAE, do you feel if you were to speak your native language in higher education settings, would there be an unspoken or spoken dislike of that language? If so, what does that look like?
3. Do you feel White mainstream English grants access to opportunities? If so, how has this played out in your life?
4. Do you feel that AAE denies you access to opportunities? If so, how have you seen this play out in your life?

All of these questions were designed to elicit Charlie's personal experiences. This conversation identified experiences, with both colleagues and students, where Charlie flexed his linguistic dexterity to appeal to a certain group, which garnered a sense of respect based on the language variety used and the group. For the purpose of this chapter, I will discuss three clips from the conversation that showcase situations when Charlie demonstrated the use of different language varieties — one when speaking with colleagues during his job interview and two when helping students navigate course assignments. During the interview, Charlie shared experiences from actual events as well as hypothetical ones, in which he describes his typical or envisioned linguistic behavior in an imagined scenario. In both cases, the constructed dialogue showcased Charlie's language practices as a Black male professional in higher education. The way Charlie constructed dialogue further allowed him to create his own flow and authentic interview experience that was true to him, further excluding any potential bias based on a prior relationship we, the participant and the researcher, held. Charlie was able to work to exclude potential bias because he focused on his own experience at the university where he worked during this study and made sure to stay true to those experiences, not ones where we both, the participant and the researcher, were members.

Construction of Dialogue

Before diving deeper into the transcript examples, it is important to note how I have set up these transcription conventions for display. I have adapted the transcript conventions outlined by Tannen, Kendall, and Gordon (2007) to develop my own layout in an attempt to continue and clearly define and illuminate the unique voices of Black men in higher education. To better reflect these voices, line numbers were marked to notate a change in speaker or a change in utterance or points expressed. There are, therefore, some lines with no numbers, and these serve as a continuance of the remarks within one thought of a single speaker. I have also included "---" before a word that was spoken simultaneously with another. While Tannen, Kendall, and Gordon's (2007) transcription utilizes brackets to showcase simultaneous talk, I opted to utilize "---" as a marker, instead of brackets "[]", as an attempt not to close off the speech of marginalized populations in brackets but rather welcome in the voice without the constraints that I feel brackets may suggest. Given the nature of this research and of how the Black voice has long been silenced, it was intentional for me to include such markings within the already limiting confines of standardized transcription conventions.

FINDINGS

It is vital to reiterate that I utilized CDA as a methodological approach that aids in reinforcing the importance of centering race, language, and culture as key concepts that are intertwined. Because race, language, and culture all play critical roles in understanding the construction of dialogue through multiple varieties, I was able to locate themes (*legitimacy*, *connection*, and *sharing*) from the data gathered, which was instrumental in recognizing the experiences of Charlie. As a Black male professional in higher education, it is essential to recognize when to utilize certain language varieties. Specifically, for AAE speakers, it is important to understand when and to whom AAE can be spoken without fear or worry of degradation or disrespect, mainly from White colleagues who feel that AAE is not an appropriate language variety to utilize in the work environment. For example, in Excerpt One, lines 8-11, Charlie spoke about his experience when interviewing for his current role at a university among primarily White peers.

Excerpt One

> 8   C: *Uhmm.. because the interview process wasn't easy. Uhm. Being the—I think it was only one other Black male in the room when I did the interview. Umm but being*
> 9   L: *--oh, wow*
> 10   C: *able to still… present myself in a professional manner, but I knew at the same time… the way I was talking there was gon' be different than five minutes soon's I lef' the call you, for example.*
> 11   L: *RIGHTT! Haha*
> *--right.*

Specifically, Charlie mentions in Line 8 that he was one of, maybe, two Black men who were in the room during his interview. This provides us with some understanding of the racial composition of the higher education context. By Charlie mentioning the fact that there were a majority of non-Black people in the interview, the statement alone suggests that he observed there was a lack of racial representation. But the most important piece to note is that there are only two Black, male, higher education professionals in the space. Because of this underrepresentation, the need to impress and showcase a different linguistic variety, other than AAE, could be viewed as essential in order for a Black man to feel valued by his predominantly White evaluators during the interview. Charlie continues in Line 10 with how he expressed himself: *"able to still... present myself in a professional manner, but I knew at the same time... the way I was talking there was gon' be different than five minutes soon's I lef' to call you, for example"*. Expressing oneself in what Charlie calls a "professional manner" is used to communicate the need to speak in standard English, or what I refer to as White mainstream English.

Through the utilization of White mainstream English, Charlie was able to use his repertoire to express himself in an environment of colleagues who did not look like him while also appearing knowledgeable and competent. Also in Line 10, we notice the shift in language variety even when constructing dialogue of this experience. When Charlie communicated that "the way [he was] talking there was gon' be differ'nt than five minutes soon's I lef' to call you", this dialect form and intonation switch in the conversation further highlights that Charlie's need to express himself in higher education as a Black man involved a conscious shift to White mainstream English when speaking with colleagues. By speaking in AAE during the interview, however, Charlie strategically connected with his intended audience – me, another Black, male professional – in a more intentional way.

Not only does Charlie's language variety shift when speaking to colleagues, but also when speaking to students. Charlie makes note of this change in Excerpt Two, Lines 18-24:

Excerpt Two

18   *C: And I knew that how... I communicate and learn, I think most my students will communicate in the exact same way, but people don't actually take that into consideration.*

19   *C: Because I don't want you sending me a long email; I'm not gon' read it.*

20   *L: hhh*

21   *C: R-r Read it. I'm gon'. I'm gon' read Instagram, TikTok, uhm. Gossip News. You kno' I mean. Uh-Shaderoom, That's what I'm gon' read.*

22   *L: haha*

23   *L: yeah*

24   *C: I'm not reading email ok. I barely wanna do schoolwork. So I know that's where our students are coming from.*

Charlie makes a connection with his students by identifying with them on the basis of race and language variety. Because the university he served was a racially diverse institution, it was vital for Charlie to form a connection with his students to build trust within their shared identity and language variety. He did so by bringing in relevant media platforms that most of his students may reference as a source of digital communication media. In Line 18 he mentions how he connects with the students because he was once the same way when it came to communication: *"And I knew that how... I communicate and learn, I think most my students will communicate in the exact same way, but people don't actually take that into consideration"*. In this statement, he shares that he relates to his students and the way they continue to learn at that stage of their life. He mentions that "people don't actually take that into consideration". It can be inferred that this statement is aimed at his White colleagues who do not consider that students require more than just White mainstream English when in academic settings: Students require a connection and a way of communicating that lends well to their own demographic and population. In Charlie's case, not

Construction of Dialogue

only was he able to connect on the level of digital media communication, but he was also able to connect with students using their language variety of Black English. This potentially helps students to feel a deeper sense of support, which, in turn, may create a more comfortable environment for his students.

In keeping with the theme of meeting students where they are, Charlie notes in Line 21 that students are more willing to read *"Instragram, Tiktok, uhm. Gossip News. You kno' I mean. Uh-Shaderoom. That's what I'm gon' read."* These all pertain to culture and language in a way that appeals to the students' understanding and scope of gathering information. While social media is not always a connection point for all students, specifically those who do not use such devices, it still serves as a tool to connect with those who do maintain their social media presence. In addition, social media can serve as a connection point for all students, not just Black students. However, the language variety spoken, in this case Black English, seems to be a hallmark of understanding and connecting to Charlie's students around topics of social media. This shared sense of connectedness helps to create a bond, which serves as a contributing factor in depicting the Black community in positive ways. While it is important to recognize that the Black experience is not monolithic, there seems to be a positive, community reinforcement when establishing cultural ties, which reifies Black well-being and solidarity as a community (Tomlin & Davis, 2022). Through Charlie's understanding and connection to the common digital communication media outlet of his students, he was able to utilize his voice as a Black, male, professional that could potentially garner a deeper connection with his students. Since these are the resources students utilize in their daily lives, Charlie's understanding and grasp of such devices and apps, coupled with his racial, gender, and professional identity and communication in a language variety he shares with his students, help to build connections with his students and understand where they are coming from. Moreover, these connections then begin to create a shared dialogue construction.

For example, in Excerpt Three, Charlie lays out an example of how he constructs a shared dialogue of a Black student who needs help submitting an assignment.

Excerpt Three

28   *C: uhm. So with that, you have to meet the students where they are. Uhm. If John is emailing you telling you he can't submit an assignment, your first question back to John would be, "how are you trying to submit the assignment?"*

29   *C: Don't tell John saying, "you got the assignment." John already said the instructor said it has to be uploaded through the course.*

30   *C: Therefore, you should check helping John. 'cause it sound like John slow.. OK. So uhm. So by that being said—and I've been doing it long enough where I'm asking John how are you submitting the assignment. John say he using is phone, so John first of all, you can't do school from your phone, but hey. You been doing it. I-I'm meeting you where you are, son. Okay*

31   *C: So.. I'm more educated on how to use technology, so I'm showing John how to submit his assignment from his phone.*

32   *C: Uploading the uh.. So I say are you using the Microsoft word? He say, "yep." I say, "Ok. Good. That the first step. You got dat!"*

33   *L: hahaha*

34   *C: And I'm talkin' jus' like how I would I'm talking now to John*

35   *L: -yeah.*

36 C: Soo.
37 L: right.
38 C: John is- is uhm. That stress of submitting that assignment is now lifted off of John.
39 L: mmm
40 C: --So John now feels like he can talk with someone he can relate to.
41 C: So that was just one example.
42 C: Most of the time students feel like they can come talk to MEE versus going to talk to.. someone else. And when—whe I can't answer their question, I ca- I can't help you, baby!
43 L: yeah
44 C: I can't help you, suga. Uhm. But what I can do is making sure that you are prompted, unfortunately, uhm how to navigate and be successful in the course.
45 L: yeah. yeah.

In this constructed dialogue, Charlie changes his language variety to Black English to indicate how he connects more deeply to his students, thus meeting the students where they are. He does this first by walking the student through how to submit an assignment saying, "*I've been doing it long enough where I'm asking John how are you submitting the assignment. John say he using is phone, so John first of all, you can't do school from your phone, but hey. You been doing it. I-I'm meeting you where you are, son. Okay.*" Charlie shows an understanding at a deeper level by anticipating problems without potentially making the student feel vulnerable when they appear to be struggling with understanding how to submit assignments, along with experiencing a lack of resources, something that may be a point of contention and intimidation had they been talking to a White professional. Charlie also meets the student where they are by changing his language variety to form a connection. He does this through copula deletion in phrases such as "*You been doing it.*" In AAE, copula deletion of the verb "to be" is a common feature, which in this example would be "have". He is also utilizing a common AAE construct – r-lessness. He says, "*I can't help you, suga.*" Dropping the r in his phonetic vocalization depicts the use of a feature of AAE as well. This framing is a common linguistic phrase utilized in Black culture as an endearing tool as well. This utilization of Black English features not only refers to Charlie's own epistemic values, but also alludes to his perception of how he wants to achieve his communicative goals by code-switching between Black English and White mainstream English, since most of his students do not come to the classroom having learned White mainstream English. Charlie expresses in Line 34 how his language changes for his students, particularly his Black students: "*And I'm talkin' jus' like how I would I'm talking now to John*". Once again, Charlie constructs dialogue, and through that construction, speaks in AAE to express his point further. This could also potentially speak to Charlie's comfort level by being more "himself" in these environments as it relates to race, his profession, and other factors that potentially impact Black, male, professionals working in higher education at PWIs. Moreover, all three examples support the conclusion that, for Black, male, higher education professionals, being able to shift language varieties in certain settings and to certain people becomes an important part of creating successful learning environments and workplace interactions with colleagues and students alike.

Construction of Dialogue

DISCUSSION AND CONCLUSION

When understanding the importance of how environments shape the way people – particularly Black people – behave, it is clear that language plays a critical role. As presented in this chapter, the ways that Charlie, a Black male professional working in higher education, constructs language in his workplace suggests that there is a need to curate connections with marginalized populations where they can show up more authentically. We know that there are certain language varieties that are often viewed as illegitimate, thus diminishing the voice of those who speak those varying varieties. AAE is one of those language varieties commonly viewed as illegitimate. McCluney et al. (2021) write, "The 'effectiveness' of racial code-switching in professional settings hinges on how well it is received by others" (p. 2). This understanding shapes the way the Black community may choose to communicate or flex their linguistic repertoire. McCluney et al. (2021) continue, "The decision to code-switch or not elicits numerous costs. Code-switching requires Black people to suppress their cultural identity, which is emotionally, psychologically, and physically draining" (p. 2). Because of this, the way some Black, male, higher education professionals speak about and within their workplace may involve the fact that they must shift their language or code-switch in order for them to be validated, respected, and offered further opportunities for growth and development, which Charlie alluded to when he spoke about his interview for this particular role as a higher education professional.

More specifically, Charlie, a Black, male, higher education professional, depicted his use of various language varieties – White mainstream English and AAE – within his workplace through scenarios of constructed conversations about marginalized students and his experience around his own interview for the role he currently holds, working primarily with White colleagues. With those depictions in mind, raciolinguistic ideologies were at play. There were multiple examples of Charlie speaking about his students utilizing AAE, which employed certain subtractive leanings within higher education spaces. In Charlie's AAE or Black English language variety choices, he chose to strengthen the community bond of the Black students through his construction of dialogue.

After taking a deeper dive within the analysis, I found three main themes that emerged in the coding – *legitimacy*, *connection*, and *sharing* – which are evident in the three examples shared. When Charlie spoke about the use of White mainstream English in his workplace, it was communicated as a tool to maintain a sense or feeling of *legitimacy*. I name that we must educate and assert boldly that all language varieties have meaning, value, and positively add to the fabric and culture of any given institution. I also found that *connection* was a theme throughout Charlie's articulation of his workplace. In the way Charlie spoke about his use of AAE in the workplace with the students, the majority of whom were Black and also spoke AAE, there was a sense of connectedness that showcased a level of shared understanding and culture. I interpret the connection Charlie forged with his students as an attempt to create a bond where students are made to feel more supported. And lastly, the concept of *sharing* became a theme embedded throughout our semi-structured interview. Charlie communicated in ways that brought light to how he spoke about both White mainstream English and AAE in his workplace. Through the utilization of both these varieties of English, he was able to share resources and outcomes not only with his students but also with his colleagues, which helped to form a bridge that linked the two varieties in order to fulfill a common goal among higher education professionals – student success formation.

While this research is needed in the field, the limitations posed within this work must be noted as well. One limitation of this chapter is that I only conducted one semi-structured interview. To gain a better picture and to create a more developed toolbox, more interviews could be conducted. Another limitation to this research is that, because of the one interview held, there was also only one institutional type discussed. Given the landscape of institutions, the way Black men who work professionally in higher education speak about and within their work environments may look and feel different based on their language construction and variety. Not all Black men who work as professionals in higher education share the same experience. It is important to note that the Black experience, on any front, is not monolithic. In selecting this participant, I was able to identify some of the ways in which the language varieties of a Black man working in higher education prove vital for connection. By selecting another candidate, these themes would likely change or expand given the second person's lived experiences. Nevertheless, any research that documents these unique lived experiences helps further the notion that the language we as Black men bring into higher education reifies culture and creates an environment to support linguistic diversity.

REFERENCES

Alim, H. S., Rickford, J. R., & Ball, A. F. (Eds.). (2016). *Raciolinguistics: How language shapes our ideas about race*. Oxford University Press. doi:10.1093/acprof:oso/9780190625696.001.0001

Baker-Bell, A., Paris, D., & Jackson, D. (2017). Learning black language matters. *International Journal of Qualitative Research, 10*(4), 360–377. doi:10.1525/irqr.2017.10.4.360

Baugh, J. (2005). *Out of the mouths of slaves: African American language and educational malpractice*. University of Texas Press.

Cameron, D. (1996). *Verbal hygiene*. Routledge.

Ed, A. M., Ed, G. L., & Au, W. E. (2011). *The Routledge International Handbook of Critical Education*. Routledge.

Fairclough, N., & Kress, G. (2001). Critical discourse analysis. *How to analyze talk in institutional settings: A casebook of methods*, 25-38.

Flores, N., & Rosa, J. (2015). Undoing appropriateness: Raciolinguistic ideologies and language diversity in education. *Harvard Educational Review, 85*(2), 149–171. doi:10.17763/0017-8055.85.2.149

Harper, S. R. (2012). Race without racism: How higher education researchers minimize racist institutional norms. *Review of Higher Education, 36*(1), 9–29. doi:10.1353/rhe.2012.0047

Harper, S. R., Patton, L. D., & Wooden, S. O. (2009). Access and equity for African American students in higher education: A critical race historical analysis of policy efforts. *The Journal of Higher Education, 80*(4), 389–414. doi:10.1080/00221546.2009.11779022

Charity Hudley, A. H., Mallinson, C., & Bucholtz, M. (2022). *Talking college: Making space for Black language practices in higher education*. Teachers College Press.

Ladson-Billings, G. (2006). From the achievement gap to the education debt: Understanding achievement in U.S. schools. *Educational Researcher, 35*(7), 3–12. doi:10.3102/0013189X035007003

Ladson-Billings, G., & Donnor, J. K. (n.d.). Waiting for the call: The moral activist role of critical race theory scholarship. Handbook of Critical and Indigenous Methodologies, 61-84. doi:10.4135/9781483385686.n4

Ladson-Billings, G., & Tate, W. F. (1995). Toward a critical race theory of education. *Teachers College Record*, *97*(1), 47–68. doi:10.1177/016146819509700104

Liu, W. (2017). White male power and privilege: The relationship between white supremacy and social class. *Journal of Counseling Psychology*, *64*(4), 349–358. doi:10.1037/cou0000227

Mallinson, C., Charity Hudley, A., Strickling, L. R., & Figa, M. (2011). A conceptual framework for promoting linguistic and educational change. *Language and Linguistics Compass*, *5*(7), 441–453. doi:10.1111/j.1749-818X.2011.00289.x

McCluney, C. L., Durkee, M. I., Smith, R. E. II, Robotham, K. J., & Lee, S. S. L. (2021). To be, or not to be… Black: The effects of racial code-switching on perceived professionalism in the workplace. *Journal of Experimental Social Psychology*, *97*, 104199. doi:10.1016/j.jesp.2021.104199

Milroy, J. (2001). Language ideologies and the consequences of standardization. *Journal of Sociolinguistics*, *5*(4), 530–555. doi:10.1111/1467-9481.00163

Ngunjiri, F. W., Hernandez, K.-A. C., & Chang, H. (2010). Living autoethnography: Connecting life and research. *Journal of Research Practice*, *6*(1), E1.

Plano Clark, V. L., & Creswell, J. W. (2010). *Understanding research: A consumer's guide*. Pearson.

Rickford, J. R., & King, S. (2016). Language and linguistics on trial: Hearing Rachel Jeantel (and other vernacular speakers) in the courtroom and beyond. *Language*, *92*(4), 948–988. doi:10.1353/lan.2016.0078

Smitherman, G. (1973). "God don't Never change": Black English from a Black perspective. *College English*, *34*(6), 828. doi:10.2307/375044

Straaijer, R. (2016). Attitudes to prescriptivism: An introduction. *Journal of Multilingual and Multicultural Development*, *37*(3), 233–242. doi:10.1080/01434632.2015.1068782

Tannen, D., & Trester, A. M. (2013). The Medium is the metamessage: Conversational style in new media interaction. In *Discourse 2.0: Language and new media* (pp. 99–117). Georgetown University Press.

Tomlin, A. D., & Davis, L. (2022). Linguistic liberation: The experiences of Black higher education professionals. In S. E. DeCapua & E. B. Hancı-Azizoglu (Eds.), *Global and Transformative Approaches Toward Linguistic Diversity* (pp. 66–79). IGI Global. doi:10.4018/978-1-7998-8985-4.ch004

Tomlin, A. D., Moss, L. V., & Price, N. S. (2023). Supporting Students of Color in Language Learning Environments: Approaches From Black Community College Faculty. In Promoting Diversity, Equity, and Inclusion in Language Learning Environments (pp. 130-144). IGI Global.

APPENDIX

Tannen Transcription Convention

Tannen, Deborah, Shari Kendall, and Cynthia Gordon (eds.) (2007). *Family Talk: Discourse and Identity in Four American Families.* New York: Oxford University Press. Pp. xiii-xiv.

((*words*))	Double parentheses enclose transcriber's comments, in italics.
(words)	Single parentheses enclose uncertain transcription.
carriage return	Each new line represents a new intonation unit.
→	An arrow indicates that the intonation unit continues onto the next line.
—	A dash indicates a truncated intonation unit.
-	A hyphen indicates a truncated word or adjustment within an intonation unit.
?	A question mark indicates a relatively strong rising intonation.
.	A period indicates a falling, final intonation.
,	A comma indicates continuing intonation.
..	Dots indicate silence (more dots indicate a longer silence)
:	A colon indicates an elongated sound.
CAPS	Capitals indicate emphatic stress.
<laughs>	Angle brackets enclose descriptions of vocal noises, e.g., *coughs, clears throat*
<*manner*>words>	Angle brackets enclose descriptions of the manner in which an utterance or part of an utterance is spoken, e.g., *high-pitched, laughing, creaky voice.*
words [words] [words]	Square brackets enclose simultaneous talk.

Additional conventions used:
= The equal sign indicates latching between two utterances.
" " Quotation marks indicate constructed dialogue (Tannen 2007).

Section 8
Speaker Agency

Chapter 15
Turkish Heritage Speakers' Reasons for Code-Switching in the United States

Didem Koban Koç
İzmir Democracy University, Turkey

ABSTRACT

The present study explores first- and second-generation Turkish speakers' reasons for code-switching in the United States (U.S.) as well as the effects of social variables (age of arrival and length of residence in the U.S.) on the speakers' reasons for code-switching. The speeches of Turkish speakers were analyzed via interviews, focusing on their reasons for code-switching. A total of 20 Turkish speakers participated in the study. The study adopted a qualitative research approach to determine the reasons for code-switching. The data were based on spontaneous corpus data consisting of 10 hours of interviews with the Turkish speakers. According to the results, the participants used code-switching for the following reasons: lexical need, emphasizing and clarifying a particular point, and filling a gap in speech. Significant effects of length of residence on the use of code-switching were also observed suggesting that the longer the speakers lived in the U.S., the less items they recalled in Turkish.

INTRODUCTION

The emergence of Turkish communities in the United States (U.S.) dates back to the 1820s when almost 300,000 Turkish people emigrated to the U.S. from what was then called the Ottoman Empire (Karpat, 2004). Since this period, the number of Turkish immigrants in the U.S. has continued to rise due to social, political, economic, and educational reasons, resulting in over one million Turks and the maintenance of Turkish. The continuous growth of the Turkish population in the U.S. and the maintenance of Turkish to a large extent, therefore, make the U.S. an ideal place to study language contact between Turkish and English.

There is now a large body of studies about Turkish as an immigrant language in contact with Dutch, German, Danish and English. For almost three decades, scholars in Europe have been inquiring into

DOI: 10.4018/978-1-6684-8761-7.ch015

the changes that occur in the speech of bilingual Turkish speakers, largely seeking possible explanations for how and why different generations and age groups code-switch. For instance, Backus (e.g. 1996, 1998, 2005, 2009, 2010, 2012), who has written several books and countless articles on diaspora Turkish, analyzed the code-switching patterns in the speech of Turkish immigrants in the Netherlands; Pfaff (2000) in Germany, Jørgensen (2010) in Denmark, Kurtböke (1998) in Australia, Türker (2000, 2005) in Norway; and Boeschoten and Verhoeven (1987) in the Netherlands as well. The scholars also examined topics such as ethnic identity, maintenance of Turkish and the degree of proficiency in Turkish and host languages. Despite the considerable number of studies conducted in Europe, particularly in the Netherlands, Germany, France, and Norway, there is a lack of grammatical and sociolinguistic studies of code-switching found in the speech of Turkish speakers living in the U.S.

The present study thus aims to fill this gap by focusing on a highly important and recurring topic in contact linguistics, code-switching. The study explores Turkish heritage speakers' reasons for code-switching from a sociolinguistic perspective. The paper is organized as follows. The following section provides a brief history of Turkish immigration to the U.S. and the current Turkish communities in the U.S. while section 3 provides an overview of functions of code-switching followed by research questions and methodology. Section 5 offers an analysis of the functions of code-switching found in the speech of Turkish-English bilingual speakers followed by a discussion of the findings. The study concludes with recommendations for further research on Turkish-English code-switching.

Turkish Communities in the U.S.: A Brief History

A detailed account of Turkish immigration to the U.S. has been provided by scholars (e.g., Akçapar, 2009; Karpat, 2004). In summary, Turks migrated to the U.S. in three consecutive periods due to social, political, educational, and economic reasons. The largest immigration movement from the Ottoman Empire to the U.S. occurred in the 1820s. It involved Turks, as well as Armenians, Jews, and Greeks. Most of the immigrants in this group were low-skilled men. They generally lived in Boston, New York City, Los Angeles, Houston, Detroit and Chicago. Although the majority of Turks went back to Türkiye after 1923, some settled in the U.S. for good but due to their lack of English skills, they could not integrate into the society. Their children, on the other hand, were able to assimilate into the American society socially and culturally as they did not have strong connections with acquaintances in Türkiye and got married with men and women of ethnic groups other than Turkish (Karpat, 2004).

The end of 1940 marked the beginning of another period of immigration, which, unlike the first group of immigrants, involved open-minded, high-skilled workers such as academics, engineers, and doctors as well as students who went to the U.S. for educational purposes. In this period, nearly 15,000 Turks immigrated to the U.S. This group was able to visit Türkiye mostly during summer holidays. The last period of immigration to the U.S. occurred in the late 1980s and increased rapidly in the 1990s. This group included Turks from different educational, demographic, and socio-economic backgrounds, migrating through the Diversity Visa Immigrant program to obtain permanent residency, scholarship programs for master's or doctorate degrees and family reunification. There were also Turks who emigrated to the U.S. to seek asylum (Karpat, 2004).

Today, there are, conservatively, 350,000 Turks living in the U.S., although numbers that also include Turkmen, Uzbeks, Uyghurs, Azerbaijanis and other Turkic ethnic groups estimate them to be close to 500,000 ("The Turkish-American Community," 2020). The former United States Secretary of Commerce John Bryson estimated this number to be at least 1,000,000 ("U.S. Agrees to Cash Transfer to Help Stabilize Tunisian Economy," 2012). Identified as a "Key Heritage Community" ("The Turkish-American Community," 2020) by the U.S. government, the Turkish community includes about 300 associations of which Assembly of Turkish American Associations, Federation of Turkish American Associations, and the Turkic American Alliance are the most important. According to the American Community Survey (2014), the majority of Turks reside in the state of New York, but they also live in considerable numbers in New Jersey, California, Florida, Texas, Massachusetts, Pennsylvania, Virginia Ohio, and Maryland. Some Turks stick to their own group and live in communities with low socio-economic status, running small businesses such as grocery stores, supermarkets, and restaurants. Those with higher socio-economic status tend to live in city centers and socialize with people of different backgrounds.

Motivations for Code-Switching From a Sociolinguistic Perspective

Language contact, which has been defined as the interaction between two or more languages resulting from migrations, colonialism, the use of technology, travelling, and globalization (Grosjean, 1982; Myers-Scotton, 2002; Sankoff, 2001; Thomason, 2001), leads to several linguistic outcomes, one of which is code-switching. Code-switching is a frequently used activity found in situations of language contact. Many similar definitions of code-switching have been provided over the years. According to Weinreich, (1953, p. 73) code-switching occurred "from one language to the other according to appropriate changes in speech situation". Gumperz (1982, p. 59) defined code-switching as "the juxtaposition within the same speech exchange of passages of speech belonging to two different grammatical systems or subsystems." Similarly, Heller (1988, p. 4) defined code switching as "the use of more than one language in the course of a single communication episode" and Milroy and Muysken (1995, p. 7) as "the alternative use by bilinguals of two or more languages in the same conversation". According to Auer, (1998, p. 1) code-switching was the "alternating use of two or more codes within one conversational episode". In a similar vein, Myers-Scotton (2006, p. 239) defined it as "the use of two language varieties in the same conversation". An example of code-switching between Spanish and English is provided in the following interaction where Lolita alternated between English and Spanish within the same sentence.

(1) Lolita: *Tengo frío, me voy a poner una suera.*

'I'm cold, I'm going to put on a sweater'
Mother: *Una suera, y sube ya mismo que van a ser las diez.*
'A sweater, and come up right away because it's going to be teno'clock.' Lolita: I'm goin' with um este ('um') Ana. She's coming up at ten
- she's leaving at ten.
Mother: *Pero quítate eso.*
'But take that off.'
(Zentella, 1997, p. 38)

Ever since the first definition of code-switching was provided in the 1950s, a significant number of studies have explained code-switching from a sociolinguistic perspective. One of the most important models that focused on the social motivations of code-switching is the *markedness model* proposed by Myers-Scotton (1993). According to this model, one language is the unmarked language and the other one is the marked language. Bilingual speakers are aware of this distinction because they know from birth that there are social meanings attached to marked and unmarked languages. Thus, speakers switch to either language in a conversation for specific social purposes. Myers-Scotton referred to this as the *markedness metric*, which is "part of the innate cognitive faculty of all humans. It enables speakers to assess all code choices as more or less marked or unmarked for the exchange type in which they occur" (1993, pp. 79-80). For instance, in her analyses of code-switching, which included data collected in east Africa, Myers-Scotton found that bilingual speakers switched to the marked language to express anger, authority, and annoyance.

From a sociolinguistic perspective, which is the focus of the present study, a review of literature concerning motivations for code-switching in contact situations has revealed that bilingual and multilingual speakers codeswitch for a variety of other reasons depending on the type of discourse and sociolinguistic factors. (Bentahila & Davies, 1992; Blom & Gumperz, 1972; Hill & Hill, 1977; Myers-Scotton, 1993). According to scholars, bilingual speakers alternate between languages to raise status (Grosjean, 1982), create social distance (Baker, 2011; Grosjean, 1982), exclude someone from a conversation (Appel & Muysken, 2006; Baker, 2011; Grosjean, 1982), request or command (Baker, 2011; Grosjean, 1982), emphasize or clarify a certain point in a conversation (Appel & Muysken, 2006; Baker, 2011; Gumperz, 1982; Malik, 1994), integrate humour into a conversation (Appel & Muysken, 2006; Baker, 2011), alleviate tension (Baker, 2011), report direct speech (Baker, 2011; Gumperz, 1982), comment on another language (Appel & Muysken, 2006) introduce a topic in a conversation (Baker, 2011), address a particular speaker (Gumperz, 1982; Malik, 1994), attract attention (Malik, 1994), use formulaic sequences, use filler words such as like (Gumperz, 1982; Malik, 1994), show the friendship and family bonding that the speakers share (Baker, 2011), show a change of attitude or relationship (Baker, 2011), and imitate friends or adults (Baker, 2011). In addition, speakers code-switch when an equivalent word does not exist or when they cannot recall words in the other language (Appel & Muysken, 2006; Baker, 2011; Malik, 1994).

For instance, in their analysis of code-switching by Arabic-French Moroccan children, Bentahila and Davies (1994) found that children alternated between languages because one of the languages did not have the concept that the children wanted to express, which Meisel (1990, p. 147) referred to as "relief strategy". Other reasons that children code-switched were to utter a quotation and make an urgent appeal. Cal and Turnbull (2011) analyzed the informal interactions of two Spanish-English bilingual speakers of Mexican origin to determine the functions of their code-switching and how using those functions shaped their identities. The speakers had a high socio-economic background; analyses of the speakers' conversations showed that the speakers switched to English to take the role of the people that the speakers referred to in their conversations. For instance, when one of the speakers was talking about her interaction with a nurse in her workplace, she took the role of the nurse by switching to English. The speakers also code-switched to English or Spanish based on the language used by other speakers. In addition, they code-switched to evaluate a situation, give direct or indirect orders, change the topic of a conversation, and exclude themselves from people with low-socioeconomic background. In a longitudinal study, Migge (2007), using Myers-Scotton's markedness model, explored how members of the highly multilingual Eastern Maroon community of Suriname and French Guiana alternated between Eastern Maroon Creole and Sranan Tongo and vice versa to construct social identities. Data included observations of speakers and recordings of informal social interactions among men, among women, and between men and women. The results showed that the speakers switched between the two varieties depending on the audience, topic, location, prestigiousness of a language, and the social group that speakers belonged to.

In his study of code-switching between Standard Arabic and Dialectal Arabic in contexts such as religious speeches, political debates and soccer commentaries, Albirini (2011), based on the data collected through audio and video recordings, found that the speakers switched to Standard Arabic to introduce formulaic expressions and direct quotations, show pan-Arab or Muslim identity, produce rhyming stretches of discourse, change the tone, mention the importance of a discourse segment, emphasize a unit, and give unnecessary details. The speakers switching to Dialectal Arabic had different motivations such as introducing daily life sayings, producing fillers and indirect quotes, simplifying a preceding idea, giving examples, changing the tone, mentioning issues that are disparaging and unacceptable, and scolding and insulting. These motivations occurred in all three types of discourse. Studying types of code-switching as well as reasons for code-switching by first-generation Bulgarian speakers living in Canada, Yankova and Vassileva (2013) analyzed the extent to which the speakers integrated English and French words, phrases, and sentences in their speech when speaking in Bulgarian. Data were collected from 16 speakers via interviews, questionnaires, and observations. The results showed that the speakers referred to English and French when an equivalent did not exist in Bulgarian. They also code-switched to create an emotional effect and draw the listeners' attention to a particular topic.

In a recent study, Al Abdely (2016) analyzed the code-switching patterns occurring between doctors and patients. The results showed that the doctors switched to English for social, communicative and psychological purposes. The majority of the doctors stated that they preferred to use English because they could not easily recall certain lexical items related to diseases and medicines in Arabic. Moreover, more than half of the doctors reported that they studied medicine in English and thus it made more sense for them to speak English in this type of formal context. Another reason that the doctors switched to English was they did not want to hurt their patients' feelings by telling them their real health conditions.

Other researchers have focused on online discourse environments such as social media. For example, Sergeant, Tagg, and Ngampramuan (2012) examined the situational and pragmatic motivations of language choices of Thai speakers in social media. An analysis of the exchanges among the speakers indicated that although Thai was the default language that was expected to be used in the interactions, switching to English occurred to a wide extent. The speakers switched to English to end a conversation, include their friends who cannot read in Thai, express names for technological products, express concepts that do not have any equivalents in Thai, and refer to certain locations. According to the authors, by switching from Thai to English and vice versa, Thai speakers expressed their local and global identities by establishing "a trans-local community operating in an online, semi-public space" (2012, p. 529).

The Present Study

This chapter builds on previous studies that focused on functions of code-switching by closely examining the reasons why Turkish-English bilingual speakers code-switch, as well the effects of social variables such as age of arrival and length of residence on the speakers' reasons for code-switching. The study aims to answer the following research questions:

1. What are the Turkish-English bilingual speakers' reasons for code-switching?
2. Do age of arrival and length of residence in the U.S. have an effect on the speakers' reasons for codeswitching?

METHODOLOGY

Instrument and Setting

The present study adopted a mixed-method research approach to determine the reasons of code-switching used by Turkish speakers living in the U.S. The data were based on 10 hours of interviews with 20 Turkish speakers. The interviews were semi-structured. The data were elicited for the purposes of identifying code-switching cases and analyzing the frequency of their occurrences. The main topic of the interviews was how the speakers have spent their lives in the U.S. If the speakers finished talking about this topic before 30 minutes were over, then they were also asked to talk about their jobs, if they worked, family, children and their favorite movie.

Each interview, during which the researcher took notes of the code-switched items, lasted for about 30 minutes. Interviews with participants who lived outside of New York City were conducted on the phone whereas those with participants who lived in the city were conducted face-to-face. The interviews were recorded by the researcher. After the interviews, the researcher asked the participants to provide reasons for their code-switching.

The participants were informed that the interviews would be used for a linguistic study but were not told the specific purpose of it so as not to influence the Turkish-English code-switching behavior of the participants. The researcher spoke only Turkish with the participants. To have a better understanding of the informants' socio-demographic characteristics and analyze whether or not social variables have an influence on code-switching, the participants were also asked to fill in a questionnaire which included questions related to their gender, age, profession, as well as age of arrival and length of residence in the U.S. The participants also reported their level of Turkish and English skills on a 5-point Likert scale (1 poor to 5 very good). The participants signed consent forms for participating in the study.

Participants

Of the 20 speakers who participated in the study, 10 were first-generation and the other 10 were second-generation speakers. One participant lived in Ohio, one in New Jersey, one in Pennsylvania, one in California and the rest of the participants lived in New York City. The researcher used the snowball sampling procedure, which is defined as identifying a few people who meet the criteria of a particular study and then asking them to identify further participants appropriate for the study and refer the participants to the researcher (Mackey & Gass, 2012). The researcher first contacted the participants through her acquaintances. Table 1 provides socio-demographic information regarding the participants. Pseudonyms were given to the participants to protect their confidentiality.

Table 1. Participants' socio-demographic information

Pseudonym	Age	Gender	Years of residence in U.S.	Age of arrival in U.S.	Profession
First Generation Speakers					
Ayşe	40	F	25	15	Unemployed
Derya	30	F	26	4	Accountant
Duygu	46	F	35	11	Attorney
Gül	27	F	15	12	Flight attendant
Nihat	45	M	26	19	Limousine driver
Seçil	24	F	12	12	Graduate student
Serdar	55	M	41	14	Professor
Tansu	57	F	40	17	Pianist
Vedat	38	M	25	13	Accountant
Yasin	32	M	19	13	Shop owner
Second Generation Speakers					
Beril	27	F	27	0	Graduate student
Berke	20	M	20	0	Undergraduate student
Ekin	32	F	32	0	Data analyst
Emin	37	M	37	0	Attorney
Esra	30	F	30	0	Event planner
James	25	M	25	0	Financial advisor
Mehmet	40	M	40	0	Broker
Mustafa	40	M	40	0	Graduate student
Serin	26	F	26	0	Graduate student
Teoman	42	M	42	0	Engineer

All first-generation speakers were born in Türkiye. Their parents were Turkish and so was their native language. Coming from a well-educated Turkish family, Tansu was born and raised in Türkiye until the age of 17. Until then, she went to a private secondary and high school where she learned English as a foreign language. Then she went to New York City to get an undergraduate degree in music at the Juilliard School. She is married to an American man. She lived in Ohio at the time of the interview. Tansu visited Türkiye almost every year. Duygu arrived in New Jersey when she was 11 years old when her father was assigned to a military base in the U.S. She did not know any English when she arrived in the U.S. She is also married to an American man. Ayşe is married to a Turkish-American man who was born to Turkish parents living in the U.S. She had a beginner level of English language proficiency when she arrived in the U.S. Nihat did not have any knowledge of English when he arrived in the U.S. He is married to an American woman. Likewise, Vedat did not speak any word of English when he arrived in New Jersey. He was single and had his own business. Among the speakers in this group, Derya was the youngest to arrive in the U.S. Serdar, Gül, Yusuf, and Seher arrived in the U.S. in their teens. Serdar and Seher were married to Turks. Nihat, Vedat, Serdar, Gül, Yasin, and Seher entered the U.S.

with an immigrant visa and lived in close-knit Turkish communities and interacted with Turkish speakers on a daily basis. Tansu, Duygu, and Derya were the only speakers who travelled to Türkiye frequently.

All second-generation speakers were born to Turkish parents living in the U.S. Except for Mehmet, Emin, and Mustafa, all second-generation speakers were single. Mehmet and Emin were married to Turkish women whereas Mustafa's wife was Mexican. This group interacted with mostly non-Turkish speakers. The following section presents the results.

Data Analysis and Results

In the present study, the term code-switching was used as a general term covering all three types: inter-sentential, intra-sentential, and tag-switching (Poplack, 1980). Inter-sentential code-switching refers to switches that occur at a clausal or sentential level. Each sentence can be in one or another language. Using inter-sentential code-switching requires the speaker to have equal competences in both languages because the speaker has to follow the linguistic rules of both languages. In the following example, the speaker uses inter-sentential code-switching from Turkish to Dutch.

(2) *Niye ora-ya gönder-iyor-lar? Arm man*

Why there-DAT send-PROG-3PL poor man
'Why are the sending him there? the poor man'
(Backus, 1992, p. 91)

Intra-sentential switching occurs within a single sentence at sentential, clausal or word level, e.g. "Sometimes I'll start a sentence in English y termino en español" ('sometimes I'll start a sentence in English and finish in Spanish') (Poplack, 1980) and tag-switching occurs when a speaker inserts single words or phrasal tags from one language into another, e.g. I mean, you know, like etc.

In the present study, the recorded interviews were transcribed by the researcher to identify occurrences of code-switching, which were then coded according to their functions following Grosjean (1982), Baker (2011), Gumperz (1982), and Appel and Muysken (2006). The data were analyzed using the Statistical Package for the Social Sciences (SPSS) version 26. The data showed that code-switching served four main functions in the participants' speech: lexical need, clarification of a point in another language, emphasizing a point made, and filling a gap. Below are some examples representing each function of code-switching used by first- and second-generation speakers in the present study.

Lexical Need

The most dominant pattern of code-switching from Turkish to English relates to lexical need; that is, the speakers switched to English when they were unable to retrieve Turkish words or phrases even though they exist in Turkish, as Examples 3, 4, 5 and 6 show. The code-switched items are shown in bold.

(3) *Biliyorsun Julliard'da **entry audition** yapıyorsun.*
Know-IMPF-2SG Julliard-LOC entry audition do-IMPF-2SG
'You know you do an entry audition at Julliard' (first-generation speaker)

(4) *Bizim burada yani operamız var, tiyatro,*
We-POSS here I mean opera-POSS-1PL exist-3SG theatre
var, her şey var, ama tabi bir yerde
exist-3SG everything exist-3SG but of course one place-LOC **country**
'country'
'We have an opera, theatre and everything but of course it is country after all.' (first-generation speaker)

(5) *New York'da Queens'de yaşlı bir kadının*
New York-LOC Queens-LOC old one woman-3SG.POSS
*evini **rent** etmiş.*
house-3SG POSS-ACC rent et-PF
'He rented an old woman's house in Queens, New York.' (first-generation speaker)

(6) *Ben okula git-tiğ-im zaman, yedi sene önce,*
I school-ABL go-VN-POSS-1SG time seven years ago
***engineering** oku-yor-du-m.*
engineering study-IMPF-PF-1SG
'When I went to school seven years ago, I studied engineering.' (second-generation speaker)

In fact, some participants requested to speak in English because they could not recall the Turkish equivalents of the English words and phrases. Examples 7 and 8 illustrate this point.

(7) *Biz shareholderları bir grup olarak temsil ediyoruz.*
We shareholder-PL-ACC one group be-GER represent do-IMPF-1PL.
Çok sıkılıyorum bazen Türkçe konuşurken.
Very bored-IMPF-1SG sometimes Turkish speak-GER.
Doğru kelimeler aklıma gelmiyor.
Right word-PL mind-1SG-DAT come-NEG-3SG.
'We represent the shareholders as a group. I get very uncomfortable when I am speaking in Turkish. The right words do not come to my mind' (first-generation speaker)

(8) *Opportunity cost var diyebilirsin İngilizcesi.*
Opportunity cost exist say-PSB-AOR-2SG English-POSS
Türkçesi ne olduğunu bilmiyorum
Turkish-POSS what be-VN-3SG.POSS know-NEG-IMPF-1SG
ama
but
'In English you can say that there is an opportunity cost, but I do not know what it is called in Turkish.' (second-generation speaker)

Filling a Gap

One of the most predominant functions concerns the use of filler words, which were mostly used by second-generation speakers. The most frequently used filler word was 'so'.

(9) So, o bakımdan New York'ta kalıyoruz.
     So for this reason New York-LOC stay-IMPF-1PL.
     'So, for this reason we stay in New York.' (second-generation speaker)

(10) Sonra belki you know oraya yaşa-ma-(y)a git-ti.
     After maybe you know there live-VN-DAT go-PF-3SG
     'After maybe you know he went to live there.' (first-generation speaker)

Clarification of a Point

A third important motivation for switching to English was to clarify a point. Here the speaker in (11) inserted joint muscles to clarify the gap between the bones, and the speaker in (12) used the English word hammer to clarify the key in a piano.

(11) Evrende sorun böbrekleri, kol
     Evren-LOC problem kidney-PL-3SG.POSS arm
     kemiklerinin arası, joint muscles öyle
     bone-PL-ACC-3SG.POSS between-ACC joint muscles like
     şeyler.
     thing-PL
     'Evren's problem is his kidneys and areas between the arm bones,
     joint muscles, things like that.' (first-generation speaker)

(12) ...tuş yani hammer denilen olay var.
     ...key I mean hammer called case exist-3SG
     'Key, I mean there is a case called hammer.' (second-generation speaker)

Emphasizing a Point Made

A fourth motivation for switching to English was to emphasize a point made during speech. This can be seen in (13) where the speaker stressed the fact that she was a suburban mother.

(13) Çocuklar okuldayken ben ya alışverişe

     Children-PL school-LOC-COP I either shopping-ABL
     go-IMPF-1SG
     gidiyorum, ya da gym'e gidiyorum, tam

go-IMPF-1SG or gym-ABL go-IMPF-1SG exactly suburban mother suburban mother.
'When the kids are at school, I either go shopping or to the gym, just like a suburban mother.'
   (first-generation speaker)

There were a total of 734 instances of code-switching occurring in Turkish as the matrix language. Of these instances, 673 (91%) switches occurred when the speakers could not recall the items in Turkish, 14 (2%) occurred when the speakers needed to clarify a point, 10 (1%) occurred when they wanted to emphasize a point and 37 (5%) consisted of filler words. 262 switches were used by the first-generation and 472 by the second-generation speakers. Table 2 shows the means and standard deviations of functions of code-switching for all participants.

Table 2. Descriptive statistics: Means and standard deviations of functions of code-switching for all participants

	Functions of code-switching	M	SD	N
Participants	Lexical need	33.6	24.47	20
	Clarification of a point	.07	1.12	20
	Emphasizing a point	.05	1.53	20
	Filling a gap	1.85	3.68	20

As can be seen in Table 2, when the whole sample is taken into consideration, participants used the lexical need function (M= 33.6 SD = 24.47) at a higher rate than the clarification of a point (M= .070 SD = 1.12), emphasizing a point (M= .050 SD = 1.53), and filling a gap (M= 1.85 SD = 3.68) functions. Given this result, repeated measures analysis of variance was also conducted to find out if the mean differences among the functions were statistically significant.

Table 3. Bonferroni comparison for functions of code-switching for all participants

Comparisons	Mean Difference	Std. error	Lower bound	Upper bound
95% CI				
Lexical need vs. clarification of a point	32.95*	5.43	16.95	48.94
Lexical need vs. emphasizing a point	33.15*	5.46	17.07	49.22
Lexical need vs. filling a gap	31.80*	5.44	15.78	47.81
*p =< 0.01				

Table 3 shows a significant effect of functions, Wilks' Lambda = .33, $F(3,57) = 35,27$, p = < 0.01 multivariate partial eta squared = .65. There were significant differences between lexical need and clarification of a point, lexical need and emphasizing a point and lexical need and filling a gap. No significant differences among clarification of a point, emphasizing a point, and filling a gap were identified.

The relationship between age of arrival and each function of code-switching and between length of residence and each function of code-switching was also investigated. Table 4 presents the results.

Table 4. Pearson correlations: length of residence and lexical need

	N speakers	r	p
Length of residence*lexical need p = .05*	20	.44	.05

There was a significant positive correlation between length of residence and the lexical need function. No significant correlations were found between age of arrival and lexical need (r=-.27, p=.25, α=0.33); age of arrival and clarification of a point (r=-.1, p=-0.11, α=-0.07); age of arrival and emphasizing a point (r = -.04, p=0.87, α=-0.03); age of arrival and filling a gap (r=-.37, p=-0.37, α=-0.90); length of residence and clarification of a point (r=.135, p=0.13, α=0.06); length of residence and emphasizing a point (r=.063, p=0.06, α=-0.04); and length of residence and filling a gap (r =1, p=0.26, α=0.31).

DISCUSSION

The purpose of the study was to identify the functions of code-switching used by Turkish speakers in the U.S. and determine whether or not social variables such as age of arrival and length of residence played a role in their use of code-switching. According to the results, the participants used code-switching with four functions: lexical need, clarifying a point, emphasizing a point, and filling a gap.

As indicated, the production data had Turkish as its matrix language and had a predominance of switches to English because the participants could not recall the Turkish equivalents, which can be considered as an indication of an incompetency in the Turkish language. Therefore, the participants referred to English words to continue the conversation. This function was used at a significantly higher rate than the others, when the whole sample is taken into consideration. Previous studies (Appel & Muysken, 2006; Baker, 2011; Malik, 1994) that explored the use of this function of code-switching also gave similar results. Recall that when Al Abdely (2016) investigated the code-switching patterns occurring between doctors and patients, he found that most of the doctors used English instead of their native language, Arabic, when communicating with their patients because they could not recall lexical items in Arabic. The author attributed this result to the doctors' high proficiency in the English language. The second most commonly used function was the filling a gap function. The participants used English fillers such as "you know" and "so" to continue conversations. This may also result from the fact that the participants had high competences in English. Previous studies also showed that the participants used "like" as a filler when they code-switched to English (Gumperz, 1982; Malik, 1994).

Regarding the social variables, the only significant correlation was between length of residence and lexical need, suggesting that the longer the speakers lived in the U.S., the longer they were exposed to English, the more they may have interacted with non-Turkish speakers, the more code-switching they used, and the less items they recalled in Turkish. Second-generation speakers, in particular, were exposed to English formally and informally starting from a very young age. In previous studies (Morales, 2003; Veltman, 1990), length of residence in the host country was found to be a strong predictor of bilingualism. In these studies, the longer the immigrants lived in the host country, the more competent they became in target language.

The present study raises questions about understanding code-switching as a unitary repertoire or two separate linguistic systems. In linguistics, the traditional concept of bilingualism is that more than one grammar is represented in the bilingual brain (MacSwan, 2017; Myers-Scotton, 1993) and a bilingual speaker's linguistic repertoire includes "language-specific internal differentiation" (MacSwan, 2017, p. 181). However, recently, certain researchers argued for a unitary grammar consisting of one unified set of linguistic features (Otheguy et al., 2015). According to Otheguy et al. (2015), bilinguals possess "unitary collections of features, and the practices of bilinguals are acts of feature selection, not of grammar switch" (p. 281). Thus, when bilinguals switch from one language into another, they are in fact selecting features from a unitary mental grammar and they not only refer to their first language, but they also make use of other linguistic resources that exist in their repertoire. To give an example, in Turkish the ablative is formed by attaching the suffixes '-den' or '-dan' to the nouns and upon hearing "okuldan" (from school), Turkish-English bilingual speakers know that it is a Turkish construction. They would also know that "from school" is an English construction because in English the ablative is formed via prepositions. These rules, according to Otheguy et al. (2015), exist in the internal linguistic system of bilingual speakers and not in separate systems.

CONCLUSION AND LIMITATIONS

The present study identified several functions of code-switching used by first and second-generation Turkish speakers living in the U.S. and also determined that length of residence had a significant effect on the participants' use of code-switching. The most commonly used function was the lexical need function, that is, the participants switched to English because they could not recall the items in Turkish. Length of residence was found to have a significant effect on this result as the longer the participants lived in the U.S, the less items they retrieved in Turkish. The study contributes to the literature on Turkish-English code-switching, particularly in the U.S. as there is a lack of studies investigating this topic.

There are several limitations of the study. The first one has to do with data collection. In contrast to many code-switching studies that analyzed in-group conversations among speakers belonging to the same speech community (e.g., Poplack, 1980; Zentella, 1997), the present study examined data collected from interviews conducted with one speaker at a time, which makes it difficult to directly compare the results with those of previous studies involving speakers interacting with one another in spontaneous conversations. Interactions in in-group or out-group contexts can result in a substantial increase in the number of switches and in the use of different functions of code-switching. As Blom and Gumperz (1972) found, speakers' code-switching behavior varies depending on the type of context and whom they speak to. The second limitation concerns the language used in the interviews. Because the participants were asked to speak in Turkish during the interviews, this may have prevented the speakers from switching to English as much as they needed to. Using both Turkish and English would have led to the use of different functions of code-switching. Further research can include interactions in in-group or out-group contexts and allow the use of both Turkish and English in the interviews.

Finally, future studies can also focus on the influence of participants' attitudes on their motivations towards code-switching. While some studies found a significant effect of attitude on linguistic behavior, some did not find such an effect. For instance, Redinger (2010) found a significant effect of language attitude on language behavior of students and teachers in multilingual classrooms in Luxembourg. However, in a study that investigated the code-switching behavior in the oral and written narratives of Spanish speakers in California, Montes-Alcalá (2000) found that although the speakers had negative attitudes towards code-switching, they still switched between the languages. Similar results were reported in a study (Koban-Koç, 2016) involving Turkish-English bilingual speakers living in the U.S. It was found that although the majority of first- and second-generation Turkish-English bilingual speakers' attitudes towards switching to English were neutral, they used code-switching to a great extent. In addition, the speakers thought that code-switching led to the loss of Turkish and thus they gave importance to maintaining the status of Turkish in the U.S. Despite its limitations, this study contributes to filling the gap in studies on Turkish-English code-switching in the U.S. context.

REFERENCES

Akçapar, S. K. (2009). Turkish associations in the United States: Towards building a transnational identity. *Turkish Studies, 10*(2), 165-193. https://doi.org/ doi:10.1080/14683840902863996

Al Abdely, A. (2016). Types and functions of code-switching in the English language used by Iraqi doctors in formal settings. *International Journal of Advanced Research and Review*, *1*(8), 10–18.

Albirini, A. (2011). The sociolinguistic functions of *codeswitching* between standard Arabic and dialectal Arabic. *Language in Society*, *40*(5), 537–562. doi:10.1017/S0047404511000674

Appel, R., & Muysken, P. (2006). *Language contact and bilingualism*. Amsterdam University Press.

Auer, P. (1998). *Code-switching in conversation: Language, interaction and identity*. Routledge.

Backus, A. (1992). *Patterns of language mixing: A study in Turkish –Dutch bilingualism* (Vol. O). Harrassowitz.

Backus, A. (1996). *Two in one: Bilingual speech of Turkish immigrants in the Netherlands*. Tilburg University Press.

Backus, A. (1998). The intergenerational codeswitching continuum in an Immigrant community. In G. Extra & L. Verhoeven (Eds.), *Bilingualism and migration* (pp. 261–279). Mouton de Gruyter.

Backus, A. (2005). The interplay between lexical and pragmatic motivations for codeswitching: Evidence from Dutch-Turkish. In J. N. Jørgensen & S. Talayman, C. (Eds.). Languaging and language practices (pp. 96-111). University of Copenhagen, Faculty of the Humanities.

Backus, A. (2009). Codeswitching as one piece of the puzzle of language change: The case of Turkish *yapmak*. In L. Isurin, D. Winford, & K. de Bot (Eds.), *Interdisciplinary approaches to codeswitching* (pp. 307–336). John Benjamins Publishing Company.

Backus, A. (2010). The role of codeswitching, loan translation and interference in the emergence of an immigrant variety of Turkish. *Working Papers in Corpus-based Linguistics and Language Education, 5*, 225-241.

Backus, A. (2012). Turkish as an immigrant language in Europe. In T. K. Bhatia & W. C. Ritchie (Eds.), *The handbook of bilingualism and multilingualism* (pp. 770–790). Blackwell. doi:10.1002/9781118332382.ch31

Baker, C. (2011). *Foundation of bilingual education and bilingualism* (5th ed.). McNaughton & Gunn Ltd.

Bentahila, A., & Davies, E. (1992). Codeswitching and language dominance. In R. J. Harris (Ed.), *Cognitive processing in bilinguals* (pp. 443–458). Benjamins. doi:10.1016/S0166-4115(08)61510-1

Bentahila, A., & Davies, E. (1994). Patterns of code-switching and patterns of language contact. *Lingua, 96*(2-3), 75–93. doi:10.1016/0024-3841(94)00035-K

Blom, J., & Gumperz, J. (1972). Social meaning in linguistic structure: Codeswitching in Norway. In J. Gumperz & D. Hymes (Eds.), *Directions in sociolinguistics: The ethnography of communication* (pp. 407–434). Holt.

Boeschoten, H., & Verhoeven, L. (1987). Language-mixing in children's speech: Dutch language use in Turkish discourse. *Language Learning, 37*(2), 191–215. doi:10.1111/j.1467-1770.1987.tb00565.x

Cal, A., & Turnbull, M. (2007). Code-switching in Spanish/English bilingual speech: The case of two recent immigrants of Mexican descent. *Working Papers in TESOL Applied Linguistics, 7*(2), 1-52.

Grosjean, F. (1982). *Life with two languages: An introduction to bilingualism*. Harvard University Press.

Gumperz, J. J. (1982). *Discourse strategies*. Cambridge University Press. doi:10.1017/CBO9780511611834

Heller, M. (1988). *Codeswitching: Anthropological and sociolinguistic perspectives*. Mouton de Gruyter. doi:10.1515/9783110849615

Hill, J., & Hill, K. (1977). Language death and relexification in Tlaxcalan Nahuatl. *International Journal of the Sociology of Language, 12*, 55–69.

Jørgensen, J. N. (2010). Languaging. Nine years of poly-lingual development of young Turkish-Danish grade school students. *Copenhagen Studies in Bilingualism*. University of Copenhagen.

Karpat, K. H. (2004). *The Turks in America: Historical background: From Ottoman to Turkish immigration. Studies on Turkish politics and society: Selected articles and essays*. Brill.

Koban-Koç, D. (2016). Attitudes towards Oral Code-switching among Turkish-English Bilingual Speakers in New York City. *Hacettepe University Journal of Turkish Studies, 24*, 151–172.

Kurtböke, P. (1998). *A corpus-driven study of Turkish-English language contact in Australia*. [Doctoral dissertation, Monash University].

Mackey, A., & Gass, S. M. (Eds.). (2012). *Research methods in second language acquisition: A practical guide*. Blackwell.

MacSwan, J. (2017). A Multilingual perspective on translanguaging. *American Educational Research Journal*, *54*(1), 167–201. doi:10.3102/0002831216683935

Malik, L. (1994). *Sociolinguistics: A study of code-switching*. Anmol Publications.

Meisel, J. M. (Ed.). (1990). *Two first languages: Early grammatical development in bilingual children* (Vol. 10). Walter de Gruyter. doi:10.1515/9783110846065

Migge, B. (2007). Code-switching and social identities in the Eastern Maroon Community of Suriname and French Guiana. *Journal of Sociolinguistics*, *11*(1), 53–72. doi:10.1111/j.1467-9841.2007.00310.x

Milroy, L., & Muysken, P. (1995). Introduction: Code-switching and bilingualism research. In L. Milroy & P. Muysken (Eds.), *One speaker two languages: Cross-disciplinary perspectives on code- switching* (pp. 1–14). Cambridge University Press. doi:10.1017/CBO9780511620867.001

Montes-Alcalá, C. (2000). Attitudes towards oral and written code-switching in Spanish-English bilingual youth. In A. Roca (Ed.), *Research on Spanish in the United States: Linguistic issues and challenges* (pp. 218–227). Cascadilla Press.

Myers-Scotton, C. (1993). *Social motivations for code-switching: Evidence from Africa*. Oxford University Press.

Myers-Scotton, C. (2002). *Contact linguistics. Bilingual encounters and grammatical outcomes*. Oxford University Press. doi:10.1093/acprof:oso/9780198299530.001.0001

Myers-Scotton, C. (2006). *Multiple voices. An introduction to bilingualism*. Blackwell Publishers.

Otheguy, R., Otheguy, G., & Reid, W. (2015). Clarifying translanguaging and deconstructing named languages: A perspective from linguistics. *Applied Linguistics Review*, *6*(3), 281–307. doi:10.1515/applirev-2015-0014

Pfaff, C. W. (2000). Development and use of et- and yap- by Turkish/German bilingual children. *Studies on Turkish and Turkic languages, Proceedings of the Ninth International Conference on Turkish Linguistics*. CUNY.

Poplack, S. (1980). Sometimes I'll start a sentence in Spanish y termino en Espanol?: Toward a typology of code-switching. *Linguistics*, *18*(7-8), 581–618. doi:10.1515/ling.1980.18.7-8.581

Redinger, D. (2010). *Language attitudes and code-switching behaviour in a multilingual educational context: The case of Luxembourg*. [Doctoral dissertation, University of York].

Sankoff, G. (2001). Linguistic outcomes of language contact. In P. Trudgill, J. Chambers, & N. Schilling-Estes (Eds.), *Handbook of sociolinguistics* (pp. 638–668). Basil Blackwell.

Saville-Troike, M. (1982). *The ethnography of communication: An introduction*. Blackwell.

Sergeant, P., Tagg, C., & Ngampramuan, W. (2012). Language choice and addressivity strategies in Thai-English social network interactions. *Journal of Sociolinguistics*, *16*(4), 510–531. doi:10.1111/j.1467-9841.2012.00540.x

The United States Census Bureau. (2021). *American Community Survey. Data profiles*. USCB. https://www.census.gov/acs/www/data/data-tables-and tools/data-profiles/2014/

Thomason, S. G. (2001). *Language contact: An introduction*. Edinburgh University Press.

Thomason, S. G., & Kaufman, T. (1988). *Language contact, creolization, and genetic linguistics*. University of California Press. doi:10.1525/9780520912793

Türker, E. (2000). *Turkish-Norwegian code-switching. Evidence from intermediate and second-generation Turkish immigrants in Norway*, [Unpublished doctoral dissertation, University of Oslo].

Türker, E. (2005). Resisting the grammatical change: Nominal groups in Turkish-Norwegian codeswitching. *The International Journal of Bilingualism, 9*(3 & 4), 453–476. doi:10.1177/13670069050090030801

Turkish Coalition of America. (2021, March 24). *The Turkish-American Community*. TC America. https://www.tc-america.org/turkish-american-community/

Weinreich, U. (1953). *Languages in contact*. Mouton.

Yankova, D., & Vassileva, I. (2013). Functions and mechanisms of code-switching in Bulgarian Canadians. *Etudes Canadiennes. Canadian Studies*, (74), 103–121. doi:10.4000/eccs.254

Zentella, A. C. (1997). *Growing Up Bilingual*. Blackwell Publishers.

KEY TERMS AND DEFINITIONS

Bilingualism: The ability to use two languages.
Code-switching: Code-switching refers to changing dialects or languages at word or sentential level.
Functions of codeswitching: Reasons for code-switching
Heritage speaker: Heritage speaker refers to a person who has learned a language during childhood at home in an informal way.
Inter-sentential code-switching: Switching to another language at a sentence level.
Intra-sentential code-switching: Switching to another language at a word level.
Tag switching: Inserting a tag from one language into another.

Chapter 16
Interrogating "Filter Bubbles" Within Content Areas and Language Choices for Multilingual Learners in US Classrooms

Karen L. Terrell
https://orcid.org/0000-0003-1094-5940
Loyola University Maryland, USA

Luciana C. de Oliveira
https://orcid.org/0000-0003-0296-4316
Virginia Commonwealth University, USA

Allessandra Elisabeth dos Santos
https://orcid.org/0000-0002-9057-2955
Sergipe Federal University, Brazil

Joy Beatty
Virginia Commonwealth University, USA

Tara Willging
https://orcid.org/0000-0001-8390-5304
Virginia Commonwealth University, USA

Silvia Hoyle
Virginia Commonwealth University, USA

Jia Gui
Clarkson University, USA

ABSTRACT

Filter Bubbles refer to a state of intellectual isolation that can result from people becoming encapsulated in streams of data. When considering factors that contribute to the language choices of multilingual learners (MLs), specifically in the primary content areas of schooling, the Filter Bubble concept easily transposes into the field of education. According to Quintos, "multicultural educators focus on an education for a more democratic and socially just society" (p. 238). However, standards of learning chosen by states and their school districts represent the values of those who sit in positions of power and govern the concepts to which students are exposed. This chapter endeavors to respond to these questions within the intersections of societal constructs and the schooling contexts of English language arts, science, social studies, and mathematics, and to determine possibilities in which MLs can be provided optimal language choices and afforded the spaces to exercise these choices.

DOI: 10.4018/978-1-6684-8761-7.ch016

INTRODUCTION

Filter bubbles (Srba et al., 2023) refer to a state of "intellectual isolation" (p. 4) that can result from people becoming encapsulated in streams of data. This includes news or social network updates, that are personalized to reader interests because of algorithm-based searches. Furthermore, people tend to join groups that share their narratives and world views. This phenomenon presents the danger that critical issues will get filtered, leaving people unexposed to views different from their own. Thus, online users may operate under misperceptions shaped by their *echo chambers*, in which users are selectively served information based on personal information (Rhodes, 2022). Such an environment is conducive to increasing biases, notably "confirmation bias" (Bozdag, 2015, p. 39) – a term that connotes seeking or interpreting evidence in ways that are partial to existing beliefs, expectations, or hypotheses at hand. Exposure to filter bubbles can hinder pluralistic dialogue and thus jeopardize democracies in modern society. Various studies have shown the impact of filter bubbles on the creation of polarization and extremism (Srba et al., 2023). These consequences lead to the generation of racist, sexist, or other prejudiced views that might lead one to experience desensitization and further spread of discriminatory materials (Rhodes, 2022). Furthermore, polarization in its extreme form may also lead to social and/or national fragmentation and even civil war (Sanín & Wood, 2014).

When considering factors that contribute to the language choices of multilingual learners (MLs), specifically in the primary content areas of K-12 schooling, the filter bubble concept easily transposes into the field of education. According to Quintos et al. (2001), "multicultural educators focus on an education for a more democratic and socially just society" (p. 238). However, standards of learning chosen by states and their school districts represent the values of those who sit in positions of power and govern the concepts to which students are exposed. Thus, a number of questions arise: What language norms exist within content texts in schooling? How do these text spaces perpetuate or challenge societal language norms? What is the role of the teacher in interrogating these norms in order to ensure equitable learning opportunities for diverse students, especially MLs? This chapter endeavors to respond to these questions within the intersections of societal constructs and the schooling contexts of social studies, science, English language arts, and mathematics, and to determine possibilities in which MLs can be provided optimal language choices and afforded the spaces to exercise these choices.

INTERSECTIONS OF SOCIAL STUDIES AND MISINFORMATION

Artificial Intelligence (AI) has been impacting and transforming the way people interact and communicate in society (Levy, 2021; Lewis et al., 2019). Due to the empowerment of computers as well as the availability of big data, data produced especially by social media platform users, the phenomenon of mass personalization of communication content is a reality (Hermann, 2022). In this online environment in which people are only exposed to opinions and information that conform to their existing beliefs, the prevalence of such misinformative content leads to false beliefs or manipulated perceptions of reality, the so-called filter bubbles, known for the decrease of diversity (Srba et al., 2023).

The term "filter bubble" was first coined by Eli Pariser in 2010, an Internet activist (Santaella, 2020) and refers to a phenomenon in which personalized internet searches dictate and predict the kind of information a social media platform user might be interested in accessing. This context can be described as if users were confined to their "own information digital world" and confined within a "safe information digital net". According to this theory, algorithms from social media companies provide users with information that is based on data acquired from their interaction on a certain platform: likes, search history, past click behavior, the type of computer, and also the location. When situating this concept within a social studies classroom, filter bubbles shield teachers and students from understanding the value of diverse perspectives and the need to interrogate historical text. Diverse perspectives include those from diverse cultural backgrounds, historically minoritized groups and even diverse languages and proficiencies. Social studies teachers who are not trained in digital literacies and concepts may not understand the close relationship between filter bubbles and the production of false content in online spaces as filter bubbles are characterized as "misinformative content" and "states of intellectual isolation in false beliefs or manipulated perception of reality" (Srba et al., 2023, p.5).

The concern raised by Pariser is a consequence of personalization algorithms, as these function by limiting access to new information, subjects and ideas outside users' interests and perspectives (Santaella, 2020). The consequence of personalization algorithms could result in having serious ethical implications within a social studies classroom. In the K-12 setting, social studies teachers who are currently unaware of the existence of filter bubbles and how these bubbles filter out diverse perspectives may only expose students to the opinions and beliefs that conform to and reinforce a dominant belief, maintaining prevailing norms. It is at these critical moments that intellectual isolation can thrive, and ideological segregation can exist. Thus, these teachers should be trained to teach their students about the importance of reflecting on and interrogating online sources and text, as the production of and access to objective online content is decentralized mainly due to the consequence of personalization algorithms. If multilingual learners, in particular, are not taught to engage in questioning the validity of sources and the need to corroborate text, they will continue to engage with homogenous perspectives and states of manipulated perceptions of reality as a result of misinformative filter bubbles (Srba et al., 2023). In this instance, "the algorithms learn what the user likes, then display more agreeable items and fewer disagreeable news items" (Rhodes, 2022, p.2). If this behavior is continued, MLs can develop the same beliefs and perspectives echoing in the existing systems, becoming a part of the systems of oppression as opposed to being contributors to the intellectual liberation of all (Freire, 2005).

While observing these phenomena, Pariser explains that these algorithms work as curators of the world (Santaella, 2020). In addition, since they do not differentiate in the quality of information presented to users, they create echo chambers where users are shielded from encountering disagreeable messages. These disagreeable messages are important counter narratives that help to balance, diversify, and challenge traditional and homogenized thinking patterns. If these messages are not included and interrogated in social studies classrooms, this leads us to question how ethical these functions actually are and to reflect upon the following: Do algorithms limit our own views and the value of diverse perspectives? Are we able to learn anything new? Are social studies teachers equipped to teach MLs about these concepts in a way that helps them to interrogate dominant narratives bolstered in misinformative filter bubbles by reflecting, and then deconstructing?

Based on these questions, researchers (e.g., Pennycook et al., 2018) state that there are important societal implications for the proper functioning of democracy. The terms Filter Bubble and/or Echo Chamber were associated with the 2016 U.S. Presidential Election (DiFranzo & Gloria-Garcia, 2017) due to the spread of fake news and misinformation shown by several studies. The development of algorithms, which enhanced markets financially as well as power relations, also impacted the Brexit elections in the United Kingdom, and for president of Brazil, in 2018. The association of filter bubble and echo chamber phenomena with these political contexts highlights the role of fake news and misinformation in shaping public opinion and voting behavior. The prevalence and impact of this misinformation was made possible by the personalized algorithms of social media platforms and search engines. These algorithms, designed at first to enhance users' engagement in order to increase advertising revenue, ended up feeding users content that aligns with their existing beliefs and preferences, limiting exposure to diverse views. Moreover, this isolates users within their own informational bubbles making them more susceptible to misinformation, sustaining current norms. In both elections, algorithms created a highly polarized information environment, enabling the spread of misinformation and potentially influencing the results.

The use of smartphones and their ubiquitous nature in our daily lives scales the formation of informational bubbles in social media as a result of AI and improved algorithms. They lead us to interact with and access content primarily from people who have consensual lines of reasoning and opinions. This is intrinsically connected to political contexts, a scenario whose leading actors are politicians who persistently propagate untrue statements that can achieve some level of success in convincing people of their truthfulness. Consequently, the implications are significant for the proper functioning of a democratic society. This phenomenon is defined as post-truth, in which truth loses its relevant character in the formation of public opinion and has a preference for information whose basis lies in beliefs and emotions. It is relevant to bear in mind the possible steps to combat the acceptance of incorrect information disseminated as fake news as well as burst filter bubbles since they offer broader implications beyond the realm of fake news on social media (Santaella, 2018).

Educating students to be critical and digitally literate consists of providing them with the basis to interrogate dominant narratives, reflect, and deconstruct ideas regardless of their context so that this is embraced as a skill and social practice. It is imperative that social studies teachers help MLs, and all students, to sharpen their critical thinking skills by reflecting, interrogating, and deconstructing the origin and influence of misinformation. Through this skillset, students can develop their capabilities to problematize the filter bubble and then to curate diverse perspectives while employing their critical thinking skills.

INTERSECTIONS OF SCIENCE AND MEDIA

The COVID-19 pandemic impacted public health at a national and international level. The World Health Organization recognized the effect of misleading communications with the term "infodemic," which prevents the dissemination of scientific information related to the coronavirus and represents a risk to public health (Eysenbach, 2020). This infodemic made managing the pandemic even more complicated due to the difficulty of finding trustworthy sources of information, contributing to the politicization of the virus and shifting the influence of traditional media and social networks (La Bella et al., 2021). In addition, the proliferation of true and false information made it more difficult for people to make decisions regarding their health during the height of the COVID-19 period. The use of the internet and social networks for the rapid transmission of fake news and rumors caused people to develop anxiety and depression, affecting the performance of their daily activities (Kim & Kim, 2020). Viewer trust in fake news was influenced by the frequency of online activity, use of information on media and social networks, and psychological and personal factors, as well as political ideologies (Halpern et al., 2019).

Online communications are identity-driven processes because people search for validation from like-minded individuals. As such, the identity bubble reinforcement model (IBRM) offers a socio-psychological perspective through social-media selectivity studies (Keipi et al., 2017). An individual's involvement in social media identity bubbles can be measured using the identity bubble reinforcement scale (IBRS) (Kaakinen et al., 2020). Studies have explained the relationships between individuals and groups online using the IBRM. Homophily has been increasing in the interactions of individuals online which build credibility in the social media publications of the person's group supporting the social media identity bubbles. Social interactions with only people who have similar identities and attitudes can increase biased mindsets that reinforce risky behaviors among online communities (Keipi et al., 2017). Widespread availability of connectivity and training for the digital management of information should be considered for all members of society as the change to remote instruction contributes to the participation of a greater number of people. However, people with limitations in language and digital data management are left behind. For this reason, it is important that they receive training in the development of digital tools to increase confidence in technologies and the participation of more diverse communities (Handley et al., 2023).

Many of the preventive actions for COVID-19 used data visualization that did not consider the language or the literacy level of the audience – another prevalent norm. Some academics think that data literacy is acquired individually with an emphasis on understanding in the same way as digital literacy or health literacy (Börner et al., 2019). Other academics use the visualization of data in images as instruments to communicate preventive health measures to patients and to encourage the use of medication (Pack et al., 2019; Roosan et al., 2020; Toscos et al., 2020). Data visualization contributes to the production of knowledge in communities. Researchers are interested in involving communities in the creation and interpretation of data, following a participatory approach that has been used in the area of environmental justice (Sandhaus et al., 2019; Wong et al., 2019). According to D'Ignazio and Bhargava (2016), there is a large gap between who can store and use data, and who may obtain the data but is unable to utilize it. This disparity primarily affects communities known to be "Limited English Proficient" and who have suffered the most from the COVID-19 pandemic (Handley et al., 2023). However, Davies (2018) challenges the presentation of science in media and the messages they deliver by using the language of science and technology to redefine the concept of the "Filter Bubble Effect" and present it as a socio-technical resource.

Research studies have shown that inequalities in access to care and exposure risk are contributing factors in Hispanic and Black populations having the highest rates of COVID-19-related infection and mortality (Mackey et al., 2021). As people in our present society tend to analyze health information they receive through diverse media, including auditory, oral, visual, and printed images, we must consider and analyze the average person's data literacy skills. Evidence shows that people move from one medium to another without having a specific preference for language; however, that movement between different languages and modalities contributes to the understanding of risk and gives confidence to individual comprehension abilities (Handley et al., 2023).

In the United States, 43% of the approximately 1.1 million adult learners enrolled in publicly funded adult education programs are multilingual learners (Handley et al., 2023). This population is comprised of immigrants, refugees, workers, underemployed, or young people who have aged out of the K-12 system. Many of these individuals may have limited skills in reading and writing in the languages that they speak (Bigelow & Vinogradov, 2011). The context of adults learning English is not normally related to the scientific transmission of data; however, it is important that populations of linguistically marginalized students acquire the knowledge and information that allows them to have preventive health care. The healthcare experiences of linguistically marginalized students support the interrelationships between health, power, language, and the way of perceiving health risks. Adult English learners develop their own interpretations of health information that they are rarely able to share with other students or communities. Literature has given little attention to the adult English learner classroom as a space in which linguistically diverse communities can make valuable contributions through the interpretation and production of data (Handley et al., 2023). Language teaching can contribute to the knowledge of data science by asking open questions that enable students to develop their curiosity for the understanding of data, describe data using visual means (e.g., data graphs, categories, shapes, and abnormal values), and allow students to demonstrate their learning (D'Ignazio & Bhargava, 2016).

INTERSECTIONS OF ENGLISH LANGUAGE ARTS AND MISEDUCATION

Public education classrooms in America with global students and communities deserve a wider range of instruction and texts. However, English Language Arts (ELA) classes generally develop students' interpretation and comprehension of texts, through a "standardized, academic English" language. Applying the idea of filter bubbles (Pariser, 2011; Srba et. al, 2023), educators can recognize that English-only instruction is isolated by choice and historically steeped in whiteness that has led to racist policies and the erasing of multilingualism and identity in schools, especially in English language arts classrooms (Walker, 2020). Miseducation about language can be revealed with the filter bubble. For example, many educators say they require students to use "correct" grammar, not aware that they could instead teach that all human language consists of systemic patterns (Smitherman, 2017). To marginalize a particular language (e.g., Haitian Creole), besides only using the language of academic English in the classroom, some educators would take measures, such as silencing and policing students if they use their home languages (Baker-Bell, 2020). Because of these actions, multilingual students may develop negative attitudes toward their cultural, linguistic, and racial identities if their native languages are discouraged in the classroom (Baker-Bell, 2013). For students who internalize negative beliefs about their home language, the exclusion of their native tongues in the classroom can lead to a sense of linguistic inadequacy and a loss of confidence in their ability to learn, as well as in their teachers and the educational system as a whole (Charity Hudley & Mallinson, 2014). Eventually, the way teachers require students of color to reject their language and culture to acquire White Mainstream English converts learning to be one-sided, monolingual, and oppressive. Language policies in schools develop from social demands on linguistically marginalized speech communities to "change their language so they don't sound like who they are" (Smitherman, 2017). Academic English in schools may be seen as a filter bubble to mediate racist language ideologies and become an internalized social narrative. Academic English creates a false dichotomy and socializes students in one way, while ignoring the rich language practices that the students already have (Souto-Manning et al., 2022). Identifying the filter bubble of literature and language in ELA classes can reveal opportunities for bursting the filter bubble, welcoming all students to belong, participate, and learn with each other.

Teachers can burst the filter bubble by guiding students to explore and critically examine their own language and community dialects by implementing critical language awareness methods. This approach serves as a powerful tool, enabling students to critically assess language policies and attitudes that may disempower them and their communities (Smitherman, 2017). Language arts classrooms can be environments that nurture healthy, multilingual communities through culturally relevant texts and experiences with literature that honors students' knowledge and language (Walker, 2020) and adding academic English to students' already rich linguistic repertoires. A print-rich environment with authentic, even co-constructed word walls and anchor charts can reflect student languages. Schools can also choose forms of literature outside the norm, starting with the students' experiences and strengths. The use of literary and historical texts from indigenous communities and communities of color highlights and contextualizes concepts of power, racial issues, and anti-colonialism, exemplifying one way in which educators can employ an ethnic studies approach (de los Ríos et al., 2019). Alternatively, the use of primary sources from these minority communities that provide counternarratives also represents a different ethnic studies teaching strategy. Teachers can use multilingual texts that encourage critical metalinguistic awareness and translanguaging beyond utilizing it as simply a scaffold for teaching English, to embrace critical translingual approaches. ELA classrooms using a critical translingual approach can dispute monolingualism as the norm. All language minoritized students should utilize their full language repertoires (de los Ríos et al., 2019). Through a translanguaging pedagogy, students can develop a greater metalinguistic awareness and linguistic consciousness, including a critical sociolinguistic consciousness (García, 2017). Enacting a pedagogy of communicative belonging positions students as stakeholders of their ever evolving knowledge and language. With this approach, schools and teachers can recognize that academic language is not a precursor to knowledge (Souto-Manning et al., 2022); rather, it is another addition to their language repertoire.

INTERSECTIONS OF MATHEMATICS AND GATEKEEPING

Historically, the notion of *gatekeeping* has indicated protection and security. With regard to the Internet and filter bubbles, "gatekeeping barriers that have traditionally curtailed the dissemination of false news relative to legitimate news have been dramatically reduced" (Napoli, 2018, p. 71). In education, gatekeeping barriers have had a more negative effect, preventing culturally, linguistically, and intellectually diverse students from accessing higher order and/or higher level content. How does this affect manifest in the realm of mathematics? Consider the demographics of professional mathematicians in the United States. According to careerexplorer.com (Sokanu Interactive Inc., 2023), the ethnic mix of practicing mathematicians in 2019 was 8% African American, 9% Latinx, 3% Arab, and 0% Native American/Pacific Islander; as opposed to 25% Asian and 46% White. This is disproportionate to the population of this country, which is 13% African American, 19% Latinx, and 2% Native American/Pacific Islander and 6% Asian and 59% White (U.S. Department of Commerce, 2023). Further, of 669 doctoral graduates in mathematics at one American university, 86 total were people of color – African American, Latinx, Native American, or Asian (Walker, 2014). This is a clear indication that the field of mathematics tends to be more accessible to Whites versus more diverse populations (i.e., another filter bubble), and it implies the isolation of the language of mathematics from the latter groups as well.

Change-Bacon (2022) discusses that the latest literature on the intersectionality of language and race reveals that "the language practices of students of color continue to be stigmatized, even when they conform to the supposed norms of English usage that are privileged in school contexts" (p.8). Delpit (2006) situates teachers as gatekeepers, providing or denying children access to the languages of power. She purports, "... pretending that gatekeeping points don't exist is to ensure that many students [primarily diverse children] will not pass through them" (p.39). Thus, it is up to teachers to decode and teach their students the "codes of power" in order to push against as many gatekeeping points as possible, breaking down walls of intellectual isolation in every content area – including mathematics.

Planas et al. (2018) suggest that it is necessary for educators to move beyond thinking simply about the language of the student, teacher, and content; but rather, progress to the conceptualization of "language as system, language as culture and language as discourse" (p. 218). Typically systems are multiple items, pieces, or even people, working together for a common aim. When considering *language as system*, the researchers define these "pieces" as expressive rules, texts (both written and oral), and also contexts. These components work together towards interpretive goals such as communication and understanding. Quintos et al. (2001) suggest that "students learn to use mathematics to understand their context and learn that these mathematical discourses can be key in the transformation of themselves, the environment, and their communities" (p. 238). Thus, children need access to gates and systems that may otherwise be closed to them. This necessity, in turn, assigns mathematics teachers the responsibility to not only teach algorithms and computations, but more importantly, to "reverse the patterns of oppression that disenfranchise students" (p. 253). According to Anderson (2007), students must be able to "participate within mathematical communities in such *a way as to see themselves* [emphasis added] and be viewed by others as valuable members of those communities" (p. 8).

Teachers convey how they view and value their students by engaging them in the discourse of their classrooms. In particular, student participation in mathematics dialogue can be supported through strategies such as "modeling consistent norms for discussions, revoicing student contributions, building on what students say and probing what students mean" (Moschkovich, 1999, p. 18). Freire (2005) states that "dialogue cannot occur between those who want to name the world and those who do not wish this naming [the gatekeeping barriers] – between those who deny others the right to speak their word and those whose right to speak has been denied them" (p. 88). "Dismantling existing echo chambers and linguistic obstacles in mathematics and other content areas "involves sustained effort, reflection, and engagement" (Chang-Bacon, 2022, p. 20) at all levels of instruction. Thus, educators must encourage the participation and contributions of their students in classroom discourse in order to enable students to make meaning of the world through mathematics and to honor the humanity of their students (Quintos et al., 2001), thereby combatting more oppressive practices to create a more just society.

CONCLUSION

The concept of filter bubbles (Srba et al., 2023) is useful for us to reflect on what may act as such in different content areas. This chapter connected various types of filter bubbles in each content area – social studies, science, English, and mathematics. In social studies, filter bubbles prevent teachers and students from understanding the value of diverse perspectives and the need to interrogate what they read. To address this, social studies teachers need to understand digital literacies and teach students to identify false content in online spaces as misinformative content. In science, we described the connections between the COVID-19 pandemic, data visualization, and the effects of "infodemic" preventing the dissemination of scientific information as representing a risk to public health. The infodemic is the filter bubble in science as we described the complications of managing the pandemic due to the difficulty of finding trustworthy sources of information.

In English language arts, Academic English may be seen as a filter bubble by creating a false dichotomy and socializing students in one way. We support the idea that Academic English be added to the rich language practices that students already have so it is not seen as a filter bubble, but rather as an added part of students' existing linguistic repertoires. In mathematics, filter bubbles include gatekeeping barriers preventing culturally, linguistically, and intellectually diverse students from accessing higher order and/or higher-level content and the explicit instruction in the language of mathematics that is critical for opening the "gates" for these students.

There are many ways we can conceptualize filter bubbles in the content areas. What we have in common in this chapter is that filter bubbles have isolated students from content, information, and perspectives, making it possible for them to miss out on concepts and ideas that are important for them to have as they develop as more informed individuals. Freire (2005) purports, "The teacher's thinking is authenticated only by the authenticity of the student's thinking" (p. 77). Thus, today's educators have the unique opportunity to combat the inequities caused by the transposed components of filter bubbles, allowing multilingual students optimal choices within language and in life.

REFERENCES

Baker-Bell, A. (2013). "I never really knew the history behind African American language": Critical language pedagogy in an advanced placement English language arts class. *Equity & Excellence in Education*, *46*(3), 355–370. doi:10.1080/10665684.2013.806848

Baker-Bell, A. (2020). Dismantling anti-black linguistic racism in English language arts classrooms: Toward an anti-racist black language pedagogy. *Theory into Practice*, *59*(1), 8–21. doi:10.1080/00405841.2019.1665415

Bigelow, M., & Vinogradov, P. (2011, March). Teaching adult second language learners who are emergent readers. *Annual Review of Applied Linguistics*, *31*, 120–136. doi:10.1017/S0267190511000109

Börner, B. A., & Ginda, M. (2019). Data visualization literacy: Definitions, conceptual frameworks, exercises, and assessments. *Proceedings of the National Academy of Sciences - PNAS*, *116*(6), 1857–1864. https://doi.org/10.1073/pnas.1807180116

Bozdag, E. (2015). *Bursting the filter bubble: Democracy, design, and ethics*. [Master's thesis, Technische Universiteit Delft]. doi:10.4233/uuid:87bde0a2-c391-4c77-8457-97cba93abf45

Chang-Bacon, C. K. (2022). We sort of dance around the race thing: Race-evasiveness in teacher education. *Journal of Teacher Education*, *73*(1), 8–22. doi:10.1177/00224871211023042

D'Ignazio, C., & Bhargava, R. (2016). DataBasic: Design principles, tools and activities for data literacy learners. *The Journal of Community Informatics*, *12*(3), 83–107. doi:10.15353/joci.v12i3.3280

Davies, H. C. (2018). Redefining filter bubbles as (escapable) socio-technical recursion. *Sociological Research Online*, *23*(3), 637–654. doi:10.1177/1360780418763824

de los Ríos, C. V., Martinez, D. C., Musser, A. D., Canady, A., Camangian, P., & Quijada, P. D. (2019). Upending colonial practices: Toward repairing harm in English education. *Theory into Practice*, *58*(4), 359–367. doi:10.1080/00405841.2019.1626615

Delpit, L. (2006). *Other people's children: Cultural conflict in the classroom* (2nd ed.). The New Press.

DiFranzo, D., & Gloria-Garcia, K. (2017). Filter bubbles and fake news. *XRDS: Crossroads. The ACM Magazine for Students.*, *23*(305), 32–35. doi:10.1145/305515

Eysenbach, G. (2020). How to fight an infodemic: The four pillars of infodemic management. *Journal of Medical Internet Research*, *22*(6), e21820. https://www.jmir.org/2020/6/e21820. doi:10.2196/21820 PMID:32589589

Freire, P. (2005). *Pedagogy of the oppressed, 30th anniversary edition*. The Continuum International Publishing Group, Inc.

García, O. (2017). Translanguaging in schools: Subiendo y bajando, bajando y subiendo as afterword. *Journal of Language, Identity, and Education*, *16*(4), 256–263. doi:10.1080/15348458.2017.1329657

Handley, M. A., Santos, M. G., & Bastías, M. J. (2023). Working with data in adult english classrooms: Lessons learned about communicative justice during the COVID-19 pandemic. *International Journal of Environmental Research and Public Health*, *20*(1), 696. doi:10.3390/ijerph20010696 PMID:36613016

Hermann, E. (2022). Artificial intelligence and mass personalization of communication content—An ethical and literacy perspective. *New Media & Society*, *24*(5), 1258–1277. https://doi-org.proxy.library.vcu.edu/10.1177/14614448211022702. doi:10.1177/14614448211022702

Kaakinen, M., Sirola, A., Savolainen, I., & Oksan, A. (2020). Shared identity and shared information in social media: Development and validation of the identity bubble reinforcement scale. *Media Psychology*, *23*(1), 25–51. doi:10.1080/15213269.2018.1544910

Keipi, T., Näsi, M., Oksanen, A., & Räsänen, P. (2017). *Online hate and harmful content: Cross-national perspectives*. Routledge.

La Bella, E., Allen, C., & Lirussi, F. (2021, December). Communication vs evidence: What hinders the outreach of science during an infodemic? A narrative review. *Integrative Medicine Research*, *10*(4), 100731. doi:10.1016/j.imr.2021.100731 PMID:34141575

Levy, R. (2021). Social media, news consumption, and polarization: Evidence from a field experiment. *The American Economic Review*, *111*(3), 831–870. doi:10.1257/aer.20191777

Lewis, S. C., Guzman, A. L., & Schmidt, T. R. (2019). Automation, journalism, and human–machine communication: Rethinking roles and relationships of humans and machines in news. *Digital Journalism (Abingdon, England)*, *7*(4), 409–427. doi:10.1080/21670811.2019.1577147

Mackey, K., Ayers, C. K., Kondo, K. K., Saha, S., Advani, S. M., Young, S., Spencer, H., Rusek, M., Anderson, J., Veazie, S., Smith, M., & Kansagara, D. (2021, March). Racial and ethnic disparities in COVID-19-related infections, hospitalizations, and deaths: A systematic review. *Annals of Internal Medicine*, *174*(3), 362–373. doi:10.7326/M20-6306 PMID:33253040

Moschkovich, J. N. (1999a, March). Supporting the participation of English language learners in mathematical discussions. *For the Learning of Mathematics*, *19*(1), 11–19.

Napoli, P. M. (2018). What if more speech is no longer the solution: First Amendment theory meets fake news and the filter bubble. *Federal Communications Law Journal*, *70*, 55–104.

Pack, G., Golin, C. E., Hill, L. M., Carda-Auten, J., Wallace, D. D., Cherkur, S., Farel, C. E., Rosen, E. P., Gandhi, M., Asher Prince, H. M., & Kashuba, A. D. M. (2019). Patient and clinician perspectives on optimizing graphical displays of longitudinal medication adherence data. *Patient Education and Counseling, 102*(6), 1090–1097. doi:10.1016/j.pec.2018.12.029 PMID:30626550

Pariser, E. (2011). *The filter bubble: What the Internet is hiding from you.* Penguin UK.

Pennycook, G., Cannon, T. D., & Rand, D. G. (2018). Prior exposure increases perceived accuracy of fake news. *Journal of Experimental Psychology. General, 147*(12), 1865–1880. doi:10.1037/xge0000465 PMID:30247057

Planas, N., Morgan, C., & Schütte, M. (2018). Mathematics education and language: Lessons and directions from two decades of research. In T. Dreyfus, M. Artigue, D. Potari, S. Prediger, & K. Ruthven (Eds.), *Developing research in mathematics education. Twenty years of communication, cooperation and collaboration in Europe* (pp. 196–210). Routledge. doi:10.4324/9781315113562-15

Quintos, B., Civil, M., & Torres, O. (2001). Mathematics teaching with a vision of social justice: Using the lens of communities of practice. In K. Téllez, J. N. Moschkovich, & M. Civil (Eds.), *Latinos/as and mathematics education: Research on learning and teaching in classrooms and communities* (pp. 233–258). Information Age Pub.

Rhodes, S. C. (2022). Filter bubbles, echo chambers, and fake news: How social media conditions individuals to be less critical of political misinformation. *Political Communication, 39*(1), 1–22. doi:10.1080/10584609.2021.1910887

Roosan, C., Chok, J., Karim, M., Law, A. V., Baskys, A., Hwang, A., & Roosan, M. R. (2020). Artificial intelligence–powered smartphone app to facilitate medication adherence: Protocol for a human factors design study. *JMIR Research Protocols, 9*(11), e21659–e21659. doi:10.2196/21659 PMID:33164898

Sandhaus, S., Kaufmann, D., & Ramirez-Andreotta, M. (2019). Public participation, trust and data sharing: Gardens as hubs for citizen science and environmental health literacy efforts. International Journal of Science Education *Part B, 9*(1), 54–71. PMID:31485378

Sanín, F. G., & Wood, E. J. (2014). Ideology in civil war: Instrumental adoption and beyond. *Journal of Peace Research, 51*(2), 213–226. doi:10.1177/0022343313514073

Santaella, L. A. (2018). *Pós-verdade é verdadeira ou falsa?* Estação das Letras e Cores.

Santaella, L. A. (2020). A educação e o estado da arte das tecnologias digitais. In *SALES, M. S. (Org.). Tecnologias digitais, redes e educação: perspectivas contemporâneas* (pp. 149–163). Edufba.

Smitherman, G. (2017). Raciolinguistics, "mis-education," and language arts teaching in the 21st century. *Language Arts Journal of Michigan, 32*(2), 3. doi:10.9707/2168-149X.2164

Sokanu Interactive Inc. (2023). *Mathematician demographics in the United States.* Career Explorer. https://www.careerexplorer.com/careers/mathematician/demographics/#:~:text=The%20largest%20ethnic%20group%20of,13%25%20and%2012%25%20respectively

Souto-Manning, M., Martinez, D. C., & Musser, A. D. (2022). ELA as English language abolition: Toward a pedagogy of communicative belonging. *Reading Research Quarterly*, *57*(4), 1089–1106. doi:10.1002/rrq.464

Srba, I., Moro, R., Tomlein, M., Pecher, B., Simko, J., Stefancova, E., Kompan, M., Hrckova, A., Podrouzek, J., Gavornik, A., & Bielikova, M. (2023). Auditing YouTube's recommendation algorithm for misinformation filter bubbles. *ACM Transactions on Recommender Systems*, *1*(1), 1–33. doi:10.1145/3568392

Toscos, D., Daley, C., Wagner, S., Coupe, A., Ahmed, R., Holden, R. J., Flanagan, M. E., Pfafman, R., Ghahari, R. R., & Mirro, M. (2020). Patient responses to daily cardiac resynchronization therapy device data: A pilot trial assessing a novel patient-centered digital dashboard in everyday life. *Cardiovascular Digital Health Journal*, *1*(2), 97–106. doi:10.1016/j.cvdhj.2020.09.003 PMID:35265880

United States Department of Commerce. (2023). *QuickFacts: United States*. United States Census Bureau, United States Department of Commerce. https://www.census.gov/quickfacts/fact/table/US/PST045222

Walker, E. N. (2014). *Beyond Banneker: Black mathematicians and the paths to excellence*. State University of New York Press. doi:10.1353/book32767

Walker, K. (2020). The English language arts classroom as a multilingual literacy community. *The Clearing House: A Journal of Educational Strategies, Issues and Ideas*, *93*(6), 284–289. doi:10.1080/00098655.2020.1789038

Wong, W., Wu, H.-C., Cleary, E. G., Patton, A. P., Xie, A., Grinstein, G., Koch-Weser, S., & Brugge, D. (2019). Visualizing air pollution: Communication of environmental health information in a Chinese immigrant community. *Journal of Health Communication*, *24*(4), 339–358. doi:10.1080/10810730.2019.1597949 PMID:31030632

Conclusion

By way of a conclusion to this edited volume, we three editors decided to meet and critically reflect on the project. We felt it was important to revisit our initial motivations in crafting an edited volume on multilingual language practices: we decided to discuss the themes we had originally envisioned as well as the themes that emerged from the contributing authors, while considering the various ways in which multilingualism and language norms have impacted us as individuals. This turned into an approximately 90-minute audio-recorded conversation, which we then transcribed and collaboratively coded for emerging themes. Following this, we collected and collated excerpts from the transcript, loosely following the emergent thematic strands. What follows is a constructed dialogue based on that conversation as well our subsequent discussions thereof.

In this constructed dialogue, we explore and juxtapose our reflections on the themes in this book, the process of collecting and curating its contributions, and questions we are taking away from the experience. We share this in a narrative form as it reflects the ongoing impacts of the book's themes on our lived experiences as well as the collaborative creative process we engaged in throughout the development of this edited volume. We end with a remaining unanswered question in order to invite future dialogue, encouraging the reader to consider their own responses to this exploration and how multilingualism and language norms are enacted in their own language practices.

Julie:

So, to conclude, let's revisit the title of our book, *Reconceptualizing Language Norms in Multilingual Contexts*. "Reconceptualizing," meaning there was a conceptualization before that we felt didn't fit, or needed revisiting, right? What are some of the norms that we felt needed to be discussed in the book?

Rebecca:

Well, this idea that monolingualism has been a norm, despite the reality of multilingualism, I think this definitely came out in the chapters – the idea that a lot of language norms, a lot of research, a lot of classroom practices are based on this norm of monolingualism. Even though I wouldn't necessarily see it that way, people might look at a society or classroom or culture and deem it monolingual. Monolingualism as a norm can be a useful frame of reference.

Julie:

Yeah, in terms of reconceptualizing norms, it just helped me to appreciate that a norm is not a norm; it's not an objective thing. It really depends a lot on what one's needs are, what one is trying to communicate, and who one is trying to communicate with. So, monolingualism and multilingualism, they're very subjective. What one person can perceive as being monolingual can be perceived by someone else as being multilingual.

Sarah:

That was the big thing too, for me, taking multilingualism as the norm, as opposed to, I think, 50 years ago. You two would have been our traditional polyglots, whereas today I think, to some extent, that conversation around what it means to be multilingual, that's shifting. There's a bit more fluidity in terms of multicompetence and not having to know each language perfectly to be considered multilingual, as well as recognizing the connection between language and culture.

Julie:

And I think too, there are sectors of society, or possibly stratifications, where multilingualism is frosting on the cake, and others where multilingualism is the core, necessary instrument that makes things work.

Sarah:

Absolutely. The chapters in the book show a variety of contexts, from public-facing messages to intimate speech, of multilingualism having a high-stakes impact on people's lives.

Rebecca:

It's true, it really stood out to me in several chapters how, sometimes, monolingualism is the idealized norm, but multilingualism ends up being the reality. Even in contexts like target-language-medium instruction, one single language is rarely used, and the mix of languages is the actual normative practice.

Sarah:

And turning the conversation to the use of English, I think some chapters showed that, even within a single language like English, there is an incredible amount of diversity in the ways that people are actually communicating in daily language practices. And those practices, when documented, really defy these traditional conceptions of homogenous, siloed languages, and of language use.

Julie:

Yeah, and although the book is in English, I was really pleased by the diversity of international contexts represented by the chapters.

Sarah:

Conclusion

I agree. I feel like English does take center stage in terms of it being a prevalent theme, but it's not the only one. One of my fears with the call for chapters for this book was that everybody would want to talk about English. And that has not been my experience curating this book. When English is being discussed, it's about how people are bringing other languages into an English-speaking environment; how people are orienting to English in their own environment.

Rebecca:

We can't ignore the role of English, of academic English, as a norm in this book. I was a bit concerned about how we would be able to balance a diversity of voices and ways of writing in academic English with our overall objective of reconceptualizing normative language practices, and whether that would become a tension for us in the editorial process. We touched on this in the preface, but the authors seem to have found ways to somehow still embody but also play with and resist norms of academic English. I don't know. It's complex.

Julie:

And the power dynamics are just so, so there.

Sarah:

It's true. Especially in the chapters that talked about classroom practices. I think there is this traditional idea about using other languages where the learner meets the language; in other words, the language is seen as this static, standardized norm, and the learner's goal is to meet that norm, so it is entirely the learner's responsibility to achieve that language standard. One thing, though, that we tried to touch on in our approach to the book and that a lot of the chapters have looked at is how people learning languages and people speaking languages are actually changing the language, right? So language is being changed by the people who speak it, and not the other way around. And I think that does mark a significant change.

Julie:

Yeah, and yet, it is still so indicative of power, in terms of *who* gets to determine language use and language choices.

Rebecca:

I think that's something that goes back to how it's all about language norms. And I think that's where intersectionality and complexity, although those terms were not explicitly mentioned in the chapters, I think those terms are really useful to this conversation, which, for me, centres around issues of language and power and access. I think that's another central contribution of the book: Reframing the use of learners' multiple languages, and also students' use of technology as part of their meaning-making repertoires, as part of their language repertoires, as a norm that already exists and that should be supported in education.

Sarah:

I agree. While a few of the chapters seek to provide guidance on how multilingualism can be supported, or celebrated, in education, the themes really do point to a new and, to me, more equitable orientation to language learning and language learners. And, in my own teaching contexts, I'm witnessing teachers discuss multicompetence with their students, using digital technologies to support learning, and encouraging linguistic diversity in the classroom. I see it in my own teaching and I see it reflected in many of the chapters in this book. And all this, to my mind, is reflective of the complexity and multiplicity and plurality that already exists in both societies and classrooms.

Julie:

This also brings us back to the idea of multilingualism as a choice versus multilingualism as a necessity. We spoke earlier about societies that valued multilingualism as an asset and those that used multilingualism as a core feature of communication, but I am also thinking of individuals learning and using languages. If you're learning a language, then drawing on your multilingual resources is sometimes necessary to convey what you want to convey. It's about being understood at a basic level. Whereas if you're able to communicate what you want to communicate in one language, using more than one language is a nuance or an aspect, you know, a way of possibly communicating solidarity or some cultural values, for example, but it's not a necessity for understanding; it goes beyond that.

Rebecca:

Well, I think multilingual necessities and multilingual choices can happen at the same time in teaching and learning. And I've noticed that, for example, two different teachers can have a completely different view of the same class. So I might get a group of students who all have the same nationality, and another teacher might get another group from a single country, and then they might look at that group and say, I have a homogenous class. And I might look at the group and say, this class has regional diversity, and different language varieties and personalities and communication styles. So, you might be able to view something through a different lens, just by resisting monolingual ideologies and engaging with the idea of multilingualism as a norm. And so I think that's part of the book's reconceptualization.

Julie:

So, at what point in the discourse will we stop saying reframing and reconceptualizing, and just say framing and conceptualizing?

Afterword

A plurality of voices, embodying the growing diversity of our collective academic thinking, characterises this volume, which offers interesting food for thought for researchers and students in the field of languages in the broadest sense. The title of the book *Reconceptualizing Language Norms in Multilingual Contexts* announces from the outset the tone and purpose of the work, which seeks to help us reflect on the multiplicity of factors that come into play when we talk about languages, their teaching and learning, language policies, identity, and epistemological reflections on all these dimensions. The book aims to provide us with a rich variety of different perspectives, seeking to reflect in its structure the multiplicity that the various contributions deal with.

We live in complex societies that witness linguistic and cultural diversity increasing year by year under the "crust" of an often imposed monolingualism/monoculturalism, which in most cases coincides with a neo-colonial vision that has at its core the domination of English and Anglo-American culture. Although this domination is very powerful, diversity still emerges, manifesting itself in different forms and – fortunately – proving difficult to stifle. It is therefore increasingly urgent to dig deep beneath that very crust and really put in question, on the one hand, what exactly that diversity is and what it entails and, on the other hand, the forms in which this monolingual/monocultural vision manifests itself.

At the very moment that one begins this process, one is confronted with a richness and multiplicity of perspectives and dimensions that may seem impossible to come to grips with, as if one were venturing into an unexplored land; yet it is precisely this journey that Proustianally opens the eyes of the traveller and allows them to see with new eyes what they have always had the opportunity to see (and hear), but have often not actually seen (or heard).

This is exactly what this book sets out to do, offering the reader a collection of voices that transport them across a multiplicity of languages and cultures, continents and contexts, actors and decision-makers.

In this journey of (re)exploration in which the various papers that make up the volume accompany us, certain key concepts serve as a guide and at the same time stimulate us to go further and to question implications and facets that are not automatically obvious.

The first of these concepts is the vision of **the norm**: What is a norm? How can we – or should we? – define it? How can it be both so elusive and so powerful and constraining?

If the norm is seen as a static boundary that distinguishes what is standard from what is not, what is right from what is wrong, it automatically becomes a way of creating a distinction between what is accepted from what is not, and by extension between who is accepted and who is not, between "us" and "them". But by extension the norm also becomes a cage for those who accept it, who are part of it, a cage that does not allow them to see multiplicity and that constrains them in an eternal present, an idealised and therefore to some extent invented present.

We are faced, on the one hand, with the opposition between a linear, monolingual vision that seeks at all costs to delimit, to cage language, its use, its teaching and learning – but also the identity of individuals and the language policies that affect them – and on the other hand, a complex vision that, in contrast, questions the very nature of individuals, of societies, the historical development of languages and their teaching/learning, but also the phenomenon of language itself, which it sees as a complex dynamic system in continuous transformation, a phenomenon that is by its very nature the bearer of difference and multiplicity. Discovering, for example, the multifaceted nature of a dominant language such as English, becoming aware of the dialects and the variety of languages – of 'Englishes' that are encapsulated in the same language, that exist, that are used by different communities – is the necessary though not sufficient condition to begin to break out of the cage of monolingualism. Becoming aware of this and of the fact that variety is present in all languages, even those that are used in more local contexts and by a limited number of speakers, almost as if in a fractal, is not yet the same as appreciating the richness of difference per se, but it allows one to enter into the complexity, to enter into it mentally. In this respect it is interesting, for example, that the book emphasises the importance of the feelings of teachers and learners, that it speaks of teacher mindset, of teacher and learner attitudes.

The monolingual and linear vision of the norm appears increasingly narrow to us because it does not allow us to take reality into account; indeed, it refuses to see reality: there is the language – standard or considered as such – and then there is everything that does not correspond to that standard, which is "Other" and as such must be rejected, or corrected. In the plurilingual and complex vision, it is precisely linguistic and cultural diversity that becomes the norm, not a norm-cage, but rather a plural, fluid and dynamic dimension that includes instead of excluding, that explores instead of rejecting, that allows itself to be moulded, in a perspective of dialogue/confrontation with the Other, instead of correction and sanctioning of the Other.

The idea of the standardisation of a language – or a culture, or a worldview – is inevitably accompanied by stigmatisation, and a consequence of this stigmatisation is a sense of malaise, of never being good enough, of feeling devalued, which ultimately leads to the loss of language and also of identity, and/or perhaps the renunciation of both. Opposing this idea of standardisation, there is a plural identity, a linguistic and cultural enrichment that does not oppose languages and cultures but values them as nourishment, as humus to make fertile arid lands out of "no-man's lands" of suspicion, of distrust, and of fear.

The notion of a cage is related to that of **"filter bubble"**, another key concept that this volume offers to help us along the way. Locked in their own bubbles, individuals often find themselves in a state of intellectual isolation that prevents them from coming into contact with different ways of thinking and seeing, and that consequently confirms them in their monocular vision, making them insensitive to any form of pluralism.

As well as helping us to reflect on all that blocks us in this way, all that nurtures the monolingual disposition of our institutions, policies and practices, this book offers us other concepts and tools that together provide what one might call a "line of hope" in that they help us to think beyond the cages, to break through the suffocating crust of monolingualism/monoculturalism, of the norm, to overcome linear vision and one-track thinking.

One of the conceptual tools that can help on this path of openness, and which is discussed in this volume, is **mediation**. For years a key concept in studies that have adopted sociocultural theory as their theoretical framework (Lantolf, 2000), mediation has recently received further attention, becoming a focal point of the new edition of the CEFR (Council of Europe, 2020). Not only does mediation complete the organisation of language proficiency in four modes of communication, (reception, production,

Afterword

interaction, and mediation), definitively breaking down the rigidity of the four skills – cages that have done much damage in language teaching, and still continue to do so, but in addition, mediation shows above all the way in which at every level – textual, conceptual and communicative – the work to be done is always to accept the complexity, the "messiness" that naturally exists with living phenomena such as languages and cultures. Mediation offers a way to leverage this complexity and enter into a new culture of openness, of diversity, and navigate hybrid spaces and cross boundaries.

In adopting this perspective in relation to mediation, we become increasingly aware of our **translingual and transcultural identities** – another of the book's key concepts – and of the fact that they are ever-changing, and plural. As Lahire already pointed out several years ago (1998), we are plural beings: we are not beings that have one single nature and then take on various roles, we are on the contrary complex beings that are continuously constructed in multiple processes of socialisation. Such a perspective has a liberating character and invites us to continuously exercise our **agency**.

The concept of agency emerges in the volume in relation to **digital reality/artificial intelligence** (AI) on one side and to the **action-oriented approach** on the other. The former positions technological tools as more "knowledgeable others," capable of offering reformulations, and thus representing an opportunity for metacognitive awareness. This process requires mediation and agency on the part of the learner. The latter, the action-oriented approach, focuses on agency in teaching/learning methodologies themselves. In this approach, not only do learners find themselves exercising their agency at every step of their learning process, but they are continually involved in unpredictable yet enjoyable interactions, which lead them to accept risk-taking as a natural and inevitable process, in a virtuous circle that also involves the teachers in risk-taking. In this sense, technologies amplify the complex dimension: agency, joy, and creativity are integrated in action-oriented digital use. Accepting the inevitable "noise" when working with technologies, when engaging in the fine-tuned delicate work that they require but also rejoicing in the freedom from the pressure to memorise that they offer, not only increases learners' motivation but also accustoms them to non-linearity, to the acceptance of complexity at all levels, in a loop that further fosters agency.

The open and dynamic perspective that appears throughout the book shows the discrepancy between multilingual realities and monolingual policies that are common at the level of languages of schooling, additional languages, and even heritage languages – both in and also far beyond the specific examples mentioned. This discrepancy is in fact another of the obstacles to the acceptance of complexity. It is one of the manifestations of the rigid, constraining vision of the norm that I mentioned at the beginning.

Such a narrow perspective is the exact opposite of a plurilingual vision, another concept the volume evokes in relation to language learning, including in the context of English for Academic Purposes. The dynamic and open lens of **plurilingualism** offers an inclusive and liberating perspective within which individual and collective agency can flourish.

One of the beautiful features of the book is that it encourages the reader to see between the lines and beyond the controversies, including the terminological controversies that are often so detrimental to the development of collective reflection, creating further barriers instead of helping to remove the – very serious – ones that already exist.

Even the mainstream media are beginning to realise the dual significance of languages. Languages are no longer seen just from the utilitarian point of view of being able to communicate in a particular context. There is increasing awareness of the profound importance of languages for the individual and the communities in which this individual finds themselves acting.

Taking AI as a starting point, *The Economist* of August 17th offers an interesting reflection contrasting those who see languages only as a means to easily order a beer and a carbonara and "those who want to stretch their minds, immerse themselves in other cultures or force their thinking into new pathways". And immediately afterwards they point out that "this is largely an Anglophone problem, since native English-speakers miss out on the benefits of language-learning most acutely. In many countries, including Britain and America, schools' and universities' foreign-language departments have been closing."

This brings us back to the monolingual and linear vision mentioned earlier: If languages are only seen as a means to do something practical then their value is diminished. If we reason in terms of political-economic power and neo-colonial vision, then English has already won. If we follow the path of one-track thinking, with a linear vision of individuals and of our collective existence – in which we are by default monolingual, monocultural and mono-identitarian – then multilingualism is reduced to a patchwork of languages/cultures living side by side without even getting to know one another, and plurilingualism is resisted as disturbing and even suspect. But in a complex vision all this changes and the perspective is reversed. As this book shows so well, in a complex vision, identities become translingual/transcultural; the norm is understood as merely a common denominator under which there is a great intrinsic diversity at all levels; language teaching becomes action-oriented and plurilingual. And, last but not least, policies are finally modelled on the nature of the societies and individuals for which they are intended instead of being designed in relation to imagined and imaginary societies and individuals, so that as a result our togetherness is shaped in the arduous yet exciting (co)construction of meaning, relationships, and authentic communication. Because, as even *The Economist* recognises, "the best relationships do not require an intermediary."

Enrica Piccardo
University of Toronto, Canada

REFERENCES

Council of Europe. (2020). *Common European Framework of Reference for Languages: Learning, teaching, assessment.* Strasbourg: Council of Europe. https://rm.coe.int/16809ea0d4

Lahire, B. (1998). *L'Homme pluriel. Les ressorts de l'action.* Nathan.

Lantolf, J. P. (Ed.). (2000). *Sociocultural theory and second language learning.* Oxford University Press.

The Economist. (2023, August 17th). Yo hablo AI. *The Economist.* https://www.economist.com/culture/2023/08/17/ai-could-make-it-less-necessary-to-learn-foreign-languages?utm_source=pocket_reader

Compilation of References

Adedimeji, M. A. (2010). Language question and the constitutional challenges of development in a multilingual country. *Journal of Research in National Development*, *8*(2). Advance online publication. doi:10.4314/jorind.v8i2.66801

Adegbija, E. (1994). *Language attitudes in Sub-Saharan Africa: A sociolinguistic overview*. Multilingual Matters. doi:10.21832/9781800418141

Adegbite, A. B. (2010). English language usage, uses and misuse(s) in a non-host second language context, Nigeria. *Inaugural lecture series 231*. Obafemi Awolowo University Press.

Adu, O. O. (2020). Women in higher education institutions in Ghana: Discourse on colonial legacies and cultural norms. *Brock Journal of Education*, *8*(6), 18–26. doi:10.37745/bje/vol8.no6.p18-26.2020

Ahluwalia, J. (2020). Both not half: How language shapes identity. *TED talk: Ideas worth spreading*. [Youtube]. https://www.youtube.com/watch?v=SP0bAQ8J6C0

Ahmad, R. (2020). Multilingual resources key to fighting COVID-19. *Language on the move.*. https://www.languageonthemove.com/multilingual-resources-key-to-fighting-COVID-19/

Aizawa, I., & Rose, H. (2019). An analysis of Japan's English as medium of instruction initiatives within higher education: The gap between meso-level policy and micro-level practice. *Higher Education*, *77*(6), 1125–1142. doi:10.100710734-018-0323-5

Akande, A. T. (2016). Multilingual practices in Nigerian Army barracks. *African Identities*, *2*(14), 38–58. doi:10.1080/14725843.2015.1100108

Akande, A. T., & Okesola, S. O. (2021). Morpho-syntactic features of Nigerian Pidgin on Radio programmes rendered in Naija. In A. T. Akande & O. Salami (Eds.), *Current trends in Nigerian Pidgin English: A sociolinguistic perspective* (pp. 201–220). De Gruter Muoton. doi:10.1515/9781501513541-008

Akçapar, S. K. (2009). Turkish associations in the United States: Towards building a transnational identity. *Turkish Studies,* *10*(2), 165-193. https://doi.org/ doi:10.1080/14683840902863996

Akinnaso, F. N. (1991). The development of a multilingual language policy in Nigeria. *Applied Linguistics*, *12*(1), 29–61. doi:10.1093/applin/12.1.29

Akyay-Engin, E. (2019). Effective foreign language teaching: ELT students' and teachers' beliefs. *International Language Teacher Education Research Group (ILTERG) Conference Proceedings* (pp. 75-85). Antalya, Turkey. www.iltergconference.org

Al Abdely, A. (2016). Types and functions of code-switching in the English language used by Iraqi doctors in formal settings. *International Journal of Advanced Research and Review*, *1*(8), 10–18.

Alamu, G., & Iloene, J. (2003). On multilingualism and the medium of construction. In O. Ndimele, (Ed.) The linguistic paradise for E. Nolue Emenanjo, Aba: NINLAN, 319-336.

Albirini, A. (2011). The sociolinguistic functions of *codeswitching* between standard Arabic and dialectal Arabic. *Language in Society*, *40*(5), 537–562. doi:10.1017/S0047404511000674

Alboim, N. & MacIsaac, E. (2007). Making the connections: Ottawa's role in immigrant employment. *IRPP Choices, 13*(3).

Alim, H. S., Rickford, J. R., & Ball, A. F. (Eds.). (2016). *Raciolinguistics: How language shapes our ideas about race*. Oxford University Press. doi:10.1093/acprof:oso/9780190625696.001.0001

Almusharraf, N. M., & Bailey, D. (2021). Online engagement during COVID-19: Role of agency on collaborative learning orientation and learning expectations. *Journal of Computer Assisted Learning*, *37*(5), 1285–1295. doi:10.1111/jcal.12569 PMID:34226784

Alstad, G. T., & Tkachenko, E. (2018). Teachers' beliefs and practices in creating multilingual spaces: The case of English teaching in Norwegian early childhood education. In M. Schwartz (Ed.), *Preschool Bilingual Education* (pp. 245–282). Springer International Publishing. doi:10.1007/978-3-319-77228-8_9

Altavilla, J. (2020). How technology affects instruction for English learners. *Phi Delta Kappan*, *102*(1), 18–23. doi:10.1177/0031721720956841

Althusser, L. (1968). *Ideology and ideological state apparatuses in Lenin and philosophy and other essays*. New Left Books.

Alvarez, S. (2014). Translanguaging tareas: Emergent bilingual youth as language brokers for homework in immigrant families. *Language Arts*, *91*(5), 326–339.

Amaral, L., & Meurers, D. (2008). From recording linguistic competence to supporting inferences about language acquisition in context. *Computer Assisted Language Learning*, *21*(4), 323–338. doi:10.1080/09588220802343454

Amin, K. (2022). We are all nonbinary: A brief history of accidents. *Representations (Berkeley, Calif.)*, *158*(1), 106–119. doi:10.1525/rep.2022.158.11.106

Amzat, J., Aminu, K., Kolo, V. I., Akinyele, A. A., Ogundairo, J. A., & Danjibo, M. C. (2020). Coronavirus outbreak in Nigeria: Burden and socio-medical response during the first 100 days. *International Journal of Infectious Diseases*, *98*, 218–224. doi:10.1016/j.ijid.2020.06.067 PMID:32585282

Anarfi, J., Kwankye, S., Ababio, O. M., & Tiemoko, R. (2003). *Migration from and to Ghana: A background paper*. University of Sussex: DRC on Migration, Globalisation and Poverty. http://www.sussex.ac.uk/Units/SCMR/drc/publications/working_papers/WP-C4.pdf

Anchimbe, E. A. (2018). *Offers and offer refusals: A postcolonial pragmatics perspective on world Englishes*. John Benjamins. doi:10.1075/pbns.298

Anderman, L. H., & Freeman, T. (2004). Students' sense of belonging in school. In M. L. Maehr and P. R. Pintrich, (Eds.) Advances in motivation and achievement, volume 13: Motivating students, improving schools; The legacy of Carol Midgley, (pp. 27-63). Greenwich, CT: JAI.

Anderson, B. (2006). *Imagined communities. Reflections on the origin and spread of nationalism* (Revised Edition). Verso.

Andrei, E. (2019). Adolescent English learners' use of digital technology in the classroom. *The Educational Forum (West Lafayette, Ind.)*, *83*(1), 102–120. 10.1080/00131725.2018.1478474

Compilation of References

Androutsopoulos, J. (2014). Languaging when contexts collapse: Audience design in social networking. *Discourse, Context & Media*, *4*, 62–73. doi:10.1016/j.dcm.2014.08.006

Angay-Crowder, T., Choi, J., Khote, N., & Shin, J. H. (2023). Embedding multilingualism in undergraduate courses: A need for heteroglossia in US TESOL teacher preparation programs. In K. Raza, D. Reynolds, & C. Coombe (Eds.), *Handbook of multilingual TESOL in practice* (pp. 445–460). Springer. doi:10.1007/978-981-19-9350-3_29

Antaki, C. (2012). Affiliative and disaffiliative candidate understandings. *Discourse Studies*, *14*(5), 531–547. doi:10.1177/1461445612454074

Antaki, C., & Webb, J. (2019). When the larger objective matters more: Support workers' epistemic and deontic authority over adult service-users. *Sociology of Health & Illness*, *41*(8), 1549–1567. doi:10.1111/1467-9566.12964 PMID:31215067

Antalya Bilim University. (2023, August 12). *Language of education*. Antalya. https://antalya.edu.tr/tr/fakulte-ve-enstituler/bolumler/elektrik-ve-bilgisayar-muhendisligi-tezli-ingilizce/icerik/hakkimizda-1/egitim-dili

Anyidoho, A., & Dakubu, M. E. K. (2008). Ghana: Indigenous languages, English, and an emerging national identity. In A. Simpson (Ed.) Language and National Identity in Africa (pp. 141 – 157). Oxford University Press

Anzaldúa, G. (1987). *Borderlands/La frontera: The new mestiza*. Aunt Lute.

Appel, R., & Muysken, P. (2006). *Language contact and bilingualism*. Amsterdam University Press.

Apple, M. (2005). Are new markets in education democratic? In M. Apple, J. Kenway, & M. Singh (Eds.), *Globalizing education: Policies, pedagogies, & politics* (pp. 209–230). Peter Lang.

Arar, K., Kondakci, Y., Kaya Kasikci, S., & Erberk, E. (2020). Higher education policy for displaced people: Implications of Turkey's higher education policy for Syrian migrants. *Higher Education Policy*, *33*(2), 265–285. doi:10.105741307-020-00181-2

Arkın, E., & Osam, N. (2015). English-medium higher education. A case study in a Turkish university context. In S. Dimova, A. K. Hultgren, & C. Jensen (Eds.), *English-medium instruction in higher education in Europe* (pp. 177–199). Mouton de Gruyter. doi:10.1515/9781614515272-010

Arno, E. (2012). The role of technology in teaching languages for specific purposes courses. *Modern Language Journal*, *95*(s1), 88–103. doi:10.1111/j.1540-4781.2012.01299.x

Aronin, L., & Yelenevskaya, M. (2022). Teaching English in multilingual Israel: Who teaches whom and how. A review of recent research 2014–2020. *Language Teaching*, *55*(1), 24–45. doi:10.1017/S0261444821000215

Auer, P. (1998). *Code-switching in conversation: Language, interaction and identity*. Routledge.

Austin, J. L. (1975). *How to do things with words: The William James lectures delivered at Harvard University in 1955* (2nd ed.). Harvard University Press. doi:10.1093/acprof:oso/9780198245537.001.0001

Avramidou- Αβραμίδου, B. (2014). Diachirisi tis polipolitismikotitas sto scholio: Mia empiriki erevna. [Managing multiculturalism in school: An empirical study.] *Πολύδρομο*, *7*, 18-25.

Awumbila, M. (2015). Women moving within borders: Gender and internal migration dynamics in Ghana. *Ghana Journal of Geography*, *7*(2), 132–145.

Aydemir, A., & Skuterud, M. (2004). Explaining the deteriorating entry earning of Canada's immigrant cohorts: 1966 – 2000. *Analytical Studies Branch Research Paper Series*. Statistics Canada.

Ayentimi, D. T. (2023, March 23). Women occupy very few academic jobs in Ghana. Culture and society's expectations are to blame. *The Conversation.* https://theconversation.com/women-occupy-very-few-academic-jobs-in-ghana-culture-and-societys-expectations-are-to-blame-200307

Backus, A. (2005). The interplay between lexical and pragmatic motivations for codeswitching: Evidence from Dutch-Turkish. In J. N. Jørgensen & S. Talayman, C. (Eds.). Languaging and language practices (pp. 96-111). University of Copenhagen, Faculty of the Humanities.

Backus, A. (2010). The role of codeswitching, loan translation and interference in the emergence of an immigrant variety of Turkish. *Working Papers in Corpus-based Linguistics and Language Education, 5,* 225-241.

Backus, A. (1992). *Patterns of language mixing: A study in Turkish –Dutch bilingualism* (Vol. O). Harrassowitz.

Backus, A. (1996). *Two in one: Bilingual speech of Turkish immigrants in the Netherlands.* Tilburg University Press.

Backus, A. (1998). The intergenerational codeswitching continuum in an Immigrant community. In G. Extra & L. Verhoeven (Eds.), *Bilingualism and migration* (pp. 261–279). Mouton de Gruyter.

Backus, A. (2009). Codeswitching as one piece of the puzzle of language change: The case of Turkish *yapmak*. In L. Isurin, D. Winford, & K. de Bot (Eds.), *Interdisciplinary approaches to codeswitching* (pp. 307–336). John Benjamins Publishing Company.

Backus, A. (2012). Turkish as an immigrant language in Europe. In T. K. Bhatia & W. C. Ritchie (Eds.), *The handbook of bilingualism and multilingualism* (pp. 770–790). Blackwell. doi:10.1002/9781118332382.ch31

Bahari, A. (2022). Affordances and challenges of technology-assisted language learning for motivation: A systematic review. *Interactive Learning Environments,* 1–21. doi:10.1080/10494820.2021.2021246

Bailey, B. (2012). Heteroglossia. In M. Martin-Jones, A. Blackledge, & A. Creese (Eds.), *The Routledge handbook of multilingualism* (pp. 499–507). Routledge.

Bailey, D., Almusharraf, N., & Hatcher, R. (2021). Finding satisfaction: Intrinsic motivation for synchronous and asynchronous communication in the online language learning context. *Education and Information Technologies, 26*(3), 2563–2583. doi:10.100710639-020-10369-z PMID:33169066

Baines, C. (2015). Seven rules for not being 'one of those' expats in Berlin. *Xtra*.* https://xtramagazine.com/travel/seven-rules-for-not-being-one-of-those-expats-in-berlin-68725

Bak, Ç. (2023). *Effects of foreign language-medium instruction on content courses in higher education.* [Unpublished doctoral dissertation, Boğaziçi University].

Baker-Bell, A. (2013). "I never really knew the history behind African American language": Critical language pedagogy in an advanced placement English language arts class. *Equity & Excellence in Education, 46*(3), 355–370. doi:10.1080/10665684.2013.806848

Baker-Bell, A. (2020). Dismantling anti-black linguistic racism in English language arts classrooms: Toward an anti-racist black language pedagogy. *Theory into Practice, 59*(1), 8–21. doi:10.1080/00405841.2019.1665415

Baker-Bell, A., Paris, D., & Jackson, D. (2017). Learning black language matters. *International Journal of Qualitative Research, 10*(4), 360–377. doi:10.1525/irqr.2017.10.4.360

Baker, C. (2011). *Foundation of bilingual education and bilingualism* (5th ed.). McNaughton & Gunn Ltd.

Baker, M. (2018). Playing, talking, co-constructing: Exemplary teaching for young dual language learners across program types. *Early Childhood Education Journal, 47*(1), 115–130. doi:10.100710643-018-0903-0

Compilation of References

Bakhtin, M. M. (1981). Discourse in the novel. In M. Holquist (Ed.), *The dialogic imagination: For essays by M. M. Bakhtin* (pp. 259–422). University of Texas press.

Bakhtin, M. M. (1981). *The dialogic imagination: Four essays* (C. Emerson & M. Holquist, Eds. & Trans.). University of Texas Press.

Balam, O. (2021). Beyond differences and similarities in codeswitching and translanguaging research. *Belgian Journal of Linguistics*, *35*(1), 76–103. doi:10.1075/bjl.00065.bal

Bamgbose, A. (1999). African language development and language planning. *Social Dynamics. Journal of African Studies*, *25*(1), 13–30.

Bamgbose, A. (2014). The language factor in development goals. *Journal of Multilingual and Multicultural Development*, *35*(7), 646–657. doi:10.1080/01434632.2014.908888

Bandura, A. (1997). *Self-efficacy: The exercise of control*. Freeman.

Barrette, C. (2001). Students' preparedness and training for call. *CALICO Journal*, *19*(1), 5–36. doi:10.1558/cj.v19i1.5-36

Barrón, N. G. (2003). Dear saints, dear stella: Letters examining the messy lines of expectations, stereotypes, and identity in higher education. *College Composition and Communication*, *55*(1), 11–37. doi:10.2307/3594198

Barrón, N. G., & Gruber, S. (2007). Diversity reconsidered: Teaching U.S. heterogeneity in a border state. *The International Journal of Diversity in Organisations, Communities and Nations*, *7*(4), 195–208. doi:10.18848/1447-9532/CGP/v07i04/58023

Barrón, N. G., Gruber, S., & Grimm, N. (Eds.). (2006). *Social change in diverse teaching contexts: Touchy subjects and routine practices*. Peter Lang.

Barrot, J. S. (2023). Using automated written corrective feedback in the writing classrooms: Effects on L2 writing accuracy. *Computer Assisted Language Learning*, *36*(4), 584–607. doi:10.1080/09588221.2021.1936071

Baugh, J. (2005). *Out of the mouths of slaves: African American language and educational malpractice*. University of Texas Press.

Bauman, R. (1999). Genre. *Journal of Linguistic Anthropology*, *9*(1/2), 84–87. doi:10.1525/jlin.1999.9.1-2.84

Bauman, R., & Sherzer, J. (1975). The ethnography of speaking. *Annual Review of Anthropology*, *4*(1), 95–119. doi:10.1146/annurev.an.04.100175.000523

Baumgartinger, P. P. (2007). Geschlechtergerechte Sprache? Über queere widerständige Strategien gegen diskriminierenden Sprachalltag. *Stimme von und für Minderheiten*, *62*, 16–17.

Bax, S. (2003). CALL—Past, present and future. *System*, *31*(1), 13–28. doi:10.1016/S0346-251X(02)00071-4

Baxter Magolda, M. B. (2004). Evolution of a constructivist conceptualization of epistemological reflection. *Educational Psychologist*, *39*(1), 31–42. doi:10.120715326985ep3901_4

Baynham, M. (2020). Comment on Part 1: Collaborative Relationships. In E. Moore, J. Bradley, & J. Simpson (Eds.), *Translanguaging as Transformation* (pp. 15–22). Multilingual Matters.

Bell, A. (1984). Language style as audience design. *Language in Society*, *13*(2), 145–204. doi:10.1017/S004740450001037X

Belz, J. (2002). The myth of the deficient communicator. *Language Teaching Research*, *6*(1), 59–82. doi:10.1191/1362168802lr097oa

Bender, E. M., Gebru, T., McMillan-Major, A., & Shmitchell, S. (2021). On the dangers of stochastic parrots: Can language models be too big? *FAccT 2021 - Proceedings of the 2021 ACM Conference on Fairness, Accountability, and Transparency*, (pp. 610–623). ACM. 10.1145/3442188.3445922

Bensekhar Bennabi, M., Simon, A., Rezzoug, D., & Moro, M. R. (2015). Les pathologies du langage dans la pluralité linguistique. *La Psychiatrie de l'Enfant*, *58*(1), 277–298. doi:10.3917/psye.581.0277

Benson, C., & Elorza, I. (2015). Multilingual education for all (MEFA): Empowering non-dominant languages and cultures through multilingual curriculum development. In D. Wyse, L. Hayward & J. Zacher Pandya (Eds.), The SAGE Handbook of Curriculum, Pedagogy and Assessment (pp. 557-574). Sage. doi:10.4135/9781473921405.n35

Benson, C. (2010). How multilingual African contexts are pushing educational research and practice in new directions. *Language and Education*, *24*(4), 323–336. doi:10.1080/09500781003678704

Bentahila, A., & Davies, E. (1992). Codeswitching and language dominance. In R. J. Harris (Ed.), *Cognitive processing in bilinguals* (pp. 443–458). Benjamins. doi:10.1016/S0166-4115(08)61510-1

Bentahila, A., & Davies, E. (1994). Patterns of code-switching and patterns of language contact. *Lingua*, *96*(2-3), 75–93. doi:10.1016/0024-3841(94)00035-K

Berens, Charlie [Username]. (2019, October 22). *Midwest Voice Translator* [Video]. YouTube. https://www.youtube.com/watch?v=7OR7yPK4wEw

Berthele, R. (2011). On abduction in receptive multilingualism: Evidence from cognate guessing tasks. *Applied Linguistic Review*, *2*, 191–220. doi:10.1515/9783110239331.191

Besnier, N. (2002). Transgenderism, locality and the Miss Galaxy beauty pageant in Tonga. *American Ethnologist*, *29*(3), 534–566. doi:10.1525/ae.2002.29.3.534

Besnier, N. (2004). Consumption and cosmopolitanism: Practicing modernity at the secondhand marketplace in Nuku'alofa, Tonga. *Anthropological Quarterly*, *77*(1), 7–45. doi:10.1353/anq.2004.0002

Besnier, N., & Philips, S. U. (2014). Ethnographic methods for language and gender research. In S. Ehrlich, M. Meyerhoff, & J. Holmes (Eds.), *The Handbook of Language, Gender, and Sexuality* (2nd ed., pp. 123–140). Wiley-Blackwell. doi:10.1002/9781118584248.ch6

Bhugra, D., & Becker, M. A. (2005). Migration, cultural bereavement and cultural identity. *World Psychiatry; Official Journal of the World Psychiatric Association (WPA)*, *4*(1), 18–24. PMID:16633496

Bidens, D. (2005). What is internalized racism. In M. Potapchuk, S. Leiderman, D. Bivens, & B. Major, (Eds.), Flipping the script: White privilege and community building, pp. 43-52. Silver Spring, MD, and Conshohocken, PA: MP Associates and CAPD.

Bigelow, M., & Vinogradov, P. (2011, March). Teaching adult second language learners who are emergent readers. *Annual Review of Applied Linguistics*, *31*, 120–136. doi:10.1017/S0267190511000109

BirkelandA.BlockA.CraftJ. T.SedarousY.WuA.NamboordiripadS. (2022). Towards a linguistics free of "native speakerhood". Psyarxiv. https://psyarxiv.com/ektmf/ doi:10.31234/osf.io/ektmf

Blackledge, A., & Creese, A. (2014) Heteroglossia as practice and pedagogy. In A. Blackledge & A. Creese (Eds.), *Heteroglossia as practice and pedagogy* (pp. 1–20). Springer.

Blizzad, B., & Batalova, J. (2020). *Cuban immigrants in the United States*. Migration Policy Institute, Washigton D.C. https://www.migrationpolicy.org/article/cuban-immigrants-united-states

Block, S., & Galabuzi, G. E. (2011). *Canada's colour coded labour market: The gap for racialized workers*. Policy Alternatives. http://www.policyalternatives.ca/

Block, D. (2007). Second Language Identities. *Continuum*.

Block, K., Cross, S., Riggs, E., & Gibbs, L. (2014). Supporting schools to create an inclusive environment for refugee students. *International Journal of Inclusive Education*, *18*(12), 1337–1355. doi:10.1080/13603116.2014.899636

Blom, J., & Gumperz, J. (1972). Social meaning in linguistic structure: Codeswitching in Norway. In J. Gumperz & D. Hymes (Eds.), *Directions in sociolinguistics: The ethnography of communication* (pp. 407–434). Holt.

Blom, J., & Gumperz, J. J. (1972). Social meaning in linguistic structure: Code-switching in Norway. In J. J. Gumperz & D. Hymes (Eds.), *Directions in Sociolinguistics. The Ethnography of Communication* (pp. 407–434). Holt, Rinehart and Winston.

Blommaert, J. (2010). *The sociolinguistics of globalization*. Cambridge University Press., doi:10.1017/CBO9780511845307

Blommaert, J. (2012). Supervernaculars and their dialects. *Dutch Journal of Applied Linguistics*, *1*(1), 1–14. doi:10.1075/dujal.1.1.03blo

Blommaert, J., & Backus, A. (2013). Superdiverse repertoires and the individual. In I. Saint-Georges & J. J. Weber (Eds.), *Multilingualism and multimodality: Current challenges for educational studies* (pp. 11–32). Sense Publishers., doi:10.1007/978-94-6209-266-2_2

Boeschoten, H., & Verhoeven, L. (1987). Language-mixing in children's speech: Dutch language use in Turkish discourse. *Language Learning*, *37*(2), 191–215. doi:10.1111/j.1467-1770.1987.tb00565.x

Bohr, C., & Acar, S. (2021). Supporting language acquisition and peer interaction through guided play in a multilingual classroom. *Young Exceptional Children*, *XX*(X), 1–10.

Bolitho, R., Carter, R., Hughes, R., Ivanic, R., Masuhara, H., & Tomlinson, B. (2003). Ten questions about language awareness. *ELT Journal*, *57*(3), 251–259. doi:10.1093/elt/57.3.251

Borg, S. (2011). The impact of in-service teacher education on language teachers' beliefs. *System*, *39*(3), 370–380. doi:10.1016/j.system.2011.07.009

Borjian, A., & Padilla, A. (2010). Voices from Mexico: How U.S. teachers can meet the needs of immigrant students. *The Urban Review*, *42*(4), 316–328. doi:10.100711256-009-0135-0

Börner, B. A., & Ginda, M. (2019). Data visualization literacy: Definitions, conceptual frameworks, exercises, and assessments. *Proceedings of the National Academy of Sciences - PNAS*, *116*(6), 1857–1864. https://doi.org/10.1073/pnas.1807180116

Bourdieu, P. (1986). The forms of capital. In J. Richardson (Ed.), Handbook of theory and research in the sociology of education (pp. 241-258). Greenwood Press.

Bourdieu, P. (1977). *Outline of a theory of practice*. Harvard University Press. doi:10.1017/CBO9780511812507

Bourdieu, P. (1984). *Distinction: A social critique of the judgment of taste*. Harvard University Press.

Bo, W. V., Fu, M., & Lim, W. Y. (2022). Revisiting English language proficiency and its impact on the academic performance of domestic university students in Singapore. *Language Testing*, 1–20. doi:10.1177/0265532221106462

Bowles, S., & Gintis, H. (1975). The problem with human capital theory – A Marxian critique. *The American Economic Review*, *65*(2), 74–82.

Bown, J. (2008). Locus of learning and affective strategy use: Two factors affecting success in self-instructed language learning. *Foreign Language Annals*, *39*(4), 640–659. doi:10.1111/j.1944-9720.2006.tb02281.x

Boyd, M., & Cao, X. (2009). Immigrant language proficiency, earnings, and language policies. *Canadian Studies in Population*, *36*(1–2), 63–86. doi:10.25336/P6NP62

Boyle, P., Halfacree, K., & Robinson, V. (2014). *Exploring contemporary migration*. Routledge. doi:10.4324/9781315843100

Bozdag, E. (2015). *Bursting the filter bubble: Democracy, design, and ethics*. [Master's thesis, Technische Universiteit Delft]. doi:10.4233/uuid:87bde0a2-c391-4c77-8457-97cba93abf45

Braun, V., & Clarke, V. (2006). Using thematic analysis in psychology. *Qualitative Research in Psychology*, *3*(2), 77–101. doi:10.1191/1478088706qp063oa

Braun, V., & Clarke, V. (2019). Reflecting on reflexive thematic analysis. *Qualitative Research in Sport, Exercise and Health*, *11*(4), 589–597. doi:10.1080/2159676X.2019.1628806

British Council & TEPAV. (2015, November). *The state of English in higher education in Turkey: A baseline study*. British Council. https://www.britishcouncil.org.tr/sites/default/files/he_baseline_study_book_web_-_son.pdf

Brudermann, C., Grosbois, M., & Sarré, C. (2021). Accuracy development in L2 writing: Exploring the potential of computer-assisted unfocused indirect corrective feedback in an online EFL course. *ReCALL*, *33*(3), 248–264. doi:10.1017/S095834402100015X

Bryfonski, L., & Ma, X. (2020). Effects of implicit versus explicit corrective feedback on mandarin tone acquisition in a SCMC learning environment. *Studies in Second Language Acquisition*, *42*(1), 61–88. doi:10.1017/S0272263119000317

Bucholtz, M., & Hall, K. (2005). Identity and interaction: A sociocultural linguistic approach. *Discourse Studies*, *7*(4/5), 585–614. doi:10.1177/1461445605054407

Buck, B. (2016). Culturally responsive peace education: A case study at one urban Latino K-8 Catholic school. *Journal of Catholic Education*, *20*(1), 32–55. doi:10.15365/joce.2001022016

Burgess, R. (1984). *In the field: An introduction to field research researching human geography*. George Allen and Unwin.

Burke, K. (1954). *Permanence and change: An anatomy of purpose*. University of California Press.

Burke, K. (1965). Terministic screens. *Philosophy and the Arts*, *39*, 87–102.

Burke, K. (1966). *Language as symbolic action: Essays on life, literature and method*. University of California Press. doi:10.1525/9780520340664

Burke, K. (1969). *A rhetoric of motives*. University of California Press.

Burton, J., & Rajendram, S. (2019). Translanguaging-as-resource: University ESL instructors' language orientations and attitudes toward translanguaging. *TESL Canada Journal*, *36*(1), 21–47. doi:10.18806/tesl.v36i1.1301

Busch, B. (2015). Expanding the notion of the linguistic repertoire: On the concept of Spracherleben—the lived experience. *Applied Linguistics*, *36*(4), 1–20. doi:10.1093/applin/amv030

Butler, J. (2011). Critically queer. In *Bodies that matter: On the discursive limits of sex* (pp. 169–185). Routledge. doi:10.4324/9780203828274-15

Byram, M., & Parmenter, L. (Eds.), *The Common European Framework of Reference: The Globalization of Language Education Policy*. Multilingual matters.

Compilation of References

Byron, P., Robards, B., Hanckel, B., Vivienne, S., & Churchill, B. (2019). "Hey, I'm having these experiences": Tumblr use and young people's queer (dis)connections. *International Journal of Communication*, *13*, 2239–2259.

Cai, Y., Pan, Z., & Liu, M. (2022). Augmented reality technology in language learning: A meta-analysis. *Journal of Computer Assisted Learning*, *38*(4), 929–945. doi:10.1111/jcal.12661

Cal, A., & Turnbull, M. (2007). Code-switching in Spanish/English bilingual speech: The case of two recent immigrants of Mexican descent. *Working Papers in TESOL Applied Linguistics, 7*(2), 1-52.

Calafato, R. (2021). "I feel like it's giving me a lot as a language teacher to be a learner myself": Factors affecting the implementation of a multilingual pedagogy as reported by teachers of diverse languages. *Studies in Second Language Learning and Teaching*, *11*(4), 579–606. doi:10.14746sllt.2021.11.4.5

Cameron, D. (1996). *Verbal hygiene*. Routledge.

Canadian Bureau of International Education. (2023). *International Students in Canada*. CBIE. https://cbie.ca/infographic/

Canagarajah, S. (2011). Translanguaging in the classroom: Emerging issues for research and pedagogy. *Applied linguistics review, 2*(1), 1-28.

Canagarajah, A. S. (2013). Negotiating translingual literacy: An enactment. *Research in the Teaching of English*, 40–67.

Canagarajah, S. (2011). Codemeshing in academic writing: Identifying teachable strategies of translanguaging. *Modern Language Journal*, *95*(3), 401–417. doi:10.1111/j.1540-4781.2011.01207.x

Canagarajah, S. (2013). *Translingual practice: Global englishes and cosmopolitan relations*. Routledge. doi:10.4324/9780203120293

Canagarajah, S. (2018). Translingual practice as spatial repertoires: Expanding the paradigm beyond structuralist orientations. *Applied Linguistics*, *39*(1), 31–54. doi:10.1093/applin/amx041

Carroll, K. S., & Sambolín Morales, A. N. (2016). Using university students' L1 as a resource: Translanguaging in a Puerto Rican ESL classroom. *Bilingual Research Journal*, *39*(3-4), 248–262. doi:10.1080/15235882.2016.1240114

Castles, S. (2016). Understanding global migration: A social transformation perspective. In A. Amelina, K. Horvath. & B. Meeus (Eds.), An anthology of migration and social transformation: European perspectives (pp. 19-41). Springer. doi:10.1007/978-3-319-23666-7_2

Cazden, C., Cope, B., Fairclough, N., Gee, J., Kalantzis, M., Kress, G., & Nakata, M.The New London Group. (1996). A pedagogy of multiliteracies: Designing social futures. *Harvard Educational Review*, *66*(1), 60–92. doi:10.17763/haer.66.1.17370n67v22j160u

Celic, C., & Seltzer, K. (2011). *Translanguaging: A CUNY-NYSIEB Guide for Educators*. CUNY-NYSIEB.

Cennetkuşu, N. G., & Ölmez, M. (2022). Transition and adaptation to higher education: Syrian immigrant students in Turkey within cultural, social, and linguistic context. *Socrates Journal of Interdisciplinary Social Studies*, *20*, 1–19.

Cenoz, J., & Gorter, D. (2013). Towards a plurilingual approach in English language teaching: Softening the boundaries between languages. *TESOL Quarterly*, *47*(3), 591–599. doi:10.1002/tesq.121

Center for New American Media (CNAM) (Producer), & Alvarez, L., & Kolker, A. (Directors) (1988). *American tongues* [Video file].

Cerezo, L. (2021). Corrective feedback in computer-mediated versus face-to-face environments. In H. Nassaji & E. Kartchava (Eds.), *The Cambridge Handbook of Corrective Feedback in Second Language Learning and Teaching* (pp. 494–519). Cambridge University Press., doi:10.1017/9781108589789.024

Chachu, S. (2022). Implications of language barriers for access to healthcare: The case of francophone migrants in Ghana. *Legon Journal of the Humanities*, *32*(2), 1–36. doi:10.4314/ljh.v32i2.1

Chang-Bacon, C. K. (2022). We sort of dance around the race thing: Race-evasiveness in teacher education. *Journal of Teacher Education*, *73*(1), 8–22. doi:10.1177/00224871211023042

Chapelle, C. A. (2003). *English language learning and technology*. John Benjamins Publishing., doi:10.1075/lllt.7

Charity Hudley, A. H., & Mallinson, C. (2011). *Understanding English language variation in U.S. schools*. Teachers College Press.

Charity Hudley, A. H., Mallinson, C., & Bucholtz, M. (2022). *Talking college: Making space for Black language practices in higher education*. Teachers College Press.

Chateau, A., & Tassinari, M. G. (2021). Autonomy in language centres: Myth or reality? *Language Learning in Higher Education*, *11*(1), 51–66. doi:10.1515/cercles-2021-2002

Chen, C. (2020). AR videos as scaffolding to foster students' learning achievements and motivation in EFL learning. *British Journal of Educational Technology*, *51*(3), 657–672. doi:10.1111/bjet.12902

Chen, C., Hung, H., & Yeh, H. (2021). Virtual reality in problem-based learning contexts: Effects on the problem-solving performance, vocabulary acquisition and motivation of English language learners. *Journal of Computer Assisted Learning*, *37*(3), 851–860. doi:10.1111/jcal.12528

Chen, L. (2019). Problematising the English-only policy in English for Academic Purposes: A mixed-methods investigation of Chinese international students' perspectives of academic language policy. *Journal of Multilingual and Multicultural Development*, *41*(8), 718–735. doi:10.1080/01434632.2019.1643355

Chiswick, B. R., Cohen, Y., & Zach, T. (1997). The labour market status of immigrants: Effects of the unemployment rate at arrival and duration of residence. *Industrial & Labor Relations Review*, *50*(2), 289–303. doi:10.1177/001979399705000206

Chitadze, N. (2022). The main principles of democracy and its role in global development. In N. Chitadze (Ed.), *Global dimensions of democracy and human rights: Problems and perspectives* (pp. 1–40). IGI Global. doi:10.4018/978-1-6684-4543-3.ch001

Choi, Y., Tomita, Y., Ko, K., & Komuro-Lee, I. (2022, May). *Understanding students' perception of online language learning*. Paper presented at the annual meeting of Canadian Association of Applied Linguistics, (online).

Choi, P. L., & Tang, S. Y. F. (2009). Teacher commitment trends: Cases of Hong Kong teachers from 1997 to 2007. *Teaching and Teacher Education*, *25*(5), 767–777. doi:10.1016/j.tate.2009.01.005

Cho, Y., & Bridgeman, B. (2012). Relationship of TOEFL iBT scores to academic performance: Some evidence from American universities. *Language Testing*, *29*(3), 421–442. doi:10.1177/0265532211430368

Christel, K. (2020). Gender disparities in Ghana's tertiary education system. *Journal of Student Affairs, New York University*, *16*, 34–39.

Christian, D. (1997). *Vernacular dialects in US schools. ERIC Document Reproduction Services No. ED406846*. ERIC. https://files.eric.ed.gov/fulltext/ED406846.pdf

Compilation of References

Citizenship and Immigration Canada. (2012). *Canadian language benchmark: English as a second language for adults.* CIC. https://www.cic.gc.ca/english/pdf/pub/language-benchmarks.pdf

Coelho, D., & Ortega, Y. (2020). Pluralistic approaches in early language education: shifting paradigms in language didactics. In S. Lau & S. Van Viegen (Eds.), *Plurilingual Pedagogies. Critical and creative Endeavors for equitable language in education* (pp. 145–160). Springer. doi:10.1007/978-3-030-36983-5_7

Coelho, E. (1998). *Teaching and learning in multicultural schools: An integrated approach.* Multilingual Matters. doi:10.21832/9781800417953

Cohen, J. L. (2008). 'That's not treating you as a professional': Teachers constructing complex professional identities through talk. *Teachers and Teaching, 14*(2), 79–93. doi:10.1080/13540600801965861

Cole, M. W. (2019). Translanguaging in every classroom. *Language Arts, 96*(4), 244–249. doi:10.58680/la201930003

Collins, C., Dennehy, D., Conboy, K., & Mikalef, P. (2021). Artificial intelligence in information systems research: A systematic literature review and research agenda. *International Journal of Information Management, 60,* 102383. doi:10.1016/j.ijinfomgt.2021.102383

Cope, B., & Kalantzis, M. (2023). Education 2.0. In Z. Xudong & M. Peters (Eds.), *The future of teaching* (pp. 276–291). Brill., doi:10.1163/9789004538351_015

Cosgun, G. (2020). Investigating the perceptions of students on the use of L1 in departmental courses in a Turkish EMI university. *The Journal of Language Teaching and Learning, 10*(2), 30–40.

Costa, F., & Coleman, J. A. (2013). A survey of English-medium instruction in Italian higher education. *International Journal of Bilingual Education and Bilingualism, 16*(1), 3–19. doi:10.1080/13670050.2012.676621

Council of Europe. (2001). *Common European Framework of Reference for Languages.* Council of Europe Publishing. https://rm.coe.int/1680459f97

Council of Europe. (2001). *Common European Framework of Reference for Languages: Learning, teaching, assessment.* Cambridge University Press.

Council of Europe. (2001). *Common European Framework of Reference for Languages: Learning, Teaching, Assessment.* Cambridge University Press.

Council of Europe. (2011). *European Language Portfolio.* Council of Europe. www.coe.int

Council of Europe. (2018). *Common European Framework of Reference for Languages: Learning, teaching, assessment-companion volume with new descriptors.* Council of Europe Publishing. https://rm.coe.int/cefr-companionvolume-with-new-descriptors-2018/1680787989

Council of Europe. (2020). *CEFR Companion Volume.* Council of Europe Publishing.

Council of Europe. (2020). *Common European Framework of Reference for Languages: Learning, teaching, assessment – Companion volume.* Council of Europe.

Council of Europe. (2022). *Enriching 21st-century language education: The CEFR Companion volume in practice.* Council of Europe.

Council of Europe. (n.d.). *Common European Framework of Reference for Languages (CEFR).* The Council of Europe. https://www.coe.int/en/web/common-european-framework-reference-languages

Council of Higher Education. (2017). *Yükseköğretimde uluslararasılaşma strateji belgesi 2018-2022 [Internationalization strategy document in higher education 2018-2022].* Council of Higher Education. https://www.yok.gov.tr/Documents/AnaSayfa/Yuksekogretimde_Uluslararasilasma_Strateji_Belgesi_2018_2022.pdf

Council of Higher Education. (2021). *Yükseköğretimde hedef odaklı uluslararasılaşma [Target-oriented internationalization policy in higher education].* Council of Higher Education. https://www.yok.gov.tr/Documents/Yayinlar/Yayinlarimiz/2021/yuksekogretimde-hedef-odakli-uluslararasilasma.pdf

Council of Higher Education. (2023a). *Study finder.* Council of Higher Education. https://www.studyinturkiye.gov.tr/StudySearch/List

Council of Higher Education. (2023c). *Uyruğa göre öğrenci sayıları raporu [Student numbers report by nationality].* Council of Higher Education. https://istatistik.yok.gov.tr/

Coyle, D., Hood, P., & Marsh, D. (2010). *CLIL: Content and language integrated learning.* Cambridge University Press. doi:10.1017/9781009024549

Creese, A., & Blackledge, A. (2010). Translanguaging in the bilingual classroom: A pedagogy for learning and teaching? *Modern Language Journal, 94*(1), 103–115. doi:10.1111/j.1540-4781.2009.00986.x

Creese, A., & Blackledge, A. (2015). Translanguaging and identity in educational settings. *Annual Review of Applied Linguistics, 35,* 20–35. doi:10.1017/S0267190514000233

Creswell, J. (2015). *30 essential skills for the qualitative researcher.* SAGE.

Creswell, J. W. (1994). Research design: Qualitative & quantitative approaches. *Sage (Atlanta, Ga.).*

Criado, R., Garcés-Manzanera, A., & Plonsky, L. (2022). Models as written corrective feedback: Effects on young L2 learners' fluency in digital writing from product and process perspectives. *Studies in Second Language Learning and Teaching, 12*(4), 697–719. doi:10.14746sllt.2022.12.4.8

Crompton, H. (2013). A historical overview of mobile learning: Toward learner-centered education. In Z. Berge & L. Muilengurg (Eds.), *Handbook of mobile learning* (pp. 3–14). Routledge., doi:10.4324/9780203118764.ch1

Crystal, D. (2003). *English as a global language* (2nd ed.). Cambridge University Press. doi:10.1017/CBO9780511486999

Cserni, R. T., & Talmud, I. (2015). To know that you are not alone: The effect of internet usage on LGBT youth's social capital. In L. Robinson, S. R. Cotton, & J. Schulz (Eds.), *Communication and information technologies annual: Politics, participation, and production* (pp. 161–182). Emerald. doi:10.1108/S2050-206020150000009007

Csikszentmihalyi, M. (2014). *The systems model of creativity: The collected works of Mihaly Csikszentmihalyi.* Springer Netherlands., doi:10.1007/978-94-017-9085-7

Cummins, J. (1984). *Bilingualism and special education: Issues in assessment and pedagogy.* Multilingual Matters.

Cummins, J. (2007). Rethinking monolingual instructional strategies in multilingual classrooms. *Canadian Journal of Applied Linguistics, 10*(2), 221–240.

Cummins, J. (2008). Total immersion or bilingual education? Findings of international research on promoting immigrant children's achievement in the primary school. In J. Ramseger & M. Wagener (Eds.), *Chancenungleichheit in der Grundschule* (pp. 45–55). VS Verlag für Sozialwissenschaften. doi:10.1007/978-3-531-91108-3_4

Cummins, J. (2009). Multilingualism in the English-language classroom: Pedagogical considerations. *TESOL Quarterly, 43*(2), 317–321. doi:10.1002/j.1545-7249.2009.tb00171.x

Compilation of References

Cummins, J., & Early, M. (2015). *Big ideas for expanding minds: Teaching English language learners across the curriculum.* Rubicon Publishing.

Curzan, A., & Adams, M. (2012). *How English works: A linguistic introduction* (3rd ed.). Longman.

Cushman, E. (2016). Translingual and decolonial approaches to meaning making. *College English, 78*(3), 234–242.

Czaika, M., & Reinprecht, C. (2022). Migration drivers: Why do people migrate. In P. Scholten (Ed.), *Introduction to migration studies: An interactive guide to the literatures on migration and diversity* (pp. 49–82). Springer. doi:10.1007/978-3-030-92377-8_3

D'Agostino, S. (2023, January 19). AI writing detection: A losing battle worth fighting. *Inside Higher Education.* https://www.insidehighered.com/news/2023/01/20/academics-work-detect-chatgpt-and-other-ai-writing

D'Ignazio, C., & Bhargava, R. (2016). DataBasic: Design principles, tools and activities for data literacy learners. *The Journal of Community Informatics, 12*(3), 83–107. doi:10.15353/joci.v12i3.3280

Dafouz, E., & Smit, U. (2016). Towards a dynamic conceptual framework for English-medium education in multilingual university settings. *Applied Linguistics, 37*(3), 397–415. doi:10.1093/applin/amu034

Dam, L. (1995). *Learner autonomy 3: From theory to classroom practice.* Authentik.

Danso-Wiredu, E. Y., Dadson, Y. I., & Amoako-Andoh, F. O. (2016). Social, economic and environmental impacts of the recent electricity crisis in Ghana: A study of Winneba. *Journal of Social Sciences, 49*(3-1), 277-288.

Danso-Wiredu, E. Y., & Brako, I. (2021). Regionalism, ethnicity, and politics in Ghana. *Ghana Journal of Geography, 13*(3), 278–303.

Darwall, S. (2009). *The second-person standpoint: Morality, respect, and accountability.* Harvard University Press. doi:10.2307/j.ctv1bzfp0f

Dashtestani, R., & Krajka, J. (2020). A call for reconciling EAP and CALL. *Teaching English with Technology, 20*(5), 1–5.

Davies, B., & Harré, R. (1990). Positioning: The discursive production of selves. *Journal for the Theory of Social Behaviour, 20*(1), 43–63. doi:10.1111/j.1468-5914.1990.tb00174.x

Davies, H. C. (2018). Redefining filter bubbles as (escapable) socio-technical recursion. *Sociological Research Online, 23*(3), 637–654. doi:10.1177/1360780418763824

De Angelis, G. (2011). Teachers' beliefs about the role of prior language knowledge in learning and how these influence teaching practices. *International Journal of Multilingualism, 8*(3), 216–234. doi:10.1080/14790718.2011.560669

De Costa, P. I., & Norton, B. (2017). Introduction: Identity, transdisciplinarity, and the good language teacher. *Modern Language Journal, 101*(S1), 3–14. doi:10.1111/modl.12368

De Costa, P. I., Singh, J. G., Milu, E., Wang, X., Fraiberg, S., & Canagarajah, S. (2017). Pedagogizing translingual practice: Prospects and possibilities. *Research in the Teaching of English,* 464–472.

de los Ríos, C. V., Martinez, D. C., Musser, A. D., Canady, A., Camangian, P., & Quijada, P. D. (2019). Upending colonial practices: Toward repairing harm in English education. *Theory into Practice, 58*(4), 359–367. doi:10.1080/00405841.2019.1626615

DeardenJ.Akincioglu M.MacaroE. (2016). *EMI in Turkish universities: Collaborative planning and student voices.* Oxford: Oxford University Press. doi:10.13140/RG.2.2.15435.39204

Delgado Hellester, M. (2013). *English skills and wages in a non-English speaking country: Findings from online advertisements in Mexico*. Cite Seer. https://citeseerx.ist.psu.edu/viewdoc/ download?doi=10.1.1.406.6883&rep=rep1&type=pdf.

Delpit, L. (2006). *Other people's children: Cultural conflict in the classroom* (2nd ed.). The New Press.

Delpit, L. (2006). What should teachers do? Ebonics and culturally responsive instruction. In S. J. Nero (Ed.), *Dialects, Englishes, creoles, and education* (pp. 93–101). Routledge.

Denney, S. C., & Daviso, A. W. (2012). Self-determination: A critical component of education. *American Secondary Education*, *40*(2), 43–51. http://www.jstor.org/stable/43694129

Dereli, B. (2018). *Refugee integration through higher education: Syrian refugees in Turkey. Policy Report, UNU Institute on Globalization, Culture and Mobility*. UNU-GCM.

Derwing, T.M., & Waugh, E. (2012). Language skills and the social integration of Canada's adult immigrants. *IRPP Study*, *31*.

Deuber, D. (2005). *Nigerian Pidgin in Lagos: Language contact, variation and change in an African urban setting*. Battlebridge.

Dewaele, J.-M., & Pavlenko, A. (2002). Emotion vocabulary in interlanguage. *Language Learning*, *52*(2), 263–322. doi:10.1111/0023-8333.00185

Di Meo, S., & van den Hove, C. Serre-Pradère, G., Simon, A. Moro, M., R. & Thierry Baubet, T. (2015). Le mutisme extra-familial chez les enfants de migrants. Le silence de Sandia. *L'Information Psychiatrique*, *91*(3), 217–224.

Diakogeorgiou- Διακογεωργίου. A. (2016). Η ένταξη των αλλοδαπών και των παλιννοστούντων μαθητών στο Δημοτικό Σχολείο. [The inclusion of non-natives and repatriated students in the Primary School]. In the *Proceedings of the 8th Conference of the Greek Institute of Applied Pedagogy and Education*.

Dicker, S. J. (2003). *Languages in America: A pluralist view* (2nd ed.). Multilingual Matters. doi:10.21832/9781853596537

DiFranzo, D., & Gloria-Garcia, K. (2017). Filter bubbles and fake news. *XRDS: Crossroads. The ACM Magazine for Students.*, *23*(305), 32–35. doi:10.1145/305515

Directorate General of Migration Management. (2023a). *Temporary protection. General of Migration Management. (2023b). Residence permits*. Directorate General of Migration Management. https://en.goc.gov.tr/residence-permits

Djite, P. G. (2008). *The sociolinguistics of development in Africa*. Multilingual Matters Limited. doi:10.21832/9781847690470

Dogancay-Aktuna, S. (1998). The spread of English in Turkey and its current sociolinguistic profile. *Journal of Multilingual and Multicultural Development*, *19*(1), 24–39. doi:10.1080/01434639808666340

Dörnyei, Z. (2001). *Motivational strategies in the language classroom*. Cambridge University Press. doi:10.1017/CBO9780511667343

Drew, P., & Heritage, J. (1992). *Talk at work: Interaction in institutional settings*. Cambridge University Press.

Dubois, B. L., & Crouch, I. (1975). The question of tag questions in women's speech: They don't really use more of them, do they? *Language in Society*, *4*(3), 289–294. https://www.jstor.org/stable/4166832. doi:10.1017/S0047404500006680

Duden. (n.d.). Queer. *Duden online*. https://www.duden.de/rechtschreibung/queer

Duff, P. A., & Uchida, Y. (1997). The negotiation of teachers' sociocultural identities and practices in postsecondary EFL classrooms. *TESOL Quarterly*, *31*(3), 451–486. doi:10.2307/3587834

Compilation of References

Duman, G., Orhon, G., & Gedik, N. (2015). Research trends in mobile assisted language learning from 2000 to 2012. *ReCALL*, *27*(2), 197–216. doi:10.1017/S0958344014000287

Duranti, A., & Goodwin, C. (Eds.). (1992). *Rethinking context: Language as an interactive phenomenon (No. 11)*. Cambridge University Press.

Dweck, C. S. (2006). *Mindset: The new psychology of success*. Random House.

EACEA/Eurydice. (2012). Key Data on Teaching Languages at School in Europe 2012. *The Education, Audiovisual and Culture Executive Agency* (EACEA P9 Eurydice and Policy Support). Brussels: EACEA P9 Eurydice. doi:. doi:10.2797/83967

Eckert, P. (2008). Variation and the indexical field. *Journal of Sociolinguistics*, *12*(4), 453–476. doi:10.1111/j.1467-9841.2008.00374.x

Eckert, P., & McConnell-Ginet, S. (1992). Think practically and look locally: Language and gender as community-based practice. *Annual Review of Anthropology*, *21*(1), 461–490. doi:10.1146/annurev.an.21.100192.002333

Ed, A. M., Ed, G. L., & Au, W. E. (2011). *The Routledge International Handbook of Critical Education*. Routledge.

Egbokhare, F. O. (2021). The accidental lingua franca: The paradox of the ascendancy of Nigerian Pidgin in Nigeria. In A. T. Akande & O. Salami (Eds.), *Current trends in Nigerian Pidgin English: A sociolinguistic perspective* (pp. 67–114). De Gruter Muoton. doi:10.1515/9781501513541-004

Ege, F., Yuksel, D., & Curle, S. (2022). A corpus-based analysis of discourse strategy use by English-Medium Instruction university lecturers in Turkey. *Journal of English for Academic Purposes*, *58*, 58. doi:10.1016/j.jeap.2022.101125

ElevenLabs. (2023). High quality AI voice cloning. https://elevenlabs.io/voice-cloning

Ellis, C. S., & Bochner, A. P. (2000). Autoethnography, personal narrative, reflexivity: Researcher as subject. In N. K. Denzin & Y. S. Lincoln (Eds.), *Handbook of Qualitative Research* (pp. 733–768). Sage.

Ellis, E. (2013). The ESL teacher as plurilingual: An Australian perspective. *TESOL Quarterly*, *47*(3), 446–471. doi:10.1002/tesq.120

Ellis, E. M. (2008). Defining and investigating monolingualism. *Sociolinguistic Studies*, *2*(3), 311–330. doi:10.1558ols.v2i3.311

Ellis, R. (2003). *Task-based language learning and teaching*. Oxford University Press.

Ellis, R., Skehan, P., Li, S., Shintani, N., & Lambert, C. (2020). *Task-based language teaching: Theory and practice*. Cambridge University Press.

Erdoğan, A., & Erdoğan, M. M. (2020). Syrian university students in Turkish higher education: Immediate vulnerabilities, future challenges for the European higher education area. In A. Curaj, L. Deca, & R. Pricopie (Eds.), *European higher education area: Challenges for a new decade*. Springer. doi:10.1007/978-3-030-56316-5_16

Errington, J. (2001). Ideology. In A. Duranti (Ed.), *Key Terms in language and culture* (pp. 110–112). Blackwell.

Escobar, C. F. (2016). Challenging the monolingual bias in EFL programs: Towards a bilingual approach to L2 learning. *Revista de Lenguas Modernas*, *24*, 249–266.

Esen, O. (2022, February 5). University study offers way to integrate Syrian refugees. *University World News*. https://www.universityworldnews.com/post.php?story=20220203061816422

Espinet, I., Aponte, G. Y., Sánchez, M. T., Cardenas Figueroa, D., & Busone-Rodríguez, A. (2020). Interrogating language ideologies in the primary grades: A community language inquiry unit. In City University of New York-New York State Initiative on Emergent Bilinguals (Ed.), Translanguaging and transformative teaching for emergent bilingual students: Lessons from the CUNY-NYSIEB Project (pp. 219-237). Routledge.

Esser, H. (2006). Migration, language and integration. *Research Review 4*. Programme on Intercultural Conflicts and Societal Integration (AKI), Social Science Research Center Berlin. http://193.174.6.11/alt/aki/files/aki_research_review_4.pdf

Essien, O. (2003). National development, language and language policy in Nigeria. In Essien, O. & Okon, M. (Eds.) Topical issues in sociolinguistics: The Nigerian perspective. Aba: National Institute for Nigerian Languages, 21-42.

Essien, O. (2006). Language and the Nigerian reforms agenda. In O. Ndimele, C. Ikekeonwu, & B.M. Mbah, (Eds.) Language and economic reforms in Nigeria. Ethnologue: Languages of the World (22nd ed.), Dallas.

Extra, G., & Yagmur, K. (Eds.). (2012). Language rich Europe: Trends in policies and practices for multilingualism in Europe. British Council/Cambridge University Press.

Eyles, J. (1988). *Research in human geography*. Basil Blackwell.

Eysenbach, G. (2020). How to fight an infodemic: The four pillars of infodemic management. *Journal of Medical Internet Research*, *22*(6), e21820. https://www.jmir.org/2020/6/e21820. doi:10.2196/21820 PMID:32589589

Fair Access to Regulated Professions and Compulsory Trades Act. (2006). Service Ontario. e-Laws. http://www.e-laws.gov.on.ca/html/statutes/english/elaws _statutes_06f31_e.htm

Fairclough, N., & Kress, G. (2001). Critical discourse analysis. *How to analyze talk in institutional settings: A casebook of methods*, 25-38.

Fairclough, N. (1989). *Language and power*. Longman.

Fairclough, N. (1992). *Discourse and social change*. Polity Press.

Fairclough, N. (1992). Introduction. In N. Fairclough (Ed.), *Critical language awareness* (pp. 1–30). Routledge.

Fairclough, N., & Wodak, R. (1997). Critical discourse analysis. In T. Van Dijk (Ed.), *Discourse in social interaction* (pp. 258–284). Sage.

Faraclas, N. (2008). Nigerian Pidgin. In B. Kortmann, E. W. Schneider, K. Burridge, & R. Mesthrie (Eds.), *Varieties of English* (Vol. 3, pp. 340–367). Mouton.

Faraclas, N. (2021). Naija: A language of the future. In A. T. Akande & O. Salami (Eds.), *Current trends in Nigerian Pidgin English: A sociolinguistic perspective* (pp. 9–38). De Gruter Muoton. doi:10.1515/9781501513541-002

Farmer, T., Hamm, J., Dawes, M., Barko-Alva, K., & Cross, J. (2019). Promoting inclusive communities in diverse classrooms: Teacher attunement and social dynamics Management. *Educational Psychologist*, *54*(4), 286–305. doi:10.1080/00461520.2019.1635020

Farrell, E. (2019). Language, economy, and the international artist community in Berlin. In T. Heyd, B. Schneider, & F. v. Mengden (Eds.), *The Sociolinguistic Economy of Berlin. Cosmopolitan Perspectives on Language, Diversity and Social Space* (pp. 145–166). De Gruyter. doi:10.1515/9781501508103-007

Farr, M., & Song, J. (2011). Language ideologies and policies: Multilingualism and education. *Language and Linguistics Compass*, *5*(9), 650–665. doi:10.1111/j.1749-818X.2011.00298.x

Ferreira, F. (2021). Inequality and COVID-19. *International Monetary Fund. Finance & Development*, 20–23. https://www.imf.org/external/pubs/ft/fandd/2021/06/pdf/inequality-and-covid-19-ferreira.pdf

Figueras, N. The impact of the CEFR. *ELT Journal, 66(4)*, 477-85

Fishman, J. A. (1965). Who speaks what language to whom and when? *La Linguistique* 1(2), 67–88. https://www.jstor.org/stable/30248773

Fishman, J. A. (1967). Bilingualism with and without diglossia; diglossia with and without bilingualism. *The Journal of Social Issues*, *23*(2), 29–38. doi:10.1111/j.1540-4560.1967.tb00573.x

Flavell, J. (1976). Metacognitive aspects of problem-solving. In L. Resnick (Ed.), *The Nature of Intelligence* (pp. 231–235). Lawrence Erlbaum Associates.

Flores, N., & García, O. (2013). Linguistic Third Spaces in education: Teachers' translanguaging across the bilingual continuum. In D. Lile, C. Leung, & P. Van Avermaet (Eds.), Managing diversity in education: Key issues and some responses (pp. 243–256). Clevedon, U.K.: Multilingual Matters.

Flores, N. (2013). The unexamined relationship between neoliberalism and plurilingualism: A cautionary tale. *TESOL Quarterly*, *47*(3), 500–520. doi:10.1002/tesq.114

Flores, N., & Rosa, J. (2015). Undoing appropriateness: Raciolinguistic ideologies and language diversity in education. *Harvard Educational Review*, *85*(2), 149–171. doi:10.17763/0017-8055.85.2.149

Flores, N., & Schissel, J. L. (2014). Dynamic bilingualism as the norm: Envisioning a heteroglossic approach to standards-based reform. *TESOL Quarterly*, *48*(3), 454–479. doi:10.1002/tesq.182

Fotiadou, G., Prentza, A., Maligkoudi, C., Michalopoulou, S., & Mattheoudakis, M. (2022). Investigating teachers' beliefs, attitudes and practices regarding the inclusion of refugee and immigrant students in Greek state schools. *Journal of Applied Linguistics*, *35*, 36–58.

Freire, P. (2007). Pedagogy of the oppressed, translated by Myra Bergman Ramos. New York: Continuum.

Freire, P. (2005). *Pedagogy of the oppressed, 30th anniversary edition*. The Continuum International Publishing Group, Inc.

Gagné, M., & Deci, E. L. (2005). Self-determination theory and work motivation. *Journal of Organizational Behavior*, *26*(4), 331–362. http://www.jstor.org/stable/4093832. doi:10.1002/job.322

Galani, M., & Stavrinidis, P.- Γαλάνη, Μ. & Σταυρινίδης, Π. (2022). Antilipsis ke praktikes ton ekpedeftikon protovathmias ekpedefsis schetika me ti diachirisi tis psychikis hygias pedion prosfigon pou fitoun stis domes ipodochis ke ekpedefsis prosfigon stin Ellada. [Perceptions and practices of primary school teachers regarding the management of the mental health of refugee children attending Refugee Reception and Education Facilities in Greece]. *Erevna stin Ekpedefsi*, *11*(1), 197–216.

Galante, A. (2018). *Plurilingual or Monolingual? A mixed methods study investigating plurilingual instruction in an English for Academic Purposes program at a Canadian university.* [Unpublished doctoral dissertation, University of Toronto]. https://hdl.handle.net/1807/91806

Galante, A. (2019). "The moment I realized I am plurilingual": Plurilingual tasks for creative representations in English for Academic Purposes at a Canadian university. *Applied Linguistics Review.*, *11*(4), 551–580. doi:10.1515/applirev-2018-0116

Galante, A. (2020). Pedagogical translanguaging in a multilingual English program in Canada: Student and teacher perspectives of challenges. *System*, *90*, 1–10. doi:10.1016/j.system.2020.102274

Gao, J., & Ma, S. (2022). Instructor feedback on free writing and automated corrective feedback in drills: Intensity and efficacy. *Language Teaching Research*, *26*(5), 986–1009. doi:10.1177/1362168820915337

García, O. (2008). Multilingual language awareness and teacher education. Encyclopedia of language and education, 6, 385-400.

García, O., & Leiva, C. (2014). Theorizing and enacting translanguaging for social justice. *Heteroglossia as practice and pedagogy*, 199-216.

García, O., Bartlett, L., & Kleifgen, J. (2007). From biliteracy to pluriliteracies. Handbook of multilingualism and multilingual communication, 5, 207-228.

García, O. (2009). *Bilingual education in the 21st Century: A Global Perspective*. Wiley-Blackwell.

García, O. (2011). *Bilingual education in the 21st century: A global perspective*. Wiley and Blackwell.

García, O. (2012). Theorizing translanguaging for educators. In C. Celic & K. Seltzer (Eds.), *Translanguaging: A CUNY-NYSIEB guide for educators* (pp. 1–6). City University of New York.

García, O. (2017). Critical multilingual language awareness and teacher education. In J. Cenoz, D. Gorter, & S. May (Eds.), *Language awareness and multilingualism* (3rd ed.) (pp. 263–280). Springer.

García, O. (2017). Translanguaging in schools: Subiendo y bajando, bajando y subiendo as afterword. *Journal of Language, Identity, and Education*, *16*(4), 256–263. doi:10.1080/15348458.2017.1329657

García, O. (2020). Translanguaging and Latinx bilingual readers. *The Reading Teacher*, *73*(5), 557–562. doi:10.1002/trtr.1883

García, O., Johnson, S. I., & Seltzer, K. (2017). *The translanguaging classroom: Leveraging student bilingualism for learning*. Caslon.

García, O., & Kleifgen, J. A. (2020). Translanguaging and literacies. *Reading Research Quarterly*, *55*(4), 553–571. doi:10.1002/rrq.286

García, O., & Kleyn, T. (2016). *Translanguaging with multilingual students. Learning from classroom moments*. Routledge. doi:10.4324/9781315695242

García, O., & Lin, A. M. Y. (2017). Translanguaging in bilingual education. In O. García & A. M. Y. Lin (Eds.), *Bilingual and multilingual education* (pp. 1–14). Springer. doi:10.1007/978-3-319-02258-1_9

García, O., Lin, M. Y., & May, S. (2017). Bilingual and multilingual. *Springer International Publishing*, *10*, 978–3.

García, O., & Sylvan, C. E. (2011). Pedagogies and practices in multilingual classrooms: Singularities in pluralities. *Modern Language Journal*, *95*(3), 385–400. doi:10.1111/j.1540-4781.2011.01208.x

García, O., & Torres-Guevara, R. (2010). Monoglossic ideologies and language policies in the education of U.S. Latinas/os. In E. G. Murillo Jr, S. A. Villenas, R. T. Galván, J. S. Muñoz, C. Martínez, & M. Machado-Casas (Eds.), *Handbook of Latinos and education: Theory, research, and practice* (pp. 182–193). Routledge.

García, O., & Wei, L. (2014). *Language, bilingualism and education*. doi:10.1057/9781137385765_4

Gardner, R. C. (1985). *Social psychology and second language learning: The role of attitudes and motivation*. Edward Arnold.

Garmon, M. (2004). Changing preservice teachers' attitudes/beliefs about diversity: What are the factors? J. *Journal of Teacher Education*, *55*(3), 201–213. doi:10.1177/0022487104263080

Compilation of References

Gee, J. P. (1987). What is Literacy? *Journal of Teaching and Learning, 2*(1), 3–11.

Gee, J. P. (1999). *Introduction to discourse analysis: Theory and method*. Routledge.

Gee, J. P. (2000). Identity as an analytic lens for research in education. In W. Secada (Ed.), *Review of Research in Education* (Vol. 25, pp. 99–126). American Educational Research Association. doi:10.2307/1167322

Genc, E., Yuksel, D., & Curle, S. (2023). Lecturers' translanguaging practices in English-taught lectures in Turkey. *Journal of Multilingual Theories and Practices, 4*(1), 8–31. doi:10.1558/jmtp.23945

George Brown College. (2023, August 30). *English for Academic Purposes Program Overview*. George Brown College. https://www.georgebrown.ca/preparatory-liberal-studies/english-as-a-second-language- esl/english-for-academic-purposes-eap-program-overview

George, E. B. (2006). *A profile of multilingual skills of young adult Xhosa mother tongue speakers* [M.Phil Thesis, University of the Western Cape].

Geremia, C., White, P. J., Hoeting, J. A., Wallen, R. L., Watson, F. G., Blanton, D., & Hobbs, N. T. (2014). Integrating population-and individual-level information in a movement model of Yellowstone bison. *Ecological Applications, 24*(2), 346–362. doi:10.1890/13-0137.1 PMID:24689146

Gershon, T. (2018, June 25). *Quantum Computing Expert Explains One Concept in 5 Levels of Difficulty*. [Video]. YouTube. https://www.youtube.com/watch?v=OWJCfOvochA

Gevers, J. (2018). Translingualism revisited: Language difference and hybridity in L2 writing. *Journal of Second Language Writing, 40*, 73–83. doi:10.1016/j.jslw.2018.04.003

Gibb, T. L. (2008). Bridging Canadian adult second language education and essential skills policies, approach with caution. *Adult Education Quarterly, 58*(4), 318–334. doi:10.1177/0741713608318893

Gilyard, K. (2016). The rhetoric of translingualism. *College English, 78*(3), 284–289.

Gkaitartzi, A., Kiliari, A., & Tsokalidou, R. (2015). 'Invisible' bilingualism – 'Invisible' language ideologies: Greek teachers' attitudes towards immigrant students' heritage languages. *International Journal of Bilingual Education and Bilingualism, 18*(1), 60–72. doi:10.1080/13670050.2013.877418

Gkaravelas, K. & Koutoussi, A. (2018). I stasis ton ekpedeftikon protovathmias ekpedefsis gia tin entaksi diglosson pedion sta dimosia scholia tis Atikis. [The attitudes of primary education teachers towards the inclusion of bilingual students in the Public Primary Schools of Attica]. *Theoria kai erevna stis epistimes tis agogis, 31*, 45-58,

Godefroidt, A., Langer, A., & Meuleman, B. (2016). *Towards post-modern identities in Africa? An analysis of citizenship conceptualizations in Ghana*. Centre for Research on Peace and Development. https://soc.kuleuven.be/crpd/files/working-papers/WP%2051%20Towards%20post-modern%20identities%20in%20Africa.pdf

Goffman, E. (1967). *Interaction ritual: Essays on face behavior*. Pantheon Books.

Goffman, E. (1981). *Forms of talk*. University of Pennsylvania Press.

Gogolin, I. (1997). The "monolingual habitus" as the common feature in teaching in the language of the majority in different countries. *Per Linguam, 13*(2), 38–49. doi:10.5785/13-2-187

Gogolin, I. (2006). Linguistic habitus. In K. Brown (Ed.), *Encyclopedia of language & linguistics* (2nd ed., pp. 194–196). Elsevier. doi:10.1016/B0-08-044854-2/05270-6

Gong, Y., Ma, M., Hsiang, T. P., & Wang, C. (2020). Sustaining international students' learning of Chinese in China: Shifting motivations among New Zealand students during study abroad. *Sustainability (Basel)*, *12*(15), 6289. doi:10.3390u12156289

González-Cruz, B., Cerezo, L., & Nicolás-Conesa, F. (2022). A classroom-based study on the effects of WCF on accuracy in pen-and-paper versus computer-mediated collaborative writing. *Studies in Second Language Learning and Teaching*, *12*(4), 623–650. doi:10.14746sllt.2022.12.4.5

González, N., Moll, L. C., & Amanti, C. (2005). *Funds of knowledge: Theorizing practices in households, communities, and classrooms*. Routledge.

Gonzalez, V. (2009). *Young learners, diverse children: Celebrating diversity in early childhood*. Corwin Press.

Goo, J. (2020). Research on the role of recasts in L2 learning. *Language Teaching*, *53*(3), 289–315. doi:10.1017/S026144482000004X

Gorter, D., & Arocena, E. (2020). Teachers' beliefs about multilingualism in a course on translanguaging. *System*, *92*, 1–10. doi:10.1016/j.system.2020.102272

Government of Ontario (2014). *Strengthening immigration in Ontario: New legislation to help attract more skilled immigrants, boost economic growth*. http://news.ontario.ca/mci/en/2014/02/strengthening-immigration-in-ontario.html

Green, D., & Worswick, C. (2004). *Earnings of immigrant men in Canada: The roles of labour market entry effects and returns to foreign experience*. University of British Columbia Press.

Grgurović, M., Chapelle, C. A., & Shelley, M. C. (2013). A meta-analysis of effectiveness studies on computer technology-supported language learning. *ReCALL*, *25*(2), 165–198. doi:10.1017/S0958344013000013

Grosjean, F. (1982). *Life with two languages: An introduction to bilingualism*. Harvard University Press.

Gruber, S. (2007). *Literacies, experiences, and technologies: Reflective practices of an alien researcher*. Hampton Press.

Gruber, S. (2021). I am an immigrant: Cultural multiplicities in U.S. educational systems. In H. Ostman, H. Tinberg, & D. Martínez (Eds.), *Teaching writing through the immigrant story* (pp. 13–35). Utah State University Press. doi:10.7330/9781646421664.c001

Gruber, S., & Barrón, N. G. (2020). Redirecting failure: Controlling a sense of self. In A. D. Carr & L. R. Micciche. Failure Pedagogies: Learning and unlearning what it means to fail (pp. 83–95). Peter Lang.

Gruber, S., & Barrón, N. G. (forthcoming). Transcultural endeavors: Boundary crossers and writing transfer. In L. Tremain & L. Miller (Eds.), *Radical frameworks for writing transfer: Epistemological justice in the writing classroom*. Peter Lang.

Guba, E. G., & Lincoln, Y. S. (1994). Competing paradigms in qualitative research. In N. Denzin & Y. Lincoln (Eds.), Handbook of qualitative research (pp. 105-117). Sage Publications.

Guerra, J. C. (2016). Cultivating a rhetorical sensibility in the translingual writing classroom. *College English*, *78*(3), 228–233.

Guest, G., MacQueen, K. M., & Namey, E. E. (2012). *Applied thematic analysis*. Sage. doi:10.4135/9781483384436

Gülle, T. (2023). Language challenges in English medium higher education and translingual assessment as an alternative tool. [Unpublished doctoral dissertation]. Boğaziçi University.

Gumperz, J. J. (1972). Introduction. In J. J. Gumperz & D. Hymes (Eds.), *Directions in Sociolinguistics. The Ethnography of Communication* (pp. 1–26). Holt, Rinehart and Winston.

Gumperz, J. J. (1982). *Discourse strategies*. Cambridge University Press. doi:10.1017/CBO9780511611834

Gumperz, J. J. (1992). *Language and social identity*. Cambridge University Press.

Güngör, H., & Soysal, T. (2021). Türk yükseköğretiminde Suriyeli mülteciler [Syrian refugees in Turkish higher education]. *Milli Eğitim Dergisi*, *50*(1), 1245–1264.

Gürtler, K., & Kronewald, E. (2015). Internationalization and English-medium instruction in German higher education. In S. Dimova, A. K. Hultgren, & C. Jensen (Eds.), *English-medium instruction in higher education in Europe* (pp. 89–114). Mouton de Gruyter. doi:10.1515/9781614515272-006

Gutmann, A. (2004). Unity and diversity in democratic multicultural education: Creative and destructive tensions. In J. A. Banks (Ed.), *Diversity and citizenship education: Global perspectives* (pp. 71–96). Jossey-Bass.

Hall, J., & Horner, B. (2023) (Eds.), Toward a transnational university: WAC/WID across Borders of language, nation, and discipline. The WAC Clearinghouse; University Press of Colorado.

Hall, K. (2009). Boys' talk: Hindi, moustaches and masculinity in New Delhi. In P. Pichler & E. Eppler (Eds.), *Gender and Spoken Language in Interaction* (pp. 139–162). Palgrave MacMillan. doi:10.1057/9780230280748_7

Hall, S. (Ed.). (1997). *Representation: Cultural representations and signifying practices*. Sage Publications.

Hamers, J. F., & Blanc, M. H. A. (2000). *Bilinguality and bilingualism* (2nd ed.). Cambridge University Press. doi:10.1017/CBO9780511605796

Hammersley-Fletcher, L., & Hanley, C. (2016). The use of critical thinking in higher education in relation to the international student: Shifting policy and practice. *British Educational Research Journal*, *42*(6), 978–992. doi:10.1002/berj.3246

Hampel, R., & Hauck, M. (2006). Computer-mediated language learning: Making meaning in multimodal virtual learning spaces. *The JALT CALL Journal*, *2*(2), 3–18. doi:10.29140/jaltcall.v2n2.23

Hampel, R., & Stickler, U. (2005). New skills for new classrooms: Training tutors to teach languages online. *Computer Assisted Language Learning*, *18*(4), 311–326. doi:10.1080/09588220500335455

Handley, M. A., Santos, M. G., & Bastías, M. J. (2023). Working with data in adult english classrooms: Lessons learned about communicative justice during the COVID-19 pandemic. *International Journal of Environmental Research and Public Health*, *20*(1), 696. doi:10.3390/ijerph20010696 PMID:36613016

Hanna, F., Oostdam, R., Severiens, S. E., & Zijlstra, B. J. (2020). Assessing the professional identity of primary student teachers: Design and validation of the Teacher Identity Measurement Scale. *Studies in Educational Evaluation*, *64*, 100822. doi:10.1016/j.stueduc.2019.100822

Harker, R. K. (1984). On Reproduction, habitus and education. British Journal of Sociology of Education, 5(2), 117-127.

Harper, S. R. (2012). Race without racism: How higher education researchers minimize racist institutional norms. *Review of Higher Education*, *36*(1), 9–29. doi:10.1353/rhe.2012.0047

Harper, S. R., Patton, L. D., & Wooden, S. O. (2009). Access and equity for African American students in higher education: A critical race historical analysis of policy efforts. *The Journal of Higher Education*, *80*(4), 389–414. doi:10.1080/00221546.2009.11779022

Harré, R., & Moghaddam, F. M. (2015). Positioning theory. The Wiley handbook of theoretical and philosophical psychology: Methods, approaches, and new directions for social sciences, 263-276. Wiley.

Hart, R. (2009). Child refugees, trauma and education: Interactionist considerations on social and emotional needs and development. *Educational Psychology in Practice*, *25*(4), 351–368. doi:10.1080/02667360903315172

Haukås, Å. (2015). Teachers' beliefs about multilingualism and a multilingual pedagogical approach. *International Journal of Multilingualism, 13*(1), 1–18. doi:10.1080/14790718.2015.1041960

Haukås, Å., & Mercer, S. (2022). Exploring pre-service language teachers' mindsets using a sorting activity. *Innovation in Language Learning and Teaching, 16*(3), 221–233. doi:10.1080/17501229.2021.1923721

Hayward, M. (2017). Teaching as a primary therapeutic intervention for learners from refugee backgrounds. *Intercultural Education, 28*(2), 165–181. doi:10.1080/14675986.2017.1294391

Hazen, K. (2001). Teaching about dialects. *ERIC Document Reproduction Services No. ED456674*. ERIC. https://files.eric.ed.gov/fulltext/ED456674.pdf

Hazen, K. (2002). Identity and language variation in a rural community. *Language, 78*(2), 240–257. doi:10.1353/lan.2002.0089

Hazen, K. (2017). Variationist approaches to language and education. In K. A. King, Y.-J. Lai, & S. May (Eds.), *Research methods in language and education* (3rd ed.) (pp. 145–157). Springer International Publishing. doi:10.1007/978-3-319-02249-9_10

Heath, S. B. (1988). Protean shapes in literacy events: Ever-shifting oral and literate traditions. In E.R. Kintgen, B. M. Kroll, & M. Rose. (Eds.), Perspectives on literacy, 348-70. Carbondale and Edwardsville: Southern Illinois University Press.

Heath, S. B. (1983). *Ways with words: Language, life and work in communities and classrooms*. Cambridge University Press. doi:10.1017/CBO9780511841057

Heller, M. (1988). *Codeswitching: Anthropological and sociolinguistic perspectives*. Mouton de Gruyter. doi:10.1515/9783110849615

Hellerman, J., & Thorne, S. L. (2022). Collaborative mobilizations of interbodied communication for cooperative action. *Modern Language Journal, 106*(S1), 89–112. doi:10.1111/modl.12754

Henderson, C. (2021). The effect of feedback timing on L2 Spanish vocabulary acquisition in synchronous computer-mediated communication. *Language Teaching Research, 25*(2), 185–208. doi:10.1177/1362168819832907

Henly-Shepard, S., Gray, S. A., & Cox, L. J. (2015). The use of participatory modeling to promote social learning and facilitate community disaster planning. *Environmental Science & Policy, 45*, 109–122. doi:10.1016/j.envsci.2014.10.004

Henne–Ochoa, R., Elliott–Groves, E., Meek, B. A., & Rogoff, B. (2020). Pathways forward for Indigenous language reclamation: Engaging indigenous epistemology and learning by observing and pitching in to family and community endeavors. In S. Canagarajah (Ed), Rethinking mobility and language: From the global south (p. 580). Springer.

Heritage, J. (2012). The epistemic engine: Sequence organization and territories of knowledge. *Research on Language and Social Interaction, 45*(1), 30–52. doi:10.1080/08351813.2012.646685

Hermann, E. (2022). Artificial intelligence and mass personalization of communication content—An ethical and literacy perspective. *New Media & Society, 24*(5), 1258–1277. https://doi-org.proxy.library.vcu.edu/10.1177/14614448211022702. doi:10.1177/14614448211022702

Herzog-Punzenberger, B., Le Pichon-Vorstman, E., & Siarova, H. (2017). *Multilingual education in the light of diversity: Lessons learned*. NESET II Report, Luxembourg: Publications Office of the European Union. https://data.europa.eu/doi/10.2766/71255

Compilation of References

Heyd, T., & Schneider, B. (2019). Anglophone practices in Berlin: From historical evidence to transnational communities. In R. Hickey (Ed.), *English in the German-Speaking World* (pp. 143–164). Cambridge University Press. doi:10.1017/9781108768924.008

Hiatt, M. A., McLetchie, A., Bagasra, A. B., Laufersweiler-Dwye, D. L., & Mackinem, M. (2019). Perceptions of diversity, inclusion, and belongingness at an HBCU: Implications and applications for faculty. In R. Jeffries (Ed.), *Diversity, equity, and inclusivity in contemporary higher education* (pp. 175–193). IGI Global. doi:10.4018/978-1-5225-5724-1.ch011

Hickling-Hudson, A. (2004). South-south collaboration: Cuban teachers in Jamaica and Namibia. *Comparative Education*, *40*(2), 289–311. http://www.jstor.org/stable/4134653. doi:10.1080/0305006042000231392

Hilal, M., & Varatharajah, S. (2022). *Englisch in Berlin. Ausgrenzungen in einer kosmopolitischen Gesellschaft/English in Berlin. Exclusions in a Cosmopolitan Society*. Wirklichkeit Books.

Hillier, L., & Harrison, L. (2007). Building realities less limited than their own: Young people practicing same-sex attraction on the Internet. *Sexualities*, *10*(1), 82–100. doi:10.1177/1363460707072956

Hill, J., & Hill, K. (1977). Language death and relexification in Tlaxcalan Nahuatl. *International Journal of the Sociology of Language*, *12*, 55–69.

Hinkel, E. (2018). Descriptive versus prescriptive grammar. In H. Nassaji (Ed.), *TESOL Encyclopedia of English Language Teaching*. Wiley. http://www.elihinkel.org/downloads/Descriptive%20v%20Prescriptive.pdf doi:10.1002/9781118784235.eelt0053

Hockly, N. (2023). Artificial intelligence in English language teaching: The good, the bad and the ugly. *RELC Journal*, *54*(2), 445–451. doi:10.1177/00336882231168504

Holliday, A. (2005). *The struggle to teach English as an international language*. Oxford University Press.

Hong, J. Y. (2010). Pre-service and beginning teachers' professional identity and its relation to dropping out of the profession. *Teaching and Teacher Education*, *26*(8), 1530–1543. doi:10.1016/j.tate.2010.06.003

Hornberger, N. H., & Link, H. (2012). Translanguaging and transnational literacies in multilingual classrooms: A biliteracy lens. *International Journal of Bilingual Education and Bilingualism*, *15*(3), 261–278. doi:10.1080/13670050.2012.658016

Hornberger, N. H., & Skilton-Sylvester, E. (2000). Revisiting the continua of biliteracy: International and critical perspectives. *Language and Education*, *14*(2), 96–122. doi:10.1080/09500780008666781

Hoyle, E., & John, P. (1995). *Professional knowledge and professional practice*. Cassell.

Hsu, H., & Lin, C. (2022). Extending the technology acceptance model of college learners' mobile-assisted language learning by incorporating psychological constructs. *British Journal of Educational Technology*, *53*(2), 286–306. doi:10.1111/bjet.13165

Hsu, L. (2013). English as a foreign language learners' perception of mobile assisted language learning: A cross-national study. *Computer Assisted Language Learning*, *26*(3), 197–213. doi:10.1080/09588221.2011.649485

Hu, G., Li, L., & Lei, J. (2014). English-medium instruction at a Chinese University: Rhetoric and reality. *Language Policy*, *13*(1), 21–40. doi:10.100710993-013-9298-3

Hult, F. M., & Hornberger, N. H. (2016). Revisiting orientation in language planning: Problem, right, and resource as an analytical heuristic. *The Bilingual Review/La Revista Bilingüe*, *33*(3), 30-49.

Hurd, S. & Lewis, T. (Eds.). (2008). *Language Learning Strategies in Independent Settings*. Multilingual Matters. doi:10.21832/9781847690999

Hymel, S., & Katz, J. (2019). Designing classrooms for diversity: Fostering social inclusion. *Educational Psychologist, 54*(4), 331–339. doi:10.1080/00461520.2019.1652098

Hymes, D. (1974a). *Foundations in sociolinguistics: An ethnographic approach*. University of Pennsylvania Press.

Hymes, D. (1974b). Ways of Speaking. In R. Bauman & J. Sherzer (Eds.), *Explorations in the Ethnography of Speaking* (pp. 433–451). Cambridge University Press.

Igboanusi, H. (2008). Empowering Nigerian Pidgin: A challenge for status planning? *World Englishes, 27*(1), 68–82. doi:10.1111/j.1467-971X.2008.00536.x

Igboanusi, H., Odoje, C., & Ibrahim, G. (2017). The modernization of HIV and AIDS' nomenclatures in Nigeria's major languages. *Terminology. International Journal of Theoretical and Applied Issues in Specialized Communication, Vol., 2*(23), 238–260.

Immigration, Refugees and Citizenship Canada. (2022). *An immigration plan to grow the economy*. Immigration, Refugees and Citizenship Canada. https://www.canada.ca/en/immigration-refugees-citizenship/news /2022/11/an-immigration-plan-to-grow-the-economy.html

Inoue, A. B. (2019). How do we language so people stop killing each other, or what do we do about white language supremacy. *College Composition and Communication, 71*(2), 352–369. doi:10.58680/ccc201930427

Irie, K., Ryan, S., & Mercer, S. (2018). Using Q methodology to investigate pre-service EFL teachers' mindsets about teaching competences. *Studies in Second Language Learning and Teaching, 8*(3), 575–598. doi:10.14746sllt.2018.8.3.3

Irizar, T. (2001). English language education in Cuba. *ESL Magazine, 4*(1), 26–28.

Irvine, J. T., & Gal, S. (2000). Language ideology and linguistic differentiation. In P. V. Kroskrity (Ed.), *Regimes of Language: Ideologies, Polities, and Identities* (pp. 35–84). School of American Research Press.

Istanbul Technical University. (2023, August 12). *Management Engineering (100% English)*. Istanbul Technical University. https://islmuh.itu.edu.tr/en/academic/education/undergraduate-programs/management-engineering

Jacewicz, E., & Fox, R. A. (2016). Acoustics of regionally accented speech. *Acoustics Today, 12*(2), 31–38.

Jakobson, R. (Ed.). (1976). *Metalanguage as a linguistic problem* (pp. 113–121). Akadémiai Nyomda.

Japan Foundation. (2021). *Nendo kaigai nihongo kyoiku kikan chosa kekka gaiyou [Results of the survey on fiscal year 2021 Japanese language education]*. Japan Foundation. https://www.jpf.go.jp/j/about/press/2022/dl/2022-023-02_1228.pdf

Japan Foundation. (December 15, 2022). *JF special stories: Language*. Japan Foundation. https://jf50.jpf.go.jp/en/story/learning_japanese_changed_my_life/

Jarvis, H. (2009). Computers in EAP: Change, issues and challenges. *Modern English Teacher, 18*(2), 51–54.

Jenkins, J. (2006). Current perspectives on teaching World Englishes and English as a lingua franca. *TESOL Quarterly, 40*(1), 157–181. doi:10.2307/40264515

Jenkins, J. (2013). *English as a Lingua Franca in the international university: The politics of academic English language policy* (1st ed.). Routledge., doi:10.4324/9780203798157

Jenkins, J. (2019). English medium instruction in higher education: The role of English as a lingua franca. In X. Gao (Ed.), *Second handbook of English teaching* (pp. 91–108). Springer.

Jenkins, J. (2020). Red herrings and the case of language in UK higher education. *Nordic Journal of English Studies, 19*(3), 59–67. doi:10.35360/njes.577

Compilation of References

Jenkins, S. (2000). Cultural and linguistic miscues: A case study of international teaching assistant and academic faculty miscommunication. *International Journal of Intercultural Relations, 24*(4), 477–501. doi:10.1016/S0147-1767(00)00011-0

John, P., & Wolf, N. (2020). Using grammar checkers in an ESL context: An investigation of automatic corrective feedback. *CALICO Journal, 37*(2), 169–196. doi:10.1558/cj.36523

Johnstone, B. (2006). A new role for narrative in variationist sociolinguistics. *Narrative Inquiry, 16*(1), 46–55. doi:10.1075/ni.16.1.08joh

Johnstone, B., Andrews, J., & Danielson, A. E. (2006). Mobility, indexicality, and the enregisterment of "Pittsburghese". *Journal of English Linguistics, 34*(2), 77–104. doi:10.1177/0075424206290692

Jones, Chris [Username]. (2012, April 18). *Southern accent, North Carolina* [Video]. YouTube. https://www.youtube.com/watch?v=gAqm5ls8Ep8

Jones, E. (2017). Problematising and reimagining the notion of 'international student experience'. *Studies in Higher Education, 42*(5), 933–943. doi:10.1080/03075079.2017.1293880

Jones, F. R. (1994). The lone language learner: A diary study. *System, 22*(4), 441–454. doi:10.1016/0346-251X(94)90001-9

Jordan, J. (2022). *Grounded literacies in a transnational WAC/WID ecology: A Korean-U.S. study*. WAC Clearinghouse & University Press of Colorado. doi:10.37514/INT-B.2022.1503

Jørgensen, J. N. (2010). Languaging. Nine years of poly-lingual development of young Turkish-Danish grade school students. *Copenhagen Studies in Bilingualism*. University of Copenhagen.

Juvonen, J., & Bell, A. N. (2018). Social integration of refugee youth in Europe: Lessons learnt about interethnic relations in U.S. schools. *Polish Psychological Bulletin, 49*(1), 23–30.

Juvonen, J., Lessard, L. M., Rastogi, R., Schacter, H. L., & Smith, D. S. (2019). Promoting social inclusion in educational settings: Challenges and opportunities. *Educational Psychologist, 54*(4), 250–270. doi:10.1080/00461520.2019.1655645

Kaakinen, M., Sirola, A., Savolainen, I., & Oksan, A. (2020). Shared identity and shared information in social media: Development and validation of the identity bubble reinforcement scale. *Media Psychology, 23*(1), 25–51. doi:10.1080/15213269.2018.1544910

Kalantzis, M., Cope, B., & Harvey, A. (2003). Assessing multiliteracies and the new basics. *Assessment in Education: Principles, Policy & Practice, 10*(1), 15–26. doi:10.1080/09695940301692

Kamaşak, R., Rose, H., & Sahan, K. (2021). Quality of instruction and student outcomes in English-medium programs in Turkey. New Connections in EMI Turkey Research Partnership Fund 2020. Turkey: British Council.

Kanno, Y., & Norton, B. (2003). Imagined communities and educational possibilities: Introduction. *Journal of Language, Identity, and Education, 2*(4), 241–249. doi:10.1207/S15327701JLIE0204_1

Kanno, Y., & Stuart, C. (2011). Learning to become a second language teacher: Identities-inpractice. *Modern Language Journal, 95*(2), 236–252. doi:10.1111/j.1540-4781.2011.01178.x

Karakaş, A. (2019). A critical look at the phenomenon of 'a mixed-up use of Turkish and English' in English-medium instruction universities in Turkey. *Journal of Higher Education and Science, 9*(2), 205–215. doi:10.5961/jhes.2019.322

Karakaş, A. (2023). Translanguaging in content-based EMI classes through the lens of Turkish students: Self-reported practices, functions and orientations. *Linguistics and Education, 77*, 101221. doi:10.1016/j.linged.2023.101221

Karakaş, A., & Bayyurt, Y. (2019). The scope of linguistic diversity in the language policies, practices, and linguistic landscape of a Turkish EMI university. In J. Jenkins & A. Mauranen (Eds.), *Linguistic diversity on the EMI campus: Insider accounts of the use of English and other languages in universities within Asia, Australasia, and Europe* (pp. 96–122). Routledge. doi:10.4324/9780429020865-5

Karakaya, K., & Bozkurt, A. (2022). Mobile-assisted language learning (MALL) research trends and patterns through bibliometric analysis: Empowering language learners through ubiquitous educational technologies. *System (Linköping)*, *110*, 102925–. doi:10.1016/j.system.2022.102925

Karimi, M. N., & Abdollahi, S. (2022). L2 learners' acquisition of simple vs. complex linguistic features across explicit vs. implicit instructional approaches: The mediating role of beliefs. *Language Teaching Research*, *26*(6), 1179–1201. doi:10.1177/1362168820921908

Karpat, K. H. (2004). *The Turks in America: Historical background: From Ottoman to Turkish immigration. Studies on Turkish politics and society: Selected articles and essays*. Brill.

Kasneci, E., Seßler, K., Küchemann, S., Bannert, M., Dementieva, D., Fischer, F., Gasser, U., Groh, G. L., Günnemann, S., Hüllermeier, E., Krusche, S., Kutyniok, G., Michaeli, T., Nerdel, C., Pfeffer, J., Poquet, O., Sailer, M., Schmidt, A., Seidel, T, & Kasneci, G. (2023). ChatGPT for good? On opportunities and challenges of large language models for education. *Learning and Individual Differences*, *103*, 2–9. doi:10.1016/j.lindif.2023.102274

Kasonde, A. (2015). Language and identity in general education in Zambia. In E. Khachaturyan (Ed.), *Language-Nation-Identity: The" Questione della Lingua" in an Italian and Non-Italian Context* (pp. 96–119). Cambridge Scholars Publishing.

Kataoka, Y., Thamrin, A. H., Van Meter, R., Murai, J., & Kataoka, K. (2023). Investigating the effect of computer-mediated feedback via an LMS integration in a large-scale Japanese speaking class. *Education and Information Technologies*, *28*(2), 1957–1986. doi:10.100710639-022-11262-7 PMID:35967830

Katz, J. (2016). *Speaking American: How y'all, youse, and you guys talk: A visual guide*. Houghton Mifflin Harcourt Publishing.

Keipi, T., Näsi, M., Oksanen, A., & Räsänen, P. (2017). *Online hate and harmful content: Cross-national perspectives*. Routledge.

Kelly, P. F. (2006). Filipinos in Canada: Economic dimensions of immigration and Settlement. *CERIS Working Paper No. 48*. http://www.ceris.metropolis.net/wp-content/ uploads/pdf/research_publication/working_papers/wp48.pdf

Kelly, P. F., Astorga-Garcia, M., & Esguerra, E. F. (2009). Explaining the deprofessionalized Filipino: Why Filipino immigrants get low-paying jobs in Toronto. (CERIS Working Paper No. 75). CERIS. http://ceris.metropolis.net

Kemp, C. (2007). Strategic processing in grammar learning: Do multilinguals use more strategies? *International Journal of Multilingualism*, *4*(4), 241–261. doi:10.2167/ijm099.0

Kerekes, J. A. (2005). Before, during, and after the event: Getting the job (or not) in an employment interview. In K. Bardovi-Harlig and B. Hartford (Eds.), Interlanguage pragmatics: Exploring institutional talk (pp. 99-131). Lawrence Erlbaum.

Kerestecioğlu, F., & Bayyurt, Y. (2018). *English as the medium of instruction in universities: A holistic approach*. Symposium conducted at the meeting of Kadir Has University, Istanbul.

Khote, N. (2018). Translanguaging in systemic functional linguistics: A culturally sustaining pedagogy for writing in secondary schools. In R. Harman (Ed.), *Bilingual Learners and Social Equity* (pp. 153–178). Springer. doi:10.1007/978-3-319-60953-9_8

Kim, E. G., Kweon, S. O., & Kim, J. (2017). Korean engineering students' perceptions of English-medium instruction (EMI) and L1 use in EMI classes. *Journal of Multilingual and Multicultural Development*, *38*(2), 130–145. doi:10.1080/01434632.2016.1177061

Kırkgöz, Y., İnci-Kavak, V., Karakaş, A., & Panero, S. M. (2023). Translanguaging practices in Turkish EMI classrooms: Commonalities and differences across two academic disciplines. *System*, *113*, 102982. doi:10.1016/j.system.2023.102982

Kırkgoz, Y., Moran Panero, S., Karakas, A., & Inci Kavak, V. (2021). *Classroom discourse in EMI courses in Turkey: On the dynamics of translanguaging practices*. British Council.

Kleyn, T., & García, O. (2019). Translanguaging as an act of transformation: Restructuring teaching and learning for emergent bilingual students. The Handbook of TESOL in K-12, 69-82.

Ko, C.-J. (2022). Online individualized corrective feedback on EFL learners' grammatical error correction. *Computer Assisted Language Learning*, 1–29. doi:10.1080/09588221.2022.2118783

Koban-Koç, D. (2016). Attitudes towards Oral Code-switching among Turkish-English Bilingual Speakers in New York City. *Hacettepe University Journal of Turkish Studies*, *24*, 151–172.

Kohnke, L., Moorhouse, B. L., & Zou, D. (2023). ChatGPT for Language Teaching and Learning. *RELC Journal*, 3368822311628–. doi:10.1177/00336882231162868

Kohnke, L, Moorhouse, B. L, & Zou, D. (2023). ChatGPT for Language Teaching and Learning. RELC Journal, 54(2), 537-550. doi:10.1177/00336882231162868

Koltovskaia, S. (2020). Student engagement with automated written corrective feedback (AWCF) provided by Grammarly: A multiple case study. *Assessing Writing*, *44*, 1–12. doi:10.1016/j.asw.2020.100450

Kormos, J., & Csiér, K. (2014). The interaction of motivation, self-regulatory strategies, and autonomous learning behavior in different learner groups. *TESOL Quarterly*, *48*(2), 275–299. http://www.jstor.org/stable/43268052. doi:10.1002/tesq.129

Korsgaard, C. M. (2007). Autonomy and the second person within: A commentary on Stephen Darwall's the second-person standpoint. *Ethics*, *118*(1), 8–23. doi:10.1086/522019

Koukoula, A. (2017). *Attitudes and opinions of teachers regarding refugee and immigrant integration in the Greek educational system. The case of the municipality of Lesvos and of Serres* [Dissertation, Hellenic Open University].

Kovinthan, T. (2016). Learning and teaching with loss: Meeting the needs of refugee children through narrative inquiry. *Diaspora, Indigenous, and Minority Education*, *10*(3), 141–155. doi:10.1080/15595692.2015.1137282

Kramsch, C. (1993). *Context and culture in language teaching*. Oxford University Press.

Krashen, S. D. (1985). *The input hypothesis: Issues and implications*. Addison-Wesley Longman Limited.

Kress, G., & van Leeuwen, T. (2001). *Multimodal discourse: The modes and media of contemporary communication*. Edward Arnold.

Kurt, Y. & Bayyurt, Y. (forthcoming). English Medium Instruction in Higher Education in Turkey. In K. Bolton, W. Botha and B. Lin (Eds.), The Routledge Handbook of English-medium instruction (EMI) in higher education. Routledge.

Kurtböke, P. (1998). *A corpus-driven study of Turkish-English language contact in Australia*. [Doctoral dissertation, Monash University].

Kwankye, S. O., Anarfi, J. K., Tagoe, C. A., & Castaldo, A. (2009). Independent North-South child migration in Ghana: The decision-making process. *University of Sussex: DRC on Migration, Globalisation and Poverty*. http://www.sussex.ac.uk/Units/SCMR/drc/publications/working_papers/WP-T29.pdf

Kyriakou, M. (2019). A critical review of the theory of diglossia: A call to action. *International Journal of Linguistics. Literature and Translation*, 2(5), 334–340.

La Bella, E., Allen, C., & Lirussi, F. (2021, December). Communication vs evidence: What hinders the outreach of science during an infodemic? A narrative review. *Integrative Medicine Research*, 10(4), 100731. doi:10.1016/j.imr.2021.100731 PMID:34141575

Ladson-Billings, G. (2006). Yes, but how do we do it? Practicing culturally relevant pedagogy. In J. Landsman & C. W. Lewis (Eds.), White teachers/diverse classrooms: A guide to building inclusive schools, promoting high expectations and eliminating racism (pp. 29–42). Sterling, VA: Stylus Publishers.

Ladson-Billings, G., & Donnor, J. K. (n.d.). Waiting for the call: The moral activist role of critical race theory scholarship. Handbook of Critical and Indigenous Methodologies, 61-84. doi:10.4135/9781483385686.n4

Ladson-Billings, G. (2006). From the achievement gap to the education debt: Understanding achievement in U.S. schools. *Educational Researcher*, 35(7), 3–12. doi:10.3102/0013189X035007003

Ladson-Billings, G., & Tate, W. F. (1995). Toward a critical race theory of education. *Teachers College Record*, 97(1), 47–68. doi:10.1177/016146819509700104

Lakoff, R. (1973). Language and woman's place. *Language in Society*, 2(1), 45–80. https://www.jstor.org/stable/4166707. doi:10.1017/S0047404500000051

Laquian, E., & Laquian, A. (2008). *Seeking a better life abroad: A study of Filipinos in Canada 1957–2007*. Anvil Press.

Larsen-Freeman, D. (2011). A complexity theory approach to second language development/acquisition. In D. Atkinson (Ed.), *Alternative approaches to second language acquisition* (pp. 48–72). Routledge.

Larsen-Freeman, D., & Anderson, M. (2011). *Techniques and principles in language teaching* (3rd ed.). Oxford University Press.

Lasagabaster, D. (2013). The use of the L1 in CLIL classes: The teachers' perspective. *Latin American Journal of Content & Language Integrated Learning*, 6(2), 1–21. doi:10.5294/laclil.2013.6.2.1

Lasagabaster, D. (2015). Different educational approaches to bi- or multilingualism and their effect on language attitudes. In M. Juan-Garau & J. Salazar-Noguera (Eds.), *Content-based Language Learning in Multilingual Educational Environments. Educational Linguistics* (Vol. 23, pp. 13–30). Springer. doi:10.1007/978-3-319-11496-5_2

Lasagabaster, D. (2015). Multilingual language policy: Is it becoming a misnomer at university level. In S. Dimova, A. K. Hultgren, & C. Jensen (Eds.), *English-medium instruction in higher education in Europe* (pp. 115–136). Mouton de Gruyter. doi:10.1515/9781614515272-007

Lasagabaster, D. (2016). Translanguaging in ESL and content-based teaching: Is it valued? In D. Lasagabaster & A. Doiz (Eds.), *CLIL experiences in secondary and tertiary education: In search of good practices* (pp. 233–258). Peter Lang. doi:10.3726/978-3-0351-0929-0/13

Lasagabaster, D. (2017). Language learning motivation and language attitudes in multilingual Spain from an international perspective. *Modern Language Journal*, 101(3), 583–596. http://www.jstor.org/stable/44981007. doi:10.1111/modl.12414

Compilation of References

Lavender Sky [Username]. (2014, September 23). *Accent challenge – Midwest – Iowa Minnesota Wisconsin USA – Mother & Daughter* [Video]. YouTube. https://www.youtube.com/watch?v=XUrpH0JedO0

Lawrence, G., Ahmed, F., Cole, C., & Johnston, K. P. (2020). Not more technology but more effective technology: Examining the state of technology integration in EAP Programmes. *RELC Journal*, *51*(1), 101–116. doi:10.1177/0033688220907199

Le Pichon, E., Cummins, J., & Vorstman, J. (2021). Using a web-based multilingual platform to support elementary refugee students in mathematics. *Journal of Multilingual and Multicultural Development*, 1–17. doi:10.1080/01434632.2021.1916022

Le Pichon, E., & Kambel, E. R. (2022). The Language friendly school: An inclusive and equitable pedagogy. *Childhood Education*, *98*(1), 42–49. doi:10.1080/00094056.2022.2020538

Le Pichon-Vorstman, E., & Ammouche-Kremers, M. (2022). Education, mobility and higher education: Fostering mutual knowledge through peer feedback. In R., Supheert, G., Cascio & J. D. ten Thije (Eds.) The Riches of Intercultural Communication (pp. 93-110). Brill. doi:10.1163/9789004522855_007

Le Pichon-Vorstman, E., De Swart, H., Ceginskas, V., & Van Den Bergh, H. (2009). Language learning experience in school context and metacognitive awareness of multilingual children. *International Journal of Multilingualism*, *6*(3), 258–280. doi:10.1080/14790710902878692

Leap, W. L. (2005). Finding the centre: claiming gay space in Cape Town, South Africa. In M. van Zyl & M. Steyn (Eds.), *Performing Queer: Shaping Sexualities 1992–2004* (pp. 235–266). Kwela Press.

Leap, W. L. (2010). Globalization and gay language. In N. Coupland (Ed.), *The Handbook of Language and Globalization* (pp. 555–574). Wiley-Blackwell. doi:10.1002/9781444324068.ch25

Leap, W. L. (2015). Queer linguistics as Critical Discourse Analysis. In D. Tannen, H. E. Hamilton, & H. Schiffrin (Eds.), *The Handbook of Discourse Analysis*. Wiley-Blackwell. doi:10.1002/9781118584194.ch31

Lechner, F. J., & Boli, J. (Eds.). (2020). *The globalization reader*. John Wiley & Sons.

Lee, E., & Canagarajah, A. S. (2019a). The connection between transcultural dispositions and translingual practices in academic writing. *Journal of Multicultural Discourses*, *14*(1), 14–28. doi:10.1080/17447143.2018.1501375

Lee, E., & Canagarajah, A. S. (2019b). Beyond native and nonnative: Translingual dispositions for more inclusive teacher identity in language and literacy education. *Journal of Language, Identity, and Education*, *18*(6), 352–363. doi:10.1080/15348458.2019.1674148

Lee, N. (2015). Migrant and ethnic diversity, cities and innovation: Firm effects or city effects? *Journal of Economic Geography*, *15*(4), 769–796. doi:10.1093/jeg/lbu032

Lee, S.-M., & Park, M. (2020). Reconceptualization of the context in language learning with a location-based AR app. *Computer Assisted Language Learning*, *33*(8), 936–959. doi:10.1080/09588221.2019.1602545

Lenoir, Y. (1996). Médiation cognitive et médiation didactique. In C. Raisky & M. Caillot (Eds.), Le didactique au delà des didactiques. Débats autour de concepts fédérateurs (pp. 223–251). Bruxelles: De Boeck Université.

Lentz, C., & Nugent, P. (2000). *Ethnicity in Ghana: A comparative perspective*. doi:10.1007/978-1-349-62337-2

Levinson, S. C. (1988). Putting linguistics on a proper footing: Explorations in Goffman's participation framework. In *Goffman: Exploring the interaction order* (pp. 161–227). Polity Press.

Levy, R. (2021). Social media, news consumption, and polarization: Evidence from a field experiment. *The American Economic Review*, *111*(3), 831–870. doi:10.1257/aer.20191777

Lewis, E. G. (1971). Migration and language in the USSR. *The International Migration Review*, 5(2), 147–179.

Lewis, G., Jones, B., & Baker, C. (2012). Translanguaging: Origins and development from school to street and beyond. *Educational Research and Evaluation*, 18(7), 641–654. doi:10.1080/13803611.2012.718488

Lewis, S. C., Guzman, A. L., & Schmidt, T. R. (2019). Automation, journalism, and human–machine communication: Rethinking roles and relationships of humans and machines in news. *Digital Journalism (Abingdon, England)*, 7(4), 409–427. doi:10.1080/21670811.2019.1577147

Li, M. (2018). The effectiveness of a bilingual education program at a Chinese university: A case study of social science majors. *International Journal of Bilingual Education and Bilingualism*, 21(8), 897–912. doi:10.1080/13670050.2016.1231164

Lin, A. M. Y., & Martin, P. (2005). (Eds.). Decolonisation, globalisation: Language-in-education policy and practice. Clevedon, U.K.: Multilingual Matters.

Lin, A. (2013). Classroom code-switching: Three decades of research. *Applied Linguistics Review*, 4(1), 195–218. doi:10.1515/applirev-2013-0009

Lin, A. (2013). Toward paradigmatic change in TESOL methodologies: Building plurilingual pedagogies from the ground up. *TESOL Quarterly*, 47(3), 521–545. doi:10.1002/tesq.113

Li, S. (2010). The effectiveness of corrective feedback in SLA: A meta-analysis. *Language Learning*, 60(2), 309–365. doi:10.1111/j.1467-9922.2010.00561.x

Li, S. (2015). The association between language aptitude and second language grammar acquisition: A meta-analytic review of five decades of research. *Applied Linguistics*, 36(3), 385–408. doi:10.1093/applin/amu054

Little, D. (2007). Language learner autonomy: Some fundamental considerations revisited. *Innovation in Language Learning and Teaching*, 1(1), 14–29. doi:10.2167/illt040.0

Little, D. (2020). Plurilingualism, learner autonomy and constructive alignment: A vision for university language centres in the 21st century. *Language Learning in Higher Education*, 10(2), 271–286. doi:10.1515/cercles-2020-2019

Little, D. (2022). Language learner autonomy: Rethinking language teaching. *Language Teaching*, 55(1), 64–73. doi:10.1017/S0261444820000488

Little, D. G. (1991). *Learner autonomy: Definitions, issues and problems*. Authentik.

Little, D., Dam, L., & Legenhausen, L. (2017). *The Linguistic, social and educational inclusion of immigrants: A new challenge for language learner autonomy*. Multilingual Matters., doi:10.21832/LITTLE8590

Liu, S., Volcic, Z., & Gallois, C. (2019). *Introducing intercultural communication: Global cultures and contexts* (3rd ed.). SAGE.

Liu, W. (2017). White male power and privilege: The relationship between white supremacy and social class. *Journal of Counseling Psychology*, 64(4), 349–358. doi:10.1037/cou0000227

Llurda, E., & Lasagabaster, D. (2010). Factors affecting teachers" beliefs about interculturalism. *International Journal of Applied Linguistics*, 20(3), 327–353. doi:10.1111/j.1473-4192.2009.00250.x

Loadsman, J. A., & McCulloch, T. J. (2017). Widening the search for suspect data – is the flood of retractions about to become a tsunami? *Anaesthesia*, 72(8), 931–935. doi:10.1111/anae.13962 PMID:28580657

Loewen, S. (2020). *Introduction to instructed second language acquisition* (2nd ed.). Routledge. doi:10.4324/9781315616797

Loewen, S., Crowther, D., Isbell, D. R., Kim, K. M., Maloney, J., Miller, Z. F., & Rawal, H. (2019). Mobile-assisted language learning: A Duolingo case study. *ReCALL*, *31*(3), 293–311. doi:10.1017/S0958344019000065

Loewen, S., Isbell, D. R., & Sporn, Z. (2020). The effectiveness of app-based language instruction for developing receptive linguistic knowledge and oral communicative ability. *Foreign Language Annals*, *53*(2), 209–233. doi:10.1111/flan.12454

Lou, N., & Noels, K. (2019). Promoting growth in foreign and second language education: A research agenda for mindsets in language learning and teaching. *System*, *86*, 102–126. doi:10.1016/j.system.2019.102126

Lu, M. Z., & Horner, B. (2013). Translingual literacy, language difference, and matters of agency. *College English*, *75*(6), 582–607.

Lu, M. Z., & Horner, B. (2016). Introduction: Translingual Work. *College English*, *78*(3), 207–218.

Lundberg, A. (2019). Teachers' beliefs about multilingualism: Findings from Q method research. *Current Issues in Language Planning*, *20*(3), 266–283. doi:10.1080/14664208.2018.1495373

Luque-Agulló, & Almazán-Ruiz, E. (2023). A checklist proposal for assessing the potential of language teaching apps. In Suárez, M.-M., & El-Henawy, W. M. *Optimizing Online English Language Learning and Teaching* (pp. 357-382). Springer International Publishing. doi:10.1007/978-3-031-27825-9

Lyiscott, J. (2014). 3 ways to speak English. *TED talk: Ideas worth spreading.* Retrieved from https://www.ted.com/talks/jamila_lyiscott_3_ways_to_speak_english

Lyster, R., & Saito, K. (2010). Oral feedback in classroom SLA: A meta-analysis. *Studies in Second Language Acquisition*, *32*(2), 265–302. doi:10.1017/S0272263109990520

Macaro, E., Tian, L., & Chu, L. (2020). First and second language use in English medium instruction contexts. *Language Teaching Research*, *24*(3), 382–402. doi:10.1177/1362168818783231

Mackey, A., & Gass, S. M. (Eds.). (2012). *Research methods in second language acquisition: A practical guide.* Blackwell.

Mackey, K., Ayers, C. K., Kondo, K. K., Saha, S., Advani, S. M., Young, S., Spencer, H., Rusek, M., Anderson, J., Veazie, S., Smith, M., & Kansagara, D. (2021, March). Racial and ethnic disparities in COVID-19-related infections, hospitalizations, and deaths: A systematic review. *Annals of Internal Medicine*, *174*(3), 362–373. doi:10.7326/M20-6306 PMID:33253040

MacSwan, J. (2017). A Multilingual perspective on translanguaging. *American Educational Research Journal*, *54*(1), 167–201. doi:10.3102/0002831216683935

Magos, K., & Margaroni, M. (2018). The importance of educating refugees. [Editorial]. *Global Education Review*, *5*(4), 1–6.

Magos, K., & Simopoulos, G. (2020). Teaching L2 for students with a refugee/migrant background in Greece: Teachers' perceptions about reception, integration and multicultural identities. *Global Education Review*, *7*(4), 59–73.

Maher, F. A., & Tetreault, M. A. T. (2001). *The feminist classroom: Dynamics of gender, race, and privilege.* Rowman and Littlefield Publishers.

Maine Video Canal [Username]. (2021, November 9). *How to talk like a Maine-ah, 9 great words to mispronounce* [Video]. YouTube. https://www.youtube.com/watch?v=p3L5czFvyCc

Maligkoudi, C., Tolakidou, P., & Chiona, S. (2018). "It is not bilingualism. There is no communication". Examining Greek teachers' views towards refugee children's bilingualism: A case study. *Dialogoi, Theory &. Praxis Educativa (Santa Rosa)*, *4*, 95–107.

Malik, L. (1994). *Sociolinguistics: A study of code-switching*. Anmol Publications.

Mallinson, C., Charity Hudley, A., Strickling, L. R., & Figa, M. (2011). A conceptual framework for promoting linguistic and educational change. *Language and Linguistics Compass, 5*(7), 441–453. doi:10.1111/j.1749-818X.2011.00289.x

Malmgren, S. (2011). Gentrification: Stop blaming foreigners! *Exberliner*. Retrieved on August 4, 2023 from https://www.exberliner.com/berlin/gentrification/

Marcel, F. (2020). *Mobile mixed reality technologies for language teaching and learning*. [Unpublished doctoral dissertation, University of Toronto]. http://hdl.handle.net/1807/103360

Marshall, S., & Moore, D. (2013). 2B or not 2B plurilingual: Navigating languages literacies, and plurilingual competence in postsecondary education in Canada. *TESOL Quarterly, 47*(3), 472–499. doi:10.1002/tesq.111

Marshall, S., & Moore, D. (2018). Plurilingualism amid the panoply of lingualisms: Addressing critiques and misconceptions in education. *International Journal of Multilingualism, 15*(1), 19–34. doi:10.1080/14790718.2016.1253699

Marshall, S., Moore, D., James, C. L., Ning, X., & Dos Santos, P. (2019). Plurilingual students' practices in a Canadian university: Chinese language, academic English, and discursive ambivalence. *TESL Canada Journal, 36*(1), 1–20. doi:10.18806/tesl.v36i1.1300

Martin, I. (2007). Some remarks on post-1990 English language teaching policy in Cuba, language policies and TESOL: perspectives from practice. *TESOL Quarterly, 41*(3), 551–557. doi:10.1002/j.1545-7249.2007.tb00085.x

Mary, L., & Young, A. (2017). Engaging with emergent bilinguals and their families in the pre-primary classroom to foster well-being, learning and inclusion. *Language and Intercultural Communication, 17*(4), 455–473. doi:10.1080/14708477.2017.1368147

Mary, L., & Young, A. (2020). Teachers' beliefs and attitudes towards home languages maintenance and their effects. In A. C. Schalley & S. A. Eisenchlas (Eds.), *Handbook of Home Language Maintenance and Development: Social and Affective Factors* (pp. 444–463). De Gruyter Mouton. doi:10.1515/9781501510175-022

Massad, J. (2002). Re-Orienting desire: The gay international and the Arab world. *Public Culture, 14*(2), 361–385. doi:10.1215/08992363-14-2-361

Matras, Y. (2009). *Language contact*. Cambridge University Press. doi:10.1017/CBO9780511809873

Matsuda, A. (2020). World Englishes and pedagogy. In C. L. Nelson, Z. G. Proshina, & D. R. Davis (Eds.), *The handbook of World Englishes* (2nd ed.) (pp. 686–702). John Wiley & Sons, Inc.

Mattheoudakis, M., Chatzidaki, A., & Maligkoudi, C., (2017). Greek teachers' views on linguistic and cultural diversity. *Selected papers on theoretical and applied linguistics, 22*, 358-371.

Mazak, C. M., & Herbas-Donoso, C. (2014). Translanguaging practices at a bilingual university: A case study of a science classroom. *International Journal of Bilingual Education and Bilingualism, 18*(6), 1–17.

McAllister, G., & Irvine, J. J. (2002). The role of empathy in teaching culturally diverse students: A qualitative study of teachers' beliefs. *Journal of Teacher Education, 53*(5), 433–443. doi:10.1177/002248702237397

McCarty, T. L. (1980). Language use by Yavapai-Apache students with recommendations for curriculum design. *Journal of American Indian Education, 20*(1), 1–9.

McCluney, C. L., Durkee, M. I., Smith, R. E. II, Robotham, K. J., & Lee, S. S. L. (2021). To be, or not to be… Black: The effects of racial code-switching on perceived professionalism in the workplace. *Journal of Experimental Social Psychology, 97*, 104199. doi:10.1016/j.jesp.2021.104199

Compilation of References

McDonald, T., & Worswick, C. (1997). Unemployment incidence of immigrant men in Canada. *Canadian Public Policy*, *23*(4), 353. doi:10.2307/3552069

Mckay, D. (2002). *Filipina identities: Geographies of social integration/exclusion in the Canadian Metropolis* (Working Paper Series, No. 02-18). Vancouver: Center of Excellence, Research on Immigration in the Metropolis.

Meier, G. S. (2017). The multilingual turn as a critical movement in education: Assumptions, challenges and a need for reflection. *Applied Linguistics Review*, *8*(1), 131–161. doi:10.1515/applirev-2016-2010

Meisel, J. M. (Ed.). (1990). *Two first languages: Early grammatical development in bilingual children* (Vol. 10). Walter de Gruyter. doi:10.1515/9783110846065

Mendoza, M. (2011). Neukölln Nasties. Foreigners Feel Accused in Berlin Gentrification Row. *Spiegel International*. https://www.spiegel.de/international/germany/neukoelln-nasties-foreigners-feel-accused-in-berlin-gentrification-row-a-750297.html

Mendoza-Fierro, L. E. (2020). *The Digital Literacy Practices of Transfronterizx ESOL College Students: Los De ESOL* [Doctoral dissertation, The University of Texas at El Paso].

Mensah, R. O., Quansah, C., Oteng, B., & Nii Akai Nettey, J. (2023). Assessing the effect of information and communication technology usage on high school student's academic performance in a developing country. *Cogent Education*, *10*(1), 2188809. doi:10.1080/2331186X.2023.2188809

Merriam, S. B. (1998). *Case study research in education: A qualitative approach*. Jossey-Bass.

Merriam, S. B. (2009). *Qualitative research: A guide to design and implementation*. Jossey-Bass.

Meyer, J. P., & Herscovitch, L. (2001). Commitment in the workplace: Toward a general model. *Human Resource Management Review*, *1*, 61–89. doi:10.1016/1053-4822(91)90011-Z

Meyer, O., & Coyle, D. (2017). Pluriliteracies teaching for learning: Conceptualizing progression for deeper learning in literacies development. *European Journal of Applied Linguistics*, *5*(2), 199–222. doi:10.1515/eujal-2017-0006

Migge, B. (2007). Code-switching and social identities in the Eastern Maroon Community of Suriname and French Guiana. *Journal of Sociolinguistics*, *11*(1), 53–72. doi:10.1111/j.1467-9841.2007.00310.x

Miles, M. B., & Huberman, A. M. (1994). *Qualitative data analysis*. Sage.

Miles, M. B., Huberman, A. M., & Saldaña, J. (2014). *Qualitative data analysis: A methods sourcebook* (3rd ed.). SAGE.

Milroy, J. (2001). Language ideologies and the consequences of standardization. *Journal of Sociolinguistics*, *5*(4), 530–555. doi:10.1111/1467-9481.00163

Milroy, J., & Milroy, L. (2012). *Authority in language: Investigating standard English*. Routledge. doi:10.4324/9780203124666

Milroy, L., & Muysken, P. (1995). Introduction: Code-switching and bilingualism research. In L. Milroy & P. Muysken (Eds.), *One speaker two languages: Cross-disciplinary perspectives on code-switching* (pp. 1–14). Cambridge University Press. doi:10.1017/CBO9780511620867.001

Ministerio de Educación Nacional de Colombia. (2014). *Colombia, Very Well!: Programa Nacional de Inglés, July, 2015 – 2025*. Colombia Aprende. http://www.colombiaaprende.edu.co/html/micrositios/1752/articles-343287_recurso_1.pdf

Ministerio de Educación Perú. (2016). *Inglés, puertas al mundo*. Ministry of Education, Peru. http://www.minedu.gob.pe/inglés-puertas-al-mundo/pdf/infografia.pdf.

Ministry of Migration Policy. (2019). *National strategy for inclusion*. Ministry of Migration Policy.

Minning, H. (2004). Qwir-English code-mixing in Germany: constructing a rainbow of identities. In T. Boellstorff & W. Leap (Eds.), *Speaking in Queer Tongues. Globalization and Gay Language* (pp. 46–71). University of Illinois Press.

Mitchell, C. B., & Vidal, K. E. (2001). Weighing the ways of the flow: Twentieth century language instruction. *Modern Language Journal*, *85*(1), 26–38. doi:10.1111/0026-7902.00095

Mockler, N. (2011). Beyond "what works": Understanding teacher identity as a practical and political tool. *Teachers and Teaching*, *17*(5), 517–528. doi:10.1080/13540602.2011.602059

Mogi, K. (2008). *Nou to souzousei* [Brain and creativity]. PHP.

Mogli, M., Kalbeni, S., & Stergiou, L. (2019). "The teacher is not a magician": Teacher training in Greek reception facilities for refugee education. *International e-Journal of Educational Studies. 4,* 42-55.

Molina, S. G. (2013). *Linguistics for teaching English in multilingual classrooms*. CreateSpace Independent Publishing Platform.

Montes-Alcalá, C. (2000). Attitudes towards oral and written code-switching in Spanish-English bilingual youth. In A. Roca (Ed.), *Research on Spanish in the United States: Linguistic issues and challenges* (pp. 218–227). Cascadilla Press.

Moodie, I., & Feryok, A. (2015). Beyond cognition to commitment: English language teaching in South Korean primary schools. *Modern Language Journal*, *99*(3), 450–469. http://www.jstor.org.jpllnet.sfsu.edu/stable/43651977. doi:10.1111/modl.12238

Moons, C. (2010). *Kindergarten teachers speak: Working with language diversity in the classroom*. MA thesis. McGill University

Moore-Jones, P. J. (2015). Linguistic imposition: The policies and perils of English as a medium of instruction in the United Arab Emirates. [JELTAL]. *Journal of ELT and Applied Linguistics*, *3*(1), 63–72.

Moorhouse, B. L., & Wong, K. M. (2021). Blending asynchronous and synchronous digital technologies and instructional approaches to facilitate remote learning. *Journal of Computers in Education*, *9*(1), 51–70. doi:10.100740692-021-00195-8

Moran, L. (2019). *Belonging and becoming in a multicultural world: Refugee youth and the pursuit of identity*. Rutgers University Press.

Morrison, B. (2008). The role of the self-access centre in the tertiary language learning process. *System*, *36*(2), 123–140. doi:10.1016/j.system.2007.10.004

Moschkovich, J. N. (1999a, March). Supporting the participation of English language learners in mathematical discussions. *For the Learning of Mathematics*, *19*(1), 11–19.

Murray, G. (2018). Self-access environments as self-enriching complex dynamic ecosocial systems. *Studies in Self-Access Learning Journal*, *9*(2), 102–115. doi:10.37237/090204

Myers-Scotton, C. (1995). *Social motivations for code-switching: Evidence from Africa*. Oxford University Press.

Myers-Scotton, C. (2002). *Contact linguistics. Bilingual encounters and grammatical outcomes*. Oxford University Press. doi:10.1093/acprof:oso/9780198299530.001.0001

Myers-Scotton, C. (2006). *Multiple voices. An introduction to bilingualism*. Blackwell Publishers.

Myers-Scotton, C. (Ed.). (1998). *Codes and consequences: Choosing linguistic varieties*. Oxford University Press.

Nakeyar, C., Esses, V., & Reid, G. J. (2018). The psychosocial needs of refugee children and youth and best practices for filling these needs: A systematic review. *Clinical Child Psychology and Psychiatry*, *23*(2), 186–208. doi:10.1177/1359104517742188 PMID:29207880

Napoli, P. M. (2018). What if more speech is no longer the solution: First Amendment theory meets fake news and the filter bubble. *Federal Communications Law Journal*, *70*, 55–104.

Narváez, F. R., Vallejo, D. F., Morillo, P. A., & Proaño, J. R. (2020). Corrective feedback through mobile apps for English learning: A review. In Smart Technologies, Systems and Applications (Vol. 1154, pp. 229–242). Springer International Publishing AG. doi:10.1007/978-3-030-46785-2_19

National Center for Education Statistics. (2022). Racial/ethnic enrollment in public schools. *The condition of education*. NCES. https://nces.ed.gov/programs/coe/pdf/2022/cge_508.pdf

Navarro, F. (2023). Afterword. Translingual lives and writing pedagogy: Acculturation, enculturation, and emancipation. In J. Hall, & B. Horner, (Eds.), Toward a transnational university: WAC/WID across Borders of language, nation, and discipline, 261-278. The WAC Clearinghouse; University Press of Colorado.

Ngunjiri, F. W., Hernandez, K.-A. C., & Chang, H. (2010). Living autoethnography: Connecting life and research. *Journal of Research Practice*, *6*(1), E1.

NHK. (2022, March 17). *Kurozu appu gendai [A close-up view of today]*. NHK. https://www.nhk.or.jp/gendai/articles/4646/

Noddings, N. (2013). *Caring: A relational approach to ethics and moral education*. University of California Press.

Norris, J. M., & Ortega, L. (2000). Effectiveness of L2 instruction: A research synthesis and quantitative meta-analysis. *Language Learning*, *50*(3), 417–528. doi:10.1111/0023-8333.00136

North, B. (1992). European Language Portfolio: Some options for a working approach to design scales for proficiency. In Council of Europe *Transparency and coherence in language learning in Europe: Objectives, assessment and certification*. (pp. 158–174). Strasbourg: Council for Cultural Co-operation.

North, B. (2023). The CEFR companion volume and the action-oriented approach. *Italiano LinguaDue*, 1-23.

North, B., & Piccardo, E. (2016). Developing illustrative descriptors of aspects of mediation for the Common European Framework of Reference (CEFR): A Council of Europe project. *Language Teaching*, *49*(3), 455–459. doi:10.1017/S0261444816000100

Norton Peirce, B. (1995). Social identity, investment, and language learning. *TESOL Quarterly*, *29*(1), 9–31. doi:10.2307/3587803

Norton, B. (2006). Identity: Second language. Encyclopedia of Language & Linguistics, 5, 502–508.

Norton, B. (2000). *Identity and language learning: Gender, ethnicity, and educational change*. Longman.

O'Grady, W., Archibald, J., Aronoff, M., & Rees-Miller, J. (2017). *Contemporary linguistics: An introduction* (7th ed.). Bedford/St. Martin's.

Ochiai, Y. (2015). *Mahoo no seiki [Century of Magic]*. Planets.

Ochiai, Y. (2018). *Dejitaru neicha: seitaikei wo nasu hanshinkashita keisanki ni yoru wabi to sabi [Digital nature: wabi and sabi of ecological digital technology]*. Planets.

Ochs, E. (1992). Indexing gender. In A. Duranti & C. Goodwin (Eds.), *Rethinking Context: Language as an Interactive Phenomenon* (pp. 335–358). Cambridge University Press.

OECD. (2018). *The resilience of students with an immigrant background: factors that shape well-Being*. OECD. https://www.oecd-ilibrary.org/docserver/9789264292093en.pdf?expires=1556025290&id=id&accname=guest&checksum=13625606919D4245C468D06156AEB392

OECD. (2022). International and foreign student mobility in tertiary education (2015 and 2020): International or foreign student enrolment as a percentage of total tertiary enrolment. In *Education at a Glance 2022: OECD Indicators*. OECD Publishing. doi:10.1787/b6a69272-

Ohta, A. S. (2017). Sociocultural theory and second/foreign language education. In N. Van Deusen-Scholl & S. May (Eds.), *Second and foreign language education, encyclopedia of language and education* (Vol. 4, pp. 57–68). Springer. doi:10.1007/978-3-319-02246-8_6

Okafor, L. E., Khalid, U., & Burzynska, K. (2022). The effect of migration on international tourism flows: The role of linguistic networks and common languages. *Journal of Travel Research*, *61*(4), 818–836. doi:10.1177/00472875211008250

Olatunji, M. (2007). Yabis: A phenomenon in the contemporary Nigerian music. *Africology*, *1*(9), 26–46.

Olivar-Tost, G., Valencia-Calvo, J., & Castrillón-Gómez, J. A. (2020). Towards decision-making for the assessment and prioritization of green projects: An integration between system dynamics and participatory modeling. *Sustainability (Basel)*, *12*(24), 10689. doi:10.3390u122410689

Olwig, K. F. (2013). 'Integration': Migrants and refugees between Scandinavian welfare societies and family relations. In O. Abingdon (Ed.), Migration, family and the welfare state (pp. 1-16). Routledge.

ONeill, R, & Russell, A. (2019). Stop! Grammar time: University students' perceptions of the automated feedback program Grammarly. Australasian Journal of Educational Technology, 35(1). doi:10.14742/ajet.3795

Ontario Human Rights Commission. (2013). *Policy on removing the Canadian experience barrier*. OHRC. http://www.ohrc.on.ca

Open A.I. (2022). Introducing ChatGPT. *OpenAI*. https://openai.com/blog/chatgpt

Open A.I. (2023). ChatGPT. *OpenAI*. https://openai.com/blog/chatgpt/

Orellana, M. F. (2009). *Translating childhoods: Immigrant youth, language, and culture*. Rutgers University Press.

Osoba, J. B. (2014). The use of Nigerian Pidgin in media adverts. *International Journal of English Linguistics*, *4*(2), 26–37. doi:10.5539/ijel.v4n2p26

Otheguy, R., Otheguy, G., & Reid, W. (2015). Clarifying translanguaging and deconstructing named languages: A perspective from linguistics. *Applied Linguistics Review*, *6*(3), 281–307. doi:10.1515/applirev-2015-0014

Owu-Ewie, C. (2017). Language, education and linguistic human rights in Ghana. *Legon Journal of the Humanities*, *28*(2), 151–172.

Oxford, R. (1990). *Language learning strategies: What every teacher should know*. Newbury House.

Oxford, R. L., & Shearin, J. (1994). Language learning motivation: Expanding the theoretical framework. *Modern Language Journal*, *78*(1), 12–28. doi:10.1111/j.1540-4781.1994.tb02011.x

Oyebode, O. O., & Okesola, S. O. (2020). #Take responsibility: Non-verbal modes as discursive strategies in managing COVID-19 public health crisis. *Language and Semiotic Studies*, *6*(4), 21–45. doi:10.1515/lass-2020-060401

Oyetade, S. O. (2003). Language planning in a multi-ethnic state: The majority-minority dichotomy in Nigeria. *Nordic Journal of African Studies*, *12*(1), 105–117.

Özdemir-Yılmazer, M. (2022). Direct access to English-medium higher education in Turkey: Variations in entry language scores. *Dil Eğitimi ve Araştırmaları Dergisi, 8*(2), 325–345. doi:10.31464/jlere.1105651

Pack, G., Golin, C. E., Hill, L. M., Carda-Auten, J., Wallace, D. D., Cherkur, S., Farel, C. E., Rosen, E. P., Gandhi, M., Asher Prince, H. M., & Kashuba, A. D. M. (2019). Patient and clinician perspectives on optimizing graphical displays of longitudinal medication adherence data. *Patient Education and Counseling, 102*(6), 1090–1097. doi:10.1016/j.pec.2018.12.029 PMID:30626550

Padilla, A. M., & Borjian, A. (2009). Learning and teaching foreign languages (pp. 541-544). Psychology of Classroom Learning: An Encyclopedia. Macmillan Reference USA.

Palmer, D. K., Martínez, R. A., Mateus, S. G., & Henderson, K. (2014). Reframing the debate on language separation: Toward a vision for translanguaging pedagogies in the dual language classroom. *Modern Language Journal, 98*(3), 757–772. doi:10.1111/j.1540-4781.2014.12121.x

Pariser, E. (2011). *The filter bubble: What the Internet is hiding from you*. Penguin UK.

Park, M. S. (2013). Code-switching and translanguaging: Potential functions in multilingual classrooms. Working Papers in *TESOL & Applied Linguistics, 13*(2), 50–52.

Parker, C., Scott, S., & Geddes, A. (2019). Snowball sampling. SAGE Research Methods Foundations., 10.4135.

Parsazadeh, N., Cheng, P.-Y., Wu, T.-T., & Huang, Y.-M. (2021). Integrating computational thinking concept into digital storytelling to improve learners' motivation and performance. *Journal of Educational Computing Research, 59*(3), 470–495. doi:10.1177/0735633120967315

Pauwels, A. (2010). *Immigrant dialects and language maintenance in Australia: The case of the Limburg and Swabian dialects* (Vol. 2). Walter de Gruyter.

Pauwels, A. (2014). The teaching of languages at university in the context of super-diversity. *International Journal of Multilingualism, 11*(3), 307–319. doi:10.1080/14790718.2014.921177

Pavlenko, A., & Norton, B. (2007). Imagined communities, identity, and English language learning. In J. Cummins & C. Davison (Eds.), *International Handbook of English Language Teaching* (pp. 669–680). Springer. doi:10.1007/978-0-387-46301-8_43

Pehl, T. & Dresing, T. (2015b). *f4analyse*. Audio Transkripition. https://www.audiotranskription.de

PehlT.DresingT. (2015a). *f4transkript*. Audio Transkription. https://www.audiotranskription.de

Pendakur, K., & Pendakur, R. (2012). Colour by numbers: Minority earnings in Canada 1996–2006. *Journal of International Migration and Integration, 12*(3), 305–329.

Penning de Vries, B. W., Cucchiarini, C., Strik, H., & van Hout, R. (2020). Spoken grammar practice in CALL: The effect of corrective feedback and education level in adult L2 learning. *Language Teaching Research, 24*(5), 714–735. doi:10.1177/1362168818819027

Pennington, M. C., & Richards, J. C. (2016). Teacher identity in language teaching: Integrating personal, contextual, and professional factors. *RELC Journal, 47*(1), 5–23. doi:10.1177/0033688216631219

Pennycook, A. (2001). *Critical applied linguistics: A critical introduction*. Lawrence Erlbaum Associates, Inc. doi:10.4324/9781410600790

Pennycook, A. (2021). *Critical applied linguistics: A critical re-introduction*. Routledge. doi:10.4324/9781003090571

Pennycook, G., Cannon, T. D., & Rand, D. G. (2018). Prior exposure increases perceived accuracy of fake news. *Journal of Experimental Psychology. General*, *147*(12), 1865–1880. doi:10.1037/xge0000465 PMID:30247057

Pérez, L. (1982). The imperial design: Politics and pedagogy in occupied Cuba, 1899- 1902. Cuban Studies/Estudios Cubanos, 12, (pp.1-18).

Perinelli, M. (2019). Triggerwarnung! Critical Whiteness und das Ende antirassistischer Bewegung. In E. Berendsen, S.-N. Cheema, & M. Mendel (Eds.), *Trigger Warnung. Identitätspolitik zwischen Abwehr, Abschottung und Allianzen* (pp. 77–90). Verbrecherverlag.

Peters, C. (2011). *The bridging education and licensure of international medical doctors in Ontario: A call for commitment, consistency, and transparency.* [Dissertation, Ontario Institute for Studies in Education of the University of Toronto, Canada].

Peters, M. A. (2016). Language attitudes and identity construction. A case study among two L2 attritors. In M. Fernández-Villanueva & K. Jungbluth (Eds.), *Beyond Language Boundaries. Multimodal Use in Multilingual Contexts* (pp. 179–199). De Gruyter. doi:10.1515/9783110458817-011

Pfaff, C. W. (2000). Development and use of et- and yap- by Turkish/German bilingual children. *Studies on Turkish and Turkic languages, Proceedings of the Ninth International Conference on Turkish Linguistics*. CUNY.

Phillipson, R. (1992). *Linguistic imperialism*. Oxford University Press.

Piccardo, E. (2018). Plurilingualism: Vision, conceptualization, and practices. In P. Trifonas, & T., Aravossitas, (Eds.) Springer International Handbooks of Education. Handbook of Research and Practice in Heritage Language Education (pp. 207-226). Springer International Publishing. doi:10.1007/978-3-319-44694-3_47

Piccardo, E. (2010). From communicative to action-oriented: New perspectives for a new millennium. *CONTACT TESL Ontario*, *36*(2), 20–35.

Piccardo, E., & North, B. (2019). *The action-oriented approach: A dynamic vision of language education* (Vol. 72). Multilingual matters.

Piccardo, E., & North, B. (2019). *The action-oriented approach: a dynamic vision of language education*. Multilingual Matters.

Picot, G., & Hou, F. (2012). How successful are second-generation visible minority groups in the Canadian labour market? *Canadian Diversity*, *9*(1), 17–21.

Pieterse, J. N. (2003). Social capital and migration: Beyond ethnic economies. *Ethnicities*, *3*(1), 29–58. doi:10.1177/1468796803003001785

Piller, I. (2016). *Linguistic diversity and social justice*. Oxford University Press. doi:10.1093/acprof:oso/9780199937240.001.0001

Pinter, A. (2017). *Teaching young language learners* (2nd ed.). Oxford University Press.

Pintrich, P. (2003). A motivational science perspective on the role of student motivation in learning and teaching contexts. *Journal of Educational Psychology*, *95*(4), 667–686. doi:10.1037/0022-0663.95.4.667

Pitkänen-Huhta, A. (2021). Multilingualism in Language Education: Examining the Outcomes in the Context of Finland. In P. Juvonen & M. Källkvist (Eds.) Pedagogical Translanguaging: heoretical, Methodological and Empirical Perspectives (pp. 226-245). Multilingual Matters. https://doi.org/10.21832/9781788927383-014

Compilation of References

Planas, N., Morgan, C., & Schütte, M. (2018). Mathematics education and language: Lessons and directions from two decades of research. In T. Dreyfus, M. Artigue, D. Potari, S. Prediger, & K. Ruthven (Eds.), *Developing research in mathematics education. Twenty years of communication, cooperation and collaboration in Europe* (pp. 196–210). Routledge. doi:10.4324/9781315113562-15

Plano Clark, V. L., & Creswell, J. W. (2010). *Understanding research: A consumer's guide*. Pearson.

Plastina, A. F. (2003). CALL-ing EAP Skills. *Teaching English with Technology, 3*(3), 16–30.

Plonsky, L., & Ziegler, N. (2016). The CALL–SLA interface: Insights from a second-order synthesis. *Language Learning & Technology, 2*(20), 17–37.

Poehner, M. E., & Swain, M. (2017). L2 development as cognitive-emotive process. *Language and Sociocultural Theory, 3*(2), 219–241. doi:10.1558/lst.v3i2.32922

Pollock, K. (2010). Marginalization and the occasional teacher workforce in Ontario: The case of Internationally Educated Teachers (IETs). *Canadian Journal of Educational Administration and Policy, 100*. http://www.umanitoba.ca/publications/cjeap/ pdf_files/pollock-iet.pdf

Poplack, S. (1980). Sometimes I'll start a sentence in Spanish y termino en Espanol?: Toward a typology of code-switching. *Linguistics, 18*(7-8), 581–618. doi:10.1515/ling.1980.18.7-8.581

Prajapati, R., & Gupta, S. (2023). Engaging students: The assessment of professional identity and emotional intelligence of language teachers. In S. Karpava (Ed.), *Handbook of research on language teacher identity* (pp. 116–130). IGI Global. doi:10.4018/978-1-6684-7275-0.ch007

Pratt, M. L. (1991). Arts of the contact zone. *Profession, 91*, 33–40.

Prentice, F. M., & Kinden, C. E. (2018). Paraphrasing tools, language translation tools and plagiarism: An exploratory study. *International Journal for Educational Integrity, 14*(1), 1–16. doi:10.100740979-018-0036-7

Provencher, D. (2017). *Queer Maghrebi French*. Liverpool University Press.

Quinio, A. (2015). *From Policy to Reality: A Study of Factors Influencing the Employment Trajectories of Internationally Educated Professionals* [Doctoral dissertation, University of Toronto]. TSpace Repository Database. https://hdl.handle.net/1807/71591

Quintos, B., Civil, M., & Torres, O. (2001). Mathematics teaching with a vision of social justice: Using the lens of communities of practice. In K. Téllez, J. N. Moschkovich, & M. Civil (Eds.), *Latinos/as and mathematics education: Research on learning and teaching in classrooms and communities* (pp. 233–258). Information Age Pub.

Raimes, A. (1983). Tradition and revolution in ESL teaching. *TESOL Quarterly, 17*(4), 535–552. doi:10.2307/3586612

Reagan, T., & Schreffler, S. (2005). Higher education language policy and the challenge of linguistic imperialism: A Turkish case study. In A. Lin & P. Martin (Eds.), *Decolonisation, globalisation: Language-in-education policy and practice* (pp. 115–130). Multilingual Matters. doi:10.21832/9781853598265-009

Reager, S. E. (2022, November 30). Voice cloning: A breakthrough with boundless potential. *Speech Technology*. https://www.speechtechmag.com/Articles/ReadArticle.aspx?ArticleID=156129

Reaser, J. (2014). Dialects and education in Appalachia. In A. D. Clark & N. M. Hayward (Eds.), *Talking Appalachian: Voice, identity, and community* (pp. 94–109). The University Press of Kentucky.

Reaser, J., Adger, C. T., Wolfram, W., & Christian, D. (2017). Appendix: An inventory of distinguishing dialect features. In *Dialects at school: Educating linguistically diverse students* (pp. 268–292). Routledge. doi:10.4324/9781315772622

Redinger, D. (2010). *Language attitudes and code-switching behaviour in a multilingual educational context: The case of Luxembourg*. [Doctoral dissertation, University of York].

Reeves, J. (2018). Teacher Identity. Framing the Issue. In J. I. Liontas (Ed.), *The TESOL Encyclopedia of English Language Teaching* (pp. 1–7). Wiley-Blackwell. doi:10.1002/9781118784235.eelt0268

ReganB. P. (2017). *The effect of dialect contact and social identity on fricative demerger*. University of Texas at Austin. https://doi.org/ doi:10.15781/t2rf5kx7s

Reinders, H., & Pegrum, M. (2015). Supporting language learning on the move: An evaluative framework for mobile language learning resources. In B. Tomlinson (Ed.), *SLA research and materials development for language learning* (pp. 116–141). Taylor & Francis. https://hdl.handle.net/10652/2991

Reis, D. S. (2011). Non-native English-speaking teachers (NNESTs) and professional legitimacy: A sociocultural theoretical perspective on identity transformation. *International Journal of the Sociology of Language*, *208*(208), 139–160. doi:10.1515/ijsl.2011.016

Reitz, J. G. (2001). Immigrant success in the knowledge economy: Institutional change and the immigrant experience in Canada, 1970-1995. *The Journal of Social Issues*, *57*(3), 579–613. doi:10.1111/0022-4537.00230

Reitz, J. G. (2007a). Immigrant employment success in Canada, Part I: Individual and contextual causes. *The International Migration Review*, *8*(1), 37–62. doi:10.100712134-007-0002-3

Rettberg, J. W. (2022, December 6). ChatGPT is multilingual but monocultural, and it's learning your values. *jill/txt*. https://jilltxt.net/right-now-chatgpt-is-multilingual-but-monocultural-but-its-learning-your-values/

Reynolds, B. L., & Kao, C.-W. (2021). The effects of digital game-based instruction, teacher instruction, and direct focused written corrective feedback on the grammatical accuracy of English articles. *Computer Assisted Language Learning*, *34*(4), 462–482. doi:10.1080/09588221.2019.1617747

Rhodes, S. C. (2022). Filter bubbles, echo chambers, and fake news: How social media conditions individuals to be less critical of political misinformation. *Political Communication*, *39*(1), 1–22. doi:10.1080/10584609.2021.1910887

Richards, J. C., & Rodgers, T. S. (2014). *Approaches and methods in language teaching* (3rd ed.). Cambridge University Press. doi:10.1017/9781009024532

Richards, L. (2006). Thinking research. *Sage (Atlanta, Ga.)*.

Rickford, J. R., & King, S. (2016). Language and linguistics on trial: Hearing Rachel Jeantel (and other vernacular speakers) in the courtroom and beyond. *Language*, *92*(4), 948–988. doi:10.1353/lan.2016.0078

Rienties, B., McFarlane, R., Nguyen, Q., Lewis, T., & Toetenel, L. (2018). Analytics in Online and Offline Language Learning Environments: The Role of Learning Design to Understand Student Online Engagement. *Computer Assisted Language Learning*, *31*(3), 273–293. doi:10.1080/09588221.2017.1401548

Robinson, P. (2001). Task complexity, cognitive resources, and syllabus design: A triadic framework for examining task influences on SLA. In P. Robinson (Ed.), *Cognition and Second Language Instruction* (pp. 287–318). Cambridge University Press. doi:10.1017/CBO9781139524780.012

Rodriguez, R. M. (2010). *Migrants for export: How the Philippine state broker labor to the world*. University of Minnesota. doi:10.5749/minnesota/9780816665273.001.0001

Rogerson, A. M. (2020). The use and misuse of online paraphrasing, editing and translation software. In T. Bretag (Ed.), *A Research Agenda for Academic Integrity* (pp. 163–174). Edward Elgar Publishing. doi:10.4337/9781789903775.00019

Compilation of References

Rogerson, A. M., & McCarthy, G. (2017). Using Internet based paraphrasing tools: Original work, patchwriting or facilitated plagiarism? *International Journal for Educational Integrity*, *13*(2), 2. doi:10.100740979-016-0013-y

Romani, L., Holck, L., & Risberg, A. (2019). Benevolent discrimination: Explaining how human resources professionals can be blind to the harm of diversity initiatives. *Organization*, *26*(3), 371–390. doi:10.1177/1350508418812585

Rooke, A. (2010). Queer in the field: On emotions, temporality, and performativity in ethnography. In K. Browne & C. J. Nash (Eds.), *Queer Methods and Methodologies. Intersecting Queer Theories and Social Science Research* (pp. 25–41). Ashgate. doi:10.1080/10894160802695338

Roosan, C., Chok, J., Karim, M., Law, A. V., Baskys, A., Hwang, A., & Roosan, M. R. (2020). Artificial intelligence–powered smartphone app to facilitate medication adherence: Protocol for a human factors design study. *JMIR Research Protocols*, *9*(11), e21659–e21659. doi:10.2196/21659 PMID:33164898

Rubin, J. (1975). What the good language learner can teach us. *TESOL Quarterly*, *9*(1), 41–51. doi:10.2307/3586011

Rudwick, S., Sijadu, Z., & Turner, I. (2021). Politics of language in COVID-19: Multilingual perspectives from South Africa. *Politikon: South African Journal of Political Studies*, *48*(2), 2, 242–259. doi:10.1080/02589346.2021.1917206

Ruiz, R. (1984). Orientations in language planning. *Bilingual Research Journal*, *8*(2), 15–34.

Ruíz, R. (1984). Orientations in language planning. NABE. *The Journal for the National Association for Bilingual Education*, *8*(2), 15–34. doi:10.1080/08855072.1984.10668464

Rumbaut, R. G. (2004). Ages, life stages, and generational cohorts: Decomposing the immigrant first and second generations in the United States. *The International Migration Review*, *38*(3), 1160–1205. doi:10.1111/j.1747-7379.2004.tb00232.x

Ruusuvuori, J. (2012). *Emotion, affect and conversation. The handbook of conversation analysis*. Wiley-Blackwell.

Ryan, R. M., & Deci, E. L. (2000). When rewards compete with nature: The undermining of intrinsic motivation and self-regulation. In C. Sansone & J. M. Harackiewicz (Eds.), *Intrinsic and extrinsic motivation: The search for optimal motivation and performance* (pp. 13–55). Academic Press. doi:10.1016/B978-012619070-0/50024-6

Ryle, G. (2000). Courses of action or the uncatchableness of mental acts. *Philosophy (London, England)*, *75*(3), 331–344. doi:10.1017/S0031819100000437

s_he (2010). Performing the Gap. Queere Gestalten und geschlechtliche Aneignung. *arranca! 28*(7).

Sabates-Wheeler, R., Sabates, R., & Castaldo, A. (2008). Tackling poverty-migration linkages: Evidence from Ghana and Egypt. *Social Indicators Research*, *87*(2), 307–328. doi:10.100711205-007-9154-y

Sadeghi, K. (2023). *Technology-assisted language assessment in diverse contexts : lessons from the transition to online testing during COVID-19* (K. Sadeghi, Ed.). Routledge.

Sahan, K., & Rose, H. (2021). Translanguaging or code-switching? Re-examining the functions of language in EMI classrooms. *Multilingual perspectives from Europe and beyond on language policy and practice*, 45-62.

Sahan, K. (2020). ELF interactions in English-medium engineering classrooms. *ELT Journal*, *74*(4), 418–427. doi:10.1093/elt/ccaa033

Sahan, K., & Rose, H. (2021). Problematising the E in EMI: Translanguaging as a pedagogic alternative to English-only hegemony in university contexts. In B. Paulsrud, Z. Tian, & J. Toth (Eds.), *English-medium instruction and translanguaging* (pp. 22–33). Multilingual Matters. doi:10.21832/9781788927338-005

Sahan, K., Rose, H., & Macaro, E. (2021). Models of EMI pedagogies: At the interface of language use and interaction. *System*, *101*, 102616. doi:10.1016/j.system.2021.102616

Sahan, K., & Şahan, Ö. (2022). Content and language in EMI assessment practices: Challenges and beliefs at an engineering faculty in Turkey. In Y. Kırkgöz & A. Karakaş (Eds.), *English as the medium of instruction in Turkish higher education* (pp. 155–174). Springer. doi:10.1007/978-3-030-88597-7_8

Sakamoto, I. (2013). Tearing down the 'Canadian experience' roadblock. *The Star*. http://www.thestar.com/opinion/commentary/2013/07/16/tearing_down_the_canadian_experience_roadblock.html

Saldaña, J. (2016). *The coding manual for qualitative researchers*. SAGE.

Sandhaus, S., Kaufmann, D., & Ramirez-Andreotta, M. (2019). Public participation, trust and data sharing: Gardens as hubs for citizen science and environmental health literacy efforts. International Journal of Science Education *Part B*, *9*(1), 54–71. PMID:31485378

Sanín, F. G., & Wood, E. J. (2014). Ideology in civil war: Instrumental adoption and beyond. *Journal of Peace Research*, *51*(2), 213–226. doi:10.1177/0022343313514073

Sankoff, G. (2001). Linguistic outcomes of language contact. In P. Trudgill, J. Chambers, & N. Schilling-Estes (Eds.), *Handbook of sociolinguistics* (pp. 638–668). Basil Blackwell.

Santaella, L. A. (2018). *Pós-verdade é verdadeira ou falsa?* Estação das Letras e Cores.

Santaella, L. A. (2020). A educação e o estado da arte das tecnologias digitais. In SALES, M. S. (Org.). *Tecnologias digitais, redes e educação: perspectivas contemporâneas* (pp. 149–163). Edufba.

Sato, M., & Loewen, S. (2022). The research–practice dialogue in second language learning and teaching: Past, present, and future. *Modern Language Journal*, *106*(3), 509–527. doi:10.1111/modl.12791

Saturday Night Live [Username]. (2019, October 18). *Every Californians ever (part 1 of 2)* [Video]. YouTube. https://www.youtube.com/watch?v=dCer2e0t8r8

Sauntson, H. (2022). Reflexivity and the production of shared meanings in language and sexuality research. In S. Consoli & S. Ganassin (Eds.), *Reflexivity in Applied Linguistics Research: Opportunities, Challenges and Suggestions*. Routledge. doi:10.4324/9781003149408-10

Sauro, S., & Thorne, S. L. (2020). Pedagogically mediating engagement in the wild: Trajectories of fandom-based curricular innovation. In V. Werner & F. Tegge (Eds.), *Pop culture in language education* (pp. 228–239). Routledge.

Saville-Troike, M. (1982). *The ethnography of communication: An introduction*. Blackwell.

Sayer, P. (2013). Translanguaging, TexMex, and bilingual pedagogy: Emergent bilinguals learning through the vernacular. *TESOL Quarterly*, *47*(1), 63–88. doi:10.1002/tesq.53

Schegloff, E. A. (1987). Analyzing single episodes of interaction: An exercise in conversation analysis. *Social Psychology Quarterly*, *50*(2), 101–114. doi:10.2307/2786745

Schegloff, E. A. (2005). Discourse as an interactional achievement III: The omnirelevance of action. In D. Schiffrin, D. Tannen, & H. E. Hamilton (Eds.), *The handbook of discourse analysis* (pp. 229–249). Blackwell Publishing Ltd. doi:10.1002/9780470753460.ch13

Schieffelin, B. B., & Ochs, E. (1986). Language socialization. *Annual Review of Anthropology*, *15*(1), 163–191. doi:10.1146/annurev.an.15.100186.001115

Compilation of References

Schildkrout, E. (2007). *People of the Zongo: The transformation of ethnic identities in Ghana*. Cambridge University Press.

Schneider, B. (2012). Is English a local language in Berlin? In *Language on the Move*. https://www.languageonthemove.com/is-english-a-local-language-in-berlin/

Schneider, B. (2020). Language in transnational communities of consumption. Indexical functions of English in third-wave coffee culture. In S. Rüdiger & S. Mühleisen (Eds.), *Talking about Food. The Social and the Global in Eating Communities* (pp. 79–96). Benjamins. doi:10.1075/impact.47.05sch

Scholze, A., Potkonjak, S., Marcel, F., Folinazzo, G., & Townend, N. (2022). Scenarios for learning – scenarios as learning: A design-based research process. In *E. Piccardo, G. Lawrence, A. Germain-Rutherford, & A. Galante Activating Linguistic and Cultural Diversity in the Language Classroom* (pp. 113–140). Springer. doi:10.1007/978-3-030-87124-6_6

Selting, M., Auer, P., Barth-Weingarten, D., Bergmann, J.R., Bergmann, P., Birkner, K., Couper-Kuhlen, E., Deppermann, A., Gilles, P., Günthner, S., Hartung, M., Kern, F., Mertzlufft, C., Meyer, C., Morek, M., Oberzaucher, F., Peters, J., Quasthoff, U., Schütte, W., Stukenbrock, A. & Uhmann, S. (2011). A system for transcribing talk-in-interaction: GAT 2 (E. Couper-Kuhlen & D. Weingarten, Trans.). *Gesprächsforschung. Online-Zeitschrift zur verbalen Interaktion* 12, 1–51. (2009)

Selvi, A. F. (2022). Resisting English medium instruction through digital grassroots activism. *Journal of Multilingual and Multicultural Development*, *43*(2), 81–97. doi:10.1080/01434632.2020.1724120

Sergeant, P., Tagg, C., & Ngampramuan, W. (2012). Language choice and addressivity strategies in Thai-English social network interactions. *Journal of Sociolinguistics*, *16*(4), 510–531. doi:10.1111/j.1467-9841.2012.00540.x

Sgoura et al.- Σγούρα, Α., Μάνεσης, Ν., & Μητροπούλου, Φ. (2018). Diapolitismiki ekpedefsi ke kinoniki entaksi ton pedion prosfigon. Antilipsis ekpedeftikon. [Intercultural education and social integration of refugee children: Teachers' perceptions.] *Dialogi! Theoria ke praksi stis epistimes tis agogis ke ekpedefsis*, *4*, 108-129.

Shafirova, L., & Araújo e Sá, M. H. (2023). Multilingual encounters in online video practices: the case of Portuguese university students. *International Journal of Multilingualism*. doi:10.1080/14790718.2023.2205142

Shapiro, S. (2022). *Cultivating critical language awareness in the writing classroom*. Routledge.

Sheen, Y. (2008). Recasts, language anxiety, modified output, and L2 learning. *Language Learning*, *58*(4), 835–874. doi:10.1111/j.1467-9922.2008.00480.x

Shohamy, E. (2006). *Language policy: Hidden agendas and new approaches*. Routledge. doi:10.4324/9780203387962

Shortt, M., Tilak, S., Kuznetcova, I., Martens, B., & Akinkuolie, B. (2021). Gamification in mobile-assisted language learning: A systematic review of Duolingo literature from public release of 2012 to early 2020. *Computer Assisted Language Learning*, 1–38.

Shotter, J., & Gergen, K. J. (1994). Social Construction: Knowledge, Self, Others, and Continuing the Conversation. *Annals of the International Communication Association*, *17*(1), 1, 3–33. doi:10.1080/23808985.1994.11678873

Sierens, S., & Van Avermaet, P. (2014). Language diversity in education: Evolving from multilingual education to functional multilingual learning. In D. Little, C. Leung, & P. Van Avermaet (Eds.), *Managing diversity in education: Languages, policies, pedagogies* (pp. 204–222). Multilingual Matters., doi:10.21832/9781783090815-014

Silverstein, M. (1976). *Shifters, linguistic categories, and cultural description. Meaning in anthropology*. University of New Mexico Press.

Silverstein, M. (1985). The functional stratification of language and ontogenesis. In J. V. Wertsch (Ed.), *Culture, communication, and cognition: Vygotskian perspectives* (pp. 205–235). Cambridge University Press.

Silverstein, M. (1993). Reflexive language: Reported speech and metapragmatics. In J. Lucy (Ed.), *Metapragmatic Discourse and Metapragmatic Function*. Cambridge University Press Cambridge.

Silverstein, M. (2003). Indexical order and the dialectics of sociolinguistic life. *Language & Communication*, 23(3-4), 193–229. doi:10.1016/S0271-5309(03)00013-2

Silverstein, M. (2022). *Language in Culture: Lectures on the Social Semiotics of Language*. Cambridge University Press., doi:10.1017/9781009198813

Simonsen, H. K. (2021). AI writers in language learning. *2021 International Conference on Advanced Learning Technologies (ICALT)*, (pp. 238–240). IEEE. 10.1109/ICALT52272.2021.00078

Simopoulos, G., & Magos, K. (2021). Approaching the education of young refugees. Teachers' perceptions and students' voices. In A. Chatzidaki & R. Tsokalidou (Eds.), *Challenges and Initiatives in Refugee Education: The Case of Greece* (pp. 37–56). Cambridge Scholars Publishing.

Singh, G., & Richards, J. C. (2006). Teaching and learning in the language teacher education course room: A critical sociocultural perspective. *RELC Journal*, 37(2), 149–175. doi:10.1177/0033688206067426

Sleeter, C. E. (2011). An agenda to strengthen culturally responsive pedagogy. *English Teaching*, 10(2), 7–23.

Smith, J. S. (2016). Cuban voices: A case study of English language teacher education. *The International Education Journal: Comparative Perspectives*, 15(4), (pp. 100-111). http://openjournals.library.usyd.edu.au/index.php/IEJ.index

Smitherman, G. (1973). "God don't Never change": Black English from a Black perspective. *College English*, 34(6), 828. doi:10.2307/375044

Smitherman, G. (2017). Raciolinguistics, "mis-education," and language arts teaching in the 21st century. *Language Arts Journal of Michigan*, 32(2), 3. doi:10.9707/2168-149X.2164

Smit, U., & Dafouz, E. (2012). Integrating content and language in higher education: An introduction to English-medium policies, conceptual issues and research practices across Europe. *AILA Review*, 25, 1–12. doi:10.1075/aila.25.01smi

Sokanu Interactive Inc. (2023). *Mathematician demographics in the United States*. Career Explorer. https://www.careerexplorer.com/careers/mathematician/demographics/#:~:text=The%20largest%20ethnic%20group%20of,13%25%20and%2012%25%20respectively

Souto-Manning, M., Martinez, D. C., & Musser, A. D. (2022). ELA as English language abolition: Toward a pedagogy of communicative belonging. *Reading Research Quarterly*, 57(4), 1089–1106. doi:10.1002/rrq.464

Spada, N. (2022). Reflecting on task-based language teaching from an instructed SLA perspective. *Language Teaching*, 55(1), 74–86. doi:10.1017/S0261444821000161

Spada, N., Jessop, L., Suzuki, W., Tomita, Y., & Valeo, A. (2014). Isolated and integrated form-focused instruction: Effects on different types of L2 knowledge. *Language Teaching Research*, 18(4), 453–473. doi:10.1177/1362168813519883

Spada, N., & Lightbown, P. (2022). In it together: Teachers, researchers, and classroom SLA. *Modern Language Journal*, 106(3), 635–650. doi:10.1111/modl.12792

Spada, N., & Lightbown, P. M. (2013). Instructed SLA. In P. Robinson (Ed.), *The Routledge encyclopedia of SLA* (pp. 319–327). Routledge. doi:10.4324/9780203135945

Compilation of References

Spada, N., & Tomita, Y. (2010). Interactions between type of instruction and type of language feature: A meta-analysis. *Language Learning*, *60*(2), 263–308. doi:10.1111/j.1467-9922.2010.00562.x

Spahn, J. (2017). Berliner Cafés: Sprechen Sie doch deutsch! In *ZEIT online*. Retrieved on March 13, 2023, from https://www.zeit.de/2017/35/berlin-cafes-hipster-englisch-sprache-jens-spahn

Speechify. (2023). *AI voice cloning: Clone your voice instantly*. Speechify. https://speechify.com/voice-cloning/?landing_url=https%3A%2F%2Fspeechify.com%2Fblog%2Fchat-gpt-4-text-to-speech%2F

Spenser-Oatey, H., & Žegarac, V. (2019). Pragmatics. In N. Schmitt & M. P. H. Rodgers (Eds.), *An introduction to applied linguistics* (3rd ed., pp. 72–90). Routledge. doi:10.4324/9780429424465-5

Srba, I., Moro, R., Tomlein, M., Pecher, B., Simko, J., Stefancova, E., Kompan, M., Hrckova, A., Podrouzek, J., Gavornik, A., & Bielikova, M. (2023). Auditing YouTube's recommendation algorithm for misinformation filter bubbles. *ACM Transactions on Recommender Systems*, *1*(1), 1–33. doi:10.1145/3568392

Stake, R. E. (1995). The art of case study research. *Sage (Atlanta, Ga.)*.

Statistics Canada (2023). *Canada's population estimates, first quarter of 2023*. https://www150.statcan.gc.ca/n1/daily-quotidien/230628/dq230628c-eng.htm

Statistics Canada. (2005). Knowledge of official languages among new immigrants: How important is it in the labour market? *Catalogue No. 89-624-XIE*. http://www.statcan.gc.ca/pub/89-624-x/89-624-x2007000-eng.pdf

Steinert, Y. (2006). *Building on diversity: A faculty development program for teachers of international medical graduates*. The Association of Faculties of Medicine of Canada.

Stergiou, A. (2019). The contribution of the University of Ioannina to refugee education. In K. Plakitsi, E. Kolokouri, & A.-C. Kornelaki (Eds.), *ISCAR 2019 Crisis in Contexts, E-proceedings* (pp. 173–186). University of Ioannina.

Stern, H. H. (1975). What can we learn from the good language learner? *Canadian Modern Language Review*, *31*(4), 304–318. doi:10.3138/cmlr.31.4.304

Stevanovic, M., & Peräkylä, A. (2012). Deontic Authority in Interaction: The Right to Announce, Propose, and Decide. *Research on Language and Social Interaction*, *45*(3), 297–321. doi:10.1080/08351813.2012.699260

Stille, S., & Cummins, J. (2013). Foundation for learning: Engaging plurilingual students' linguistic repertoires in the elementary classroom. *TESOL Quarterly*, *47*(3), 630–638. doi:10.1002/tesq.116

Stollznow, K. (2020). Not that there's anything wrong with that. In On the Offensive: Prejudice in Language Past and Present (pp. 96–123). Cambridge University Press. doi:10.1017/9781108866637.004

Straaijer, R. (2016). Attitudes to prescriptivism: An introduction. *Journal of Multilingual and Multicultural Development*, *37*(3), 233–242. doi:10.1080/01434632.2015.1068782

Strauss, A., & Glaser, B. G. (1967). *The discovery of grounded theory: Strategies for grounded theory research*. Aldine Publishing.

Sun, Y., & Gao, F. (2020). An investigation of the influence of intrinsic motivation on students' intention to use mobile devices in language learning. *Educational Technology Research and Development*, *68*(3), 1181–1198. doi:10.100711423-019-09733-9

Svensson, G. (2021). 5. Developing Pedagogical Translanguaging in a Primary and Middle School. In P. Juvonen & M. Källkvist (Eds.) Pedagogical Translanguaging: Theoretical, Methodological and Empirical Perspectives (pp. 76-94). Multilingual Matters. https://doi.org/10.21832/9781788927383-007

Swain, M., Kinnear, P., & Steinmann, L. (2015). *Sociocultural theory in second language education: An introduction through narrative* (2nd ed.). Multilingual Matters. doi:10.21832/9781783093182

Tan, J. P. L. (2008). Closing the gap: A multiliteracies approach to English language teaching for 'at-risk' students in Singapore. In A. Healy (Ed.), *Multiliteracies and diversity in education: New pedagogies for expanding landscapes* (pp. 144–167). Oxford University Press.

Tannen, D., & Trester, A. M. (2013). The Medium is the metamessage: Conversational style in new media interaction. In *Discourse 2.0: Language and new media* (pp. 99–117). Georgetown University Press.

Taquini, R., Finardi, K. R., & Amorim, G. B. (2017). English as a medium of instruction at Turkish state universities. *Education and Linguistics Research*, *3*(2), 35–53. doi:10.5296/elr.v3i2.11438

Tassinari, M. G. (2017). A self-access centre for learners and teachers: Promoting autonomy in higher education. In M. Jiménez, J. J. Martos, & M. G. Tassinari (Eds.), *Learner and teacher autonomy in higher education: Perspectives from modern language teaching* (pp. 183–208). Peter Lang.

Tatzl, D. (2011). English-medium masters' programmes at an Austrian university of applied sciences: Attitudes, experiences and challenges. *Journal of English for Academic Purposes*, *10*(4), 252–270. doi:10.1016/j.jeap.2011.08.003

Teddlie, C., & Yu, F. (2007). Mixed methods sampling: A typology with examples. *Journal of Mixed Methods Research*, *1*(1), 77–100. doi:10.1177/1558689806292430

ten Have, P. (2007). *Doing conversation analysis: A practical guide* (2nd ed.). SAGE. doi:10.4135/9781849208895

Teo, T., Hoi, C. K. W., Gao, X., & Lv, L. (2019). What Motivates Chinese University Students to Learn Japanese? Understanding Their Motivation in Terms of "Posture.". *Modern Language Journal*, *103*(1), 327–342. doi:10.1111/modl.12546

Terry, G., Hayfield, N., Clarke, V., & Braun, V. (2017). Thematic analysis. In C. Willig & W. Stainton (Eds.), *The SAGE Handbook of Qualitative Research in Psychology* (pp. 17–37). SAGE. doi:10.4135/9781526405555.n2

The Guardian. (n.d). Top 20 countries for international students. *The Gurardian*. https://www.theguardian.com/higher-education-network/blog/2014/jul/17/top-20-countries-international-students

The United States Census Bureau. (2021). *American Community Survey. Data profiles*. USCB. https://www.census.gov/acs/www/data/data-tables-and tools/data-profiles/2014/

Thirteen / WNET, & MacNeil-Lehrer Productions (Producers), & Cran, W. (Director) (2005). *Do you speak American?* [Video file].

Thomason, S. G. (2001). *Language contact: An introduction*. Edinburgh University Press.

Thomason, S. G., & Kaufman, T. (1988). *Language contact, creolization, and genetic linguistics*. University of California Press. doi:10.1525/9780520912793

Thornton, K. (2016). Evaluating language learning spaces: Developing formative evaluation procedures to enable growth and innovation. *Studies in Self-Access Learning Journal*, *7*(4), 394–397. doi:10.37237/070407

Tien, C. Y., & Li, C. S. D. (2014). Codeswitching in a university in Taiwan. In R. Barnard, R., & J. McLellan (Eds), Codeswitching in university English-medium classes: Asian perspectives (pp. 24-42). Bristol: Multilingual Matters.

Time Association. (2022, November 28). *International student mobility at a Glance 2022*. Top International Managers in Engineering. https://timeassociation.org/2022/11/28/international-student-mobility-key-numbers-2022/

Compilation of References

Tomlin, A. D., Moss, L. V., & Price, N. S. (2023). Supporting Students of Color in Language Learning Environments: Approaches From Black Community College Faculty. In Promoting Diversity, Equity, and Inclusion in Language Learning Environments (pp. 130-144). IGI Global.

Tomlin, A. D., & Davis, L. (2022). Linguistic liberation: The experiences of Black higher education professionals. In S. E. DeCapua & E. B. Hancı-Azizoglu (Eds.), *Global and Transformative Approaches Toward Linguistic Diversity* (pp. 66–79). IGI Global. doi:10.4018/978-1-7998-8985-4.ch004

Toscos, D., Daley, C., Wagner, S., Coupe, A., Ahmed, R., Holden, R. J., Flanagan, M. E., Pfafman, R., Ghahari, R. R., & Mirro, M. (2020). Patient responses to daily cardiac resynchronization therapy device data: A pilot trial assessing a novel patient-centered digital dashboard in everyday life. *Cardiovascular Digital Health Journal*, *1*(2), 97–106. doi:10.1016/j.cvdhj.2020.09.003 PMID:35265880

Townend, N., Bartosik, A., Folinazzo, G., & Kelly, J. (2022). Teachers implementing action-oriented scenarios: realities of the twenty-first century classroom. In *E. Piccardo, G. Lawrence, A. Germain-Rutherford, & A. Galante Activating Linguistic and Cultural Diversity in the Language Classroom* (pp. 179–234). Springer. doi:10.1007/978-3-030-87124-6_8

Trent, J. (2010). Teacher education as identity construction: Insights from action research. *Journal of Education for Teaching*, *36*(2), 153–168. doi:10.1080/02607471003651672

Tsaliki, E. (2017). Teachers' views on implementing intercultural education in Greece: The case of 13 primary schools. *International Journal of Comparative Education and Development*, *19*(2/3), 50–64. doi:10.1108/IJCED-07-2017-0013

Tsung, L. (2015). Multiple identities and second language learning in Hong Kong. In D. N. Djenar, A. Mahboob, & K. Cruickshank (Eds.), *Language and Identity Across Modes of Communication* (pp. 107–124). De Gruyter Mouton. doi:10.1515/9781614513599.107

Türegün, A. (2008). The politics of access to professions: Making Ontario's Fair Access to Regulated Professions Act, 2006. [CERIS Working Paper No. 70]. CERIS. http://www.ceris.metropolis.net/

Türker, E. (2000). *Turkish-Norwegian code-switching. Evidence from intermediate and second-generation Turkish immigrants in Norway*, [Unpublished doctoral dissertation, University of Oslo].

Türker, E. (2005). Resisting the grammatical change: Nominal groups in Turkish-Norwegian codeswitching. *The International Journal of Bilingualism*, *9*(3 & 4), 453–476. doi:10.1177/13670069050090030801

Turkish Coalition of America. (2021, March 24). *The Turkish-American Community*. TC America. https://www.tc-america.org/turkish-american-community/

Turner Martí, L., & Pita Cespedes, B. (2001). *A pedagogy of tenderness*. Asociación de Educadores de Latinoamerica y el Caribe.

Tüzela, A. E. B., & Akcan, S. (2009). Raising the language awareness of pre-service English teachers in an EFL context. *European Journal of Teacher Education*, *32*(3), 271–287. doi:10.1080/02619760802572659

Tzakosta, M. (2022). Language variation placed in the center of language teaching: The example of dialectical teaching in tertiary education. In S. Karpava (Ed.), *Handbook of research on multilingual and multicultural perspectives on higher education and implications for teaching* (pp. 1–41). IGI Global. doi:10.4018/978-1-7998-8888-8.ch001

UNESCO. (2008). Student achievement in Latin America and the Caribbean, Santiago, Chile. OREALC, UNESCO.

UNESCO. (2023, August 12). *Definition of "International (or internationally mobile) students"*. UNESCO. https://uis.unesco.org/glossary

UNHCR. (2023). *Tertiary Education.* UNHCR. https://www.unhcr.org/tertiary-education.html.

United States Department of Commerce. (2023). *QuickFacts: United States.* United States Census Bureau, United States Department of Commerce. https://www.census.gov/quickfacts/fact/table/US/PST045222

University of Toronto. (2023, September 10). *Generative Artificial Intelligence in the classroom.* University of Toronto. https://teaching.utoronto.ca/resources/generative-artificial-intelligence-in-the-classroom/

Us, P.L. – The CNAM Channel [Username]. (2017, March 8). *#Real thick accent: Boston North End Italian* [Video]. YouTube. https://www.youtube.com/watch?v=omVFxtbZoyw

Ushida, E. (2005). Role of students' attitudes and motivation in Second language learning in online language courses. *CALICO Journal, 23*(1), 49–78. doi:10.1558/cj.v23i1.49-78

Ushida, E. (2017). The impact of global English on motivation to learn other languages: Toward an ideal multilingual self. *Modern Language Journal, 101*(3), 469–482. http://www.jstor.org/stable/44981000. doi:10.1111/modl.12413

Van Dijk, T. A. (1998). *Critical discourse analysis.* HUM. https://www.hum.uva.nl/teun/cda.htm

Van Dijk, T. A. (Ed.). (1997). *Discourse as social interaction.* Sage.

van Kleeck, A., & Schuele, C. M. (1987). Precursors to literacy: Normal development. *Topics in Language Disorders, 7*(2), 13–31. doi:10.1097/00011363-198703000-00004

van Lier, L. (2007). Action-based teaching, autonomy and identity. *Innovation in Language Teaching and Learning, 1*(1), 1–19.

van Lier, L. (2010). The ecology of language learning: Practice to theory, theory to practice. *Procedia: Social and Behavioral Sciences, 3*, 2–6. doi:10.1016/j.sbspro.2010.07.005

Varghese, M. M., Motha, S., Park, G., Reeves, J., & Trent, J. (2016). In This Issue. TESOL Quarterly on Language Teacher Identity, 50(3), 545-571.

Varghese, M., Morgan, B., Johnston, B., & Johnson, K. A. (2005). Theorizing language teacher identity. *Journal of Language, Identity, and Education, 4*(1), 21–44. doi:10.120715327701jlie0401_2

Vázquez-Montilla, E., Just, M., & Triscari, R. (2014). Teachers' dispositions and beliefs about cultural and linguistic diversity. *Universal Journal of Educational Research, 2*(8), 577–587. doi:10.13189/ujer.2014.020806

Velasco, P., & García, O. (2014). Translanguaging and the writing of bilingual learners. *Bilingual Research Journal, 37*(1), 6–23. doi:10.1080/15235882.2014.893270

Vergou, P. (2019). Living with difference: Refugee education and school segregation processes in Greece. *Urban Studies (Edinburgh, Scotland), 56*(15), 3162–3177. doi:10.1177/0042098019846448

Vikøy, A., & Haukås, Å. (2021). Norwegian L1 teachers' beliefs about a multilingual approach in increasingly diverse classrooms. *International Journal of Multilingualism,* •••, 1–15.

Vonkova, H., Jones, J., Moore, A., Altinkalp, I., & Selcuk, H. (2021). A review of recent research in EFL motivation: Research trends, emerging methodologies, and diversity of researched populations. *System (Linköping), 103*, 102622–. doi:10.1016/j.system.2021.102622

Vygotsky, L. (1978). *Mind in society: The development of higher psychological processes.* Harvard University Press.

Waldinger, R. (2015). *The cross-border connection: Immigrants, emigrants, and their homelands.* Harvard University Press. doi:10.4159/harvard.9780674736283

Walker, E. N. (2014). *Beyond Banneker: Black mathematicians and the paths to excellence*. State University of New York Press. doi:10.1353/book32767

Walker, K. (2020). The English language arts classroom as a multilingual literacy community. *The Clearing House: A Journal of Educational Strategies, Issues and Ideas*, *93*(6), 284–289. doi:10.1080/00098655.2020.1789038

Wang, J.-S., Lan, J. Y.-C., Khairutdinova, R., & Gromova, C. (2022). Teachers' attitudes to cultural diversity: Results from a qualitative study in Russia and Taiwan. *Frontiers in Psychology*, *13*, 976659. doi:10.3389/fpsyg.2022.976659 PMID:36467240

Warner, C., & Dupuy, B. (2018). Moving toward multiliteracies in foreign language teaching: Past and present perspectives…and beyond. *Foreign Language Annals*, *51*(1), 116–128. doi:10.1111/flan.12316

Warren, C. A. (2014). Towards a pedagogy for the application of empathy in culturally diverse classrooms. *The Urban Review*, *46*(3), 395–419. doi:10.100711256-013-0262-5

Warschauer, M. (2000). The death of cyberspace and the rebirth of CALL. *English Teachers'. Journal*, *53*(1), 61–67.

Wei, L. (2011). Moment analysis and translanguaging space: Discursive construction of identities by multilingual Chinese youth in Britain. *Journal of Pragmatics*, *43*(5), 1222–1235. doi:10.1016/j.pragma.2010.07.035

Weinreich, U. (1953). *Languages in contact*. Mouton.

Wenger, E. (1998). *Communities of practice: Learning, meaning, and identity*. Cambridge University Press. doi:10.1017/CBO9780511803932

Werner, V., & Tegge, F. (2020). *Pop culture in language education theory, research, practice* (V. Werner & F. Tegge, Eds.). Routledge. doi:10.4324/9780367808334

Whitebread, D. (Ed.). (1996). *Teaching and learning in the early years*. Routledge. doi:10.4324/9780203436493

White, C. (1995). Autonomy and strategy use in distance foreign language learning: Research findings. *System*, *23*(2), 207–221. doi:10.1016/0346-251X(95)00009-9

White, D. E., Oelke, N. D., & Friesen, S. (2012). Management of a large qualitative data set: Establishing trustworthiness of the data. *International Journal of Qualitative Methods*, *11*(3), 244–258. doi:10.1177/160940691201100305

White, M. J. (Ed.). (2016). *International handbook of migration and population distribution* (Vol. 6). Springer. doi:10.1007/978-94-017-7282-2

Wigfield, A., & Eccles, J. S. (2000). Expectancy-value theory of achievement motivation. *Contemporary Educational Psychology*, *25*(1), 68–81. doi:10.1006/ceps.1999.1015 PMID:10620382

Williams, M., & Burden, R. (1997). *Psychology for language teachers*. Cambridge University Press.

Wilson, J., & González, M. G. (2017). Tackling the plurilingual student/monolingual classroom phenomenon. *TESOL Quarterly*, *51*(1), 207–219. doi:10.1002/tesq.336

Winke, P., & Goertler, S. (2008). Did we forget someone? students' computer access and literacy for CALL. *CALICO Journal*, *25*(3), 482–509. doi:10.1558/cj.v25i3.482-509

Wodak, R., & Meyer, M. (Eds.). (2009). *Methods of critical discourse analysis*. John Benjamin.

Wolfram, W. (2013). Sounds effects: Challenging language prejudice in the classroom. *Education Digest*, *79*(1), 27–30.

Wolfram, W., & Schilling, N. (2015). Why dialects? In *American English: Dialects and variation* (3rd ed.) (pp. 27–58). Blackwell.

Wong, M. (2014). Navigating return: The gendered geographies of skilled return migration to Ghana. *Global Networks*, *14*(4), 438–457. doi:10.1111/glob.12041

Wong, W., Wu, H.-C., Cleary, E. G., Patton, A. P., Xie, A., Grinstein, G., Koch-Weser, S., & Brugge, D. (2019). Visualizing air pollution: Communication of environmental health information in a Chinese immigrant community. *Journal of Health Communication*, *24*(4), 339–358. doi:10.1080/10810730.2019.1597949 PMID:31030632

World Population Review. (2022). *Countries*. World Population Review. https://worldpopulationreview.com/countries/ (accessed 5th October, 2022).

Wright, T. (2002). Doing language awareness: Issues for language study in language teacher education. In H. Trappes-Lomax & G. Ferguson (Eds.), *Language in language teacher education* (pp. 113–130). John Benjamins Publishing Company. doi:10.1075/lllt.4.09wri

Wright, T., & Bolitho, R. (1993). Language awareness: A missing link in language teacher education? *ELT Journal*, *47*(4), 292–304. doi:10.1093/elt/47.4.292

Xu, L. (2012). The role of teachers beliefs in the language teaching-learning process. *Theory and Practice in Language Studies*, *2*(7), 1397–1402. doi:10.4304/tpls.2.7.1397-1402

Yağmur, K. (2001). Turkish and other languages in Turkey. In G. Extra & D. Gorter (Eds.), *The other languages of Europe* (pp. 407–428). European Cultural Foundation.

Yankova, D., & Vassileva, I. (2013). Functions and mechanisms of code-switching in Bulgarian Canadians. *Etudes Canadiennes. Canadian Studies*, (74), 103–121. doi:10.4000/eccs.254

Yeung, M. Y., Cheng, H. H., Chan, P. T., & Kwok, D. W. (2023). Communication technology and teacher–student relationship in the tertiary ESL classroom during the pandemic: A case study. *SN Computer Science*, *4*(2), 202–202. doi:10.100742979-023-01667-7 PMID:36789247

Yıldız, A. (2019b). *Suriye uyruklu öğrencilerin Türkiye'de yükseköğretime katılımları [Participation of Syrian students in higher education in Türkiye]*. Yaşar Üniversitesi Yayınları.

Yıldız, A. (Ed.). (2019a). *Integration of refugee students in European higher education: Comparative country cases*. Yaşar University Publications.

Yıldız, M., Soruç, A., & Griffiths, C. (2017). Challenges and needs of students in the EMI (English as a medium of instruction) classroom. *Konin Language Studies*, *5*(4), 387–402.

Yıldız, M., & Yeşilyurt, S. (2017). Use or Avoid? The Perceptions of Prospective English Teachers in Turkey about L1 Use in English Classes. *English Language Teaching*, *10*(1), 84–96. doi:10.5539/elt.v10n1p84

Yin, R. (2003). *Case study research: Design and methods* (3rd ed.). Sage.

Yoro, T. (2014). *Jibun no kabe [The wall of oneself]*. Shinchosha.

Young, A. S. (2014). Unpacking teachers' language ideologies: Attitudes, beliefs, and practiced language policies in schools in Alsace, France. *Language Awareness*, *23*(1–2), 157–171. doi:10.1080/09658416.2013.863902

Young, R. F. (2008). *Language and interaction: An advanced resource book*. Routledge.

Young, R. F. (2009). *Discursive practice in language learning and teaching*. Wiley Blackwell.

Compilation of References

Zachos, D. T., Papadimitriou, N. T., & Sideri, E. (2020). Minority education in Greece: Thrace Muslim teachers' approaches and views. *Preschool and Primary Education*, *8*(2), 144–157. doi:10.12681/ppej.21897

Zarrinabadi, N., & Afsharmehr, E. (2022). Teachers' mindsets about L2 learning: Exploring the influences on pedagogical practices. *RELC Journal*, 1–15. doi:10.1177/00336882211067049

Zentella, A. C. (1997). *Growing Up Bilingual*. Blackwell Publishers.

Zhang, T. (2021). The effect of highly focused versus mid-focused written corrective feedback on EFL learners' explicit and implicit knowledge development. *System (Linköping)*, *99*, 102493–. doi:10.1016/j.system.2021.102493

Zhang, R., & Zou, D. (2022). Types, purposes, and effectiveness of state-of-the-art technologies for second and foreign language learning. *Computer Assisted Language Learning*, *35*(4), 696–742. doi:10.1080/09588221.2020.1744666

Zheng, Y., & Yu, S. (2018). Student engagement with teacher written corrective feedback in EFL writing: A case study of Chinese lower-proficiency students. *Assessing Writing*, *37*, 13–24. doi:10.1016/j.asw.2018.03.001

Zhu, H., & Li, W. (2020). Translanguaging, identity, and migration. In J. Jackson (Eds.), The Routledge handbook of language and intercultural communication (2nd ed.) (pp. 234–248). Routledge.

About the Contributors

Sarah Jones is a seasoned language educator currently working as a course instructor and doctoral candidate at the University of Toronto. Her research interests include interlanguage pragmatics, interactional sociolinguistics, and phatic communion in multilingual spaces.

Rebecca Schmor is a PhD candidate, graduate research assistant, and course instructor at the University of Toronto. She has taught and conducted research with higher education institutions, ministries of education, and private language schools in Canada, China, Cuba, Germany, and Italy. Her main research interests centre around inclusive language education and plurilingual teacher identity.

Julie Kerekes is an Associate Professor in Language and Literacies Education at OISE. Her research and teaching focus on language and power in intercultural institutional settings, and on the professional development of second language educators.

* * *

Nancy G. Barrón served as the Director of the Interdisciplinary Writing Program and is a Professor of Rhetoric, Writing, and Digital Media Studies at Northern Arizona University. She teaches courses in the rhetoric and climate change content, media design, history of rhetoric, science writing, and professional writing. Professor Barrón participates as a faculty adviser for English undergraduate students with attention to career planning. She has held various student support administrator roles such as faculty adviser for Sigma Tau Delta (student honor society), faculty adviser for the Language Lair (Learning Community), mentor for new faculty, and she has provided numerous workshops, and individual consultations on integrating research, writing, media, and presentation skills across the disciplines. Dr. Barrón's work on her position as a Latina faculty member, and her work on confronting identity issues experienced by non-mainstream students (particularly Latine students) in higher education can be found in journals such as College Composition and Communication, The Writing Center Journal, Literacy in Composition Studies, Across the Disciplines, The Journal of Literacy and Technology, Computers and Composition, The International Journal of Technology, Knowledge and Society, Environmental Humanities, The International Journal of Diversity in Organisations, Communities and Nations, and International Journal of Educational Management.

Ingrid Barth has an M.A. in Curriculum Design and Evaluation and a Ph.D. in Educational Technology from Bar Ilan University and is a graduate of the Feuerstein Institute's Instrumental Enrichment

About the Contributors

and Dynamic Assessment programs. Her main areas of interest include designing software to support acquisition of high-frequency vocabulary, and using mediation to adapt academic content courses to needs of EMI (English Medium Instruction) students. Ingrid has been affiliated with The Open University of Israel's English Unit and Tel Aviv University's Division of Languages, and as a teacher educator, is currently working on developing national level professional development modules for tertiary level English teachers as well as for content lecturers who teach EMI students. She recently completed a Horizons 2020 project to bridge high school – university gaps and recently won a Ministry of Education grant for utilizing Researcher-Practitioner Partnerships to design online professional development to support CEFR-aligned curriculum reform.

Joy Beatty is a doctoral student in the Ph.D. program in Education (Curriculum, Culture, and Change concentration) in the School of Education at Virginia Commonwealth University. She is a Southern Regional Education Board (SREB) Doctoral Scholars program fellowship recipient and a Holmes Scholar. She was a curriculum writer for CodeVA and taught history and English for over ten years in Virginia and Maryland. Additionally, Joy taught English in South Korea as part of a sponsorship by the Rotary Club. Her passion is developing curriculum for teachers so they can challenge dominant narratives as a way to support diverse learners.

Ali Borjian is Professor and Chair of Department of Elementary Education at San Francisco State University. He is a Fulbright scholar and has conducted research in Mexico. Dr. Borjian's primary field of interest focuses on teacher education and teacher professional development. His areas of specialization are second language acquisition, immigration, and teacher education. Much of his training has focused on issues of teaching and learning as it relates to language acquisition and cultural diversity.

Leor Cohen earned a Ph.D. at Bar-Ilan University, Israel in Sociolinguistics. Post-doctorate at King's College, London in Narrative and Identity. Research interests include Discourse Analysis, Conversation Analysis, Linguistic Ethnography, Language Socialization, Ethnomethodology, Narrative and Identity. Currently Head of the English Unit at the Open University Israel, and Chair of H-INET, a professional association representing all tertiary level English language practitioners in Israel.

Eftychia Damaskou is a French teacher in the Greek public secondary education She is currently preparing her doctoral thesis on teaching material design for multilingual primary classes. Since 2015, she has been appointed as external expert in matters of teaching material design at the Greek Institute of Educational Policy. Her published research work focuses on teaching material design, young foreign language learners' language attitudes, and multilingual competence development within young learners.

Elena Danilina is a PhD candidate in Language and Literacies Education at the Ontario Institute for Studies in Education (OISE) and a sessional instructor at the Graduate Centre for Academic Communication (GCAC) at the University of Toronto. Her research focuses on plurilingualism, AI-based technology, and learner autonomy. Elena's teaching experience in higher education spans over fifteen years in the UAE, Morocco, USA, and Canada.

Esther Yeboah Danso-Wiredu is an associate professor at the Department of Geography Education. She is the immediate past Acting Head of Department of Geography Education at the University of Education, Winneba. She had her Bachelor's Education in Geography and Resource Development at the University of Ghana, Legon and obtained her Master of Philosophy in Social Change at Norwegian University of Science and Technology (NTNU), Norway. She has a Post Graduate Diploma in Higher Education at the University of Education, Winneba. And a PHD in Geography at the Katholieke Universiteit, Leuven (KULeuven). She has experienced working with a number of NGOs within and outside Ghana and in teaching as well.

Lavon Davis is a current PhD student at the University of Maryland Baltimore County in the Language, Literacy, and Culture program. He also teaches courses in Academic Literacies, American Studies, and English. Working for nearly 10 years as a scholar practitioner in higher education, Lavon considers himself a lifelong learner whose talents and skills led him to the body of scholarship and research. Through his passion for teaching and working with students, faculty, and staff, his unwavering curiosity for language and how one's linguistic dexterity grants access or denies access in higher education, or other settings, became a critical point of interest. Lavon received his Bachelor of Arts in English with Honors from Francis Marion University, his Master of Education in Higher Education from the University of North Carolina Wilmington, and his Master of Arts in Linguistics: Language and Communication from Georgetown University.

Luciana C. de Oliveira, Ph.D., is Associate Dean for Academic Affairs and Graduate Studies and a Professor in the School of Education at Virginia Commonwealth University. Her research focuses on issues related to teaching multilingual learners at the K-12 level, including the role of language in learning the content areas and teacher education, advocacy and social justice. Currently, Dr. de Oliveira's research examines scaffolding in elementary classrooms. She has authored or edited 24 books and has several and has over 200 publications in various outlets. Dr. de Oliveira has over 25 years of teaching experience in the field of TESOL. She served as President (2018-2019) of TESOL International Association and was a member of the Board of Directors (2013-2016). She was the first Latina to ever serve as President of TESOL.

Allessandra Elisabeth dos Santos is a Ph.D. student from the Federal University of Sergipe (UFS), Brazil. Her research focuses on artificial intelligence and its impact on English language writing. She holds a Master's degree in Education from UFS and a Post-Baccalaureate Diploma in Education from the University of Winnipeg, Canada. She has 26 years of teaching experience in the field of TESOL/TEFL and also taught college students. Allessandra was a teacher educator and academic coordinator for 10 years in an Elementary and Middle Years bilingual school in Brazil. Currently, she holds a CAPES scholarship and is an affiliate of the Multilingual Learners in Schools (VCU) and TECLA: Technologies, Education and Linguistics (UFS) research groups.

Emma Sarah Eshun is a Senior Lecturer at The Basic Education Department and her research interest is in English Language. She holds an M.Phil and Bachelor of Education from the University of Education, Winneba and her PhD from the University of Ghana, Legon.

Sibylle Gruber is a professor of Rhetoric, Writing, and Digital Media Studies at Northern Arizona University. She has published on intersectionality, justice, equity, diversity, feminist rhetorics, technological literacies, composition theories and practices, translingualism, and transnational rhetorics. Her

About the Contributors

teaching practices are influenced by her international experiences and her experiences as a second-language learner, especially in terms of the social and cultural aspects of communicative practices. Her current work focuses on projects that explore the complexities of intersectionality, transculturalism, and transnational identities in a global knowledge society.

Jia Gui is a recent Ph.D. graduate in Education, with a concentration in Curriculum, Culture, and Change in the School of Education at Virginia Commonwealth University. She was a TESOL teacher and taught college students and secondary school students in China. She taught the World Language course in U.S. elementary schools. Her current research interests include the Language-Based Approach to Content Instruction (LACI) and teacher education for multilingual learners.

Talip Gülle holds a Ph.D. in English Language Teaching from Boğaziçi University, where he has also obtained his B.A. and M.A. degrees. He works as a research assistant at the Department of Foreign Language Education at Bartın University. His current research brings together English Medium Instruction, multilingualism, and assessment, with a focus on the potential implications of the English-only policy, and of translanguaging, in content assessments for L2-English users in tertiary-level English-medium programs in Türkiye.

Brian Hibbs, Ph.D., is an associate professor of education at Dalton State College, USA. He teaches courses in applied linguistics, language teaching methodology, and culture and education to prepare pre-service elementary education teacher candidates to work with English learners in their own instructional contexts. His scholarly interests include applied linguistics, faculty development, intercultural competence, language teaching methodology, second language acquisition, study abroad, and teacher research.

Didem Koban Koç is currently working as an Associate Professor in the Faculty of Education/Department of Foreign Languages Education at İzmir Democracy University, İzmir, Türkiye. She is also the Department Chair. She received a Ph.D. degree in Linguistics from the City University of New York, USA, an M.A. degree in Teaching English to Speakers of Other Languages (TESOL) from New York University, USA, and a B.A. degree in Teaching English as a Foreign Language (EFL) from Middle East Technical University, Türkiye. She taught in a variety of institutions such as the City University of New York, Pace University, the College of New Rochelle in the United States and Hacettepe University in Türkiye. She gave lectures in Denmark, Germany, Italy and Poland via the Erasmus+ staff mobility program. Her research interests are bilingualism/multilingualism, sociolinguistics and teacher education. She has numerous publications in these areas.

Yavuz Kurt is an assistant professor in the English Language Education Program of the Foreign Language Education Department at Marmara University, İstanbul. His research focuses on English medium instruction in higher education, English as a lingua franca, English as an international language, and the assessment of Turkish as a second language. He co-authored articles published in national and international refereed journals. Recently, he has been involved in national and international research projects about English-medium instruction in multilingual settings.

Emmanuelle Le Pichon is head of the Centre de Recherches en Éducation Franco-Ontarienne (CRÉFO) and Assistant Professor at the Ontario Institute for Studies in Education, University of Toronto,

Canada. Her research revolves around plurilingual education. She is the co-creator of the Language Friendly School network.

Ariel Quinio earned a Ph.D. in Curriculum, Teaching and Learning, and M.A. in Measurement and Evaluation at the Ontario Institute for Studies in Education at the University of Toronto (OISE/UT). He was a former University Researcher from the Philippines and a Lecturer in Methods of Research and Statistics for over 10 years. His research interests focus on mixed methods designs, high-stake testing and measurement, classical test theory and Rasch scale modeling, program evaluation, equity studies in education and the critical pedagogy He is currently a Continuing Adult Education Instructor at Monsignor Fraser College in Toronto, Canada.

Karen L. Terrell, Ph.D., is an English Language Specialist for the U.S. Department of State, an Assistant Professor of Mathematics Education at Loyola University Maryland, and the CEO/Owner of the Terrell Educational Foundation. Her research interests include mathematics education and content- and-language integration, as well as genre pedagogy and technology integration for diverse learners. Dr. Terrell has over 22 years of educational experience, including teaching and coaching in secondary schools, consulting for both charter and private schools as well as the Massachusetts Department of Youth Services, and lecturing for over 15 years in higher education. She currently serves as the 2nd Vice President of Georgia TESOL

Yasuyo Tomita is a Sessional Lecturer at the Ontario Institute for Studies in Education at the University of Toronto. In her research and teaching, she is interested in instructed second language acquisition (e.g., form-focused instruction, corrective feedback), teaching methodologies (e.g., action-oriented approach), and learner identity and investment. Currently, she is collaborating on several research projects, including a meta-analysis of native/non-native speaking teachers, classroom research on learner perceptions towards online and in-person language learning, and a systematic review of integrated and isolated form-focused instruction. Her latest publication focuses on second-language acquisition theory and practice in online language learning contexts.

Tara M. Willging is a doctoral student at the Virginia Commonwealth University in Richmond, Virginia. She is a member of the Multilingual Learners in Schools research group at VCU, contributing to book chapters, articles, and presented at VATESOL 2021, SETESOL 2022 and VATESOL 2023. She is an adjunct professor for the graduate and undergraduate teaching and learning courses at VCU. This is her eighth year as a practicing ESOL teacher. Her research interests include translanguaging in education and other assets- based pedagogies.

Vroni Zieglmeier is a second-year graduate student in linguistics at Freie Universität Berlin. Their research interests are at the intersection of linguistics and anthropology and include language and gender/sexuality, language contact, language ideologies, linguistic landscapes, phonological variation and change, and sociophonetics.

Index

A

action-oriented approach 108, 111-112, 119-121, 126-127, 134, 148
African American English (AAE) 270, 273
age of arrival 284, 288-289, 295
AI 88, 90, 93-97, 99-100, 102, 106, 109, 124, 128, 302, 304
Awareness Campaigns 227-228, 242-243

B

Bilingualism 19, 55-57, 59, 65, 149-150, 153, 157, 159-161, 181-182, 201, 204-205, 207, 265, 284, 296-300
Black English 269-270, 272, 277-279, 281
Bourdieu 23, 25-26, 40-43, 46

C

Codeswitch 3, 269, 287
Code-switching 2-3, 14, 18, 20, 55-57, 66, 99, 159, 197, 207, 211, 278-279, 281, 284-289, 291, 294-300
Collaboration 44, 50, 68-69, 74, 79, 81, 86, 132, 135, 151, 161, 311
Community of Practice 1-2, 16, 23-27, 42, 50
content areas 301-302, 308-309
Context 1-2, 5, 9-11, 14-17, 20-21, 24-26, 28, 33, 36, 40-43, 50, 62, 66, 70, 74-76, 80, 82, 90, 92-93, 104-105, 112, 117, 119, 121, 123, 125, 131-133, 135, 138-147, 149-151, 153, 159, 166-169, 171-173, 175-176, 178, 188, 197, 200, 203-204, 213, 222, 227, 229-232, 243, 248, 256, 267, 269, 271, 275, 288, 296-297, 299, 302, 304-305, 308
Critical Language Awareness 69, 81-82, 85, 252-253, 265, 306
Critical Perspectives 23, 65
Cultural Identity 23, 25-26, 28-29, 33, 37-38, 40-43, 50, 80, 152, 173, 221, 253, 279
Culturally Relevant Pedagogies 54, 61-63
Culturally Relevant Pedagogy 66, 161

D

Dialect 73, 75, 212, 220, 223, 247-248, 253-258, 260-261, 263, 267-270, 276
Dialectical Variation 247-250, 252-259, 261-264, 268
digital nature 108, 111, 116-123, 126
digital technology 108-123, 126
Discourse Analysis 20, 23, 26, 28, 47, 49, 83, 148, 231, 269, 273, 280
Discursive Practices 4, 68, 70-71, 73-74, 86
Diversity 6-10, 19, 30, 33-34, 45, 47-49, 58, 60, 63-64, 73-74, 77, 79, 81-82, 85, 90-91, 103, 106, 118-119, 122, 128-129, 150, 160, 165-169, 171-172, 175, 178, 180-184, 186-187, 199, 203, 206, 214, 222-223, 225-234, 243, 245, 248-249, 251, 253-257, 266, 272-273, 280-281, 285, 302

E

EAP 88-100, 102-105
ecological system 108, 111, 117, 119
Educational Technology 88, 98, 105, 123, 125, 128
Emergent Bilingual 64-65, 67, 265
EMI in Türkiye 189
Employment 23-34, 36, 38-46, 48-50, 91, 149, 156, 159
English in Berlin 2, 7, 9-10, 19
English-Medium Instruction 186, 203-209
ESL 37, 39, 41-42, 54-55, 57-58, 62, 64, 66, 102-103, 125, 129, 161, 207
ESOL 66, 247, 256, 268
Ethnicity 5, 20, 26, 28, 30-31, 37, 41, 71-73, 77, 82, 212, 222-223, 255, 274

F

Filipinos 23, 36, 38, 48

filter bubbles 301-304, 306-309, 311-312
Flexible Language Use 186
functions 21, 43, 57, 61, 66, 93, 95, 134, 197-198, 202, 206, 226-227, 234, 284-285, 287-288, 291, 293-297, 300, 303
Functions of codeswitching 297, 300

G

Gender and Sexuality 1
Ghana 211-216, 221-224

H

Heritage speaker 300
Heteroglossia 54, 57, 65, 247, 249, 251-252, 264
Heteroglossic Ideologies 54, 57
Higher Education 36, 59, 80, 82, 85-86, 89, 91, 101-102, 104, 106, 135, 186-189, 191-192, 194, 198, 203-209, 215, 221, 256, 265-267, 269-276, 278-281

I

immigration 15, 23, 26-27, 31, 33-34, 43-48, 52, 131, 284-285, 298
Inclusiveness 30, 225-226, 230, 234, 236, 239, 243
Indexical Field Construction 1
Indexicality 1, 3, 7, 15, 19
inequity 71, 80, 254, 301
instructed SLA 108, 112, 128
Integration 24, 26-29, 31-36, 38, 40-41, 43-50, 57, 62, 78, 84, 88, 91-93, 96, 98-99, 104, 125, 167, 170-171, 175, 181-183, 194-195, 205, 209, 213, 223
International Student 89, 191, 199, 206, 208-209, 265
Internationally Educated Professionals (IEPs) 23
Inter-sentential code-switching 291, 300
inter-sentential switching 284
Intra-sentential code-switching 300
intra-sentential switching 284, 291

L

L2 Identity 1, 15
Language 1-7, 9-21, 23-30, 33-47, 49-52, 54-86, 88-112, 114-129, 132-142, 145-163, 166-175, 177, 179-191, 193, 195-209, 211-212, 214-215, 217-228, 230-232, 234-237, 239-245, 247-257, 261, 263-270, 272-281, 284, 286-288, 290-291, 294-302, 305-312
Language Acquisition 15, 70, 82, 90, 92, 108, 111-112, 115, 121, 123, 125-126, 131, 139, 152, 154-155, 179, 256, 298
Language and Identity 1, 21, 42, 71, 213, 222
Language Autonomy 68, 86
Language Contact 1, 3, 17, 20, 244, 284, 286, 297-300
Language Diversity 73-74, 79, 106, 183, 186-187, 255, 280
Language Dynamics 211, 213, 221
Language Ideology 2, 7, 12, 16, 19, 68, 71, 76, 86, 250
language learning 15, 18, 20-21, 59, 70, 74, 76, 82, 89-95, 97-99, 101-112, 114-129, 148-150, 152, 155, 158-159, 161-162, 166-167, 179, 181-182, 222, 249, 252, 281, 298
Language Norms 23-26, 44-45, 131, 227, 230, 247, 249, 253, 268, 302
Language Policy 44, 52, 66, 101, 103, 159, 186, 206-208, 244, 253
Language Socialization 139, 148
Language Subordination 68, 71, 79, 81, 86
Language Use 10, 15-17, 23, 26, 33, 39, 50, 65, 69-71, 74, 76-78, 109, 114, 136, 186, 197, 207-208, 211, 217, 227-228, 230, 239, 241-242, 248, 250-252, 254, 257, 264, 272
Language Variation 71, 247-249, 254-256, 261, 263-268
Language Variety 250, 254, 257, 269-270, 274-279
Language-Friendly Pedagogies 88, 90
Learner Autonomy 88, 91-93, 96, 99, 102, 104
length of residence 284, 288-289, 295-296
Levels of Job Satisfaction 42, 50
Linguistic Diversity 33, 60, 81, 90, 165, 167-169, 171-172, 184, 199, 203, 206, 225-234, 243, 245, 248-249, 251, 254, 256-257, 272-273, 280-281
Linguistic Repertoire 2, 55, 62, 67, 90-91, 101, 169, 197, 203, 248, 251, 255, 271-273, 279, 296

M

Metapragmatics 148
Migration 24, 44, 47-49, 85, 89, 160, 166, 183, 193-194, 203, 205, 209, 211-213, 215, 218-224, 297
Mindsets 165-167, 169, 179, 181-182, 185, 305
Monoglossic Ideologies 57, 205
Monoglossic Ideology 67, 186-188, 202-203
Monoglossic Perspective 187, 200, 209
Motivation 15-16, 94, 109, 116, 119, 121, 123-124, 127-129, 149-153, 155-157, 159-163, 176, 190, 193, 293
Movements of Integration 42, 50
Multicultural 23, 26, 30, 33, 35, 37, 40, 42, 44-45, 47, 61, 66, 84-85, 101, 104, 159, 171, 175, 178, 180, 182, 187, 203, 205-206, 208-209, 230, 232, 244,

Index

267, 281, 301-302
Multidialecticalism 268
Multilingual 1, 6, 16-17, 21, 54-55, 57, 61-66, 83, 86, 89, 101-106, 109-112, 116-117, 121-122, 127-128, 131, 146, 148, 159-161, 163, 165-168, 170-172, 174-175, 179-182, 184, 186-187, 199-200, 202-209, 213, 222, 225-233, 238-239, 243-245, 250, 253-254, 264-267, 281, 287, 297, 299, 301-303, 305-307, 309, 312
Multilingualism 1, 44, 54-55, 57-58, 63-66, 74, 101-105, 110, 128, 150-151, 159-160, 165-167, 172, 175, 178, 180-182, 184, 186-187, 189, 201, 203, 225-231, 243-244, 248, 250, 264-265, 298, 306

N

Named Language 56, 198, 209
Negatively Downward 29-30, 50
Negatively Upward 29-30, 50
Norm 5, 8, 55, 70, 74-75, 77, 80, 187, 205, 209, 227-228, 233, 243, 248, 250, 252, 268, 305, 307

O

Obstacles to Learning 149
Ofelia García 55

P

Periphery Country 50
Plurilingualism 88, 90-91, 104-105, 110, 134, 173, 205
Pluriliteracies 55, 58-59, 65, 67, 207
Positively Downward 29-30, 50
Positively Upward 29-30, 50
Positivist Approach 24, 50
Public Health 225, 227-234, 238-243, 245, 304, 308, 310

S

social variables 255, 284, 288-289, 295
society 16, 18-19, 23-24, 33-34, 36, 45-46, 60, 70, 76, 85, 91, 106, 110, 116, 118, 121, 141, 143, 146, 174, 201, 212, 221, 225, 227, 230, 232, 234, 237-239, 250-255, 260, 271-272, 285, 297-298, 301-302, 304-305, 308, 310
Sociolinguistics 2-3, 18-19, 33, 101, 135, 147, 244, 281, 298-299

T

Tag switching 300
Teacher Candidate 268
Teacher Identity 84, 162, 165, 181, 183-184
Teachers of English in the Global South 149, 153
Teaching Practices 73, 77-78, 81, 88, 92, 99-100, 149, 153, 157, 159, 166-167, 174, 180, 199-200
technology 62, 88, 93, 98, 100-102, 104-105, 108-123, 125-129, 151, 160, 277, 286, 301, 305
Transculturalism 69, 73-75, 81, 86
Translanguaging 44, 47, 54-67, 76, 85, 101-103, 166, 181, 187, 197-209, 265, 299, 307, 310
Translingual Agency 81, 86
Turkish-Medium Instruction 187

W

Winneba 211, 213-222

Recommended Reference Books

IGI Global's reference books are available in three unique pricing formats:
Print Only, E-Book Only, or Print + E-Book.

Order direct through IGI Global's Online Bookstore at
www.igi-global.com or through your preferred provider.

ISBN: 9781799897064
EISBN: 9781799897088
© 2022; 302 pp.
List Price: US$ **215**

ISBN: 9781799889854
EISBN: 9781799889878
© 2022; 383 pp.
List Price: US$ **215**

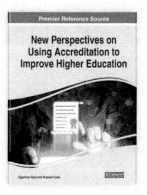

ISBN: 9781668451953
EISBN: 9781668451960
© 2022; 300 pp.
List Price: US$ **195**

ISBN: 9781799852001
EISBN: 9781799852018
© 2022; 355 pp.
List Price: US$ **215**

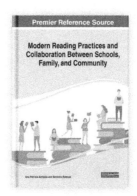

ISBN: 9781799897507
EISBN: 9781799897521
© 2022; 304 pp.
List Price: US$ **215**

ISBN: 9781799868293
EISBN: 9781799868316
© 2022; 389 pp.
List Price: US$ **215**

Do you want to stay current on the latest research trends, product announcements, news, and special offers?
Join IGI Global's mailing list to receive customized recommendations, exclusive discounts, and more.
Sign up at: **www.igi-global.com/newsletters.**

Publisher of Timely, Peer-Reviewed Inclusive Research Since 1988

www.igi-global.com | Sign up at www.igi-global.com/newsletters | facebook.com/igiglobal | twitter.com/igiglobal | linkedin.com/igiglobal

Ensure Quality Research is Introduced to the Academic Community

Become an Evaluator for IGI Global Authored Book Projects

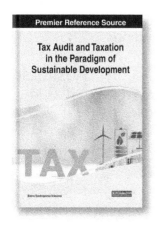   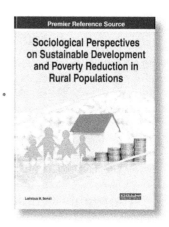

The overall success of an authored book project is dependent on quality and timely manuscript evaluations.

Applications and Inquiries may be sent to:
development@igi-global.com

Applicants must have a doctorate (or equivalent degree) as well as publishing, research, and reviewing experience. Authored Book Evaluators are appointed for one-year terms and are expected to complete at least three evaluations per term. Upon successful completion of this term, evaluators can be considered for an additional term.

If you have a colleague that may be interested in this opportunity, we encourage you to share this information with them.

Easily Identify, Acquire, and Utilize Published Peer-Reviewed Findings in Support of Your Current Research

IGI Global OnDemand

Purchase Individual IGI Global OnDemand Book Chapters and Journal Articles

For More Information:
www.igi-global.com/e-resources/ondemand/

Browse through 150,000+ Articles and Chapters!

Find specific research related to your current studies and projects that have been contributed by international researchers from prestigious institutions, including:

- Accurate and Advanced Search
- Affordably Acquire Research
- Instantly Access Your Content
- Benefit from the InfoSci Platform Features

"It really provides an excellent entry into the research literature of the field. It presents a manageable number of highly relevant sources on topics of interest to a wide range of researchers. The sources are scholarly, but also accessible to 'practitioners'."

- Ms. Lisa Stimatz, MLS, University of North Carolina at Chapel Hill, USA

Interested in Additional Savings?

Subscribe to **IGI Global OnDemand Plus**

Learn More

Acquire content from over 128,000+ research-focused book chapters and 33,000+ scholarly journal articles for as low as US$ 5 per article/chapter (original retail price for an article/chapter: US$ 37.50).

7,300+ E-BOOKS.
ADVANCED RESEARCH.
INCLUSIVE & AFFORDABLE.

IGI Global e-Book Collection

- **Flexible Purchasing Options** (Perpetual, Subscription, EBA, etc.)
- Multi-Year Agreements with **No Price Increases** Guaranteed
- **No Additional Charge** for Multi-User Licensing
- No Maintenance, Hosting, or Archiving Fees
- Continually Enhanced & Innovated **Accessibility Compliance Features** (WCAG)

Handbook of Research on Digital Transformation, Industry Use Cases, and the Impact of Disruptive Technologies
ISBN: 9781799877127
EISBN: 9781799877141

Handbook of Research on New Investigations in Artificial Life, AI, and Machine Learning
ISBN: 9781799886860
EISBN: 9781799886877

Handbook of Research on Future of Work and Education
ISBN: 9781799882756
EISBN: 9781799882770

Research Anthology on Physical and Intellectual Disabilities in an Inclusive Society (4 Vols.)
ISBN: 9781668435427
EISBN: 9781668435434

Innovative Economic, Social, and Environmental Practices for Progressing Future Sustainability
ISBN: 9781799895909
EISBN: 9781799895923

Applied Guide for Event Study Research in Supply Chain Management
ISBN: 9781799889694
EISBN: 9781799889717

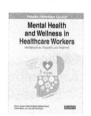

Mental Health and Wellness in Healthcare Workers
ISBN: 9781799888130
EISBN: 9781799888147

Clean Technologies and Sustainable Development in Civil Engineering
ISBN: 9781799898108
EISBN: 9781799898122

Request More Information, or Recommend the IGI Global e-Book Collection to Your Institution's Librarian

For More Information or to Request a Free Trial, Contact IGI Global's e-Collections Team: eresources@igi-global.com | 1-866-342-6657 ext. 100 | 717-533-8845 ext. 100

Are You Ready to Publish Your Research

IGI Global offers book authorship and editorship opportunities across 11 subject areas, including business, computer science, education, science and engineering, social sciences, and more!

Benefits of Publishing with IGI Global:

- Free one-on-one editorial and promotional support.
- Expedited publishing timelines that can take your book from start to finish in less than one (1) year.
- Choose from a variety of formats, including Edited and Authored References, Handbooks of Research, Encyclopedias, and Research Insights.
- Utilize IGI Global's eEditorial Discovery® submission system in support of conducting the submission and double-blind peer review process.
- IGI Global maintains a strict adherence to ethical practices due in part to our full membership with the Committee on Publication Ethics (COPE).
- Indexing potential in prestigious indices such as Scopus®, Web of Science™, PsycINFO®, and ERIC – Education Resources Information Center.
- Ability to connect your ORCID iD to your IGI Global publications.
- Earn honorariums and royalties on your full book publications as well as complimentary content and exclusive discounts.

Join Your Colleagues from Prestigious Institutions, Including:

 Australian National University Massachusetts Institute of Technology

 Johns Hopkins University

 Harvard University

 Columbia University IN THE CITY OF NEW YORK

Learn More at: www.igi-global.com/publish
or Contact IGI Global's Aquisitions Team at: acquisition@igi-global.com

Individual Article & Chapter Downloads
US$ 29.50/each

 Easily Identify, Acquire, and Utilize Published Peer-Reviewed Findings in Support of Your Current Research

- Browse Over **170,000+ Articles & Chapters**
- **Accurate & Advanced** Search
- Affordably Acquire **International Research**
- **Instantly Access** Your Content
- Benefit from the **InfoSci® Platform Features**

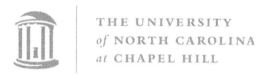

THE UNIVERSITY *of* NORTH CAROLINA *at* CHAPEL HILL

" *It really provides* an excellent entry into the research literature of the field. *It presents a manageable number of* highly relevant sources *on topics of interest to a wide range of researchers. The sources are* scholarly, but also accessible *to 'practitioners'.* "

- Ms. Lisa Stimatz, MLS, University of North Carolina at Chapel Hill, USA

Interested in Additional Savings?

Subscribe to
IGI Global OnDemand *Plus*

Learn More

Acquire content from over 137,000+ research-focused book chapters and 33,000+ scholarly journal articles for as low as US$ 5 per article/chapter (original retail price for an article/chapter: US$ 29.50).

Printed in the USA
CPSIA information can be obtained
at www.ICGtesting.com
LVHW082346150324
774517LV00005B/758